MAXIM LITVINOFF

MAXIM LITVINOFF

MAXIM LITVINOFF

BY

ARTHUR UPHAM POPE

L. B. FISCHER · NEW YORK

To *the memory of*

WILLIAM WENDT

RICHARD MONTAGUE

HERMAN LATHROP TUCKER

Acknowledgments

A BOOK OF THIS KIND which had to be done quickly with only meagre material available is in no small degree the product of teamwork and I am most grateful to the following colleagues and associates for loyal and effective help.

Curt Riess was very helpful in the initiation of the book, organized a great part of the research, assembled and arranged material and suggested various ideas. *Ladislas Farago* supplied some critical information from recondite sources and many facts out of his exceptional knowledge of European politics in the last ten years. *Mrs. Valerie Engelsrath* was in charge of research from German and Italian sources. *Dr. Tibor Koeves* was most helpful in criticism of the text, checking documents and making useful suggestions. *Harriet Moore* of the American Russian Institute read the entire manuscript with greatest care and provided constructive criticism and good judgment. *William Mandel* of the same office also read the manuscript and made useful corrections. *Walter Duranty, Sir Bernard Pares, Maurice Hindus* and *Max Lerner* were kind enough to read the complete text and I have profited by their friendly help. *Lorraine Meyer* has done more for the book than could be asked of any secretary. *Sidney Wallach,* my immediate taskmaster, tempered his firmness with sympathy and patience, for which I am most grateful. And finally, *Dr. Phyllis Ackerman* set aside important work to read the manuscript and proof several times, provided both critical and constructive ideas of greatest value and reviewed many documents and publications.

I am especially grateful to *Moritz Braun,* who nearly forty years ago interested me in Russia's struggle for freedom and justice—a struggle which I have followed with sympathetic interest ever since, and to *Albert Rhys Williams and his wife,* who introduced me to Moscow many years ago, to *Walter Duranty* with whom I have had many illuminating conversations, and to *Ambassador Davies* for information and sympathetic encouragement. To *Louis Fischer* I owe many facts and helpful ideas. *Ferdinand Kuhn, Jr.,* has been for years a delightful, inspiring and instructive companion on many an excursion in political thinking. In February, 1936, Mr. Kuhn predicted the Munich appeasement which he already was convinced had been decided upon in principle.

I am also indebted to a number of Ambassadors, Ministers and Secretaries stationed in Moscow over a long period of years. Their knowledge and judgment have been invaluable. Naturally they should remain anonymous; I also owe to other foreign correspondents than those named and to various American engineers and specialists working in a great many parts of Russia significant first hand information. My obligations to Russian friends and colleagues including unknown chance acquaintances in Russia are beyond recounting. I am especially indebted to *Academician Joseph Orbeli* and *Professor Camilla Trever,* with whom I have spent many memorable hours, who have proven how happy and productive co-operation between Americans and Russians can be.

Finally, I am indebted to the *Woodrow Wilson Memorial Library* in New York, which put at my disposal the text of all the speeches that Litvinoff made in Geneva. As journalistic sources the *New York Times,* the *London New Statesman and Nation* have been most useful.

While all those mentioned and others who are not, are in no small degree responsible for whatever merit the book may have, no one of them can be charged with any of its deficiencies.

A. U. P.

Preface

THE LAST TWENTY-FIVE YEARS have been unspeakably disastrous to the whole human race. Peace and reconstruction, a determined and creative effort for a decent and humane civilization can bring hope and salvation. The alternative is a new and final disaster for all. Who will lead? Whom shall we trust? To whom shall we listen?

One thing is clear—the statesmanship of the last thirty years is bankrupt. It was powerless to stay the disaster that all feared. The Foreign Offices which demanded to be let alone to arrange affairs as they saw fit can no longer request, "leave it to us." Their policy of appeasement led straight to catastrophe, a lesson too slowly learned.

It is the people of the world who pay in frustration, anguish and death for the mistakes of government. Twenty-five years ago the peoples of all countries passionately wanted some type of international organization to defend them against the holocaust and to provide them with an assured opportunity for self-realization and productive living. It was not forthcoming. The common man wants to know why. He insists that there shall be a new and resolute attempt to organize the world for order, security and progress and he is determined to find leaders who can provide it. He is now studying leaders and leadership, seeking new ways to permanent peace. Moreover, if the democratic concept which affirms that the public will alone can validate policy still holds, then the public is entitled to the fullest account possible of the leaders who are trying to shape its destiny.

Among the leaders Maxim Litvinoff is of outstanding importance. He represents one of the greatest nations, one that with its more than 10,000,000 dead and its devastated provinces has quantitatively at least suffered most in this war, and measured by the damage it has inflicted on the German war machine, done most to win it. Furthermore, it is Maxim Litvinoff who not merely foresaw the debacle, as did many others, but made the most consistent and intelligent effort to avert it, striving over a long period, with courage, tenacity and constructive imagination to build up a defense—the only one possible—collective security. That "Peace is Indivisible" was his wise insight—too long ignored. He has combined in a remarkable way realism and idealism. He has understood each crisis as it came, predicted with unbelievable accuracy what was going to happen next, and fought for a vision against complacency, inertia, selfishness. He is a statesman above all others in our time or perhaps in any other, of whom it could be said with reasonable justice, "he was always right." It is necessary to understand the sources of his character, the essential quality of his motives, the discipline and experience that gave him such insight and power.

This attempt to present, for the first time, a coherent account of his career does not pretend to be a definitive, scientific biography with an exhaustive paraphernalia of documentation such as some day must be written—much of it by Litvinoff himself. The life of a statesman cannot be fully recorded while he is still at the height of his career with historical finality or with full justice to the events. Important documents are still locked up in official archives or in memoirs yet to appear, and certain critical questions are still unresolved so that even a preliminary discussion of them might easily be harmful.

But this book undertakes to recount conscientiously the major features of Litvinoff's life and of the times with which they are inextricably interwoven, a task for which the writer has some, if insufficient, qualifications; and if a responsible biography is not offered now, frivolous or sensational accounts will usurp the place. Indeed, Litvinoff has had occasion to discourage more than a score of proposals to write his life, and the material already published in books and magazine articles, consists largely of distortions, misstatements and downright inventions.

Despite, therefore, the inevitable limitations, a Litvinoff biography is long overdue. Litvinoff would prefer to remain anonymous, as the industrious servant and representative of a great people. He is by both temperament and conviction completely absorbed in his work and holds that every statesman ought to be only the instrument of his State. He thinks of himself not as an individual but merely the focus of a great idea and the movement which it has inspired; he would much prefer that no life be written of him, but he has become so completely a public character that this preference cannot weigh against the public need for more information about him.

A few statements have been made in the text which are based on the author's personal experience or on sources to which he had special access but cannot now cite, partly because some of them were off-the-record comments by public officials still in responsible positions and others would involve individuals who are now living in a dangerous environment.

It is said that in our hurried age few serious books are read through; if any part of this book is to be skipped, it should not be the great speeches of Litvinoff himself:

His speech at London in March, 1936, on the Occupation of the Rhineland (p. 381).

His speech at Geneva in June, 1936, on the betrayal of Ethiopia (p. 369).

His speech of November 28, 1936, on Intervention in the Spanish Civil War (pp. 393, 405).

His famous speech at Geneva, September 21, 1938 (p. 6).

These are among the ablest and most significant political documents of our time, models of strictly controlled facts, sound principle, rigorous logic, political idealism and moral integrity. They should be read and reread. They reveal some of the fallacies that have vexed international politics since the first World War and have cost us so heavily. The precision and validity of the predictions are proof that these utterances are firmly grounded on realities, and such a control of realities may stand us well in the future.

CONTENTS

	PAGE
ACKNOWLEDGMENT	vii
PREFACE	ix
PART ONE: *The Practical Revolutionary*	1
Chapter One: The End of an Epoch	3
Two: Youth and Early Development	32
Three: Civil War in Russia	57
Four: The Bolsheviks Fight World War I	98
Five: Coming to Power	119
PART TWO: *The Fight for Recognition*	139
Chapter Six: Gradual Approach	141
Seven: A New Type of Diplomat	189
Eight: Disarmament	223
Nine: Foreign Minister	256
Ten: Litvinoff in Washington	288
PART THREE: *Peace Is Indivisible*	313
Chapter Eleven: Collective Security	315
Twelve: What Price Peace?	351
Thirteen: Into the Abyss	396
Fourteen: Back at Work	440
POSTSCRIPT	475
BIBLIOGRAPHY	500
DOCUMENTATION	503
INDEX	510

PART ONE

THE PRACTICAL REVOLUTIONARY

CHAPTER ONE

The End of an Epoch

THE LAST HALF of September, 1938, was tense with dread. Statesmen, now thoroughly alarmed, pathetic in their impotence, were busy contriving desperate expedients to avert impending war. The memory of eleventh-hour rescues from previous crises sustained a flickering hope, but made only darker the prospect and more intolerable the suspense. The situation was shot through with confusions and violent contrasts. A powerful nation demanded the life of a little one, while the League of Nations, potentially infinitely more powerful, yet now infirm and faltering, looked on in a mood of vague anxiety quite the opposite of that fury of purpose which inflamed the savage aggressor. The policies and ambitions of many nations were in conflict; their individual advantage and temporary security seemed to be in direct contrast to their real and permanent interest—peace for all. The League at Geneva was talking, talking and accomplishing nothing, more intimidated by immediate and conventional difficulties than by more remote but universal dangers; enfeebled by compromises and evasions, sabotaged by its sworn protectors, still holding with phantoms unprofitable strife. Its unrealistic discussions contrasted strangely with that melancholy session in Prague, where in Hradshin Castle on the night of the 20th, grappling with grim and bitter reality, the victim nation marked for death was summoning its courage to make the blood sacrifice that the Allied appeasers demanded to feed to the ravening aggressor, now hot for the kill.

Adolf Hitler and Neville Chamberlain faced each other—another contrast as great as was known to history: one shouting, savage, hysterical, with a lust for violence; the other uncertain, of gentle speech and mild manners—dreading conflict, hoping, pleading. There was a third, less conspicuous figure in this crisis, who contrasted with both but more especially with Chamberlain—Maxim Litvinoff, clear-headed,

resolute, coolly audacious. Chamberlain, conventional, timid, complacent and unimaginative, differed from Litvinoff in every respect and
for years had opposed him on every issue. Litvinoff staying in Geneva,
accurately gauged the whole situation in terms of fact and principle;
Chamberlain rushing to Berchtesgaden, to Godesberg, to Munich, was
baffled by the volcanic forces before which he was pitifully inadequate,
trying with the profit-and-loss conceptions of a Birmingham company-
director, to appease and divert a fanatical ruffian whose neurotic com-
pulsions and wild ambitions were to him quite strange and wholly
incredible. Chamberlain, the sensible business man, was seeking to
reason with the unreasonable, to appease the unappeasable, to extract
mercy from the merciless. The whole attempt was fatuous in conception, inept in execution and foredoomed to dismal failure. Litvinoff's
plan, on the other hand, was reasonable, technically sound, universal
in scope and might have succeeded if given a chance.

Chamberlain had had the power but not the understanding. He had
hopes, especially that his problems might be automatically solved in
the end by a German-Russian war and for this he worked and contrived but he had no real clarity of purpose and no constructive program. Litvinoff, on the other hand, having long ago taken the exact
measure of Hitler, thoroughly understood and had long predicted just
what was happening, but he was helpless. He had a program which
looked to the welfare of all, which he had urged for ten years and
which could have forestalled the disaster, had it not been frustrated
by the indifference, selfishness and downright incompetence of those
charged with the destiny of nations. Now, while Chamberlain was
shuttling back and forth, Litvinoff could do nothing but sum up and
offer, as one last forlorn hope, one more plan that even then could
have saved the world from disaster, had only the Allied statesmen
responded with the speed and the sovereign resolve that the danger to
civilization demanded.

Now Chamberlain and his sinister alter ego, Sir Horace Wilson,
together with the confused and frightened Daladier, were beginning
their final retreat. To no avail they abandoned nations, threw away
honor, surrendered precious power and paved the way to the abyss.
For this complete defeat they were acclaimed as few have ever been.
A fatuous claque in the Tory Party hailed Chamberlain as "one of the

supreme figures in history," "the greatest statesman of all time"; one writer even referred to him as "the noblest figure since Christ." Many resolute English like Winston Churchill thought otherwise, seeing straight through to the grim facts. As Churchill said: "We have sustained a total, unmitigated defeat. . . . We are in the presence of a disaster of the first magnitude. Do not suppose that this is the end. It is only the beginning. . . ." But at the same time in Paris Daladier was welcomed by a semi-hysterical crowd, roaring their gratitude and delight for a timely rescue, greeting with huzzas the prelude to calamity.

Litvinoff, meanwhile, unacclaimed, still regarded with skepticism and indifference, still derided, faced the great questions of the hour with complete understanding and steady courage.

There was nothing new in the threat of war. Chamberlain himself confessed that the dread of it had long been his constant nightmare. The forces of destruction had been gathering for more than twenty years; thousands the world around had seen a world-destroying conflict daily crowding closer. Why this fatuous dallying with disaster? How was it that the great hopes for which so many had died, hopes which alone could justify the sufferings and sacrifice of the first World War, were set so frivolously at naught? Was man incapable of controlling his own destiny? Was some mysterious fate driving the nations to self-destruction?

Chamberlain was not the sole architect of the calamitous complex that now threatened everything; Stanley Baldwin and preceding Tory governments had contributed much. Indeed, each of the Great Powers had played a sorry part. The United States bears a heavy burden of guilt. Her desertion of the League and refusal to participate in the World Court, the economic merry-go-round of the 1920's, the obtuse demand for the payment of international debts in gyrating currencies blocked by unscalable tariff walls, which of course made for embittered politics, a falling standard of living and mounting despair in many countries; the failure of America to heed the warnings of impending economic disaster, to see its implications or to deal with it adequately when it came—all this had made for fears, tensions, hatreds, which the powers of aggression were, by the early 30's, exploiting to their own ends. Britain's rejection of the Protocol in 1924, its quibbling and obstruction at Geneva just at the critical moment when there was a rising tide of hope and determination in the League itself, the failure of both the United States and England to give guarantees of protection to France, understandably agitated and alarmed, the inability of Britain and France to keep step—these and a score of other conflicting currents repeatedly thwarted healing and constructive forces that might have forfended the catastrophe.

On the psychological side, the evils were rooted in group selfishness, in intellectual indolence, a neurasthenic timidity, a sheer want of faith. Unwilling to move with the spirit of the times, indifferent to the legitimate and imperative demands for social and economic justice for all, part of the world was trying to escape its moment in history, trying to return to national isolation and live by its own powers for its own ends in a system that had become inseparably one—and could no longer be held apart. Evasive, obstructionist when or if they could, they threw the international political and economic machinery out of gear until it was whirling and thrashing itself into ruin. Chamberlain and all who held with him tried, with eyes averted from the meaning of the vast energies out of control, to tinker with this and that. Litvinoff was convinced that the structure itself would have to be renovated and redesigned.

With cold logic, with a devastating analysis that laid bare all the maladies of international politics, with courage born of his own character and profound experience, with unflinching realism that minimized no fact, with a self-confidence that came from uncompromising sincerity and a passion for the welfare of humanity, the whole speech resonant with a grim humor and edged with sarcasm, Litvinoff pronounced his terrible indictment in the Assembly Hall of the League of Nations.

It was at four o'clock on the afternoon of September 21 that Litvinoff arose to an audience that was restless, anxious, skeptical of all fundamentals, paralyzed by its own conventions, self defeated by its own self-interests. The order of the day was the annual report of the Secretary-General on the League's work during the last twelve months. But Maxim Litvinoff proceeded to expose to the indifferent delegates the processes and forces by means of which the League of Nations, that one great hope of man, had been rendered frustrate and impotent, to show why, in the hour of humanity's greatest danger, it was helpless to avert the disaster all dreaded, and what still might be accomplished to save the nations from massacre and devastation, from impoverishment and demoralization, if only they could seize on the realities and courageously do the obvious. He was speaking to the delegates but addressing the world.

"The subject before us," Litvinoff began, "is the annual report of the Secretary-General on the League's work during the past twelve months. Quite naturally and rightly, however, the speakers so far have dealt, not with what the League has done during this year, but with what it has not done this year or in previous years. Evidently everyone recognizes that the League of Nations was not set up for the activity recounted in the report presented by the League's Secretary-General. It must not be forgotten that the League was created as a reaction to the World War and its countless horrors; that its object was to make that the last war, to safeguard all nations against aggression, and to replace the system of military alliances by the collective organization of assistance to the victim of aggression. In this sphere the League has done nothing. Two States—Ethiopia and Austria—have lost their independent existence in consequence of violent aggression. A third State, China, is now a victim of aggression and foreign invasion for the second time in seven years, and a fourth State, Spain, is in the third year of a sanguinary war, owing to the armed intervention of two aggressors in its internal affairs. The League of Nations has not carried out its obligations to these States.

"At the present time, a fifth State, Czechoslovakia, is suffering interference in its internal affairs at the hands of a neighboring State, and is publicly and loudly menaced with attack. One of the oldest, most cultured, most hardworking of European peoples, which acquired its independence as a State after centuries of oppression, today or tomorrow may decide to take up arms in defense of that independence. I am sure that the sympathies, if not of all Governments, then at any rate of all peoples represented at the Assembly, go out to the Czechoslovak people in this its terrible hour of trial; that we all remember the most active part played by Czechoslovakia and its present President, M. Beneš, in the organization and development of the League of Nations; and that all our thoughts are so occupied with the events in Czechoslovakia and around it that we delegates find it difficult to give the necessary attention to the Assembly's agenda—in which Czechoslovakia is not mentioned. There is nothing surprising, therefore, in the fact that the general discussion has centered on what the League of Nations ought to have done, but did not do.

"Unfortunately, our discussion has not been limited to the recording and explanation of the League's blunders and mistakes, but has included attempts retrospectively to justify them, and even to legalize them for the future. Various arguments have been used, among them the most favored being a reference to the absence of universality. The shallowness of this argument has been pointed out more than once. The League of Nations was not any more universal during the first twelve years of its existence than it is today. From the outset it lacked three of the largest Powers and a multitude of smaller States. Furthermore, some States left it; others joined it; and up to the time of the first case of aggression it never crossed anyone's mind—or, at all events, no one expressed such views in the League—that the League could not fulfill its principal functions, and that therefore its Constitution should be altered and those functions, the function of guardianship of peace, withdrawn.

"No one has yet proved, and no one can prove, that the League of Nations refused to apply sanctions to the aggressor in this case or in that because States were absent from its ranks, and that this was the reason why sanctions, applied in one case, were prematurely brought to an end. Even composed as it is today, the League of Nations is still strong enough by its collective action to avert or arrest aggression. All that is necessary is that the obligatory character of such actions be confirmed, and that the machinery of the League of Nations be at least once brought into action in conformity with the Covenant. This requires only the goodwill of the States' Members, for there are no objective reasons of such a character as to prevent the normal functioning of the League: at any rate, no such reasons as could not be foreseen by the founders of the League and by those States which later joined it.

"If the complaints of lack of universality be carefully examined, they will be found to reveal considerations of quite a different nature. When the League was being set up, or when it was receiving new accessions, no one seriously anticipated that any State would defy Articles X and XVI of the Covenant and undertake aggression, and that there would arise the necessity of applying those articles in practice, thereby disturbing one's own tranquillity as a State, and sacrificing one's immediate interests."

The man speaking looked, not like the conventional diplomat, but rather like a successful middle-class business man, who had perhaps had some international contacts. Dark hair, already thinning and graying, was brushed back from a high, prominent brow. Behind glasses set on a fleshy yet firmly modeled nose, the gray-green eyes were quick and sharp, but the broad mouth seemed ready for laughter and the general effect was benevolent. This, and the weight that he had already put on, made him appear easy-going and a bit slow, but those who had to deal with him promptly revised any such impression.

Litvinoff continued, timely sarcasm now giving a biting edge to his argument:

"Now that aggression has become a reality, it is apparently necessary to eliminate collective methods of combating aggression in order to avert it from oneself. A fire-brigade was set up in the innocent hope that, by some lucky chance, there would be no fires. Things turned out differently, however. Fires have broken out in defiance of our hopes, but luckily not in our immediate vicinity; so let us dissolve the fire-brigade—of course not forever, but merely temporarily. Directly the danger of any fire disappears, we shall reassemble the fire-brigade without a moment's delay.

"Careful study of the case presented by the opponents of sanctions will reveal yet another argument. Aggression has raised its head too high; its forces have been multiplied and are growing daily. The exponents of aggression today are several, and fairly powerful; moreover, they have joined forces in mutual defense (true, so far principally with the help of printing ink and radio). These facts cannot be contested. The aggressor States have grown immensely during the last three years. They have formed a bloc in order to defend the principle of aggression. For the triumph of that principle they defend and justify one another, even when one of them is infringing the vital interests of another. There are cases, too, of their joint aggression."

Litvinoff's great speech was aimed squarely at those willing to sabotage the League itself in order to appease the aggressors. It was the sequel to a proposal that he had made six months earlier to halt the viciously accelerating onrush of aggression: an international conference to deal with the mounting menace. Had his suggestion been accepted and followed by resolute concerted action of the nations that wanted peace—and they were in an overwhelming majority—the war might have been averted. The responsibility for frustrating this plan rested primarily on one man—Neville Chamberlain, who, as Prime Minister of England, held the decisive power.

The first critical moment in the series of European crises had been marked by Hitler's annexation of Austria (March 12, 1938). Just before the long-threatened invasion was set in motion, Anthony Eden, England's Secretary of State for Foreign Affairs, urged direct action to forestall it, but Chamberlain, proclaiming peace as his motive, rejected Eden's suggestion and instead, accepted his resignation (February 20, 1938), just as the die was cast. Three weeks later, Hitler's legions rolled triumphantly into Austria. Although Lord Halifax, Eden's successor, was deeply shocked, Chamberlain merely looked on apathetically. When Litvinoff presented his plan for the anti-aggression conference, Chamberlain promptly rejected it in a speech before the House of Commons (March 24, 1938) that was not even courteous.

Assuming that Hitler would need a year, perhaps two, to absorb his new territory, European politicians believed that he would not make any further move in the near future; the non-aggression pacts which he offered to many countries, during or just after the rape of Austria, strengthened this belief. Actually, however, he drove ahead with furious impatience, and only two months later was vehemently exploiting the Sudeten German "problem." Here was a pretext for an assault against Czechoslovakia, a State that had long irked Hitler, for were it left independent, it would be a constant threat to the flank or rear of a German army invading France, Poland or Russia, but if it could be seized, it would considerably enrich Germany's economic resources, especially in the heavy industries. To be sure, Hitler had solemnly pledged his word to respect Czechoslovakian sovereignty, and on the other hand, his generals had anxiously warned him that the army was in no condition to undertake an operation that might easily prove dangerous. But megalomania does not defer to either honor or prudence, and England's inertia in the Austrian crisis had given Hitler the measure of the one serious potential barrier to his program of conquest, for while France had repeatedly made formal assurances of aid to Czechoslovakia, France was dependent upon England, and England meant Chamberlain.

Hitler's contemptuous estimate of Chamberlain was almost immediately confirmed. The Prime Minister, blindly committed at all costs to his peace-and-the-status-quo policy for Britain, was obviously ready to make any concession to keep trouble at a distance, even if it meant toying with the dubious and exceedingly dangerous project of encouraging hostility between Germany and Russia and actually opening the way to such a conflict. He not only advised Czechoslovakia to make an arrangement with the Fuehrer, but even received his Sudeten-German satellite, Konrad Henlein, a professional trouble-maker, who was sent to England to make doubly sure that Chamberlain and the men around him could be counted on to offer no serious obstacle to Nazi plans. In the end, although the Prague government made suggestions for compromise, Hitler, sure of his ground and intent on seizing the country, refused all adjustments.

A second critical moment came on May 20 when Hitler had concentrated a considerable part of his army on the Czechoslovakian border. It was clear that despite Nazi denials, an invasion was pending. But this time the Fuehrer was checked by an unexpected show of resistance. On the advice of Russia, the Czechs swiftly mobilized. Enraged at the unexpected challenge, Hitler proclaimed this an "unheard of humiliation," but nonetheless recalled his troops, which, it was explained, had only been engaged on normal spring maneuvers. America and a majority of the British hailed Germany's rebuff with downright glee, which still further infuriated Hitler, but Chamberlain seemed not to relish the incident and instructed his Ambassador to Berlin, Nevile Henderson, to suggest an international conference, *omitting Russia.*

Hitler, however, was no more interested in a British conference than he had been in Czechoslovakian compromises. Nothing would suit him short of control. Chamberlain, vaguely uneasy, tried again. On August 3 he sent to Prague, as an adviser, Lord Runciman, a shipping magnate, who had a reputation in England as negotiator and conciliator but had no knowledge of the Czechoslovakian problem, if indeed there was one, and lacked also the impartiality and firmness needed for the dangerous and difficult task. Runciman, spending most of his time with the Henlein group, dealt only perfunctorily and briefly with

the accredited democratic government, gradually and relentlessly forc-
ing it, under threat of Britain's displeasure, to give way on almost every
point. Hitler's patience was fast being exhausted. At Nuremberg on
September 12, the last session of the Nazi Party Congress, he slammed
the door to all proposals for Sudeten-German self-determination and
demanded instead outright incorporation of the area into Greater
Germany.

Chamberlain's maneuvers had served only to encourage violence
and give notice that he would sacrifice almost anything rather than
fight, and it was against this policy of appeasement that Litvinoff thun-
dered nine days later in the Geneva Assembly Hall:

"But the responsibility for this regrettable fact lies with those States
which restrained the League from resistance to the aggressors when
they were still weak and divided, and were still making only their first
timid attempts to break the peace. They have grown stronger thanks
to the fact that these attempts were allowed to reach a successful conclusion; thanks to the tolerance, and indeed impunity, of one breach
of international treaties after another, and of the propaganda of aggression; thanks to the policy of concessions, fruitless negotiations and
backstairs intrigues with them. They are still weaker, even yet, than
the possible bloc of peaceable States. But the policy of non-resistance to
evil and of humoring the aggressors, which we are being recommended
to adopt by the opponents of sanctions, will have no other end than the
further strengthening and expansion of the forces of aggression, the
further extension of the scope of their activities. Then the moment may
really arrive at which they have grown so strong that the League of
Nations—or what remains of the League of Nations—will be unable
to deal with them, even should it desire.

"We have heard here the naive suggestion that we should renounce
sanctions and instead take up afresh the study of the question of disarmament. Is it not clear that the less the hopes of collective action,
the more attention every State will be forced to give to strengthening
its own armaments? Is it not clear that, as the aggressor States will not
lag behind, the unrestrained armaments race now going on will reach
quite Homeric dimensions, and that one of the reasons for this will have
been the abandonment of sanctions? But success in this armaments
race is open only to the Great Powers, while the smaller States will

have nothing left but to prepare for suicide, chloroforming themselves as a preliminary with the new narcotic—neutrality."

The big hall was filled to the last seat with attentive listeners from many nations, but it was the show, not the substance of concerted power; the men who really controlled policy were away in London, nervously awaiting Hitler's next ultimatum, for, thanks to his unscrupulous audacity, the initiative was now, and for a long time to come would be, completely in his hands. The anxious representatives of the smaller nations, huddled together in Geneva, tried in vain to look important. They knew that they weren't; they were sitting there just for the record, and it was principally for the record that Litvinoff was speaking, for, while he was doing his utmost to rouse the nations to some intelligent and resolute action in the face of the common onrushing peril, he had scant hopes.

"There are inside and outside the League two tendencies," he continued, "two conceptions of how best to preserve peace. There exists an opinion that when some State announces a foreign policy based on aggression, on the violation of other peoples' frontiers, on the violent annexation of other peoples' possessions, on the enslavement of other nations, on domination over entire continents, the League of Nations has not only the right, but also the duty of declaring loudly and clearly, that it has been set up to preserve universal peace; that it will not permit the realization of such a program; and that it will fight that program by every means at its disposal. Within the framework of such declarations, individual members of the League can and must constitute special groups for the joint defense of individual sectors of the threatened peace front.

"It is presumed that States which openly denounce the principles underlying the League Covenant and the Briand-Kellogg Pact, which extol aggression and ridicule international obligations, are inaccessible to persuasion or argument—save the argument of force—and that there is no room for bargaining or compromise with them. They can be restrained from carrying their evil designs into effect only by a demonstration of the force which they will encounter, should they make the attempt.

"Naturally, at the least attempt to carry out aggression in practice, there should be brought into play in appropriate measure, and according to the capacities of each Member of the League, the collective action provided by Article XVI of the Covenant. In other words, the aggressor should be met with the program laid down by the League Covenant, resolutely, consistently and without hesitation. Then the aggressor himself will not be led into temptation, and peace will be preserved by peaceful means.

"There is, however, another conception, which recommends as the height of human wisdom, under cover of imaginary pacifism, that the aggressor be treated with consideration and his vanity be not wounded. It recommends that conversations and negotiations be carried on with him, that he be asssured that no collective action will be undertaken against him, and no groups or blocs formed against him—even though he himself enters into aggressive blocs with other aggressors—that compromise agreements be concluded with him, and breaches of those very agreements overlooked; that his demands, even the most illegal, be fulfilled; that journeys be undertaken, if necessary, to receive his dictates and ultimatums; that the vital interests of one State or another be sacrificed to him; and that, if possible, no question of his activity be raised at the League of Nations—because the aggressor does not like that, takes offense, sulks. Unfortunately, this is just the policy that so far has been pursued towards the aggressors; and it has had as its consequence three wars, and threatens to bring down on us a fourth. Four nations have already been sacrificed, and a fifth is next on the list.

"In view of such lamentable results of this policy, we had the right to expect that there would be recognition of its mistaken character, and of the necessity of replacing it by some other policy. Instead we have heard proposals here to make the old policy permanent. Hitherto, the aggressor reckoned with the possible reaction of the League of Nations, and showed a certain hesitation in preparing his aggression, carrying it out gradually and in proportion to his growing certainty that there would be no reaction at all. But now we are asked to reassure him beforehand that he need fear nothing at the hands of the League, and that the League henceforward will not apply to him either military or even economic and financial sanctions. At the very worst, he is threatened with moral condemnation, and that, in all probability, clothed in appropriately courteous diplomatic forms.

"I have already had the occasion to point out in another place that

Articles X and XVI, with the latent threat of international sanctions contained in the latter, constitute a powerful potential of peace. It is now suggested that we destroy that potential. Hitherto, in spite of the paralysis of the League, in spite of its non-fulfillment of its obligations in many cases, the aggressor still might fear that a moment would come when the League would nevertheless do its duty and rap him over the knuckles. He therefore carried on a tireless campaign against Article XVI through his friends, inside and outside the League. But henceforth he need not worry: he need fear no obstacles, at all events so far as Geneva is concerned.

"If anyone should wish to realize the importance for the aggressive countries of the proposed nullification of Article XVI, let him study the comments of the Press of those countries on the speeches made at the Assembly on the subject, and the praise lavished on the speakers. Furthermore, we know that certain small countries have been subjected to direct pressure by one aggressive State, which by threats and promises was endeavoring to persuade them to join the movement for the abolition of Article XVI.

"I shall probably hear the reply that no one has any designs on Article XVI, or even on sanctions, and that all that is proposed is to eliminate their obligatory and automatic character. I hope my colleagues will forgive me if I tell them that such a reply can be intended only for very naive people.

"Is it not obvious that the whole value of Article XVI lies in its obligatory character, that is, in the objective character of sanctions, which enables every Member of the League to rely on universal aid if it is attacked? But if such aid is to depend on a separate decision in each individual case, if assistance is to be granted to some States and not to others, there can be no question of a feeling of security. And who will agree to make sacrifices and to grant altruistic aid to another State, if the latter declares beforehand that it is under no obligation of reciprocity? Will anyone pay premiums to an insurance company if he is not guaranteed the automatic payment of benefit in cases provided beforehand, if that payment depends on the quite arbitrary decision of the management of the company?

"Yet we are flatly told that every Member of the League is to judge for itself whether its participation in sanctions coincides with its interests. But to grant aid to another State in one's own interest requires no League of Nations. It was the practice long before the League existed. Did not twenty-five States combat the Central Empires during the World War because their interests coincided? Did not pre-war blocs and alliances serve the same end of the joint defense of their common interests by groups of States? But we were told that the League of Nations was to put an end to the system of private alliances and agreements, and to replace them by the principles of collective security, based on the common interest of all peoples in the maintenance of peace!

"We are also put off with assurances that the measures proposed will be of a purely temporary character, and that in some indeterminate future it will be possible once again to return to the obligatory and automatic character of sanctions. No indication is given, however, of what conditions will be necessary for such a change.

"If the reason for the modus vivendi now proposed is the absence of universality, why must we think that a League of Nations completely withered away as to its contents and retaining a mere shell outside will present any attraction to new Members, or that those States which remained outside the League on account of the compulsory character of sanctions will enter it in order to restore that compulsory character, once it has been abolished? If, on the other hand, the obligatory application of sanctions is considered impossible because aggressions have appeared on the political horizon, what grounds have we for believing that the phenomenon will disappear? If it does disappear, there will be no need of sanctions."

Litvinoff was again directing his words to Chamberlain and his entourage of appeasers, for even after Hitler's violent and completely revealing speech of September 12, Chamberlain had continued, with weak and unrealistic stubbornness, to attempt placation. By now, however, events were developing with alarming speed. Henlein had tried a revolt, had failed, and the Government in Prague had ordered martial law. The French had begun to man the Maginot Line, and the British fleet was "on the alert." In the meantime, Mussolini's paper, *Popolo d'Italia,* had declared that Czechoslovakia had ceased to exist. Hitler, apparently, took a more realistic view and again ordered troop concentrations along the Czech border "to prevent further incidents."

Even thus confronted with the failure of his policy, however, Chamberlain could see no way out except still more appeasement. On September 15 he rushed to Berchtesgaden for a consultation with the Fuehrer, in the course of which Hitler abruptly declined any compromise, and demanded immediate self-determination for the Sudeten Germans, even at the cost of world war. Chamberlain's pleas could secure no more than Hitler's promise not to take further action until the British Government had convened.

On September 16, Chamberlain was back in London, and on the 18th, at a joint session of the British and French cabinets he proposed that Czechoslovakia cede to Germany the Sudeten German territories. The decision was made without consulting or notifying Russia, or, for that matter, any other country. Three days after that Litvinoff made his famous Geneva address, roundly denouncing Hitler, and at the same time Chamberlain, for their defiance of international usage and their affront to the basic principle of international co-operation.

"Are we, perhaps, being told," he asked, "that the present master of world destiny cannot yet rise to the heights of international solidarity, but that in the future they themselves, or their successors, will reach that elevated level? We know, however, that those heights were already reached by the founders and first leaders of the League of Nations, and that the people who have replaced them are calling us back to a revision of the original intentions of those who founded the League. Here too, consequently, it is rather a case of retrogression. I fear we must draw the conclusion that it is not a question of a moratorium for the League, but of a radical change in its character.

"The bitter taste of the remedy we are offered seems to be realized by the doctors themselves, since they propose to dilute it with syrup, in the shape of the suggestion that the unanimity rule be abolished in respect of the first paragraph of Article XI, dealing with what the League must do in the event of war or threat of war. Such a suggestion might have been welcomed if Article XVI were maintained, with its list of practical measures which the League can take. But when we are asked to nullify Article XVI, the aggressor will not be frightened of Article XI, which makes it possible only morally to condemn him.

"One of those who spoke here of Article XVI had the courage to tell us that his statement applied to Article X as well. That position

seems to me to be entirely logical. After all, if we are to renounce collective measures for combating aggressors, Article X, which speaks of
the undertaking 'to respect and preserve as against external aggression
the territorial integrity and existing political independence of all members of the League,' remains an empty declaration, deprived of all
practical significance."

The force of Litvinoff's speech, the importance and weight of his
words seemed in strange contrast to any practical effect that they could
have; his appeal was still to the international public and the verdict of
history. He knew better than anyone else that the fate of Europe was
being decided, not there in Geneva, but in the little town of Godesberg
and in the purlieus of 10 Downing Street. Litvinoff must have felt the
irony of the situation doubly as he took in the imposing picture of the
great Assembly Hall—a large, high, somewhat theatrical room in
bright colors, filled with delegates, and lined with impressive murals,
brilliantly illuminated by indirect lighting. In the three galleries journalists and public listened with intense absorption, either directly to
Litvinoff who was speaking English, or, with earphones, to the inter-
preters who were translating his words simultaneously into French:

"The supporters of what amounts to the abolition of Article XVI, in
their speeches from this tribune, assured us of their loyalty and devotion to League principles. I may be permitted to ask: if the principle
of collective security and joint struggle against attacks·on the territorial
integrity and political independence of League Members are eliminated
from the League, to what other principles of the League are they
pledging their loyalty? Is it, possibly, the League's decisions regarding
the drug traffic, assistance to refugees, establishment of an international
system of signaling at level-crossings, or to the results of the statistical
and other researches of our various commissions? But what have all
these questions, important as they are in themselves, in common with
the maintenance of peace, with that main object for which the League
was set up? Could they not be considered by some organization with
a more modest and less pretentious title? Is it for this that the tax-
payers of various countries have to spend vast sums, totaling thirty
million francs a year? If we are to be realists, and to declare the idea
of the League of Nations to be a 'great illusion,' then there is no need
to create new illusions—the more so because they will deceive nobody.

"I am not saying this at all in order to try to convince those Governments and statesmen who have adopted decisions reflected in some of the speeches we have heard here. The mistakenness and harmfulness of those decisions for the whole of humanity, and first and foremost for those States which have attempted to defend them, will be shown by history.

"At a moment when the mines are being laid to blow up the organization on which were fixed the great hopes of our generation, and which stamped a definite character on the international relations of our epoch; at a moment when, by no accidental coincident, decisions are being taken outside the League which recall to us the international transactions of pre-war days, and which are bound to overturn all present conceptions of international morality and treaty obligations; at a moment when there is being drawn up a further list of sacrifices to the god of aggression and a line is under the annals of all post-war international history, with the sole conclusion that nothing succeeds like aggression—at such a moment, every State must define its role and its responsibility before its contemporaries and before history. That is why I must plainly declare here that the Soviet Government bears no responsibility whatsoever for the events now taking place, and for the fatal consequences which may inexorably ensue."

Those who listened to his statement are unanimous that Litvinoff seemed unusually dispassionate while delivering it. The Russian Foreign Commissar habitually started his speeches slowly and clearly, but accelerated until, as he became excited, he ended so rapidly, carried away by what he was saying, that he was almost impossible to follow word by word. But this time as he neared the end, his utterance became more spaced and unemphatic. Had he perhaps said these things to himself too often to be stirred by them any more? Or was his poise now rather apathy in the face of the approaching end?

For Litvinoff had foreseen this day and now quite aware that disaster had overwhelmed all his hopes, was consciously delivering his valedictory, resuming his whole diplomatic policy, summarizing all that he had done during a lifetime, fighting for peace. It was his political last will and testament. He was also speaking as public prosecutor, delivering a terrible and unanswerable indictment of the folly, selfishness, the plain incompetence of statesmen of the Great Powers, and

at the same time pronouncing as judge the verdict of guilty on a world
that had supinely connived at its own destruction.

Correspondents, bored but schooled by years of listening to official
addresses, leaned forward in their gallery, breathless with attention.
They were absorbed by the majestic marshaling of facts, the shrewd
diagnosis of the ills that vexed the heart of Europe, the robust refusal
to be humbugged by the slogans and conventions of this pretentious
institution, the clear and implacable logic. The audacious *J'accuse*
moved all of them by the tragedy, the prophetic power, the deep moral
fervor that infused these words, freighted as they were with the sense
of the impending doom now gathering over the peoples of Europe,
dreary with the feeling of defeat in the face of unspeakable catastrophe, relieved only by the sense of heavy duty honorably discharged,
and a quiet sense of pride in the record he and his country had made
as sincere and stanch defenders of peace and collaboration.

"After long doubts and hesitations, the Soviet Union joined the
League in order to add the strength of a people of a hundred and seventy millions to the forces of peace. In the present hour of bitter dis-
illusionment, the Soviet Union is far from regretting this decision, if
only because there would undoubtedly have otherwise been attempts
to attribute the alleged impotence and collapse of the League to its
absence.

"Having entered the League, the Soviet Union has been unfailingly
loyal to the League obligations which it undertook, and has faithfully
carried out, and expressed its readiness to perform, all the decisions
and even recommendations of the League which were directed to preserving peace and combating the aggressors, irrespective of whether
those decisions coincided with its immediate interests as a State.

"Such was its attitude during the attack on Ethiopia. The Soviet
delegation invariably insisted that the League should do its duty to
Spain, and it is not the fault of the Soviet Union that the Spanish
problem was withdrawn from the League of Nations and transferred
to the so-called London Non-Intervention Committee, which, as we
now all know, considers its object to be to avoid intervening in the
intervention of the aggressive countries in Spanish affairs. The activity
of the Soviet Government in relation to the Spanish events, both in the
London Committee and outside it, has been permeated with the spirit

of League of Nations principles and the established standards of international law. The same can be said likewise of the Chinese question. The Soviet delegation always insisted that the League of Nations should afford the maximum support to the victim of Japanese aggression, and those modest recommendations which the League of Nations adopted are being fulfilled more than loyally by the Soviet Government.

"Such an event as the disappearance of Austria passed unnoticed by the League of Nations. Realizing the significance of this event for the fate of the whole of Europe, and particularly of Czechoslovakia, the Soviet Government, immediately after the *Anschluss,* officially approached the other European Great Powers with a proposal for an immediate collective deliberation on the possible consequences of that event, in order to adopt collective preventive measures. To our regret, this proposal, which, if carried out, could have saved us from the alarm which all the world now feels for the fate of Czechoslovakia, did not receive its just appreciation.

"Bound to Czechoslovakia by a pact of mutual assistance, the Soviet Union abstained from any intervention in the negotiations of the Czechoslovak Government with the Sudeten Germans, considering this to be the internal business of the Czechoslovak State. We abstained from all advice to the Czechoslovak Government, considering quite inadmissible that it should be asked to make concessions to the Germans, to the detriment of its interest as a State, in order that we should be set free from the necessity of fulfilling our obligations under the treaty bearing our signature. Neither did we offer any advice in the contrary direction. We valued very highly the tact of the Czechoslovak Government, which did not even enquire of us whether we should fulfill our obligations under the pact, since obviously it had no doubt of this, and had no grounds for doubt. When, a few days before I left for Geneva, the French Government for the first time enquired as to our attitude in the event of an attack on Czechoslovakia, I gave in the name of my Government the following perfectly clear and unambiguous reply:

"'We intend to fulfill our obligations under the pact and, together with France, to afford assistance to Czechoslovakia by the ways open to us. Our War Department is ready immediately to participate in a conference with representatives of the French and Czechoslovak War Departments, in order to discuss the measures appropriate to the moment. Independently of this, we should consider desirable that the question be raised at the League of Nations if only as yet under Article XI, with the object, first, of mobilizing public opinion and, secondly, of ascertaining the position of certain other States, whose passive aid might be extremely valuable.' It was necessary, however, to exhaust all means of averting an armed conflict, and we considered one such method to be an immediate consultation between the great powers of Europe and other interested States, in order if possible to decide on the terms of a collective démarche.

"This is how our reply was framed. It was only two days ago that the Czechoslovak Government addressed a formal enquiry to my Government as to whether the Soviet Union is prepared, in accordance with the Soviet-Czech pact, to render Czechoslovakia immediate and effective aid if France, loyal to her obligations, will render similar assistance, to which my Government gave a clear answer in the affirmative.

"I believe it will be admitted that both were replies of a loyal signatory of an international agreement and of a faithful servant of the League. It is not our fault if no effect was given to our proposals, which, I am convinced, could have produced the desired results, both in the interest of Czechoslovakia, and in those of all Europe and of general peace. Unfortunately, other steps were taken, which have led, and which could not but lead, to such a capitulation as is bound sooner or later to have quite incalculable and disastrous consequences.

"To avoid a problematic war today and receive in return a certain large-scale war tomorrow—moreover, at the price of assuaging the appetites of insatiable aggressors and of the destruction or mutilation of sovereign States—is not to act in the spirit of the Covenant of the League of Nations. To grant bonuses for saber-rattling and recourse to arms for the solution of international problems—in other words, to reward and encourage aggressive super-imperialism—is not to act in the spirit of the Briand-Kellogg Pact.

"The Soviet Government takes pride in the fact that it has no part in such a policy, and has invariably pursued the principles of the two pacts I have mentioned, which were approved by nearly every nation in the world. Nor has it any intention of abandoning them for the future, being convinced that in present conditions it is impossible otherwise to safeguard a genuine peace and genuine international justice. It calls upon other Governments likewise to return to this path."

2

Litvinoff had worked with unusual care on the speech, yet he knew that words could no longer arrest the fatal international processes and had openly said as much to several people. On September 16 he had told Louis Fischer, for instance: "They [the English and French] have sold out Czechoslovakia"; * and he had made a similar remark to the former American Ambassador in Moscow, Joseph E. Davies.†

That Litvinoff's speech was one of the greatest of our time, a document which will find high place in any history of the twentieth century, the correspondents fully realized as they listened, yet outside Russia, the text took only a secondary place in the world's newspapers. Much "hotter" news was spread across the front pages.

For Chamberlain had conferred the next day, September 22, in Godesberg with Hitler, who had again raised his price for what Chamberlain persisted in calling "peace in our time." The Fuehrer now, among other cruel and unreasonable demands, insisted on the immediate occupation of Sudetenland by German troops; nor would he even guarantee the new frontiers of Czechoslovakia.

The English Prime Minister was annoyed, but he was even more disturbed when Hitler showed on a map that he wanted much more land than originally had been considered Sudetenland. Chamberlain left Godesberg on September 23. Prague mobilized once more. The French Premier, Edouard Daladier, came out openly against Hitler's Godesberg demands.

Events were moving faster and faster. By September 25 the English and French Cabinets had met in London, and France was assured of British help if she should be involved in war. Chamberlain sent one of his friends on a flying trip to Berlin hoping to calm Hitler, as he was scheduled for a speech the next day in the Berlin *Sportpalast.* President

* Louis Fischer, *Men and Politics*, p. 561, New York, 1941.
† Joseph E. Davies, *Mission to Moscow*, p. 1, New York, 1941.

Roosevelt spoke out, appealing to those in authority to settle their differences without resorting to war.

In the *Sportpalast* speech the Fuehrer was not quite so violent as London had feared. He demanded his pound of flesh, but he added that, aside from Sudetenland, he had no further territorial claims in Europe.

Mussolini, prompted by the French Foreign Minister, Georges Bonnet, now moved for a conference to settle everything among the five powers: England, France, Germany, Italy and Czechoslovakia. But Hitler would agree to only a four-power conference. Czechoslovakia was not to be invited, though it was her fate that was going to be decided.

Russia was conspicuously omitted from both proposals, though she was the one power ready to defend Czechoslovakia, despite the fact that she had less obligation to do so than any of the others. In the first place, when Czechoslovakia was created after World War I by the other Allied governments, Russia had not participated in the councils. In the second place, Czechoslovakia had not only been one of the last countries to recognize the Soviet Union, but it had been the seat of active hostility against the Soviets. This was in part due to the influence of France, where, since the fall of Blum and the disintegration of the Popular Front, a succession of governments and the most powerful elements in finance, industry, the Church and social life, to say nothing of the odious Laval, had all been anti-Soviet. But it was also in part due to elements inside Czechoslovakia—the reactionary Agrarian Party, and the National Democratic Party which had maintained close friendly relations with anti-Bolshevik Social Revolutionaries in Russia. Czech State funds had even been used to subsidize publications of anti-Soviet-Russian groups, and Czech leaders had repeatedly shown such interest in exiled Russian youths, grooming them to become intellectual leaders after the fall of Communism in Russia, that there had even been a serious question of State support for a White Russian University in Prague. Other Czech circles encouraged certain East Galician political groups which could be played against Moscow.

Edouard Beneš, on the other hand, though he may have been involved in some of these activities to a certain degree, had hoped to make his country the mediator between Russia and the rest of the world and had done everything in his power to bring the Soviet Union into the League of Nations and in general to act as intermediary between the Soviets and the West European cultures, but without much result.*

Throughout this sequence of fatal events, despite the hopelessness of the situation, Litvinoff continued to make every effort. On September 23 he declared in a session of the Sixth Commission in Geneva that even after Beneš had accepted the British-French conditions, Soviet Russia would still be willing to aid Czechoslovakia if she were attacked. On the same day the Soviet Ambassador in Prague, M. Alexandrovski, had given Beneš the same assurance, adding that Soviet Russia would help even if France would not help at all, although Russia was under no legal obligation to participate until France had begun the discharge of her responsibilities. Immediately after delivering this note, Alexandrovski went to Moscow to get more specific instructions.

In the meantime, Beneš, who speaks Russian well, telephoned to Stalin, and also several times to Litvinoff in Geneva, and the Czech envoy in Moscow, Zdenek Fierlinger, was in constant touch with the Narkomindel (Soviet Russian Foreign Office—*Narodnyi Komissariat Inostrannykh Del*).

Hitler, Mussolini, Chamberlain and Daladier met on September 29 and 30, in Munich. This time Hitler got everything that he had demanded at Godesberg. At one o'clock on the morning of September 30, Chamberlain and Daladier gave in completely and, in effect, signed what Hitler dictated.

In the Hradshin Castle in Prague the Czech Government was in permanent session. It could not reach a decision, even after Chamberlain let it be known that England and France would not fight for Czechoslovakia if she rejected the Munich settlement. So the French and the British Ambassadors in Prague went to work on Beneš, informing him during the fatal night of September 29 to September 30, that he must accept the Munich settlement. Otherwise France and England not only would leave Czechoslovakia to her fate, but would actually participate on Germany's side in imposing military sanctions against her.

* Louis Fischer, *The Soviets in World Affairs*, II, pp. 505 ff., London and New York. 1930.

Beneš said: "This is blackmail," and it was.

Alexandrovski meanwhile rushed back from Moscow with a detailed note on how Soviet Russia would help Czechoslovakia. He arrived at Prague in the middle of the night, dashed to the Hradshin and sent his note into the Government conference. A few minutes later the Chief of Protocol, Smitly, came back, and reported sadly:

"It is too late; the voting is all over."

Daladier, returning to Paris with some apprehension lest the French population rise against him, was astonished at the large crowds roaring approval for having (as they thought) saved France from the dreaded horrors of war. Mr. Chamberlain was still full of illusions. Stepping out of the plane in Croydon, he was jubilantly certain that he had achieved "peace in our time."

Litvinoff knew better. The Moscow press knew better. It wrote: "Munich is a crime against real peace." The American press was also scornful and skeptical.

The Czechoslovakian Government had been forced to accept the Munich agreement by pressure, not only from those who had helped formulate it, but also from within, especially from the Anti-Soviet Agrarian Party which urged that occupation of the country by Hitler would be better than its defense by Voroshilov. The Minister of Interior, Gerny, and the Minister of Defense, Machnik, were both members of that party and they had joined in demanding that the Government repudiate Russian help and accede to Hitler's demands. Associated with them was Yaroslav Preiss, one of the leaders who had had a meeting at his house during the day, of big industrialists and representatives of important banks.

Bonnet's crooked stratagems were also a large factor in the tragedy. Chamberlain may have honestly believed that he was promoting peace, but Bonnet cannot be credited with any noble motives. During a long conference with Litvinoff in Geneva in September, even before Chamberlain's trip to Berchtesgaden, he had been assured that Russia would help Czechoslovakia. Yet the very next day Bonnet informed the French cabinet that Russia *would not* help Czechoslovakia and, furthermore—another untruth—that Rumania would not give Russia permission to march troops through its territory. When Bonnet's colleagues found out that he had lied, it was already too late. And, of course, the scandal was hushed up.

Bonnet falsified facts in other ways also. When the English Government told the French Government (on September 26) that it would come to the aid of France if France would fight for Czechoslovakia, Bonnet immediately announced to the French press that this communiqué had not yet been confirmed. When the English confirmation finally appeared, it was too late to make much impression on the French people. The very next day, September 27, Hitler mobilized. Bonnet took steps to have the news denied in the Paris press that evening.

Yet though Bonnet's maneuvers had been grossly dishonest, and Mr. Chamberlain might claim good intentions in his own defense, the latter was primarily responsible for the tragic blunder. For the French could hardly resist any determined pressure from Britain; the Bank of France was too dependent upon the Bank of England. Moreover, Chamberlain's purposes were somewhat devious and his sympathies curiously constricted. He gave no evidence of caring one way or the other about Czechoslovakia; but he was certainly very much concerned about Russia, which in his heart he feared and deeply disliked.

Dreadful as were the consequences of Munich and the Chamberlain policy of appeasement, it did achieve one not inconsiderable value—it demonstrated to the whole world that England wanted peace. It convinced the English public that every conceivable effort and risk had been undertaken to safeguard the peace and demonstrated to the entire nation that Hitler was the aggressor, on his head the guilt and on his hands the blood for all that followed. On the other hand, members of his own party could see no advantage in the transaction and Mr. Dalton quotes the comment of a well known Conservative on the Munich appeasement: "The Government had to choose between war and shame; they chose shame and they'll get war too."

Czechoslovakia, as Litvinoff knew, was for Chamberlain never more than a pawn. Litvinoff was entirely convinced, as were many others, both at the time and since, that Chamberlain's basic policy was to save England by inducing Germany to fight Russia. That was why he did not wish to have Litvinoff at Munich. Litvinoff saw and understood too much and talked much too plainly.

Litvinoff has said more than once that he realized perfectly that he was left in an impossible position in Geneva, and having always prided himself on being a political realist, it was small comfort for him to know that the world's sympathy was on his side. He was sure that if the question had been put to a vote, he would have carried at least the Anglo-Saxon countries, and he thinks possibly he might even have carried Germany, since her people were at the time definitely and unmistakably against war. The spontaneous demonstration for Chamberlain in Munich proved it. The cool reception of Hitler's *Sportpalast* speech, September 26, proved it again, while the sullen and hostile reception of the military demonstration, the fake "march through" in Berlin on the night of September 27, alarmed even Hitler, and a number of his leading generals, among them General Beck, were decidedly anxious. Germany was not ready for war.

But Litvinoff also knew that in this case the people had very little voice in the decisions. Public sentiment could not help Czechoslovakia or Europe. Litvinoff knew that Hitler was not bluffing, that he was determined to go to war if his demands were not met. Only a supreme alliance against the Nazis by all the nations involved would perhaps check Hitler's plan. Litvinoff knew, too, that England and France were bluffing and that they had no intention of fighting for Czechoslovakia. Why otherwise, as Winston Churchill wrote on December 1, 1938, should Hitler at the time of Munich have concentrated three-quarters of his army along the Czechoslovakian border, leaving the Western frontier almost unprotected? Hitler likewise was perfectly sure that France and England had no intention of fighting. His foreign minister, Joachim von Ribbentrop, had brought him convincing assurances. Thus Litvinoff was faced with the fact that everything he had fought for since he had arrived in Geneva was about to collapse.

3

In spite of all this, Litvinoff did not give up. He still sought some means to help Czechoslovakia. Poland, as he said to friends, would never agree to the passage of Russian troops. Therefore, he concentrated on Rumania.

A sufficient army could not go from Russia to Czechoslovakia over

Rumania's existing roads and bridges. A new two-way railroad was being built to the eastern part of Czechoslovakia and then into Rumania which would have been useful, but though construction had been in progress for many years, it was not yet finished. Now, work went ahead throughout the twenty-four hours, with giant searchlights during the night. It was a race against time, against the inevitable, like Litvinoff's last efforts in Geneva.

In any case, Litvinoff felt that Russia could send planes to Czechoslovakia via Rumania, but Rumania would have to consent. He worked hard to secure her permission, though without much hope of success. He took the matter up with the Rumanian Foreign Minister, Cafencu. To his surprise and encouragement, Cafencu said that Rumania might grant everything he wanted. King Carol, approached by both Cafencu and Beneš, agreed to permit transportation of troops across Rumania if he were satisfied that the Russians would not leave any forces in Rumania, and if Rumania handled the administration of all transportation.

But shortly afterwards—on September 14—King Carol held a Crown Council and Litvinoff was notified that the decision was reversed. Nothing could be done at that late hour. However, the King suggested that a conference take place in Bucharest. Litvinoff agreed to go there—perhaps, as he remarked with bitter irony, to show Chamberlain and Daladier that he, too, had a conference to attend.

King Carol evidently had hoped that some hitch would develop at the last moment. When none occurred, he informed Litvinoff that the conference would have to be postponed. There might, he said, be one in October. But by that time everything was over. Czechoslovakia had been dismembered, and Hitler was preparing his next stroke.

Litvinoff packed his trunks. He bade good-by to his few real friends in Geneva. He told them that he thought he would not be back, that he had already lost too much time there. Now he was sure, as was Stalin, that no English or French policy remained on which to base a Russian policy for peace.

On January 16, 1939, the *New York Times* was advised from Geneva: "Among the League luminaries not present at this time is Maxim M. Litvinoff, and his absence is taken to underline Russia's partial withdrawal into her shell as far as international politics are concerned."

A few months later, on May 3, newspaper headlines all over the world reported Litvinoff's resignation.

For a few days this was a sensation. What had happened? Had he been purged? Was he to disappear forever from the political stage? On one thing all commentators were agreed: that Litvinoff's retirement from the political scene was effective long before his actual resignation. Since France and England had succumbed to Hitler, there had been no place for Litvinoff or his policy of collective security, which they had rejected and sabotaged.

Litvinoff had left Geneva on September 25, 1938. His last days there were void of special events. Only minor officials of minor countries were present. The big-wigs of international politics were either preparing to go to Munich or were watching Munich from their capitals.

He went away in a melancholy mood. But even at the end, his sense of humor did not desert him altogether. He commented dryly on the fact that at the station only newspaper men waited for him. This was ironic, because Litvinoff had never altogether liked newspaper men. He termed them "evils, but necessary evils." On the other hand, newspaper men had always liked Litvinoff immensely, recognizing immediately that he made good copy. They had hailed his first sensational speeches in Geneva, and fully understood and appreciated his last and greatest speech. Now they came to see him off. No matter what they thought of his politics or of Communism in general, they admired without reserve his courage, consistency, his firm and brilliant mind, his vision and his realism. Besides, he had a wonderful sense of humor, and he had never let them down.

4

Litvinoff's trip from Geneva to Moscow was to be his last for a long time. How many he had made during the preceding ten, twenty years! How often had he raced from one end of Europe to the other! Once he had visited the United States. The nights and days spent on international express trains and planes, added together, would total many months: London, Warsaw, Berlin, Paris, Brussels, Rome, Ankara, Geneva, Copenhagen, Stockholm, the Hague, Genoa and Geneva and always Geneva again.

Sometimes he traveled alone, sometimes he headed delegations whose members filled many reserved compartments: staff from the Narkomindel, experts, translators, secretaries, couriers. There were so many frontiers, so many countries in Europe, so many representatives of governments to talk to, so many treaties to be discussed, to be drawn up, to be signed, to be ratified—treaties of neutrality, of guaranty and of non-aggression; settlements of disputes; treaties of mutual assistance and of friendship; provisional agreements and agreements on trade relations and navigation.

He had not always been welcome when he undertook these trips. Many countries, at one time, had not even allowed a representative of the Soviet Union to enter. In others, people were suspicious and grossly discourteous, apparently even afraid of Soviet diplomats, or at least acting as if they expected them to be unshaven, shabby, ill-mannered and downright offensive.

Litvinoff speaks Russian, French, English and German and reads and understands another half-dozen languages. Nicholas Titulescu once said jokingly that he could not make out which was Litvinoff's native tongue. He had needed all these languages to do his work in those last twenty years, while he traveled over Europe.

CHAPTER TWO

Youth and Early Development

LITVINOFF WAS BORN on July 17, 1876, in Belostok, which is on the Moscow-Warsaw railway where it crosses the Prussian frontier line. His father was Moses Wallach, his mother, Anna née Perlo, and he was named Meer Genokh Moisseevitch Wallach. The family had been settled in Belostok for generations, and the grandparents on both sides are buried in the huge Jewish cemetery there.

His father was a produce merchant who traveled through the region buying up the local crops, and into Prussia, his chief market, but later he took a position in the town bank. He was an intelligent man interested in contemporary literature, especially Turgenev, Dostoevski and Tolstoi, with a well-stocked library, so that in a way the house was a center for the Belostok intelligentsia. People would drop in to borrow a book and sit down round the samovar to talk over the latest news from St. Petersburg or Moscow, or the most recent publication of Alexander Herzen or Mikhail Bakunin. The discussion, often prolonged, in the typical Russian way, until late into the night, frequently turned to the possibility of some kind of revolution. But it was only mild middle-class talk: things had to be changed; things should be thus and so; Russia would be better off with this or that; and the feeling spent itself in volubility. Not one of them would have dreamed of doing anything about it.

Anna Perlo, a hard-working little woman with a kind face and big heart, had been married before, as had Wallach, and there were three groups of children: hers by her first husband, his by his first wife, and those of their own marriage, in all, in addition to Meer, later to be called Maxim, two daughters and two other sons.

Belostok was a small city but had been growing since the first textile mills were established there in 1845, until in 1876 its population had increased to about 60,000—approximately 75 per cent Jewish, the rest

Russians, White Russians and Lithuanians; and it was quite a busy place, for the peasants round about sold their produce there: chiefly potatoes, rye, oats, wheat, flax and hemp. Moreover, new industries were springing up about the time of Litvinoff's birth—woolen, silk and felt hat factories—in a well-marked wave of prosperity.

The city was proud of an immense park of conifers and large peat bogs where wild oxen had been kept for more than 150 years, a jealously preserved tradition which made the town famous in a small way, and it also boasted the provincial Governor's palace; but the average citizen living there, year in and year out, would have been more aware of the dismal winter months and the cold wet days of spring and autumn, with the long main street crowded with carriages slogging through the deep mud.

2

When the little Meer (today Maxim) was five years old—in 1881—the quiet, comfortable life of the Wallach family was sharply interrupted. In the dead of night special police agents of what was then called the Third Section, demanded admittance to the house. They ransacked the living-room, went through all the books and papers in the library, and finally took the father away, though they had not found anything incriminating. He was thrown into prison and accused of having foreign connections with elements hostile to Russia.

Little Meer, awakened by the turmoil, cried when his father was taken away, and though he could not understand what was happening, he has never forgotten the midnight visitation—which must have been for so young a child a terrifying experience.

The father was kept in prison for about six weeks, most of the time incommunicado. Not even his wife could see him. Once she took the little boy, as he still vividly remembers, to the office of the public prosecutor, probably, he now thinks, to arouse sympathy, for his mother wept there in the public prosecutor's office. Later the child visited his father in prison, and this made a lasting impression on him.

Finally, the authorities admitted that the charges against Wallach were without foundation—they had, as it turned out, been concocted by a commercial rival, one of his very few enemies—and he was released. His friends were numerous and loyal and a crowd waited for hours in the square before the prison in order to welcome him.

Soon all was again normal in the Wallach household, but from that time on the arrest and imprisonment were an oft-told family tale, and at last Wallach wrote it all down for his descendants to read.

It was the cruel and unjust execution of Lenin's brother, to whom he was profoundly devoted, that gave to Lenin's whole life a focus and drive that made of him one of the most potent figures of recent times.

Did the memory of the terrifying midnight raid, the peril to a loved father, the threat to the security of the home and the gross injustice of it all contribute a similar even though less conscious motivation to Litvinoff's life, that helped to give it concentration, unity and continuity in his fight for freedom and justice?

The children were naturally divided somewhat into three groups, with conscious differences and competing loyalties. It was an instructive miniature world with normal tensions and conflicts but in this case resolved by good will and the orderly government of wise parents. It was a good education for young Wallach and perhaps encouraged in him faith that different groups of human beings can and must learn to live together.

3

The family was devoutly religious, and it was the boy's duty to go with his father to the Temple on Friday evenings and Saturday mornings, but he went merely as a duty imposed by his parents, without considering the inner meaning of religion. "Going to the synagogue," Litvinoff says, "was something like doing homework." Yet Litvinoff was not unresponsive to the religious inspiration normal to adolescent youth. It was for him a passing phase of idealism to be replaced by faith in works. It survived half-unconsciously in loyalty to over-individual values, to the sense of a great cause that, without sentimentality, exacts of each his uttermost service, which is likely to give direction, consistency and driving power to a clear-minded, robust personality.

For years Litvinoff took for granted that everyone was Jewish; when he found out how many religions there were, even in a small place like Belostok, he was at first bewildered, then he began to think. Something, he concluded, must be wrong for so many religions to compete, and gradually he left the formal Jewish faith.

Jews had been in a difficult and unhappy position in Russia since 1796. Prior to that the Jewish population had been negligible, only a few thousand in the Ukraine, but the Third Partition of Poland brought under Russian sovereignty for the first time a great number of Jews. The result was a law forbidding them to live outside the West Russian provinces.

In 1804 restrictions were enacted which, with modifications, remained in force until the abdication of the Czar in 1917: Jews were not to own land or attend schools of higher learning. After 1850 merchants wealthy enough to pay certain taxes could live where they wished; later, Jewish artisans were permitted to settle in a number of provinces; in 1879 a small proportion of Jews was admitted to schools of higher learning, and thereafter a good many exceptionally gifted and prominent Jewish scholars and artists were accepted socially. Russian liberals and intellectuals were always opposed to anti-Semitism.

Indeed, the Jewish persecutions under the Czars, such as the pogroms of the 80's and 90's and the abominable massacre at Kishinev in 1903 when scores were killed, several hundred wounded and 700 houses destroyed, and the wave of pogroms after the 1905 revolution, were inspired by Government agents in an effort to divert popular discontent, and with the rising tide of revolution, the masses came to understand this. Jews and revolutionaries, moreover, were victims of the same persecution from the *Ochrana,* the secret political police, and the Black Hundred (*Chernaia Sotnia*) shot down starving workers, assassinated liberal leaders, organized pogroms and other forms of illegal violence.

4

Young Meer Wallach went to a *Realschule*—in Belostok the German term was used—which was next best to a *Gymnasium,* and began reading books, though at first without any deep interest. The family and their friends spoke Yiddish, so that Russian was none too easy for him, which perhaps for the time being impeded his response.

When he was in his mid-teens a young man whom he knew decided to emigrate to the United States, and he explained his plans to the adolescent Meer. He would, he said, cut all ties, leave everything behind. Only by breaking with the past could one succeed in a new life, by forgetting the old standards, ideas, laws, even family bonds. The youthful Wallach listened, remembered, and years afterwards took heed.

A little later, when he was seventeen—in 1893—he left school and went into the army, the only available way to break out of the narrow confines of a provincial town. He hoped that he would be sent to a big city, perhaps even St. Petersburg or Moscow, but he was disappointed. He was sent south to Baku and he still remembers the journey vividly, his first trip outside Belostok. It took nine days, with a whole day's stop-over at several junctions, and for the first time he saw and felt the vastness of Russia.

Young Wallach, a good-looking, husky lad, judging from a photograph taken then—was assigned to the 17th Caucasian Regiment, and the examining medical officer was immediately impressed with his energy and robustness.

The commander, Colonel Aleksander Aleksandrovitch Fell, son of a Russianized German, was ambitious to have his regiment chosen as a guard regiment, with all the prestige and privileges which that entailed. Consequently he was very strict with his men, was indeed noted for his rigorous discipline. Young Wallach was anxious lest he could not measure up to the requirements.

But in the five years that he stayed in the army, though he was never promoted, he made a satisfactory record, enjoyed the experience and profited greatly by it, learning to take orders and to lead a well-regulated life—virtues that he would hardly have acquired in his own family.

He profited most, he is now convinced, from friendship with his Captain, a Bulgarian named Slugov who had joined the Russian army because his parents wanted him to fight the Turks. When Slugov explained this to him, Wallach was struck by the number of nations and races that felt called on, for ambiguous reasons, to fight each other.

Slugov, a man of intellectual bent, took an interest in Wallach, and held long conversations with the lad which opened his mind to new ideas. He introduced him to many books, especially by liberals of the time, who were struggling to find some way out of the deepening misery of the Russian people, which was largely due to the incompetence and heartlessness of the Russian autocracy. At first the boy's old feeling of inadequacy in the Russian language embarrassed him, but that was soon surmounted and he began to read avidly. He devoured almost any book that came his way, but in literature the writers who counted most with him were Vissarion Belinski, the great critic; Nicholas Gabrilovich Chernishevski, the Nihilist author of the propaganda novel *Chto Delat* (*What Is To Be Done*); Herzen, Dostoevski and, perhaps most of all, Turgenev. Later, Slugov gave the boy some French lessons and introduced him to French literature. But he did not limit his reading to belles lettres by any means. Already he was reading Nihilist publicists like Dmitri Pisarev and Nikolai Dobroliubov and studying Marx and the history of Socialism.

Meanwhile he was learning, too, from concrete experience. His handwriting was satisfactory and having perfected his Russian, he soon qualified for clerical duty. He was assigned as bookkeeper to a sergeant in the Service of Supplies named Andrei. Here he had a chance to see just how his superior had, in a few years, appropriated for himself thousands of rubles—an accepted practice. Everyone who could was enriching himself in such ways, and however much Andrei might embezzle, he did at least feed and clothe the regiment well. Slugov encouraged Wallach to think that, if he stayed in the army, he might even some day get Andrei's place.

But before the five years of his enlistment were up—in 1898—his army career came to a sudden end. In one of the Baku factories—Litvinoff has forgotten which—there was a fairly large strike of workers who were just beginning to organize, which involved clashes with the police, and finally required military intervention. The 17th Regiment was called out and Colonel Fell was delighted. Now he could demonstrate the efficiency of his regiment and his superiors would see why the 17th should be made a guard regiment. Slugov, on the contrary, was depressed at the prospect of having to shoot workers, and Wallach so completely shared this view that, when the order was given to fire into a crowd of some 300 strikers, he held his fire. He was already aware of his solidarity with the working people. He was sent back to barracks, but Slugov never reported the matter to the Colonel, rather hushing it up and eventually getting Litvinoff a discharge for some petty violation of regulations. These are the facts out of which Nazi propaganda concocted a crude story of desertion.

Today Litvinoff shows little outward sign of having been a soldier; but the 17th Regiment in Baku is called the Maxim Litvinoff Regiment.

5

After leaving the army, the twenty-two-year-old Wallach went to Kiev where he worked as a clerk, progressively changing jobs until he found a place in a sugar factory owned by Baron Ginsburg, one of the richest industrialists in Russia. Here he advanced so rapidly that soon he was manager of the factory, drawing a high salary, for he had considerable talent for business, being exact, orderly, clearheaded and sensible. He would doubtless have been very successful had he been content to be a business man.

But he was already moving out of that sphere. The only external signs were, first, that his reading, more intense and industrious than ever, had shifted wholly from literature to books on economics, sociology, and politics, including pamphlets of every aspect and tinge; and second, that—to his friends' perplexity—though he was making good money and living with great frugality, he seemed never to be in funds.

He could not explain, for his money was going into an underground political group recently organized, one of many then active in Russia, the Social Democratic Labor Party. It was an outlawed organization and if any leader was discovered and identified he had to flee Russia on the instant, usually to Switzerland. Otherwise, he would certainly be imprisoned, or exiled to Siberia. For reasons of safety the Party was subdivided into small groups who knew each other but no one outside that "cell," so that the secret police or *Ochrana* would not be likely to get more than one cell at a time.

Litvinoff, having finally chosen the Social Democratic Labor Party from among a number of possible affiliations, applied for membership late in 1898 and was accepted almost at once, with a summons to the home of a man whom he knew as Yankel Gordon, who gave him his Party pass. His "cell" consisted of seven members.

Litvinoff himself considers that his real history begins at this moment, or possibly five years later when he met Lenin in London, for on becoming an underground party member, he followed the course recommended years before by his friend emigrating from Belostok, likewise taking a cue from his hero Bazarov in Turgenev's *Fathers and Sons*. He cut all ties, even the most intimate, and obliterated the past so successfully that he has practically forgotten his younger years, so that now he is sometimes entertained to have others recall childhood anecdotes which he pushed out of his mind nearly a half century ago. He is proud of his parents—the faithful mother who died a few years after he became a revolutionary, the courageous upright father, who died in 1909; but he chose what seemed to him the greater duty—to be a good revolutionary rather than a good son, so he refuses to sentimentalize over the long-since severed family relations, the more so as he thinks those early years had little or no bearing on the significant part of his life—a denial of early formative influences that few psychologists would accept as valid.

Wallach was determined to further the Party by every means in his power without regard to his personal interests. He meant business and committed himself to his new career with complete devotion, apparently without reservations of any kind, so when he heard that the Kiev branch badly needed a printing press, he immediately offered not only his entire savings, but also as much more as he could borrow. The press was bought and he spent his night hours turning out leaflets and pamphlets. One night, after Wallach had been in the Party about two years, while he and his friends were busy operating the press, the police raided their hiding place. There had been a traitor in their group. Litvinoff thinks that it was a man named Pudken who had arrived with credentials from the Moscow Party organization and been admitted without further investigation. Litvinoff and his comrades were arrested, tried and sentenced to two years in prison.

Political prisoners were allowed to read, so Litvinoff used his time in the Kiev Prison to improve his knowledge of English, learned to play chess and tap his moves on the wall of his cell to his neighbors, and extended his acquaintance with Socialist principles and the history of the movement. Among the literature that reached him were the first numbers of a new revolutionary paper called *Iskra* (*The Spark*), just getting started by Russian émigrés in Geneva, and in one of these he read, in an article signed "Lenin":

"We shall have to form men who not only devote to the revolution their free evenings, but their whole life. We must form an organization so large that we can carry through a definite specialization of duties for the different kinds of our work."

Wallach rededicated his life to the revolution.

6

Liberal and revolutionary ideas had been increasingly influential in Europe for nearly a hundred years when Karl Marx and Friedrich Engels, in their *Communist Manifesto,* written in 1847, launched the slogan: "Workers of the World, Unite." The first step towards complying came in 1862 when, during the London World Exhibition, English labor unions called French and German delegations to a conference. Another conference the next year prepared for a permanent organization, and on September 26, 1864, was founded the Committee of the First International, headed by Marx, Giuseppe Mazzini and Louis Auguste Blanqui. Two years later the first congress was held in Geneva, with sixty delegates from Belgium, Italy, Portugal, the United States, Denmark, Holland, Austria and Germany. Three years later another congress assembled at Eisenach, Germany.

The movement was checked in 1871 by the defeat of the Paris Commune, and the next year the international organization fell apart, owing chiefly to a conflict between Bakunin and Marx, who moved the headquarters from London to New York.

No further action to unite the workers of the world was attempted for seventeen years, then two congresses met in Paris (1889), one called by the anti-Marxist English union, the other composed of Marxist unions of various countries, constituting the first assembly of the Second International. This was the organization which established May First as the international workers' holiday.

Thereafter yearly congresses considered Socialist Party problems, especially tactics, usually proposing compromise solutions, and the movement grew rapidly. In 1904, 444 delegates met at Amsterdam; in 1910 at Copenhagen 896 representing twenty-three countries. But no real cohesion was developed. The strength was merely numerical and therefore largely illusory.

In Russia in the middle of the nineteenth century, practical political and social thinking was still almost a hundred years behind that of the rest of Europe. The economic system was based on peasant serfdom, but 'after the severe defeat of Russia in the Crimean War, in 1856, about the time Alexander II succeeded to the throne, a new trend became gradually apparent, although it had its roots in earlier thinking and aspiration. Intelligentsia—university professors and students and especially writers who had traveled abroad—sincere, generous and compassionate minded thinkers, came back to denounce Russian conditions. They founded many protest parties, none of them, however, immediately effective, for they had no practical experience and there were no indigenous traditions to guide them. Outstanding among these leaders were Herzen, the liberal writer of genuine power whose ideas were markedly in advance of his time, and Bakunin, the founder of Russian Nihilism, a party and doctrine that have been misunderstood in the West, owing chiefly doubtless to the name, which was not of the adherents' own choice, but a sobriquet affixed to them by Turgenev in *Fathers and Sons* (1864). The doctrine represented an attempt to apply to social questions the method of natural science, which the later nineteenth century found so impressively successful, and was consequently, like all Positivism, energetically opposed to religion. Other major tenets were government by a federation of independent communes, and economic collectivism.

Literary realists without specific political aims were more influential in waking up the people. Tolstoi and Turgenev, neither of whom was a revolutionary, and Dostoevski, who after a revolutionary youth became quite reactionary, described so specifically and vividly governmental corruption and the merciless conditions which were grinding the mass of the people that increasing thousands were moved to pity, indignation and protest. The spirit of revolt was being kindled, and the smoldering flame could not be extinguished by the most savage repression of the ensuing decade.

Alexander II tried at first a few half-hearted reforms such as elective representative assemblies, Zemstva, but these were only in certain provinces and they had few powers. Then in 1861 he liberated the serfs, a really important step; but not long after that he showed himself just as reactionary and cruel as his predecessors, ruthlessly crushing a Polish revolt, establishing strict censorship throughout Russia, reducing education to a minimum, and increasing the secret police, the "Third Section."

These repressive measures rallied recruits to the ranks of the Nihilists and Anarchists, and promoted a terrorism, which focussed first on the Czar himself. On March 12, 1881, while Alexander was returning to the palace from inspecting troops and driving along the Catharine Canal, one of a group of conspirators threw a bomb at him. It missed and he exclaimed, "Thank God, I am untouched." Another conspirator, named Grinevitsky, shouted, "It is too soon to thank God," and threw another bomb which tore open the Czar's abdomen, shattered his legs and terribly disfigured his face. In a few hours he was dead.

His son, Alexander III, by continuing to fight stubbornly and cruelly against any reform, greatly augmented the revolutionary movement—now reinforced, especially in the larger cities, by the urban working class that was rapidly developing with the new industrialization, for cheap labor had attracted foreign capital and factories were springing up in many of the great cities.

Concomitantly, trade unionism was coming in from England and Germany, and the first Marxist group in Russia, called the "Emancipation of Labor" (*Osvobozhdenie Truda*), was formed in 1883 by Georg V. Plekhanov. An émigré living in Geneva, he and his friends translated into Russian the works of Marx and Engels, and got them printed and smuggled into Russia. They also circulated simple expositions of Socialism in many brochures and leaflets. Thereby, as Lenin afterwards said, they "laid the theoretical foundation for the Social Democratic movement and took the first step towards the working-class movement."

On October 20, 1894, Nicholas II, son of Alexander III, who had married the daughter of the King of Denmark, assumed control of all the Russias. Nicholas was a thoroughly inferior character. Former Czars had been perhaps as ill-equipped, ill-prepared and unprincipled, but Nicholas II had more difficult problems to face than most of them had had, for in some respects Russia was coming abreast now of the rest of Europe, and meanwhile her own sins—the neglect of the peasantry, lack of education, corrupt, cruel and incompetent administration and a reactionary State Church—were catching up with her with a vengeance. By 1902 the working class numbered nearly 7,000,000— 5,500,000 men, the rest women—roughly, half urban and half rural laborers. The latter included about a million landless peasants, most of whom went after the harvest to the towns, where they worked during the winter and picked up revolutionary ideas, for the movement was growing fast in many classes—students, writers, artists, factory workers, and members of the Zemstva, who, despite their lack of administrative or legislative powers, were a strong and beneficent influence in rural life and did exercise some restraining and directive influence on local governments.

The itinerant workers took their new and exciting notions back to the country in the Spring and there they found listeners made sympathetic to suggestions of reform or even revolt by their desperate circumstances. Only about 4 per cent of the landed peasantry owned as much as a dozen acres each. Of the remainder, nearly half had only about three to ten acres, while the rest—approximately half of the total —had to try to grub out a livelihood on two and a half acres or less. Not 2 per cent had as many as twenty head of cattle, and nearly two-thirds did not have even a single cow.

Thus revolutionary flames were creeping through the land, and to deal with the increasing distress and proportionately increasing peril, Nicholas II had in his entourage only one promising man, the Prime Minister, Sergius Witte. Formerly a journalist, then a railway and financial expert, Witte had some understanding of the situation and of the palliatives without which there would be disaster. But in 1903 the Czar dismissed him because V. K. von Plehve, a reactionary of incredible cruelty, and the Third Section thought him too progressive.

Thereafter the Czar was surrounded entirely by reactionaries blind enough to think that they could arrest progress and maintain the status quo by repressive measures of the utmost severity. This policy only piled up grievances, increased bitterness and steadily undermined a government already utterly inadequate to the demands of the time. The Czar, by his ignorance and conceit, by his suspicions, vacillation and caprice, began with blind obstinacy to dig his own grave and write the doom of his dynasty.

This is the Russia in which was formed the Social Democratic Party in 1898. The Party itself was created by uniting scattered groups already functioning without correlation in St. Petersburg, Moscow, Yekaterinoslav and various other towns including Kiev where, that same year, Wallach became a member. Nine men constituted its first congress, at Minsk in 1898. Neither Plekhanov nor Ulianov (Lenin) attended, since one was in Geneva, the other exiled in Siberia. A "Credo" was issued, limiting the Party program to economic questions and eschewing political problems. All present were arrested and the Party organization was destroyed, but the movement was not halted.

7

The Russian revolutionaries practically all did their work and became famous under pseudonyms. They had to drop their real names when they were blacklisted by the Czarist police—often when they were still mere schoolboys, and were marked down just for reading or distributing revolutionary literature. The strict passport control in Russia required that a traveler register with the authorities in every city or town in which he arrived. Thus by changing their names frequently as they moved about, the revolutionaries could keep a step ahead of the blacklist. Otherwise they could hardly have survived and certainly could have accomplished nothing politically. When it was necessary, false passports and other legal papers were readily fabricated. Sometimes these maneuvers were facilitated by sympathizers within the police organization; otherwise bribery was an ever potent help in time of need, for the whole government organization was riddled with corruption, and bribery was fairly safe and simple.

Ulianov became in this way Lenin—the man from the River Lena. Dzugashvili is now Stalin—the man of steel. We know Scriabin as Molotov—the hammer.

Wallach in the following years assumed various pseudonyms: Gustav Graf, Ludwig Vilhelmovitch Nietz, Maxim Harrison, Engineer Tech; but at the same time he was known as Maxim Maximovich Litvinoff. Wallach took the name "Litvinoff" from a novel by his favorite author, Turgenev. Various legends have circulated as to the origin of the name—for instance, that he took it from the town Litvina because he had organized there a successful strike—but Litvinoff says that he never led any strike anywhere.

8

When Litvinoff decided to devote his whole life to the revolution, his sentence still had eleven months to run. He could not wait. He had to get out; and nine other political prisoners, including Zinoviev and Kamenev, felt the same way. Planning the escape was entrusted to the clear-headed and practical Litvinoff, and he went about it methodically, restraining his friends' impatience so that he would have time for the most thorough preparation.

Certain circumstances were propitious: political prisoners could receive visitors, and they had daily exercise in a small courtyard separated from the street only by a twenty-five-foot wall.

Litvinoff made a rope ladder out of sheets. Then a girl came to see one of the conspirators, bearing a huge bunch of flowers. Had a guard bothered to pick up that bouquet, he would have found it strangely heavy. It contained an iron hook.

On August 18, 1902, when the prisoners went out in the court for their walk, someone proposed that, to get more exercise, they play a game, and the guard did not object. It involved much running about, laughter, and calling back and forth so that only Litvinoff, who stayed close to the street wall, heard a signal from the other side. Immediately he jumped on the guard and one of the other plotters whisked out from under his coat a thin blanket that had been hidden there, and threw it over the head of the guard, who was then gagged and bound. Meanwhile another of the group pulled out the sheet-rope ladder which had been wrapped round his body, and at the fourth or fifth attempt they succeeded in catching the iron hook on the top of the wall. One after another—Litvinoff the last—they swarmed over to freedom.

Looking back on the exploit, Litvinoff believes that the guards, who interposed only a half-hearted resistance, were more or less sympathetic to the escape. They had all been guarding political prisoners for some years, had learned a lot about their programs and sympathy for the common man.

Litvinoff stayed for a while right in Kiev, working under an assumed name in a twine and cord factory. But soon he decided to leave
Russia for Geneva to try to meet the man who published *Iskra*. He
wrote to Lenin but got no reply. So he started out to find him.

9

Vladimir Ilich Ulianov was born in 1870 in Simbirsk, son of a
teacher, who later became an inspector of public schools—one of a
family of six, four girls and two boys, of which he was the younger.
When he entered Kazan University his older brother, Alexander, was
already active in a revolutionary organization called the "People's
Will," and Vladimir, following suit, was soon expelled from the University for membership in a radical group. He returned later, however, to finish his studies and then went to St. Petersburg where he
passed his bar examinations at the age of 21, in 1891. That same year
his brother was arrested, convicted and executed, charged with having
plotted the assassination of Czar Alexander III.

Vladimir meanwhile was studying Marx, so that when he went to
Samara (now Kuibyshev) to practice law shortly after being admitted
to the bar, he was really more interested in the social and economic
problems of the working classes than in his own profession, and not
long thereafter he went back to St. Petersburg to devote himself to the
propagation of the Marxian doctrine.

In 1895 he went to Geneva to meet Plekhanov, who twelve years before, when Lenin was still a lad, had formed the first Russian Marxist
group. Plekhanov was impressed by him, predicting for him a great
future. Lenin returned to St. Petersburg, founded an underground
organization—the Union for the Liberation of the Working Class—
was soon arrested by the secret police, and spent a year in prison awaiting trial. This gave him an opportunity to read more revolutionary
literature, and he studied especially the development of Russian capitalism.

When he was finally tried, he was sentenced (in 1897) to three years
exile in Eastern Siberia "under constant police supervision." He lived
in a peasant's hut in a dreary little town named Shushenskoe on the
Lena River near the Mongolian border, but he was surrounded by

revolutionary friends serving similar sentences. (Nadezhna Konstanti-novna Krupskaya, who arrived shortly after he did, a fellow exile in another region, was permitted to come to Shushenskoe in order to marry Lenin. She was a woman of the noblest character, generous, brave, wise, absolutely devoted. She was indispensable to Lenin's life.) He had his books, received newspapers and was busy on one of his most important works, *The Development of Russian Capitalism.*

Even in Siberia he was able to follow every phase of the first Russian Social-Democratic Congress in the second year of his exile, and was dismayed by the rejection of political action in the "Credo," as was also Plekhanov many miles away in Switzerland; both did all they could to counteract what they regarded as a timid and short-sighted policy.

On the completion of his Siberian sentence, Lenin left Russia, going to Switzerland expressly to found a paper that would differ from all the other Russian exile publications in that it would be addressed, not to other exiles, but to readers inside Russia—*Iskra.*

Starting the paper presented many problems. The plan was to have it printed in Stuttgart, but in the end, it actually went to press in Munich. In 1902 Lenin spent some time in London doing research work in the British Museum for a stipend of £6 a month, and later the offices of *Iskra* were transferred there.

10

The young Maxim Maximovich who left Russia for the first time looked far more like the conventional revolutionary of popular imagi-nation than did the Litvinoff of later years, but even then he did not go around unshaven for days, which was supposed in the West to mark the real revolutionary, nor did he meet any of the other popular expectations of personal dishevelment. A photograph of him during that period shows a wiry young man with a mop of unruly black hair, a long, almost frightening mustache with drooping ends, keen eyes under bushy brows—altogether an intense, courageous, even some-what demonic young man, a revolutionary right out of a novel by Zola or Flaubert.

He had left a Russia which was a world apart, to go into a Europe sparkling with vivid activity. The British Empire was at the zenith of its power, reflected in Queen Victoria's dramatic Jubilee. The Paris World Exhibition of 1900, which had just closed after receiving, so the papers said, almost 50,000,000 visitors, had reaffirmed in splendor France's cultural leadership of the Western World.

The arts were flourishing brilliantly. Theaters were full: Sarah Bernhardt was enthusiastically acclaimed; Eleanora Duse made everyone, from loges to gallery, weep. Opera houses, impressive with sumptuous gowns and jewels, were ringing with the golden voices of singers like the de Reszkes, Nordica, Melba. Paderewski was the pianist sensation, and concert goers were beginning to speak of a young violinist named Kreisler. Ibsen, Björnson, Strindberg, Tolstoi, Dostoevski, Gerhart Hauptmann were widely read. In England, Kipling and his imperialism were still the rage, but H. G. Wells was commanding increasing attention, and the audacious George Bernard Shaw was challenging a growing audience. Impressionistic painting had already taken its place in the great tradition; Cézanne, frustrated, had toiled with his own highly personal adaptations; and the striking expressionism of Gauguin, Van Gogh and their contemporaries was provoking controversy.

But the chief developments were in industrial techniques. The New York subway was begun. The horseless carriage still caused comment —and doubt. The Zeppelin was succeeding in its first test. The Curies were hard at work on significant problems. Röntgen had received the Nobel Prize in Physics for his discovery of the X-ray. Fridtjof Nansen was about to start for the North Pole. Marconi had signaled the letter "s" across the Atlantic. In a few years the Wright brothers would astonish the world with their first successful flight in a heavier-than-air machine.

Henri Dunant, who had inspired the formation of the Red Cross, had received the first Nobel Peace Prize, but Europe was far from an established peace. Underneath the pleasant surface trouble was brewing everywhere. France was still tense over the affair of Captain Alfred Dreyfus, which had started in 1894 and dragged on into 1906. Shortly before the end of the last century the Boer War had distressed British hearts and minds. Kaiser Wilhelm II, making rash anti-British propaganda out of that war, had aroused a furor of resentment that had alarming reverberations and increased tension throughout the world. A little later the Kaiser became greatly excited by the so-called Yellow Peril, imagining himself leader and perhaps savior of the White nations. All he accomplished was to embitter relations with the Orient and to divert a certain amount of attention from the real discontents that were threatening the stability of Europe.

Nicholas II, of all people, had proposed a permanent world peace conference, which finally convened in the Hague and led to the establishment of a permanent international court. But there was no peace. There was a general illusion of security, but actually there were conflicts the world round. In addition to the Boer War there had been the Italo-Abyssinian War (1896), the Turkish-Greek War (1897), the Spanish-American War (1898), the Philippine-American War (1899–1901) and the Boxer Rebellion in China (1900).

Assassination was almost a political commonplace. The Queen of Korea had been killed by Japanese political agitators in 1895. General Antonio Maceo, leader of the Cuban revolution, had been murdered in 1896. Empress Elizabeth of Austria-Hungary was stabbed by an anarchist at Geneva in 1898. Umberto, King of Italy, was done away with in 1900. President William McKinley died in Buffalo in 1901 from an assassin's bullet. King Alexander and Queen Draga of Serbia were killed two years later in Belgrade.

The conflict between labor and capital was growing in intensity. The obvious luxury of the now thoroughly industrialized world kindled burning resentment among the under-privileged. Ambition, envy, gross injustices, exploitation, graft and waste were all feeding hidden fires. No, despite the triumphs of art and literature, the progress of science, the plethora of enormous fortunes, the luxury and gaiety of life —all was not well with the world. It had seemed as if civilization was now entering on its final and supreme phase—achievement, prosperity, security, permanence. It could claim to be the heir to all the ages, firmly founded on all that had gone before. Yet the tremor of its bases underground gave warning to the discerning few of the coming earthquake. The young Maxim Maximovich was destined to play a great part in the ultimate catastrophe—and in the subsequent reconstruction.

In the Russia from which the young Litvinoff had fled, the reactionary elements—court, Church and nobles—the political liberals, and industrialists, and the Revolution now growing in uncompromising power, were wrestling for the body and soul of the country. Conditions were getting worse under the morbid Czarina and the incompetent Czar, who, having advocated a permanent peace conference, was accessory to a permanent, bloody and cruel war against his own people. The prisons were full. Executions of political prisoners were a matter of course. Political assassinations were multiplying, but no serious remedy was even attempted.

Night lay dark over Russia, but just below the horizon the Revolution was gathering force, ablaze with passion and hope, and in the midst of it was Maxim Maximovich Litvinoff.

II

When Maxim Maximovich arrived in Geneva, he wrote again to Lenin, a brief, businesslike note offering his services, and again got no reply. But he did meet Plekhanov who suggested that he help smuggle copies of *Iskra* into Russia, and for this purpose Litvinoff went to Berlin (he already spoke German) where, as Gustav Graf, he took a room in a cheap little lodging house in the Neustaedtische Kirchstrasse. The Prussian police, at the request of the Czarist police, assigned a detective, Karl Woltz, who was already keeping track of a number of Russian exiles, to watch Litvinoff, also.

Litvinoff, however, went about his business, full of ideas as to how to get copies of *Iskra* into Russia, and succeeded in organizing underground deliveries, partly with the help of German Social Democrats. This kept him busy through the rest of 1902 and 1903, and whether or not Detective Woltz knew what he was doing only the Prussian police records for that period would show; but in any case the German authorities never interfered.

Meanwhile Litvinoff, undiscouraged, wrote several more times to Lenin but still without success. Lenin was too busy to bother with letters from unknown young men, and too canny to take up with an unrecommended person who might be a police informer.

In July, 1903, Lenin called the Second Congress of the Russian Socialist Congress to meet in Brussels. The "Credo" of the First Congress
had aroused controversies among Party members and sympathizers on
many points, and a Second Congress was necessary to deal with these.

Litvinoff thought he would now have a chance to meet Lenin so
he went to Geneva, but got there a few hours after Lenin had left
for Brussels. Undaunted, Litvinoff took the next train to Brussels and
found the empty warehouse on the outskirts of the city where the
Congress was supposed to assemble; but no one was there. Enquiry
revealed that the Belgian police had suggested to the Russians that if
they did not want to be arrested they would do well to move on, so
they had all gone over to London.

Still undeterred, Litvinoff made the trip—train, channel steamer, and
train again—to London, where he met a man named Blumenfeld who
took him to the British Museum reading room where Lenin worked
many hours every day. And so at last Litvinoff met Lenin.

Lenin, short, stocky, disproportionately broad shouldered, with the
shrewd, tight face of a peasant, and reddish hair, bristly mustache
and beard, did not make, on most people, any great effect. His entrance
into a room never attracted attention and many who became admirers
or followers have admitted that they did not even remember their first
contacts with him. Yet to the more observant, Lenin's fine high brow
and steely eyes, his alertness and capacity for intense concentration,
belied the superficial peasant aspects and implied not only an exceptional intellect, but a personality beyond the intellectual, and on even
slight acquaintance he revealed a convincing human simplicity and
directness that carried with it real charm. Litvinoff was deeply impressed and will never, could never forget the moment. The deep
sympathy, a friendship founded on common aims, which developed
between the two men, was never even temporarily disturbed for the
rest of Lenin's life.

Lenin went with Litvinoff to Hyde Park Corner to listen to some
of the speeches, then Lenin took him home—to two shabby little rooms
at 30 Holford Square, so meagerly furnished that there were not
enough chairs for those present. There he met Lenin's wife, Krupskaya.

12

The second Russian Social Democratic Congress marked a great advance over the first: forty-three delegates represented twenty-six organizations, and both Plekhanov and Lenin were present.

The first vote on the first paragraph of the new program, concerning the Marxian concept of the proletarian dictatorship was decisive. Lenin and his *Iskra* group had a majority and consequently from then on called themselves Bolsheviki ("those of the majority"), while the opponents became the Mensheviki ("those of the minority").

The oppression of the Jews, their deliberate persecution (largely in the hope of diverting the rest of the populace from their own sufferings) by the *Ochrana,* which also persecuted political reformers, together with the idealism deeply inbred in large sections of the Jewish people, combined to attract Russian Jews into reform movements, but comparatively few of them allied themselves with the Bolsheviki. Many joined the Mensheviki, and the "Bund," a Jewish Socialist group, were responsible for Lenin's set-back at this very Congress.

Lenin refused to recognize a group defined as Jewish because to him, as to every Marxian, religion was an intellectual soporific that hampered realistic thinking and prevented fundamental social changes. The "Bund," in turn, along with others, voted against Lenin's proposal that every Party member also join an underground, actively fighting organization, and it was defeated. This almost split the Party, but for the time being, compromise adjustments were contrived, though with considerable difficulty.

Litvinoff stood unwaveringly with Lenin, profoundly convinced that he was right, not always perhaps at this stage correctly understanding the sources and implications of the conflicts and decisions swirling around him, but committed to the leader who offered the best chance for a real revolution. So he offered his services to Lenin who accepted and kept him at the job, at which he had proved successful, of smuggling contraband literature into Russia—"transport," in the Russian revolutionary vocabulary. Shortly after the London Congress, Lenin left the *Iskra* staff and began to edit a new paper in Geneva, *Vpered* (*Forward*). This was of major importance in the activities of Lenin and his group in the following years, and every effort was made to keep it going. Thus somewhat later (December 4, 1904) Lenin wrote of it in a letter to one of his associates in a burst of rhetorical exaggeration, "We must have our paper and money. You must send money here. Kill if need be, but send money," a passage often quoted subsequently out of context, and deliberately misinterpreted by enemies of the new Russia.

Litvinoff undertook the "transport" of the new journal, and his notable success is measured in a comment by Lenin himself, in a letter to one of the women workers, Zemliachka (December 26, 1904): "There will be transport as long as we have Papasha [Litvinoff]. Let him take the most energetic measures for handing over his inheritance in case of failure."

Litvinoff's usefulness to his Party increased steadily. Stationed now in Riga and co-operating closely with Leonard B. Krassin, he carried on "Frontier Administration"—Bolshevik argot for arranging the arrivals and departures of illegal agents smuggling over the border forbidden literature and secret letters, and he was also busy organizing underground printing shops.

Lenin found his young assistant practical, competent, dependable and above all so invariably calm that he nicknamed him *Papasha*— the father of the family who is a good provider, established, settled, substantial—and that is how Litvinoff's friends felt about him, even at that early age.

13

The years 1904–1905 were active and difficult for the leading Russian émigré revolutionaries. The dissensions within the Party had been only precariously patched up at the London Congress and soon broke out in innumerable more or less acrimonious discussions which involved extensive correspondence in many directions.

By August, 1904, it was obvious that another congress was needed to work some order out of the conflicts. Lenin proposed that it be held in London, but the Mensheviks decided to hold a congress of their own in Geneva. Lenin's reaction was instantaneous: two congresses, two parties; and in October of that year his group began to select the Committee for Organization of the Bolshevik Party. Lenin wrote

from Geneva that he did not want to designate the members himself,
but he would like to recommend a few particularly trustworthy comrades who had already done some preliminary work and would be
the right people to continue work for the revolution in such a committee. He named seven men, among them (under the agreed pseudo-
nym "Felix") Litvinoff.

The work of organizing the Congress went on, but amidst considerable difficulties. On the one hand, there were disagreements within
the ranks, on the other, constant need of money, for arranging a congress was an expensive business. Lenin's letters at this time are full
of the quarrels in the Party and he was unsparing in condemnations
of various members, but there is never a single word of criticism for
Litvinoff. And Litvinoff was evidently of help also with the financial
problems, for a letter from Lenin to Zemliachka (December 26, 1904)
expressing enthusiastic appreciation of successful fund raising specifically includes Litvinoff in his congratulations.

Only one letter of this period from Lenin directly to Litvinoff is
available, owing to an odd mischance. Litvinoff had a number of letters from Lenin which he valued greatly. When, after the 1917 Revolution, he was appointed Ambassador from the Soviet Union to the Court
of St. James, he took these with him, but knowing that the British authorities might ransack his office, with consequent loss of the letters, he
stowed them away in a safe. When His Majesty's Government expelled
Litvinoff late in the summer of 1918, he took the letters out of the safe
and gave them to a friend in London to guard.

In the following two years Litvinoff was constantly working hard
and steadily, with important absorbing responsibilities, but finally in
1919 he settled down to live in Moscow and decided to get back his
precious letters. But he could not recall to whom he had given them.
To at least twenty friends in London he made enquiries, but none
knew anything about the letters. Litvinoff has no suspicion that the
correspondence has been misappropriated, only he cannot imagine
where it can be.

All the letters, he knows, were, like the one remaining example, impersonal, concerned only with general political questions and the ad-
visability of various tactics: *

* Here published in English for the first time.

Geneva, December 1904

Dear Friend,

I hasten to answer your letter which has pleased me very much. You are right, a thousand times right, that we must act decisively, in a revolutionary way, that we must forge the iron while it is still hot. I am also of your opinion that we must unite the committees of the majority (Bolsheviks). The necessity of a center in Russia and of an organ outside Russia has become clear to us all. For the latter, we have already done everything we can. Riadovoi is trying everything. He has been able to win collaborators. He is now devoting himself entirely and with all his energies to the search for a millionaire—not without some chance of success.

Finally, you are a thousand times right that we must act, act openly. The only question at issue between us concerns a detail, and this detail must be thought over cold-bloodedly, namely: a conference of committees, or a direct formation of a "Bureau of Bolshevik Committees." (We should like this name better than the name of Committee of Organization though, of course, the name does not matter.) The Bureau would be recognized in the beginning by some and later by all committees. You are for the first possibility, we are for the second one. If a conference abroad were possible, I should be for it. In Russia, however, it would be extremely dangerous, long drawn-out and not very productive. In the meantime, Odessa, Nikolaev and Yekaterinoslav have got together and asked the "Twenty-two" to name a Committee of Organization. In our answer we have proposed the name "Bureau of Committees of the Majority" and also seven candidates [Russalka, Felix, Zemliachka, Pavlovich, Gusev, Alexeyev, Baron]. We are writing about it to Odessa and St. Petersburg. Alexeyev has already left to join you. Would it not be better to have Riga, St. Petersburg and Moscow make the choice of the candidates than to publish this immediately, then to go to the Committee of the North, to the Caucasus, to Saratov, Nizhnyi, etc. and to ask them to join the Bureau and to complete the Bureau in a liberal manner with some of their candidates? (though it is not very likely that the joining committees will demand many additions in the composition of the Bureau). I simply cannot imagine that we'll have difficulties with the composition of the Bureau.

The advantages of such a procedure are: speed, not many expenses, no danger. These advantages are very important, for now everything depends on speed. The Bureau will be the official organ of the united committees and will replace the central committee in case of a split. The composition of the literary group for our future central organization is also already planned. (Five or six: Riadovoi, Galerka, I, Schwarz, plus Lunacharsky, perhaps with Barsov.) The transport you will have to take in hand and as energetically as possible. We have won over a former member of the "Bund" who has done much work at two frontiers; he promises to do the work for us, for two hundred to three hundred rubles a month. We are only waiting for the money, then we'll have him get together with you.

The disadvantage of your procedure is delay. I think there is no sense in putting ultimatums to the Central Committee or the Party Council. The Central Committee plays the hypocrite. I don't doubt for one moment that it has sold itself to the minority (Mensheviki) and that they will try to betray the Party Congress. We should not have any illusions. Now with the entire central machinery in their hands they'll have a thousand means to betray the Party Congress. They have already begun with it. We will prove this in the press by analyzing the decisions of the Party Council. Of course, we are all for a Congress and we shall go on being for one, but we must shout everywhere that they betray this Congress and that we are going to prove their betrayal.

I now put the Party Congress in the ninth place and in the first place our organ and the Russian center. If they accuse us of being disloyal, they are ridiculous. They pushed us by settling with the Mensheviks. It is not true that the secret organization of the Mensheviks has been dissolved. No, three members of the Central Committee have joined the secret organization—that is all. The whole machinery now is a secret organization against the Party. Only fools don't see that. We must answer by building an open organization and unmasking this conspiracy.

Please build up belief in our organization and in our future organ. Only we must have a bit of patience till Riadovoi has completed his arrangements. Collect letters and send them to us (always marked for Lenin), and material especially from workers. There is only one detail on which we do not agree with you. I really should have been glad to have a conference. But believe me, it wouldn't pay. It is much better that we come out immediately with a communiqué about a Bureau. We shall easily come to an agreement about its composition, and conflicts in this respect are not likely. As soon as the Bureau makes known its existence it will be recognized rapidly. And it will then begin to speak in the name of all Committees. Please think this over once more and answer me as quickly as possible.

CHAPTER III

Civil War in Russia

MEANWHILE THE GENERAL situation in Russia under the misrule of
Nicholas II had been steadily moving towards tumult, disaster, and
a new birth. In 1902–1903 a wave of strikes swept with mounting force
from one end of the country to the other, from the Obukhov munitions
plant in St. Petersburg in 1902, to Rostov and Batum, where there were
numerous demonstrations then and again in 1903, when the epidemic
spread to Baku, Tiflis, Odessa, Kiev and Yekaterinoslav.

War with Japan was imminent, too. The Japanese were convinced
that it was a life-and-death matter to arrest at once the onward drive
of Russian imperialism which was on its way to take control of
Korea. Once Korea was in Russian hands, the island empire itself
would be imperiled. The Japanese were united, enthusiastic and ardently determined to settle accounts. But there was no enthusiasm for
the war in Russia, save among the military and some of the nobles,
who had questionable timber interests in Korea from which they expected great profits, if only Japan could be kept at arm's length. People
in general were suspicious, apprehensive and resentful. No one believed that war was necessary or that any fundamental interests of the
country were threatened by Japan.

The Government, however, was not worried, and conducted its
negotiations with Japan in a most contemptuous manner. General
Alexei Nikolaievich Kuropatkin, Minister of War, returning that same
year from a trip to Japan, reported to the Czar: "Japan is not a formidable enemy. We are perfectly ready and could in the space of
thirteen days have four hundred thousand men on the Japanese frontier. This is three times as many as would be needed to repulse the
army of our adversary. The war would be a simple military promenade
and no necessity could arise for moving any of our troops from the
German or Austrian frontier." And indeed important men in the

57

Government thought that a war would be useful to divert the populace from its growing resentments and from its now menacing hostility.

The war began February 6, 1904. It was over in nineteen months. On January 2, 1905, Port Arthur fell to the Japanese. Between February 25 and March 10 Marshal Oyama defeated General Kuropatkin in a long battle for the possession of Mukden, ending all hope of Russian victory, but not the possibility of stalemate. The Black Sea fleet had been refused passage through the Dardanelles by the Turks, so the main Baltic fleet started for the Far East, promptly making a sorry exhibition of its lack of discipline and good sense by shooting up some English trawlers in the North Sea, a fatuous blunder that nearly involved Russia in war with Britain and alienated world sympathy. The fleet, burdened with ill omen, continued on its way. Since passage through the Suez Canal had been refused by the English, the Russians had to sail all the way round the Cape of Good Hope, only to fall, on May 27, 1905, into a trap prepared by Admiral Hihashi Togo, at Tsushima Straits, where they were out-maneuvered, out-shot and practically annihilated.

By the time the peace treaty was signed (September 5, 1905) the "simple military promenade" had cost 6,000,000,000 rubles and more than 400,000 lives, and had shown to the world the weakness of the Czar, the inadequacy of his Government, and the incompetence of the Army and Navy commands.

The people were deeply humiliated, for although they had opposed the war, they had assumed a Russian victory was inevitable. Now, disillusioned and thoroughly angry, mourning their dead, struggling with a serious business depression, and burdened by increased taxes, they resented more than ever the increasing tyranny from which they daily suffered. The great majority hated and despised the autocracy for its corruption, its cruelty and utter incompetence, while all were chagrined by the taunts or patronizing sympathy of the rest of the world. The revolutionaries took a grim if not gleeful satisfaction in this indecent exposure of Czarism. As Lenin said: "Not the Russian people but the Russian Czarist regime has suffered a shameful defeat. The Russian people have won by the military defeat." There was a general agreement that the Government of the Czar had forfeited the allegiance of the country and that it was doomed.

The disastrous war with Japan and all the new tribulations which it brought merely precipitated and magnified what was already long in process, and even before the war was over the storm broke. The growing discontent of the people was everywhere finding expression: revolutionary forces were moving towards a climax of some kind. In December, 1904, the Congress of the Zemstva (Provincial Assemblies) resolved that a popular assembly should be established, and a petition to that effect was presented to the Czar. The Czar was as usual evasive —then abusive. A "ukase" was issued rebuking the impudence of those who had dared press for reforms. New and severer restrictions were clapped on the press, the prisons again were jammed. That same month the Barristers' Association also presented a petition demanding reforms. The Czar merely published an Imperial Manifesto making vague promises and stating: "Autocratic power is immutable over the fundamental laws of the Empire."

But protests continued to pour in—for the first time from the industrialists who began to see that arbitrary and incompetent government was very bad for big business. The Moscow Manufacturers' Association complained of the disordered financial system, the precarious political order, the backward state of public education, which all seriously interfered with proper productivity; and without more efficient production Russia could not reach the world markets. Both were essential for her prosperity.

The Ural manufacturers protested that Russia lacked both civic freedom and a firmly established legal order and that this was the cause of the disturbances in their industrial system.

The sugar manufacturers of Kiev announced that the sugar industry "is directly interested in the welfare of the great masses, which are the main consumers of its product," and complained of the absence of freedom of speech, press and public assembly, "the inalienable rights of every citizen in every modern country, a deprivation that hampers the full development of the productive forces of our country."

"We cannot live any longer under such conditions!" declared the Nizhnyi-Novgorod Chamber of Commerce in October, 1905. "We need order as we need air to breathe!" *

The industrialists were not particularly moved by humanitarian con-

* M. J. Olgin, *The Soul of the Russian Revolution,* p. 130, New York, 1917.

siderations; indeed, they were fearful lest the intolerable conditions of
the workingmen should be alleviated at the expense of business. And
when the Government replied to these petitions, suggesting economic
concessions to the workingmen, they answered that they could neither
run their business at a loss nor was their business a charity, that the
basic difficulty was political not economic and that if political rights
were granted, the workingmen would be satisfied and amenable. But
their protests and debates are significant as an indication that even this
class was aware that the Government's tyranny and its daily demonstration of incapacity to govern were creating conditions hostile to
Russia's progress or even elemental welfare.

More sinister and alarming were the demonstrations, disorders and
revolts taking place throughout the country. They were a grim en-
dorsement of the complaints and a fair warning that catastrophe was
in the making. A terroristic repression was soon in full swing. In Moscow and St. Petersburg General Dmitri Trepov wielded knout and
saber with random cruelty on all and sundry who dared to engage in
political activity or even to express opinions.

2

The working classes in St. Petersburg had, not long since, found a
new leader, a Christian Socialist priest, Father George Gapon, who
became the subject of still unresolved controversies. It has been asserted, but never proved, that he was an *agent provocateur* in the service of the Third Section, and he is definitely known to have taken
money from the police; but this he explained as a trick to quiet their
suspicions, and claimed that he used the money to arm the workers.
The police did apparently deliberately ignore his political activities, but
this does not necessarily mean that he was collaborating with them.
They may have believed that he would never lead a real revolution,
but by his somewhat capricious activities would rather split the ranks
of the revolutionaries; and Gapon, while he may have been hunting
with the hounds and running with the hare, may equally well have
sincerely believed, with the muddled fanaticism of an hysteric, that a
revolution was Russia's only solution. In any event he did organize the
workers in the great Putilov munitions works in St. Petersburg, and

on January 15, 1905, they struck, demanding a national constitution. Gapon accompanied a delegation that submitted their case to the Ministry of the Interior. As there was little hope in this quarter they then decided to present, the next Sunday, January 21, a written petition to the Czar in person, asking for elementary justice, for tolerable living conditions, for some voice in their destiny. It was a humble and moving plea of joint authorship, but unified by common suffering and common hope:

"We, the workingmen of St. Petersburg, our wives, our children and our helpless old parents, have come to Thee, our Sovereign, to seek truth and protection. We are poverty-stricken, we are oppressed, we are burdened with unendurable toil; we suffer humiliation and are not treated like human beings. . . . We have suffered in patience, but we are being driven deeper and deeper into the slough of poverty, lack of rights and ignorance; we are being strangled by despotism and tyranny. . . . Our patience is exhausted. The dreaded moment has arrived when we would rather die than bear these intolerable sufferings any longer. . . . We have only two ways open to us, 'either the way to liberty and happiness or the way to the grave'." Preliminary letters to the Minister of the Interior and a pathetic one to the Czar informing them of the plans to present the petition were not even acknowledged.

The long procession of marchers led by Gapon started to move from the Pedagov Highroad to the Palace Square, formed by the somber dark red Winter Palace on the north, the General Staff headquarters on the south, and on the west the stately Admiralty with its classic façade of yellow and white, and golden spire. They carried banners, icons and portraits of the Czar, and despite their misery and despair, they had no thought of revolution. So they were horrified, then panic-struck to be met, not by the Czar, who had fled to Tsarskoe Selo, but by a charge of cavalry, gendarmes and imperial guards stationed round the palace, and salvos of murderous volleys from the adjacent streets. In five minutes that bitter cold winter day had become Bloody Sunday, and a humble demonstration had turned into a chaos of terrified men struggling in flight over their dead and wounded comrades. Street urchins who had climbed up the trees in Alexander Park to see the sights were shot like sparrows—a sporting test of the soldiers' marksmanship. The hurricane of fire ceased. Five hundred had been killed, nearly three thousand wounded.

Gapon, the most shocked and startled of all, stood bewildered amidst the spattering bullets, but a young Jew, Pincus Ruthenberg, ran up, threw his overcoat over the priest, and guided him away to safety. That evening, deeply agitated by the dreadful deeds of the day, Gapon penned a terrible and prophetic letter to the Czar:

"The innocent blood of workers, their wives and children, lies forever between thee, O soul destroyer, and the Russian people. Moral connection between thee and them may never be any more. . . . A sea of blood—unexampled—will be shed. Because of thee, because of thy whole family, Russia may perish. Once for all, understand this and remember, better soon with all thy family abdicate the throne of Russia and give thyself up to the Russian people for trial. Pity thy children and the Russian lands, O thou offerer of peace for other countries and blood drunkard for thine own!

"Otherwise let all blood which has to be shed fall upon thee, Hangman, and thy kindred!

"Postscriptum—Know that this letter is the justifying document of the coming revolutionary terroristic occurrences in Russia."

Then he wrote a manifesto to the Russian Socialist Parties:

"I summon all the Socialist parties of Russia to enter immediately into agreement among themselves and to begin the business of armed uprising against Czarism. All the forces of every party should be mobilized. The technical plan of conflict should be a common one for all. Bombs and dynamite, terror by individuals and by masses—everything which may contribute to the national uprising. . . . Let us repeat the cry of the St. Petersburg workingmen on January 9th, 'Liberty or death!' "

He demanded that a parliament be created and called on the workers to strike—his last decisive act. He disguised himself by cutting his long hair and beard, fled the country, finding temporary refuge in Viborg. His manifestos may have been desperate attempts to revive his now discredited leadership but whatever the motive and whoever mysterious Gapon really was, these utterances are memorable because of their timeliness; their authority was derived from the suffering of the Russian people.

Father Gapon's abortive appeal to the Czar and its bloody repulse was evaluated a year later by a conservative journal, *Courier of Europe:* "January 22, 1905, is a historic day in the life of Russia; few equal it in the past; few, probably, will equal it in the future. . . . January 22 . . . was a critical day, critical for the form of government that had outlived itself, still more critical for the political consciousness and the faith of the people. . . . On January 22 hundreds of thousands of mystically inclined workingmen discovered that their idea of the Czar as an omnipotent source of truth on earth and love for the people, was quite incompatible with reality. Their faith in the Czar, the father of the oppressed and the wronged, was shaken." *

As a leader Gapon was by now completely discredited. He returned to Russia, resumed his old relations with some of the higher officials of the Government, and, in general, played a mysterious, ambiguous role. Socialists of all shades distrusted him, the Social Revolutionists adjudged him a traitor and "by order of Secret Tribunal" he was killed in 1906 by the same Pincus Ruthenberg who had once saved him.

The Czar thought to end "the disturbance" by a fatuous pronouncement that showed he had learned nothing from the shocking events of the day. A Commission was appointed "to investigate the causes of labor unrest in St. Petersburg and its suburbs and to find means of avoiding them in the future." The Commission, without authority or competence, was a complete futility and served only to prove that the maladies of Russia could no longer be cured by such means.

But meanwhile the tide of revolt was sweeping on. The day after Bloody Sunday the International Socialist Bureau also published a manifesto predicting that the Czar, in having peaceful workers shot, had written his own death sentence.

Both documents—the one showing the weakness of the Government, the other the growing strength of the revolution—were widely circulated with effective results. General strikes broke out in many cities of the outlying regions: Riga, Libau, Warsaw, Lodz, Vilna, Tomsk and Batum. The intellectuals now began to make full common cause with labor. The revolutionary forces were suddenly augmented by recruits and funds. Ultimately the rural areas participated. In January, 450,000

* Cf. M. J. Olgin, *op. cit.,* p. 112.

workers struck, more than the total number of strikers in the ten preceding years; in February 293,000 more, and while bloody suppression
by the police reduced the strikes in March and April, altogether in the
year 1905 there were more than 13,000 strikes and probably more than
3,000,000 walked out—a remarkable figure for a young industrial country like Russia. There was a shocking total of civilians killed and
maimed during these disorders.

Even the Government, arrogant as it was, saw that some concessions
had to be made. By the middle of February, 1905, the Czar began to
yield. The argument that seems to have counted with him was the
assassination of his cousin—the cruel Grand Duke Sergei—on February 4, 1905. His bomb-mangled remains apparently affected the Czar
more than the pitiful corpses that littered the Palace Square on Bloody
Sunday, a scant four weeks before. The Revolution began to seem more
real and more dangerous. Two weeks later he granted the right of
petition, a long delayed elemental right universally acknowledged even
in semi-barbarous countries. At the same time (February 18) he announced his intention of creating a representative body—a more substantial though still only vague, half-hearted concession, that had been
urged eighty years earlier and with increasing force and unanimity
thereafter. The Zemstva addressed the Czar early in June, boldly charging that "the criminal negligence and corruption of your advisers has
plunged Russia into a disastrous war. . . . For the sake of Russia's
safety, for the sake of order and internal peace, we beg you to issue
an order calling representatives of the people, elected equally and without discrimination by all your subjects." The Czar apparently accepted,
but his well-known evasiveness, insincerity and infirmity of will robbed
his declaration of its full effect.

Meanwhile way off in London that April, Lenin was holding his
Third Congress where he established the Bolsheviks as the only legitimate representatives of the Social Democratic Labor Party (see p. 38).
This split was perhaps a decisive factor in the failure of the revolt then
in progress in Russia. And Litvinoff, during this period, was indus-
triously stoking the revolutionary furnace with inflammatory literature.

May 1, celebrated in Russia for the first time, saw enormous demonstrations, more than 200,000 in the streets of the two capitals alone
and eleven days later the 70,000 textile workers of Ivanovo-Vosnyes-

sensk initiated a strike that lasted three weeks, despite such violent efforts to suppress it that hundreds were wounded, and twenty-eight killed. The revolters were forming many organizations, unions were recruiting heavily, not only among artisans, but also in the white-collar ranks—engineers, accountants, railway men; and on May 8 was founded the Union of Unions (*Soyus Soyusov*), whose leaders originated the slogans for the revolt.

But though the leadership was thus industrial, part of the revolt, in the Baltic provinces, Poland and the Caucasus, was purely political and in many areas it was soon difficult to separate the two factors.

On June 13, during an Odessa strike, several workers were killed by the Cossacks. There was furious resentment. Odessa had many times felt the brutal hand of repression. Revolt flared up, and the next day the crew of the armored cruiser *Potemkin,* in the harbor, objected en masse to the decayed meat that was being regularly served them. Thirty were court-martialed and shot, whereupon another crew member, Vakulinchuk, protested the wholesale murder and was killed by an officer. A general mêleé ensued, in which many officers were killed and the rest thrown into the sea. When, on June 17, the body of Vakulinchuk was buried with honor and thousands attended, the police dared not interfere. Troops arrived the next day but could not prevent the *Potemkin* from leaving port. After ten days' cruising in the Black Sea, it landed on the coast of Rumania, whose Government decided, contrary to international law, to return the crew to Russia. Most of them, however, escaped.

By this time the revolution had spread through rural districts where peasants waged more than 7,000 independent struggles in the course of the year, expressions of blind exasperation, without political support or direction. The peasants could wait no longer. For generations they had seen their holdings shrink, their land increasingly impoverished, the indifference and neglect of the Government march apace. Now everywhere homes of the rich, aristocrats and farmers alike, were burned and plundered by a desperate and aroused peasantry. Everywhere the Government responded with punitive expeditions that tortured, killed and burned without discriminating. Outrages on women were particularly numerous and revolting, and mere lads of sixteen or seventeen were not infrequently hung, generally without trial. Whole villages were exterminated. Troops were formally instructed to be merciless, and merciless they were.

The Government organized the Black Hundreds—groups of criminals, sadists and ruffians whose business it was to make ruthless and illegal war on all liberal or revolutionary movements and persons. Their techniques were breaking up of meetings, beatings, assassinations, arson, pogroms; the latter was their specialty. Intellectuals and labor leaders were favorite victims of their outrages. The Black Hundreds worked hand in glove with the secret police and were immune from prosecution. Pogroms became frequent, especially in the Baltic, Polish and Ukrainian provinces.

But what of the Czar, the autocrat of all the Russias, charged by fundamental law with the sole and indisputable responsibility for the government of those vast populations and territories? All that happened and all that followed in the next dozen years was in definite part a consequence of his incapacity, inferior intelligence and infirm will—combined, as is not infrequent, with stubbornness and conceit. Even his personal amiability was poisoned by a streak of vindictive cruelty common in weak men. He knew about and approved the deeds of the Black Hundreds—indeed, both he and the little Czarevitch wore the emblem of that infamous organization. All but a few sentimental, semi-hysteric monarchists recognized his utter inadequacy. Even his own mother acknowledged it. Once she replied to the Prime Minister, Witte: "You mean to say that my son lacks both character and will power? I am afraid, my dear Witte, you are absolutely right."

The terms "drunkard" and "wastrel," frequently applied to him in Russia, will seem excessive in the West, where his worst traits were little known and his amiability in personal and family relations tended to disarm or mitigate criticism. But he was certainly indolent, irresponsible, ill-educated, with an illiterate credulity that made him an eager victim of superstitions, pseudo-mysticism, and similar pious frauds. His youth had been spent in trivial amusements and heavy drinking.

Actually Nicholas was evidently riven with fears. He was afraid lest his ministers or advisers become too popular, so he flattered and tried to charm them, then suddenly dismissed them. He was afraid, sensing his own weakness, lest they dominate him, so if in a crisis he had to take a minister's advice, immediately afterwards he would often get rid of him. He was afraid of the whole complex in which he found himself, so he took refuge in mild exercise—walking, bicycle riding, sea bathing—which gave him the reputation of an amiable country gentleman, and in family sociabilities, consuming in the meanwhile vast quantities of champagne and making a minute account of his trivialities in diaries that are hardly more than a ludicrous record of futilities. He felt at ease only with inferiors, so he hedged himself in with men even more commonplace than he, or those apt at flattery, or others who advanced themselves by intrigue and deception.

He feared equally his people and his own impotence to deal with them, so he descended to brutality—fictitious strength—exulting in his feeble way in pogroms and killings. Examples are uncountable and all hideously similar in revealing a repulsive lust for inflicting suffering, a moral deficiency due in part no doubt to a vague and abstract imagination. There was, for instance, the young girl prisoner whom a Cossack killed because she looked out of a window instead of keeping her eyes fixed on a blank wall, and the Czar commended him for his service and sent him a handsome money reward.

Nicholas has given a damning revelation of himself in his diaries, posthumously published in 1920. Day after day they reveal a man who seemed interested in drinking more than in any other one thing, and lacked not only understanding but a really serious interest in his people or in the business of government:

"May 10, 1884: Yesterday we emptied 125 bottles of champagne and I tasted champagne from every one of them.

"October 21, 1889: Today I have a bad hangover because we drank for two days and I personally drank myself into a complete stupor.

"November 11, 1889: Yesterday I tested six different sorts of port wine. No wonder I became somewhat befuddled.

"May 9, 1893: Completely drunk, but had a good time."

Page after page is filled with such notations, with never an indication that the Czar had done anything worth while. Sentences like "Walked a long way and killed two crows, drank tea by daylight . . ." are characteristic. There were walks, there were rides in a boat, there were drinking parties and more drinking parties.

Even in the year 1905, when the whole country was in a state of upheaval, he did not seem to be disturbed: "Took a long walk in a thin shirt and took up paddling again ... had tea on the balcony. .... Had Marie and Dimitri to dinner ... drove them home to the palace. ...."

The mysterious stubbornness with which he resisted all attempts at reform and every suggestion that any part of the royal power be shared with any representatives of the people was due not merely to weakness and fear, but also to a deeply grounded religious conviction, artfully solidified and enhanced by his religious preceptors from youth on, especially by the able but fanatically narrow-minded Procurator of the Holy Synod, Pobiedonatzev. The Czar actually felt that he had made a pledge more important than life itself to protect and maintain the autocracy.

This conviction the Czarina was incessantly harping upon, reminding him that, while he had all power over his people, God and his oath had all power over him personally. The Czarina's religiosity, which verged on mania, was greatly intensified by her desperate and genuine maternal anxiety over her ill son. The lad was a hemophiliac, whose life was in constant jeopardy, the slightest bruise causing agonizing internal hemorrhage. The Czarina sought to take on herself the burden of guilt for this affliction, to atone for the misfortune and to appease heaven by the most exhausting religious vigils and supplications. This anxiety, compounded with piety and vulgarized by an illiterate credulity which the Czar fully shared, encouraged them both in the most commonplace superstitions, and rendered them an easy prey for the quacks, charlatans, mystics and sundry soothsayers that clustered round the court.

3

On Saturday, July 8, 1905, a man appeared at Litvinoff's hideout in Riga, where he was still busy with "transport" and "frontier administration" under the name of "Felix," introduced himself as Burenin, presented credentials as a courier of the Party, and told Litvinoff that the Social Revolutionaries (a leftist party which approved of terrorism) led by Father Gapon, had succeeded in buying large quantities of weapons in England which had been loaded on a steamer called the *John Grafton* in a Scottish port, but the men around Gapon had become too frightened to do anything about getting the arms to Russia.

Burenin had a letter suggesting that Litvinoff undertake the job, adding that only he could carry the venture through.

Up to this time Litvinoff had managed the transport of literature or agents but had had nothing to do with arms, yet without hesitation he plunged into this new and more difficult enterprise.

To unload the contraband in any of the regular Russian ports was out of the question. He must find a secluded harbor fit for landing the cargo and within reasonable reach of St. Petersburg and Moscow. He selected an excellent natural harbor on the island of Nargo near Reval, where frontier guards were few, and ordered the *John Grafton* to proceed there. Then he wrote asking that a number of reliable students and workers go to Reval to take the arms into Russia. These would-be smugglers arrived in good time, but the *John Grafton* did not show up. It had disappeared. It had run on a drifting mine off Finland and sunk.

Consequently, the arms on the *John Grafton* never got into the hands of the revolutionaries. Litvinoff wrote to Lenin that he would try to make up for the loss, and between July and September of 1905, he did succeed in getting into Russia, most of it going to St. Petersburg, some 15,000 rifles (Mausers and Mannlichers), 3,000 revolvers and several tons of dynamite. But the last did not interest him much. He wrote to Lenin that he could get it in Russia any time.

This is the famous tale of the *John Grafton* as told by those who claim to know. But it has never been properly authenticated.

4

At last, on August 3, 1905, after decades of struggle, defeat and hope for a representative assembly, an Imperial Manifesto was published, announcing the establishment of the Duma. The Duma had no real legislative authority but could only advise. The complicated electoral system by which it was chosen was artfully planned to restrict voting almost wholly to the propertied minority.

The thinking minority was disappointed; the unions and all the political parties, except those of the extreme right, were at once in active opposition, but by the nation as a whole the Manifesto was greeted with popular rejoicing. Yet at the very moment, the Government, as if in spiteful revenge for the concessions that had been extracted from it, started a new wave of repression and persecutions. Meetings were broken up with bloodshed, the jails were again filled and brutal officials did their worst.

A new wave of organized protest began September 19 with a strike of the printers' union, and when it was suppressed, the Union of Unions called a general strike. Thus the first Russian general strike was inspired, not by the Social Democratic Labor Party, but by a purely industrial organization.

The general strike, which began October 7, included railway employees, so the capital was almost immediately isolated. In three days it had spread throughout the country, with centers at Kharkov, Reval, Smolensk, Minsk, Yekaterinoslav, Kursk, Poltava, Belgorod, Saratov and Samara. In the face of so vast a movement, the Government was helpless, and forty delegates from striking factories were able to hold, on October 13 in St. Petersburg, the first session of the Workers' Soviets (Council of Representatives of the Workers), the inception of the type of organization that in 1917 would determine the structure of the revolutionary government.

On October 17, the Czar attempted to regain control of the dangerous situation by issuing another manifesto, assuring his people rather effusively that their grief was his grief, and promising:

1. To grant . . . unshakeable foundations of civil freedom on the principles of real inviolability of persons, freedom of conscience, speech, assembly and associations.

2. Without stopping the appointed elections to the State Duma, to bring to participation in the Duma, as far as possible in the short time left before its summons, those classes of the population which at present are altogether deprived of electoral rights, leaving the further development of universal suffrage to the newly established Legislative Order.

3. To establish as an unshakeable principle that no law could become binding without the consent of the State Duma, and that to the representatives of the people there should be guaranteed the possibility of actual participation in supervision of the legality of the actions of the authorities appointed by us. . . .

NICHOLAS.

If the Czar had conceded these things a year, or even a few months earlier, bloodshed could have been averted. Now he could not even get his manifesto printed immediately. It took five days because of the printers' strike.

Witte was made Premier—an able, forceful man, who did his best to mitigate the severities of the autocratic regime. Popular excitement was somewhat calmed by several of his decrees, notably a general amnesty for 70,000 or 80,000 political prisoners, which included some of the ablest and most devotedly patriotic men in the country; and the promise of wide suffrage was hopeful. He made conciliatory appeals to the workers, but his expressions of solicitude and the fair promises were received with scorn and sarcasm. Labor was now thoroughly cynical.

Late in October, before any of these pledges could be put into effect, the sailors at Kronstadt mutinied. For the first time men in the armed forces, taking a leaf out of economic and political struggles, attempted collective bargaining, demanding more pay and decent conditions of living. The mutiny was repressed with shocking bloodshed. Many hundreds were arrested and several hundreds executed. Bitterness deepened resolution, anger; hope mounted.

Thus while the leaders of the Social Democratic Labor Party had for years fomented the revolutionary spirit among the Russian masses, the Party had little to do with the actual revolt of 1905, and it was indeed in no position to lead since its very existence was threatened by internal dissensions. Plekhanov and the more conservative Mensheviki or minority who met in Geneva, were convinced that a revolution could be successfully carried through in Russia by the bourgeoisie, with city workers helping, but without counting on the peasants because they were "not yet ripe for revolt." Lenin and the Bolsheviki or majority, working from London, knew that it must be a workers' *and* peasants' revolution, and the grim uprisings of 1905, abortive though they were, proved their point. The Third Congress in London that same year saw the Mensheviki-Bolsheviki break made definite and final.

Armed with a false passport, Lenin returned to Russia secretly, since a public appearance would have been very risky. He wanted to test his theories about revolutionary strategy and tactics by first-hand, factual-minded observation. He watched the conduct of the strikers down to minute details, interviewed hundreds of workers, peasants and soldiers, made extensive notes, sat in the back row, unrecognized, through many sessions of the Soviets. Perhaps for a moment, during the crucial Kronstadt uprising, when no one knew whether or not the majority of the army and navy would join, he hoped or even believed that the Revolution would succeed right then. When the movement failed to spread in the armed services, Lenin was one of the first to realize that the time had not yet come. But he felt sure that the next time the Czarist Government lost a war, the real Revolution would succeed, and when that did occur twelve years later, his careful studies during those months— of how a revolution works itself out, how the hated Czarist power operated under various conditions—would be of inestimable value to him and his generation. Lenin saw and persuaded others that the Revolution could be guided by thoroughly planned and tested techniques. Passion and accident played diminishing roles. Thus revolution was destined to succeed at last.

5

Maxim Litvinoff in 1905 was still in Riga, organizing the smuggling of revolutionary literature into Russia. In August, Krassin urged him to come to St. Petersburg to start a newspaper, and after the Czar's manifesto of October 17 Litvinoff and his friends, as well as all the other hitherto suppressed parties, had the novel experience of publishing openly. The Bolsheviks and the Mensheviks, each anxious to influence the masses, especially in the coming Duma elections, raced to be the first to get out a daily paper, and Litvinoff succeeded with the *Novaya Zhizn* (*The New Life*) which appeared on the streets on October 27, only ten days after the manifesto which made it possible, beating the Menshevik *Nachalo* (*The Beginning*) by several days.

But the paper was short-lived. On December 3 it was suppressed and its offices closed. Litvinoff himself has written of his part of the venture in a "Mémoire" published with reprints of the thirty-odd issues, long since great rarities, which the Soviet Government issued in 1925:

Memories of Maxim Litvinoff
(written on November 25, 1924)

"At the beginning of November, 1905 (this means during the last third of October, old style), I was asked unexpectedly by Krassin to take over the administrative direction of our legal Social Democratic paper, *Novaya Zhizn*.

"Shortly before, I had gone from St. Petersburg to Riga in order to do illegal work. I was carrying a passport made out in the name of Engineer Ludwig Vilhelmovitch Nietz. For I was as skeptical of the working of the October amnesty, as all Bolsheviki were. Furthermore, I was not quite sure whether my whole past was to fall under the amnesty, since the *Ochrana* had charged me with attacking a guard during the flight from the Kiev prison.

"An illegal underground worker as the publisher of a great factual daily—this was the situation, which was, at least, piquant. Before that time I had often had access to illegal, hand-worked presses, and connections with small printing shops, and I had also directed the shipping department of the *Iskra* in Geneva. It tempted me now to build up the first legal Social Democratic paper, and I accepted Krassin's proposal. Incidentally, this proposal had been made a few days before to Gukovski, but it had not worked out. Therefore, he was made editorial secretary and I was charged with the administration and the publishing of the newspaper.

"It would have taken much too long to get permission to publish a new daily. Therefore, we used the permit owned by the poet, Minski, who thus had to function as 'responsible editor.' We also had to find an official publisher who was leading a legal existence. We found it in F. M. Andreyeva.* The financing was taken over by Gorki.

"I went immediately to Moscow to discuss a number of financial questions and to get power of attorney from Andreyeva. When I returned from Moscow on November 8 (October 26, old style) I was asked to bring out the first number the very next day.

"We had a contract with the Narodnaya Polza, a printing shop, and we had office space on the Nevsky Prospect. But there was no furniture, there were no employees, no set-up for a circulation department, nothing, absolutely nothing had been prepared. Some essential furniture had to be bought in a hurry, and collaborators—especially from among our comrades in the suburbs of St. Petersburg—had to be

* The actress wife of Maxim Gorki.

brought in. The circulating department was taken over by the Party accountant, who unfortunately had not the slightest knowledge or qualification for this type of work. . . .

"The workers of St. Petersburg and the general public awaited the first issue of the first legal Social Democratic paper with impatience. This impatience became even greater when it was announced that with the first number there would be a gratis section—the program of the Party. From the early morning our offices on the Nevsky Prospect were surrounded by crowds."

That the office should have been on the Nevsky Prospect, a magnificent boulevard, is interesting, for no address in St. Petersburg could have carried greater prestige. Establishing the newspaper there meant erecting revolutionary headquarters near the very heart of the enemy. Litvinoff seems to have scored a good point here, and must have keenly relished the situation.

"The printing shop worked very slowly and, during the first night, could turn out only 15,000 copies, which were practically torn from the hands of our messengers. We had to go on printing all day long and the copies were distributed as soon as they got to our office.

"In this confusion it was impossible to send out newspaper vendors with the first edition. Workers from the factories in the suburbs had to send delegates to the Nevsky Prospect in order to get the paper. It was the same during the next few days. The printing facilities could not turn out enough papers to satisfy the demand, the shipping department did not function, and subscribers in the provinces did not receive the first issue. New subscriptions came in daily—thousands of new subscriptions. Money orders were brought in in baskets. Telegrams from the provinces begged for the newspaper. Since nobody knew the subscription price, many people wired hundreds of rubles and asked for the newspaper—at any price.

"In the office many Party members who had no inkling of the technique of getting out a newspaper worked busily, but the amount of useful work they did was small. . . . I myself had to work twenty, sometimes twenty-four hours a day. In any case, by the next day we succeeded in satisfying the demand. We got hold of a second printing shop, reorganized the circulation department, made changes in the office personnel, and got a few real experts to work for us.

"Still, the arrangements did not work smoothly yet. . . . The subscribers complained that the mailmen and letter carriers removed the wrappers from the newspapers in order to read them themselves. In the provinces, groups were formed in order to subscribe for and read the *Novaya Zhizn* collectively. Speculators enjoyed a little windfall—in the country the price for one number rose to more than one ruble.

"After a month all hitches were eliminated, and the organization worked so smoothly that when the editors and administrators of all the daily newspapers met in St. Petersburg in order to discuss steps to take in the steady fight against the postal administration, the distributing companies and even against the police, it was I who was elected chairman."

This also was an amusing situation: a "Mr. Nietz," as representative of all the St. Petersburg newspapers, discussing administrative questions with the authorities and the police, who would have liked nothing better than to arrest Mr. Litvinoff, if only they could have found him.

"This choice meant, of course, general recognition on the part of experts, of the smooth organization of our newspaper.

"The original capital of our newspaper was the 15,000 rubles given me by Gorki. This whole sum was needed for the initial costs of getting the paper started, but after that the newspaper paid for itself through its subscriptions and through advertisements. . . . The newspaper not only could exist without further outside aid, but even made money for the Party—and this, in spite of the high salaries which were paid to the partly bourgeois editorial staff and to the collaborators.

"The newspaper soon became the center of the Party activities in Petersburg. Meetings of the Party were held in its offices. . . . Eventually these offices became too small and we had to seek new ones. Often workers and peasants, and even bourgeois came in with complaints about arbitrary actions on the part of Czarist bureaus. Officials, officers, even policemen came to admit their old sins and to assure us of their sympathies for the Social Democratic Labor Party. When the Government had decided to surround the building in which the deputies of the Workers' Soviet were in session and to arrest them, I was informed of it by an officer of the Guard, who came to my office quite openly.

"When Lenin arrived in Petersburg, great changes took place on the

editorial staff. Vladimir Ilich did not approve of the influence demanded by the Minski group, which stood on its formal rights of possession. He insisted on a clear separation, and the editorial power was
put into the hands of the Central Committee. Vladimir Ilich, from
that day on, collaborated actively, and sometimes I saw him at two or
three o'clock in the morning reading his last proofs in the printing
shop.

"After printing the 'Party Manifesto' the newspaper was banned."

This manifesto appeared in Number 27 on December 2. It was very
forcible and began with the words: "The government is on the verge
of bankruptcy. It has changed this country into a mass of ruins and
covered it with corpses. . . ."

"The police order was brought into the printing shop late at night,
and we decided with the typesetters to publish the last number in
spite of the order. The directors of the printing shop protested, and we
got them out of the way by simply shutting them into a room of the
printing shop for the night. The printed newspaper was not sent to
the shipping office but went directly out to the suburbs through confidential members of the Party who had been hastily assembled. The
next morning, all the police could do was to take cognizance of the
distribution of that forbidden number.

"The offices on the Nevsky Prospect went on working for some time
in order to liquidate the whole business. One day when I arrived at the
office, the doorman whispered into my ear that a detective who wanted
to talk to me had been around earlier. I asked what he had wanted,
and the doorman answered that he had left a sheet of paper containing
the names of a few suspicious characters. The detective wanted to
know if these people worked at our office. I looked at the list and found
my real name there, along with the name of my secretary, and the real
name of an illegal woman collaborator whom we called 'The Mouse.'
Evidently, to the very last, the *Ochrana* had not suceeded in identifying me. It wanted to get informaion from me about myself!

"Anyhow, I decided not to trifle with my luck. I told the doorman
to send away the detective when he came back. Then I went to my
office, gathered together all the documents, and went out through the
back door.

"After a few days I received a new order from the Central Committee, and left St. Petersburg."

6

The suppression of Litvinoff's newspaper, and with it the dissolution of the Party structure, marked the end of the "days of liberty" (the *Dni Svobody*) and the beginning of the end of the revolt. The same day the Workers' Soviet was dissolved and 200 members were arrested and deported. Lenin called for a general strike and for armed resistance—the first summons to active revolt. But it was too soon, the Party was too weak. Funds were exhausted by preceding strikes, and there was not enough money on hand to carry the strikers through. In St. Petersburg the strike never really got started, and in Moscow, while fighting continued behind hastily flung up barricades for four weeks and much blood was spilled, the revolutionaries never had a chance.

Passion was spent, the people exhausted and frustrated. There had been no plan, no cohesion—just a general convulsion. Nothing much had happened, except the creation of a precarious and largely impotent Duma—and some plain writing on the wall, which the autocracy, morally and politically illiterate, could not read.

The Czarist Government, recovered from their confusion and near panic, resumed severe control and began sending out savage punitive expeditions from city to city, town to town, village to village, burning, torturing, killing in a most atrocious and reckless way. By the spring of 1906 more than 14,000 people had been killed, more than 18,000 had been wounded and more than 70,000 were under arrest. The reaction was in full swing, led by the Minister of Interior, Peter A. Stolypin, who even in Czarist Russia would be ranked as a ruthless reactionary. He was himself energetic, industrious and courageous. He had some real ideas but believed that killing plus other forms of practical terrorism would restore "order." Order first, reforms afterwards, he insisted—an old plea to gain time and a free hand to impose his own kind of reforms. The revolutionary leaders had to flee the country, but some were caught and exiled to Siberia. Still, in a few parts of Russia sporadic fighting went on for many months, in some cases for years. In reprisal, the University of Warsaw, for instance, was closed for three years.

The Duma promised in the Czar's Manifesto of October 17 was finally convened on April 27, 1906, but drastic and fraudulent changes had been made in the electoral system to give the urban populace only 26 per cent of the Duma seats, while 47 per cent went to large estate owners and the peasants, who, the Government mistakenly hoped, would support its policy.

The time had been very short for organizing effective parties, much less settling on policies or representatives, yet twenty-six different parties, and sixteen representing national minorities put up candidates. The Bolsheviki boycotted the first three Duma elections, because Lenin believed that they would accomplish nothing, and that Bolshevik participation would even give the Czarist regime an alibi for whatever might happen. Lenin felt it would be most unwise to allow the Government to claim that the Duma represented all classes and parties.

To everybody's surprise, the most important conservative party, the "Union of the Genuine Russian People," formed by anti-Semitic reactionaries, monarchists and those who financed the Black Hundreds, did not win a single seat. Then came, from right to left, first the "Octobrists," named for the October 17 Manifesto, supporting a constitutional monarchy, and led by Alexander I. Guchkov, a very able man, and Michael Rodzianko, who were to play a decisive part in Russian politics prior to the first World War; second, the "Cadets," short for "Constitutional Democratic Party," representing the liberal bourgeoisie (with quite a number of Jewish members), led by Professor Paul Miliukov, who played an important part during the first half of the 1917 Revolution; third, the Social Revolutionaries, the only group that had already had something of an organization, descendants of the "Narodniki" ("Populists") founded in 1901. Definitely not Marxist, they stood for continuance of private property under a Socialist leadership, and, contrary to the Communists, believed in acts of individual terrorism. During World War I they supported the Czarist Government. Fourth in order of liberalism came the Mensheviki, the so-called "right wing" of the Social Democratic Labor Party.

The "Cadets" were the strongest party in the First Duma, the Mensheviki and Social Revolutionaries formed the second largest group, and the entire Right had only twenty-six deputies out of the 524. In spite of having tampered with the election law, the Government had suffered a complete defeat. The body was dissolved after only seventy-two days, on July 20, 1906.

It had shown itself remarkably capable and courageous, had given evidence of surprising political judgment itself and contributed a lot to the political education of the country which now had a new rallying point that competed with the previously unique authority of the Czar.

On the fateful day in 1906 when it was decided to dissolve the Duma, the Czar merely wrote in his diary:

"July 7 [old calendar]: Very busy morning. Half hour late to breakfast with the officers . . . a storm came up and it was very muddy . . . we walked together. . . . Signed a decree dissolving the Duma . . . dined with Olga and Petya. Read all evening."

The following day, the Tavricheski Palace where the Duma met was surrounded by soldiers and the Duma was declared dissolved. Thus ended the first Russian experiment in representative government; thus was extinguished a Duma that had shown surprising capacity, dignity and courage in facing, with the slender power permitted them, Russia's desperately urgent problems. All Russia was thrown into a turmoil; 200 deputies, a majority, went to Viborg, whence they issued a manifesto challenging the Government, insisting that they were the only lawful representative body and urging the people to refuse to pay taxes or to report for military duty.

One sentence in this manifesto is of historic importance: "If the government contracts loans to secure funds, such loans contracted without the approval of the people's representatives will be invalid; the Russian people will never acknowledge them and will not pay them." This was a statement signed by 200 legally elected members of a representative body that by law had been charged with the supervision of appropriations, a body that had been illegally and improperly dissolved. It was the authentic voice of Russia, and although the document was wanting in strict legality, nevertheless it spoke with moral authority and should have been a fair warning to bankers in other countries who sought to make profitable loans to the Russian Government, with which most of them sympathized rather than with the people.

The Czar, in the face of these events, with his usual fatuity could only comment:

"July 9, Sunday: The Duma was closed today. At breakfast after mass, long faces were noticeable among many . . . the weather was fine. On our walk we met Uncle Misha who came over yesterday from Gatchina. Was quietly busy until dinner and all evening. Went paddling in a canoe."

"July 14: Got dressed and rode a bicycle to the bathing beach and bathed enjoyably in the sea."

"July 15: Bathed twice. It was very hot. Only us two at dinner. A storm passed over."

"July 19: Bathed in the morning. Received at the farm. Uncle Vladimir at Chagin lunched with us. . . ."

Was this aloofness, the product of self-discipline, the detachment of an assured superiority? It was nothing of the sort. The indifference was real. The Czar as a personality was a near-zero, a man without real interest in any significant subject or problem, let alone in the welfare of his country or his own people. Conventional phrases, a few emotional attitudes, mostly superficial, pleasant family relations, a little playing at life, obstinate ignorance and evasion, the shadowy gestures of imperial government—these comprised the bulk of a life on which Fate had concentrated the most grievous responsibilities, and equally prodigious opportunities. To both he was wholly inadequate. Revolutionaries counted it as good fortune; a powerful, informed, liberal-minded Czar might have indefinitely bolstered up the rapidly disintegrating system of autocracy, whereas in the person of Nicholas II the whole country saw the institution exposed, indicted and condemned.

The second Duma, from March, 1907, to June, 1907, was elected during the dictatorship of Stolypin. His regime somewhat weakened the parties of the Center and helped those of the Left, for when he tried to deprive sixty-five Mensheviks of their parliamentary immunity, the Duma refused to comply with his demand. Stolypin used this incident as an excuse for dissolving the second Duma.

Stolypin then decreed a new electoral law according to which the peasants, now considered unreliable by the Government, were reduced to 22.2 per cent, the workers and poorer urban classes to 12 per cent, while the big estate owners were now given 50 per cent of the votes.

Only then did Stolypin succeed in getting a Duma with which he could "collaborate," and it continued "working" from the autumn of 1907 till June, 1912. The plan was clear, to favor the privileged and well-to-do who, thus receiving favors, would the more willingly endure or support governmental tyranny. By Stolypin's policy there were certain economic ameliorations and some actual progress, but the class division was accentuated: the rich were getting richer, the poor poorer. It was hoped that the new Duma would validate the process.

When the call was issued for the Fourth Duma which endured from 1912 to the 1917 Revolution, the Bolsheviks finally decided to name candidates. By that time the working masses of Russia were convinced that there was no chance for a liberal or mildly leftist revolution. Indeed, the arrogant and illegal way in which the Government disposed of the Dumas which were not to its liking was proof that the Czar and his advisers were only trifling with the people's needs and hopes and that they had not the slightest intention of yielding any power or privilege. This plain fact at first seemed to the Bolsheviks to compromise every party that had put up candidates for election and made them appear as accessories to fraud and unrepentant tyranny. The repeated but futile attempts of the Mensheviks to oppose the Czarist regime within the Duma had probably brought a great number of workers, peasants and intellectuals over to the Bolsheviks, though regardless of that, since 1907 the Bolsheviks had had a clear majority over the Mensheviks in all congresses which had taken place outside Russia.

7

Before the revolt of 1905 the Party had been very small, with hardly any real organization, so that it had needed money only for illegal printing shops. Most of the members, though they lived illegally, had some trade or profession which took care of their individual necessities. The printing presses were nearly always provided by a few rich men who either sympathized with the Party or hoped through lavish contributions to forestall unpleasant consequences and get protection if the Revolution should succeed. Leonard Krassin, an engineer in the Putilov works, was especially skillful in locating these millionaires and extracting their money. Lenin was entirely willing to take their cash without promising anything in return.

Those revolutionaries who fled abroad, like Lenin, required next to nothing or took little jobs to keep themselves alive, but large amounts were essential for publications, especially for *Iskra,* for which Lenin frantically asked for money in many letters, and those sums were usually paid by millionaires or by liberal intellectuals brought around by Krassin.

These conditions, however, gradually changed after the failure of the 1905 revolt, for now the Party was getting large, with more than 100,000 members, so that an organization had to be maintained, and rebuilt again and again each time it was destroyed by the police. Moreover, for at least eighteen months after the collapse of the revolt, a succession of local civil wars, guerrilla fights, continued in Poland, in the Baltic, and in the Caucasus, and these, too, cost money.

Krassin could no longer get together sufficient amounts. Some millionaires had lost their taste for the Revolution after the bloody events of 1905, and others thought that it was finished once and for all so that they would never need an alibi. Liberal intellectuals would have liked to help but were afraid, because the Czarist police cruelly punished even sympathizers. Maxim Gorki gave the Party all the money he earned by his books, plays and lecture tours, but could not carry the entire expenses alone.

Some rather chimerical plans for raising money were proposed, incorrigibly theoretical and typically Russian. For instance, good-looking young Party members were to marry rich girls and then turn over their fortunes to the Party. However, this and similar notions did not work. Their very impracticality was a witness to political frustration, to lack of organizational experience as well, even though evidence of theatrical talent.

"Expropriation" was the most important proposal, the organized robbery of banks and revenue offices. The guerrilla bands, especially those under Stalin, never admitted that they were defeated. They were in the midst of civil war. The Czarist regime was the enemy. The enemy had to be attacked and beaten wherever and whenever possible. Nobody would consider it wrong if the army of a country at war confiscated moneys belonging to the enemy. The Russian guerrillas felt exactly the same way about the money in Russian banks, especially in State-controlled banks or in Treasury branches—taxes paid by people who had had no voice in determining the amounts.

Expropriation can be judged only in relation to the exigencies of civil warfare. This was why Lenin himself declined to discuss the question. He felt that it was a basic revolutionary right to expropriate the capital of the State, but he was against the expropriation of private capital before the Socialist state was organized. He was for the partisans, but against bandits. The Party decided against expropriations in its conference at Stockholm in 1906, but this did not commit Lenin, or the Bolshevik wing, since the majority there was Menshevik.

Litvinoff was against expropriation from the beginning. He felt that it would do the Party more harm than good, especially since the Russian public and the outside world would not recognize the difference between expropriation and theft.

However, since no official stand had been taken against expropriation by the Bolshevik group, the practice became more prevalent throughout 1906. In October alone there were 362 incidents. The preferred plan was to get hold of the money while it was in transport. The expropriation "Commandos" were called "Boyeviki," "fighters," a name taken from the Polish partisan groups, who were highly proficient in expropriation, under the leadership of Pilsudski, later Marshal and dictator of Poland.

Soon afterwards Lenin decided that Litvinoff and the others who had come out against expropriation were right. Many dubious elements had entered the Party through these expropriation adventures. Since the police had destroyed the Party structure, no control was possible. Consequently, Lenin asked, during the Party conference of 1907 in London, for another and stronger resolution against expropriation. This time the Bolsheviks were in the majority and it was they who voted against expropriation.

Expropriations were especially numerous in the Caucasus, where Stalin continued a desultory warfare after the failure of the 1905 revolt, and an anti-Communist legend asserts that Stalin himself, together with a few friends, robbed many banks, but this is quite untrue. Stalin was no Russian revolutionary Jesse James. He had even at that time too responsible a position to indulge in such adventures.

8

Litvinoff had seen a great deal of Lenin during the "days of liberty" in St. Petersburg. Subsequently, Lenin stayed for some time in a place near St. Petersburg; then for a while he lived in Finland. Two years later he returned to Switzerland. During this period Litvinoff was often in and out of Russia, for he was again the "transport" man, whose task it was to smuggle newspapers, pamphlets, agents into Russia. But now there was something much more important to transport into Russia than even Lenin's articles or the *Proletariat,* the illegal organ of the Moscow and Petersburg Party committees.

Now the most important thing was arms.

Ever since Bloody Sunday in January, 1905, the conviction was everywhere growing that only an armed revolution could succeed—the power of the autocracy was too great, and its military and police agents too ruthless for demonstrations or appeals to effect anything. These could only result in frustration and merciless repression. "We need arms." Millions had struck, but only a few thousand had been able to shoot. Stalin, the only Bolshevik leader who had been able to develop the revolt into a sustained civil war, in his Caucasus district, had said in a speech on October 17, 1905: "What we need for a decisive victory is three things: first—arms; second—arms; third—arms; and arms again." In January, 1906, Lenin had complained: "We should have taken to arms more resolutely, energetically and aggressively. We should have explained to the people that it was impossible to confine ourselves to a peaceful strike and that a fearless and relentless armed strike was indispensable." He was furious with Plekhanov who, after the call for armed resistance, had declared: "They should not have taken arms."

Both Lenin and Stalin decided that the revolt had failed because there had not been enough armed resistance, and both concluded that if a revolt were ever to have a chance, a great quantity of arms would have to be sent into Russia. Lenin for years had expressed, in writing and speaking, his approval of the workers who had taken up arms, and railed against those who "were contemptuous of Brownings." The logical man for such "transport," the man who, according to Lenin, guaranteed transport as long as he was alive, was Litvinoff.

Litvinoff, before he finally disappeared from Russia—because eventually even the *Ochrana* found out who Nietz really was—had been offered by the Central Committee the choice between two important assignments: to go to America to prepare a lecture tour for Gorki, who hoped by this means to bring in new funds for the Party; or to organize the purchase of weapons and ammunition abroad and their transport into Russia. Litvinoff preferred the latter.

Buying arms for Russian revolutionaries had become very difficult. The affair of the *John Grafton,* Father Gapon's attempt to smuggle weapons, in which Litvinoff had been involved, had led to a sharp official protest by the Russian Embassy in London, which made the English police extremely watchful. The Russian Government had financed during the summer of 1906 an enormous press campaign in France to facilitate placing a Russian loan with the big banks. As a result revolutionary arms traffic was under the ban there, too. In Germany, the political police collaborated with the *Ochrana* without any attempt at concealment. When Litvinoff went abroad, all his friends and comrades told him that the time was not at all propitious, that it would be impossible to ship arms and it might be better to wait a while. Litvinoff, however, having received his assignment from the Central Committee, characteristically went ahead. Later he wrote of this period: "Ilich has taught us that nothing is impossible, and that one must simply ignore difficulties. And that's why I just went to work." During the next two years Litvinoff was connected in one way or another—usually as the organizer—with many gun-running expeditions, mostly of small consignments of which not even Litvinoff himself can recall the details, though he does remember very well one wholesale undertaking.

His work took him all over Europe. He stayed a while in Paris and in Berlin, to study the kinds of arms available there, and especially the kinds that would be most useful in the sporadic warfare which Stalin, back in the Caucasus, was still maintaining. He inspected a great number of models, discussed dozens of proposals before he made a decision. Later, he said jokingly that in those days he really became the father of all Soviet Russian "imports"—fifteen years before there was a Soviet Russia.

He decided to buy Mauser rifles and machine guns, which could be purchased most readily from the State munition factories of Denmark. So one day the management of the Mauser works received a letter requesting that a representative be sent to Hamburg to meet a representative of the Army of Ecuador. When the Danish gentleman appeared in Hamburg he met Litvinoff who blandly ordered machine guns for the South American Republic.

Shortly afterwards he ordered guns and ammunition from a German factory, using as agents the firm of Schroeder & Company, and pretending this time to represent a Belgian company. On this occasion he was aided in making his selection by a man who knew a good deal more about guns, Semyon Arshakovitch Ter-Petrosian, who, under the name of Kamo, became one of the most celebrated daredevils of the Russian Revolution. Kamo came, not from the intellectual circles of the Party, but from a guerrilla organization in the Caucasus, where he had co-operated closely with Stalin. Kamo had just staged a dramatic escape from the Tiflis prison, and in September, 1906, he was chosen to go abroad to arrange with Litvinoff the details of the arms shipment. He went to St. Petersburg where he obtained a false passport, and from there proceeded to Liége where he met Litvinoff, who was still playing the role of a representative of a Belgian firm. Kamo was very excited. Litvinoff and his revolutionary friends, enjoying the situation thoroughly, got themselves up like regular bourgeois. Together, they visited a number of factories. Then Kamo returned to Russia for a time, while Litvinoff went to Karlsruhe in Southern Germany, still as a Belgian representative, to take over the munitions ordered.

The director of the factory in Karlsruhe told the "Belgian" that a number of Russian officers had just arrived to buy arms, too, and asked if he would like to watch the tests along with them. Litvinoff, who was always up to any situation, said that he would be pleased with such an arrangement. After all, Belgium had always been a friend of Russia, so why should he not co-operate with the Russian officers? He met them, became quite friendly with them, and they gave him many valuable pointers as to new weapons used in the Russian army. Litvinoff even went so far as to ask his Russian acquaintances to look over the matériel which he had ordered. They pointed out to him that two or three of the types were no good, and at least in Russia would not be acceptable. Litvinoff promptly refused to take delivery of the matériel in question.

The problem of getting the arms into Russia remained. Again he crossed Europe, visiting Dutch, Belgian, French and Austrian ports. Many local Socialist organizations tried to help him, but he could not find a boat for the cargo. Finally, at the little port of Varna in Bulgaria, where authorities did not supervise things too carefully, he felt he could load his arms on a boat; but how was he to get the arms across Germany and Austria into Bulgaria? Surely, this could not be done without the Bulgarian authorities getting wind of the affair. Then it occurred to him to use the rather complicated Balkan political situation of those days for his purposes, and he intimated to the Bulgarian authorities that the weapons were intended for Macedonian revolutionaries who were eager to free themselves from the Turks. This rather appealed to the Bulgarians, so they closed their eyes and let the shipment pass to Varna.

Litvinoff has described the whole episode in a contribution to the biography of Kamo by Bibineyshvili, published in Moscow in 1934:

"I established relations with the Macedonian revolutionaries and found a very willing though not quite altruistic agent named Naum Tyufektsheyev. . . . After consultation with him I decided to ask permission of the Bulgarian Government to ship to Varna arms which allegedly were to be sent as contraband into Turkish Armenia. The affair was represented to the Bulgarian Government in such a way that it appeared that the Macedonian revolutionaries wanted to help the Armenians revolt against the common enemy, the Turks.

"Since the Macedonians at that time were fully aided by the Bulgarian Government, Tyufektsheyev did not doubt that we would succeed with this method and he was right.

"I will not pretend that the Bulgarian officials who put seals on the freight cars filled with arms acted from sheer patriotism. They had other motives too, and not quite unselfish ones." Litvinoff then recounts that not only did the duty have to be paid twice, but that bribes also had to be paid to the Bulgarian petty officials.

"The difficulty of getting the arms from Belgium and Germany across Austria was taken care of admirably through the internationally known German shipping firm of Schenker and Company. The arms arrived at the Bulgarian frontier after we had paid duties in other countries, and we had to pay duty again in Bulgaria. But what did it matter, since we finally had our material in the port?

"Two-thirds of the difficulties thus were solved. Now came the question of getting the arms out of Varna. The Bulgarians had no large ships and the few steamship companies definitely declined to consider the transport of arms without a specific point of delivery. For if the weapons were to be unloaded somewhere as contraband, such a shipment might endanger their boats as well as their men. Here, appeal to patriotism and the mention of the Macedonians' fight against the Turks was quite in vain.

"So, I decided to buy a ship and have a Russian crew. Finally I found a small yacht—the *Sarya*—in Fiume and bought her for 30,000 francs. The *Sarya* had just made a trip from America to Europe and seemed to be adequate for our purposes. I bought the yacht in my own name. She was undergoing repairs at a small wharf in Fiume, and she was brought over to Varna by her own crew. This was done only after I had bought return tickets from Varna to Fiume for the entire crew."

On September 25, 1906, Kamo and three other men left St. Petersburg and traveled to Berlin via Finland, Stockholm and Stettin. There they found a telegram from Litvinoff asking them to go on to Sofia, where they met Litvinoff who told them all about the boat and the arms. They all went to Varna, where they expected the rest of the money for the boat to arrive at any moment.

However, the money did not arrive, and for a very good reason: the Central Committee of the Party was now, after the collapse of the 1905 revolt, predominantly Menshevik, and they did not believe—or, at least, could not easily be convinced—that armed resistance was necessary. Valuable weeks went by and nothing happened. Litvinoff then decided to go to St. Petersburg himself, where he appeared before the Central Committee, created a scene, and finally got the money.

In the meantime, Kamo took on a number of sailors to man the *Sarya*. He was not too happy about the crew, and did not really trust even the captain, Kovtunenko, though he was a former sailor from the *Potemkin,* and a Party member. So Kamo and his three friends decided to keep an eye on the crew throughout the whole trip.

Neither was Litvinoff happy after he inspected the crew, but he still felt that Kamo would succeed in getting the cargo through. He wrote about their departure:

"With a much lighter heart I stood on the beach and saw the yacht sailing away. I hoped that soon the revolutionary task on which I had worked for ten months would be carried through successfully. But three days later I learned in Sofia that the *Sarya* had run aground— perhaps on account of a storm, perhaps on account of the cowardice or inexperience of the captain."

Indeed, a storm did blow up immediately after the *Sarya* left. Kamo became seasick but recovered shortly. In his cabin he had constructed an infernal machine with which he planned to blow up the boat if it should be stopped by a Russian warship or the Russian authorities. Kamo, however, never made use of his infernal machine. When the boat foundered on a sandbank his cabin filled with water, and put the machine out of order. For twenty hours the *Sarya* had to wait, until Rumanian fishermen came along and rescued the crew.

The sailors were afraid of being arrested by the Rumanian police and simply ran away. Kamo and his friends could do nothing alone, and besides, they were, of course, in constant danger of being thrown into prison. While they were still discussing what to do, Rumanian fishermen stole the arms and made away with them.

Litvinoff immediately went to Bucharest, but he was helpless, since the Russian Minister had heard about the affair and had roused the Rumanian police. He could only send a harsh note of protest to the Central Committee for having lost so much time. In later years Litvinoff was to become famous for his harsh notes of protest, but he says that this was unquestionably the sharpest he ever wrote.

The affair could not be hushed up. All Rumania chattered about the "adventure of the Russian students." Kamo and his three friends were finally arrested and sent to Constanza. To save them, Litvinoff used all his connections with Bulgarian revolutionaries. Finally, he succeeded in getting the Bulgarian Government to make a semi-official statement that the *Sarya* had been loaded with arms for the Macedonian Committee. Thus the Government saved its face and let the arrested comrades go, and one by one they returned to Russia.

Later, Kamo himself often spoke about that disastrous affair and, according to his biographer, he always emphasized the unique organizing genius and the shrewdness of Litvinoff. "His face would light up and he would tell about a dozen large and small details, proving the exceptional talents of Papasha as an underground worker and a revolutionary organizer.

"The *Ochrana,* of course, finally found out everything. Captain Kovtunenko, who had returned to Russia and was living illegally in Odessa under another name, was arrested in May, 1907. He was grilled for days, but he revealed nothing. Nevertheless, there was a little entry in one of the dossiers of the political police found after the Revolution:

" 'With the money robbed from the revenue department of Kviril in 1905—allegedly 200,000 rubles—Kamo and the emigrant Meer Wallach, who had escaped from the Kiev prison, bought arms abroad and wanted to bring them on a yacht *Sarya,* bought for this purpose, from Varna to Russia.' "

9

After returning from Bulgaria, Kamo began systematically to lay the groundwork for some expropriations, choosing as objectives two money transports—one to Julfa, the other destined for Baku. Kamo led both enterprises, both failed, he was seriously wounded and lost the sight of one eye.

But even before he had fully recovered, on June 13, 1907, he successfully managed the "Tiflis expropriation." A rumor had circulated through half the population of the city that a considerable sum of money was to be brought to the State Bank from St. Petersburg. A letter-carrier passed the story on to Kamo, giving him his first intimation of the transfer.

The Police Commissioner of Tiflis discounted the whole matter as groundless, but on June 13 towards 11 o'clock in the morning, two sacks of money did arrive, and were loaded into a carriage. The cashier and accountant of the State Bank and two armed guards got in with them and five Cossack cavalrymen surrounded the vehicle.

Revolutionaries had been stationed at various points along the route that the carriage would take, and communicated its passage to each other by previously arranged signals. When the chief conspirators, who were waiting in the Tileputchuri Restaurant, got the signal, they went out and took their stations in the square where the bank stood.

Kamo himself meanwhile, disguised as an officer, had been strolling about the square dropping hints to passers-by that it might be better to get out of that neighborhood, and thanks to this, few people were around. When the time drew near for the bank carriage to come, he got into an elegant phaeton, where he sat to watch the proceedings, smoking one cigarette after another.

The sign to make the attack was given by one of the conspirators standing on the pavement unfolding a newspaper. Six others then threw bombs at the carriage; there was a close series of deafening reports, two guards and one Cossack were killed, the other Cossacks hurled from their horses, the cashier and accountant thrown out bodily to the ground. The horses bolted, dragging the carriage after them. At this instant, on which everything depended, one of the revolutionaries stationed close by threw his bomb, reserved for the purpose, into the careening carriage. A confederate with quick presence of mind pulled one of the two sacks out of the vehicle and raced away. The square was filled with smoke. Everyone was too panic-stricken to prevent his escape.

When Kamo heard the explosion and saw the now empty carriage racing along, he realized at once that something had gone wrong. He ordered his driver to follow the carriage, took out his revolver, fired several shots, and altogether acted the officer who was pursuing the bandits. This added to the general confusion. Finally, his phaeton caught up with the conspirator who was trying to get the money sack to safety. Kamo, without a moment's hesitation, struck his driver over the head with the butt of his revolver, threw him off the phaeton, helped his friend to get the sack into the vehicle and then drove on. Away from the scene of violence, people merely thought him an officer having his morning drive. The troops, which by now were streaming towards the scene Kamo had left, saluted and allowed him to proceed. Three people were killed and a number were slightly wounded, but all the conspirators got away.

Kamo hid the money, 250,465 rubles, in a friend's apartment and later it was transferred by employees of a moving firm to the study of the Director of the Tiflis Observatory, who knew nothing of what was going on. Naturally, nobody thought of looking for it in the quarters of this highly esteemed gentleman.

Four weeks later, Kamo, again disguised as an officer and traveling in a first-class carriage, carried all the 500-ruble notes to St. Petersburg. During the trip he seemed extremely anxious lest the hat which he was taking to his wife should be crushed. The other people in the compartment understood his worry and treated the big hat box with special consideration. In St. Petersburg Kamo delivered the money to the Central Committee, which had already arranged for its transfer to other countries for safekeeping.

Both Stalin and Litvinoff have been blamed or credited, according to the point of view, with participation in the Tiflis exploit, but while Stalin as Chairman of the Tiflis Committee must have known the plan in advance and probably put Kamo in charge of it, there is no reason to suppose that he himself was actively engaged, while Litvinoff, despite the oft-repeated legend depicting him as a gun-man storming through the streets of Tiflis, was really several thousand miles away in Paris.

Some time later Kamo was arrested in Berlin for carrying a weapon without permission, and it was discovered that he had some connection with the Tiflis affair. When the German authorities ordered his extradition to Russia, he simulated insanity, and kept up the pretense for four years. This he could do, even under the supervision of German psychiatrists, because, doubtless, of the marked neurotic trend in his personality. After his release and return to Russia he was arrested many times by the Czarist police, sent to different prisons, confined in various asylums, and sentenced to death no less than four times. Yet he always managed to escape and was still alive and at large when the Party came into power. Now, however, that his comrades were carrying the responsibility for government reorganization, there was little place for a romantic adventurer like Kamo. But he died a hero's death in 1921, for when he was plunging down a steep hill in Tiflis on his bicycle, a little girl rushed out into his path. It was his life or hers, and he deliberately swerved into the bank and was rather badly smashed up.

The day had passed for the flaming revolutionary with his fantastic plots, incredible audacity and slightly unbalanced mind. The hard, slow, systematic work necessary to establish and operate the new regime would hardly have been congenial to his ardent soul. Kamo might have proven an embarrassment to the Bolsheviks.

10

Meanwhile Litvinoff left Paris, in August, 1907, and went to Stuttgart as a Bolshevik delegate to the Twelfth International Socialist Congress, which opened there on August 18, with Plekhanov and Martov representing the Mensheviks. It was an impressive affair, with 884 delegates representing 25 different nations in Europe, Asia, America, Australia and Africa; and, outwardly at least, it was a perfect picture of international solidarity, with everything on the surface extremely friendly.

August Bebel, the grand old man of German socialism, opened the meeting. Delegates from England, France, Holland and Belgium each had his say. The French delegate, Hervé, claimed that the famous discipline of the German Socialists was a discipline of stagnation and death. There had been a time, he said, when German Socialists were not afraid to speak up and were not silenced even by the very real threat of prison. Now that they had 3,000,000 followers, they had grown timid and were always afraid of compromising their party. Vaillant and Jean Jaurès also scored the timidity of the German Socialists.

All the sessions were much the same. People talked, quarreled and argued over many problems, but nothing real happened. Resolutions were adopted, one protesting against the expulsion and the persecution of Rumanian Jews, another extending the sympathy of the Congress to the Russian Revolution. But none of these resolutions was of any importance. In vain did Litvinoff try to get some formula adopted which, in the event of war, would cripple the contesting governments and make actual fighting between peoples impossible, even if it was necessary to foster a revolution for the purpose. But all his attempts were stopped either by Bebel himself or by other members of the German Socialist Party. They were against war—to be sure; but they did not want to use the means within their power to combat war. They wanted to fight war with talk and the obvious propaganda weapons.

Watching the famous Socialist leaders of all countries exhaust themselves in this make-believe parliament, and try to evade the significant questions instead of solve them, Litvinoff became increasingly bored and disillusioned. It seemed to him that this was more a bourgeois than a Socialist gathering. He felt that the leaders of the Second International had put on too much weight—in a figurative sense as well as in avoirdupois—to be able still to act as revolutionaries. This was especially true of the German Socialists, who were becoming more and more German and less and less Socialist.

The Stuttgart Congress, Litvinoff has said, was "only a fleeting incident. It didn't mean very much to me at that time or any time afterwards, except that I was disgusted and saw doubly clearly how right Lenin was not to compromise."

But actually it was a very instructive episode for Litvinoff and his disparagement of its significance is a result of his characteristic objectivity and almost complete lack of interest in himself. What counted for Litvinoff, and consequently what he afterwards recalled, was not what *he* said, thought or felt, but the simple fact that the Congress got nowhere. A few years later Litvinoff was again confronted by the same kind of international gathering that again failed in an hour of international danger, failed then even more miserably. But that time, Litvinoff was in a position to fight, and he fought.

II

Kamo's Berlin arrest was in November, 1907, and in January, 1908, a Russian student, Sarah Ravitch, was arrested in Munich for passing ruble notes expropriated at Tiflis, which were identified by their serial numbers. During the next few days there were arrests in Rotterdam, Stockholm and Geneva. And on January 18, Litvinoff was arrested in Paris.

Later reports, of which there were many, described Litvinoff's Paris stay in the lurid formulae of commonplace romantic fiction:

"He was swimming in money." "He was elegantly though grotesquely dressed (yellow waistcoat, long rolled collars with flowing red neckties, hats with enormous brims, dark green shoes)."

"He lived extremely well, ate only in the best restaurants, insisted that his champagne be very dry and cold, invited his hungry comrades and always paid their bills." When arrested—so the legend has it—

hundreds of thousands of francs were found in his wallet, the proceeds of a series of highway robberies and holdups. "He was also [probably in his spare time!] the head of a band which counterfeited money."

Of course there is no word of truth in all this. The report was not merely irresponsible, it was specifically dishonest, and was written not by any reporter but in an editorial office as part of a policy. The simple facts are that the Munich police found that Sarah Ravitch had come from Geneva, hence the Geneva arrests. Then other Tiflis notes were found in the possession of people who had just come from Paris. Therefore, the police concentrated on Litvinoff, who had been shadowed for some time, because the police knew of his revolutionary activities.

The conservative journal *Figaro* in three reports (January 19, 22, 23, 1908) gave a straightforward account covering the essential facts. Litvinoff, posing as a law student and calling himself Dethiarsk, had been living at 33 Rue des Ecoles, and working with a Russian woman student twenty-seven years old named Freda Yanpolska, who lived at 15 Avenue des Gobelins. After Litvinoff had returned from a trip to Lausanne, he and Mlle. Yanpolska were arrested at the Gare du Nord while they were buying tickets for London, and twelve 500-ruble notes were found on him, bearing numbers on the Tiflis list. Litvinoff gave the name Abraham Borissouck and said that he had been born in Kaminetz in 1877, but afterwards "admitted" that he was Dethiarsk and in the end was identified as Meer Wallach. They were sent to prison and Litvinoff said—quite truthfully—that he had been in France when the Tiflis robbery took place, had had nothing to do with it, had been given the notes by the Russian revolutionary treasury and not asked their origin, was on his way to England to sell them, and Mlle. Yanpolska had no connection with the affair. The Paris police had acted at Russian behest and were clearly not anxious to be involved. Litvinoff and Mlle. Yanpolska were therefore released but were ordered expelled and were escorted by the police to the frontier.

The *Figaro,* however, did not tell the whole story. Pressure had been brought to bear by the Russian authorities for extradition. Similar requests made in other countries had been refused. Clearly, whatever else the Tiflis expropriation may be called, it was a political crime, and France had always considered herself an asylum for political refugees. Nonetheless, the insistence of the Czarist Government was so great that the matter was finally referred to the Minister of Justice. The Ministry of Justice had been taken over only two weeks before by a man, formerly Minister of Education, who prevented the French police from turning Litvinoff over to the Czarist police. Whether he actually saved Litvinoff, or whether Litvinoff had no real need of a savior, will probably never be known.

Litvinoff was to meet that French Minister of Justice twenty years later under quite different circumstances. His name was Aristide Briand.

12

After his release, the French authorities escorted Litvinoff to Boulogne, whence he crossed to England, arriving in January, 1908. There he was destined to stay for a long time, much longer than he had expected.

Through a letter of introduction from Maxim Gorki, Litvinoff made friends with the director of the London Library, a Mr. Charles Hagleberg Wright, who obtained a job for him with a London publisher, Williams & Norgate.

As clerk in the foreign department, Litvinoff started at a salary of 25 shillings a week, but he rapidly showed that he could do anything and had excellent judgment, and so his responsibilities expanded until he was called in to participate in important conferences regarding the entire policy of the firm. His pay was gradually increased until, when he left Williams & Norgate in 1914, he was getting £3 10s a week, nominally $17.00, but in purchasing power far more, and a good salary for the time and the job.

During the period, for business convenience, he used the name Maxim Harrison, but this was only in the office, and in general he was still known as Litvinoff. Indeed after taking that name, Litvinoff never really changed it. When later he became an English subject, he was naturalized as Litvinoff.

When Litvinoff arrived in England, he was no longer a youngster. He was thirty-two years old. And psychologically he had never been young; he had always been a "Papasha," a calm, settled man, quite without the characteristics of the traditional wild, romantic revolutionary of fiction; and now in the six years that he was with Williams & Norgate, to 1914, those traits became more marked.

His business associates found him competent and hardworking, indistinguishable from thousands of London middle-class respectable employees. His friends knew him to be gentle and amiable, and mammas with daughters to marry off looked on him with a friendly eye as a most eligible bachelor. He was especially fond of children, and while in the boarding house in Hampstead where he lived, he could not keep a pet, he was always ready to stroke a friendly dog.

His friends and acquaintances, who were legion, were chiefly Russian exiles, also living in boarding houses in Hampstead, and he spent most of his free hours, usually evenings, seeing and talking to them. They were not all Party members, by any means, and many were as ignorant of his political activities as were his British business associates, who would probably have rejected as absurd any assertion that the quiet little man was actually a revolutionary.

But social incidents were soon swept off the board by the cyclone of war. An Austrian archduke was murdered in Serbia. Ultimatums were issued. The great European Powers mobilized. On August 1, 1914, Germany declared war on Russia. Three days later Great Britain and France were at war with Germany. A week later millions of men were killing and being killed.

CHAPTER FOUR

The Bolsheviks Fight World War I

WHEN World War I broke out, Lenin had been living for some time in the little village of Poronino in the Galician Province of the Austro-Hungarian Empire, near the Russian frontier, so near, indeed, that from time to time he walked into Russian territory. He was in constant touch with the Russian leaders of the movement, especially through his work on *Pravda,* the first Party newspaper to appear legally inside Russia since 1905. Lenin had no illusions about the reactionary and capitalist forces in all the European countries which wanted war, and few about the strength and determination of the Socialist parties, whose leaders had become too complacent for dangerous revolutionary activities, yet he could not bring himself to believe that the working masses would permit themselves to be led meekly to the slaughter.

Now the war had come, and the Austrian police immediately arrested the "enemy alien," Lenin, the very man who had used all his influence to persuade the Russian people to stay out of the war. The local police were deluged with denunciations from residents of Poronino of the strange little man who went on extended walks near the frontier and must, therefore, they felt sure, be a dangerous spy. Furthermore, when searching Lenin's shack, the police found a mass of statistical material, and since they could not make out the figures, they jumped to the conclusion that these were coded messages. Ambitious agents even declared that Lenin "had inspected the surrounding hills and had made topographic reports on the roads."

Lenin was not idle even in prison. There he found numbers of peasants, who had been rounded up for one reason or other or no reason at all, and could not secure release for the simple reason that they had no idea of what was going on. Many could neither read nor write. So Lenin undertook to counsel them and even write applications for them. The peasants, liking and trusting him, made him their confidant.

In the meantime Lenin's friends and others belonging to the Austrian Party overwhelmed members of the Austrian parliament and various people of influence with telegrams and letters demanding the immediate liberation of Lenin. They made it clear to government officials, who had never heard of Lenin and considered that a Russian was a Russian, that the Socialist leader was not exactly a friend of the Czar—that, on the contrary, he could be counted upon as an ally in defeating the Czar. Consequently, after only a few days, Lenin was freed and allowed to cross Austria to Switzerland, which under normal circumstances took about twenty-four hours but took him, in the confused international situation, a fortnight.

By the time Lenin was released from prison, the policy of the Socialist parties of Europe was no longer in doubt: they were all for war. The German Socialist Democratic Party in particular, the largest of the Second International, became quite chauvinistic. Its members not only voted for the war credits, but its principal newspaper, the *Vorwaerts,* in Berlin, of which Friedrich Stampffer was the editor, came out for the exaggerated rightist program of annexation of foreign territories. The French were not much better. Their greatest leader, Jean Jaurès, had been assassinated, perhaps because he would not have endorsed France's entry into the war. But the others did, and Hervé, who only a short time before had held a strong anti-war policy, now became one of the wildest of nationalists. The English Labor Party finally gave the war its blessing, too, though in this party, even in the exciting and confusing hours as war broke out and primitive instincts surged over the barriers of reason, John Burns and a few others spoke up with the courage of their convictions. In Italy, which had an alliance with Germany and Austria, the unions and the Socialists, seconded by one of their leading men, Benito Mussolini, had gone on record against getting involved on that side and Mussolini came out strongly against war; but a few months later he became one of the most aggressive advocates of Italy's entrance on the side of the Allies.

In Russia the situation, from the Socialist point of view, was much better. In the Duma the seven Mensheviks as well as the five Bolsheviks declared themselves against the war, against war credits and one

Menshevik even read publicly an anti-war manifesto written by Lenin. But the Russian masses felt differently. They were distressed over the plight of their little brothers, the Serbs, and were soon inflamed by the war fever. There was no talk of revolution or revolt. Tens of thousands went to the gates of the Winter Palace, knelt, prayed and sang patriotic songs. The Czar appeared on the balcony. All the sins of the regime were forgotten in the upsurge of patriotism. With the enemy "at the gates," the Czar once more became the Little Father, the God-sent savior.

Because of this general feeling, after the war had started, Plekhanov and the majority of the Mensheviks asked the workers to co-operate with the Czarist Government in the war. This meant a complete and final break between Plekhanov and Lenin.

For Lenin no compromise was possible. He was against this war or any war which was not either a working class war or a war of national defense. On the day of his arrival in Berne he summoned the Bolsheviks living there, and read them his theses on the war, which from that time on were the basis of future Bolshevik tactics:

"Propaganda for the Socialist Revolution: The demand not to take arms against brother-workers or the proletarians of enemy countries, but only against the bourgeois government at home. To fight without compromise against chauvinism and against the leaders of the Second International who have betrayed socialism."

Lenin settled in Zurich. From November, 1914, to the beginning of 1917, he and his assistant, Grigori Zinoviev, edited a Russian newspaper there called *Sozialdemocrat*.

From the very beginning, Lenin was convinced that the war would bring about a Russian revolution. He propagandized for a defeat of the Czarist Government, not merely because it was bad and unjust, but because he believed that this was the only way to revolution. According to Lenin, the Russian proletariat had to break with all who had supported the war or had even favored a truce with the Czarist regime. He sharply attacked not only the Mensheviks, but also the small group around Leon Trotsky. Trotsky was against the truce, too, but he had refused to join a fight to the finish against the Russian Socialists and Democrats who favored a truce because they did not want to split the workers' movement at that time. The Mensheviks believed themselves the representatives of the Russian workers, while the Bolsheviks considered themselves the leaders of the coming Revolution.

In Russia the Bolsheviks could not speak out. Most of their leaders were either in prison or exiled in Siberia. A strong and promising leader, Stalin, had been arrested in 1913, and confined to the distant area of Turushansk.

On October 13, Lenin published eleven directions for the revolutionary work in Russia. First, he declared that the slogan, "Call a Constitutional National Assembly" was no longer pertinent. Now everything depended upon who would call such an assembly. If the Czar were allowed to do so, it would frustrate the Revolution. Lenin urged that three demands should be incorporated in such a summons: There must be a democratic republic, the large estates must be expropriated, and the eight-hour day established.

In the second thesis he insisted that the workers take no part in the war industry committees which had been formed to hasten arming.

The third thesis advocated the spread of Social-Democratic propaganda among the peasants and soldiers. Every strike movement should be extended, and an immediate termination of the war demanded. Also, the liberation of the Bolshevik Duma delegates had to be pressed.

His fourth thesis stated that workers' delegations and similar groups must be considered organs of the Revolution.

The fifth and sixth theses had to do with the social character of the coming Russian Revolution. Lenin was still convinced that the Revolution would have to be a liberal bourgeois revolution and not one involving the expropriation of private capital. This would follow later.

In theses seven and eight, Lenin took pains to make clear why he had changed his ideas since 1905 about a coalition: "We still hold possible the participation of the Social Democrats in a provisional government, together with the democratic petty bourgeoisie, but not with the revolutionary chauvinists. Revolutionary chauvinism is based on the condition of the petty bourgeoisie as a class. This always sways between the bourgeoisie and the proletariat. Now it sways between chauvinism, which prevents its being revolutionary even in the sense of a democratic republic, and proletarian internationalism. A coalition with the democratic parties is still permissible for the Bolsheviks, but only if these parties declare themselves against chauvinism, that is, against the imperialistic system." Practically, under the circumstances then existing, this meant the rejection of a coalition, because the Democratic parties (as well as the Socialists under Plekhanov) were for national defense.

Thesis nine affirmed: "If the revolutionary chauvinists win in Russia, we should be against the defense of their country in this war. Our slogan is: Against the chauvinists (even if they are revolutionary or republican) and for association with the international proletariat, in the name of the Socialist revolution."

Thesis ten explained: "To the question whether the proletariat can have a leading part in the Russian bourgeois revolution we answer: 'Yes, this is possible, if the petty bourgeois will go to the left at the decisive moment.' "

The eleventh and last thesis contained the entire program of so-called world revolution: "To the question, what will the party of the proletariat do if a revolution should bring it to the helm during this present war, we answer: 'We would offer peace to all warring people, under the condition of the liberation of colonies and the liberation of all enslaved and oppressed nations.' Neither in Germany nor in England nor in France would the present government accept such conditions. Then we would have to prepare the revolutionary war and lead it; that is, we would not only carry through our entire minimum program with all the means at our command, but we would also incite the peoples of all nations now oppressed by Great Russia and all colonies and dependent nations in Asia: India, China, Persia, etc. And, above all, we would incite the Socialist proletariat of Europe to revolt against their own governments, in spite of their social chauvinists."

This statement that Lenin made at the very beginning of World War I remained the program of the Bolsheviks during the war, and was the basis for everything Litvinoff was to do in that period.

2

Litvinoff, as a successful employee of a publishing firm, was, in the eyes of his employers and business friends, establishing himself as a conventionally useful member of society, but in his own opinion his real work was that which he did out of hours for the Socialist Party.

In 1912 he became the representative of the Bolshevik Party in the International Socialist Bureau in London—a kind of ambassador or foreign minister of the Party.

It was an important post. Among Lenin's letters of this period, there are many to different Party members in which he again and again insists that Litvinoff was the man with whom to get in touch about all international organization questions. For instance, he wrote to Alexander Shliapnikov in Stockholm (October, 1914) that he could not agree with Shliapnikov's taking steps without consulting Litvinoff. "Litvinoff is our legal representative in the International Socialist Bureau," Lenin said.

His use of the word "legal" is interesting. Even in those fighting years, Lenin thought of himself as chief of a governmental organization. Two months later, in December, 1914, he wrote to Shliapnikov almost menacingly: "Have you finally come to a written understanding with Litvinoff?"

In the summer of 1915 he wrote sharply to Karl Radek: "Not I, but Maximovich has been the representative of the Central Committee in the International Bureau in London since 1912."

How great was Litvinoff's authority can be seen from a letter written on February 9, 1915, in Berne, Switzerland, to the Menshevik newspaper *Nashe Slovo* (*Our World*) published in Paris. The *Nashe Slovo* had suggested directly to Lenin a united front against the official Social Democratic Labor Parties in all countries, which helped the warring governments. Lenin was wholly in favor of such a move but reminded them: "You know, of course, that Litvinoff is the official representative of our Central Committee in the International Socialist Bureau. We sent him your letter and our answer and ask you to turn to him in all pressing matters. For he decides by himself all questions about these and other tactical changes, about steps to take, negotiations etc. We can only express our full solidarity with this comrade in all important questions."

It was inevitable that Litvinoff should represent the Bolsheviks at the first wartime international Socialist Congress, called by the Party of Independent English Workers, to take place in London on February 14, 1915. This party demanded, first, that German and Austrian workers' delegations should be invited, too. It felt—as did the Bolsheviks—that to assemble only the Socialists of one side at war would be basically wrong, a contradiction of the very principle of international socialism. But the French Socialists declared that they would not take part in a conference at which German or Austrian delegates were present, and consequently, the Congress was composed exclusively of representatives from the Allied countries. About forty well-known Socialists from France, England, Belgium and Russia met—among them Keir Hardie, Ramsay MacDonald and Arthur Henderson from England; Marcel Sembat, Jean Longuet, Vaillant, Albert Thomas and Léon Jouhaux from France; Emil Vandervelde from Belgium. From Russia there was Ivan Maisky; the Menshevik, L. Martov, had not been able to obtain a passport. Litvinoff had not been invited at first, and getting him an invitation, which came only a few hours before the meeting opened, took a lot of wire-pulling. If the other Socialists hoped that he would not appear they were mistaken. This meeting was much too important for the Bolsheviki to allow any question of etiquette to interfere.

The French and English Socialists could not have been uncertain about what Litvinoff would say or do at such a conference. Lenin had left no doubt. In his letter of February 9, 1915, to *Nashe Slovo,* he developed eight basic points for future Bolshevik policy. He:

1. was against any truce or any national bloc.

2. believed in invoking the class struggle and revolutionary action.

3. urged the rejection of all military credits.

4. insisted that Socialists retire from the bourgeois cabinets of Belgium and France.

5. appealed for collaboration with the German Socialists who had voted against war credits [Liebknecht and Rosa Luxemburg].

6. wanted organization of soldiers at the front.

7. encouraged women to start a general anti-war agitation.

8. stressed the need for aid to the Russian revolutionaries in their fight against Czarism.

The situation was clear, painfully clear. The demands of the Party, as Lenin and Litvinoff knew very well, would never be accepted. Therefore, Litvinoff's appearance at the Congress would be only a demonstration against the social chauvinists of all countries, for the united proletarians of all countries.

Litvinoff's invitation to the Congress was on an ambiguous basis but he would have gone without even that grudging notification for he had a demonstration to make, and he started to make it with his first words. "Citizens," he greeted the English, French and Belgian delegates, used to being addressed as "Comrades," and provoked them quite as successfully as he had intended.

Litvinoff's own report of the meeting appeared in the Russian paper *Sozialdemocrat,* the Party organ, appearing in Paris, on March 3, 1915 (Number 39).

"London, February 14, 1915.

"Last night I received from the Secretary of the British Section of the International the address of the conference, in reply to a letter in which I gave my address without asking for an invitation. I decided to go in order to attempt to read a declaration. I met Rubanovitch of the Social Revolutionaries [the Social Chauvinists], Tchernoff and Bob Rov of the Mysl, Maisky of the Organization Committee. He had been delegated along with Martov, who could not appear because he did not obtain a visa. There were eleven delegates from England (Keir Hardie, as Chairman, MacDonald, etc.), sixteen from France (Sembat, Vaillant, etc.), three from Belgium (Vandervelde, among others).

"The Chairman opened the conference with the announcement that its purpose was an exchange of opinion, not the formulation of resolutions. One of the Frenchmen made an additional move: Why not confirm the opinion of the majority with a resolution? This was accepted in silence.

"On the program: No. 1. The rights of the nations, Belgium, Poland. 2. The Colony. 3. Guarantees of peace. A commission to test the mandates was elected (among others Rubanovitch). It was voted that one representative from every country should talk briefly about its stand on the war. I took the floor and protested against the fact that the official representative of our Party in the International Socialist Bureau was not invited.

"The Chairman interrupted me, arguing that all have been invited who have 'well-known' names. I protested for a second time that our representative was not notified. Then I referred to our manifesto 'The War and the Russian Social Democracy,' which indicates our general stand on the war and which has been sent to the International Socialist Bureau. I pointed out that before we can talk about peace conditions, one must be clear as to the means with which we can work to bring about peace, and to this end we must decide whether there was a general revolutionary social democratic basis, and whether we conferred as chauvinists and pacifists or as social democrats. I read our declaration, but the Chairman did not let me finish. He declared that my position as a delegate was not even assured, and that they had not assembled 'to criticize different parties.' I declared that I should continue my speech after the report of the commission on the mandates.

"Short declarations about the general stand were made by Vaillant, Vandervelde, MacDonald, Rubanovitch. On the basis of the report of the commission testing the mandates, it was proposed that Maisky himself decide whether he would represent the organization's committee alone, also I was 'permitted' to participate at the conference. I thanked the conference for this 'kindness' and continued where I left off in my declaration in order to find out whether I could stay. The Chairman interrupted me. He would not allow me to make 'conditions.' Then I requested permission to announce the reasons why I would not participate in the conference. This was turned down. Then I asked permission to say that the Social Democratic Workers' Party of Russia did not take part in this conference. I left a written declaration with the Chairman about the reasons. I gathered up my papers and left. . . ."

In its first publication, in *Nashe Slovo* of February 27, 1915, Litvinoff's statement which he had not been permitted to finish at the Congress was mutilated by censorship, but a month later, March 29, 1915, it was printed in full in the *Sozialdemocrat* (No. 40):

"Citizens:

"Your conference calls itself a conference of Socialist parties of the Allied warring states, Belgium, England, France and Russia. Permit me to direct your attention to the fact that the Social Democracy of Russia, as an organization represented by the Central Committee which is accredited to the International Socialist Bureau, has not received an invitation from you.

"The Russian Social Democracy whose opinion has been expressed by the members of the Russian Social Democratic Workers' fraction in the Duma (they are now arrested by the Czarist Government)—is not represented at your conference. We hope that you will declare this officially lest we accuse you of tampering with the truth.

"Permit me now to say a few words about the goal of your conference, that is to say, what the organized Social Democratic workers of Russia expect from you.

"We think it our Socialist duty, before we can approach any conversations about the reconstruction of the International and before we attempt to rebuild international alliances among Socialist workers, to request the following:

"1. That Vandervelde, Guesde and Sembat immediately leave the bourgeois governments in Belgium and France.

"2. That the Belgian and French Socialist parties destroy the so-called 'national bloc,' which is a betrayal of the Socialist flag and which is only a front behind which chauvinist orgies of the bourgeoisie can go on.

"3. That all Socialist parties abandon a policy of ignoring the crimes of Russian Czarism and begin again to aid the fight led by the workers of Russia without regard to the cost to Czarism.

"4. That, in conformity with the decisions of the Congress of Basle, it will be declared that we hold out our hands to those revolutionary Social Democrats of Germany and Austria who have answered the declaration of war with the preparation of propaganda for revolutionary action. The acceptance of war credits must be absolutely condemned.

"The Social Democrats of Germany and Austria have committed a horrible crime against Socialism and the International in voting for war credits and in coming to a 'truce' with the Junkers, the Church and the bourgeoisie. But the Belgian and French Socialists have done no better. We understand very well that circumstances can arise which force the Socialist minority to submit to a bourgeois majority, but under no circumstances must Socialists cease being Socialists, and sing in the chorus of the bourgeois chauvinists, and forget the cause of the workers, and enter bourgeois governments.

"German and Austrian Socialists commit a horrible crime against Socialism if they, following the example of the bourgeoisie, declare hypocritically that the Hohenzollerns and the Hapsburgs are conducting a war 'of liberation from Czarism.'

"But no less a crime is committed by those who pretend that Czarism is becoming more democratic and more civilized, by those who conceal the fact that Czarism chokes and destroys unhappy Galicia economically, just as the German Kaiser has choked and destroyed Belgium. And by those who conceal the fact that a Czarist gang has thrown into prison the parliamentary representative of the Russian workers, and that only a short time ago the Czarists sentenced several workers from Moscow to six years of forced labor for the sole reason that they belonged to the Social Democratic Labor Party. And by those who conceal the fact that Czarism has oppressed Finland worse than ever, that workers' newspapers and workers' organizations are shut down in Russia, that the billions necessary to make war are squeezed by a Czarist clique from hungry peasants and penniless workers.

"The workers of Russia offer with comradely feelings their hand to those Socialists who act as do Karl Liebknecht, the Socialists of Serbia, Italy and the English comrades of the Independent Labor Party, a few members of the English Labor Party and our arrested comrades of the Russian Socialist Democratic Labor Party.

"We call on you to follow on this road, the road of Socialism! Down with the chauvinism that betrays the cause of the proletariat! Long live international Socialism!"

"(Signed) Maxim Maximovich."

Lenin himself later testified that Litvinoff did a thoroughly competent job. The conference in London, at which he scarcely was allowed to speak, became an important milestone in the annals of the Party. Litvinoff saw to that by pointing out the differences between the Bolsheviki and the other Socialists and by showing that it was not the Bolsheviki who were responsible for the continuation of the war.

Lenin wrote: "The task of our adversaries, the Social chauvinists, at the London Conference was clear. It was necessary to leave this conference, held in the name of very clear anti-chauvinist principles, without becoming a lover of Germany. For the Germanophiles, while opposing the conference, too, had only chauvinist and no other motives. Comrade Maximovich understood and fulfilled his task by speaking clearly about the betrayal of the German Socialists and turning down a resolution where a sentence to this effect was to be omitted." (Evidently Lenin is referring here to an attempt by the German Socialists to use Litvinoff's declaration for their own purposes.)

The Congress members finally did come to a resolution of sorts. They made clear that the Socialists of the Allied countries were not making war against the German and Austrian peoples but only against the governments of those countries. They demanded that Belgium be liberated and compensated and that the question of Poland be settled in accordance with the wishes of the Polish people. They also endorsed a United States of Europe and even of the world, and declared they were for uniting the workers' classes of all industrial countries in an effort to do away with diplomacy, militarism, and the manufacture of arms.

But these were words and nothing more. It was decided at London not to make public the discussions at the conference. But the news leaked out that even this meaningless resolution had not been accepted unanimously.

So nothing had been achieved at all. No way to end the war or to unite the workers of all countries had been shown, let alone any plan to do away with secret diplomacy and arms manufacturing. On the contrary, there was still talk about the "war of liberation" against Prussia—which in so many words meant that the Allied Socialists continued to sanction the war.

Words in the resolution decried the guilt of "all governments." But French Socialists came out against such a formulation, and neither the French nor the Belgian Socialist ministers felt impelled to resign from their cabinets, to demonstrate the common war guilt of which they had vaguely spoken.

All in all, it was a declaration of complete bankruptcy on the part of the Second International. The Second International had not been willing or able to prevent the war, as Litvinoff had foreseen; at London in 1915 it showed that it was neither willing nor able to do anything to stop the war, or even to prevent future wars.

Litvinoff's departure, announcing that the Russian Social Democratic Labor Party would have no part in such a business, marked the beginning of a split which was to be decisive in the history of the next quarter century, for it was a major precondition of the Russian separate peace of 1917, forced by the workers, of the long, determined struggle thereafter of the Western powers to throttle the new Russia, of the ambiguity of aims in the international policies of the British Conservatives, and the equivalent groups in associated countries, which gave Fascism and Nazism a chance, sacrificed Ethiopia, wrecked Spain, and made possible if not inevitable the present worldwide slaughter.

Yet the group that Litvinoff left was already dead. The Second International would continue to meet, it would be publicized all over the world as representing the workers, but its activities, however busy, would be only the futile gestures of a ghost.

3

About this time Litvinoff left Williams & Norgate and took a job with another publisher, the old conservative house of John Murray. Then he moved on to another publishing firm called Bassington House, then went back to Williams & Norgate. In between he taught Russian in Berlitz schools in both London and Rotterdam. The revolutionary Litvinoff was interrupting the life of the business man, Maxim Harrison. Maxim Harrison had every so often to give up his job, because Litvinoff was called away, especially to Holland where he met German revolutionaries who could not enter England. But despite his increasing revolutionary responsibilities (of which his British associates remained blandly unsuspecting), Litvinoff still wanted his alter ego Maxim Harrison to earn his living, so that he would not have to draw on the meager Party funds, contributed at such cost by ill-paid, ill-fed workers.

And in the end Maxim Harrison's business became of considerable use in Litvinoff's politics, for Harrison got a new student of Russian, Rex Leeper, a high official of the British Foreign Office, in charge of the Russian Department, and as teacher and pupil got better acquainted they discussed current Russian affairs. Thus Litvinoff learned a good deal about the British official attitude towards Russia, and as he says himself, was able to influence Leeper, to a certain extent, about Russia, and thereby affect the ideas of the men around Leeper. Then finally, through Leeper and Williams & Norgate he got a job with the Purchasing Commission of the Russian Delegation in London, where he soon was considered one of their most faithful employees. In this way considerable information of value was transmitted direct to the Bolshevik Party.

Politics, moreover, was not the only topic of conversation between Leeper and Litvinoff. Through Leeper, Litvinoff got to know Ivy Low, a girl whom he had met in 1914 at a house party, where she persuaded her host's father-in-law to make it possible for his son-in-law to stay in London to pursue a literary career. Later, Litvinoff had come across his friend again, found him converted into a prosperous business man, his change of status symbolized by a change of residence from the literary purlieus of Bloomsbury to the eminent solidity of Hyde Park, and learned that Ivy Low had again played the decisive part in this situation. For the girl, a little startled at her success, concluded that her host probably had no great literary contribution to make, so he might as well go into the carpet business. To balance accounts with her own sense of responsibility, she went to him, and persuaded him in turn to give up the notion of writing and accede to his father-in-law's wishes. His success had already proved her point.

The girl's unusual sense of justice and duty, and energetic effectiveness, interested Litvinoff, and he told the story to Leeper, who said that he knew Miss Low, and soon arranged to have Litvinoff meet her at a literary party. Not long afterwards Leeper was called on to act as witness at their marriage at Hampstead Town Hall.

Ivy Low was born in the Bloomsbury section of London in 1889. Her father was one of three brothers, all in journalism, though he had himself started as a teacher. The other two won the distinction of knighthood—Sir Sydney and Sir Morris Low—and though Ivy's father died young of pneumonia, he had already had a promising career: as collaborator, with H. G. Wells, on the *Educational Times,* which they edited and also largely wrote; as editor of a number of English textbooks; and as translator into English of the works of Björnstjerne Björnson.

But despite these accomplishments, they were poor and both he and his wife, who also wrote, eked out a living by reviewing books, which brought in a little money, not so much from the reviews, as from the sale of the review copies. After Low's death his wife continued to write, and later married H. J. Herbert of the British Museum staff, well known for his work on illuminated manuscripts.

When Ivy was thirteen she went to live with one of her uncles and promptly announced that she also was going to be a journalist. Her uncle suggested that she was a little young to have made such a decision, but when she showed him some of her scripts, he had to admit that they revealed talent, though they seemed a bit radical. Only two years later she began publishing, and in the following years she sold stories to the *Manchester Guardian, The New Statesman,* the *Evening Standard,* and *Country Life,* including articles on the appalling conditions in the slums of London's East End, with suggestions for remedies—education, organization, and even revolt.

In her early twenties she brought out a novel, *Growing Pains,* and subsequently one called *The Questing Beast,* which she once described to a friend as, "It makes me blush but it won't make you." A third, published in London in 1943, as *His Master's Voice,* and in New York as *Moscow Mystery,* is a mystery story with a Moscow background.

The Ivy Low who married Litvinoff was an unusually good-looking girl: tall, with deep dark eyes in a calm, serious face framed by beautiful brown hair, a high forehead and a firm chin that contrasted with a small, delicate mouth.

The day of the marriage both Leeper and Litvinoff were much pressed for time, the one leaving immediately to get back to the Foreign Office, the bridegroom rushing off to attend to some business which was urgent then, but now none of those concerned can recall what it was.

The bride had counted on a wedding luncheon in her favorite teashop in Baker Street, and being left alone did not modify her plans. She went and ate it by herself, and from that time on showed the same reasonable adaptability in adjusting herself to the necessities of Litvinoff's often difficult life. She knew about her husband's political activities, and having since childhood been intensely aware of the injustices of the social system and the need for drastic action to right them, was completely in sympathy and helped him in no small degree, especially when he was called away to the Continent. They lived in far from comfortable circumstances, in the house where he had roomed before, and even when he gave a considerable proportion of his earnings to the Party, she never demurred.

In 1917 the first child, Misha, was born, and in 1918 the second, Tanya. Litvinoff, always interested in children, has been a devoted father.

4

Lenin and Krupskaya lived in Zurich under difficult conditions during the war. Their one room at 14 Spiegelgasse, rented from a woman interested in their revolutionary work, was scantily furnished with two beds, a table, a few chairs and a sewing machine; they could rarely open a window because of the unbearable smells from a sausage factory in the same building. Poor as they were, they could have managed to live in better quarters, but they would not leave their sympathetic landlady. Lenin worked all day in the library, seeing few people because most of his former collaborators found his views too extreme and believed that his refusal to compromise would finally isolate him completely.

Lenin, on the contrary, was convinced that the war could have been avoided if the Socialists had held with unswerving loyalty to the program he advocated: if they had acted resolutely and promptly to expel all opportunists, chauvinists, and narrow-minded nationalists. He pointed out repeatedly that only Russian Socialists, and only those among them who were stanchest and most objective, had actually contested participation in the war.

The war had begun for Russia with the shocking disaster of Tannenberg, August 29, 1914, a defeat that cost several hundred thousand men, deliberately risked in response to frantic appeals from the French for a second front in the East to stay the German rush on Paris. The Germans, alarmed by the invasion of East Prussia, at the critical moment dispatched divisions drawn from their army in France. Paris was saved, Tannenberg lost. Joffre made handsome acknowledgment of this sacrifice and service.

Meanwhile, the Russian southern army was advancing on Lvov, which they succeeded in entering on September 2. Prematurely elated by the virtual rout on that sector of the Austro-Hungarians, the Russians became a bit patronizing towards their English and French allies who had not yet made any such sensational advance. The manic moment, however, reacted into a depression when soon thereafter they ran into a series of heavy defeats. Morale throughout the country began to sag steadily as the people realized that the war, instead of ending in a few weeks, might go on for years. In St. Petersburg (now officially Petrograd) and Moscow only close observers would have noted the gradual deterioration of the national spirit, but in rural areas and the provinces the disillusion was rapid. Before the first year was up, soldiers on furlough were reluctant to return to their units, peasants were openly protesting against leaving their fields, and minor riots were frequent.

After the initial fervid protestations of loyalty, the masses began to see that it was the same old Government with which they had to deal, the same stiff-minded bureaucrats, the same incompetence, heartlessness and corruption. Repression and terrorism were renewed; the press was muzzled by a political censorship, the labor unions were suppressed, new outrages against the Jews were fomented, arrests and banishment continued. The enthusiasm and desire of the people to contribute to the great enterprise were chilled and repulsed by the official contempt or inertia. Three days of rioting shook Moscow in June, 1915, after rumors circulated that Government members, in German pay, were preventing the authorities from exerting the maximum efforts against the enemy. Shops were plundered, houses demolished, anyone with a German name was in danger of attack, many were killed. The people began to realize something of their power.

Following the fall of Warsaw that summer, the wealthy classes also began to feel the depression keenly. Everyone knew that the Czar was surrounded by the wrong men, but a large majority still believed that he could lead them to victory. They wanted only modest and entirely reasonable concessions; assurance that the army was being properly led and supplied, guarantees against the perfidy and even treason in high places, minor administrative and electoral reforms. No satisfaction was forthcoming, but the continued defeats in the Carpathians, the fearful losses of the army, its sufferings and its heroism, its magnificent tenacity, finally moved the Czar to action. A proper supply commission was appointed, some reactionary ministers were removed, and the Duma summoned.

Yet all this was only temporary and superficial. The Empress was interfering more and more in the government. Rasputin's power was growing. German infiltration in both the Government and the military command continued to increase the danger. The common soldiers—incredibly brave and long-suffering, fighting by night with bayonets instead of by day with ammunition, because there was no ammunition —began to feel that they were being betrayed.

At the end of August, 1915, the Czar, contrary to the unanimous advice of his ministers, dismissed Grand Duke Nicholas, who had been Commander-in-Chief since the opening of the war and was trusted by the whole nation and greatly respected by his enemies. The Czar, urged by the Czarina with her characteristic want of judgment, then took over the high command himself. It was a costly mistake, for he could now be held responsible for all the errors hitherto attributable to ministers and generals, but still no word was uttered against him personally.

Meanwhile, in the Duma both Professor Paul Miliukov, an outstanding liberal, and Alexander F. Kerenski, who was somewhat more to ,the Left, demanded a new system of government, giving a decisive voice to the people. Denunciations of the crimes of the authorities and demands for real power for the people poured ominously in from radical and conservative alike. The Duma was suspended on September 3.

5

At the end of that summer (September 5 to 8, 1915), about thirty men constituting the International Conference of Opponents of the Truce—left-wing Socialists who opposed compromises for the sake of the war—met in a small room in the inn of Zimmerwald, a little Swiss village. Among the Germans present were Georg Ledebour and Adolf Hoffmann. Two men came for France, and there were delegates from Italy, Norway, Sweden, Holland, Bulgaria and Rumania, but none from England. Lenin and Zinoviev represented the Bolsheviki, Martov and Axelrod the Mensheviki, and Leon Trotsky one of a number of smaller groups. Secret agents and journalists were too numerous for comfort.

The great Socialist congresses of the past, impressive demonstrations of the power that the workers of the world might exert, had produced no real results at all. This small gathering in an obscure village did represent a revival of international planning, though Lenin was again disappointed. Karl Kautsky, a German Independent Socialist, led the large majority of twenty-three in denouncing any truce, but continuing adherence to the Second International and opposing revolutionary action. The seven votes on Lenin's side, counting his own, included none from France or Italy. The manifesto finally issued merely stated that the Zimmerwald congress was against the war, a world catastrophe.

Zinoviev criticized the meeting: "The conference took only a first shy, uncertain step in the direction of international Socialism. Above all, the conference did not want to advocate a precise and clear resolution about the crisis. . . . The development moves slowly, but it moves forward."

It did move when the group met a second time, in the village of Kienthal in April, 1916, comprising again German radicals, French, Italians, a Serb, a few Swiss Party members and representatives of various Russian and Polish groups. The situation had now definitely changed. Millions of Socialists the world over, weary of the war, felt that the leaders who had voted for it had led them astray. Yet the manifesto issued here still did not adopt the Bolshevik program of converting the war into a civil war, with the aim of furthering world revolution by the overthrow of existing governments. This meeting served, however, to draw somewhat closer together international elements in Socialist parties and was, in certain respects, the first in a long series of steps leading to the Third International.

6

In 1916 in Russia anti-government resolutions grew bolder in tone and the Social Democrats and Social Revolutionaries were openly distributing revolutionary propaganda in the factories. The situation became more serious under the virtual dictatorship of the thoroughly hated Protopopov, stubborn, perverse and merciless—a former liberal who had become one of the fiercest of the reactionaries. He had been in the Duma and was now Minister of the Interior, an appointment that provoked the Provincial Assemblies (Zemstva), which were by no means radical, to an angry protest. In this highly important post he based most of his policies on astrological advice. Maurice Paléologue, the poised, penetrating French Ambassador, weighed him coolly in the balance: "Behind his expansive bravado and restless activity there is nothing but cerebral erethism. He is a monomaniac who will soon be under restraint." * Such was the regime that Litvinoff was working to overthrow.

By October the Government had again demonstrated its complete incompetence. Indolent, confused, irresponsible, cruel, it had brought the nation to the verge of disaster. At the very time when it needed the cordial support of the people, who were ready with their various economic and social agencies to help carry the burdens of the time, the Government, with an obtuseness and perversity hard to match in the annals of maladministration, suppressed or destroyed them all. The machinery of government remained, but it was scarcely operating. Many departments were in complete chaos; fraud and speculation disorganized the major services; as a result of bureaucratic incompetence and corruption, the transport system was thoroughly disrupted; fuel was insufficient in the cities, which meant suffering to millions; whole urban populations were stricken with food shortages that amounted to near famine, while foodstuffs rotted in freight cars shunted onto sidings, or, through administrative blundering, were immobilized in areas of abundance.

The people were miserable with the dread of an impending debacle, but they were angry as well as alarmed, thoroughly exasperated with the Government, which, in turn, felt for them only hatred, contempt and, above all, fear. Occasionally, the authorities were moved to gestures of conciliation, but these proved deceptive and were immediately followed by more acts of repression. The Black Hundreds sought to bolster the Government by its own methods. Thus Dr. Dubrovin, their leader, privately offered two hundred rubles for the assassination of Paul Miliukov. The rumble of approaching revolution was clearly audible.

In December both Government officials and representatives of the special reactionary groups, like the Black Hundreds, pressed the Czar for a separate peace with Germany. They realized that State authority

* Maurice Paléologue, *Memoirs*, III, p. 115. New York, 1924.

had broken down and revolution was inevitable, if not imminent, and urged that the military power be conserved to bolster the autocracy and repress rebellion. An end to war would doubtless have been welcomed by peasants, soldiers and workers. Above all, they wanted bread and peace. But the liberal bourgeoisie thought it essential to continue the war against Germany, convinced that, with Germany victorious, Russia would have no future of any kind. All were united in wanting drastic changes in government, and by this time most of them wished to get rid of the Czar himself.

On December 30, 1916, Prince Felix Yusupov, the Grand Duke Dmitri and Purishkevich, leader of the Extreme Right in the Duma, hoping to ameliorate the situation, assassinated the bizarre priest Rasputin, an illiterate, thoroughly disgusting, and criminal debauchee, who, through his almost hypnotic influence over the Czarina, as her letters to the Czar clearly show, was deciding, and deciding calamitously, all major policies. It was Rasputin who, by appointing henchmen of similar base character to the most holy and responsible offices of the Church, added to the rancor of the later campaigns against religion. His elimination, however, had no practical effect other than the retirement of the Czarina from the political scene. The paretic Protopopov continued to consult his ghost.

By the beginning of 1917 disorders were breaking out everywhere, the Czar and Czarina were being blamed for the chaos, and the public tension increased when the opening of the Duma was postponed. Yet just at that time Lenin, addressing a group of young Swiss workingmen, said: "We old ones shall perhaps not live to see the decisive battle of the coming revolution," adding his hope that the young Socialist generation of Europe would be victorious.

Lenin was only forty-seven, but he was tired. He was depressed by the indecisive results of the Kienthal meeting. For years he had overworked, writing innumerable letters, articles, brochures, books, aided only by the faithful Krupskaya. Now she had undergone a dangerous operation and they had been separated for weeks.

Lenin was finding it darkest just before the dawn.

CHAPTER FIVE

Coming to Power

At the end of February, 1917, the Government was in a chaos of internal conflict, while the people were united in their determination that the Government should go. In the imperial family there was discord, resulting dissension rent the Cabinet and multiple conflicts kept the Duma in an inner turmoil, but the public was unanimous that the time had come to end the old regime.

Disorders multiplied all over Russia; especially in Petrograd there were demonstrations, parades; everywhere the unplanned gatherings of vast and excited crowds had the threatening character of a spontaneous mass convulsion which nothing could withstand. By February 23 a movement was under way for a general strike.

Increasing hunger added a dangerous quality of desperation to the mobs. On March 8 the looting of bakeries began, and continued with mounting excitement on the 9th. Troops were patrolling the main streets of the capital, but they were not grim and hostile, as in Father Gapon's day; they were fraternizing with the crowds and soon began going over to their side in such rapidly increasing numbers that by Monday the 12th only one regiment of the Petrograd garrison remained loyal to the Government. In the three days, however, numbers still uncounted had been killed in street fighting, factories were stopped, business was paralyzed, and a number of public buildings were in flames. The Czar ordered additional troops to Petrograd to restore law and order; they never arrived; the railway men refused to transport them.

Meanwhile, the Duma was attempting to organize a provisional government, quiet the outburst, and obtain food and fuel supplies, and to this end the Council of Elders appointed a committee of thirteen. The same day (March 12) a second nucleus also coalesced, representing the Socialists, the Soviet of Workers' and Soldiers' Deputies. The first wished to avoid revolution, the second to carry through the revolt actually in progress; but both recognized the necessity of an immediate abdication of the Czar, and the Soviet was in agreement that the Duma should carry the responsibility for reorganizing the government.

Three days later (March 15) a new Provisional Government was formed under Prince George E. Lvov, who had been President of the All-Russian Zemstva Union. In the Cabinet of eleven was one Socialist, as Minister of Justice, Kerenski, who had been the most effective liaison between the Duma committee and the Soviet in the three preceding days and was now supposed to watch the Provisional Government on behalf of the Soviet, which expected to be the power behind the scenes.

The very first act of the new Cabinet was to secure the abdication of the Czar. The plan called for the recognition of the Czarevitch as monarch, with Grand Duke Michael as Regent, but when the Duma emissaries presented this request to Nicholas II on the evening of March 15, he pleaded his son's ill-health and abdicated directly in favor of Michael—an act for which actually he had no legal authority.

The Soviet, however, would have none of Michael. They had had enough of Czars, above all, enough of Romanovs. The issue offered the test of power between the two constitutive factions of the Government, and there was scarcely a moment's doubt where the decision lay. The Soviet was master. Michael abdicated after a stormy conference in his presence on the morning of March 16.

The Revolution had won. It had been nearly a hundred years under way—a hundred years crowded with dark tribulation, with the slow acquisition of political education, with sacrifice, aspiration and many bloody defeats. It was not a theoretical revolution, but it had far more of leadership and program than the abortive revolution of 1905 and '06. The Duma, which had been a sounding board for the affirmation of the people's rights against an opaque tyranny, had acquainted them with the necessity and something of the character of a people's government. Unrepresentative though it was and deprived of legislative or executive authority, it had nonetheless given the people a rallying point, and there had been a vast amount of instruction, thinking, discussion. The revolutionary parties with their underground literature and their secret meetings had trained and disciplined tens of thousands for the great effort. The rest was spontaneous. The unspeakable stupidities, cruelties and incompetence of the Government had assured the Revolution a relatively easy victory. The Government had itself collapsed—one might almost say abdicated, for it had all but abdicated the essential functions of government. An angry people pushed it over the brink, but it had already doomed itself to destruction.

2

Litvinoff, alone in his Hampstead apartment because his wife was still in a nursing-home with her three-weeks-old infant Misha, awoke on a misty London morning and, still in bed, began reading his morning paper. The Russian Revolution had begun! He dashed out of bed, into the bathroom, jumped into the tub, leaped out and began to rub himself dry—only to realize that in a veritable trance of excitement he had been "bathing" in a dry and empty tub. He flung on clothes and got to a telephone by half-past eight.

Madame Litvinoff, in the nursing home, was awakened as usual at eight by a nurse coming in and opening the curtains. When she asked for morning papers the nurse brought them but said: "There is hardly anything in them this morning. Another Zeppelin raid over the East End, but it was driven back. All quiet on all fronts, they say." So Madame Litvinoff did not bother with the news. Then a telephone message came from her husband: "Czar abdicated, Provisional Government."

News of the Russian Revolution was brought to Lenin by a friend, and a few hours later Swiss papers published the reports, and dispatches were being posted on the bulletin boards. Lenin, characteristically the calmest of the calm, was on this day in such a fever of excitement that he could only roam the Zurich streets, neither seeing nor talking to anyone. His conviction that the war would bring about the Revolution had been more quickly and completely proved true than even he had ever dared hope.

The Provisional Government announced to the émigrés that "it would gladly recall all those who had suffered for the good of the country." Lenin and his associates started to pack for an immediate return.

But the English and French governments, which had promptly recognized the new Russian regime (March 24), thought otherwise. Their one interest was in keeping Russia in the war. Hence they were indeed glad to have corrupt, unpopular Russian officials supplanted by leaders who, they thought, could command the loyalty of the masses, but they were not willing to permit the return home of émigrés who were opposed to Russia's continued participation in a non-working-class war. Lenin and the other Bolsheviki in Europe had to remain on the outside.

At first Lenin conceived schemes to thwart the Allies—either by getting professional smugglers to pass him through Germany, or by traveling on the passport of a mute Swede. But Krupskaya thought both impractical, and to discourage the latter and more apparently feasible project pointed out that Lenin might dream about his political opponents and call out in his sleep in Russian: "Criminal! Criminal!" If he thus proved that he was neither mute nor Swedish, arrest was certain.

So he settled down to writing letters trying to influence the Revolution from afar. He had never thought of Soviets, which had been created spontaneously by the masses, as the form of the new government, yet he saw at once, even at that distance, that they were the logical framework. He was now determined, as soon as the liberal Provisional Government was abolished, to concentrate all power in the Soviets. This conviction, the product of his own political insight, he supported by quotations culled from Marx's writings on the Commune of 1871, and scattered broadcast letters to Party members, both inside Russia and out, announcing that he would break relations with any of them who wanted to continue the war or collaborated with the Provisional Government. Among those disagreeing with him was Leo Kamenev, the editor of *Pravda,* who had been liberated by the Revolution and was very much opposed to giving power to the Soviets.

Less than a fortnight after the Czar's abdication, the Soviet's first manifesto announced that they were ready to make peace (March 27). This was directly contrary to the Provisional Government's policy of continuing to fight alongside the Allies.

Two weeks later (April 9) a second Soviet statement declaring that the war must result in permanent peace on the basis of "no annexations, no indemnities and the free development of the nations," was sent to all Russian Ambassadors, but the Provisional Government's accompanying letter reaffirmed adherence to the Allies. The Soviet-Provisional Government rift was widening.

Meanwhile someone—it probably will never be determined who—realized that the Germans would be glad to help get into Russia a man intent on stopping Russo-German hostilities. General Ludendorff, the real master of German policy, and some of Lenin's Swiss comrades may have had the idea about the same time. At any rate, the German Minister to Switzerland began negotiations and various friends of Lenin worked to the same end. Lenin foresaw that political enemies would denounce him for trafficking with German imperialists, so he informed Party members all over Europe what he was doing and got their written approval.

Lenin and thirty comrades left Switzerland for Russia via Germany on April 8. Friends tried to dissuade Lenin from the dangerous trip up to the moment of starting. Without even answering, Lenin walked with his wife into the third-class car and the train sped towards Germany. While the other émigrés, excited, talked and sang, Lenin remained silent, even when at Stuttgart a German Union representative wished to meet him. Lenin refused, wanting only to get to Petrograd.

In Stockholm, Swedish Socialists who provided the Russian group with luncheon beginning with the characteristic table full of smörgasbord, were startled to see every dish promptly cleaned up by their long-underfed guests. While there, Radek, insisting that the future leader of Russia should not enter his domain wearing shabby shoes, got him to buy a new pair, but when he urged him to buy a few shirts and a new overcoat, Lenin retorted that he was not turning haberdasher.

The last few miles to the Russian frontier the party drove in sleighs. At the border a few soldiers met them. While waiting for the train to Petrograd, Lenin was intensely absorbed in the last issue of *Pravda,* making extensive notes of the criticisms he wanted to discuss with Kamenev.

Lenin was plunging into a darkly confused and unstable situation. The actual administrative machinery was in complete disarray. The old police organization had disintegrated and could no longer exercise authority. Elementary order was maintained by the Soviets, who patrolled the streets with soldiers and armed workers. Only executives of the old regime knew how to run the departments and not enough of these remained at their posts, for many had fled or been arrested. At the front, soldiers' soviets and officers were fighting for power, and through-

out the country the peasants were rioting, burning and plundering, and
the revolutionary elements were furiously disputing and scheming.

The conservative classes—nobility, landowners, officers, high officials
—supported the liberals; an overwhelming majority of peasants and
soldiers were in favor of the Mensheviki; and a considerable proportion, perhaps a majority, of the industrial workers, were on the side of
the Social Revolutionaries, undeterred by their terroristic policies. These
last two parties wanted to terminate the war on the basis of no annexations and no reparations, and were anxious to convert to active revolutionary Socialism the masses on both sides, but neither party wished
to assume the difficult and politically dangerous task of taking over the
government of the country. Both believed that only a liberal bourgeois
government could carry on.

The Bolsheviki were split. Kamenev led one section that aimed at a
coalition with the Social Revolutionaries seeking to develop the liberal
government into a pure democracy. Lenin, on the other hand, was opposed to any coalition, as he had been since 1914, when the other parties had supported the war.

Lenin thought he might be arrested, perhaps by the guards on the
Petrograd train, and when friends boarded the train some miles outside
the city, the first question he asked them was: "Will they arrest me?"
When on April 16 at nine o'clock they pulled into the Finland Station
in Petrograd, music blared and spotlights played on packed thousands,
including the Chairman of the Workers' Soviets and representatives
from every regiment—all assembled to greet Lenin.

Though such acclaim was beyond his most hopeful expectations,
Lenin's poise was unshaken as he addressed the crowd: "Soldiers, sailors, workers! I see in you the advance guard of the proletarian world
army. Everywhere civil war will follow imperialist war. Already we
see the dawn of the world revolution."

For more than an hour Lenin was borne slowly through the main
streets atop an armored motorcar, saying a few words at every corner.

Lenin addressing his people was as deeply impressive as Lenin, when
first met as a private individual, was unimpressive—as if he were exem-
plifying in his own person one aspect of the complex Bolshevik theory of
the individual as such in history, his subordination to the social whole
in which he plays his part. As a leader before his adherents Lenin be-

came the visible embodiment of the power that carried the Revolution to success through so many tribulations. Even at the decisive moment that turned the Revolution into his hands he was the undramatic person, but the dramatically transmuted embodiment of his function:

. . . a thundering wave of cheers announced the entrance of . . . Lenin —great Lenin. . . . A short, stocky figure, with a big head set down in his shoulders, bald and bulging. Little eyes, a snubbish nose, wide, generous mouth, and heavy chin. . . . Dressed in shabby clothes, his trousers much too long for him. Unimpressive, to be the idol of a mob, loved and revered as perhaps few leaders in history have been. A strange popular leader—a leader purely by virtue of intellect; colourless, humourless, uncompromising and detached, without picturesque idiosyncrasies—but with a power of explaining profound ideas in simple terms, of analysing a concrete situation. And combined with shrewdness, the greatest intellectual audacity . . . his voice was hoarse—as if it had hardened that way after years and years of speaking—and went on monotonously, with the effect of being able to go on forever. . . . For emphasis he bent slightly forward. No gestures. And before him, a thousand simple faces looking up in intent adoration.*

And this magic continued to work for the reshaping of Russia from then on—not merely to his death, but on and on:

A small, busy, thick-set man . . . greeted by applause like thunder . . . their faces were shining, like men who looked on God . . . 500 faces can light up and shine at the sight of him.†

His little cortège proceeded amidst his people; turning chaos into purpose, until it arrived at the Bolshevik headquarters—in the palace of the former Prima Ballerina of the Opera, the Czar's mistress.

But Maxim Maximovich was not there for this triumphant arrival.

3

Lenin immediately made his position clear by announcing ten theses:

1. Regardless of the Czar's abdication, the war, as far as Russia was concerned, was still imperialistic.

---

* John Reed, *Ten Days That Shook the World*, pp. 125, 127, New York, 1926.
† Walter Duranty, *Duranty Reports Russia*, p. 190.

2. The Russian Revolution must advance from the first to the second stage (from the overthrow of the Czar to the overthrow of capital).

3. The Provisional Government should not be supported.

4. The Soviets of the Workers' Deputies constituted the only possible revolutionary government.

5. All large estates should be expropriated.

6. All banks should be merged, control to be vested in the Soviets.

7. The Soviets should take over production and distribution.

8. The Bolsheviki should immediately hold a congress to alter their program and name in accordance with the new turn of revolutionary events and the disrepute into which the name Social Democrat had fallen.

9. The name "Social Democrat" should be changed to "Communist."

10. The International should be re-established.

The Provisional Government was getting into constantly deepening difficulties. The Soviets, invited to enter the government on May 10, declined, but the Social Revolutionaries and Mensheviki accepted on May 12. Miliukov, Minister of Foreign Affairs, and Guchkov, Minister of War, were replaced, respectively, by Tereshchenko and Kerenski (May 18).

The Allies pressed Kerenski to undertake an offensive to prove the new Russia's strength, and Kerenski, though somewhat dubious, felt military successes might save the internal situation. So on July 1 he actually started an offensive. After initial local gains, it failed completely, seriously compromising the Provisional Government. Lenin had predicted just such an outcome.

On July 16 and 17 disorders, especially among naval personnel at Kronstadt, provoked government action against the Bolsheviki. Trotsky was arrested and Lenin had to disappear for a while. The unstable conditions also precipitated another revision of the governing heads, in which Kerenski became Premier (July 21). By September, however, Kerenski's position was so weakened by the growing opposition of the people that Lenin could publish *State and Revolution,* a pamphlet announcing his program, largely repeating his earlier theses.

The confused and precarious situation was now rapidly resolving.

With accelerating momentum events rushed towards catastrophe. General Lavr Kornilov, with the tacit support of at least some of the Allies, attempted a coup d'état on September 8, staging himself as "the man on horseback." Kerenski had to turn for support to the Soviets, thereby strengthening them; and the near success, then grotesque failure of Kornilov's enterprise destroyed the people's and especially the soldiers' remaining faith in the rulers. The compromise coalition was breaking up, an epoch was closing, a new world struggling to be born.

Kerenski made one more anxious effort: he resolved the Government into a Directorate of five and without waiting for a Constituent Assembly, proclaimed a republic (September 15). But the Russians wanted more than the conventional government form. At the end of October he tried a more desperate halfway step and now spoke of peace, and the land for the peasants. It was too little and too late. His popular support was irretrievably gone. On November 3 a meeting of soldiers' delegates refused further obedience to the General Staff, recognizing only the Military Revolutionary Committee, a resolution that went even further than Trotsky had wished; Kerenski's request that it be rescinded was ignored; the Bolsheviki took over the government of Petrograd (November 6). The specifically Jewish group, the "Bund," which had opposed Lenin in the Party congress, fought him up to the last minute (November 7).* Kerenski went to the front (November 7) hoping to meet troops that he had ordered to march on the capital, expecting them to put the Bolsheviki in their place and restore him to real power. His power was gone beyond recovery. On November 8 the Council of People's Commissars was founded, with Lenin as president. His assumption of authority prevented complete chaos and anarchy. The next day the Bolshevik Government sent a peace offer to all warring nations, and less than a month later (December 5) Russia and Germany declared an armistice.

But still Maxim Maximovich was not there.

4

Litvinoff's absence from the final scenes of the Bolshevik battle and triumph was consistent with both his character and his function. He

* John Reed, *op. cit.,* p. 93.

was and is primarily a thinker and adjudicator, not an abstract theorist, like other outstanding members of his group, but a concrete, practical rationalist; and secondarily he is an organizer and administrator. He is not at all the adventurer type, though he never shirked effort or danger to further his ideas and ideals. His major contribution to his cause was in its external relations, as intermediary between his Party, now his country, and the other nations. Lenin, with his usual perspicacity, had discerned and correctly appraised these values and designated Litvinoff as a link with the Western world.

Consequently, on January 3, 1918, he was appointed the first Soviet Ambassador to the Court of St. James, a responsibility for which his ten years of work in England had well prepared him. Learning his assignment through the newspapers, he wrote to the British Foreign Office, but his letter was returned, unopened. As always, patiently persistent, he wrote to demand immediate transfer to him of the Czarist Embassy in Chatham House, and prepared to move there. But Downing Street would not oust the Czarist diplomat, for he was still accounted the accredited Russian representative, though the Czar who had accredited him was gone. Lord Robert Cecil, Undersecretary for Foreign Affairs, and the men around him, were sincere in their belief that Lenin, Trotsky and the other leading Communists were paid German agents. That there was no evidence whatever for such a view did not matter. The British disappointment over the loss of a second front in the East, the deep distrust of revolutionaries in general, old prejudice against Russia—these, not facts, controlled opinion.

So Litvinoff opened the "People's Embassy" in offices at 21 Victoria Street, run with the help of his wife and friends who volunteered, making a living meanwhile on the side as best he could. Litvinoff summarized the situation in a letter to Trotsky, who had been appointed Commissar for Foreign Affairs. Litvinoff had asked the British Foreign Office for a meeting in order to regulate certain practical questions (the visaing of passports, use of codes, military conventions and similar necessary details), but the letter was not answered. "I presume," Litvinoff wrote, "the question of my recognition will not be settled until the arrival of Buchanan." And further:

The reception accorded by the Press is quite satisfactory. I am making the acquaintance of the representatives of the Labor movement. I have issued an appeal in all the Socialist papers to the English working men. Even the bourgeois press readily accords me its pages to explain our position.

I shall write more fully by the first courier. I have not received an answer from you to my telegram of January 4th, new style, No. 1. I request you very much to confirm the receipt of all telegrams and to number your telegrams.

The codes will, I trust, be delivered to me by the courier. Greetings to Lenin and all friends. I press your hand warmly.

Yours,

(Signed) M. Litvinoff.

Litvinoff's personal circumstances at the time are described in an anonymous Narkomindel (Soviet Foreign Office) report, which Litvinoff himself came across in the files some years later—made perhaps at the behest of a potential enemy, or perhaps only as a routine verification:

"On a cold January night, with the rain streaming down, I went to the distant northern suburb of London, seeking the house where the newly appointed representative of Soviet Russia was living.

"Before me stretched an endless row of deadly monotonous, small, two-story houses, and as I jumped across puddles and mudholes I was forced to think of the very different circumstances under which I had paid a visit to the Ambassador of Czarist Russia.

"Finally, in the pale light of blacked-out lanterns, I found the house and knocked. A young, simply dressed woman with bobbed hair opened the door. A moment later I was in the small, poorly furnished room whose only decoration, aside from a burning fireplace, was a bookshelf with the *Encyclopaedia Britannica,* the *History of the Paris Commune* and a few other books.

"The representative of the Soviet Republic, dressed in a shabby brown coat, was drinking tea and serving himself from a teapot which stood on the hearth.

"The young woman with the bobbed hair who had opened the door for me came into the room after me and without any pretense she began to stir the dough for a *piroge* (Russian pie). That was Mrs. Litvinoff. The house, the furnishings, the whole setup of the home of the new Ambassador of the Soviet Russian Republic was in no way different from the home of an English worker's family.

"Litvinoff stayed in this distant suburb till summer and then moved to another suburb where he rented an equally modest little house and where, on the other side of a small park, his secretary had taken lodgings. I could not find out that during that time anything in the exterior of our Ambassador had changed. I saw him in the same shabby, brown suit at the workers' conference in Nottingham at the moment of his highest triumph, when he made a speech (see page 133) in the presence of Vandervelde, Long, Renaudel and Huysmans, who appeared on that important occasion either in tails or, at least, in frock coats."

Litvinoff was surprised by Trotsky's first instructions: to get released from Brixton jail a Russian long resident in England, George Chicherin, who had been arrested by Scotland Yard's Alien Squad for making a pacifist speech in Hyde Park. Litvinoff, who had met him from time to time, respected his intellectual integrity and courage, but did not like a certain ambiguity of mind and purpose or his pallid Menshevik views. He was shocked, therefore, to learn that Chicherin had been chosen by Trotsky as his first assistant in the Foreign Office. Trotsky was convinced—rightly, as it proved—that Chicherin had been genuinely converted to Bolshevism, and he was the only man available with Russian Foreign Office experience, having worked in the archives there some years before.

The British authorities, having quite failed to grasp the significance of the Russian Revolution, refused short-sightedly to release Chicherin. Litvinoff therefore announced that no Englishman would leave Russia. Within twenty-four hours Chicherin was released, and he returned at once to Russia, where, after being Trotsky's first assistant, he soon himself became Foreign Commissar (when Trotsky was made Commander-in-Chief of the Red Army), and remained Litvinoff's chief for thirteen years.

Litvinoff, though officially unrecognized, was very busy, principally answering, always personally, letters from comrades asking aid, for as Kornev, his Russian biographer, has noted:

"This man, who knows no sentimentality, can be very sensitive when confronted with the needs of fighters for the working-class cause."

Other letters had to be dealt with, too, such as one from an Oxford student enquiring what the Soviet Union would do about self-determination, to which Litvinoff replied: "Soviet Russia will be a federation of republics. It will be, on a smaller scale, what a genuine League of Nations should be."

The League of Nations did not yet exist but already Litvinoff was implicitly critical of it, just as a possibility. As to Russia, it was a sound forecast.

By Christmas, 1917, even Downing Street realized that Great Britain would have to be represented in Russia, for many business interests were involved, many British subjects were in Russia, and conceivably Russia might join Germany. The British Foreign Office therefore decided to send a special mission, headed by an unofficial representative who would have full responsibility but no definite authority, and not necessarily diplomatic privileges, though the Bolshevik Government was given to understand that if it granted these, Britain would do the same for Litvinoff. The difficult post was assigned to Bruce Lockhart,* formerly British Consul at Moscow, one of the few Western diplomats who, understanding the Russian mind and situation, had foreseen the Revolution; Rex Leeper and Fedor Rothstein, a War Office translator who later became Russian Minister to Teheran, arranged a meeting between Lockhart and Litvinoff. Thus the British Government had to come to Litvinoff after all, even if unofficially.

From the beginning of the meeting, in a Lyons restaurant in the Strand, Lockhart, Leeper, and Rothstein made it clear that Soviet Russia would not be recognized, but Litvinoff realized that Lockhart's very presence there would be a step in that direction and readily agreed to write a letter of introduction to Trotsky.

At the end of the luncheon Litvinoff ordered, as his sweet, "Diplomat" pudding, but the waitress came back to report that there was no more. Smiling ruefully, he murmured: "Not recognized, even by Lyons."

5

During the Russo-German truce, Allied military experts who were quite out of touch with the facts wrote repeatedly from Russia that

* *British Agent.*

only the Communists were preventing Russia from going on with the war, thereby abolishing the second front so desired by the Allies. Their informers hoped by means of such misrepresentation to provoke Allied intervention for the restoration of the old order. Actually, no one in Russia wanted or felt able to continue the war.

The Communists especially had to have peace. On that platform they had won the chance to govern after the failure of the Kerenski offensive. So they opened negotiations with the Germans at Brest-Litovsk on December 22. Their position and policy was well stated in a *London Daily Chronicle* reporter's interview with Litvinoff, published January 2, 1918, and considered sufficiently important to be cabled to the *New York Times,* where it appeared January 6:

My task as Ambassador [said Litvinoff] will be to disseminate the truth about Russia and so dissipate the web of misunderstanding and misinterpretation of her motives. The second revolution in November was carried out with a view of taking the reins from the trembling hands of Kerenski and his associates, and handing them over to the Soviets, in which all the Socialist parties were represented.

After the second revolution, the Bolsheviki were willing to share responsibility for the management of the country with the other Socialist parties. Although this coalition plan was backed up by the powerful union of railway men and by the various army organizations, the Bolsheviks' invitation was refused by the rightists who hoped at that time for the speedy defeat of the Bolsheviks with the aid of Kornilov and Kaledin, and civil war began.

The responsibility for the resultant bloodshed must fall upon those irreconcilable elements. It is grossly malicious to represent the Bolsheviks as pro-German, or anti-Allied. They are none of those things. They realize as clearly as anyone that Kaiserism and Junkerdom are the greatest obstacles across the path of the international proletariat towards self-emancipation.

They would regard it as their highest triumph if they could carry the torch of revolution to Berlin.

I do believe, in fact, that through the negotiations now going on and the multifarious propaganda that is being pushed among the German soldiers in the east, Trotsky and Lenin are contributing towards the downfall of Kaiserism more effectively than the Allies by their fighting in the west. A separate peace would be looked upon by the Bolsheviks as a disaster and as a collapse of all their efforts.

Litvinoff realizing fully that the British Government was not making the slightest effort to understand the Soviet's situation, found occasion to appeal directly to the English people at the conference of the Trade Union Congress and the Labor Party in Nottingham, at a special session on January 23, 1918, set apart for addresses by foreign representatives.

Litvinoff said ironically that, in spite of being the representative of a government, he considered himself a political refugee; but he was sure that, the more unfriendly the attitude of the British Government was towards him, the better this conference would understand. He explained that the Russians revolted against the war not just because they were opposed to imperialist war. Speaking of negotiations at Brest-Litovsk, which were then still under way, he commented: "Even if peace does not result from the negotiations, revolution in Germany— and, may I hope, somewhere else—may come within the range of immediate possibilities."

This implied advocacy of revolution in Great Britain was warmly received by many in the audience, but the conservative Morning Post objected very strongly to the speech; the Daily Express protested that it was "the most menacing speech ever delivered by the Ambassador of a friendly country"; and Downing Street, brushing aside the fact that they had refused Litvinoff recognition as an ambassador, and ignored his many appeals, instructed its representative in Russia, Bruce Lockhart, to protest immediately to Trotsky against Litvinoff's "impossible behavior."

The negotiations at Brest-Litovsk were interrupted early in February. Trotsky, now Commander-in-Chief of the Red army, opposed acceptance of the harsh German conditions; but the Soviets had no alternative, and on February 23, 1918, the Central Executive Committee voted by 118 to 86 that the treaty be signed.

From Trotsky's note of December, inviting the Allies to define their attitude towards peace negotiations and "to openly state before the world clearly, definitely and correctly in the name of what purposes must the people of Europe bleed during the fourth year of war" * until March 14, when the Congress of Soviets finally voted for the acceptance of the cruel Treaty of Brest-Litovsk, there was better than a fight-

* Quoted by Schuman, in American Policy Toward Russia, p. 70.

ing chance to keep Russia in the war on the Allied side—at least, so David Francis, the American Ambassador, and Raymond Robins were confident, Bruce Lockhart concurring. Trotsky and Lenin promised to do their best if the Allies would extend practical military assistance to the exhausted and impoverished Russian Armies which were utterly incapable of resuming a serious offensive without substantial support and encouragement.

Immediately afterwards (March 5) Trotsky declared that he would defeat the ratification if America and the other Allies would promise aid against Germany, with a guarantee not to interfere with Russian internal policy. The Allies missed their chance, the treaty was signed, and a German Ambassador appeared at Moscow, which had been made the capital on March 9. Meanwhile, in February all the Allied diplomats had moved from Petrograd up to Vologda.

Lenin believed that the treaty would not be much help to the Germans, for while it would release some troops to serve on the Western front, he foresaw that many would still be needed in the east to guarantee the peace. He was afraid of the Germans and certain that Russia, sooner or later, would have to fight them again, a conviction reinforced by the Germans' failure to live up to the treaty terms; but he also did not trust the Allied governments, knowing full well that they wanted to collaborate with Russian reaction; and there were elements—chiefly certain Cossack regiments and wealthy peasants (kulaks), as well as many of the old aristocrats and conservatives in Moscow and Petrograd—who were ready to conspire with foreign anti-Bolsheviki. The war, however, was absorbing Allied resources to the full. They had no money or arms to spare just then for Russian counter-revolutionaries. Above all, moreover, Lenin wanted to keep all war away as long as possible from Russia, which had bled and starved to the point of exhaustion.

Lenin further promised to use his influence, which would have been decisive, to induce the Congress of Soviets, soon to meet, to reject the Brest-Litovsk terms, if the United States would extend any hope of real help. Unfortunately, in Francis' final cable of appeal to the State Department (March 9) to take advantage of the offers of Lenin and Trotsky, he included a restatement of his conviction that they were German agents. The meeting of the Soviet Congress was postponed from the 12th to the 14th at Robins' request in order to give time for Washington's answer. Lenin waited until the last moment, but Washington sent only vague generalities expressing good will and saying nothing about the matter in hand.* The Russians had no alternative. A treaty unparalleled in modern times for sheer brutality was authorized. The Western press promptly denounced the fateful but inevitable Soviet decision as a gross betrayal and Lenin and Trotsky as blackest traitors.

Litvinoff likewise hated and feared German militarism, but he also despised British capitalism. The Russian people were strongly anti-German and becoming increasingly hostile as they saw Germany establish a reactionary regime in the annexed Russian territory, and participate in the Finnish civil war on the side of the reactionary Baron Mannerheim.

In June, Litvinoff, convinced that recognition by the United States would go a long way towards solving the Soviets' international problems, proposed that he be sent there, and Lenin, agreeing, appointed him Ambassador to the United States. Boris Bakhmetev, who had been named Ambassador by Kerenski, was still in Washington. The State Department viewed him with a mild skepticism, but though the government he represented was no longer in existence, they accorded him all diplomatic privileges and allowed him to draw on previously established credits. Compared with Litvinoff he seemed to the State Department functionaries the lesser of two evils, so when Litvinoff asked for a visa, he at first received no answer at all from Washington, then finally the application was refused.

Meanwhile, the Socialists of the Allied countries met again in London and, as usual, nothing was accomplished.

Allied intervention in Russia was now being delayed only by disagreements among themselves as to the conditions. Some, like President Wilson, were willing to intervene against the Germans only with Russian permission. Others, like the British Foreign Office, proposed intervention without permission but only against the Germans, avoiding intrusion into Russian domestic affairs. Still others, like the British War Ministry, wanted to intervene against both the Germans and the Bolsheviki.

* For an excellent account of the whole transaction see Schuman, *op. cit.*, pp. 70-80.

Serious setbacks on the Western front finally forced the issue. The French General Staff demanded that the second front be reopened. On July 23, members of the Allied embassies moved from Vologda to Archangel, notifying the Russian Government that the move meant nothing, certainly not a rupture of relations. But on August 4 Allied troops landed in Archangel. The Wars of Intervention had begun.

6

The summer of 1918 was a desperately difficult one, which nearly broke the Soviet regime. Civil War, intervention and the ambiguous struggle with the Czechs was exhausting the Soviet capacity for defense. There was an epidemic of terroristic acts, directed against the Soviet Government, which the Soviets believed, and with some pretty substantial evidence too, were being directed and aided by Allied representatives who were in Russia. The German Ambassador, Mirbach, was assassinated on June 6; Field Marshal von Eichorn on July 30. There were active centers of rebellion in the Ukraine. Strikes and peasant uprisings were fomenting in widely scattered areas; plans were made for railroad sabotage, blowing up bridges and actual plots against the Soviet Government. The Soviets were sure that they had full information about bribes of Red Guard officers and plans looking to the assassination of various Bolshevik leaders. Meantime the armies of intervention were steadily coming down from Archangel. Everything was conspiring to create an explosive and frantic reaction on the part of the Soviets. On September 1, 1918, at the very moment when things seemed blackest for the Bolsheviki, Fanny Kaplan, a young girl who belonged to the Right Wing of the Social Revolutionary Party, shot Lenin. At first his death seemed inevitable. Lenin himself pleaded that the girl's life be spared * but the populace, infuriated at the outrage, let loose a terror that could not be halted until Lenin, just emerging from three months of coma, gave the order: "Stop the terror." It was stopped, but not before it had furnished anti-Soviet elements the world over with violent and easily exaggerated arguments against the new regime—arguments to which Lenin replied in an interview with Lincoln Steffens.

* Walter Duranty, *op. cit.*, p. 122, New York, 1934.

"Do you mean to tell me," he said, "that those men [in Paris] who have just generated the slaughter of seventeen millions of men in a purposeless war are concerned over the few thousands who have been killed in a revolution with a conscious aim—to get out of the necessity of war—and armed peace? ... But never mind, don't deny the terror. ... If we have to have a revolution, we have to pay the price of revolution. ... There will be a terror. It hurts the revolution both inside and out, and we must find out how to avoid or control or direct it. But we have to know more about psychology than we do now to steer through that madness. And it serves a purpose that has to be served ... We have to devise some way to get rid of the bourgeoisie, the upper classes. They won't let you make economic changes during a revolution any more than they will before one; so they must be driven out ... The only solution I see is to have the threat of a red terror spread the fear and let them escape." *

On the day Lenin was shot, the Bolshevik authorities, who never abated their conviction that the assault was connected with British activities in Russia (Fanny Kaplan was officially reported to have admitted that she approved of her Party appealing for English and French aid against the Soviet regime),† sent Cheka (secret police) agents to the British Embassy in Petrograd. The British clerks tried to resist. A Captain Cromie shot down one of the police and was himself immediately killed. The Russian authorities arrested all the British in Petrograd and they arrested Lockhart in Moscow.

Litvinoff had finally been permitted to live in the Russian Embassy in London but was by no means persona grata. He had particularly irritated the authorities—and delighted Scottish workers—by appointing as Soviet consul a Scottish teacher named McLean, an appointment which Lenin specifically approved (in a speech to the professional Soviets on June 28, 1918) as consistent with the revolutionary view.

Now the British Government put Litvinoff under police surveillance as an answer to the Russian arrests of Lockhart and the other British subjects, and Lord Robert Cecil commented: "If there were an organized government in Russia this would, of course, mean war. But as

* Lincoln Steffens, *Autobiography*, II, pp. 797-8, New York, 1931.
† *Ibid.*, p. 797.

there is no real government, no immediate steps will be taken affecting the Bolsheviki."

While Lenin hovered near death, Lockhart's position looked grave. He himself believed, as he wrote later, that if Lenin died he would be executed, and the British Government took such a serious view of the situation that they arrested Litvinoff and his staff and sent them to Brixton prison, where Litvinoff's cell bore the sign: "Reserved for the military guests of His Majesty." Madame Litvinoff had just given birth to her second child, their daughter Tanya.

As danger of Lenin's death receded, both Lockhart's and Litvinoff's prospects brightened, and finally the Russians suggested that Lockhart and his staff would be sent back to England if Litvinoff and his staff were allowed to return to Russia. The British Government, skeptical, agreed to release Litvinoff only if he stayed aboard a steamer in a neutral port until assurances were received that its subjects had crossed the Russian border. Finally everything was arranged and Litvinoff and his group went to Stockholm to wait for a steamer there. Madame Litvinoff and the two children remained in England until Litvinoff could send for them.

The tensions, bred primarily of fear intensified by herd imitation, which distorted most observation of Russia even by trained historians during these years, are typified by a presumably scholarly account of this complex episode, which reduces it to the statements: "The life of Lockhart, the British High Commissioner in Moscow, was spared only in exchange for the release of Litvinoff." ". . . his [Litvinoff's] arrest on charges of fomenting mutiny among Russians in England brought about his expulsion during the late summer of 1918." * There is no mention of the attack on Lenin or the British resistance to the Soviet police.

So ended Litvinoff's brief career as Ambassador to the Court of St. James, to the end—like his Government—unrecognized.

* A. L. P. Dennis, *The Foreign Policies of Soviet Russia*, pp. 62, 56, New York, 1924.

PART TWO

THE FIGHT FOR RECOGNITION

CHAPTER SIX

Gradual Approach

MANY FACTORS in the Russian situation conspired to mislead the Allied statesmen. The Revolution itself was not only thoroughly alarming, but also exceedingly difficult, at the time, to gauge. Its apparent suddenness, magnitude and violence, the grandiose ambitions of the revolting masses and the messianic fervor for a world revolution astonished even a close and skilled observer like Gorki, while Grand Duke Nicholas, in spite of all that was going on before his eyes, remained at first optimistic about the salvation of the Provisional Government, and Miliukov, in the midst of decisive developments, expressed the conviction that Lenin had shot his bolt, that the Soviets would have no more of him, and that the revolution would be over in a few days.*

If responsible participants could have so little grasp of the facts, small wonder that foreign officials could not, at least in the beginning, understand what was going on. Nor were most of the Allied representatives on the spot qualified to unravel and estimate the intricacies of the moment. Practically all, with the notable exceptions of Bruce Lockhart, British Consul in Moscow, and Maurice Paléologue, the French Ambassador, had almost wholly neglected to investigate behind the government façade. Most of them had "indoor minds" and were either frankly baffled or violently prejudiced, and in general they were handicapped by ignorance of the language, an almost complete insulation from the life and views of the Russian people and, on the other hand, by too close contacts with the former ruling classes. Consequently, they failed to gauge the creative energy and implacable resolution which were driving the Revolution forward.

At the same time plenty of reactionary Russian officials and officers who, by virtue of their position, were the diplomats' chief Russian acquaintances, were quick to assure them, because of either prejudice or

* Maurice Paléologue, *op. cit.,* p. 302.

misinformation, that Russia could be brought back into the war, and that the Bolsheviki did not represent the country. Even many who in their own hearts may have known better could have urged this, for the remnants of both the old regime and the moderately liberal bourgeoisie were fully aware that only foreign arms could restore them to power. As a result, most of the reports which went back to the Foreign Offices of the Allies were vague, erroneous, often gravely misleading.

Moreover, anti-Bolshevik representatives of the former Russian Government were exercising considerable pressure in foreign capitals, especially Washington, while the actual Government had no spokesmen abroad to correct the distorted reports.

The diplomats and their governmental colleagues at home were almost all ready to accept this anti-Soviet propaganda because it calmed their own anxieties. The threatened loss of a second front while Germany was still powerful and dangerous (Ludendorff's great offensive in the spring of 1918 was yet to come) was an absorbing anxiety for overburdened leaders. Furthermore, their own governmental and economic regimes were, if not threatened, at least dangerously challenged by this new upheaval, so momentous and incalculable. With a common will to disbelieve, they saw the rapidly running chain of events not as another phase in the recurrent modification of economic and social structures, but rather as a capricious and menacing eruption into world history.

The Soviets themselves did not make it any easier. They proclaimed the world revolution with crusading passion and proposed to withdraw from the war. Moreover, in the confusion of the moment, long pent-up resentments found outlet in acts of violence and meaningless cruelty which were no part of the revolutionary program but did it discredit.

The occasional voice of information and objective judgment could not make itself heard through the emotional deafness epidemic among the Soviet opponents. In Petrograd Grand Duke Nicholas said to Paléologue: "The collapse of autocracy will now mean the salvation and greatness of Russia," * but for once the astute and cultivated Frenchman lost his clear vision and was skeptical. On the other hand Albert Thomas, French labor leader, at the opposite end of the social scale, found the Revolution charged with immense significance

* *Ibid.,* p. 258.

and promise. He saw in it grandeur and beauty, and assured his government that a revision of Allied war aims which would eliminate annexations and indemnities would rally the new Russia to Allied support. His advice went unheeded.

Colonel Raymond Robins, head of the American Red Cross in Russia (though a year later he expressed opposition to the Bolsheviki), while he was actually in Russia tried to explain to the world that the only alternative to the Bolsheviki which the Russian situation could offer was control by the Social Revolutionary Party, only another version of the same thing, and counseled "generous and sympathetic co-operation" with Lenin and his group. Edgar Sisson, representing the Creel Committee in Russia, whose assignment it was to know the facts, seconded Colonel Robins's recommendation. Only the liberal minorities of France, England and the United States listened, and they too wrote and spoke to no avail.

Months passed, the Soviet organization was adjusting and consolidating itself, but still no new enlightenment came to the Foreign Offices of the Allied Powers. Indeed, they began to formulate their hostility in official communications. Thus Bainbridge Colby, Secretary of State for the United States, said on August 10, 1918, when the Soviet Government had been established almost a year: "The existing régime in Russia is based upon negation of every principle of honor and good faith and every usage and convention underlying the whole structure of international law; the negation, in short, of every principle upon which it is possible to base harmonious and trustful relations, whether a nation's or individuals'." *

And the French Government was still, five months later (January, 1919), among the false prophets: "The criminal régime of the Bolsheviks . . . does not . . . furnish any possibility whatever of developing into a government. . . ." †

Six months after that (*London Times,* July 18, 1919) General Jan Smuts asked that Russia be left alone and the blockade lifted, and predicted, in a cautious statement that should have won conservative confidence: "It may well be that the only ultimate hope of Russia is a

* G. K. Cumming and W. W. Petit, *Russian-American Relations,* pp. 280-281, New York, 1920.

† *L'Humanité,* Jan. 11, 1919 (Alfred P. Dennis, *The Foreign Policies of Soviet Russia,* New York, 1924).

sobered, purified system; and that may be far better than the Tsarism to which our present policy seems inevitably tending."

But "facts make bad witnesses when the emotions sit in judgment," especially when the emotion is fear wearing the mask of indignation or outraged virtue. And so the Powers, angry at what they deemed a betrayal, alarmed at the prospect of anti-war movements and possibly even revolution in their own strained and weary countries, contemptuous of the disorders that amounted to near anarchy at times in Russia, indifferent to the humane ideal which was the generating force of the Revolution, and concentrating instead on the threat it held to privilege and the status quo, lashed out whenever they saw a chance, determined to stop history and wipe out the Soviet Government promptly in order to prevent repetition by imitation elsewhere.

2

The Russians who had to carry most of the responsibility for protecting their country in these inimical but not officially hostile foreign relations were George Chicherin, Commissar for Foreign Affairs, and Litvinoff, Vice-Commissar in charge of European affairs—two men so diametrically contrasted that it was a question whether they would conflict with, or complement, each other.

Chicherin (1872–1936), the son of aristocratic parents, had grown up in diplomatic society and been groomed for a diplomatic career, taking a post in the Foreign Office archives to train himself in historical technique. Scanning documents, he learned about the oppression and unspeakable miseries of the common people and about the crimes of Czarism. This converted him to Socialism—though not yet to revolution; and when World War I broke out he avowed pacifism—though not yet the willingness to fight for peace.

But while alienated, as a result, from his class, outwardly he remained the aristocrat—quiet, detached, with excellent manners; and perhaps this conflict fostered a neurotic tendency, making him diffident and anti-social. Steffens saw him as "a shy, little, serious man." * He preferred to be alone, reading or listening to music, above all Mozart; and later, when diabetes developed, he became a hypochondriac, con-

* Lincoln Steffens, *op. cit.*, p. 794.

sulting innumerable doctors, taking endless cures and feeling unhappy when told that he looked better.

As Louise Bryant vividly presented him: "His aloofness is so evident that one can hardly find any concordance about the astounding decision of such an obvious aesthete to become an active part of revolution—which is sweat and blood and violence. Perhaps that explains why he wraps his vision round him like a cloak and shuts out the sun in order not to be disturbed and disillusioned by reality." *

It is not surprising that Chicherin was a somewhat disbalanced personality and that he ended his days definitely under a mental cloud—perhaps a manic depressive with a paranoidal tinge. His mother had wanted girl children and was greatly disappointed to find she had two boys to bring up. Consequently, she dressed them as girls, kept their hair in long curls until they were twelve—a bizarre but not uncommon fraud which had the usual damaging consequences.

Chicherin was thus the diametric opposite of Litvinoff, who "is hale, hearty and loves the fleshy things of life. He fairly bursts with a florid, extravagant energy, like a man who has just emerged from a hot bath, dressed in haste and is late for an appointment. He is big and burly, wearing his clothes loosely with a sort of unkempt but smooth-shaven air. He is a great worker and, when he has the opportunity, enjoys life. . . . He never looks tired and seems to begin each task with the same enthusiasm." †

Trotsky's choice of Chicherin to succeed him as head of the Narkomindel was surprising, since Chicherin had not been a Party member before the October Revolution; but Lenin acceded to the suggestion.

When Chicherin began his work in Moscow he indulged his antisocial bias unrestrainedly, isolating himself in a world of papers: state papers, accumulated documents, diplomatic notes, books—an immeasurable confusion that he was able to get under control largely because of his extraordinary memory, which later made many European diplomats fear him.

Litvinoff was at first disturbed, as he has since said himself, at the prospect of co-operating with a man who, as a Menshevik, had for years

* Louise Bryant, *Mirrors of Moscow,* p. 182, New York, 1923.
† *Ibid.,* pp. 199-200.

been an immediate adversary, the more so as Litvinoff had his own ideas on Russia's foreign policies which might not accord with Chicherin's, though he knew that Lenin would support him in his program, if need be, even against Chicherin. Moreover, the temperamental antithesis threatened problems: Chicherin introverted and tending to abstract thinking; Litvinoff realistic and practical. As Louis Fischer put it in *Men and Politics:* * "Chicherin was queer and a genius. He usually remained above the battle in a world partly of his own private construction. But Litvinoff is full-blooded, virile and tempestuous." And from this contrast resulted many specific differences: Chicherin was inflexible, as introverts are apt to be—Litvinoff ready to compromise on means in order to achieve progress towards his ends; Chicherin, unrealistic, was ready for conflict—Litvinoff anxious to avoid it as unprofitable; in short, it was a theorist versus a pragmatist. Chicherin was suspicious of any international agreement as a possible entering wedge for outside interference in Soviet affairs—a rationalized extension, perhaps, of his personal aversion to social relations; and he was reluctant to subscribe to any document not consistent with his principles. Litvinoff, on the other hand, believed that Russia should function internationally wherever possible in order to establish herself, hence should participate whenever she could in conferences and treaties. The two men's relative values in Russia's foreign relations also were opposed: Chicherin looked to the East, considering Persia and Afghanistan of primary importance; Litvinoff believed that Western Europe took precedence. Even their working habits were opposed: Chicherin functioned in a chaos of physical disorder, his desk buried beneath a progressive random accumulation into which important papers periodically disappeared, necessitating a frantic search. But Litvinoff had the makings of a good business man, had for years earned his living as such, and in addition had had valuable organizing experience in the period when he had carried on revolutionary "transport."

Yet, underlying these differences of attitudes and techniques were more fundamental agreements. Both were utterly devoted to the new order in Russia, for, as Lenin and Litvinoff soon saw, Trotsky had been right about the genuineness of Chicherin's conversion, and his political integrity was unquestionable; and both almost wholly distrusted the

* P. 128.

foreign offices and the masters of the foreign offices of other countries.

Litvinoff, concerned here as always with results, made every effort to bridge some of the superficial gaps between them: Chicherin did his best work at night (as a person of this type often feels he does), so liked to start the day late; Litvinoff had always liked to start the day early but, to accommodate his chief, he also became a night worker. Before long, the amicable relations between the two had developed as near to friendship as was possible in the case of a personality like Chicherin's.

Litvinoff has recorded his deep respect for Chicherin's capacity: "He was an extraordinary man, a mental giant, a tireless worker whose unprecedented memory permitted him a concentration second to none, and whose ascetism rendered him invulnerable to influences other than the best interests of the Soviet Union. His only weakness, perhaps, was that he found it difficult to delegate authority and wanted to execute all his ideas himself. Often he conceived a diplomatic note, drafted it himself, then translated it and went to the length of carrying it to the nearest post office. This actually happened during our stay in Berlin in 1922."

In the end it was neither man, nor was it the two together, whether in accord or opposition, that determined Russia's foreign policy, because for years this policy was imposed externally, since it consisted in the Soviet Union's adjustments to world conditions.

3

The Powers started a campaign to confine the new Russia entirely to her own domain and keep her out of the international scene as much as possible in the spring and summer of 1918. Their first moves were partially defensible as efforts to keep supplies out of German hands. British, French, and American troops landed at Archangel where considerable stores, shipped to Russia by the Allies, had accumulated. And far on the other side of the country in June of that year the Czechoslovak corps, who by then were at loggerheads with the Soviets over various mutual irritations and suspicions, were encouraged to revolt, presumably to hold the Trans-Siberian Railway, lest military matériel that had been shipped in through Vladivostok be carried to the enemy.

The corps were made up of some 45,000 men who had deserted from the Austrian army to the Russians, in order to fight their national oppressor, the Austro-Hungarian monarchy, and had been formed into a special Corps of the Russian army. When the war was over, they were to be sent home by the Soviet Government, via Siberia.

The invasion army through the north, which involved in all about 27,500 troops (not including 20,000 White Russians), more than three-quarters British and American, with some British and French naval units, occupied Murmansk (July 1, 1918), and, a month later, Archangel, staged a White Guard revolt, set up a White government of North Russia and killed quite a number of loyal Russians.

The Czechoslovak revolt set off insurrections among the Volga kulaks and resulted in temporary White governments there and in Samara and Omsk. Meanwhile, the Japanese landed troops, both in Vladivostok and as far north as Nikolaevsk, nearly 75,000 in all, who joined 8,500 American and some 15,000 French and British soldiers, all invaders, but claiming that they were "protecting" the Czechoslovaks. The Soviets there were dissolved and White counter-revolution was encouraged.

With the revolt in Germany and the consequent collapse of the enemy, the only excuse for Allied intervention into Russia was gone, and on Armistice Day Lenin appealed to the peoples of the world to stop interfering in the affairs of his country. But though the Powers could no longer claim even the semblance of a justification, and their results, moreover, had up to that time been negligible, fear of a future world that was beginning to take shape in Russia and of all that it might mean to them and theirs prevailed. They launched out into a real but undeclared, and as far as possible, unacknowledged, Russian war.

This war was waged chiefly on two fronts. In Siberia, after considerable confusion, Admiral Alexander Kolchak, of the old Russian navy, had been set up with Allied tacit consent and considerable material aid, as Dictator (November 18, 1918), and commanded a mixture of loosely knit forces, including the Czechoslovaks; in the Caucasus General Anton Denikin, with a miscellaneous entourage, was likewise aided and abetted. The hope was that the two fronts could be pushed forward to a point of consolidation, that then the combined forces could take

Moscow and set up some kind of government more to foreign taste. The problem of just what kind of government it would be was evaded, owing to the incoherent diversity of the elements involved, and the chaotic ambiguity in the anti-Soviet effort was increased by Entente participation, for Germany secretly supported Generals Peter Krasnov and Konstantin Mamontov in provoking the Don Cossacks to revolt, German and Turkish troops likewise helped cut off the Caucasus, and Tiflis and Baku were occupied. A monument in Baku today commemorates the Russians who were executed by the British authorities for resisting this occupation. Allied naval units also appeared in the Black Sea and the greater part of the old Russian navy was spirited away, eventually to Bizerte.

All this, with other scattered uprisings, and the loss of the Ukraine under the Brest-Litovsk Treaty, deprived Soviet Russia of her principal sources of raw materials, fuel, and food. Soon factories had to shut down and the cities had not even enough bread. The Soviet Government faced the critical test: would the masses defend their Revolution? They did. Hundreds of thousands volunteered for the Red army. Hundreds of thousands more volunteered to help Lenin organize the supply of arms and food to the front.

The Government took control of all industries and decreed a state monopoly of grain under which all the peasants' surplus was to be acquired by the State at a fixed price. Thus, grain stores for the army and the workers could be accumulated. Universal conscription of labor was introduced. Russia had recognized total warfare.

By this time—the end, that is, of 1918—all diplomatic representatives, both Allied and neutral, including consuls, had left territory under Soviet control. The Ambassadors and their staffs had moved from Petrograd to Vologda in February, presumably lest the Germans, then advancing into Russia, take the city; had refused to come to Moscow when the capital was moved there in March; and had then in July gone on to Archangel, hypocritically assuring the Russian Government that this did not mean a break in relations, though the Allied Ambassadors already knew of the coming Archangel invasion, which was effected only a few weeks later.

Consequently, when the Russian Government made a diplomatic

effort to end the international banditry, Litvinoff could short-cut diplomatic procedures, and on December 24, 1918, he addressed a letter
directly to President Wilson.

Stockholm, December 24th 1918

In addition to the general peace offer recently addressed by the Soviet
Government to the Allies, I formally informed today the Stockholm
Ministers of the United States and of the Allied countries that I am authorized to enter into negotiations for a peaceful settlement of all questions
making for hostilities against Russia. The principles proclaimed by you as
a possible basis for settling European questions, your avowed efforts and
intentions of making the settlement conform to the demands of justice
and humanity, induce and justify me to send you this statement, inasmuch as most points of your peace programme are included in the more
extensive aspirations of the Russian workers and peasants, now rulers
of their country.

It was they who first proclaimed and actually granted to nations the
right of self-determination, who suffered most sacrifices in fighting imperialism and militarism both at home and abroad, who dealt the severest
blow to secret diplomacy. And it is partly for these innovations in politics
that they have been fiercely attacked by the former ruling classes of Russia and their counterparts in other countries. To justify this attack a network of lies and calumnies has been woven round the activities of the
Soviets and forged documents put into circulation.

Unfortunately, Allied Statesmen accept all the monstrous accusations
against the Soviets at their face value, without taking the trouble to check
them. Whilst agents of the anti-Soviet parties are allowed and encouraged
to move freely in Allied countries and disseminate untruth, representatives
of the accused side have never been allowed to put fully their case and to
answer the charges made against them.

In fact, the chief aim of the Soviets is to secure for the toiling majority
of the Russian people economic liberty, without which political liberty
is of no avail to them. For eight months the Soviets endeavored to realize
their aims by peaceful methods without resorting to violence, adhering to
the abolition of capital punishment, which abolition had been part of
their programme. It was only when their adversaries, the minority of
the Russian people, took to terrorist acts against popular members of the
government and invoked the help of foreign troops that the laboring masses
were driven to acts of exasperation and gave vent to their wrath and bitter
feelings against their former oppressors.

For the Allied invasion of Russian territory not only compelled the Soviets against their own will to militarize the country anew and to divert their energies and resources—so necessary to the economic reconstruction of Russia, exhausted by four years of war in defense of the country—but also cut off the vital sources of foodstuffs and raw materials, exposing the population to most terrible privations, bordering on starvation. I wish to emphasize that the so-called "Red Terror"—which is grossly exaggerated and misrepresented abroad—was not the cause but the direct result and outcome of Allied intervention.

The Russian workers and peasants fail to understand how foreign countries, which never dreamed of interfering with Russian affairs when Tsarist barbarism and militarism ruled supreme, and even supported the regime, can feel justified in interfering in Russia now, when the working people themselves, after decades of strenuous struggling and countless sacrifices, succeeded in taking power and the destiny of their country in their own hands, aiming at nothing but their own happiness and international brotherhood, constituting no menace to other nations.

The Russian workers and peasants are determined to defend their dearly won power and liberties against invaders with all the means their vast country puts at their disposal, but mindful of the inevitable wanton loss of life and treasure on both sides, and wishing to avert the further ruining of Russia which must result from the continuation of internal and external fighting—they are prepared to go to any length of concessions enabling them to work out peacefully their social schemes.

I understand that the question of relations with Russia is now engaging the attention of Allied Statesmen. I venture then, to submit to you, Mr. President, that there are now only two courses open to them.

One is continued open or disguised intervention on the present or on a still larger scale, which means prolongation of war, further embitterment of the Russian masses, intensification of internal strife, unexampled bloodshed, and perhaps total extermination of the Russian bourgeoisie by the exasperated masses, final devastation of the country, and, in case of the interventionists after a long struggle obtaining their end, a White Terror eclipsing the atrocities of the Finnish White Guardists, the inevitable introduction of a military dictatorship, and the restoration of the monarchy, leading to interminable revolutions and upheavals, and paralyzing the economic development of the country for long decades.

The other alternative, which I trust may commend itself to you, is impartially to weigh and investigate the one-sided accusations against Soviet Russia, to come to an understanding with the Soviet Government, to withdraw the foreign troops from Russian territory, and to raise the economic blockade—soothing thereby the excited passions of the masses—to help Russia to regain her own sources of supply, and to give her technical advice how to exploit her natural richness in the most effective way, for the benefit of all countries badly in need of foodstuffs and raw materials.

The dictatorship of toilers and producers is not an aim in itself, but the means of building up a new social system under which useful work and equal rights would be provided for all citizens, irrespective of the class to which they had formerly belonged. One may believe in this ideal or not, but it surely gives no justification for sending foreign troops to fight against it, or for arming and supporting classes interested in the restoration of the old system of exploitation of man by man.

I venture to appeal to your sense of justice and impartiality.

I hope and trust, above all, that before deciding on any course of action you will give justice to the demand of audiatur et altera pars.

Litvinoff was now convinced that any effort to make peace would be ignored by the Allies, and said as much on January 10, but two days later Chicherin sent a formal note to the American State Department asking them to name time and place for a peace conference. Litvinoff was still in Stockholm and thither went W. H. Buckler, an attaché of the United States Embassy in London, known for his liberal views, to confer with him. Litvinoff pledged his government to an armistice at any time on the Archangel front, without prejudice to Russians who had co-operated with the Allies, and President Wilson on January 21, 1919, put these terms before the Peace Conference, already in session in Versailles. Out of this, after a certain amount of bickering and adjustment, grew a plan to have representatives of all Russian factions meet for negotiation of their differences on the island of Prinkipo in the Sea of Marmara.

On that same day Litvinoff, realizing that a major motive in all the other Governments' muddled policies in respect to Russia was their fear of revolutions stimulated by Russia, made a statement through the Associated Press in which he admitted propaganda activities in Germany, but denied any such activities in neutral or Allied countries: "This talk of propaganda is rather fantastic and does not conform to facts. While I represented the Russian Government in England, neither I nor any of my staff engaged in any illegal propaganda.

The same applies to Bolshevik diplomats in Scandinavia. Now, when the Entente nations are waging war on Russian territory, we feel justified in engaging in propaganda work among the Allied troops. Any Government in our place would do the same. With the end of hostilities and the withdrawal of these troops, there will be neither opportunity nor desire on our part to make foreign troops or citizens the object of our propaganda. In regard to Germany, we do not deny that propaganda work, despite the formal peace, continued to be the greatest danger to the Russian Revolution; and our propaganda was an act of self-defense. Even now, the Allies are attempting to make Germany a jumping-off ground for attacking Russia, and are using for this purpose even German troops with the connivance of Scheidemann's Government. This is instanced in the Baltic provinces, Lithuania and Ukraine. With the cessation of the Allied war against the Soviets and the resumption of diplomatic intercourse, relations with Germany and Russia will be put on a more formal footing, and then the German Government will have as little cause for complaint about propaganda as any other Government at peace with Russia."

Litvinoff assured the correspondent that the Bolsheviki were friends of freedom of the press and political liberty, and that the suppression of all opposition in Russia was due to the fact that other political parties there had invited foreign troops to invade the country. In concluding, he said he was sorry that Paris had been chosen for the Peace Conference, because it was the least suitable place for Soviet representatives to go, adding that it was not President Wilson's fault that the Russian Government, which had now been in power for fifteen months, was not represented at the Conference.

Only three days later (January 24, 1919), Lenin addressed the workers of the world, denouncing the conference of the Second International, called to meet in Berne the next month, attacking the leaders, and announcing that an international congress of workers would be held in Moscow beginning March 2, 1919. The Berne Conference of the Second International was thereby quashed; the Moscow Congress convened and thus was established the Third International. Thereafter the Second International held various meetings, some externally impressive, but its influence waned steadily. The Third International in this way marked an important advance in consolidating Russia's international revolutionary influence, but for that very reason it added serious difficulties to the task of consolidating her governmental international position.

The Prinkipo conference plan came to naught because, while the Soviet Government accepted and pledged itself in advance to a generous policy even in respect of foreign debts, the various anti-Soviet factions refused, with great show of moral indignation, to put their cards on the table.

But President Wilson still looked for a peaceful settlement and Lloyd George was similarly disposed, though there was strong opposition from the French, mindful of the large Czarist Russian loans that had been placed in their country. The first step was to get an outline of the proposed Soviet terms, and for this William C. Bullitt, then an assistant in the State Department attached to the Peace Commission, was sent to Russia at the end of February. Lincoln Steffens, the noted liberal journalist, accompanied him.

On the train to London Bullitt showed Steffens penciled on a sheet of paper the seven items which Philip Kerr, secretary to Lloyd George, had given him as the terms for the Bolsheviki to agree to. Bullitt's instructions were to negotiate a preliminary agreement with the Russians so that the United States and Great Britain could persuade France to join them in an invitation to a parley, reasonably sure of some results. Colonel House had proposed and Lloyd George had planned the visit; Bullitt's instructions came from House and the British Prime Minister. And the British paved their way, while in Stockholm U. S. Minister Morris put them in touch with Bolshevik agents.[*]

When they got to Russia, Bullitt conferred chiefly with Litvinoff, "now practically Assistant Secretary of Foreign Affairs."[†] Apparently there was some dispute among the Russians as to the real purposes of the Bullitt mission and whether to deal with it at all. Steffens told Chicherin that the Russians' part was to grant Bullitt, not the least of his requests, but the most that they could, since this might enable Wilson and Lloyd George to win over the French. They had to repeat this often. When Chicherin was at last convinced, he wired Lenin. They

---

[*] Lincoln Steffens, *op. cit.*, pp. 792-796.
[†] Bullitt, "Testimony Before the Committee on Foreign Relations, United States Senate," 1919.

were invited to come to Moscow to carry on under Lenin's eye. Bullitt
and Steffens accompanied Chicherin and Litvinoff to Moscow.

Bullitt, Chicherin, and Litvinoff, with Lenin near by, negotiated
daily. Bullitt found all three "full of the sense of Russia's need for
peace." Bullitt steered his way through to an agreement with Lenin
and Chicherin on the seven points of Lloyd George's memorandum,
and House's points as well were accepted with very slight verbal modifications.

The terms were very liberal on the Russians' part, providing for retention of territories of the old Russian Empire, including Finland, by
the governments then in power, with general amnesty and demobiliza-
tion, and in return requiring only evacuation of all foreign armies and
re-establishment of normal international relations. Finally—a striking
concession—all governments on Russian territory were to join in recognizing outstanding Russian debts. Bullitt was favorably impressed
with the conditions in Russia and was convinced that "no real peace
can be established in Europe and the world until peace is made with
the revolution."

Action was to be taken on the proposals by April 10, and Litvinoff
and his Narkomindel associates must have felt that the solution of their
first great international problem was coming closer. Colonel House,
who saw Bullitt immediately on his return to Paris, gauged the importance of his observations and recommendations, was, according to
Steffens, enthusiastic, and urged Bullitt to see Wilson at once.

The second day Lloyd George received Bullitt at breakfast, "listened
and was interested. Of course, Bullitt had brought back all the Prime
Minister had asked." *

Nevertheless, from that point on, everything got bogged down. Wilson declined to see Bullitt and requested a brief written report. This
was promptly submitted but still Bullitt did not get his interview. Steffens remembered that Wilson had once promised, in gratitude for
Steffens' assistance in another situation, to see him if he ever sent in
his name with the statement: "It's an emergency." Steffens felt this occasion justified calling on the pledge but Wilson still would not meet
either man. Wilson was not discriminating against Russia, for he similarly evaded Professor Archibald Coolidge of Harvard, whom he had

* Lincoln Steffens, *op. cit.*, p. 799.

sent on a somewhat comparable survey mission to Hungary. Wilson had simply reached the point of exhaustion, where he could not give attention to all the demanding questions that confronted him, nor could he willingly suffer the impact of strong personalities or compelling new ideas, and he had a theory to justify himself to himself: that the intellectual must sometimes close his mind and act.

Lloyd George's repudiation was even more brusque. He denied in Paris any acquaintance "with the young man" and when there were enquiries in London, he crossed the Channel to appear before the House of Commons to declare explicitly and at length that he knew nothing of the "journey some boys were reported to have made to Russia . . ." * And he too had a theory to justify himself: such prevarications were an old British political custom, when a Minister found himself embarrassingly entangled in one of his own trial balloons.

And embarrassing this one had become, both abroad and at home. Abroad, the French were making trouble, charging Lloyd George and Wilson with having gone behind their backs to negotiate with the Russians. At home, Northcliffe, Lloyd George's inveterate enemy, had rigged a Conservative opposition with Winston Churchill in the driver's seat, ready to throw the Prime Minister out of power if he even broached a friendly Russian adjustment.

Thus was submerged in a morass of accident, unworthy motives and political finagling, a simple reasonable arrangement, which would have saved the world incalculable trouble and financial loss and released Litvinoff's abilities as a statesman from years of struggle for normal international relations for Russia, to more constructive purposes.

In April, Kolchak had some temporary successes which the predominant antipathy to the Soviets, constantly confusing most of the world's statesmen, magnified into portents of triumph. The question of settlement with Russia was dropped by the Allied conferees, the moment passed, and Litvinoff still had ahead of him the long road to recognition along which he had now to toil, slow step by step.

The Kolchak prospects, however, were soon blasted. In April, just before reaching the Volga, he was defeated, and later he was taken prisoner and shot (February 7, 1920). General Nikolai Yudenich, stationed in the Baltic, was next designated to defeat the Soviets. He

* Lincoln Steffens, *op. cit.,* p. 800.

quickly assembled a motley crew of Letts, Latvians, Esthonians, some German units and White Russians and developed a swift attack on the famine-stricken city of Petrograd. But after initial successes that brought him to the suburbs of the city, he was blocked by the devoted resistance of Red army units, aided by ill-equipped workers including many women, who actually fought in the trenches. By the end of 1919 he, too, was defeated.

In October, 1919, General Denikin, sweeping up with almost irresistible momentum from the Caucasus, captured Orel. But shortly afterwards near Kharkov, Orel and Voronezh, he ran into a formidable trio: Stalin, Klementi Voroshilov and Semyon M. Budenny, who, at the head of furiously determined proletarian armies, defeated him decisively. By the beginning of 1920 the whole Ukraine and the Northern Caucasus had been cleared. Yudenich was driven back to Esthonia, and ultimately the interventionists in the Far East, Transcaucasia, and the Crimea were expelled.

The civil war had cost Russia dear. The White armies were guilty of senseless destruction and of savage atrocities. Great Britain, France, and Italy had already decided to lift the blockade against Soviet Russia, but shortly after the blockade was lifted, in 1920, almost without warning, Poland attacked Soviet Russia, driving deep into Russian territory before the Red armies could be rallied to throw them back to the gates of Warsaw.

And for years politicians, especially in England, continued to cherish schemes for intervention.

4

Litvinoff, pursuing his policy of forging international contacts for the Soviets, even when he had to accept unsatisfactory conditions, had arranged in November, 1919, before the Wars of Intervention were over, or the blockade was lifted, to get out of the country and establish at least personal relations in European centers. His aims were: raising the blockade, peace, and recognition; his pretext, the relatively trivial problem of prisoner exchanges.

Whether by design or accident, the way was paved for negotiations by a two-fold announcement in the *London Times* on November 10, of the terms that had been communicated eight months earlier to Bullitt without results, the second statement coming through Colonel Cecil l'Estrange Malone, a Liberal member of the House of Commons who had gone to Russia two months before. The whole question was again brought to public attention by two contributions in the *London Times* for December 4, one a communication from Malone, who claimed to be releasing a Russian Government request, the other a written comment by Litvinoff to Reuter's. Malone reaffirmed Russia's desire for peace and urged that Great Britain take official cognizance of the advances by sending a representative either to Moscow or to confer with Litvinoff in Copenhagen. Litvinoff confirmed Russia's readiness to make peace and gave assurance that the Bullitt terms were still available, though he denied that Malone had been commissioned by the Soviet Government to announce this, and he also proclaimed an "open-door" policy without discrimination in favor of or against any nation, but pointed out that what Russia needed most, machinery, was primarily available in Great Britain and the United States.

Europe's fear of the unknown new neighbor, the Soviet Government, was almost ludicrously reflected in the precautions with which Litvinoff and his delegation were surrounded. At Dorpat in Esthonia, which they reached on November 16, they were housed in a building in the suburbs, guarded by Esthonian troops, and forbidden to see anyone in private.

Yet Esthonia was disposed to be friendly. She had already joined with Finland, Latvia, and Lithuania at the beginning of October in a declaration proposing peace negotiations with the Soviets, and was the first to execute a peace and mutual recognition treaty with her big neighbor only three months later (February 2, 1920).

From Dorpat the Russian delegation went on to Copenhagen, where the Danish authorities acted in a rather crude and unreasonable manner. Litvinoff himself described the incivilities with which he was entertained there in a half-humorous letter to a friend (February, 1920):

Immediately after my arrival in Copenhagen I learned that O'Grady [the British representative with whom he was negotiating] had had the greatest difficulties to put me up, that the hotels in which he tried to rent rooms for me declined one after the other, and that finally only the Tourist Hotel had agreed to take me. This strange behavior of the hotel managers was explained as the consequence of a press campaign against us and by the intrigues of Russian White Guards.

When, after a short time, the Tourist Hotel, too, asked me to leave within a week, and when it became impossible to find a new hotel, I found out that the real reason for the behavior of the management of the Tourist Hotel, as well as of the other hotels, was that they did not want to be under continuous surveillance by the police.

I tried to rent rooms outside the city, about ten kilometers from Copenhagen. But the police let me know through O'Grady that they would not permit this because it would be too complicated to organize a police surveillance there.

The official motive for the steady presence of detectives following me wherever I went was the protection of my person against possible White Russian assaults. In vain did I try to rid myself of this protection and thus to give myself an opportunity to move into a hotel of my own choice.

Twice I sat till late in the evening on my trunks and did not know where to spend the night.

Neither the Danish government nor the English delegation lifted a finger to change this situation. I received a few invitations from private persons to put me up, but did not choose to accept them. O'Grady was either beside himself or he seemed resigned, or in any case incapable of doing anything. For he felt that the English chargé d'affaires was trying in every way to frustrate his efforts by keeping him away from direct contact with Danish authorities—allegedly for reasons of diplomatic etiquette. I personally tend to believe that the English mission was more to blame for this whole occurrence than the Danish government.

When I finally simply refused to go on negotiating before the question of lodging was taken care of, O'Grady himself found a small third-class hotel with a bad reputation, and I had to move there. A few days later the police stopped watching the place.

O'Grady begged and implored me to stay till the signing of the agreement [about the exchange of prisoners] and promised to take the negotiations about the execution of this treaty into another, more hospitable country.

An Associated Press dispatch of January 23, 1920, confirms this account:

Virtually every hotel has refused to accommodate Mr. Litvinoff, who has appealed both to Mr. O'Grady and Mr. Chicherin, Bolshevik Foreign Minister, asking that negotiations be transferred to another country. In his telegram to Mr. Chicherin, Litvinoff declared that he is under semi-arrest and is being watched constantly. Six detectives are staying in his hotel. Litvinoff accuses the Danish Government of not fulfilling the guarantees given when the negotiations were proposed.

The official representatives there of other countries were also discouraging. Just before this, in December, the Seventh Soviet Congress had passed unanimously a resolution, the draft of which had been submitted by Lenin:

The Russian Socialist Federated Soviet Republic intends to live at peace with all peoples and to concentrate all its powers on inner reconstruction in order to build up production, transport and civil administration on the basis of the Soviets—all of which has been prevented so far, first, by the pressure of German imperialism, second, by the intervention of the Allies and by the hunger blockade.

The government of the peasants and workers has proposed peace to the Allied Powers repeatedly, namely:

On August 5, 1918, through a verbal note of the Narkomindel to Mr. Poole, the American representative.

On August 24, 1918, to President Wilson.

On November 3, 1918, to all Allied governments via representatives of neutral powers.

On November 23, 1918, in a note from Litvinoff to all representatives of the Allied Powers.

Furthermore, on January 12, on January 17, and on February 4, 1919. Furthermore: draft of a treaty with Mr. Bullitt on March 12, 1919. On May 7, 1919, through Nansen.

Approving completely of all these many steps of the Sovnarkom and the Narkomindel, the Seventh Soviet Congress declares again its undiminished wish for peace and proposes again to all Allied Powers, to England, France, the United States, Italy and Japan, as well as to each power separately, to enter into peace negotiations immediately and orders the Executive Committee, the Sovnarkom, and the Narkomindel to continue the policy of peace and to do everything to expedite its success.

The phrase "first, by the pressure of German imperialism," had been inserted by Lenin at the end of the first paragraph, at the very last minute.

Litvinoff sent this resolution on December 10 to all Allied Ambassadors with the notification that he was empowered to enter into peace negotiations. It was returned the next day by the British, French, and Italian Ambassadors in Copenhagen with the statement that they were not authorized to accept communications from Litvinoff, and that to take cognizance of such a proposal would be a breach of faith with Denmark which permitted Litvinoff's presence only to discuss prisoner exchanges; hence politics was excluded. A similar reply came a few days later from the American Ambassador.

That same day the Associated Press reported:

Litvinoff discussed anything but prisoners and began giving out peace propaganda. . . . Litvinoff tried to make the exchange of prisoners dependent upon certain peace terms. This was rejected.

But Litvinoff, though deploring that peace should be shunted off as "politics," did not give up, and when, owing to the defeat of all the armies they had sent to Russia, the Supreme Allied Council decided to lift the blockade, Litvinoff immediately started another peace offensive. Now trade with Russia could begin again, so he told O'Grady on February 2, 1920, that, "Peace between Soviet Russia and the Allies was the first essential to the resumption of commerce."

Moreover, American business men (but by no means the United States Government) were considering resuming trade with Russia, which prompted Litvinoff to declare on February 7, 1920:

"Soviet Russia is also anxious to resume trade. We need large quantities of American manufactured articles, tools and machinery, especially locomotives and repairing plants. Half of Russia's locomotives are in need of repairs."

And on February 10 Lloyd George admitted in a public speech the failure of intervention and intimated that it was time to do business with Russia. To be sure, his excuse was that trade would probably alter the Soviet internal structure: ". . . We can . . . save her by trade. . . . We must fight anarchy with abundance"; * but the Russians were ready to take the trade relations and see to their own internal affairs.

* A. L. P. Dennis, op. cit., p. 383.

The Allies, including the United States, tried to circumvent recognition of the Soviets by doing business with the Co-operative Societies in Russia which, though government-controlled, could be considered by capitalist countries as "private" enterprises. Litvinoff, however, saw through this maneuver immediately and declared: "Trade with Russia through the Co-operative Societies means, of course, trade with Soviet Russia." And on February 9 the Paris Bureau of the Associated Press had to announce:

Mr. Litvinoff has been named chief director of the Russian Cooperatives. It will be difficult then to trade with the Cooperatives directed by Mr. Litvinoff without trading with the Soviet Government of which Mr. Litvinoff is the official agent.

It would, indeed, have been difficult under any circumstances; but it was doubly so with Litvinoff watching carefully for any evasion.

On February 27, 1920, Litvinoff announced that he and Krassin, Commissar for Trade and Commerce, and Viktor Nogin, who was in charge of Russia's entire textile industry, would constitute a deputation to organize Russia's foreign trade. He hoped to establish headquarters in London, but if not admitted by the Allies, they would go to a neutral country.

Still doing everything possible to reopen foreign relations, on March 23, Litvinoff made the following statement in Copenhagen:

"We have triumphed over Yudenich, Denikin, and Kolchak because they had the people against them. We do not wish either to avenge or to attack anyone. We are leaving all the little republics which have arisen round us absolute freedom to adopt whatever regime they like. We respect the right of every country to dispose freely of its own affairs. But on the other hand we claim similar treatment. We must be left in peace to work out among ourselves our social experiment. If that experiment succeeds, other peoples will follow it. If it fails, we shall be obliged to try another method. In any case, none must interfere with us. That is all we ask. . . . We are convinced pacifists. We have had to fight because war was forced on us, but we are anxious to lay down arms. We desire a renewal of normal commercial relations with other countries. Europe has need of Russian raw materials and we have need of manufactured goods in return. We are ready to recognize the

Russian debt—former loans with interest. We also solemnly declare that we will repulse any secret German advances seeking an alliance against the Entente. We do not wish to hear talk of any military combination whatever."

Litvinoff summarized the terms as follows:

"1. Recognition of the Soviets.

"2. Liberty for them to develop in peace and normally within their boundaries their social experiment.

"3. Assurance given by the Soviets that they will not interfere in the interior politics of other nations.

"4. Mutual and serious guarantees to that effect.

"5. Renewal of economic relations.

"6. Disarmament of the Red army as soon as peace is assured.

"7. Recognition of Russia's former debts and loans with interest."

The last concession was a bombshell but the Allies were still determined not to give official heed and the offer was studiously ignored for years especially by the United States.

Litvinoff was not making much progress, but at least he was in contact with an Allied representative—O'Grady—and even that was a slight step towards his goal. So he dragged out the conferences for ten months, giving the world a chance to realize that representatives of the Soviets were not unwashed bandits, making known Russia's terms, working on trade agreements, and preventing Russia from being wholly isolated. To this end he deferred consideration of the case of thirty-five English officers whom Downing Street, under socially influential pressure, was anxious to have released.

Lenin was bitter at the Allies' refusal to help re-establish peace in Europe, and when in the summer of 1920 a delegation of English workers came to Russia and attempted to arrange a bridge between the Soviets and the British working classes, Lenin replied, in a long letter published in *Pravda* on June 17, 1920:

Your delegation proposed to me to send a letter through you to the English workers and also to make an offer through you to the English Government. I answered that I gratefully accepted the first proposal, but that I could not approach the English Government through a workers' delegation, but only in the name of our Government through Comrade Chicherin.

I have turned to the English Government many times with formal proposals to begin peace negotiations. Such proposals continuously and without interruptions were made by all our representatives, by Comrade Litvinoff as well as by Comrade Krassin and others. The English Government refuses stubbornly to listen to our proposals.

Litvinoff was also negotiating while in Copenhagen for prisoner exchange with a representative of Austria, but there the situation was quite different, for Austria had automatically recognized the Soviet Government by participating in the Brest-Litovsk Treaty and that recognition held despite the nullification of the Treaty by the subsequent defeat of the Central Powers. The prisoner convention was signed July 5, 1920.

On May 17 and 18 Litvinoff's expulsion from Copenhagen had been demanded by the Danish conservative press on the ground that the exchange of prisoners had been negotiated. The statements were markedly discourteous, asserting that "his continued presence is dangerous," and in some articles suggesting that a strike of dockers and seamen then in progress had been financed by him—which the Danish Socialist Party vigorously denied.

But Litvinoff refused to be intimidated, and was even joined by Madame Litvinoff and the children. Shortly afterwards, however, on September 3, he had to leave, and speaking his mind freely about Denmark's conduct, went on to Norway to undertake trade negotiations there. He had hoped to remain there some time, but the Norwegian Government showed little interest and broke off the conversations a month later—October 4—so he returned to Russia.

Meanwhile, three other Baltic treaties had been negotiated: with Lithuania (July 12), Latvia (August 11) and Finland (October 24). All were demonstrations of Soviet liberality, for in addition to establishing peace (except in the case of Lithuania, with whom Russia had not been at war), the Soviets recognized the independence of each of these erstwhile provinces, freed it from responsibility for Russian obligations, provided for the return of properties that had previously been taken by Russia, and made grants of various economic privileges, including, for Esthonia and Lithuania, actual money. Both sides recognized the economic advantages of friendly relations, and Russia made

her large concessions the more readily because her leaders still believed
that the bourgeois democracies set up in these little states would soon
cede to the pressure of their own peoples for a Communist order. But
despite these special circumstances and despite various frictions that
developed from time to time on all sides, the Baltic treaties were a notification of Russian readiness to go more than halfway in any effort to
restore international order in Europe. Litvinoff had won his first diplomatic victory.

<h1 style="text-align:center">5</h1>

But these small successes did not mean that Russia had really been
received back in any real sense as a partner in international affairs. The
Great Powers were still determined to exclude her and were still guilty
of active aggression. Now, however, having made a fiasco of direct
intervention, they were encouraging other nations to hostile action,
particularly Poland, which was in an elated, ambitious, and chauvinistic
mood. The Polish war against the Soviets had been in the making for
some time and Litvinoff had done his utmost to halt it. But when he
found this impossible, he took up the next best course, an effort to terminate it as quickly as possible.

As one step towards this, he had exposed the driving forces behind
it in a statement on February 4, 1920, characterized by the candor
which was to be one of his major diplomatic techniques:

"Certain Allied reactionaries are working hand in hand with the
military party, the conservative elements and the Foreign Office in Germany. Rumors about the massing of Russian troops on the Polish frontier have, for the most part, come through German sources. Naturally,
Germany would wish to bring about a new war between Poland and
Russia in order to weaken the new-born state and eventually ruin her."

Marshal Pilsudski, virtual head of the Polish State, refused even to
discuss the peace that Russia repeatedly offered, for he intended to take
advantage of Russia's presumed weakness in order to extend his frontiers from Danzig to Odessa by seizing the Ukraine west of the Dnie-
per. He was ready to risk a costly military adventure despite the fact
that at that very moment Poland was in such desperate straits that the
American relief organization was feeding a million and a half Polish

children and had already given $50,000,000 for famine alleviation there.[*]

In April, 1920, while Wrangel was marching towards the Donetz Basin, Poland penetrated a hundred miles into Russian territory without any declaration of war, and took Kiev (May 6). But the Red army recaptured it and drove the Poles out of the Ukraine and Belorussia. The Poles reported this successful Soviet defensive reaction to the unprovoked invasion as a "treacherous assault" on their "brave armies."

Prince Lubomirski, Polish Minister to the United States, announced that "the war which Poland is carrying on is not one of conquest but exclusively one of defense." [†] But on February 28, the Council of Ambassadors at Paris drafted a note to Poland, calling attention to the fact that Poland's eastern boundary, as laid down by the Supreme Council on November 25, 1919, lay far to the west of the districts that Polish forces had already occupied, which she now claimed.[‡]

The Russian troops then continued towards Warsaw and, in the south, towards Lvov, but they had been too hastily organized, had advanced too rapidly, and at some points were separated from their sources of supply, so just when the Poles were on the brink of disaster, they succeeded in breaking through the Russian lines.

The French, who were behind Poland's move and expected to profit by her victory, had sent to her rescue a military mission headed by Maxim Weygand. The Russian defeat has often been credited to his generalship, but this was only a triumph of French propaganda. The Polish victory was due to the mistakes of Trotsky and Tukhachevsky, who rashly overextended a flanking movement, thereby leaving a dangerous wide gap in the Russian lines, of which Pilsudski's swift and ferocious counterattack took full advantage. Pilsudski actually found Weygand of so little help that he would not even call him "General," but spoke of him as "Monsieur," and in official unpublished documents recommended that he return to France.

Poland was in no condition to follow up her success and finally, on October 20, in the Peace of Riga, renounced her claims. After the Polish retirement, the Russians could concentrate on General Wrangel, who commanded the White forces in the South, and so drove him back,

---

[*] Stanley J. Marks, *The Bear That Walks Like a Man*, p. 29, Philadelphia, 1943.
[†] Schuman, F. L., *op. cit.*, p. 178.
[‡] *Ibid.*, p. 177.

first into the Crimea, then, in November, into the sea, thus permanently re-establishing Soviet control in Russia proper. This success was soon followed by the liberation of Transcaucasia, Azerbaijan, Georgia, and Armenia.

6

Russia's victories in the Wars of Intervention were now complete, but while direct military action against the Soviets had perforce to be abandoned, the Powers did not by any means relinquish their hostility. Litvinoff knew that there were two ways to deal with this: first, allay their fears of Soviet-prompted revolutions in their own countries; second, tempt them into actual if not diplomatic relations by playing on one of their strongest motives—the hope of profit. His guiding motto became: "Trade will be followed by recognition."

In this Litvinoff, as might be expected of a practical man, was taking a middle course. Theoretically, the Soviets were supposed to foment world revolution, and certain elements in the Party, notably Trotsky, never abandoned this as a primary aim. Lenin himself had originally held this view and a major function of the Third International was to disseminate propaganda for a Communist world. Consistent with this program, the International had subsidized propaganda campaigns in Germany just after the war and again during the inflation period, had co-operated with Communist groups in England, France, and the United States, spread arguments broadcast, especially in China, for revolution, and had also co-operated with the Hungarian Communist regime of Bela Kun.

Yet all this added up practically to very little, and of at least equal weight was the extreme opposite Bolshevik trend, later typified by Stalin's policy, towards concentration of all efforts within Russia herself. A vast country with an inherited chaos—economic, social, administrative—to reorganize, and incalculable unexploited potentialities to develop, would require immeasurable energy, skill, and financing to stabilize internal conditions, as some important members of the Party recognized. All elements agreed that none of the nation's territory or resources should be alienated. Hence Moscow's refusal to recognize Rumania's annexation of Bessarabia, and her retention, by force of arms, of the Caucasian states, whose great oil fields, moreover, were essential for Russia's ambitious program of mechanization, especially of agriculture.

Litvinoff stood between the two extremes because he believed in the primary importance for Russia's immediate future of international relations and trade. Hence, whatever might be his belief in the ultimate value of world revolution, he knew that any activity in that direction was unwise, as his press statement of January 21, 1919 (see p. 152), had implied, and later he decisively opposed Soviet aid to foreign revolutionary movements, which could be interpreted as "unwarranted aggression." Indeed, in the middle twenties he said to Louis Fischer: "The prospect of world revolution disappeared on November 11, 1918." *
On the other hand, he worked for years to impress on his colleagues the impossibility of concentrating exclusively on internal problems.

Pursuing the determination to win for Russia her normal place in the world community, he undertook to make some arrangements with the United States. He was now (March, 1921) Chief of all Soviet Legations abroad and in that capacity, on March 21, he dispatched his first note to President Harding and Congress:

From the first day of her existence, Soviet Russia has nourished the hope of the possibility of a speedy establishment of friendly relations with the great republic of North America and had firmly expected that intimate and solid ties would be created between the two republics to the greater advantage of both. . . .

There was no answer, but not long thereafter (March 28), the American consul at Reval handed Litvinoff a copy of a statement made by Secretary of State Hughes:

The Government of the United States views with deep sympathy and grave concern the plight of the people of Russia, and desires to aid with every appropriate means in promoting proper opportunities through which commerce can be established upon a sound basis. It is manifest to this Government that in existing circumstances there is no assurance of development of trade, as the supplies which Russia might now be able to obtain would be wholly inadequate to meet the needs, and no lasting good can result as long as the present causes of progressive impoverishment continue to oper-

* Louis Fischer, *Men and Politics*, p. 127, New York, 1941.

ate. If fundamental changes are contemplated, involving due regard for the protection of persons and property and the establishment of conditions essential to the maintenance of commerce, this Government will be glad to have convincing evidence of the consummation of such changes, and until this evidence is supplied this Government is unable to perceive that there is any proper basis for considering trade relations.

Litvinoff's comment was a justified rebuke:

"I am afraid the masses in Russia will interpret and resent the statement of Mr. Hughes as an attempt to interfere with the internal affairs of Russia and to dictate from the outside a scheme for the Russian social system, and that they will justly say that the conquests of the revolution for which they have fought for more than three years, and for which they underwent enormous privations, are not for sale. . . . I wish to state most emphatically in the name of my Government that due protection would be given to American citizens and their imported goods and also necessary guarantees for the observation of the laws and customs of international trade.

"I feel sure that trade relations soon will be renewed, but the acceptance of the proposal of a Russian mission to the United States would accelerate it by dispelling the misunderstandings and misconceptions which prompted Mr. Hughes's statement."

Meanwhile, in a statement of March 27 to the Associated Press, he dangled the profits-carrot:

Four steamers have already been loaded at Petrograd with flax, and other raw materials for exportation; the Foreign Trade Commissariat has $500,-000,000 worth of materials for export, including metals, minerals, fuel, lubricants, hides, furs, flax, timber, tobacco, bristles, manganese and caviar.

Fifty sawmills are working in North Russia exclusively for exports. The flax and hemp are partly at Reval and partly enroute. Russia would import railroad material, agricultural implements, electrical machinery of all kinds, tools and chemicals. Large quantities of boots and leather have already been imported and much is still due from America. Speedy importation would quicken progress and increase the amount of Russian exports. New beds of graphite have been discovered. . . . Trade with Russia offers unlimited possibilities which no other country can rival.

Again a few days later (April 6), Litvinoff played on another of his opponents' major motives—competitiveness, and continued to lecture Secretary Hughes on the error of his ways:

". . . as the United States seemed to have made up its mind that it did not wish to know the truth about Russia, it would be useless to permit American newspaper correspondents to go to Moscow. If they wrote the truth they would not be believed, and would be accused of making propaganda. . . . The effects of the British agreement are already showing, for the orders we have placed created greater confidence. The meager port facilities of Reval are congested by Russian imports and some ships are being diverted to Riga. We will make whatever reforms Russia needs to benefit the workingmen but not at the dictation of a foreign power."

During the month of March, 1921, a trade agreement with Great Britain was signed. This contained the provisions that gold sent in payment for merchandise bought by Russia in Great Britain would not be confiscated towards old debts or claims there, and each of the signatories would refrain from carrying on in the other any propaganda, or undertake "any type of hostile action" against the other. But immediately after the agreement was signed, the British Government, and even more the English press, began to complain of Communist propaganda there. Finally, the British Foreign Secretary, Lord Curzon, sent a note of protest to the Soviet Government, charging it with responsibility for intrigues against the British Government, and to this Litvinoff replied, on October 7, 1921:

"The Soviet Government feels sure that the British Foreign Office was misled by a gang of professional forgers and swindlers and had it known the dubious sources of its information its note of September 7 would never have been sent. . . . Still, the Russian Government has done its utmost to honor all its undertakings and has endeavored to obviate any causes of friction and misunderstanding."

7

As a matter of fact animosity against Russia had been aroused that year, in British official circles at least, by a very striking Russian diplomatic success in Persia (February 26, 1921). The presence of British armed forces in Persia had aroused considerable resentment there and Britain had attempted to impose a treaty (August 9, 1919), that meant the fatal impairment of Persian sovereignty and virtual British control of the country. The Soviets, on the contrary, offered the Persians terms of such unprecedented generosity that it made the British policy seem by comparison predatory and hostile.

When it became known that British ambitions had been implemented by outrageous bribes (£50,000 each to three notoriously corrupt Cabinet ministers), even the women of the country revolted and the Persian Majless (Parliament) refused to ratify the treaty. By contrast, the Russian treaty was magnanimity itself, as it gave everything and demanded almost nothing in return, renouncing without remuneration of any kind all Czarist Russian privileges in Iran, canceling the outstanding Persian debt to Russia, turning over to the Persian Government the Imperial Bank of Russia there, with all its assets and cash reserves, and the Julfa-Tabriz Railway, and even delivering Russian missionary properties there to the Government for educational uses and freeing Persia from the century-old restriction of maintaining a navy in the Caspian Sea. The Russian triumph was complete, and it resounded throughout the bazaars of the Near and Middle East.

May, 1921, saw the first provisional agreement forged between Germany and the new Russia. The Soviet leaders' lingering misgivings about the "chauvinist" Socialists in control in Germany were finally overcome by Baron Heinrich von Maltzan, Chief of the Eastern Division of the Berlin Foreign Office, despite the fact that he was a "bourgeois" with strong tendencies to the Right. Germany was still almost as much ostracized as Russia; therefore, he argued, they had best make common cause.

Lenin had adopted, in the hope of temporarily easing Russia's economic crisis, the New Economic Policy, or NEP, a compromise arrangement that permitted for the time a considerable amount of private business. Some of the dogmatists among the Bolsheviki bitterly resented this, fearing that it would be the opening wedge for compromises that would soon nullify the Revolution, but their dire predictions came to naught and the adjustment provided a much-needed breathing spell.

Germany, like other foreign countries, believed that the NEP had come to stay, a mistake in their judgment which accrued to Russia's benefit, for it made easier the execution of the provisional economic agreement. Germany hoped that the industrialization of Russia would open up opportunites for German capital and business enterprise. However, Maltzan was almost alone in the German Foreign Office in realizing how much Germany needed Russia, and he could not convince even his most intimate collaborators of what seemed to him the self-evident fact that Russia offered Germany an immediate and profitable field for the economic expansion essential to her own recovery. Since they were both surrounded by more or less hostile countries, they would do well to reinforce each other.

The rapprochement was facilitated by similarities in the characters of Litvinoff and Maltzan, despite the great differences between their backgrounds: both were indifferent to personal prestige. Maltzan had said: "I was born without prestige," and was known as "the Baron without prestige," and later even as the "Red Baron." Both were realists without illusions, unsentimental, not to say hard boiled, to a degree that shocked and alarmed other diplomats. Litvinoff undoubtedly became increasingly aware of Maltzan's merits, once describing him as "the only completely honest diplomat I had to do with at that time."

Throughout the negotiations, Maltzan received daily telegrams from Ebert warning him and Walter Rathenau against making an arrangement with Russia, and Ebert never quite forgave Maltzan for presenting him, and the rest of the world, with a fait accompli.

In the course of the year Russia effected treaties not only with Persia, but also with Afghanistan, Turkey, and Outer Mongolia (all of which were outside Litvinoff's province), and trade relations were established with Italy, while certain Austrian banks extended credits on generous terms, which the Soviets always met.

8

The United States, on the other hand, continued to cut off its nose to spite its face, though some formulated otherwise its stubborn rejections of Russia's friendly efforts. For it was widely and persistently rumored that certain British and American oil interests were behind these inimical tactics, hoping thereby to force Russia to relinquish to them valuable oil rights, and it was common knowledge that one influential figure in the background was the rabidly reactionary Sir Henry Deterding, later a friend of Adolf Hitler, who beyond doubt lavishly financed a good deal of anti-Soviet propaganda.

In August, 1921, however, American and Russian diplomats did meet. A widespread famine in southern and eastern Russia, caused by the dislocation of the Russian farming system following the Wars of Intervention, challenged American sympathy, and American relief organizations, in which Herbert Hoover was the most conspicuous personality, offered help and sent a delegation to Riga to discuss procedure with Russian representatives. Maxim Litvinoff was chairman of the Russian delegation.

On August 9, 1921, the *New York Times,* under the dateline, "Riga, August 8," reported:

Moscow announces that M. Litvinoff representing the Central Executive Committee on Famine Relief arrived in Riga Wednesday to carry on conversations with W. F. Brown, the representative of Mr. Hoover. This eleventh hour substitution of the first and foremost Bolshevist foreign plenipotentiary for non-political personages like Gorki or Tchinchuk clearly indicates the Soviets' intention to try to open negotiations with America.

This was undoubtedly one of the reasons why Litvinoff was named for the post; but there was another: the Russian Government, fully aware of Mr. Hoover's implacable, almost vindictive hostility to the Soviet Union, was suspicious of what certain members of the relief organizations might do or try to do, once they entered the country.

The first inkling of this doubt appeared in a statement which Litvinoff made to foreign press representatives in Riga on August 11: "We will gladly accept all purely humanitarian aid that may be offered to us, but to any attempts to take away the prerogatives of the Soviet Government or any of its power we reply, 'non possumus.'"

Litvinoff has said that at the time he had the impression that most of the men with whom he was negotiating were more interested in obtaining entry into Russia than being good Samaritans. His mistrust lest the Americans might include spies and agents was not without reason, for he knew that the head of the American Relief Association had used his position to discredit the Hungarian Communist regime of Bela Kun.

Eventually, Hoover's representative, Brown, lost his temper and blurted out: "After all, Mr. Litvinoff, you ought to remember that what we want is to get food into Russia."

To which Litvinoff replied: "Food can be a weapon." *

The negotiations finally ended in an agreement, signed on August 20. Litvinoff made a statement clearly indicating that what seemed to him even more important than food was an understanding with America:

"I hope this first meeting of representatives of the two great countries will be followed by others. Each fresh meeting will bring us closer together and make us understand that if we have been kept apart it is due to misunderstandings and differences that can be readjusted." But they were not to be readjusted for a long time to come.

When the first spasm of moral indignation against the Soviets—both genuine and artificially aroused—was relaxing, the Czarist debts were brought up by the United States and other Foreign Offices, and used as an excuse for further deferring recognition, despite the warning given by the Viborg Manifesto (July 10, 1906), signed by two hundred duly elected members of the Duma, which had so explicitly stated: "If the Government contracts loans to secure funds, such loans contracted without the approval of the people's representatives will be invalid. The Russian people will never acknowledge them and will not pay them." The fact that other countries were not meeting their unambiguous obligations to the United States was equally disregarded.

When a conference of Powers in the Pacific area or with special interests there was called at Washington, and the American State Department specified, not without relish, that Russia would be excluded, the Soviet Government protested (July 19, 1921), affirmed that in the interest of peace they considered it "their duty to participate in all international conferences which were aimed at a solution involving the interests of Soviet Russia," and warned that "the

---

* Litvinoff's misgiving that Americans might conceivably use relief for political purposes, a doubt that seemed so ungracious at the time, was curiously confirmed many years later by an admission of the State Department, given in defense of its Vichy policy, that the workers for American relief agencies had, under that guise, been able to gather much information of political and military value to this country.

policy tending to leave Russia outside the collective decision of various Powers on questions concerning it, not only cannot assist the settlement of conflicts at present disturbing the world, but will only render them more acute and more complicated."

Litvinoff's next attempt, made from Stockholm on November 14, 1921, was reported by the Associated Press:

The proposal that the United States guarantee all Russia's debts to other countries and the suggestion that the Washington Conference might deal with such a plan if the Russian Soviet Government were permitted to participate in the conference were made today by M. Litvinoff.

"If Soviet representatives attended the Washington Conference, America would soon discover that Russia is a country interested in the Pacific Ocean and the Far East to a greater extent than Italy or Belgium. That this discovery would aid in the proper solution of Far Eastern problems seems clear to everyone who has not a prejudiced opinion.

"The Soviet Government has hitherto scrupulously satisfied all obligations and will not conclude any new ones or pledge itself to old ones without knowing in advance ways and means to satisfy them. In their own interests the nations concerned must take part in re-establishing Russia's economic life.

"In 1919 I suggested that if America should endorse Russia's foreign debts in this way, some of the most important questions of humanity could be solved. Russia would thus have to deal with only one creditor. My personal opinion is that this scheme could be carried out now as well as previously, if only the American Government showed the necessary good-will."

M. Litvinoff pointed out that in a note to the powers the Soviet Government had pledged itself to acknowledge immediately certain categories of the national debts, consideration of which he added, "will open up the whole of the complex political questions whose solution it will be impossible to obtain if they are not dealt with according to international views. Thus we proposed the assembling of an international conference. It is not only a question of acknowledgement, but also of fulfilling our obligations."

But Russia was not invited to the conference at Washington.

9

During the summer of 1921 the Litvinoffs were at last able to establish a home together again, in Moscow. The apartment allotted to them by the Government was in a residence on the bank of the Moscow River opposite the Kremlin, with a superb view of that beautiful assemblage of old buildings. Built by a millionaire who had controlled Russia's sugar factories, and known consequently as the Sugar King's Palace, it is an enormous ornate structure, reputed to have cost more than $2,000,000, with a central hall surrounded by huge marble columns, and adorned with a tremendous chandelier. The walls were hung with huge paintings for which the Sugar King had paid handsomely, the floor carpeted with Caucasus and Turkoman rugs, and the reception rooms were full of French period furniture. Immediately after the Sugar King moved in, he was assassinated by one of his numerous illegitimate sons.

Following the Revolution, it was taken over, like all other mansions, by the Government, which later assigned it to the Biurobin (the Central Office for Foreign Service) to be used for the entertainment of foreign guests of the State, and to this end a sizable staff of servants was installed. Thus a whole series of notables who came from abroad to see the new Russia was housed there in splendor—of a kind: Enver Pasha of Turkey; the British sculptress, Clare Sheridan; the American, Sidney Hillman, of the Amalgamated Clothing Workers' Union. When Laurence Steinhardt came to Moscow as American Ambassador, was shown the building and was told that it cost $2,000,000, he looked up at the colossal chandelier in the hall and replied: "I'm sure it did; that thing must have cost a million."

In contrast to all this pretentious magnificence, the Litvinoff's three-room apartment on the second floor was relatively small, and there they lived simply, attended by only one maid—Pelagaya Afanasevna, who came into their employ when they settled in Moscow, and remained with them until 1942, when they left for the United States. Litvinoff's salary—the amount determined by the Party for members in his class of service—could not exceed 500 rubles a month plus, of course, the use of the apartment, most of his food (supplied from government stores) and an expense account, as Soviet representative, of 2,500 rubles a month—all told only a small fraction of the remuneration for an official of Litvinoff's status in any other country.

Summers, and subsequently during his retirement, the family, supplemented by various dogs, for which they have a weakness, lived in a country house or dacha, about an hour's drive from the Kremlin on a road running north, known as the Rublova Woods. Though this had been a fashionable section under the Czar, and the villas were built by rich men, they are simple. The Litvinoff villa consisted of an entrance hall, a commodious living room and a dining room downstairs, and upstairs a few bedrooms. The furniture was rather sparse, but adequate and comfortable. The whitewashed walls were bare of pictures, and ornaments quite lacking, but, in the English manner, there were always many flowers. The grounds were enclosed in a green fence behind which six or eight Ogpu guards were always on duty. The Litvinoff children still live in the dacha.

But most of Litvinoff's own life was spent in his office in the Narkomindel. This had been established in a huge old office building with two wings, rather shabby in its dull greenish-gray plaster coating, in sharp contrast to the Foreign Offices of the other important countries. On the corner of Bolshaya Lubyanka and Kusnetsky Most, in the Sokolniki District in the northeastern section of Moscow, it faced a church, but in 1924 this was torn down and the space converted into a public park. Litvinoff's rooms on the second floor next to Chicherin's (into which he moved when he succeeded his chief) look out onto this, and to an old palace beyond built by the Prince Pozharsky who in 1612 had won Moscow for the Russians in the war of liberation against Poland. He could see, too, the house that once belonged to Count Rostoptchin, Governor-General of Moscow, who appears in Tolstoi's *War and Peace*.

Litvinoff arrived at this office every day about eleven in the morning, and not uncommonly stayed until two the next morning, often without leaving even for luncheon, which would then consist of a piece of bread brought from home in his blouse pocket. For Litvinoff in his own country was completely Russian in dress and appearance, quite different from the conventional Englishman of the Hampstead days, though when he traveled abroad he resumed the international costume. Hour after hour he worked to establish and build up in favorable international connections the new order to which he had devoted his entire adult life, seeing few outside his colleagues, family and a small group of friends, shunning newspaper correspondents, so that he acquired the reputation of being more unapproachable than Stalin himself.

Madame Litvinoff was almost equally busy. Litvinoff, unlike most men in his position in Russia or elsewhere, writes all his own speeches. When they are for foreign consumption, Madame Litvinoff puts them into English, for despite Litvinoff's years of using English, he writes in Russian.

Moreover, she was doing some writing on her own, and also became very much interested in Basic English, a simplified version of the language built on a carefully selected vocabulary devised to meet the maximum range of needs with the minimum difficulty for the foreigner, so that it would be more easily available for international communication. Convinced of great possibilities in this more natural and reasonable substitute for Esperanto, she interested the Soviet Commissariat of Popular Education in the textbook by C. K. Ogden, which she herself translated into Russian, and she also taught Basic English, first in Moscow and later in Sverdlovsk.

She never, however, let these interests interfere with her attention to her children. Indeed, for the first two years in Moscow she had entire care of them, taking them to and from the kindergarten every day and also skillfully supplementing their education. Thus she would have beside their beds, when they woke up, the drawing of some motive in a tapestry, rug or curtain in the Sugar King's Palace, and this they would have to identify during the day—a game which so delighted the youngsters that they, too, began giving her designs to find. Madame Litvinoff thinks that it was perhaps these pattern-hunts which first gave Tanya the idea of studying art.

The Litvinoffs enlarged their happy family group by adopting a girl of peasant origin, Katiusha.

In the upbringing of Misha, Litvinoff had to take a hand, for, boylike, he went through an unruly stage, indulging in fights and escapades which dismayed his mother. Litvinoff was entertained rather than disturbed by these exploits, yet felt that his son had to be checked to a certain extent and did not spare the rod; but this never interfered with the loving confidence between them.

Indeed, there has always been a rare intimacy between the father and the children. They began to share their parents' enthusiasm for moving pictures when they were still so young that Litvinoff had to read the captions for them and elucidate the more complicated parts of the plots. Incidentally, Litvinoff still finds satisfactory relaxation in the cinema, preferring technicolor pictures, especially musicals, though he thinks the greatest film America has produced is Reinhardt's "Midsummer Night's Dream," which he saw at an American embassy party late in 1937; Russia's best, Litvinoff feels, is "Peter the Great."

Other amusements parents and children shared, too: the circus and the vaudeville theater, Myusik Hol. Here they saw, late in 1933, Harpo Marx, whose particular brand of comedy proved to be a riotous success with the Russians. The Litvinoff family were in the capacity audience that laughed almost to exhaustion at his first performance, and with many others went backstage to meet him after the curtain. Whereupon Harpo repeated his famous cutlery stunt, but this time produced the knives, forks, and spoons out of Litvinoff's pockets— to the delight of all concerned.

Litvinoff also played chess—learned long ago in the Kiev prison— with Misha, until the youngster reached the point where he checkmated Father regularly. Then Father, so he says, gave it up.

But he did not give up his music, for singing and playing the piano, so he says (in a frankly amateurish way), are his great delights, and among his favorite songs are two in English that his wife taught him: "Home on the Range," and "Katy Did, She Did."

As the children got older they took a great interest in Litvinoff's work, demanding to know all about the famous diplomats whom he was meeting, what they were like and how they acted.

Through all these years the Litvinoff's closest friends were the Molotovs, who had the dacha next door to theirs. Viacheslav Mihailovich Molotov is considerably younger than Litvinoff—he was born in 1890—and from a rather different milieu. He is a pure Russian—his family name was Scriabin—of the round-headed type, with broad forehead, wide nose, rather far-apart eyes behind glasses, a close-clipped mustache. His expression is serious but kindly, his manner quiet but firm. Of a family of working people, he went to work young and joined the Party when he was only sixteen.

At the time of the Revolution he was Chairman of the Bolshevik Section of the Petrograd Soviet but played an inconspicuous albeit important part in the rapid critical events of the turnover. In the interval he had lived the usual life of the Russian underground Party worker —never taking any dramatic role but persistent and faithful, and remaining always in Russia, as did Stalin, in contrast to most of the other Bolshevik leaders who during that period were émigrés. He has always been close to Stalin, a dependable and very able lieutenant. In 1927 he succeeded Uglanov as Secretary of the Moscow Party Committee, became a member of the Politburo and in 1930 assumed the duties of Prime Minister, which he carried until May 5, 1941, when they were taken over by Stalin himself.

Because he is quiet, dry, lacking in any striking personal qualities, a hard worker rather than a hero of adventure or even an orator, there has been a tendency among foreigners to dismiss him with an oft-repeated phrase attributed to Lenin—"the best filing-clerk in the Soviet Union"; but a shrewd judge like Ambassador Davies has characterized him as "an exceptional man with great capacity and wisdom." *

Madame Molotov (Pauline Semyonova Zhemchuzhna) is an exceptionally capable and very busy woman. Formerly Commissar for Fisheries, she then became Commissar for Cosmetics, which involves running four large factories as well as organizing the distribution including the organization of beauty parlors and perfume shops which, in the main cities at least, were, up to the war, really smart. To this she has since added the considerable responsibilities of Assistant Commissar of the food industries. Yet despite all these administrative absorptions, she was for years known as the best dressed woman in Russia.

10

On January 6, 1922, representatives of Great Britain and France, meeting at Cannes, decided that, in principle, diplomatic relations should be resumed with Soviet Russia. At the time, as Lloyd George revealed by implication two years later, Britain, France, Belgium, and Italy had some sort of secret agreement to take action in relation to Russia only as a group, not separately.† Shortly after the Cannes meet-

---

* Joseph E. Davies, *op. cit.*, p. 112.
† Lloyd George's statement in *The Daily Chronicle*, February 16, 1924.

ing, the liberal French Premier, Aristide Briand, was supplanted by the conservative, Raymond Poincaré (January 15). Poincaré could not reverse Briand's policy on Russian recognition, but he could make it difficult.

In accordance with the Cannes decision, Lloyd George put Russian diplomatic relations on the agenda of a conference to be held at Genoa, to which he invited twenty-nine European countries, in addition to the British Dominions, including England's recent European enemies, and also the United States. The other questions for consideration were problems of reconstruction—financial, economic, commercial—and continental transport problems.

When the Russian Foreign Office received the invitation, Chicherin, characteristically, argued that it would be no use to send anyone, as nothing would come of it. Litvinoff had no illusions as to the outcome, either. He had just made clear in an interview with Walter Duranty (January 6, 1922) the bitter depth of his mistrust of other governments:

"How can we fail to suspect the rest of the world, when we see that the first consequences of the Washington Conference—one of whose objects was the settlement of Far Eastern affairs—was the invasion of Russian territory by a Japanese army? It looks to us as if any settlement accomplished in Washington would consist of carte blanche to Japan to start land-grabbing at our expense.

"After four years as a pariah among nations the Soviet Government judges events with a pariah's distrust, a pariah's expectation of the kicks that must accompany even halfpence."

Yet despite this utter and well-founded skepticism, he was faithful to his program of maintaining Russian external contacts whenever possible, urging that the appearance of Russian delegates at an international conference was in itself important, and Lenin seems to have agreed with him.

The United States declined the invitation; Russia's acceptance, contrary to official European hopes, caused general nervousness and uncertainty. Everywhere preliminary meetings were hastily arranged. Lloyd George and Poincaré met at Boulogne on February 25; Allied economic experts on March 20. The Little Entente called its members to Belgrade; and Poland, Latvia, Esthonia, and Finland conferred at Warsaw.

When the delegates finally appeared in Genoa, they had decided to be severe with Soviet Russia and to discuss at length the restitution of foreign private property in the Soviet Union, as well as payment of the Czarist debts. But they did not intend to talk—at least not openly in the conference—about one of the most important questions in the background—petroleum—to what extent Soviet Russia would allow English, Dutch, and American companies to exploit its oil fields. If Soviet Russia were willing, everything else could easily be arranged. The moral issues could be left to take care of themselves, even the debts could be compromised; restitution of private property was of concern to the delegates in proportion to their direct or indirect financial interest; these were in themselves relatively unimportant; but the question of oil—that was something else again. If Soviet Russia felt that the oil belonged to the Russian people and was to be reserved for their use and advantage, then, of course, the situation would be most unpleasant and difficult, and negotiations would be greatly impeded.

Since this was the first important international conference in which Soviet Russia had participated, it seemed certain for a while that the Soviet delegation would be led by Lenin himself. His last-minute decision against going was the first indication that the Russians did not expect to get much out of the conference, a hint confirmed by a statement that Lenin released to the press: "We shall go to Genoa as businessmen. . . . I do not expect to conclude a political alliance." The Russian delegation was headed by Chicherin. He was accompanied by Joffe, Soviet representative in Berlin, Vorovsky, Krassin, and Litvinoff.

Lenin had asked every member of the Russian delegation to send reports to him personally; had instructed Chicherin not to conclude any treaties, but if any proposal was made to him, to flirt with the idea; and had also had a long conference with Litvinoff, in which the leader was explicit and clear: since Russia was plunging back into European affairs after five years of enforced seclusion, he counseled caution and warned Litvinoff not to be in a hurry. Moreover, as Litvinoff now recalls, he was to watch Chicherin.

Then Litvinoff asked: "And Germany?" German and Russian representatives had already made some preliminary moves towards a rapprochement in Berlin.

Lenin thought a bit, then said that if Germany were ready to sign a genuine treaty—not something worth less than the paper it was written on—Litvinoff had his blessing and should go ahead.

England was represented by Lloyd George; France by Louis Barthou, Poincaré's Minister of Justice; Italy by her last constitutional Prime Minister, Facta; Germany by her Foreign Minister, Walther Rathenau and his close collaborator, Maltzan. Of all the men who played an important part there, only Maxim Litvinoff and Lloyd George are still alive, and Lloyd George is an old man. Chicherin, Krassin, Maltzan, and Facta have long since died; Joffe committed suicide; Vorovsky, Rathenau, Barthou, and the Bulgarian Premier, Stambulisky, have been assassinated.

The conference opened on April 10. "Such a gathering had not been seen since Bismarck called the Congress of Berlin [1878] . . . the leading statesmen of Europe had assembled together, nominally in order to heal the wounds of world trade—but, in fact, to end the War. . . . It was an Oecumenical Council, comparable to those the mediaeval Church used to summon for the salvation of Christendom. And, as in the Middle Ages, a terror overhung the gathering that failure might portend catastrophe to European civilization." *

Other delegates viewed the Russians with curiosity. Outwardly they did not seem to be "different." They all appeared in morning-coats or faultless tails and top hats. Their behavior was formal, stiff, correct. Their manners were irreproachable. In short, they did not make a spectacle of themselves as the other delegates had half expected— expectations that had their roots in diplomatic reports at the time of the Revolution, describing the shabby and uncouth appearance of the rank and file as well as of certain prominent Soviet personalities.

The Russians scored the first point. After formal platitudinous opening speeches by the three chief Allied representatives, Chicherin read an address, first in French and then in English, expressing Russia's desire to co-operate in world rehabilitation, looking forward to future congresses which would embrace the whole world, then pledging her solemn word to disband the Red army whenever the other nations would really disarm; and in response to Barthou's furious protest against the introduction of the disarmament question,

* Baron Harry Kessler, *Walther Rathenau*, p. 322, London, 1929.

he pointed out—to the enthusiastic entertainment of all but the French delegation—that he had made the statement chiefly in order to reassure France, owing to M. Briand's citation at Washington of the Red army as France's main reason for her heavy rearmament program.

Then Russia scored a second point: the right, along with the four great Powers and Belgium, to have a seat and vote on every one of the subcommissions, which in effect reinstated Russia as one of the Great Powers of Europe and established a precedent for her becoming a permanent member of the Council when she joined the League of Nations. This in itself was a striking justification of Litvinoff's policy of attending the conference.

Litvinoff's role there, however, was not conspicuous, though on April 17 he made a speech that evoked considerable interest. Calmly putting up a bold front, he took the position that the Russians had come to the conference as winners and that, furthermore, they did not owe anybody anything:

"The Allies have lost their war with Russia, we are here to make peace. We have named our conditions. We must be paid for what Russia did for the Allies and we must be paid for the damage the Allies did Russia through Kolchak, Denikin, and Wrangel and by the blockade, for which America also was responsible. Russia spent in 1914–1917 for the Allies 20,000,000,000 gold rubles. We want that back. The damage through the intervention and blockade was 35,000,-000,000 gold rubles. If we are paid that we will recognize Russia's pre-war debts.

"The Allies claim 65,000,000,000 gold francs from us. We claim 125,000,000,000 gold francs. We cannot make peace and go back with less than 20,000,000,000 gold francs."

Such statements, of course, deceived nobody, least of all Litvinoff himself. Everyone knew that the Soviets, in spite of having defeated the armies of intervention, needed aid from the rest of the world much more than the rest of the world needed Russia.

She was, however, in a situation that gave her bargaining power in the diametric opposition between official French and British policies —the French concentrated on reparations and other pressure on Germany, the British aiming at a give-and-take rehabilitation for Europe as a whole. The French as part of their plan proposed that Russia collect her reparations from Germany, which would nearly double Germany's reparations burden, would check any developing co-operation between the two cold-shouldered countries, and give Russia cash that France would promptly take in payment of Russia's *pre-war* debts in France. To persuade Russia to this, Russia's *war*-debts would be canceled against her intervention claims. All this was embodied or implicit in a clause of a previously prepared proposal known as the London Agreement which was taken out of committee and discussed in private conferences, from which the Germans were excluded.

Lloyd George, on the other hand, was also ready to play up to the Russians. As Winston Churchill wrote at the time to Lord Curzon (April 26, 1922): "The great objective of the Prime Minister's policy has been Moscow, to make Great Britain the nation in the closest possible relations with the Bolshevists, and to be their protectors and sponsors before Europe." * Animus may have exaggerated Churchill's estimate, but Lloyd George certainly did realize the necessity of including Russia if Europe as a whole was to be re-established economically. And then, too, there was oil.

Meanwhile, Litvinoff, quietly in the background, was establishing useful relations. Also in the background was the German representative, Maltzan, and the two men got together. They had a bond: Russia and Germany were the poor relations at the conference; and the longer the conference lasted and the more doubtful it became whether the other delegates would deal constructively with the problems of Russia and Germany, the closer Litvinoff and Maltzan became.

A second man with whom Litvinoff became very well acquainted —the beginning of a friendship that was to last for years—was the French delegate, Louis Barthou. Barthou worked under considerable pressure. Poincaré bombarded him with telegrams because he was afraid that Barthou might conclude a treaty with Soviet Russia, which Poincaré despised. Barthou was annoyed at first, but when the telegrams kept pouring in he became amused. Once during an excursion to the Campo Santo, Barthou mentioned the telegrams to his Russian friend, and upon their return to Barthou's hotel even showed him some of them.

* Quoted by Churchill, *The World Crisis: The Aftermath*, p. 415, London, 1929.

II

But while the Barthou-Litvinoff friendship was destined to last long, and later to have very important results, the immediate benefits came from the meetings between Litvinoff and Maltzan.

By April 15 it was clear that the Allied Powers were asking too high a price for their recognition of Russia: acknowledgment of, and an effort to repay, the Czarist debts; and also admission of the right of foreign companies to exploit the oil fields. These concessions would not only have been economically disadvantageous to Russia; they would also have violated fundamental principles of the Revolution. That night the Russian delegation met to decide whether to withdraw from the conference, or to go ahead independently of Britain and France. They chose the latter, and at 1:15 the next morning—Easter Sunday— Joffe telephoned Maltzan that, if the Germans would meet them at Rapallo by noon, Russia would execute a treaty. The Russians knew better than to wait for a more seemly hour; France and Britain, having failed to come to any arrangement with them, would be opening negotiations with the Germans.

Maltzan woke Rathenau in order to report the Russian offer to him. Rathenau, who had come to Genoa expecting to co-operate with Lloyd George, hesitated, suggesting that he ought to report the situation to Lloyd George. Maltzan argued that that would be treachery to the Russians, and in the end they compromised and Maltzan was instructed to telephone the next morning to inform Mr. E. F. Wise, of the British Board of Trade, the Prime Minister's confidential lieutenant, that they were going to Rapallo to sign a treaty with the Russians.

When Maltzan telephoned, however, at 7:30 that Sunday morning, Wise was asleep and could not be disturbed (after all, it *was* the Easter week end), and when he called again, Wise had gone out. So when the Germans left for Rapallo they had informed no one. But when they got out there at noon the situation was still touch-and-go, for after lunch word came by telephone that Lloyd George was trying to reach Rathenau. Rathenau, however, had gone on to Portofino to visit a friend, leaving Maltzan to work out the terms with Litvinoff, and could not be reached.

Those terms provided that Russia and Germany renounce all claims to war indemnities, including maintenance of war prisoners. Germany renounced all claims to compensation for losses incurred by German subjects in consequence of Russian socialization of private property, "provided that the Soviet government does not satisfy similar claims of other states." Diplomatic and consular relations were resumed. Economic relations were to be regulated "with mutual feelings of good will." Of major significance was the agreement to confer before making any important decisions regarding other nations. But the big fact was the treaty itself. The two outcasts of the conference had found themselves, and within a few hours concluded a treaty while the other diplomats had been sitting round for days making speeches. And it was the first peace treaty executed between former enemies after the war, and was thus characteristic of Russia's policy in general, and Litvinoff's in particular.

The announcement of the treaty created a sensation. Lloyd George was beside himself with fury. What could now possibly come out of the conference for which he had had such high hopes, especially in the face of that paragraph in the Treaty of Rapallo about not paying compensation for socialized private property? That showed the representatives of other nations what they had to expect.

The Germans—not the Russians—were reproached by all the other delegates, accused of being tactless, perfidious; and the French delegates boycotted them socially for the remainder of the conference. Clearly the other delegates had hoped or even believed that a united front existed against, not yesterday's enemy, Germany, but yesterday's friend, Russia. The Germans had broken the tacit accord against Communism.

Louis Barthou, amused, suggested that Lloyd George call off the conference, since obviously it no longer had any reason for continuing. Lloyd George refused, however, to retreat—he considered that his personal prestige was seriously involved—and the conference went on for another month without any further important occurrence. Genoa was a fiasco.

As for Rapallo, three days after the treaty was signed the German Government sent special agents to Ruhr industrialists informing them of the concessions which the Reich had just obtained in the treaty. They took their cue, and with government credits started to develop these newly acquired Russian concessions. Probably rearmament interests influenced the Germans, too. As for the Reichswehr's relation to the Treaty of Rapallo, Litvinoff thinks that they may have had some connection with it, but he is sure that Maltzan was free of army commitments while negotiating, that the Reichswehr moved in only after the deal was completed, when it realized that here was its first opening since the Versailles Treaty.

When the Treaty of Rapallo was ratified in the autumn of 1922, Germany sent to Moscow as Ambassador, Count Brockdorff-Rantzau, a disciple of Maltzan, but a schemer with ambitions of his own. The men of the Narkomindel were not sure of his good faith.

As a minor corollary of Rapallo, Litvinoff negotiated in Prague, on June 5, 1922, a de facto recognition treaty in which Czechoslovakia agreed not to recognize any other Russian government, took cognizance of the Russian Government trade monopoly, and both signatories pledged themselves to refrain from propaganda in the other's territory. But the friendly tone of the terms did not compensate for the lack of de jure recognition, and relations between the two countries remained somewhat uneasy.

Less than three weeks later (June 24) the German Foreign Minister, Walther Rathenau, who had signed the Treaty of Rapallo, was assassinated in broad daylight while driving through the streets of a Berlin suburb, by young German nationalists, animated by multiple motives: Rathenau was a Jew; one of the most prominent and intelligent representatives of the Republic; the arch-proponent in German politics of the international view; and last, he had signed the Treaty of Rapallo.

The murderers, who committed suicide when the police were about to apprehend them, are today national heroes of Germany. Hitler has erected monuments to their memory.

CHAPTER SEVEN

A New Type of Diplomat

LITVINOFF AS A FULL-FLEDGED diplomat was decidedly unusual. Enemies have accused him of having brought into international negotiations the bazaar technique of starting discussions by demanding an exorbitant price so that even with substantial concessions he could still make a good profit. If this was Litvinoff's method, it was justified not only by both the aim and the results, but also by the conditions that other countries imposed upon him. No matter how often his proposals were rejected—for instance, in the case of the United States—he always tried again, always came back with new offers. His negotiations were not secret, and were never complicated by efforts to save face. All that mattered was to get as much as circumstances permitted for the 160,000,000 people whom he represented. The awareness of those 160,000,000 people helped him through many a difficult situation; and he was conscious also of the value of peace to all nations and the common man everywhere. Litvinoff has the typical Russian feeling for humanity as a whole.

One of Litvinoff's collaborators once said that the statesman whom Litvinoff admires most is Talleyrand, on whom he has gathered a whole library, studying his life, memoirs, and numerous treaties with great care. Externally the two appear utterly opposed. To be sure, Talleyrand represented diplomatically a revolutionary government, but he also served four other regimes—Minister of Foreign Affairs under Napoleon, Minister of Foreign Affairs in the Cabinet of Louis XVIII, leader of the opposition against Louis XVIII, Ambassador to London under Louis Philippe—and changed his political ideas repeatedly, whereas Litvinoff, through his entire life, has been loyal to one idea. Talleyrand had been a bishop, Litvinoff when still a boy grew away from organized religion, and, as a Marxian, eliminated in the end all supernatural conceptions.

But their differences are less important than their inner resemblances: intense patriotism marks both careers; both gave their lifelong efforts to the cause of liberty—each, of course, following his own interpretation, in accordance with his moment in history; and both are distinguished by exceptional self-restraint, finesse, and dexterity, reinforced by cool impersonality in negotiating. Moreover, there is a real similarity in significant circumstances: when in 1815 Talleyrand went to the Congress of Vienna, France was an outcast among the nations; before Talleyrand left Vienna, France was in power again. Russia's days as an outcast are over; Litvinoff, still at the height of his diplomatic career, serves a Russia that is a power again.

According to his Russian biographer Kornev, Litvinoff, when asked if there was a "type" of Soviet diplomat, answered: "I cannot imagine a typical Soviet diplomat and I hope there is not." He explained that the Soviet diplomat tries in peacetime to perform the task which the Red army would have to perform in wartime—a reversal of the famous sentence of Clausewitz: "War is the continuation of politics with other means." In any case, Litvinoff has always felt that no Soviet diplomat was irreplaceable.

But it is doubtful whether Litvinoff, during the first half of the 1920's, could have been replaced, though he would never admit that himself. On the whole, the Bolshevik tradition is for anonymity: the Party considers itself the custodian of the will and ideals of the nation; the individual is the worker, the agent, only; his policy and authority are derived from the group which disciplines him to its service.

Litvinoff has been one of the most anonymous among the anonymous workers. He has proved over and over again that he has no interest whatever in personal prestige and actually does detest the limelight. In 1936 while he was attending a congress in Montreux, the Central Executive Committee conferred on him the Order of Lenin. M. Kalinin, Chairman of the Central Executive Committee, wired him congratulations on his sixtieth birthday for his "outstanding achievements in the fight for peace." Molotov and Stalin wired: "On the day of your sixtieth jubilee, the Council of the People's Commissars and the Central Committee of the Communist Party of Russia greet you as one of the oldest collaborators of the Party, as the leader of Soviet diplomacy in your indefatigable fight against war and for the cause of peace in the interest of all workers."

Litvinoff answered in a telegram to Stalin, Molotov and Kalinin: ". . . If I look back I am chiefly proud of having done my whole Party work of forty years under the immediate guidance of our great leaders and teachers, Lenin and Stalin. If there are any successes in my diplomatic work they must be attributed to the strong and wise leadership of the man who is responsible for the successes in all fields of socialist reconstruction—Stalin."

Yet Litvinoff could have taken pride in the fact that, from being suspected, shunned, and snubbed, he had by sheer force of character, by superior intelligence, by tenacity, skill, and complete sincerity won the respect of all the diplomats of his day, who now unanimously recognized him as outstanding. Ambassador Davies two years later reports: "One can well understand why he should bear the reputation of being the ablest Foreign Minister in Europe," and adds, "I think he is, and had the pleasure of saying so to Stalin and Molotov." * Some of his colleagues abroad were even afraid of him, and all knew his power as a negotiator. It is always difficult, without offering substantial concessions, to get him to commit himself. He is like absorbent cotton: when pressed, he apparently gives way, conceding and retreating in a sensible and disarmingly agreeable way; yet when the time comes for final commitment, there he is in good shape; he has not given way at all. Nor has there ever been any feeling of tension or bitterness, or hint of trickery or bad faith in his dealings. His tranquil detachment, complete freedom from anxiety, his ready laughter and deliciously ironic wit all have helped. He has invariably been confident, conciliatory, unhurried, cool, giving the impression that he had all the time in the world to wait. Count Werner von der Schulenburg, the German Ambassador to Moscow, once said, "I have the toughest diplomatic job in the world and the most agreeable opposite number." In reality there was no harder fighter, no more incessant worker than Litvinoff in those years, yet in his heart he carried a heavy burden of anxiety and even dread—for he saw all too clearly the appalling holocaust that the rulers of Europe were preparing for mankind, "piling the faggots hour by doomful hour."

* Joseph E. Davies, *op. cit.*, p. 362.

2

Two months after Rapallo, Litvinoff was named chairman of the Russian delegation to the Hague Conference, which was to settle "once and for all" the international debt question. Litvinoff's attitude towards American participation, hopeful but wary, was revealed in a statement that he made in Berlin on May 28 to a correspondent for the London *Daily Herald*:

> Russia would welcome America's participation at the Hague conference on condition that she recognize Russia's sovereign rights and renounce her attempts to dictate the nature of our social and political order.
> We recognize the value of American assistance, but we are convinced that if America acts at the Hague in the manner suggested by the recent threats of Secretary Hughes she will play an even more unfortunate role than France played in Genoa.

His mistrust of the other countries, also, was made evident in a statement issued in Moscow on June 16:

"The first and most important question at the Hague Conference would be what amounts the bankers would supply to Russia's credits." He was counter-attacking before the main attack on him had started.

On June 26, at ten o'clock in the morning, Litvinoff's train pulled into the station of Scheveningen near the Hague. No Dutch Government official met the Russian delegation, which had as escort only two policemen who led Litvinoff and his assistants to the Orange Hotel, across the street, and on the way objected to his walking on the grass. The Russians were shown into a wing of the hotel shut off from the rest, and as soon as they entered, a corps of uniformed police took up positions before the door.

Litvinoff, in response to a request, sent word immediately that he would receive journalists. But the police refused them entrance.

These first few hours showed Litvinoff what he had to expect at the Hague. But just as he had not given up in Copenhagen two years before, so he persisted now. Every time he was asked what Russia would do about the debts, he replied by asking what the others would do about credits to Russia. When the others inquired into Russia's budget, he declared this to be interference with Soviet sovereignty. He was frank: on June 30, he admitted that, "whatever action Moscow took with reference to foreign claims would be done simply for the purpose of obtaining foreign credits." Later he said that this was a passing remark, but represented the attitude of the Soviet leaders.

The other delegates were particularly annoyed when Litvinoff declared that Soviet Russia did not even know whose property it had confiscated. On July 7, the English representative became indignant: "Do you really mean to say that having nationalized foreign properties and having administered them, the Soviets don't know who the former owners are?"

Litvinoff answered: "Exactly." And the New York Times added: "Half an hour of questioning failed to shake Litvinoff's claim of Soviet ignorance."

America came into the discussion repeatedly. On the same day, Litvinoff stated in conversation that the Russian delegation was expecting to negotiate with an important group of financiers which included Otto H. Kahn of Kuhn, Loeb & Company.

A week later Otto H. Kahn, who had arrived in the Hague, declared that, "The conference with the Russians will bring useful results and will presumably lead to a closer approach to unity of views and policies on the part of England, France, and the United States in respect to the Russian situation." He denied, however, that he had seen or spoken to any of the Russian delegates.

That was as near as the Russians and the Americans got to each other at the Hague Conference.

Almost from the beginning, Litvinoff felt that the conference would fail. On July 12 he declared that "the failure of the conference is now a foregone conclusion." Still he did everything he could to make himself heard. That same day he stated that the Soviet Union was the most stable country in Europe because it had had no change of government for five years: "Capital would be safer in Soviet Russia than in any capitalistic country in the world." Two days later he asked for $1,600,000,000 credits, in exchange for which Russia would immediately recognize certain former debts and repay them after a moratorium. One of the grotesque features of the conference was the unwillingness of the other Powers to let the Russians know the exact

extent of their claims. Again and again Litvinoff asked this question
without getting a satisfactory reply. In the end the English and French,
especially, caricatured the facts by claiming that the conference had
to be broken up "because the Russians refused to agree to any working
machinery or rules."

On July 23 Litvinoff and his group left for Berlin, where he put
up at the Russian Embassy on Unter den Linden, and made a statement through the press that "Europe would have to wait fifty years,
perhaps, before Russia would accept the maximum demands of
France and Belgium." He also said: "The failure of the conference
has demonstrated that the Russian question cannot be settled in a
joint conference."

3

Nevertheless, before the year was out, Litvinoff himself called
another joint conference, in Moscow in December, 1922—the first
disarmament conference after the World War. Litvinoff has explained
his motives:

"I do not hesitate to say quite frankly that the money which the
Soviet Union then was spending on the Red army was badly needed
for internal reconstruction. Our neighbors needed the money which
they were spending on their armies for better purposes, too. I had
reason, therefore, to believe that my proposals for a genuine disarmament would be welcomed by our neighbors. But strangely enough they
were not. And this, of course, made the conference a complete failure.

"Poland and at least one other state with a common frontier with
us were virtually pawns in the hands of powers, opposed, for their
own reasons, to a real reduction of armament in Europe. But the
armament burden was so heavy during those days that no government
openly dared to admit its unwillingness to disarm or to decline an
invitation to a disarmament conference.

"That was the psychological basis from which I started. I sent out
invitations for all our immediate neighbors to come to a disarmament
conference in Moscow. I knew that they had to accept. Well, they did.
But before they arrived, Poland, Latvia, Esthonia, and Finland
arranged for a secret meeting at Reval to decide on a common plan

of action for the conference—a common front against genuine disarmament, of course."

Litvinoff put his cards on the table. On December 4 he announced the proposals of the Soviet Government, which would be binding if the conference were successful: the Russian army would be reduced to 200,000 men; the military budget would be limited to a certain sum per soldier; a demilitarized zone would be established at the frontiers between Russia and her neighbors (as in a recently concluded Russo-Finnish treaty).

He finished with biting irony: "The Russian Government, to its great regret, is unable to put forward proposals as to the limitation of its naval forces. The Russian Fleet, however, is already reduced to a quarter of the strength it had in 1917." He was referring to the theft of large sections of the former Russian Navy by General Wrangel with Allied connivance. When Litvinoff spoke, those units were at Bizerte.

Litvinoff called the Moscow disarmament conference a farce, yet he did score a major diplomatic and political victory. The Poles, obviously feeling that the generosity of the Russian proposals was influencing the other nations, wanted to show themselves equally generous, so they suggested reducing their army from 373,000 to 280,000 men. The Polish representatives apparently had forgotten that shortly before, they had told the League of Nations that the Polish army consisted of only 280,000 men. But Litvinoff had not forgotten; and he told them that if they really wanted to reduce their army by 25 per cent, they would have to get down to 210,000. The Poles were caught in the net of their own misstatements. They had either falsified facts to the League of Nations or had tried to mislead Litvinoff. Perhaps they had erred in both cases. Litvinoff immediately recognized their predicament, and Russian disarmament propaganda—designed and supervised by Litvinoff personally—made the most of it.

Publicity was in the end all that Litvinoff got out of the conference, but he felt that that might prove important. By demonstrating that the other Powers did not really want to disarm, he hoped to embarrass them politically and finally shame them into some sort of action in that direction, no matter how limited. In this policy, evoked by the failure of the Moscow disarmament conference, he had full co-operation from

Lenin and Stalin (and he was still following it at the Geneva Disarmament Conference in 1927). All three men believed that no government could reject the Russian disarmament proposals and then use the excuse of a Bolshevik menace to support a militaristic program, as Briand had done at the Washington Conference.

This was a logical theory, but Litvinoff, the realist, seems to have forgotten this once that human memories are short. Just that inconsistency was successfully perpetrated: the Russian disarmament offers having been rejected, a pretense of fear of Russia was paraded as an excuse for rearming.

4

One obstacle after another was thrown up by the other countries to frustrate Litvinoff's major aim: the resumption of normal relations between Russia and the rest of the world. The stupidity and blatant intellectual dishonesty against which he had to struggle would have driven even most seasoned diplomats to bitterness and despair, but Litvinoff never faltered. His intellectual skepticism and ironic humor protected him from discouragement. The transparent falsehoods and petty meannesses that would have overwhelmed a less sophisticated mind, he could observe with amused, if contemptuous, detachment. And his intense ethical idealism would not permit him to give up.

On January 21, 1923, a new breach of international courtesies necessitated the following note to the State Department of the United States:

According to information in the possession of the People's Commissariat of Foreign Affairs, remnants of counter-revolutionary bands intend in the spring of this year to cross the Bering Straits to Alaska to dispose of furs looted on the territory of the Russian Socialist Federal Soviet Republic. It is ascertained that the Russian marauders with looted public property of the R.S.F.S.R. have obtained entrance to Alaska without let or hindrance from border or local American authorities.

The Russian Government, while taking steps to prevent in the future the efforts of criminal elements to find shelter abroad with their loot, calls the attention of the American Government to the above and expresses its firm belief that the American Government in turn will issue orders barring the admittance to Alaska of Russian citizens not in possession of the proper Russian documents issued by competent Soviet authorities.

And again on February 1, he wired:

Information has been received by the Russian Government that a number of Russian ships [14], hurried off from Vladivostok by Admiral Stark during the Japanese invasion, have gone to Manila. In a cable dated January 9, the Russian Government notified all other governments of their criminal act against the property of the Soviet Republic. In calling the attention of the American Government to the possible sale of the Russian ships by Stark or his associates, the Russian Government will urgently take the necessary steps to protect the rights of the Soviet Republic to prevent the illegal transfer of the seized property and prohibit their registration by the authorities at Manila or other ports within American jurisdiction.

This endless contest, adroitly combined with conciliation, had to be continued on all sides. The next month (March 9, 1923) it was France to whom Litvinoff had to protest "against the reported intention of the French to sell General Wrangel's ships now at Bizerte. Those ships were used by the anti-Bolshevik commander in South Russia in evacuating his troops."

In May of that same year Lord Curzon threatened to break off British-Soviet relations on the ground that Communist propaganda had continued in England, and the situation hung in the balance until the following January, when Ramsay MacDonald came into office.

During May, 1923, also, a Russian delegation was told in Switzerland that 40,000 men would throw them across the Swiss border if they did not leave immediately. Soon afterwards, on May 10, Vaslov Vorovsky, the chief Soviet delegate to the Second Lausanne Conference, while dining in the Hotel Cecil, was murdered by a Russian émigré of Swiss descent, Maurice Conradi. Conradi claimed that he was simply avenging relatives killed during the Revolution; others said he had been prompted and paid by the Imperial Russian Red Cross, a reactionary society with headquarters in Geneva. Thereafter, Switzerland was flooded with anti-Soviet propaganda—countless articles, pictures, films revealing "Soviet atrocities" to the Swiss public. One par-

ticularly lurid motion picture purported to depict the Soviet war on
religion, showing priests being murdered, Thomas-à-Becket-wise, at
the altar. Cable reports from Geneva told that, when the picture was
first shown, many of the audience rushed weeping from the theater.

In the atmosphere thus created, a fair jury was out of the question
and, as a result, Conradi's trial was a farce unworthy of the Swiss
democracy. Conradi was, of course, acquitted. Temporarily rich and
famous, he began to travel extensively, but in a few years his "wonderful" deed was forgotten. To recoup his fame and fortunes, he
decided in 1931 to murder another Russian. But he could not screw
up his courage to the sticking point, and the authorities easily thwarted
him. In the end he went into the French Foreign Legion, where he
soon died.

As a result of the Vorovsky assassination, Russia decided to boycott
Swiss goods, and Switzerland retaliated by expelling all Russians from
the country.

In the midst of all this active enmity, an occasional friendly voice
was lifted—even in the United States, where prejudice was bulwarked
by the Puritan conscience of Secretary Hughes. In April, 1923, Senator
and Mrs. Burton K. Wheeler visited Moscow and were put up in the
Sugar King's Palace, and after their return the Senator gave an interview to the New York *Evening Post* (May 28, 1923) in which he
advocated immediate resumption of diplomatic relations: "There is
absolutely no reason in the world why the United States should not
recognize Russia."

But on December 6, that same year, Coolidge said, in a message to
Congress: "The United States does not propose to enter into relations
with a regime which refuses to recognize the sanctity of international
obligations." Plymouth rock was holding firm.

5

In 1922 it was becoming increasingly difficult for Lenin to attend
to the immense amount of work which he had laid out for himself.
After a few hours at his desk, his ideas refused to take shape. Cruel
headaches followed. During January the physicians ordered him to
reduce drastically his working time, but in June his condition de-

teriorated rapidly, until there was general paralysis and loss of speech.

Cerebral hemorrhage due to arteriosclerosis was the diagnosis, and for three months he lay ill in a town named after Maxim Gorki. But gradually he regained control of his limbs, recaptured speech, and by September he believed himself well again. Everyone around him, however, knew that he was doomed; only Litvinoff refused to admit it. According to his statements, Lenin was always getting on nicely. Was he putting up a good front for Russia, reassuring the world lest the absence of Lenin's hand from the helm arouse even more distrust of the Soviets? He has been accused of such deliberate political prevarication.

Or was there a personal motive in these repeated assertions of Lenin's imminent recovery? Lenin was to Litvinoff the most important man in the world, the source of infallible decisions, the perfect leader. True, since the revolutionary victory, they had seen less of each other. Litvinoff had been much away from Moscow, and even when he was there, Lenin's foreign policy conferences were normally held with the Chief Commissar, Chicherin, and Lenin's personal surveillance was focused on men whom he could not trust as implicitly as he knew he could trust Litvinoff. But their reciprocal confidence was too secure to need reaffirmation by personal contact. It was enough for Litvinoff to know that Lenin was guiding the social development for which, together, they had given the hard and dangerous years. But if some day Lenin was no longer there? Was Litvinoff, in trying to persuade the world that Lenin still had years ahead, trying to persuade himself?

When Lenin returned to his office in the Kremlin by the middle of October, 1922, he did seem "fit as a fiddle" * and was prolific of new plans to consolidate the Soviet system, but he was no longer the old Lenin. His capacity for creative effort and for continuous hard work were both almost gone. His friends and comrades looked on, hoping and despairing and unable to do anything.

On March 12, 1923, an extra edition of *Pravda* announced that Lenin's blood circulation had again become irregular and movement was impeded in the right leg and right arm. His speech was only slightly impaired.

* Walter Duranty, *op. cit.*, p. 122.

Lenin rested again. This time he seemed to recover in a few weeks, but the man who, in the late autumn of 1923, spoke to the Soviets of Moscow on the fifth anniversary of the Bolshevik Revolution was marked by death.

Another few weeks went by, and Lenin grew more and more weary of the struggle. So he returned to Gorki. The first snow was falling and he was able to take long sleigh-rides. He thought his health was improving.

Towards evening on January 21, 1924, the end came. For an hour the fever mounted, convulsions racked his body, but Lenin no longer felt anything. Just before seven o'clock he died. The immediate cause was paralysis of the respiratory centers due to cerebral hemorrhage. Krupskaya was with him.*

Lenin's death shook his friends and collaborators profoundly. When Kalinin gave an account of it to the Soviet Congress, meeting in a Moscow theater, he wept bitterly. The hundreds of people assembled, at first dazed and speechless with sorrow, broke out in sobs and moaning.

There was passionate grief throughout Russia. All over the world people mourned him. On the day of Lenin's funeral, the international proletariat proclaimed a five-minute stoppage of work. In many places, factories, railways, communication systems, paused for those five minutes.

In the severe cold—the thermometer reached 35 degrees Fahrenheit below zero—hundreds of thousands of men and women, day after day, filed slowly past Lenin's coffin, which stood in the white columned hall of the former Nobles' Club on the Red Square in Moscow. The guards waved their arms, stamped, and tried in vain to keep warm around improvised log fires. The silent masses appeared not to feel the cold. In endless file they passed by, solemn, still. They seemed stunned.

More than 800,000 men and women gathered for the funeral. Once more it was bitter, bitter cold. Stalin, Kamenev, Zinoviev, Bukharin, Rykov, and Kalinin carried Lenin's red-draped coffin on the long march. Bands played the "International" in slow, measured beat.

Litvinoff was at the funeral, but he was not among the pallbearers.

* *Ibid.*, pp. 126-128.

"I was close to Lenin," he said, "but there were many who were closer to him."

There were many important and moving speeches. Of them all, the most deeply touching were Krupskaya's few simple words.

January 21 was designated a day of mourning for Russia, commemorating, by coincidence, two tragedies: Lenin's death and the "Bloody Sunday" of 1905.

6

Russia was in mourning, but Litvinoff had no time to mourn. Lenin was dead, Lenin's work in Russia had to be kept going.

At first the Party direction, which meant in effect the Government, was in the hands of a triumvirate, Kamenev, Zinoviev, and Stalin. There were tensions, conflicts, competition, with Trotsky in the immediate background manipulating for power and for his policy of world revolution as the primary purpose, against Stalin's growing insistence on Russian internal development as the first, all-absorbing job.

Litvinoff had lost a leader and a friend, but what counted most—and keeping this constantly in mind was the greatest tribute he could pay Lenin—was the cause: making the world safe for humanity. The Revolution had to be solidly established, and for this, foreign recognition was essential. Litvinoff was busy negotiating to this end on all sides, and in 1924 succeeded in winning recognition from most of the Powers. The United States needed another nine years to make up its mind.

On January 23, Ramsay MacDonald and the Labor Party came into power in England. Litvinoff had been working hard behind the scenes to obtain British recognition, and the Labor Party had made it one of the planks of their campaign platform, which they could safely do since not only many Liberals, but also a considerable body of Conservatives were by that time convinced of its necessity. To accelerate its actual execution, Christian G. Rakovsky, Russian Ambassador in Paris, prompted by daily telegrams from Litvinoff, kept in constant touch with MacDonald, even before he had formed his Government; and Litvinoff very cleverly stimulated a competition between Mac-

Donald and Mussolini as to who was to be the first to sign a recognition agreement with Russia. Mussolini was spurred on by regular bulletins from Litvinoff's representative in Rome, Yordansky, who was likewise fortified by daily messages from his chief. Special concessions loomed invitingly ahead as the prize.*

MacDonald crossed the line a few days ahead by extending an offer of formal recognition to the Soviet Union, as one of his first acts after coming into office, and on February 2 granting it unconditionally. A clause was, however, included, like that in the 1921 trade agreement, providing that neither carry on propaganda in the other country. For the moment no ambassadors were named, Rakovsky being charged with seeing to Russian affairs in London from his post in Paris, while the British named as their chargé d'affaires R. M. Hodgson—hardly a tactful selection since he had also represented his government in its friendly relations with Kolchak.

Discussion of both public and private debts was postponed until April, when an Anglo-Soviet conference met in London (April 14). Rakovsky represented Russia until June, when Litvinoff arrived to take his place at the head of the Russian delegation.

According to Harvey E. Fisk of the Bankers Trust Company,† Russia's public debts to Great Britain then consisted of:

Government and Railway Bonds	$ 333,000,000
Commercial Investments	261,000,000
War Debt	2,766,000,000
Total	$3,360,000,000

Litvinoff presented counter claims, based chiefly on damage during the Wars of Intervention. Two years before, at Genoa, he had asked for £4,067,226,040—that is, roughly, $20,000,000,000. Rakovsky's memorandum showed that Russia would settle for approximately $10,000,-000,000.

"More than 1,350,000 Russian lives were lost during those wars," Rakovsky argued, following Litvinoff's suggestion. "Thirty-five hundred bridges were destroyed. Entire provinces were laid waste."

* Louis Fischer, *The Soviets in World Affairs*, II, p. 468, London and New York, 1930.
† Their private publication: *The Inter-Allied Debts*, New York.

The English said that they could not be held responsible for damage caused by troops which, though armed by them, had not been under British command.

This argument Litvinoff countered with a valid and pertinent historical precedent, the case of the *Alabama* which, "though fitted out in England, did not belong to the British Government. Yet the Geneva Court of Arbitration—on September 14, 1872—ordered the British Government to pay the United States $15,500,000 for damage caused by the *Alabama*."

From the beginning it was obvious that the City, represented by a group of bankers, was determined to frustrate the negotiations, for they immediately submitted to the British Government a number of demands, and had them published at the same time in the London daily newspapers, which included all the claims that had been rejected by Litvinoff in Genoa and the Hague.

The Soviet Government in order to facilitate relations, was ready to make a certain compensation for the nationalization of private property, even though they admitted no inherent right in those claims, provided first, that they were designated as "claims," not "losses" (since the latter would both imply the illegality of nationalization and also set a precedent for demands by expropriated nationals of other countries); second, that the British Government guarantee a loan to enable the Soviets to meet such claims—a condition they consistently maintained for sound economic reasons; and third, that only claims be paid that had been admitted as valid by both governments. Since MacDonald had only a minority in the House of Commons, was not unconditionally supported even by the leaders of his own party and finally —like every British Government—had to make some gesture of deference, at least, to the antipathetic financial interests, Litvinoff was pessimistic about the outcome—justifiably, as events rapidly proved.

For on August 4, when no progress had been made after seventeen hours of continuous discussion, Captain T. C. C. Gregory of the Foreign Office, a "die-hard" Tory and implacable enemy of the Soviets, suggested at 4:00 o'clock in the morning, the moment of low vitality, to Undersecretary of State Arthur Ponsonby, that negotiations be broken off; three hours later Ponsonby succumbed, and announced that "the treaty cannot be signed and the negotiations, therefore, fall to the ground." The City had won, preventing the Labor Government from coming to a full and satisfactory understanding with the Communist regime.

Yet negotiations were resumed two days later because MacDonald and Ponsonby realized that the people who had elected them wanted an agreement with Russia. On August 10, an Anglo-Soviet general treaty was signed, but it did not decide the questions of debts and claims, and still did not embrace important features which would have made it the much-desired commercial treaty.

Yet the Opposition was furious even at this limited victory for the Labor Party and the Soviets. The King despised the Soviets; his resentment over the killing of his cousin, the Czar, never cooled. Emphatically, George V was against any understanding with the new Russian order. The Conservative press raged. The *Morning Post* wrote of British interests betrayed. The *Daily Telegraph* called it a "useless treaty." Lloyd George, though he probably had been ready at Genoa to cede to the Russians more than MacDonald now yielded, was also opposed.

The fight against the treaty was well organized, and the anti-Soviet group was determined that the Labor Cabinet must go. On October 8, MacDonald was defeated in the House, as a result, in no small part, of his Russian policy. He resigned, and general elections were fixed for the 29th.

His opponents had no time to lose. They acted promptly, and at the critical moment produced a letter bearing the purported signature of the Secretary of the Comintern, Grigori Zinoviev, which, in the opinion of many, swung the election to the Conservative Party.

7

According to this letter Zinoviev gave the British Communist Party instructions on tactics during the elections, and also advised it to work inside the British army in order to "paralyze all the military preparations of the bourgeoisie."

The letter was first published in the *Daily Mail,* which was fanatically anti-Communist. The editor, Thomas Marlowe, declared that he had received two copies of the letter from Captain Gregory, the same Gregory who had been a hostile influence in the treaty negotiations.

Marlowe had never seen the original. Neither had any official of the British Government. Three or four copies were circulating in England, but the original remained mysteriously invisible. Might the "original" have betrayed the hand of the forger?

There was ample internal evidence that the letter was a fraud. The letterhead read "Executive Committee, Third Communist International, Presidium." But there was no such thing as a "Third Communist International," there was only a "Third International." Zinoviev had allegedly signed as "President of the Presidium of the Executive Committee of Communist International." Hundreds of documents showed that he always signed as "President of the Executive Committee." There were innumerable proofs that the letter had never been written by Zinoviev, or anyone else connected with the Communist Party. Even its style was different from other communications of the Comintern.

Later, much too late, it was proved that the Zinoviev letter was indeed a forgery. It had been fabricated by a certain Druzhelovsky, a White Russian émigré and professional forger, who had worked in Berlin under instructions from the Polish secret service. Druzhelovsky had received the draft of the letter from other Russian émigrés also working for the Polish secret service. All this came out in several trials in Soviet Russia and in Germany, and through the testimony of newspaper men in other parts of Europe. Furthermore, the British Trade Union Congress sent a delegation to Moscow to examine the Comintern files. It reported: "The deputation satisfied itself that there was no . . . channel in the Comintern departments by which a letter signed by Zinoviev could have been either discussed, drafted or issued. . . . This inspection convinced the deputation, so far as the negative can be proved, that no 'Red letter' ever left the Comintern."

The Zinoviev letter might never have been published, especially not at such a decisive moment, if MacDonald had not been deceived by the permanent officials of the Foreign Office, who were Conservative, anti-Communist and, incidentally, anti-MacDonald. They held the letter in the Foreign Office, waiting to show it to MacDonald when he was busy with other pressing matters and could not promptly or clearly gauge its importance. He admitted as much himself later, expressed his regret and said that "the letter was a deliberately planned and devised concoction of deceit, artfully contrived for the purpose of deceiving the public and influencing the election. That it played a major part in the verdict no one will deny. That it was fraudulent few will dare to deny."

In any case, the Labor Party was defeated in the election and the Conservatives won. Stanley Baldwin became Prime Minister. Later, certain Conservative circles, who were not happy at having the Party charged with such a sordid trick, attempted to clear up the affair of the Zinoviev letter. But Baldwin consistently refused to investigate. He rejected an official Soviet offer to submit the question to arbitration. By then even the *Morning Post* (March 6, 1925) said that, "One finds a growing feeling among Conservatives that the government would be well advised to grant an investigation." The London *Times* seconded this opinion on the next day: "No reason seems to exist why the demand should not be granted . . . The refusal might conceivably confirm some lingering suspicion that the present government . . . has something sinister to hide."

The unwillingness of the British Government to do anything, even belatedly, about the Zinoviev letter not only proved that it had "something sinister to hide," but showed that the Government felt constrained by a strange code of honor to support, at least publicly, those who had committed the fraud, though Captain Gregory was later quietly and unceremoniously dropped. The Government's attitude throughout implied a certain degree of sanction for dubious methods as long as they were used against Russia, and a like degree of immunity for the instigators, even though they perpetrated fraud on the electorate. It was another demonstration that the leaders of the Conservative Party did not regard Soviet Russia as entitled to the basic amenities of civilized international intercourse. In short, the British Government was thoroughly and undisguisedly hostile to Russia. Of this the Foreign Office gave increasingly explicit proof. Indeed, their animosity began, in Russian eyes at least, to approach conspiracy.

8

Had the Soviets really been intent on an ambitious program of Communist propaganda abroad, as the British Government had tried to claim, Germany would have been the country in which to undertake it on a grand scale. The Treaty of Rapallo had facilitated all contacts. The combination of circumstances in late 1923 and 1924—the inflation which ruined the German middle class and, at its height, threw most of the country into utter despair about the future, and the passive resistance in the Ruhr which benefited only a few industrialists who obtained large indemnities—might well have influenced the German masses in favor of Communism, so that it would have been the moment to try to start a Communist revolution. That Moscow did nothing of the sort is good evidence that the accusations were without much foundation. Russia prevented Poland and Czechoslovakia from attacking Germany when she could not have put up any resistance in the East. Moscow also was opposed to the French occupation of the Ruhr. But French and English liberals—not to mention the Labor Party, Lloyd George, Sir John Simon, Ramsay MacDonald, Arthur Henderson—also denounced the Ruhr invasion. Even the American Secretary of State deplored it, but was persuaded by Ambassador Herrick * in Paris to withhold the intended protest.

In spite of the fact that the Soviets had not seized this obvious chance to promote a revolution in Germany, however, the elements that ruled Germany from backstage—the Junkers and industrialists—were not in favor of friendly relations with Russia. On May 3, 1924, the Berlin police raided the Soviet Trade Delegation in Berlin. The excuse was that a German Communist, whom the police had arrested, had broken away and run into the building. The two policemen who had been escorting him left the premises when informed that they were on extraterritorial ground, but that afternoon two hundred policemen forced their way through the offices, breaking open drawers and files in their presumed search for the fugitive.

The Soviet Ambassador, Nikolai Krestinsky, immediately protested to Foreign Minister Gustav Stresemann that the raid was a violation of the Trade Delegation's extraterritorial rights, which it certainly was; but it was even more: an indication of the real feelings in certain German circles towards Soviet Russia. Stresemann was furious about this stupid arbitrary interference with his policy and shouted so loudly over the telephone at the authorities responsible for it that Krestinsky, who was present, was convinced that the Foreign Office, at least, had nothing to do with the affair.

Still it was a frontal attack against Litvinoff's policy. Such an intrusion into the commercial offices of any country would have been an outrage, but in any other case it would have been less significant, for to Litivinoff trade was a step towards recognition, and after recognition a means of strengthening relations between Soviet Russia and other countries. Trade for him, therefore, definitely belonged in the sphere of politics. This was, of course, the reason that the Germans had struck against the Russian Trade Delegation.

For the Germans the raid netted exactly nothing. They found no revealing documents, and, on the other hand, Litvinoff, while exchanging several firm diplomatic notes via Chicherin and Krestinsky, closed the main office of the Trade Delegation in Berlin and the Leipzig and Hamburg branch offices, and canceled Russian participation in the Leipzig Fur Auction and the Cologne Fair. By July 29, the Germans had to give in. They stopped apologizing for the raid and offered compensation for the damage done. For a while trade relations improved again, and a commercial treaty was executed in October 1925.

But the Germans obviously no longer intended to honor the spirit of Rapallo. Field Marshal von Hindenburg, who had succeeded Ebert as President of the German Republic, certainly was even less friendly to the Soviets than his predecessor, and Stresemann was by no means overeager to improve relations with them. One of the extreme annexationists during the war, he had been moving, contrary to the general political drift in Germany, from the right towards the center; but though an able man with genuine strength of character, he did not have either the insight or the large ideas of the murdered Rathenau, and his interests centered in the West. He believed that an arrangement with France would win for Germany a respite from international pressure, a chance for reconstruction, and ultimately a genuine revision of the Versailles Treaty. In relations with Russia, he wanted to be correct, but nothing more.

Maltzan, who had become Undersecretary of State, also had lost interest in Russia, and would make no effort to improve relations with her. Indeed, he was so disappointed that the arrangement which he had promoted had produced such meager results that he developed a definitely hostile attitude, and seems even to have favored severance of Russo-German relations.

But the more Stresemann became involved in his negotiations with France, the more clearly he saw the bargaining value of friendly relations with Russia. In the meantime, however, Russia, especially in the person of Litvinoff, had been losing interest in the Treaty of Rapallo. For both sides it had been something of a political trick, valuable chiefly as a demonstration that the pariahs could forge international links. Now both countries were looking in other directions for further worlds to conquer—Russia the more willingly because of the chilly atmosphere that the German Rightists had engendered.

Thus Stresemann was forced into the anomalous situation of trying to keep the treaty from collapsing altogether. To this end Brockdorff-Rantzau, the German Ambassador in Moscow, sent daily notes to the Narkomindel, couched in sentimental terms, urging that relations be strengthened "between the two severely stricken peoples." These appeals amused Litvinoff, embarrassed Stresemann, and so annoyed Maltzan that he refused to read any more of Brockdorff-Rantzau's dispatches.

9

Finally, in October, 1925, Stresemann's temporary need of keeping Russian cards up his sleeve was terminated by his triumphant conclusion of the Locarno Treaty with France, England, Belgium, and Italy, and from then on the West predominated heavily in Germany's international policy. Symptomatic of this was the appointment of Maltzan, who had played a major part in the Treaty of Rapallo, as Ambassador to Washington.

The Locarno Treaty contained nothing beyond agreements already embodied in the Versailles Treaty, the most important section being the Rhineland Pact, comprising firm-sounding guarantees for the French, Belgian, and German frontiers. But it did console the Allied diplomats for having been outwitted at Genoa by the Russians with the Treaty of Rapallo; and it gave them an occasion to assure their peoples that at last a real move had been made towards permanent European peace, though there was little basis for such assertions, and even the temporary good will which was engendered was not implemented or maintained with any energy or conviction by Sir Austen Chamberlain, who got great credit for this achievement.

To the Germans, however, the treaty did mean that they were again explicitly accepted in the good society of the Western Powers, and they could read it as a sign that some revision of the Versailles Treaty was approaching, for the very reaffirmation of certain points in the Versailles Treaty indicated that the Western nations did not account it unchallengeable.

To the Russians, conversely, the treaty marked the beginning of isolation. Up to that point the Narkomindel, which in this respect meant chiefly Litvinoff, had chalked up a significant score of successes. Many countries had come round to recognizing and doing business with the Soviets:

> 1920: Esthonia, Lithuania, Latvia, Finland, Poland
> 1921: Persia, Afghanistan, Turkey and Outer Mongolia
> 1922: Germany
> 1923: Italy
> 1924: England, Norway, Austria, Greece, Sweden, China, Denmark, Mexico, France
> 1925: Japan, Turkey

And the following had accorded de facto recognition: Belgium, Czechoslovakia and Hungary.

Trotsky had denied that capitalist and socialist states could live in the same world; Litvinoff and his Narkomindel colleagues had been proving and making it possible. Now it looked as if the Locarno Treaty might undo a good deal of this important work. The Russians had no sentiment about Rapallo, but they could not let pass without comment a treaty that included Germany in a system of guarantees from which Russia was excluded. Chicherin made the point on December 1, 1925:

"The agreement gives the British Government an opportunity to exert powerful pressure on Germany, as a result of which Germany may be forced against her own will to change her attitude towards the Soviet Government."

The *Russian Soviet Encyclopaedia* is equally frank in its article on the Locarno Treaty: "England, by creating the guaranty system of Locarno, wanted a 'balance' on the continent . . . and hoped to play the

role of an arbiter herself. The English leaders hoped to use their growing influence in order to organize, under British leadership, a bloc of
west European states against the Soviet Union. This was the direction
of the then Conservative English government. . . ."

When Chicherin spoke of Germany's being forced "against her own
will" into a new attitude towards Russia, he was probably speaking as
a politician. Because now that Stresemann had reached his understanding with the West, he quite openly showed that he no longer cared
much about peace in the East. He refused to sign an "Eastern Locarno," that is, he would not guarantee the eastern frontiers as Chicherin
and Litvinoff suggested. Stresemann had the good excuse of the Polish
Corridor. Furthermore, the English, who certainly were not ardently
interested in keeping the Soviet frontier tranquil, were encouraging
him in his new attitude.

10

In that same month, December, 1925, the President of the League of
Nations Council invited the Soviet Government to participate in the
Preparatory Disarmament Conference. Litvinoff replied that he would
like to take part in a disarmament conference, but was amazed that it
had been called in Geneva. The Soviet Government could not send
delegates to Switzerland until the Vorovsky affair had been settled.
Several attempts were made to do this—one by the French Government, another by the German journalist Paul Scheffer, who was then
liberal but later became passionately pro-Nazi. All failed, so Russia
stayed away from the first Disarmament Conference in February, 1926.

Germany's entrance into the League of Nations in 1926 seriously increased Russia's isolation. Germany had tried in vain to join the
League immediately after the conclusion of the Versailles Treaty. Later,
on several occasions, she had been invited to join, but had refused, and
logically so, because the League and the Versailles Treaty were devised
to preserve the status quo, while the first concern of German foreign
policy was to change it. Now at Locarno, feeling that the words of
Allied statesmen promised a more lenient and co-operative attitude,
Stresemann promised that Germany would enter the League.

There was dismay in Moscow; Count Brockdorff-Rantzau, who had

been against the Locarno Treaty, again came out against Germany's
entrance into the League, sharing the views of Chicherin, with whom
by this time he was in quite close relations. Stalin, on the contrary,
claimed that Germany's presence in the League meant that Russia
would have a friend there. Stalin could hardly have had any illusions
about Stresemann's friendship, but he concluded that Stresemann, in
order to play an important part in the League, would have to revive
the bogeyman of Russia hoping to frighten the English. It turned out
exactly as Stalin had foreseen. Before entering the League, Germany
executed with Russia a new neutrality and non-aggression treaty,
drafted by Chicherin and Litvinoff, a supplement to the Rapallo pact,
to which Stresemann appended a letter declaring that "should any
move directed solely against the U.S.S.R. take shape within the League
of Nations, Germany would oppose it."

On April 24, the day the treaty was signed, Litvinoff, speaking to the
Central Executive Committee of the Soviet Union in the Kremlin,
explained the new document:

"We still feel there is animosity abroad against us and all too many
dangers of war. . . . We do not believe the League of Nations gives the
world sufficient guarantees, and we have even reason to think that it is
being used to form a hostile combination against Russia. So we have
taken steps ourselves to prevent a recurrence of the horrors of the
Great War. . . . Our treaty of mutual non-aggression with Germany,
which is the completion of work towards the friendship of the two
nations begun at Rapallo, was signed in Berlin today. . . ."

Of France, he said: "Although negotiations have as yet produced no
concrete results, we are hopeful of arrangements benefiting both countries."

Of Great Britain: "Despite the hostilities of certain members of the
Conservative government, there are now signs that business interests
are desirous of extending imperial credits to Russia."

And then Litvinoff spoke, as he did at every opportunity, of the
United States:

"There is a tendency towards a renewal of friendlier relations, although the American government has declined to change its point of
view. They insist on our recognition of the Kerenski debt, but once
negotiations begin, that point should not present great difficulty. . . .

We have repeatedly stated that we are ready to begin negotiations, but their demand that we commit ourselves beforehand seems unusual. We are anxious for the friendship of the United States . . . and despite everything, I think on the whole things are heading towards a mutual agreement before very long."

The "hostile combination against Russia" to which Litvinoff referred was a scheme of Sir Austen Chamberlain, and one of the first things that Stresemann accomplished in the League was to frustrate it. Thereafter Germany served Russia indirectly on various occasions by exploiting situations that Russia provided, for their nuisance value against the dominant Powers.

II

The hostility which had led Chamberlain to devise the scheme that Stresemann had frustrated was but a reflection of the British Tory Government's attitude. Baldwin, when he became Prime Minister in 1925, had left no doubt as to the course he intended to follow. He refused to ratify the Anglo-Russian Treaty signed by MacDonald. Except for recognition, nothing was left but the Trade Agreement of 1921.

This was a heavy blow to Litvinoff, who saw his carefully laid plans going awry. He tried to save what could be saved. He went for counsel and help to Lord d'Abernon, a diplomat of high standing and great influence in British affairs, whom he had met in Berlin in the autumn of 1925. But though he assured d'Abernon of Russia's readiness to reopen negotiations with England in the hope of establishing more friendly relations, he received no encouragement. Indeed, the British Government did not trouble to inform Moscow why it had rejected the Treaty of 1924, what changes it wished, or what new proposals it might be interested in—an act of intentional discourtesy.

As a matter of fact, the British Government did everything to make things more difficult. British Communist leaders were arrested in London in October, 1925. Again, "evidence" was published which was intended to prove a close relation between the Communist Party of Great Britain and the Third International, and the receipt of funds for the Party from Moscow. Once more the Comintern proved an almost fatal handicap to Litvinoff's plans and hopes. He had the difficult task of explaining the difference between the Soviet Government and the

Comintern. That both were in reality responsible to and guided by the Party did no' make his problem any simpler.

But Litvinoff, tenacious, flexible, and realistic as ever, did not give up, nor did he spend any time in sulking or in recriminations, but began planning how to renew negotiations. On April 25, 1926, in an address before the Central Executive Committee in Moscow he announced that he was ready to reopen discussions with Great Britain, "with a view to finding a way out of the present deadlock." There was no response from London.

In May, 1926, the Presidium of the Council of Russian Trade Unions sent the striking miners of England 250,000 rubles, and later, 2,000,000 rubles more. Local Russian trade unions augmented these sums by collecting from each worker one day's pay. There were also collections in Russian theaters, concerts and other places of public assembly. Contributions for the striking miners likewise arrived from America and Germany, but these did not excite the English as did the Russian contributions, for they knew that Russian trade unions could transfer money to England only by special permit from the Soviet Government. Permission had been granted.

On June 10, 1926, Sir Austen Chamberlain told the House of Commons that £380,000 had been sent from Russia to support the strikers. He went on to say that he had warned the Government of the Soviet Union "that continued propaganda in Britain would inevitably lead to a break in diplomatic relations." Likewise he protested in a note to the Soviet chargé d'affaires. The answer, four days later, was that the Russian Government "could not prohibit the trade unions, comprising millions of workers of Soviet Russia, from sending money abroad in aid of the trade unions of another country." When it was hinted in Conservative circles that the Soviet Government itself had contributed from its own funds to the striking miners, the Russian chargé d'affaires denied this emphatically.

But by now the miners' strike had expanded to a general strike and the feeling against Soviet Russia was steadily mounting. On June 19 Winston Churchill made a violent speech, affirming that it was quite possible to do business with the Russians without recognizing them. "I have always thought the United States' policy against Bolshevik Russia was the right one," he said. He called Russia "an ignorant slave state," and accused the Bolsheviki of believing that "the same sort of stuff with which they bamboozled their own *muzhiks* would suit Britain." He became quite specific: "Personally I hope to see the day when either there will be a civilized government in Russia, or we shall have ended the present pretense of friendly relations with men who are seeking our overthrow."

Even the conservative *Daily Express* was shocked at such extravagant and ill-tempered language. But Churchill had only put, in his characteristically forcible and vivid way, what all conservative Englishmen believed and wanted. Three days after the Churchill speech the Government hurried to publish a so-called Blue Book containing the papers which had been seized on the arrest of the British Communist leaders.

During this period the British Government had been considerably disturbed also by Communist propaganda in China, under the leadership of Leo Karakhan, and Michael M. Borodin who as Soviet representative, in southern China had taken an effective part in the Chinese revolution. Great Britain at the moment feared Communism in China far more than it did the mounting Fascism of Japan.

Nor were British Foreign Office feelings, at least, soothed by a Guarantee of Neutrality Treaty concluded the next year (October 1, 1927) between the Soviet Union and Persia, for there were functionaries who were still very sensitive about the signal defeat that they had suffered in Persia at Soviet hands in 1921 (see pp. 168-169).

It was clear to Litvinoff that Russia's relations to the Western Powers were going badly. There were many ominous indications that British foreign policy, so stubbornly hostile to the Soviets, was about to succeed. The Russians saw themselves again threatened with the dreaded isolation and encirclement. In May, 1926, Marshal Pilsudski had accomplished his semi-Fascist coup d'état which made him the Dictator of Poland. In December, 1926, there was a Fascist putsch in Lithuania. The Russians had reason to suspect that the British had had something to do with both these moves. In September, 1926, Chamberlain came to certain agreements with Mussolini in Leghorn, in which Mussolini's preposterous and theatrical flattery of Mrs. Chamberlain may have played some part.

Litvinoff realized that direct progress with Britain was unlikely, so he characteristically resorted to a detour: the friendly relations between Soviet Russia and Turkey could be profitably exploited. About a year earlier, on December 17, 1925, Litvinoff had concluded a neutrality treaty with the Turks. He had hoped that such a treaty would move other governments to seek similar agreements. Accordingly, he announced that he was ready to consider any suggestions that might contribute to peace among the nations. On December 23, he made the following statement:

"The Soviet-Turkish Peace Treaty is a sample of the compacts that Soviet Russia is ready to sign with other powers, holding that only such agreements and not League of Nations or Locarno machinations can pave the way for world peace.

"The Treaty is a serious step towards world peace because it is directed against no one and threatens nobody's interests." But no other country had responded.

Now, a year later, there still was only Turkey. But Turkey was willing to conclude a new treaty devised to improve relations still further, and the pact was duly signed in Odessa in November, 1926. The Turkish Ambassador in Berlin, possibly in response to a hint from Litvinoff, announced that his country would "on no account join in the ring of hostility with which England has tried to surround the U.S.S.R. We realize perfectly that every blow dealt the U.S.S.R. will have a most painful repercussion in Turkey."

During this same time Russia was struggling to come to a satisfactory arrangement with France, also. France, which had little intention of paying her own unconditional debts to the United States, had never ceased to bicker over the highly controversial debts which she claimed from Russia. In 1924 under the liberal Premier, Edouard Herriot, France recognized Russia, but Herriot was forced to start new negotiations on the debts. After two years of discussion, Russian and French delegates met in Paris in February, 1926, to sign a treaty. The settlement which the French demanded involved an annual payment of 125,000,000 gold francs ($25,000,000). The Russians offered 40,000,000 gold francs ($8,000,000) a year for sixty-two years, providing France made them a loan. At the end of the year the discussions were still dragging along.

The Soviets were likewise working on the problem of their American relations. In 1925 W. Averell Harriman had undertaken to organize American participation in financing Russo-German trade and Felix M. Warburg and other outstanding bankers had stood ready to co-operate in the project; but Herbert Hoover as Secretary of Commerce found reasons for obstructing it, thereby giving the equally anti-Russian elements in the State Department occasion to vent their antipathy by vetoing the arrangement—to the satisfaction and profit of German financiers.*

For a brief time early in 1926, nevertheless, it looked as if Russo-American relations would be promoted from a strange source, the Standard Oil Company. The company had done some business with the Moscow Naphtha Syndicate and saw possibilities of bigger deals ahead; consequently their public relations agent, Ivy L. Lee, was instructed to start a nationwide propaganda campaign for recognition. But Sir Henry Deterding, always quick to resume his favorite role of red-baiter, interfered. He had at least one conversation with Walter Teagle of Standard Oil (whose recent resignation was connected with somewhat dubious transactions with the I. G. Farben interests in Germany), and Ivy L. Lee was told to abandon the propaganda campaign.

Another strong force working against recognition was the American Federation of Labor, which was violently hostile to the Soviet Union. The conservative leaders of this organization seemed to be afraid that if Soviet Russia were recognized, more radical labor groups in the United States would come to the foreground and they themselves would lose influence with the working masses.

Various well-established religious organizations also threw their weight against the recognition of a "Godless nation," which was, in their view, "conducting an all-out war against religion." A number of Senators, particularly Senator Borah, had been victimized by whispering campaigns originating in England concerning Russia's plans for a world revolution, and also influenced by far-from-truthful campaigns organized by certain White Russians who, incidentally, had some effect on the State Department and even more with American representatives in Riga, Warsaw, and Berlin.

The most effective arguments advanced by those who were opposed to any official relations with the Soviet Government were: first, that it

* Louis Fischer, *The Soviets in World Affairs*, pp. 701 ff.

was an unstable regime which might collapse on short notice; second, that it was unrepresentative, established by a brutal and fortuitous seizure of power by an irresponsible minority that held the Russian people helpless in the grip of terrorism; third, that the Soviet Government by repudiating all debts owed to foreign governments, banks and individuals, and confiscating private property belonging to foreign nationals, had denied the sanctity of international obligations which was prerequisite for international intercourse; and fourth, that the Soviet Government had as its primary purpose the promotion of world revolution and that that would be facilitated by recognition and diplomatic privileges, which, as Bainbridge Colby said, "would become a channel for intrigues and . . . propaganda for revolution. . . ."

The Soviet Government repeatedly offered to discuss compensation for the debts and confiscated property and denied all the other contentions, offering to submit evidence in support of the denials, but every attempt on their part to take up all these problems in the spirit of mutual accommodation and of "mutual non-intervention in internal affairs" (note of Chicherin, December 16, 1923) was ignored. The State Department insisted, contrary to international usage, that acceptance in principle of the claims of the United States Government was the indispensable prerequisite to any negotiations.

United States Government claims were later assessed at $192,601,297 plus about $100,000,000 in interest. The total Russian war debt in the United States amounted to about $279,000,000, without interest. American sources estimated private property claims to be in excess of $300,000,000; the Russians maintained that they amounted to $61,000,000.

As to Communist propaganda, few really believed that there was any real danger. As Roy Howard of the Scripps-Howard Press, hardly a Soviet sympathizer, once commented: "Personally, I think the menace of Bolshevism in the United States is about as great as the menace of a sunstroke in Greenland or chilblains in the Sahara." William Philip Simms of the Scripps-Howard Press, said:

"If we cannot make a success of Soviet Russia, pray tell me what good it would do us to spend all those perfectly fantastic billions— which I assure you we don't have and never did have—for foreign propaganda? Conversely, if Russia blooms under our system, no propaganda will be needed." And later (December 1, 1930) Stalin in an interview with Walter Duranty dismissed the whole matter: "All this talk of propaganda is ridiculous. Propaganda doesn't do *anything*. Constitutions and systems are changed by natural causes, not by talk or books." * But the argument for years had a scare-value that constrained the timid and uninformed.

On February 23, 1927, Chamberlain warned the Soviet Government against defaming, attacking, and offending the British Empire.† "A continuation of such acts . . ." he declared, must sooner or later result in an abrogation of the Trade Agreement . . . "and even the severance of ordinary diplomatic relations." It took Litvinoff only three days to prepare and send his answer, which affirmed the fundamental right of Russians to discuss world affairs, including British policies, in their own country without having it construed as a violation of the treaty provision covering propaganda; and for every citation that Chamberlain had made from the Soviet press or personalities to show anti-British bias, Litvinoff quoted English attacks on the Soviet Union, including statements by such outstanding men as Churchill, speeches in the House of Commons, and insults even to the accredited Russian diplomats in London in British Conservative papers. And he put the responsibility for any break in relations which might ensue right at the door of the British Foreign Office.

This, of course, did not deter the Tory Government, and their determined hostility continued to manifest itself in repeated varied attacks. Thus in Peking on April 6, 1927, the police raided the Soviet Embassy and published documents said to have been confiscated there, proving Soviet revolutionary activities in China. A month later, on May 5, Litvinoff called the Moscow representatives of the foreign press to the Narkomindel and denounced these papers as frauds and forgeries.

One week later, on May 12, at 4:20 P.M., a large force from Scotland Yard entered the building of Arcos—a private British company directing exports and imports from Russia—and the Soviet Trade Delegation at 49 Moorgate and proceeded to search the premises and the employees. Only an hour afterwards, and in response to repeated demands, did they produce a warrant. They took over the telephone exchange, stationed men at all exits, detained the employees until late into the

* Walter Duranty, *op. cit.,* p. 239.
† Louis Fischer, *op. cit.,* pp. 682 ff.

night, and opened safes and steel boxes with pneumatic drills. After a hasty study of documents, they took many away. Everyone, including two women who had diplomatic passports, was forced to submit to a search of their persons.

The official reason given for this illegal raid was that a secret document had disappeared from the War Office and, according to the counterespionage agency of the British military intelligence, it had been traced to a Bolshevist secret agent. Scotland Yard was told to look for the missing document in the Trade Delegation and the Arcos, but not at the Embassy. Baldwin and Chamberlain did not want to go too far.

Baldwin was presented with an official note of protest from the Soviet Embassy, pointing out that the chairman of the Trade Delegation enjoyed immunity and diplomatic privileges by the terms of the Anglo-Russian Trade Agreement of 1921. Diplomatic immunity, according to the Russians and to all interpretations of international law, applied not only to one's pockets, but to one's papers, office, and home. This immunity had been violated. Scotland Yard had even opened sealed diplomatic mail which the addressees had not yet read. However, the British Government was unwilling to interfere with Scotland Yard's search, and in spite of the note of protest the police remained in the offices of the Trade Delegation.

At the end of the fourth day the document had not been found. Later, when Britain was forced to make public the documents found and confiscated in the raid, which, incidentally, did not lead to any arrest or even indictment, the *Manchester Guardian* said (on May 25): "There is nothing to prove that the Trade Delegation has done anything which a British Communist might not legally do or anything worse than the things of which the British government had before complained." The findings were meager—and that in spite of Scotland Yard having examined thousands of letters. Therefore, when the Government finally published its White Paper, several documents were included that had not been found in the raid, but had been obtained by means which Austen Chamberlain refused to reveal in the House of Commons, though other speakers in the House pointed out that they were evidently obtained by British agents using the same kind of espionage tactics that the Government was trying to employ as a cause of grave complaint against the Soviet Government. The Opposition made it known through its leader, Clynes, that it considered the raid "obviously a failure" and the White Paper "a bright, diverting, comic publication."

Yet since Baldwin had gone so far, he had to go a step further. On May 24, 1927, he declared that the British Government would "terminate the Trade Agreement and require the withdrawal of the Trade Delegation from London and recall the British Mission from Moscow."

The break of diplomatic relations followed automatically, notification thereof being sent by Chamberlain to Moscow on May 26, but Arcos and other Russian commercial organizations were allowed to continue. Even the Tory prejudices would not be allowed to injure British pockets.

Despite this continuation of commercial relations, there was genuine alarm in Moscow and a real fear lest England recommence the Wars of Intervention where she had left off seven years before. But Litvinoff was coolly skeptical. England, he thought, had broken off relations in the hope that other countries would follow, and she wanted nothing further than a general boycott of the Soviet Union. Britain's role in the Wars of Intervention had been costly and futile. Her more sober statesmen were not likely to allow the experiment to be repeated.

What were the chances of the boycott which Litvinoff foresaw? On the very day of Baldwin's speech, Aristide Briand told Chicherin that France was not bound by England's policy towards Russia. This was reassuring. Germany, too, indicated that she would remain strictly neutral.

In June, Soviet Minister P. Voykov was murdered in Warsaw, and Litvinoff demanded the prosecution and expulsion of all enemies of Russia from Poland. Chamberlain thought (possibly hoped) that a Russo-Polish war might result and asked Stresemann in Geneva whether Germany would permit the transfer of British and French troops to Poland. Stresemann hedged. He did not want to give an immediate answer. In fact, he never answered at all.

However, Chamberlain and his Tory associates were not easily put off. It was at this point, during the session of the League in June, 1927, that Chamberlain again tried to create a united front against Russia. He called a secret meeting of English, French, German, Belgian, Italian, and Japanese representatives to discuss the Soviet problem. Briand presided. Chamberlain emphasized the danger of Bolshevik propaganda not only to Great Britain but to all Europe and Asia as well. Briand disagreed. He said that the Bolsheviki had not proved to be disturbers of the peace but rather a barrier to chaos.

Thus, by the middle of 1927, the Soviet Union's international position, after having greatly improved in 1926, had again deteriorated, to the point where it was ambiguous if not actually alarming.

CHAPTER EIGHT

Disarmament

THE Moscow disarmament conference had been practically ignored by the Powers, but the Soviet Government, as represented by Litvinoff, had important contributions to offer on this major international problem. Geneva was the answer, and in time Stalin and Chicherin were convinced that Russia might well be represented at the disarmament conferences there. Finally in April, 1927, this was rendered possible by an apology from the Swiss Government, due to pressure from various sources, for the Conradi affair and the accompanying anti-Soviet activities.

Litvinoff made clear before he left Moscow the position that he would take in Geneva: "The Government of the Soviet Union," he said, "has never concealed its mistrust of the readiness and ability of capitalist nations to destroy the system of war among peoples, and therefore to achieve disarmament." *

When Litvinoff reached Switzerland it soon became evident that the formal amity presumably established with the Swiss Government was largely illusory. Both the authorities and the citizens showed themselves unfriendly. Visas were refused for a number of Russian journalists and Litvinoff's request for permission to establish a permanent Russian office in Geneva was rejected.

Personally, Litvinoff made himself inconspicuous, taking rooms in a family hotel, the Pension d'Angleterre, not on the lake, and too modest to have a ballroom or even tennis courts, or the facilities for giving a diplomatic dinner, had Litvinoff wished to. And in appearance he was equally unobtrusive—no red ties, just a quiet little bourgeois, eccentric only for his broad-brimmed black hat, which had no diplomatic precedent.

With his very first speech, however, he became a figure to be re-

* Louis Fischer, *op. cit.*, pp. 747-748.

marked. The delegates were startled by its tenor but genuinely impressed by the speaker's force and sincerity. This was delivered on November 30, 1927:

"The Government of the Union of Socialist Soviet Republics, having been unable to participate in the three sessions which have already been held by the Preparatory Commission of the Disarmament Conference, has entrusted its delegation to the fourth session of the Preparatory Commission to make a declaration covering all questions connected with the problem of disarmament.

"1. The Government of the Union of Socialist Soviet Republics adheres to the opinion it has always held that under the capitalist system no grounds exist for counting upon the removal of the causes giving rise to armed conflicts. Militarism and navalism are essentially natural consequences of the capitalist system. By the very fact of their existence, they intensify existing differences, giving a vast impetus to all potential quarrels and inevitably converting these into armed conflicts.

"The people in all countries, however, enfeebled and impoverished by the imperialist world war of 1914–18 are imbued with the determination to struggle against imperialist wars and for the guaranteeing of peace between the nations.

"This is precisely what has made it possible for the Soviet Government to accept the invitation of the League of Nations, the latter having expressed itself in favor of disarmament. In so doing, the Soviet Government demonstrates in the face of the whole world its will to peace between the nations and wishes to make clear to all the real inspirations and true desires of the other States with regard to disarmament.

"Despite the fact that the World War of 1914–18 was called the 'war to end war,' the whole history of post-war international relations has been one of continuous and systematic increase of armed forces in the capitalist States and a vast increase of the general burden of militarism. So far none of the solemn promises of the League of Nations has been even partially fulfilled, while in all its activities in this regard the League of Nations has systematically evaded setting the question in a practical light.

"All the work done by the Preparatory Commission in this regard has been, so far, of a purely decorative nature. Indeed, the League of

Nations only approached the question of general disarmament in 1924. It was decided to call a conference on general disarmament on May 1, 1925, but up to the present not only has the matter of general disarmament not advanced a single step but the date of the conference has not even been fixed.

"Likewise, the League of Nations has been fruitlessly engaged upon the question of the limitation of war budgets since 1920.

"The reluctance to put into practice the policy of disarmament was manifested both in the methods adopted and the alteration of the questions of disarmament and guarantees, while simultaneous attempts were made to sum up in detail all the factors determining the armed power of the various countries concerned. Such a setting of the question, evoking endless and fruitless arguments on so-called military potential, affords an opportunity for the indefinite postponement of the fundamental and decisive question: the actual dimensions of disarmament.

"There can be no doubt that by setting the question thus at the coming Disarmament Conference not only will it be impossible to achieve the curtailment of existing armaments but States belonging to the League of Nations may even receive legal sanction for increasing their armaments.

"The Soviet Government has systematically endeavored to get the question of disarmament definitely and practically formulated. Its endeavors have, however, always encountered determined resistance from the other States. The Soviet Government—the only one to show in deeds its will to peace and disarmament—was not admitted to the Washington Conference of 1921–22, devoted to questions of the curtailment of naval armaments. The proposal of general disarmament made by the Soviet delegation to the Genoa Conference on April 10, 1922, was rejected by the Conference. Despite this opposition, the Soviet Government has never relaxed in its determined endeavors with regard to disarmament. In December, 1922, a Conference was called in Moscow, by the Soviet Government, of representatives of the border States for the joint discussion of the problem of proportional curtailment of armaments. The Soviet Government agreed to a considerable diminution of its armaments despite the fact that this would not affect many Great Powers always ready, whether under the obligation of treaties or

not, to come to the assistance of the other countries represented at the
Moscow Conference should these be involved in conflicts with the
Soviet State. A definite scheme for the limitation of armaments was proposed at the Conference by the Soviet Government. This scheme was,
however, rejected."

The audience was not large. Less than fifty persons had gathered in
one of the many small conference rooms of the National Hotel in
Geneva. It was, after all, a committee meeting, only a preparatory conference for disarmament. Preparatory—and this, nine years after the
World War had ended, nine years after the first universal demand for
general disarmament, motivated equally by humane and economic reasons, though when the horrors of war slowly faded in men's memories,
economic considerations were uppermost in the minds of the representatives of the Great Powers.

That the commission, as Litvinoff said, did a lot of "decorative
work," was chiefly because the issue itself was ambiguous. Would a
partial disarmament prevent wars? Why should smaller armies de-
crease the likelihood of future conflicts?

Further complications were implicit, moreover, in the constantly
diminishing birth rate of France, in contrast to the ever-growing one of
Germany. French statesmen knew that France alone would never have
been able to defeat Germany in 1918. They had reason to doubt
whether, in a second assault by Germany, France's former allies would
come to her aid again; yet such aid would be even more essential with
the ratio of strength changing steadily in Germany's favor. America
had adopted a policy of isolation, and England, entirely misjudging
the real balance of power, was very much concerned about France as a
threat to European peace, greatly underestimating future danger from
Germany.

For this the French themselves were in part to blame. They had no
hope of genuine universal disarmament; with partial disarmament,
given their depressing population statistics, they would almost certainly be at a fatal disadvantage. They dared not present their case
frankly, because a full statement of the facts would be an admission of
weakness to both their own people and the world, and a candid avowal
of their skepticism of real world peace would only further antagonize
the English and convince them more firmly that France rather than

Germany was the menace. Thus the saber-rattling which made the English suspicious expressed the sincere and almost unanimous conviction throughout France that she would have to rely on a strong army. These facts inevitably reduced the work of the Preparatory Commission to a tissue of hypocrisy.

Litvinoff's strategy was to challenge the elaborate pantomime which the conference staged for its world audience with a specific program, and he now led up to this:

Despite the skeptical attitude of the Government of the Union of Socialist Soviet Republics towards the labors of the League of Nations, it accepted the invitation of December 12, 1925, to attend the coming Disarmament Conference, and only the Soviet-Swiss conflict, evoked by the assassination of M. Vorovsky, Minister Plenipotentiary, and the subsequent acquittal of the assassins by the Swiss Court, prevented the Union of Socialist Soviet Republics from attending the previous sessions of the Preparatory Commission.

In now sending its delegation to the fourth session of the Preparatory Commission on Disarmament, the Government of the Union of Socialist Soviet Republics has authorized it to present a scheme for general and complete disarmament.

. . . .

II. The delegation of the Union of Socialist Soviet Republics is authorized by its Government to propose the complete abolition of all land, naval and air forces.

The Government of the Union suggests the following measures for the realization of this proposal:

"(a) The dissolution of all land, sea and air forces and the non-admittance of their existence in any concealed form whatsoever.

"(b) The destruction of all weapons, military supplies, means for chemical warfare and all other forms of armament and means of destruction in the possession of troops or in military or general stores.

"(c) The scrapping of all warships and military air vessels.

"(d) The discontinuance of calling up citizens for military training either in armies or public bodies.

"(e) Legislation for the abolition of military service, either compulsory, voluntary or recruited.

"(f) Legislation prohibiting the calling-up of trained reserves.

"(g) The destruction of fortresses and naval and air bases.

"(h) The scrapping of military plants and factories of war industry equipment in general industrial works.

"(i) The discontinuance of assigning funds for military purposes both on State budgets and those of public bodies.

"(j) The abolition of military, naval and air ministries, and the dissolution of general staffs and military administrations, departments and institutions of every kind.

"(k) The legislative prohibition of military propaganda and military training of the population and of military education both in State and public bodies.

"(l) The legislative prohibition of the patenting of all kinds of armaments and means of destruction with the view to the removal of incentives to the invention of the same.

"(m) Legislation making the infringement of any of the above stipulations a grave crime against the State.

"(n) The withdrawal or corresponding alteration of all legislative acts, both of national or international scope, infringing the above stipulations."

III. The delegation of the Union is empowered to propose the execution of the above program of complete disarmament as soon as the Convention in question comes into force, in order that all the necessary measures for the destruction of military stores be completed in a year's time.

The Soviet Government considers that the above scheme for the execution of complete disarmament is the simplest and most conducive to peace.

In the case, however, of capitalist States rejecting immediate actual abolition of standing armies, the Soviet Government in its desire to facilitate the achievement of a practical agreement on complete disarmament, is prepared to make a proposal for complete disarmament to be carried out simultaneously by all contracting States, by gradual stages, during a period of four years, the first stage to be accomplished in the course of the coming year.

National funds freed from war expenditure, to be employed by each State at its own discretion, but exclusively for productive and cultural purposes.

IV. Whilst insisting upon the views just stated, the delegation of the Union of Socialist Soviet Republics is nevertheless ready to participate in any and every discussion of the question of the limitation of armaments whenever practical measures really leading to disarmament are proposed.

V. The delegation declares that the Government of the Union fully subscribes to the Convention on the prohibition of the application to military purposes of chemical and bacteriological substances and processes, expresses its readiness to sign the Convention immediately while insisting on an early date being fixed for its ratification by all States, and considers that, in order to insure the practicability of the Convention, it would be necessary to raise the question of the establishment of workers' control over those chemical industries susceptible of being rapidly converted to war purposes in States having a highly developed chemical industry.

We have laid before you our program of disarmament, but realize that its radical and exhaustive nature may make it appear at the first glance complex, difficult of realization and perhaps even Utopian. This, however, is merely because the problem of complete disarmament has always been treated as a forbidden subject and never yet thoroughly dealt with. We understand perfectly that the realization of this program may not be compatible with certain political interests, chiefly those of the Great Powers, the interests of war industries or those of the numerous groups of speculators, but I contend that in itself the problem of complete disarmament presents no difficulties and is capable of rapid and easy solution.

It is in any case a great deal simpler, and would require far less time to work out in detail, than the schemes which have so far been used as a basis for the work of the Preparatory Commission. I confess that, on acquainting myself with the findings of the Commission, I was aghast at the complexity, confusion and multiplicity of the questions with which that of disarmament had become involved. The Commission had, in effect, devoted several sessions to the discussion of the enumeration and headings of the clauses to make up an international Convention for limitation of armaments. Unanimity has only been achieved with regard to certain trivial and common points. The overwhelming majority of the clauses—or rather their headings —evoked dissensions which have so far failed to be reconciled either by the Commission itself or by private negotiations between the Governments concerned. If and when, however, these dissensions have been reconciled, the Commission still will be only at the threshold of its real difficulties. The Commission will have to agree to the satisfaction of all as to what constitutes security for each country, and, individually, the extent and importance of its international obligations, its geographical peculiarities and other special features, before the level of its effectives, technical armaments, military and air vessels, etc., can be established.

The mere enumeration of these questions will suffice to bring before us the utter helplessness—more, the Utopianism—of expecting this question to be solved within any imaginable period.

The latest manifestations of international life, various international trea-

ties recently concluded, lead not to the unification but rather to the still further division of the European and non-European countries into political
groupings, and to the intensification of their mutual antagonisms, and do
not afford the slightest grounds for optimism as to the outcome of the questions before the Preparatory Commission.

To crown all, attempts are still being made to delay for a long time to
come the work of the Preparatory Commission pending the solution of a
series of political questions not less confused and complex than those I have
already mentioned.

One thing is certain: if the present basis of the Preparatory Commission's
work is not changed, it is—even if not exploded by the abundance and
weight of its own internal differences—condemned to years, if not decades,
of work either completely sterile or productive of quite intangible results.

We live in a time in which the outbreak of fresh wars is no mere theoretical danger. This is not merely our opinion; many reasonable statesmen
in capitalist countries have expressed the same fears quite recently. The imminence of war is making itself felt everywhere. If it is to be averted, something will have to be done. In our opinion, the best guarantee of security
for all peoples and all countries is immediate complete disarmament. This
problem should be faced immediately and solved in the shortest possible
time. Those countries postponing the solution of this problem are taking
upon themselves an enormous responsibility. I therefore beg to move on behalf of the Soviet delegation the following resolution:

"Whereas the existence of armaments and the tendency they show to
growth by their very nature inevitably lead to armed conflicts between nations, diverting the workers and peasants from peaceful productive labor
and bringing in its train countless disasters;

"Whereas armed force is a weapon in the hands of Great Powers for the
oppression of peoples in small and colonial countries; and

"Whereas the complete abolition of armaments is at present the only real
means of guaranteeing security and affording a guarantee against the outbreak of war;

"The Fourth Session of the Preparatory Commission for the Disarmament Conference resolves:

"(1) To proceed immediately to the working out in detail of a draft
Convention for complete and general disarmament on the principle proposed by the Delegation of the Union of Socialist Soviet Republics;

"(2) To propose the convocation, not later than March, 1928, of a Disarmament Conference for the discussion and confirmation of the proposals
provided for in paragraph (1)."

We are fully aware that certain circles will endeavor to stigmatize our program and resolution as propaganda. We are quite ready to accept this challenge and declare that we are making propaganda for peace and shall continue to do so. If the Preparatory Commission for the Disarmament Conference is not a suitable place in which to make peace propaganda, then apparently we are here under a misunderstanding. The Soviet Government pursues, and has always pursued, a resolute peace policy which it has always shown, and is still showing in deeds as well as in words. Only a few days ago, when the clouds of war seemed to be darkening the horizon on the east of Europe more ominously than ever, everything in its power was done by the Soviet Government to avert a calamity. It brought all possible arguments to bear upon the Lithuanian Government to persuade it immediately to declare the cessation of the state of war between Lithuania and Poland. The Soviet Government was also instrumental in persuading Lithuania's other two neighbors to offer the same advice, and steps were also taken by it in Warsaw tending towards the maintenance of peace. This peace policy of my Government gives us a special right to declare that we shall not let a single opportunity slip for making the most intensive propaganda for peace and disarmament.

When Litvinoff finished, the president of the meeting remarked that "the difference existing between the points of view of the Soviet Delegation and that of the other members of the Commission, as it had hitherto appeared, consists not in regard to the aim . . . but in the methods to be used to attain it."

And there the meeting ended.

After the speech, there were three groups that had a welcome for him: The Society of Friends, a woman's organization for Peace and Reconciliation, and the representatives of the press.

It was the press who immediately realized that in Litvinoff there had emerged on the world's stage a personality of outstanding interest. The liberal press saw in him something of a prophet, opening up surprising vistas; they could not foresee the results of his policies, but they at once recognized him for a courageous and sincere man.

He understood the problems and points of view of the correspondents, spoke to them with frankness and vigor, and with a gargantuan humor which they vastly relished. The respect and good will that he won from the press included those of the most conservative papers of

Europe and even those whose editorial policy was definitely anti-Soviet. Whenever Litvinoff spoke, the press gallery was crowded. Any lunch in his honor, or evening entertainment or communication, brought the correspondents out in full force. This friendship and good will of the press provided Litvinoff and his ideas with a world-audience that would have been impossible had he followed the rather stuffy style of many of the delegates.

2

Litvinoff's speech representing Russian foreign policy should not have surprised the men of Geneva. Prime Minister Rykov had expressed the same views in his speech to the Fourth Congress of the Soviets in April, 1927:

"The League of Nations is endeavoring to prove its 'pacifism' by convening a disarmament conference. But the preparatory work of the conference indicates that it is less a disarmament conference, than a conference to discuss how to maintain, with the least expenditure, the military rule of those countries which at present still dominate the whole world. We are prepared to accept the most drastic measures for the prevention of war and competition in armaments, and we call upon the Powers to do this. We propose that the standing armies be completely abolished, that war industry be done away with and a real control be set up consisting of representatives of the people, of the workers, of the trade unions, and of the peasants."

Stalin himself had been equally clear in an article that appeared on July 28, 1927, in *Izvestia*:

The Soviet Government must pursue, firmly and unwaveringly, its policy of peace and of peaceful relations notwithstanding all the provocative moves of our enemies, notwithstanding all the pin-pricks at our prestige. The provocateurs in the camp of the enemy taunt us and will continue to taunt us that our policy of peace is the child of our weakness, of the weakness of our army. . . . We cannot and must not play into their hands. We must go our way, defending the cause of peace, demonstrating our will to peace, revealing the criminal designs, and branding them as the protagonists of war.

But though the principles that Litvinoff presented to the committee had thus been definitely formulated by members of his Government on various occasions, the delegates were shocked.

There was no mistaking their ironical, not to say contemptuous attitude. Many of the military delegates obviously thought the speech was a
joke and the diplomats put it down as nothing more serious than a
verbal demonstration; a demagogic appeal to the press and the general
public, a disingenuous attempt to confuse the issue with utter impracti-
calities. A considerable number of the delegates sought to conceal their
embarrassment or express their ill will by descending to the tricks of
schoolboy rudeness, shifting in their chairs, coughing, whispering to
each other and managing at times to make so much ill-bred noise that
Litvinoff could scarcely be heard. Despite the obvious hostility, Litvinoff spoke with ease, confidence and considerable force. He knew that
he had to reach a larger, more important audience than the group before him whose attitudes and conclusions were already made up.

Lord Halifax rather ostentatiously left the room. Sir John Simon
closed his eyes as though fast asleep, a signal to his colleagues that he
was, quite properly of course, bored, but also a good camouflage, for
actually Sir John slumbered not nor slept. He was too intelligent not
to be fully alive to what was going on, and afterwards privately congratulated Litvinoff quite warmly on the force and ability of his argument. Sir John was a connoisseur of argument.

Similarly the press, by profession good judges of news value, which
in such instances means good prophets of historical value, were aware
that here was a momentous utterance. The balcony on the left of the
hall was astir with excitement, as the reporters hung on every syllable
—or rather every one that they could follow, for Litvinoff was speaking
with a rhythm and accent that obscured some of his words; and the
minute he finished they rushed out of the room to cable summaries all
over the world.

The few spectators who had bothered to come to this meeting of the
Preparatory Commission manifested an equally tense interest. Evidently the people were more concerned with real disarmament than
were their governments, and no official instructions forbade them to
show it.

This recognition by simple people of Litvinoff's honest devotion to
the cause of peace was typified by a group of elderly American ladies
living at the Geneva Young Women's Christian Association. Nothing
could be further from their ideals than Communism, but peace was

important to them as it was to Litvinoff, and they appreciated his sincerity. They became his champions and invited him to the one dinner given in his honor during that stay in Geneva. He accepted and found himself the only man present.

The dissemination of Litvinoff's speech through the world by the press provoked angry attacks from other delegates: the Russian representatives had been interested only in making the conference appear ridiculous; it was all propaganda they insisted—an accusation that Litvinoff had explicitly predicted in the speech.

Actually, Litvinoff had simply expressed a conviction held by objectively thinking people the world over. He had, systematically and in detail, developed a self-evident proposition: disarmament means the destruction of all kinds of fighting equipment, and the abolition of its means of replacement. But he had gone deeper than that, when clearly and insistently he pointed out that in the problem of war or peace there was only one alternative: *world* war or *world* peace. Later he gave this important insight a classic formulation: peace is indivisible.

The principle that "peace is one and indivisible" had already become almost tantamount to a religion for Litvinoff, and had for years taken a central place in his policy. He had first apprehended it during his short stay at the conference of the Allied Socialists in London in February, 1915. Then, long after, while following the Russo-German negotiations at Brest-Litovsk from his post as unrecognized Ambassador in London, he found it confirmed. He coined the phrase on February 25, 1920, in a note to the Allies who were concluding peace with all their former enemies while fighting their former ally, Russia; but it was not until 1932 that it attained world currency. Sir Perceval Phillips, then representing the London *Daily Mail* at Geneva, adopted it, and the Soviet delegation used it in several statements. Litvinoff himself says of it: "This phrase and the definition of aggression and aggressor [which he was to formulate in 1933] are perhaps my contribution to the abstract science of peace." Few peace slogans have survived, but Litvinoff's "peace is indivisible" will live, because it is profoundly and enduringly true.

Yet nothing, of course, is more agitating than truth to those who have half-hidden motives for not facing it. Or as the French delegate Joseph Paul-Boncour had murmured to one of his colleagues: "It's too simple." In complexity, as politicians and lawyers have known for centuries, lies the most effective evasion.

Litvinoff, watching his colleagues' revealing agitations, finally decided to soothe them. So in a short speech he assured them that he had no intention of making the conference seem ridiculous. He had meant every word he said. Probably many of them were indeed conventional enough to accept this as an apology.

No wonder the press was interested in this man Litvinoff. Eight years before, Litvinoff, at Dorpat, had said flatly that Russia did not want any foreign correspondents within her borders because "the Soviet Union had suffered enough from the lies and calumnies of the capitalistic press." In short, on Russia's behalf he discarded international journalism as an unnecessary evil. But at Geneva in 1927 he half changed his mind; not that he thought it any less evil, but he saw it might be necessary.

Out of Litvinoff's proposals came no action whatever, only a little fable, originally credited to the Spanish delegate, Don Salvador de Madariaga: Once upon a time the animals decided to disarm in order to live at peace. All believed it a good plan and all offered proposals. The tiger suggested that the elephant disarm by giving up his trunk. The elephant suggested that the lion disarm by getting rid of his teeth. The lion suggested that the snake disarm by renouncing its poisonous fangs. Finally, the Russian bear got up and said that everyone should disarm completely and then express their friendship by everyone giving everyone else a good big hug.

3

While Litvinoff was there in Geneva, the Franco-Russian debt conferences were still being slowly shoved along their weary way in Paris, and in September Russian Ambassador Rakovsky published a report on them. The French promptly characterized it as a fraud. As a matter of fact the report was accurate—but that only made it a blacker sin, since it was thereby a stronger weapon in the hands of Poincaré's enemies who could urge the reasonableness of the terms against Poincaré's fixed determination not to settle with the Soviets in any way. The issue thus became involved in French internal politics, including obscure inner-party feuds that have never been elucidated; and also it was used as a football in complex international petroleum manipulations. As a result of these cross-currents—most of them indifferent to the interests both of the French claimants and of French economy as a whole—Rakovsky had to leave Paris (September 30, 1927), and diplomatic relations between the two countries were just saved, not without impairment.

Litvinoff, hoping to improve the relations, asked, on December 2, for an interview with Aristide Briand, and two days later they met, Litvinoff thus seeing for the first time that man who had, in 1907, been instrumental in his release from prison in France, saving him from extradition by the Czarist police.

Litvinoff, like everyone else, was impressed by Briand. He looked more artist than diplomat—the shock of long gray hair, drooping mustache, unfailing cigarette—and was an artist in oratory, playing on his voice like a musical instrument, conjuring up with masterful ease exquisite words and powerful phrases. At his best when slightly in his cups, so that cold rationality did not constrain lyricism, he composed great impromptus on humanitarianism, peace, ethical ideals. His audience, including himself, was for the time being, at least, convinced, entranced, and elevated by an eloquence that was close to fine art.

In his youth Briand had been politically well to the Left and when at the age of forty he went actively into politics, still fought for liberal principles, notably the separation of Church and State. By 1927, however, his central policies were neither liberal nor realistic, especially his major tenet of friendship with Germany, for it was providing support for the trends that were leading to another world strife. Litvinoff saw him as a traitor to his own early self, an opportunist who had sacrificed idealism to calculation, and sold out liberalism to bourgeois reaction; and Briand's support of Germany must have seemed little short of obtuse to Litvinoff, who foresaw world disaster as the inevitable outcome of German policy.

At their first conference, the two men disagreed on important specific questions. According to the *Matin* of December 5, 1927, Briand sketched the plan of an "Eastern Locarno," including frontier guarantees, neutrality obligations, and peace assurances between Russia and Poland, Rumania and the Baltic states. Litvinoff immediately saw here the dangerous possibility of a Baltic-Balkan bloc led by Poland in united opposition to Bolshevism, and voiced his dissent.

Yet though Litvinoff was never bemused by Briand, either in general or in particular, he was always—even against his better judgment—a little partial to him. Perhaps Litvinoff sensed remnants of Briand's earlier, better self, lingering deep down under the politician, a Briand who did sincerely and earnestly long for a just, enduring peace.

4

During the negotiations between Briand and Litvinoff, the diplomatic world of Geneva was speculating as to whether the Russian representative would also meet the British delegate, Sir Austen Chamberlain, in an attempt to resume the relations which Chamberlain's party had broken off with such unattractive displays of enmity. Indeed, rumors became so rife that both the Russian and English delegations had several times seen fit to deny that any such conference was planned.

The two men had sat for days in the small auditorium of the National Hotel where the Preparatory Commission was meeting, affecting to ignore each other's presence, while the rest of Geneva chuckled. Most felt that Litvinoff's cool nerves had helped him make a better figure than the bewildered, embarassed Englishman, who scarcely knew where to look.

The meeting of the Preparatory Commission drew towards its close and Litvinoff asked permission from the Swiss Government to leave the country by way of Zurich, for he wanted to visit the room where Lenin had lived throughout the war. But the Swiss Government, consistent with its inimical attitude, refused this simple personal request.

Litvinoff's departure was then announced for Saturday, December 5; Chamberlain was to leave two days later. On Friday the gulf between the two Foreign Ministers and their countries seemed as wide as ever, but gossip began circulating in the Hotel Beau Rivage, where the British delegation stopped, that Chamberlain was anxious to meet Litvinoff. It was even whispered that Chamberlain's secretary, W. Selby, had said so. The rumors reached George Slocomb, then chief correspondent of the London *Daily Herald;* he went to the Pension d'Angleterre, and induced Litvinoff to say that he would be willing to make a formal request to be received by Sir Austen, if he were privately assured that it would be granted.

In the meantime, Selby, who had been notified, denied that he had intimated that Chamberlain wanted to meet Litvinoff. Litvinoff, when he heard about it, shrugged his shoulders. Slocomb, however, did not accept the situation. He telephoned to the Beau Rivage, got through to Chamberlain himself, told him the story, and suggested that if Litvinoff were assured in advance of the response, he might still be willing to make such a request.

Later in the evening Slocomb received a cryptic telephone message that the British Foreign Secretary wanted him to know that "if a reasonable request were made to him, courtesy would dictate an appropriate reply."

Again Slocomb hurried to Litvinoff. He reached the Pension d'Angleterre at midnight and Litvinoff and his wife had already gone to bed. He woke them up and they discussed the situation in pajamas and dressing gown.

Finally, Litvinoff agreed to the experiment. Half-past midnight, Slocomb took up the telephone, called the Hotel Beau Rivage and asked for the secretary of the British delegation. Then he handed the receiver to Madame Litvinoff, who in a calm, cool voice enquired if Sir Austen would receive Mr. Litvinoff on the following morning. Sir Austen had retired for the night but a reply was promised for the next morning. Early next morning the answer came that Sir Austen would be glad to receive Mr. Litvinoff at three o'clock in the afternoon. Litvinoff had to change his reservations on the morning train for Berlin.

Thus met two men, one, who by every factor of temperament and interest, both personal and class, was committed to the effort to stop the historical economic process at the status quo, or if possible drag it backwards to a phase more favorable to his group; the other, who, at the behest of conviction, had in boyhood stripped himself of interests and ever since had marched far ahead of actual conditions, trying to clear the way for change and urge it on. The meeting could hardly be anything but a study in opposites. It took less than an hour, without witnesses. According to both Litvinoff and Chamberlain, only Comintern propaganda was discussed and no agreement was reached.

When Litvinoff returned and Slocomb asked him what had happened, Litvinoff remarked: "It was not worth postponing my departure."

Chamberlain, he said, had received him with formal courtesy, but beyond that had not been very cordial. Chamberlain had brought up the old accusations concerning the close relation between the Soviet Government and the activities of the Communist International. Litvinoff had answered that the Soviet Government could not suppress the Comintern, nor could it prevent Soviet citizens from speaking their views on developments in the capitalist world. He did not consider this propaganda. If the Soviet Government were to act as Chamberlain suggested, it would cease to be a Communist government. Litvinoff, furthermore, ventured to say that although the Conservative Party in England might be responsible for the conservative government, the conservative government was not responsible for the activities of the Conservative Party.

Sir Austen refused to see the point. At the end of the meeting the two statesmen agreed on a press release. It read:

Mr. Litvinoff having asked Sir Austen Chamberlain for an interview, a meeting took place between them at the Hotel Beau Rivage this afternoon. The meeting gave occasion for a frank exchange of views upon the relations between the Government of the Union of Socialist Soviet Republics and the British Government. It was not, however, found possible to reach any basis of agreement within the course of the interview.

Still, in spite of Litvinoff's momentary regret that he had not taken the earlier train to Berlin, he knew that the meeting had by no means been a complete failure. The fact that Chamberlain had received him sufficed to make him, and thus the Soviet Union, an even greater factor in international politics. He always believed in appearing on the international stage, even if only for the record. And to appear with Chamberlain at a time when no diplomatic relations existed between Russia and England would be noted throughout the world as an acknowledgment of Russia's status and importance.

Chamberlain had less reason to be satisfied. When he was later questioned about the episode in the House of Commons, he stated that he regretted the ineffectual meeting. He knew that what he had regarded as a gesture of diplomatic courtesy actually had helped

Litvinoff and Russia. When he was leaving Geneva and noticed Slocomb among the newspaper men at the station, he beckoned to him and said: "Do you think it was pleasant for me to shake the hand of the representative of men who killed a cousin of my sovereign?"

5

Early in 1927, before Litvinoff had forced the question of genuine disarmament out into the open, Briand had approached Frank B. Kellogg, then Secretary of State for the United States under President Coolidge, with a proposal of a two-Power pact which would substitute for the general ethical and humane condemnation of war, a specific legal prohibition. Since Sargon the Great more than 4,000 years ago, war had been accepted as a normal and legitimate means of determining international relations. Now it was to be outlawed. Such an agreement, would, first, make explicit and binding the United States' obligations in the settlement of world problems, and without active American recognition of her responsibility, as everyone knew, peace arrangements would lack the necessary scope and authority. Second, the pact would, it was thought, provide an unambiguous basis for marshaling world opinion against any aggressor, and through that promote restraining action.

There was nothing new in this convention; the principles had been formulated in the League Covenant. But pacifists and humanitarians believed or tried to believe that it offered new hope, and optimism fed on the fact that Secretary Kellogg was working to expand Briand's proposed two-Power agreement into a declaration committing the other nations also to "renouncing war as an instrument of national policy."

But how little substance it provided for honest pacifist hopes soon became evident; its very proponents were actually maneuvering it into another anti-Soviet instrument. World peace was to cloak a diplomatic offensive that would create a situation dangerous to world peace.

At the center of this new diplomatic aggression against the Russian Government was Kellogg's intense animosity. He repeated the demand that the Soviets unconditionally assume the debts of the preceding regime and also that the Soviets undertake compensation for expropriated private properties, without any chance to present their own considerable counter claims. This dogmatic ultimatum, quite contrary to international usage, the Russian Government was to take or leave, and if the latter, it had no right to complain at being cast out of such idealistic enterprises as the Briand-Kellogg Pact.

Business, of course, was another matter. Even outcast Russia would not be excluded from that as long as she offered the United States a good market. And an excellent market she was becoming. In the year preceding the Pact, the United States had bought from Russia $14,638,-500 worth of goods, but she had exported to Russia goods to the value of $96,717,000—a difference quite unusual, for the Soviets aimed to maintain an approximate trade balance with each country. The disparity was in part due to Russia's need for American goods; probably also the Russian Government—and Litvinoff in particular—wanted a closer and friendlier contact with the United States; for Litvinoff desired, above all, Washington recognition for the Soviet Union.

Kellogg and those who saw eye to eye with him seemed unaware that the nature and rights of property are inevitably a theory. Because they were accustomed to their theory, it seemed to have in their eyes the status of unchallengeable and enduring truth, and apparently they never examined the intricate debatable assumptions which it involves. They were righteously defending dogma—not to mention the advantages that that dogma assured them—against heresy. The Russians, on the contrary, saw them as blind and wicked worshipers of the golden calf.

Logically the only solution for such an impasse was to agree to differ, but none of the Powers was willing to relinquish an advantageous business connection, and Litvinoff knew that there could not be two detached units in a completely interrelated world. As usual, he was clearly aware of the futility of the proposal now before the nations, but he never forgot that the best remedy for suspicion is contact, and Soviet Russia, if she was to allay the uneasy hostility of the other nations, must whenever possible play in their games, however childish.

In this Litvinoff was supported at home only by Nikolai I. Bukharin, editor of *Izvestia*. His other Russian colleagues were so bored by the uselessness of the particular document that they refused to look beyond

it to the opportunity it offered for strengthening Russia's international standing. Chicherin was always opposed to international conferences and treaties, while Kalinin dismissed the problem by pointing out that the pact would amount only "to some more talk instead
of a real abolition of war," that it was nothing but a "huge smoke
screen put up by capitalistic powers to fool the workers and masses of
the world, to lull them into a feeling that war does not threaten."
Later, in May, 1929, Prime Minister Rykov said that "the Kellogg
Pact cannot be regarded as a preventive of war because that document contains no real guaranty against war."

True enough, in Litvinoff's opinion, but incidental; the point was,
to his mind, that it would be far easier for the Powers to resume
intervention into a Russia which was explicitly an outsider, than into a
co-signatory of a pact affirming the illegality of aggression.

Kellogg, feet firmly planted in his prejudices, which were shared
by the majority in the Government, would not budge. But finally he
had to shift his position—grudgingly and as little as possible: Russia
would be allowed to adhere, but only after the other Powers had
ratified the pact. Then he was pushed on another few inches to permitting Soviet Russia to sign immediately after the other fifteen
Powers, thus keeping Russia distinct from the "original" signatories,
and saving his own face by avoiding a meeting with any Russian
representative, for, he explained, he had "no desire to meet Chicherin
or Litvinoff in person." Yet even so, Kellogg continued to regret the
concessions that he had been forced to make.

Litvinoff was not accepting any such discrimination without protest,
but the only opening through which he could influence the situation
was Germany. On July 28, 1928, he and Krestinsky had Count
Brockdorff-Rantzau and some other German diplomats to luncheon
at the Russian Embassy in Berlin, and Litvinoff made it clear that he
also might have some objections or at least reservations.

The pact was signed in Paris on August 27, 1928—the year in which
rearmament costs among the nations reached the highest level since
the Versailles Treaty—by the representatives of fifteen States, using a
gold pen made for the occasion. That same day Jean Herbette, Ambassador of France to Soviet Russia, officially asked Litvinoff in Moscow, in the name of his Government and that of the United States,

in accordance with instructions from the State Department, if the Soviet Union wished to adhere to the pact. In reply Litvinoff requested all official correspondence pertaining to it.

The pact itself was of a kind to strike Litvinoff as almost useless, and Litvinoff's view was shared by both Stanley Baldwin and Winston Churchill. Churchill said of it: "It may well be that vague, general, pious affirmations like the Kellogg Pact do not carry much practical conviction."

Article 1 read: "The high contracting Parties solemnly declare in the name of their respective peoples that they condemn recourse to war for the solution of international controversies, and renounce it as an instrument of national policy in their relations with one another."

Article 2: "The high contracting Parties agree that the settlement or solution of all disputes or conflicts of whatever nature or of whatever origin among them shall never be sought except by pacific means."

Words without any probability, let alone guarantee of deeds, phrases without penalties; less force and conviction than in the dialogue of a Punch-and-Judy show; for there when one puppet gets obstreperous the others do at least knock him about.

Two days later Herbette again called on Litvinoff, who said that the Soviet Union would sign, but with reservations. Herbette declared that he could not accept any Soviet reservations since they would not be valid unless all the adherents accepted them. On August 31, Litvinoff summoned Herbette again and handed him the Soviet Union's note of adherence, and asked that the note be forwarded to Washington also. Both Great Britain and France had signed with reservations which almost in effect nullified the application of the pact at certain sensitive spots in their nationalist or imperialist interests. Russia therefore also included reservations in her note of adherence, chiefly rejecting the British and French reservations, and emphasized again one of Litvinoff's major theses: that the only guarantee of peace would be genuine disarmament. Then the Soviet Union was the first country to ratify the pact, the Comintern opposing it uncompromisingly to the end. It was not until September, 1930, that all sixty-one of the major States had adhered to it, and even then Brazil and Argentina still remained aloof.

6

The year that the pact was signed—1928—the Preparatory Disarmament Commission was to meet again in March, its preceding meeting having adjourned in December, 1927.

On February 20, 1928, Litvinoff announced from Moscow that he was ready to amplify and implement the proposals which he had made originally. He promised to be in Geneva by March 14, when the Preparatory Commission was to open its fifth session. He also suggested that Turkey be invited to the meeting.

He arrived punctually on March 14, for the opening session on the following day, and on March 19, the actual deliberations began on Litvinoff's proposal for immediate, complete and general disarmament, which was now presented in the form of a draft Convention, differing only in lesser points from his original statement:

The Soviet draft Convention of Immediate, Complete and General Disarmament, sent by the delegation of the Union of Socialist Soviet Republics to the Secretary-General of the League of Nations a month ago, is entirely based upon the main theses presented by the Soviet delegation at the fourth session of the Preparatory Commission in November last.

I have the honor to draw the attention of this Commission to the fact that the draft Convention provides for land, naval and air forces in all States to be put into a condition, not later than one year from its coming into force, rendering it difficult to employ them for warlike purposes, thus considerably limiting the possibilities of armed conflicts even before the carrying out of complete disarmament.

I consider it unnecessary to dwell in detail on the separate points of our draft Convention, since the latter was accompanied by a special explanatory note, sent to all members of the Commission.

I venture to remind the Commission that no attempts to give serious consideration to the Soviet proposals were made at its fourth session. During the extremely brief discussion of this question, not a single serious argument against the Soviet proposal nor any practical criticism of it was put forward. The Soviet delegation is naturally unable to accept as criticism such remarks as have been heard, namely: that the Soviet draft Convention is "too simple," or that, "even if complete disarmament were accomplished, the peoples would all the same fight among themselves in disarmed and disorganized masses with sticks, penknives, fists, etc."

The cautious attitude and the refusal to discuss our proposals, at the fourth session of the Commission, displayed by the other delegations may partly be explained by the novelty and unexpectedness of the Soviet proposals, although attempts were made to cast doubts even upon the novelty of our proposal. M. Beneš, I seem to remember, referred to a Norwegian proposal similar to ours supposed to have been made to the League of Nations. Now, I took the trouble to verify this statement, but was unable to find any traces whatsoever among the material of the League of Nations, including those with which the Disarmament Section of the League was so kind as to furnish me at my special request, of any proposals for general and complete disarmament.

At the Third Committee of the Assembly of the League in 1924, the Norwegian delegation mentioned wishes expressed by the Inter-parliamentary Union regarding the reduction of war budgets by one-half in the course of ten years. Even this was qualified by the stipulation that war expenditure incurred by individual States under the Covenant of the League of Nations should not be included in war budgets subject to reduction. There was not a word as to the abolition of the other half of war budgets, nor anything whatsoever about the reduction of armed forces and materials for war. The Danish delegation, referring to the same Inter-parliamentary Union, expressed a desire for the reduction of land armed forces in all countries in accordance with the resolutions of the Treaty of St. Germain, i.e. allowing each State the right to keep an army of 5,000 per million inhabitants, and naval armaments in accordance with the Versailles Treaty, i.e. 2,000 or 4,000 metric tons per million inhabitants. According to these calculations, the Union of Socialist Soviet Republics, for example, would be entitled to an army of almost 735,000 men, which would be an increase of 175,000 to its present standing army and 200,000 metric tons to its navy, while China would be entitled to a standing army of something like two millions. Such have been the most drastic ideas with regard to disarmament so far expressed in the League of Nations. I say "ideas," for none of these have been crystallized in the form of proposals or resolutions or made the subject of serious discussion. Lord Esher's plan, aspiring only to the reduction of land and air armed forces, had also nothing in common with the idea of complete and general disarmament. It may therefore be considered irrefutable that the proposal for complete and general disarmament has been put in a definite form before the League of Nations, and indeed brought into the sphere of international relations, for the first time, and the Union of Socialist Soviet Republics will always be proud to call this initiative its own. If, however, I dwell upon this point, it is from no motives of mere sentiment, but because it seems to me that, in certain League of Nations circles, an erroneous conception exists that the Soviet delegation is wasting the Preparatory Commission's time, on proposals already discussed and rejected by the League. Such an erroneous conception, unless corrected, might react unfavorably on the further procedure with regard to our proposal.

The Soviet delegation, anxious as it was to speed up the consideration of its draft Convention and thus bring nearer the beginning of real disarmament, nevertheless agreed to the postponement of the consideration of its proposals until the fifth (current) session, bearing in mind their novelty and desirous to give an opportunity for all members of the Commission and their Governments to make themselves ready for their practical consideration. With this aim, the Soviet delegation provided the Secretary-General of the League of Nations with the draft Convention, accompanied by an explanatory note, a month before the beginning of the fifth session of the Preparatory Commission, for despatch to the respective Governments, and now considers itself entitled to ask for the practical consideration of its proposals without further delay.

The Soviet delegation considers it essential once more to emphasize the fact that nothing but the fulfillment of the Convention for Immediate, Complete and General Disarmament proposed by the Government of the Union of Socialist Soviet Republics is capable of solving in a satisfactory manner the problem of general security and peace. This would also in itself solve a series of other vexed international problems, such as the freedom of the seas, and so on. At the same time, the execution of the Soviet scheme would not come up against the difficulties inevitably connected with partial disarmament. By way of example, I would cite the matter of control, for it is perfectly obvious that it must be infinitely easier to control total than partial disarmament.

I would further emphasize the fact that the basis of disarmament as proposed by the Soviet delegation, being uniform and applicable to all States, is therefore the most equitable and the least likely to arouse opposition from individual States. It is precisely this, in my opinion, which constitutes the obvious simplicity of our proposal, although, strange to say, some of its opponents have endeavored to make an added objection of this very simplicity.

The scheme offered for the consideration of the Preparatory Commission represents a single organic whole, which cannot be split up into separate parts. It is wholly penetrated by a single idea and therefore requires, first and foremost, consideration and acceptance of its underlying principles.

The Soviet delegation therefore considers it indispensable that general discussion should result in a reply—not merely theoretical but quite clear and definite—being given to the questions: Does the Preparatory Commission accept the principle of general disarmament during the period mentioned in the Convention? and, does it accept the proposal as to that rate of disarmament which would make war impossible in a year's time? The Soviet delegation considers that all other delegations and their Governments have had time enough, if they cared to, to study both the underlying idea of the Soviet proposal and the draft Convention in its finished form.

During the three-and-a-half months which have elapsed since the fourth session of the Preparatory Commission, the Soviet delegation has had ample opportunity to convince itself that the idea of complete disarmament has been met and accepted with enthusiasm by the broadest masses of both hemispheres and by all progressive and peace-loving elements in human society. The innumerable addresses and resolutions of sympathy from labor parties and multifarious organizations, groups and societies from all parts of the world which I am still receiving testify, among other things, to this. I will not take up your time by enumerating all of them, but will venture to read only one—a collective address I received here a few days ago, signed by representatives in thirteen countries of a hundred and twenty-four organizations (chiefly women's) whose total membership runs into many millions. This document, showing as it does the lively response among women evoked by the Soviet proposals, derives special importance from the extension of women's political rights now proceeding in some countries. Their declaration is as follows:

"On behalf of the growing world opinion, embodied in the organization which we represent, we gratefully welcome the courageous proposals of the Soviet Government for complete and general disarmament, and note with satisfaction that they are to be discussed in detail by the Preparatory Disarmament Commission at its next meeting on March 15.

"Being convinced that these proposals represent the will of the great mass of people in every country, who are determined to make an end of war, and that where the will exists practical means can be realized for giving it effect, we urge with all the strength at our command that the members of the Commission should examine the Russian proposals with the utmost care and with the determination to place before the International Disarmament Conference, when it meets, some concrete scheme for the complete disarmament of the world within a definite period of time."

This document bears one hundred and sixty-three signatures of the secretaries of the respective organizations (Annex 3).

The Soviet delegation entertains not the slightest doubt as to the acceptability and desirability of its proposals for the broad masses of the population, who now look to the Governments and the bourgeois groups and classes supporting them to make the next move.

Mere theoretical discussions and arguments about disarmament no longer meet the case—it is time to take practical steps towards the realization of disarmament. It seems to me there has been more than enough of discussion of disarmament. I shall venture to furnish members of the Commission with a few data (Annex 4) from which it will be seen that, as well as the general Assemblies of the League of Nations and the Council of the League, the thirty-eight sessions of which occupied themselves with the question of disarmament, no fewer than fourteen different commissions and other League organs devoted over a hundred and twenty sessions—not sittings, mark you, but sessions—to this question of disarmament, on which one hundred and eleven solutions have been passed by general Assemblies of the League and the Council of the League alone. Turning to the results of this vast quantity of work, the documentation of which has taken reams of paper, we are forced to the conclusion that not a single step of real importance has been taken towards the realization of disarmament. The Soviet delegation considers that an end should be put to a situation which may discredit the very idea of disarmament. It would be loath for its proposals to serve merely for the multiplication of commissions and sub-commissions or other organs, which would simply add to the existing resolutions with the same negligible results as those so far achieved. The Soviet Government has not sent its delegation to Geneva for this sort of work. Absorbed in the vast problem of rebuilding an enormous State, with a population of one hundred and fifty millions, on entirely new principles, and in the creation of a new social-economic structure in the face of the open opposition of the whole of the rest of the world and in the most unfavorable circumstances, it would never have turned aside from this work if its attitude to the problem of peace were not everything that is serious, practical and sincere and if this problem were not a keystone of its whole policy. In this connection, I may be permitted to mention, by way of illustration of the Soviet Government's serious attitude to the question under discussion here, the fact that, although it did not take part in the League of Nations Conference which passed the Protocol for the prohibition of the use in war of asphyxiating, poisonous or other gases and of bacteriological methods of warfare, only adhering to the latter at the last session of the Preparatory Commission, it was one of the States (three in all) to ratify this Protocol, still unfortunately a dead-letter owing to its non-ratification by other States, the majority of which are Members of the League.

We are aware that shallow persons and equally shallow Press organs pretend to see inconsistency between the peace-loving proposals of the Soviet Government and the maintenance and improvement of the Red Army. As a matter of fact, the Union of Socialist Soviet Republics already has a smaller army, not to mention its navy, than any other State in proportion to its population and the extent of its frontiers, while if we consider individual security—the favorite theme of this Assembly—it must be admitted that the Soviet Union is in a less favorable position than any other State. It has almost the whole of the world against it in unconcealed hostility to the new State. A glance at the Press of any country on any day—full of attacks, invectives and libels on the Union of Socialist Soviet Republics—will serve to show the extent of this hostility. A number of countries have to this day not recognized the existence of the Soviet Government, already in its eleventh year, and non-recognition can only be construed as an act of hostility. But even those countries recognizing the Soviet State not infrequently indulge, with a few exceptions, in hostile manifestations which are often grave tests of the patience and peaceableness of the Soviet Government. The new Soviet State has seen its territory invaded by foreign troops which caused detriment to the State, from the results of which it has not yet recovered. A part of the territory of the former Russian Empire, the population of which unmistakably aspires towards the Soviet Union is still occupied by foreign troops, preventing it from exercising its right of self-determination. All this notwithstanding, the Red Army has remained during the ten years of its existence, and will continue to remain, exclusively a weapon of defense. The Union of Socialist Soviet Republics does not require an army or a navy for any other purposes, all aggressive or imperialistic aims or ambitions being completely foreign to it.

In any case, the Soviet Government has declared, and still declares through its delegation in Geneva, that it is ready to abolish all the military forces of the Union in accordance with its draft Convention as soon as a similar decision is passed and simultaneously carried out by the other States. The Soviet Government declares once more that it is ready for this, and asks the other Governments represented here if they also are ready.

The Soviet Government expects a reply to this question at the present session of the Preparatory Commission at which all the more important States are represented. No sub-commissions or any other auxiliary organs—in fact, no body of a lesser composition and authority than the Preparatory

Commission—can give an answer to this question. The Soviet delegation hopes that this answer will be given quite openly, publicly, in the full light of day and under the control of public opinion. This reply should, of course, be brought up for final sanction by the International Disarmament Conference, an early date for the convocation of which is urged by the Soviet delegation.

The proposals formulated by myself in two questions are so clear as neither to demand nor admit of preliminary diplomatic negotiations and conversations between different countries and groups of countries.

In conclusion, I will venture once more to repeat the two main questions underlying our proposals:

"1. Does the Commission agree to base its further labors on the principle of complete and general disarmament during the periods proposed by us? and

"2. Is it prepared to carry out the first stage of disarmament so as to make the conduct of war, if not an absolute impossibility, of extreme difficulty in a year's time?"

Only when unequivocal and affirmative replies have been given to these questions will it be possible to enter upon the detailed consideration of the Soviet draft Convention.

The Soviet delegation considers itself entitled to count upon special support from the delegation of that Government * which is now publicly making a proposal for the prohibition of war. The sincerity of this proposal could not be more convincingly confirmed than by the adherence of its authors to the Soviet draft Convention for complete disarmament, pursuing the aim not merely of the moral prohibition but also of the abolition of the possibility of war. Since armed forces have no other raison d'être but the conduct of war, and since the prohibition of war would make them quite superfluous, it would appear that consistency and logic must dictate to the Government concerned the support of our proposal.

The Soviet delegation is convinced that all delegations here present realize the responsibility and importance of solving this great question, and realize also its vast consequences for the fate of humanity, and that, therefore, no delegation will refrain from publicly expounding the point of view of its Government.

The only two colleagues who had any sympathy at all for Litvinoff's proposals were the Turkish and German delegates. Turkey's policy

* The United States.

was, in general, pro-Soviet. Germany had her own motives. Actually the German army had been increased, but this was in disregard of the Versailles Treaty, and was therefore officially ignored; so the chief German delegate at Geneva, Count Bernstorff, felt free once again to remind the other delegates that Germany had disarmed; that she had asked for an armistice in 1918 only on the basis of Woodrow Wilson's fourteen points, which contained specific provisions for general disarmament; and that now was the time to disarm since it had not been done earlier.

Other delegates objected more or less violently to Litvinoff's proposals. The Italian representative admitted that the "scheme is designed not only to do away with war in the future but also to efface it from history," but saw practical difficulties. So did the French delegate, who at the same time admitted that Litvinoff's proposal "is undoubtedly in keeping with the ideal we all have in view."

The English delegate, Lord Cushendon, made a few conventionally appropriate remarks, but went on: "Is it practical?" He thought not, and proceeded to enumerate once again the British Government's grievances against Communists. The French, Italian, and British representatives who congratulated themselves that they were not like other men—theoretical and sentimental—but were really practical, obviously thought that, saving for a few desultory gestures, it was quite practical to allow affairs to continue to drift as they were steadily drifting, towards the ruin and horror which finally engulfed their own and every other European country. This the practical men could neither foresee nor prevent.

Perhaps the frankest was the Japanese delegate, Sato, who said that he had come to Geneva to reduce armaments, not to abolish them; that if the commission did not remain within its realm, it would act against the spirit of the League of Nations. "The draft Convention now before us," he said, "contemplates complete and total disarmament—which is not provided for in the Covenant."

Most of the delegates felt that a lack of armament or complete disarmament would not eliminate the possibilities of wars; that there should be a minimum of armament for intranational purposes, such as quelling revolts or combating strikes; and that if everybody were to disarm, the industrialized countries would be in a better position in the event of war because they could replace their arms more rapidly.

Litvinoff insisted that all such arguments were specious. He admitted that disarmament would not necessarily exclude wars, but it would help abolish them, and pointed out that, according to his plan, war industries would be done away with, and it had taken the United States twelve to twenty months in World War I to get its war production organized. As to arms for domestic troubles, Litvinoff replied that he could not discuss it at this time or place; he was afraid that if he were to bring forward his solution for social unrest, the representatives of capitalist states might not listen.

Replying to the contention that his fourteen points infringed upon the intent of the League Covenant, Litvinoff suggested that the Covenant be changed: "You are rendering your League a poor service, gentlemen, if you make a fetish of it."

The president of the commission finally submitted a resolution on March 23 that most of the members considered the Soviet draft Convention "impractical." On the same day Litvinoff, never discouraged, presented an entirely new set of proposals. The Preparatory Disarmament Commission had rejected total disarmament. Here, now, were measures for partial and gradual disarmament. While he still thought his first proposals preferable, he hoped that this new set would, if accepted, prove a step towards complete disarmament.

Again there were many speeches and beautiful words and veiled doubts, and again the other delegates thought Litvinoff's suggestions were too idealistic. During the years 1927 and 1928, none of Litvinoff's numerous proposals was accepted. Nor did he expect them to be, but the stakes were so tremendous, the perfectly clear alternative to disarmament so appalling, that the faintest prospect of success demanded the utmost effort from anyone who could serve the cause of peace. Now, however, he was becoming increasingly hopeless of achieving any practical results at Geneva, at least.

The Preparatory Disarmament Commission, which had started its work in 1926, continued deliberating up to 1929, and then resumed again in 1931 and 1932. By the spring of 1929, the League of Nations had published 14,000 pages of reports on disarmament debates. But nobody had disarmed yet, not a single soldier had been dismissed, not a single ship had been retired. Lengthy discussions were devoted to what weapons should be called defensive and what offensive, which planes could be termed civil, which military. By 1932, more than 20,000 pages of speeches and debates had been printed and published, and still nothing practical had been achieved.

By 1932 everyone knew that nothing ever would be accomplished. The factual-minded Litvinoff had known it long before, and he, who had always kept in mind that his country could use its still insufficient industrial resources for much more constructive purposes than building tanks and planes, despite his astute skepticism, must have felt deeply disappointed and frustrated. Realist that he was, by 1928 he knew that nothing was left for Soviet Russia but to rearm in order to protect her frontiers against a world which was proving itself less and less friendly, and when he returned from Geneva that year, he advised the Russian Government to hasten rearmament in every possible way.

Finally, the almost unbelievable happened. On February 2, 1932, the Disarmament Conference—no longer the Preparatory but the actual Disarmament Conference—had its first meeting. Delegates from sixty countries attended, among them Litvinoff. The first session was about to begin when it was suddenly announced that the opening would be deferred for several hours.

Something serious had happened. The Japanese had bombarded the railway station of Shanghai. Some time before, they had invaded Manchuria under the pretense of "protective operations." But Shanghai was a thousand miles from the theater of "protective operations." When the news reached Geneva, most of the delegates wanted to find out from their governments if they were going to declare war on Japan—before they discussed disarmament.

But after a few hours' delay, the first session of the Disarmament Conference got under way, with another flood of speeches.

7

In the summer of 1928, when the Soviet Union was still the only Power that had ratified the Briand-Kellogg Pact, Litvinoff saw a chance to make a more practical contribution towards peace than that exercise in elocution ever would be. Charles Dewey, American financial adviser to Poland, came to Moscow to see him and pointed out that Poland was spending 40 to 45 per cent of her budget on her army, a destructive disbalance due to fear of Russian aggression. Dewey wanted to know if there were any basis for the Poles' fear.

Litvinoff, always valuing concrete action above statements, offered Poland an agreement, usually called the Litvinoff Protocol. This was by no means the Soviet Union's first overture to her suspicious next-door neighbor. Chicherin had offered her a Russo-Polish neutrality and non-aggression treaty in 1925 and the offer had been renewed on August 24, 1926, by the Russian Ambassador to Poland, Voykov. But Poland looked to the Quai d'Orsay and Downing Street for guidance, neither of which was anxious to see Russia and Poland draw together. So Poland turned a cold shoulder on her Slavic sister.

Once again, at this third Russian gesture of reassuring friendliness, Poland's attitude was negative, however polite. Zaleski, the Polish Foreign Minister, answered that, while he would be delighted to enter into a new agreement with Russia, Rumania must participate. Rumania had not entered into diplomatic relations with the Soviet Union, so Zaleski was sure he had quenched the Litvinoff Protocol.

Litvinoff, however, answered that he would be happy to have Rumania in the Protocol, so the Rumanian delegate, Charles A. Davila, appeared in Moscow, and conversed with Litvinoff about Bessarabia, Russian territory seized by Rumania after World War I, to which Russia had never renounced claim. Litvinoff, feeling that it was short-sighted and imprudent to allow that tract of land to interfere with friendly relations with the Western Powers, had, alone in the Narkomindel, always advocated letting it go, but others in Russia, especially Stalin, maintained that national prestige was involved in Bessarabia, and Litvinoff had to give in. With Davila in Moscow, Litvinoff was obliged to protest against Rumania's seizure of Bessarabia. This he did tactfully so as not to embarrass the delegate and yet without in the least compromising Russian claims.

Finally on February 9, 1929, in a conference room of the Narkomindel, Litvinoff, honoring the occasion by wearing a dark suit with a white handkerchief showing in his breast pocket, read the Protocol text to a crowd of formally attired delegates, secretaries, and newspaper men from many different countries, and it was signed by representatives of the Soviet Union, Esthonia, Latvia, Poland, and Rumania. Finland had declined the invitation.

The Protocol renounced war between the signatories as an instrument of national policy: that is to say, it was in effect a specific regional reaffirmation of the Kellogg Pact.

Litvinoff did not suppose that these provisions would make war impossible. They were not really binding. But the Protocol did demonstrate to the adjacent countries that Russia's intentions were amicable and honorable so that war could come only from another quarter.

For Soviet Russia the Protocol marked the end of a period of constant rejection and humiliation, a period when Great Britain, the United States, China, Poland, France, even small countries like Denmark and Switzerland and Holland, had repeatedly showed their suspicion of, and contempt for, Soviet foreign policy. In the Protocol Soviet Russia had taken the initiative and assumed an important place in the diplomatic world, no matter how much Chamberlain, Kellogg, Briand, Stresemann and their coteries might dislike and resist it.

CHAPTER NINE

Foreign Minister

THE GROWING SUCCESS of Litvinoff's program was now bringing him increasing responsibility for Russia's foreign policy, and Chicherin's failing health made it easier for him to take over more authority. His policy of unflagging persistence in developing international contacts and seeking participation in international conferences and agreements, even though it meant accepting rebuffs and a certain traffic in discreet compromises, had gradually displaced Chicherin's preference for withdrawal and theoretical consistency. Litvinoff had thereby saved Russia from isolation, and probably protected her from renewed intervention. More positively, he had obtained for her formal recognitions and valuable trade treaties; however he still had important battles to fight.

Yet Russia's international situation should have been eased, for the major source of suspicion and irritation had been the fear of world Communist propaganda inspired by the Comintern, which the other governments insisted on identifying with the Russian Government, and now Stalin's policy was fast triumphing over that of the orthodox Bolsheviki like Trotsky and his satellites. This meant that all Russian interest and energy were to be directed to her own problems of internal development, and the acceptance of this program was marked by the inauguration of the first of the two Five-Year Plans (1928 to 1937).

But the chief Powers were slow in grasping the implications of the Five-Year Plan and taking reassurance therefrom. A nucleus of the permanent staff of the British Foreign Office, with a long record of excessive conservatism, would still, as late as 1928, have been glad to see the Soviet Government destroyed, and men in this group had opportunities not only for passive resistance in opposing Russia, but also for more active sabotage.

France, likewise, was overtly hostile, sometimes bitterly so, nor was the United States Government by any means friendly, and the tension was soon manifested in open diplomatic conflict. The occasion was a relatively minor affair on the other side of the world. On July 10, 1929, Chinese, as a move in the intricate game of their internal politics, seized the Chinese Eastern Railway, which despite its name was Russian property, connecting Siberia with the Pacific via Manchuria, and held it on the thin pretext of protest against Soviet propaganda activities, refusing either to return it or pay for it. Also a considerable number of Soviet citizens were jailed, and thereafter small clashes occurred on the Soviet-Chinese frontier.

The American Secretary of State, now Henry L. Stimson, under President Hoover, had no representative in Moscow from whom to get a report and he did have in the State Department individuals who were blindly and vindictively hostile to Russia and all her plans. Ignorance proved, as usual, to be dangerous however well intentioned and high minded, and Stimson began to muddy the water. As heir to the Chinese policy of John Hay and Charles Evans Hughes, he was committed to protecting China's political and territorial integrity and to maintaining the Open Door to equal opportunity there for all nations. Now he feared that Soviet Russia would use the railway contretemps as an opportunity to make war on the Chinese and violate these principles. Moreover, such action on Russia's part would contravene the Briand-Kellogg Pact, of which, as Kellogg's successor, he was also guardian.

To assemble the forces against the presumed potential aggressor, on July 25, 1929, he handed to diplomatic representatives in Washington of Great Britain, France, Japan, Germany, and Italy an aide-mémoire on the subject. Again the lack of official relations between the United States and the Soviet Union made trouble. Russia, having no diplomatic contact, heard about the communication indirectly, which aroused suspicions, always a medium for breeding resentment. In this case the resentment proved justifiable when, after more than a week's delay, she obtained a report on the contents.

For Stimson, apparently ignoring what Russia herself might be doing, had proposed that the parties to the Manchurian conflict withdraw their troops from the danger zone, and the railway be operated, pending settlement, by a commission to be composed of five Russians, five Chinese, and a neutral chairman.

Yet Russia herself in the person of Litvinoff was already working so earnestly on the problem that even other Powers, by no means partial to Russia, saw no reason for intervention. The Russians were emphatically opposed to such interference, especially since they feared that the "neutral" chairman of the proposed investigating group would be from the United States, and Russia simply did not believe that any American that would be given such a position would be really neutral. They had reasons for their distrust.

So Litvinoff continued his single-handed efforts at settlement, his first big assignment in the Far East. But Stimson persisted, invoking now the Briand-Kellogg Pact, and acting through France. This was maladroit, though undoubtedly honest on Stimson's part, for Litvinoff was acutely aware of France's dangerous enmity to Russia. As a result, he flamed into resentment and on December 3 answered a note of the preceding day from Stimson in almost undiplomatic language, sharply protesting Stimson's intrusion into the negotiations which were then progressing quite satisfactorily, asserting that: "This cannot be regarded as a friendly act," and finally pointing out that "the Paris [Briand-Kellogg] Pact does not give a single state or group of states the function of protector of this Pact."

Litvinoff's angry note ended in an expression of amazement at the United States, which presumed to give the Soviet Union advice and counsel while still refusing to recognize its existence. Stimson was offended, characterizing Litvinoff's note as extremely tactless.

According to rumor in the State Department, the note postponed recognition, but this is not likely. The State Department had never indicated any intention of recognizing Soviet Russia, and various powerful interests in the United States were still resolutely opposed to re-establishing Russo-American relations.

Outstanding among these was the Standard Oil Company of New Jersey, which was thereby only continuing the anti-Soviet policy that international oil interests had for years supported for their own reasons. As always before, a major figure in the background was the Fascist-minded Deterding. These devious forces now made a new sortie in the form of "documents" showing that the American proponents of Russian recognition, Senators Norris and Borah, were in Soviet pay, but H. R. Knickerbocker, the American correspondent in Berlin to whom they were offered, had little trouble in proving that, like so many anti-Soviet "documents," they were forgeries.

Other American big business interests, on the contrary, were now strongly supporting Russian recognition, not of course because they feared and detested Communism any the less, but because they, unlike the State Department, had to be both informed and realistic and so they knew that Russia's government was there to stay and Russia was destined to be an increasing factor in world economy. Indeed, many of the large companies had long been doing considerable business with Russia, some of them, like General Electric, Vacuum Oil, International Harvester, Singer Manufacturing, and New York Life Insurance, disregarding the fact that claims which they had entered against Russia for a total, in round numbers, of $3,000,-000,000 remained unsettled because Russia would admit only $61,000,-000 of the amount.

Meanwhile in England, the Conservative Government had been voted out of office and the Labor Party under Ramsay MacDonald had for the second time come into power. Consequently, in September, 1929, negotiations for recognition were opened, and on November 5 the House of Commons passed the Recognition Bill, though by the close vote of 324 to 319. On December 20 the first (recognized) Soviet Russian Ambassador to the Court of St. James, Gregory Sokolnikov, presented his credentials—not, however, to the King, but to the Prince of Wales. Evidently His Majesty was still mindful of the death of his cousin.

2

A Foreign Minister can be no stronger than his government. He can only inform and try to guide the central authority from which he derives his status and function. Litvinoff, in the magnificent battle that he fought for years in behalf of world order, had behind him Joseph Stalin.

Stalin was definitely established by 1930 as the leader of the Russian people and the focus and controlling power of their Government. This power had accrued to him, not through any government position (he did not become Premier until May 5, 1941), but because as General Secretary of the Party, which in turn controlled the Government, he had, with quiet tenacity, shrewdness, and severity, built up around himself and down and through the Party, especially among the younger people, a loyal organization that looked to him for direction and authority.

His final control, however, had been won only through six years of unremitting struggle against dual opposition: from the Right, or Troika, where Bukharin, Rykov and Tomsky were the outstanding personalities; and from the Left, where Trotsky, closely supported by Kamenev and Zinoviev, fought with virile animosity, both openly and underground. The Rightists were concerned to accelerate the development of internal prosperity by furthering the NEP policy of private enterprise in certain areas of production, and were especially urgent for support of the well-to-do peasantry as the best means of increasing the agricultural output. The Leftists clung tenaciously to Bolshevik orthodoxy, which held that world revolution was not only the essential condition for the success of the Russian Revolution, but, more important, was the ultimate purpose and justification of the Revolution itself; and they also hewed straight to the Marxian line in demanding that the peasantry be subordinated to the industrial workers. The Trotsky faction, moreover, was also cemented by intense loyalty to Trotsky's brilliant personality—compelling, despite his instability, egotism, and romantic addiction to extremes.

Stalin's middle course recognized, with the Rights, the primacy of internal development, but took account of the danger to the revolutionary program from both increasing private enterprise and peasant social insubordination, though he believed strongly in the possibility of ultimately absorbing the peasantry into the Socialist State. He rejected world revolution and could cite as proofs of the futility of this program its failure in Germany—where the desperate post-war conditions should have provided a perfect situation; in England—when the attempt based on the General Strike of 1926 had been a ludicrous fiasco; and in China, another presumably ideal setting, where actually, after bright Communist hopes, the situation was fast resolving into ambiguity. Stalin believed that the best way to influence the economic and social systems of other countries was by demonstrating the complete success of his form of Socialism in Russia. This thesis of the primacy of Russian socialist development he had begun advocating before Lenin's death.

Trotsky persisted in such violent and unflagging opposition that he was finally ejected from Russia, but he still carried on his plotting from outside, feeding himself and his followers both inside Russia and out, on the hope of a drastic overturn in the Soviets either through internal revolt or as the by-product of a foreign war. This Trotsky acknowledged in 1931 in an interview with Emil Ludwig on the island of Prinkipo. His party, he said, was "scattered and therefore difficult to estimate," but, asked when it could come together, he answered: "When an opportunity is presented from the outside— perhaps a war or a new European intervention when the weakness of the government would act as a stimulus."

Through all this Litvinoff was unwaveringly loyal to Stalin. Both were old Bolsheviki but neither was doctrinaire, and their common practicality led both to ready adjustments in terms of actual fact, and to medial solutions. On one point, however, they differed: Stalin in rejecting world revolution tended also to reject world relations, and to look away from Europe towards the vast extent of possibilities and problems eastward within his own borders. He was too intensely aware of the colossal task of raising upwards of 170,000,000 people to prosperity and security by the full employment of Russia's magnificent resources, to realize the dangers of isolation. Litvinoff, on the other hand, was certain that the world was indivisible, and in the end Stalin gave him full and generous support in the task of sharply turning Russia's foreign policy away from fomenting world revolution to collective security.

When Stalin emerged as the decisive individual in Russia, he was almost unheard of in the outside world, and still, largely because of the Bolshevik theory of the impersonal status of political forces, is too little known.

Joseph Visaronvich Dzugashvili was born of Georgian peasant parents in Gora, near Tiflis, in 1879. His father was a cobbler and expected his son to follow his trade, but when he was fourteen he went on a scholarship to an Orthodox Theological Seminary, probably through the influence of his mother, a religious woman, and he remained there four years. He left presumably because of impaired health; actually, it would seem, because he was expelled for insubordination, and he must have found the regime mentally as well as physically uncongenial, though he got there the foundations of a broad literary education so that he is still interested in the great classicists—Plato, Shakespeare, Goethe—and finds his most satisfactory recreation in reading.

Thereafter (1898) he went at once into revolutionary activities, became a member of the Social Revolutionary Party and of the Tiflis Committee, was an effective leader in local action in the 1905–06 revolution, and persisted for many months in guerrilla warfare, after the struggle had largely subsided almost everywhere else. Like the other outstanding revolutionists, he took a "working" name, Stalin, the "man of steel." When the 1905–06 effort was frustrated, he did not, like most of the Party leaders, flee from Russia but remained, and was arrested and sentenced to exile. He escaped, however, then and on two subsequent occasions.

In 1912 he edited a revolutionary paper in Baku in the Georgian language, and published his first book on revolutionary theory. He also represented his Party in the Duma, and became one of the editors of the Party organ, *Pravda*. In the course of all this work he had left Russia several times for a few days to attend Party congresses—at Stockholm, Cracow, Prague, London—but always went back to resume his underground activities inside the country. In 1913 Lenin wrote of him to Gorki: "We now have a fine Georgian here, who is working on a big article on the national question . . ." *—an episode which assumed importance much later, in relation to long-subsequent events. Lenin had first met Stalin about ten years earlier.

That same year he was again arrested and exiled, this time remaining in banishment up within the Arctic Circle until the success of the 1917 Revolution automatically released him. In the first Bolshevik Cabinet he was Minister for Nationalities, dealing primarily with the affairs of the exceedingly numerous and varied minority groups in Russia. He was from the first a member of the Politburo. In the

* Lion Feuchtwanger, *Moscow 1937*, p. 131, London, 1937.

Wars of Intervention he fought in the Ukraine and against Yudenich outside Leningrad, and showed great technical capacity as a military leader; the position he assumed on January 25, 1942, of Supreme Commander-in-Chief of the Russian armies is not by any means a mere formal title. His most notable exploit was the defense of Tsaritzin, subsequently Stalingrad, and he recommended to Lenin the plan that is credited with having terminated the Wars of Intervention. During this period there were constant and bitter conflicts with Trotsky. The two contrasted in every way, in temperament, methods, and policies. Stalin became General Secretary of the Communist Party in 1921, but also continued as head of the Ministry for Nationalities.

He has been married and widowed twice—once before the Revolution, once just after—and has a son by his first wife, and a son and a daughter by his second wife, none distinguished. In addition to his Kremlin apartment he has a dacha near Moscow and a winter dacha down in his own region at Sochi on the Black Sea, where a "cure" for heart ailments (he has complications from an overtired heart) has been developed around natural sulphur springs.

He plays chess, is an inveterate pipe smoker, likes music—the Georgians are famous for their passionate love of music—and can be a jovial companion (the Georgians are also famous for being hard drinkers), yet at banquets where there are many toasts to be drunk in vodka, Stalin protects himself by having his glass filled with water.

By the beginning of 1923 his position was so strong that Walter Duranty, with remarkable prescience, wrote of him: "Stalin is one of the most remarkable men in Russia and perhaps the most influential figure here today." *

The world-wide discussion, speculation, and controversy provoked by his assumption of Lenin's place, turning chiefly on the question of his real relation to Lenin, and the part played by personal ambition, have probably almost invariably oversimplified both problems, which can hardly be finally resolved, if ever, until time has provided more documentation, and more detached judgment; but there can be no doubt of Stalin's sincere devotion to fulfilling the Revolution as he sees it—assuring maximum human values by means of every resource

---

* Walter Duranty, *op. cit.,* p. 101, who, in conversation with the writer, credits Ernestine Evans with being the first foreign observer to sense the importance of Stalin.

of government. In this vast undertaking Stalin watches details even
down to trivia, but at the same time he always takes the long view,
and holds steadfastly to the ultimate objective, compromising in incidental situations but never with the ultimate purpose, shifting his
tactics as necessities require, but never losing sight of the fixed goal,
which is to create an orderly, prosperous, productive, civilized, and
powerful nation, as the framework for significant human living where
each can develop according to his needs and talents, and participate
to the measure of his capacities in the values of a cultivated community
life. He thinks of himself as a successor to Peter the Great, Russia's
pioneer builder, and it is significant that (so it is said) a portrait of
Peter the Great adorns his private study in his Kremlin apartment.

In the contest that he has had to wage he has perforce been ruthless,
and ruthlessness was necessitated also by other circumstances. Since
the Wars of Intervention, revolutionary Russia constantly feared and
expected attack from outside and, as danger from the Allies receded,
a new, more specific and terrible menace arose from the savage ambitions of Nazi Germany, made more dangerous by the complementary
threat from a chauvinistic and excitable Japan. To save the Revolution
from these imminent foreign dangers, Russia would have to rely
on herself alone—though she also would do her utmost to build up
the collective security which Litvinoff would advocate year after year.
Isolated self-defense would require development of resources and industries with a wholly unprecedented speed. Yet the Russian people
were, by old cultural pattern, intermittent in purpose, distractable,
spasmodic. The answer was discipline—and Stalin as a military leader
found the answer natural. But discipline to be imposed on a people
long habituated to caprice and irregularity of effort required ruthlessness. At the same time, ruthlessness perhaps came the more easily
to him because the Georgians, a mountain people probably descended
directly through some 5,000 years from an indigenous population,
have a tradition of relentless determination, with little mitigating
mercy.

Tardiness, absenteeism, a huge labor turnover were the order of the
day in most industries. The productive energy of the average Soviet
worker was then far below that of his American counterpart; yet the
nation's peril was clear; her needs imperative. Hence, the Government

introduced general education and specific propaganda as well as new regulations lengthening the seven-hour day to eight hours, a painful concession to necessities for they had taken special pride in the reduced hours of labor. Workmen who devised practical means of increasing production became national heroes. Competitions between factories and departments took on the excitement of our baseball rivalries; collective enthusiasm was engendered and penalties enforced. The combination worked. It is doubtful if any of Stalin's critics in or out of the country could have solved this most fundamental and urgent problem as effectively as he did.

Stalin is faithful to the Party theory that the individual is but the instrument of the group, and there is every reason to credit his honesty when he refuses personal credit for Russia's achievements under his regime, insisting on the distribution of recognition to his assistants, the Russian people, and above all to Lenin. Thus if personal ambition is involved in his motives, it is in this respect strongly qualified.

It is, moreover, in much the same way (as focus or symbol of an idea, a process and its gratifying results) that Stalin functions as the *living* national hero—for Lenin is still the national hero, and Stalin contributes in every way to maintaining the dead leader in this position, devout in his belief in Lenin's peculiar greatness. The Russians have for generations been, as a people, romantics. Much of their pre-revolutionary religiosity was primarily romantic, indulging emotions of worship for their own sake, with picturesque demonstrations intensifying the emotions and also in themselves satisfying. The Czar was for them the great and good Father. Comparable mental processes are now concentrated on Stalin, but are associated with the concrete benefits of distributed increasing prosperity, and with the confident expectation of constant future advances in standards of living and culture. Stalin, in short, is the image of a utilitarian pragmatic social faith with its concomitants in hope, of psychic dependence, and gratitude. The abstractness of his status Stalin himself emphasizes by vigorously applauding when other speakers praise Stalin, his policies, his achievements. The approbation refers, he is in effect announcing, not to any individual, but to the program, the efforts it has engendered, and all that these can mean to the human race.

Stalin is a rather short man, slight but compact in build, with the absolutely black hair of his race and brown eyes "exceedingly kindly and gentle," * and beautiful hands.† "His demeanor is kindly, his manner almost deprecatingly simple, his personality and expression of reserve strength and poise very marked" with "a simple dignity," and deliberate, soft, rather toneless speech. "He gave the impression of being sincerely modest" but "of a strong mind which is composed and wise" and "he has a very great mentality. It is sharp, shrewd, and, above all things else, wise"—"a very strong, able man who is practical, with a lot of common sense." Also "He has a sly humor," ‡ is well informed on a considerable range of subjects, and not above "doodling" while he reflects! Quentin Reynolds quotes a British correspondent who once wrote of Stalin, " 'He looks like the kindly Italian gardener you have in twice a week.' You couldn't find a better description of the Soviet leader than that." §

He is a hard, concentrated worker—as was Lenin—an exceptionally able organizer and efficient administrator, with excellent judgment in selecting lieutenants. His career has demonstrated perseverance, determination, patience, endurance, and courage, both physical bravery and the moral courage to admit his own errors, on which he lays special emphasis; and withal a certain flexibility that leads to constant adjustment to stubborn facts and the disregard of slogans or doctrinaire pronouncements which are more ideological than realistic. This last has frequently enraged orthodox Socialists and Bolsheviki, especially abroad, who hotly accuse him of betraying the Revolution and its edicts.

His greatest accomplishments have been the unification of the country, and its thoroughgoing industrialization, so essential for war as well as the general national economy—a 60-to-100-year development crowded into ten, as several observers have put it. The collectivization of agriculture likewise has been a major and difficult achievement, made more difficult and consequently more cruel by the stubbornness of certain sections of the peasantry. Yet when in the end collectivization succeeded, it brought prosperity to the peasants and banished the ever-recurrent menace of famine, has saved and will continue to

---

* Lion Feuchtwanger, *op. cit.,* pp. 92-95.
† Joseph E. Davies, *op. cit.,* p. 357.
‡ Lion Feuchtwanger, *op. cit.,* p. 126.
§ Quentin Reynolds, *Only the Stars Are Neutral,* p. 94, N. Y., 1943.

save tens of thousands from suffering and death, and has firmly established one of the essential economic bases of the Soviet State.

The Constitution is largely the work of Stalin; although he would object to the individual credit, the fact remains that he conceived it, created it and established it. Not completely democratic in all respects in accordance with Western standards, it is genuinely more democratic and progressive in others. It is the Government's contract with the people, guaranteeing them the fruits of their past and present sacrifices, their blue print for the Good Life, for all, forever, as they themselves may progressively conceive the Good Life; a contract destined to complete fulfillment. Sentimental and doctrinaire democrats have protested bitterly because the Constitution has not yet been put into full operation and have charged Stalin with perpetrating a fraud upon the people, an irresponsible condemnation that has no regard for the facts or requirements of the situation. Stalin and others in the Soviet Government well knew that the life of the nation was in definite peril from the planned attacks from the West. Hitler was kind enough to announce his destination and publish his time-table. The successful defense of the nation required furious, sustained, and wisely directed labor; it demanded continuous sacrifice on the part of all. The strictest discipline was necessary and something like martial law remained and had to remain in effect, for these were in essence war conditions, and war begins, as Hitler himself said, long before actual fighting occurs. This Stalin knew and he acted accordingly. It was no time for general debates or political dissension, * such as so often paralyze democracies in their hour of danger. It was the time for long-range, strictly controlled plans.

The Russian people only gradually accepted this last verdict. As the first Plan was inaugurated, with its severe demands and no visible benefits to the average man, there was grumbling, resistance, sabotage, and a few indulged in the idea of revolt. Some of the older Bolsheviki found the process inhumanly severe and too nationalistic to accord with the world revolutionary thesis of its founders. But the people increasingly understood and approved, as soon they saw the results appearing in a better life, as consumer's goods, from 1935 on, began to flood the cities and the countryside and mass education and social

* Lion Feuchtwanger, *op. cit.*, pp. 82-83.

benefits contributed more and more to their well-being. Everyone entertained confident hopes in still better things to come, and all felt secure behind the growing might of the Red army, which, as no force since the days of the French Revolution, was and is truly a people's army.

The people of Russia know their Constitution with an enthusiasm and thoroughness that few Western nations bring to the understanding of their basic State documents. The Constitution is everywhere honored, acclaimed, studied, remembered. With the coming of peace, it will soon become the law of the land without reserve. No government could conceivably dare to withhold it for long, even if it so wished.

Stalin is a great leader not merely because of the clarity of his ideas and that sureness of self which breeds confidence; not merely because of his prodigious industry, his courage, his realism, which all respect; not merely because he has successfully imposed a severe discipline on the whole country; but also and to a very important degree because he is in essentials only just ahead of those whom he leads, not dragging his followers into new and strange policies they cannot understand, but preceding them and marching in the direction that they themselves, in the vast majority, expect and want to go. His integration with his countrymen is the result equally of circumstances and of art —of circumstances, because he *is* one of them, a Russian workingman, with a mind far superior in vigor and decisiveness, range of information, judgment, to the average man, but still different in degree rather than kind; of art, because a well-organized intelligence service keeps him apprised not only of the general trends in the country, but even, apparently, of murmurs, minor shifts of emphasis, scarcely articulate anticipations.

The art of leadership is also fortified by a system of education and public information service, by a soundly devised, psychologically very sophisticated propaganda that keeps the people close to their leaders and to the national program. The subject of propaganda may be the stability of the family, community care of children, the necessity for a more varied diet, or the importance of recreation, the importance of becoming universally air-minded, or instructions and recruiting for the various organizations for national defense and welfare. The national education aims to eliminate race prejudice in every form, in which it has already succeeded; to instill and arouse love of the native land, its beauties, its ancient heroes and legends, the greatness of its experiences and achievements in the past, which now so confidently prophesy a glorious and inspiring future. These are the principal elements in the national propaganda, the program that Stalin believes in and directs, which brings him the loyalty of the people.

3

The temper of the anti-Stalin criticism abroad, supercharged with emotionalism and exaggeration, has had a trace of the desperation and fanaticism characteristic of Trotsky himself—and is indirectly and in part evidence of Trotsky's still potent control of his disciples.

Trotsky was a man of great force and capacity and of exceptional intelligence. He was a hard and precise worker, but also had ferocious intensity, blazing fervor, imagination, audacity, quick wit, courage, and such magnetism that he exercised an almost hypnotic hold on his followers. The army swore by him. His political friends were ready to follow him in the most rash and even fantastic adventures. Some he dominated with an almost Hitlerite influence. Such passionate loyalty is on occasion admirable and can accomplish, as it did under Trotsky's inspiration, miracles on the battlefield. His oratorical powers also were extraordinary, often carrying the day by dazzling tours de force, and his adroit, mercurial mind was especially effective in the days when the Revolution could proceed only by plotting, intrigue, and swift improvisations.

But these were not the qualities needed for construction after the Revolution had been won. A permanent society is not built by improvisation—and Trotsky's improvisations not infrequently turned into muddles, which was particularly offensive to the methodical Stalin. The Revolution must be succeeded by fundamental construction, by deliberation, experiment, revision, tenacity, and continuity of purpose. Realistic flexibility was imperative, and Trotsky was formidable as a Marxian debater, beginning his attacks against deviations demanded by

practical fact even under Lenin. Co-operation is of the essence, and
Trotsky was a rampant individualist. "Trotsky's non-Bolshevist past is
no accident," said Lenin. "He was not a consistent Menshevik either,"
he could have added, for Trotsky was in the habit of creating small
dissident groups. Under Lenin's dominant personality, Trotsky did accomplish for seven years a good deal within the framework of the Party.
It was another matter, however, when he sought to inherit Lenin's
authority.

His utility for reconstruction was further impaired by his fanatical
adherence to the old Bolshevik fundamental of world revolution, long
after it had been proved impossible, and perilous to Russia itself.
Added to all this, the bitterness of his personal feuds, his inordinate
capacity for the most venomous hate, and his incandescent ambition
made him a definite menace to the new Russia.

Consequently, despite his great services in the early days, he had to
be eliminated. He had three years (he was finally exiled in January,
1928) in which to adjust to changing problems and the changing methods that they indicated. He could only stand fixed in the Bolshevism of
ten, the theories of twenty, years earlier—with increasing bitterness and
increasing recklessness as to means and results.

He has now been dead three years (he was assassinated in August,
1940) but his ardent and dominating personality still exerts its bizarre,
almost sinister influence over many former associates and followers,
dispersed over the world. And even confronted by the justification of
Russia's course through her magnificent demonstration against the
Nazis, in morale, organization and all that goes to make fighting
power, they still prefer to hark back to the old antagonisms.

Still crusading under the impetus of Trotsky's ghost, they are willing to take chances, not merely with their own lives, but with Russia's,
not merely with Russia's future but with the whole anti-Fascist cause.
Had they succeeded in the 1930's and precipitated civil war, Russia
would have been unready for the terrific ordeal that almost engulfed
her. Her armies would have been destroyed, the country overrun and
her territories and resources in the hands of the Nazis, to employ for
their final great, perhaps irresistible, assault on civilization.

Yet still, eyes turned back to their scintillating self-defeated hero, this
scattered lost legion is frantically vocal of its inherited hatred.

4

In October, 1929, a real disaster shook the Western world: the New York Stock Market collapsed, the repercussions shaking the whole business world. The lessons which sound economists had long been expounding in vain to a "prosperity"-bedazzled people had come home with a vengeance.

The immediate effects on Russia of the depression of 1930–31 were unfortunate. Although by her own internal reorganization Russia had already eliminated the causes, both economic and psychological, which had been chiefly responsible for the debacle that now afflicted the Western Powers, nonetheless as part of the world economy she was bound to suffer. Countries where the lag of consumption in relation to production had been neglected in the paralysis of laissez-faire were now frantically struggling to hold what was left of the home market for their unsalable goods.

Hence Russian goods were taboo, and again economists' warnings went unheeded. What mattered it if disaster had confirmed their reiterated prophecy that quantity production could be sustained only by a corresponding increase in purchasing power at home? Their warning now that wealth was, generally speaking, in proportion to the rapidity of untrammeled circulation was brushed aside by the average business man as just theory. The sale of a bill of goods was practical fact, and the local manufacturer could compete with foreign competitors selling the same products under his very nose, only, if at all, by slashing prices below the profit level.

Thoroughly alarmed by the imminence of bankruptcy, the harassed industrialist or director was frequently in no mood to look with detachment at the world scene beyond his own problems, and since the majority was entangled in this hand-to-mouth psychology, trade restrictions, preferential agreements and protective tariff walls, in which the American business man especially has long had a childlike faith, were hastily thrown up, over the protests of the minority informed on the way of world trade. These, of course, retarded interchange, and exchange control further encumbered business—a fatal economic Maginot Line, which protected nothing, kept out prosperity, and made bad matters dangerously worse.

Stalin turned a cool, appraising eye on the whole muddle:

The present world economic depression [he said in an interview with Walter Duranty on December 1, 1930] is very heavy and will be heavier yet. It is the worst of the periodic crises that mark the decay of the capitalist system, but I do not think it will last or that it is the culminating crisis. Capitalism is still strong and may recover, but this last year has exposed its fatal weakness—capitalism cannot exist without markets, and the mutual rivalry of capitalist states bars them from each other's markets. . . .*

It gradually dawned on those who prescribed trade-restricting remedies that instead of curing they actually worked further mischief. Early in 1931, President Hoover saw the connection between the world economic crisis and the American depression, and in June he proposed an international moratorium of war reparations and war debts. At that time, the move, although patently necessary, seemed revolutionary— most astonishing from a Republican president. A few years later nobody seriously believed that those European debts would ever be paid.

Hoover's move, however, could not forestall panic in Europe. Partly in consequence, there was a wholesale failure of American banks. In September, 1931, 1,305 had to close, and in October, 522 more shut down. In 1932 unemployment continued to rise, until, according to conservative estimates, there were at least 12,000,000 persons out of work. Almost the worst feature of the depression was that nobody could tell when and how it would end. For example, Andrew Mellon—at that time Ambassador to the Court of St. James—admitted that he did not know.

In March, 1932, Ivar Kreuger, the Swedish match king, widely believed to be one of the richest and most powerful men in the world and accepted with fatuous credulity by some governments and many American bankers and investors, though he was suspect at home in Sweden, committed suicide, and his industrial empire crashed in complete ruin. A few weeks later the superstructure of corporations which Samuel Insull had built up by dubious methods fell apart. In the large cities there were riots and hunger marches, in the country, food and

* Walter Duranty, *op. cit.,* p. 235.

transportation strikes; everywhere there were anxiety, confusion, resentment, paralysis, and recession. Some began to think that the lights were going out all over the United States.

The situation of the farmers, a critical class in the nation's economy, grew steadily more desperate. By the middle of 1932, cotton was selling below 5 cents, wheat below 50 cents, corn at 31 cents. The gross income of farms had dwindled from 12 billions in 1929 to 5¼ billions in 1932. In many districts farmers who could not pay the interest on their mortgages were evicted, often provoking violent resistance, either forcible prevention of the sale or purchase of the livestock and tools at ridiculously low prices after prospective bona-fide buyers had been excluded.

As was inevitable, the blind consciousness that something was fundamentally and drastically wrong spawned a weird brood of economic theories—some of them sincere, most of them ignorant and impractical, not a few dishonest expedients for getting power. Prominent among them was Huey Long's share-the-wealth scheme. The Senate was busily investigating, meantime, the scandal of the enormous profits of certain Wall Street men before, during, and after the crash.

Russia had to suffer along with the societies guilty of making the unhappy mess. Her foreign trade diminished from $910,000,000 in 1930 to only $570,000,000 in 1932.

Meanwhile, Chicherin's health was gravely deteriorating, and on July 25, 1930, Litvinoff succeeded him as Foreign Minister. Chicherin went into such complete retirement that even his friends scarcely saw him. He spent the time reading widely in English, French, and German, and playing the piano, chiefly Mozart, until he died on July 7, 1936—by that time so forgotten that his passing was barely mentioned in the Soviet press and only a handful of people attended his funeral.

As Foreign Minister, Litvinoff soon undertook to counter the adverse trade trend which threatened the economic stability of the Soviet Union and jeopardized the precious Five-Year Plan. In May, 1931, he proposed an "economic non-aggression pact," but did not succeed in getting any of the restrictions upon Soviet exports mitigated. Some of the near-by smaller countries—Greece, Turkey, Iran—were glad to import Russian industrial products at reasonable rates, but the total was too small to compensate for the loss of trade with the Great Powers. This hardly made for more cordial relations with France and England.

However, the conflicts and disagreements with the Western nations began to subside into relative insignificance as Japan and Germany commenced to darken the international horizon by reckless pronouncements, threats and sinister schemes.

5

In September, 1931, Japan set off a train of explosive events by wantonly attacking China, offering only the most flimsy and dishonest excuses—the first large-scale experiment in aggression and the first serious test of the resolution and effectiveness of the governments that wanted to maintain peace and the political status quo.

Stimson, still Secretary of State, felt the necessity of doing everything possible to keep peace in the Far East, and urged Great Britain to co-operate in an effective protest. Sir John Simon, although similarly perturbed by the aggression, believed that it could probably be curbed by financial pressure when Japanese bonds came due, and was unwilling to join in the protest unless America would promise to go to war if Japan resisted. The English feared the protest might turn out to be a bluff on which they could not make good. Stimson, as the British ought to have more clearly realized, had no power to commit the United States to war, and his arguments for joint action were unsuccessful. In both the American and the British governments there were those who felt that the other one had let them down. It is obvious, however, that if each had been willing to co-operate with Russia, a combined démarche would have tended to cool even the hottest heads in Japan, and there was precedent for this in a protest in 1894, which forced the Japanese, after they had captured Port Arthur from the Chinese, to relinquish the occupied territory and retire.

Russia, evidently hoping to forestall complications in that direction, offered Japan a non-aggression pact in December, 1931, but it was refused, and a second offer in November, 1932, also met a refusal. This was suspicious, and chauvinism was flourishing mightily in Japan. The Soviet Union had good reason to fear that Russian territory might be attacked.

The Russian Government, therefore, took steps to defend itself in the Far East by strengthening its railroad communications and by increasing the number of troops stationed there. In December, 1932, diplomatic relations with China, which had been broken off in 1927, were re-established.

More important still, the Far Eastern conditions made Russia review searchingly the whole European situation. Litvinoff realized that a simultaneous attack on Russia from the East and the West must be prevented at all costs, for Russia no less than Germany understood perfectly the peril of a two-front war, and in the heart of Europe things began to look dangerous.

Germany was fast developing into a semi-Fascist country. Stresemann was dead. Despite an avowed intention to represent justly all parties and interests, President Hindenburg, as age progressively dimmed his judgment, was yielding more and more to his Junker friends, and revealing his true colors as a natural full-fledged reactionary. The threat of Hitler loomed continuously more ominous. By the autumn of 1931 his party had become the second in size in Germany. The Social Democratic Party was larger, but its leaders were getting on in years; their energies, imagination, and courage were waning in the face of discontent at home and ceaseless sabotage in official quarters, and they simply looked on while the power was usurped by the army and heavy industry. This was approximately what the perspicacious and resolute young Litvinoff had foreseen as early as 1907. The German army advocated a certain degree of friendly contact with Soviet Russia—for purely strategic reasons—but everything else pointed to the end of German-Russian friendship and collaboration.

Russia, therefore, tried first to improve relations with France. As late as June, 1930, Stalin had called France "the most aggressive and militaristic country among all the aggressive and militaristic countries in the world," echoing a similar judgment of Woodrow Wilson's in 1920. Such an unqualified condemnation was not warranted in 1930, and by 1931 not even the most suspicious Russian could see France as the great menace to European peace. In August of that year Litvinoff arranged a non-aggression treaty with France, but France delayed her signature until the Soviets could conclude similar treaties with Poland and Rumania. Poland, however, did not want any additional treaties with Soviet Russia, and it was only in January, 1932, when aggressive German intentions were unmistakable, that Poland returned to the original offer from Moscow and a few months later (July 25, 1932) a treaty was signed. No pact between Russia and Rumania was negotiated or signed, but Litvinoff made a definite promise not to use force in settling the Bessarabian question. (See p. 254.)

True to his basic precepts, Litvinoff worked to eliminate one troubled spot after another and wherever possible to replace tension and apprehension by co-operation. Although Russia's claims in Bessarabia were valid, none the less Litvinoff assured Titulescu, Rumania's able Foreign Minister, that Russia would not press her claims in any way. This was partly in acknowledgment of Titulescu's intelligent and effective work in the League; for Titulescu was a man of decidedly superior intelligence, strength of character and liberal convictions. He was one of Litvinoff's strongest supporters in all international conferences and a close friend as well; and for him Litvinoff had the highest regard. But Titulescu was something of a thorn in the flesh of King Carol. His own high standards and sense of responsibility were frequently in conflict with royal policies. And to the loss of all Europe, Titulescu was shelved and replaced by Tartarescu, who lacked all of Titulescu's special qualities. In efficient and business-like manner the latter thought he would now reduce what was only an understanding to the terms of a written pact. So he asked Litvinoff how soon he would be ready to sign the protocol: "What protocol?" asked Litvinoff. "Why, your agreement, of course, not to press Russia's claims for the return of Bessarabia." ". . . Oh! but that was just a personal arrangement between me and Titulescu!"

The implication was clear that as long as Rumania was vigorously co-operating in reasonable and liberal policies she could expect generous consideration from Russia, but not otherwise.

In the summer of 1932 Hindenburg dismissed Chancellor Bruening, the last political leader in Germany who fought the trend towards Fascism, and appointed in his stead Franz von Papen, a reactionary par excellence, ambitious, unscrupulous, clever and stupid by turns,* who represented heavy industry and the army. He also had good connections with Hitler, though at times their friendship seemed tenuous. Papen proceeded to govern Germany with complete disregard of its Constitution, and with practically no one behind him except Hinden-

* Cf. Tibor Koeves, *Satan in Top Hat*, New York, 1941.

burg and the heads of the army. The army now demanded rearmament more loudly than ever—a demand effectively seconded, behind the scenes, by the steel trusts of the Ruhr and Saar.

Edouard Herriot, once more Premier of France, appreciating the seriousness of the Nazi menace, now advocated a new rapprochement with Soviet Russia. Both Herriot and Pierre Cot, Minister of Aviation, visited Russia and brought back decidedly encouraging reports of Russia's strength and her growing value as an ally. In consequence, on November 29, 1932, the two governments signed a non-aggression pact and conciliation convention which also protected their economic relations and promised mutual abstention from propaganda. French nationalists disapproved, the reactionaries raged, the British were secretly annoyed, but the French public favored the proposal and the French parliament, despite opposition and sabotage, ratified it on February 15, 1933.

These two treaties—with Poland and with France—were part of a series of six arranged by the Narkomindel within a year and a half (Afghanistan, June 24, 1931; Finland, January 21, 1932; Latvia, February 5, 1932; Esthonia, May 4, 1932) to bulwark at least East European peace, and thereby, it was hoped—as the preamble of each document specified—contribute to world peace. Litvinoff was holding to his conviction of the indivisibility of peace, and estimating coolly its shivering instability.

6

While Franco-Soviet relations now became almost cordial, British relations with Russia continued to be disturbed, especially when the British Government was forced by the adoption of imperial preferences (Ottawa Conference, 1932) to abrogate a previous trade treaty with the Soviet Union. Then in March, 1933, all relations between Russia and Great Britain were thrown into confusion. On March 11 and 12 the Soviets arrested a group of engineers from the Metropolitan Vickers Electrical Company, whom they charged with being agents of the British secret service. Under considerable pressure one of the men confessed. Lethargic Stanley Baldwin, then President of the Council in the British National Government, always the advocate of patience in all things, with a constitutional disposition to find any action premature, on this occasion showed almost explosive energy. In a week he suspended the trade negotiations then in progress with Russia, and when on April 19 the Soviet court convicted five of the men, sentencing three to deportation and two to prison, on the very same day he secured permission from Parliament to place an embargo on 80 per cent of the goods that Russia had been buying from Great Britain and automatically opened the floodgates in England to abuse of the Soviets.

The innocence of the British engineers was adopted as a cardinal test of policy and negotiations. When Vernon Bartlett, special correspondent for the London *News Chronicle,* sincerely trying to be objective, sent dispatches that made the Soviet case appear at least reasonable, he was rebuked by an undersecretary of the British Legation in Moscow for "not playing the game." He replied that he was not playing any game but trying to report the truth. The Russians, on the other hand, were convinced that the engineers were guilty. There were all the makings of a most dangerous conflict.

Litvinoff acted promptly and with good sense, and made a genuine effort for conciliation, but the issue remained an open sore for two months. The returning British engineers were pledged by Baldwin to the most gravelike silence. The full inside story of the incident has yet to be written, although the Russians published a complete account of the hearings and the evidence, evidence that never convinced the English that the charges had any more substantial foundation than overactive Russian suspicions and some curious misunderstandings.

British-Russian relations never were as friendly as those between Russia and France. Britain's distrust of Russia was rooted in the long history of clashes between the two imperialisms in Asia, and anti-Soviet propaganda had been especially virulent and successful in Great Britain. England's news services from Russia were meager and undependable; the London *Times,* because it could not get assurances of completely free dispatches, would send no correspondent to Moscow. Consequently, it preserved its dignity and freedom of action by reprinting dangerous nonsense passed on from anti-Soviet sources by the Riga correspondent.

The Government's fear of Communist propaganda was kept on the alert by apprehensions as to its effect in the Middle East and India. On the insistence of British security agents, the Egyptian Government was reluctantly obliged to maintain stringent regulations against the entrance into Egypt, not merely of Russians, but also of anyone of any nationality who had been in Russia. No passport containing a Russian visa could be visaed for Egypt without strong diplomatic representations.

Britain's mistrust of the Soviets even led her to welcome signs of Germany's military resurgence as an offset to growing Russian strength. While the French were more than ever fearful of their Teutonic neighbor, the English saw no particular threat in Hitler's rearmament program, a tragic and costly error sustained by both good and bad motives. They had found their enemy brave and intelligent, even if unwisely governed and cruelly ambitious. Moreover, the conscience of Great Britain was chagrined by its own propaganda credulity in World War I, and rather ashamed of the falsehoods that at certain points had grossly maligned the Germans.[*]

England's sympathy with Germany was intensified also by her resentment of French intransigence during the 1920's. She was impatient of France's demands for an unreasonable settlement that Germany would never be able to carry out, and suspicious of the French pleas for security, partly because these had been shockingly exploited for individual political purposes—an abuse that really did not indict either the genuineness or the reasonableness of French fears.

Behind the British tendency to a pro-German attitude lay, too, the devout desire in Britain for peace. To fear Germany as a potential enemy implied possibility of war again; reconciliation with Germany pushed war—European war at least—into a vague future, and the English were sick of war and convinced of its ghastly futility. The Oxford Union by a dramatic vote denied the validity of the conventional appeal to war for God, King, and Country. A scandalized and vociferous demand for reconsideration by young Randolph Churchill was voted down. A vast petition for peace warned the Government of the strength of the movement. It lost a by-election (at Fulham, autumn, 1933) by 7,000 votes on a straight-out issue of pacifism.

Britain's failure to identify Germany as the real enemy, her inability to see the entire character of the Russian Revolution beneath the numerous confusions and false fronts, and her stubborn hostility have

[*] Cf. Arthur Ponsonby, *Falsehood in War Time*, New York, 1928.

been in part charged to Litvinoff. It is true that the whole situation developed under Litvinoff's eyes and at the time when he was one of the principal determining forces in Russia's foreign policy and had almost a free hand in negotiations. But it would need a good deal more specific evidence to put the blame on Litvinoff for this most plausible aberration by which the British confused potential friend and foe. Its causes were too deep in history and too perfectly in accord with the character of the British Tory Party then in power to be charged to any one foreign diplomat. When the English finally saw the light, it was too late to check the catastrophic results.

7

In this difficult situation—with Japan threatening in the East, Germany an increasing menace in the West, and Tory England somnolently misreading the total situation—Litvinoff once more looked towards the United States.

Stimson was at last ready, by the beginning of 1933, to recognize the Soviet Union and fully aware that the real danger in the Far East was not Russia but Japan. The presidential election of the preceding autumn, however, had gone by a great majority to Franklin D. Roosevelt, so Stimson had to cede his post to Cordell Hull, reluctantly, for as he realized and in effect said, he was having to give up the job just as he was beginning to learn the business.

Roosevelt had made it clear, even before his election, that he stood for recognition of Soviet Russia. During the summer of 1932 he had sent as his personal emissary to Moscow, William C. Bullitt, who had already been there for President Wilson in 1919; and Bullitt told the correspondents in Russia, off the record, that Roosevelt "will be the next President" and that "American recognition of the Soviet Government will be one of the first acts of his administration."

Bullitt's second mission was even less successful than the first had been. Litvinoff was out of town and his assistants in the Foreign Office did not realize the implications of the unofficial American envoy's visit. They put him up in a second-rate hotel, The New Moscow, on the other side of the Moskva River, and paid little attention to him. Bullitt left without having accomplished anything.

By the time Roosevelt was elected, public opinion in the United States strongly supported the recognition of Soviet Russia. In January, 1933, 800 college presidents and professors addressed a message to the President-Elect stating that "failure to recognize Russia has contributed to the serious situation in the Orient and prevented adoption of policies which might have frustrated the imperialistic ventures of Japan"—views which were identical with those held in Moscow. In the minds of most informed Americans, recognition was only a matter of time. Of this Litvinoff was fully aware.

The chief factor in this sweeping reversal of opinion, however, was the economic situation, which was by now acutely dangerous. In March, 1933—a few days before Roosevelt was inaugurated—many states had to declare a bank holiday, and on the eve of Roosevelt's election even Illinois and New York were forced to follow suit. A few months later the National Recovery Act was passed, with the idea of spreading employment by shortening hours of labor and preventing starvation by guaranteeing minimum wages. But it became more and more evident that a completely disorganized world market was among the main causes of the crisis.

President Hoover had come to believe that no American recovery could be achieved without a world recovery. President Roosevelt and his new Secretary of State, Hull, believed that too. Hull advocated as a means towards such recovery the immediate breaking down of the tariff walls around the United States which had so signally failed to protect prosperity. Closely connected with this policy was, of course, the question of stabilization of the international currencies and establishment of a steady exchange rate between them. As advocated by the platform of the National Democratic Party in 1932, "an international economic conference designed to restore international trade and facilitate exchange" was hopefully agreed upon and summoned to meet in London in June.

Litvinoff was the chief of the Russian delegation at this London Economic Conference. He arrived in London on June 10, 1933, and four days later the *New York Times* said:

It was not the address of Neville Chamberlain, British Chancellor of the Exchequer, presenting the first really concrete proposals for curing the world's economic ills that stirred the delegates most, nor was it Secretary of State Hull's discourse, in general terms on the evil of economic nationalism with the promise of concrete suggestions later. What really thrilled the conference most was a passage in an afternoon speech by Litvinoff.

The passage in question was noteworthy:

I am sure, gentlemen, that you all realize that economic peace is possible only against the background of peace in all phases of international life. However excellent may be the resolutions passed by the Economic Conference, they will have no influence whatsoever in the alleviation of the economic crisis so long as we continue in the present state of general political uneasiness and perturbation, with the uncertainty as to what the morrow will bring forth, and the fear of the outbreak at any moment of that most terrible manifestation of economic conflict—war. This sentiment of general anxiety has not only been not allayed of late, but, if anything, has increased, in spite of international consultations and the conclusion of pacts. Indeed we are now cognizant of international consultations and pacts which have actually added to political mistrust. Nothing but radical measures in the sphere of disarmament and the strengthening of security guarantees by the signing of bi-lateral and general pacts of non-aggression, could to some extent calm those fears and create the proper atmosphere for peaceful economic relations.

Going into detail, Litvinoff gave some sensational figures:

The Soviet Government as a rule draws up its import in strict accordance with its export possibilities on credit facilities. But the Soviet delegation could conceive of conditions, such as lengthened credits and normal conditions for Soviet exports and other favorable factors, which might induce its government to extend these plans to a degree which would have no small influence in alleviating this crisis. According to the calculations of our delegation, the Soviet Government, given such conditions, might agree to place orders abroad in the near future to the sum of about $1,000,000,000.

To be still more definite, the Soviet Union could in the near future absorb about $200,000,000 worth of ferrous metals; $100,000,000 worth of materials for textile, leather and rubber industries; $400,000,000 worth of machinery, including railway equipment to the value of $100,000,000; $85,-000,000 worth of agricultural goods including breed stock; $50,000,000 worth of consumer's goods such as tea, cocoa, coffee and herrings; and

$50,000,000 worth of new ships, chiefly for industrial purposes, such as fishing, seal hunting and dredging.

The significance of these figures will be more evident if it is realized that they amount to from 25 to 66 per cent of existing world stocks. . . .

It only remains for me to add that the vast majority of countries here represented might be supposed to be interested in the export of the commodities I have enumerated.

"Economic non-aggression," for which Litvinoff was here asking, was an old demand of his. He had, without much success, proposed the very same thing two years earlier in Geneva. At that time, the other nations, believing that they could solve their own problems, had not listened. The only solution that had occurred to them was an increasingly severe and more uncompromising economic warfare against one another. But by this time, they knew that at least in matters of economy peace was indivisible, and they now listened to Litvinoff when he explained:

". . . Speaking of a truce acknowledges the existence of a state of war, and armistice means cessation of all fighting, not merely abstention from the beginning of fresh battles. The same should be true of economic warfare."

Litvinoff finally proposed a simultaneous suspension in all countries of all legislative or administrative measures of economic warfare. He promised that a Russian resolution to this effect would be submitted to the conference.

It was a strong speech. While the other delegates to the London Economic Conference could bring forward only vague generalities, Litvinoff had offered a practical solution, and this made a profound impression. After this speech Litvinoff undoubtedly was the most important personality at the London Economic Conference, completely eclipsing Raymond Moley, chief of the United States delegation, though he had made a spectacular entrance.

Litvinoff also used his sojourn in London to start arrangements and negotiations pertaining to matters which did not figure on the program of the conference. Most important for him and for Soviet Russia, were his conversations with the Foreign Secretary, Sir John Simon, which resulted on July 1 in lifting the embargo on Russian purchases of British goods which England had imposed pending the outcome of the

Vickers affair, and in the liberation, the next day, of the two engineers sentenced in Russia to imprisonment.

The purpose for which the conference had been called was never achieved, chiefly because by the time Secretary of State Hull had started an arrangement for stabilizing international currencies and President Roosevelt's adviser, Raymond Moley, had committed himself to some extent in this matter, Roosevelt personally had become convinced that America should act alone. Whatever the reasons, and they have never been clearly presented to the public, the President suddenly decided—very much to the dismay of his own delegation—that America should withdraw from an international stabilization agreement.

Litvinoff, however, succeeded at the conference in at least two measures; one was or could have been of the greatest international value, the other concerned only the United States and Soviet Russia. The first, and more important, which proved his outstanding capacity as a diplomat and the unique value of a statesman who could and did think, was his definition of "aggression." For years, almost every State had concluded non-aggression pacts with other States. But all lacked a clarification of the very meaning of aggression, thus leaving a loophole for those who wanted to evade their obligations.

The Kellogg-Briand Pact renounced war but did not define aggression. Litvinoff was the only statesman who saw this crucial defect, and now he proposed to remedy it by a "Convention for the Definition of Aggression," not only with Russia's neighbors with whom he had signed the treaties of non-aggression, but also with members of the Little Entente (Czechoslovakia, Rumania, Yugoslavia), who had refused so far to recognize the Soviet Union.

On July 4, 5, and 6, definition-of-aggression conventions were signed with Rumania, Czechoslovakia, Turkey, Yugoslavia, Esthonia, Afghanistan, Persia, Poland, Latvia, and Lithuania. These conventions, originally suggested by Litvinoff to the Disarmament Conference in February of that year, won for the Soviets great sympathy throughout the Western world. Once more Soviet Russia's determination to avoid war was made manifest.

Moreover, the conventions constituted an important contribution to the "practical science" of peace, clarifying what all disarmament conferences had left obscure or had even tried to make as nebulous as possible. After Litvinoff's definition, there were still many cases in which statesmen argued whether or not a country had been attacked. But never for a moment could they create any doubt in the mind of the world at large as to what constituted aggression and who was the aggressor. Ever since Litvinoff wrote his definition, the world has known—in spite of the opinions of the appeasers—that Japan was an aggressor and not a defender, that Italy was an aggressor and that Hitler was an aggressor.

The Convention for the Definition of Aggression signed on July 4, 1933, embodied that definition:

The Central Executive Committee of the Union of Socialist Soviet Republics, His Majesty the King of Roumania, the President of the Republic of Turkey and His Majesty the King of Yugoslavia:

"being desirous of consolidating the peaceful relations existing between their countries;

"mindful of the fact that the Briand-Kellogg Pact, of which they are signatories, prohibits all aggression;

"deeming it necessary, in the interest of general security, to define aggression as explicitly as possible in order to obviate any pretext whereby it might be justified;

"noting that all States have an equal right to independence, security, the defense of their territories, and the free development of their institutions;

"animated by the desire to secure to all peoples in the interest of the general peace the inviolability of the territory of their countries;

"judging it expedient, in the interest of general peace, to bring into force, as between their countries, precise rules defining aggression, until such time as those rules shall become universal,

"have decided to this end to conclude the present Convention. . . .

ARTICLE I

"Each of the High Contracting Parties undertakes to accept in its relations with each of the other Parties, from the date of the entry into force of the present Convention, the definition of aggression as explained in the Report dated May 24th, 1933, of the Committee on Security Questions (Politis Report) to the Conference for the Reduction and Limitation of Armaments, which Report was made in consequence of the Soviet delegation's proposal.

"Accordingly, the aggressor in an international conflict shall, without prejudice to the agreements in force between the Parties to dispute, be considered to be that State which is the first to commit any of the following actions:

"1. Declaration of war upon another State;

"2. Invasion by its armed forces, with or without a declaration of war, of the territory of another State;

"3. Attack by its land, naval or air forces, with or without a declaration of war, on the territory, vessels or aircraft of another State;

"4. Naval blockade of the coasts or ports of another State;

"5. Provision of support to armed bands formed on its territory which have invaded the territory of another State, or refusal, notwithstanding the request of the invaded State, to take on its own territory all the measures in its power to deprive those bands of all assistance or protection.

"No political, military, economic or other considerations may serve as an excuse or justification for the aggression referred to in Article 2. . . ."

8

Litvinoff's other achievement at the London Economic Conference, the preparation of a basis for negotiations with the United States, ultimately was to result in recognition of Soviet Russia. On June 22 Bullitt visited Litvinoff at the Russian Embassy in Kensington Palace Gardens and talked with him for an hour, while United States Senator James Couzens had luncheon with another Soviet delegate to discuss details of recognition. On July 2 Litvinoff conferred with Assistant Secretary of State Raymond Moley. Moley went to great pains to deny that there had been any talk of recognition. The subject of discussion was, in fact, the conditions under which the United States would sell to Russia 60,000 to 80,000 bales of cotton. Two days later the purchase was concluded on a 70 per cent credit basis. Litvinoff stated, as he had done before, that Russia could use large quantities of metals and other raw materials. This, he suggested, might help recovery in the United States and bring the two countries closer together. By July 4 Litvinoff was convinced that recognition would follow. He was informed by his new American friends that "President Roosevelt looked favorably upon the re-establishment of ordinary relations with the government which then had ruled Russia for sixteen years."

The London Economic Conference thus became a high point in the career of Litvinoff, the statesman. On his return to Moscow, Stalin congratulated him, particularly on the imminent recognition by the United States, and told him quite formally that his "long fight for recognition was thus crowned by the important event now impending."

But there was still one dark cloud on the horizon: Litvinoff knew that there was dangerously little time left to organize a peace which could be preserved and defended against the new threat just being launched by the resolute fanatic, Adolf Hitler.

CHAPTER TEN

Litvinoff in Washington

WHEN MOLEY AND BULLITT returned to Washington from London they reported to President Roosevelt their talks with Litvinoff. The President reiterated his intention to recognize Soviet Russia at the earliest possible moment. Bullitt, using as a channel the Russian Information Bureau, carried out the behind-the-scene negotiations with the Narkomindel. It was finally agreed that Litvinoff would come to Washington during the first week of November. There was no time to be lost because Secretary Hull was to leave for the Pan-American Conference in Montevideo, and President Roosevelt wanted him to be present at the Russo-American negotiations.

When everything was arranged, President Roosevelt and the President of the Soviet Union, Mikhail Kalinin, exchanged letters:

Washington, Oct. 10, 1933

My dear Mr. President:

Since the beginning of my Administration, I have contemplated the desirability of an effort to end the present abnormal relations between the hundred and twenty-five million people of the United States and the hundred and sixty million people of Russia.

It is most regrettable that these great peoples, between whom a happy tradition of friendship existed for more than a century to their mutual advantage, should now be without a practical method of communicating directly with each other.

The difficulties that have created this anomalous situation are serious but not, in my opinion, insoluble; and difficulties between great Nations can be removed only by frank, friendly conversations. If you are of similar mind, I should be glad to receive any representatives you may designate to explore with me personally all questions outstanding between our countries.

Participation in such a discussion would, of course, not commit either

Nation to any future course of action, but would indicate a sincere desire to reach a satisfactory solution of the problems involved. It is my hope that such conversations might result in good to the people of both our countries.

I am, my dear Mr. President,

Very sincerely yours,

(Signed) Franklin D. Roosevelt

Moscow, Oct. 17, 1933

My dear Mr. President:

I have received your message of October 10th.

I have always considered most abnormal and regrettable a situation wherein, during the past sixteen years, two great Republics—The United States of America and the Union of Soviet Socialist Republics—have lacked the usual methods of communication and have been deprived of the benefits which such communication could give. I am glad to note that you also reached the same conclusion.

There is no doubt that difficulties, present or arising, between two countries, can be solved only when direct relations exist between them; and that, on the other hand, they have no chance for solution in the absence of such relations. I shall take the liberty further to express the opinion that the abnormal situation, to which you correctly refer in your message, has an unfavorable effect not only on the interests of the two states concerned, but also on the general international situation, increasing the element of disquiet, complicating the process of consolidating world peace and encouraging forces tending to disturb that peace.

In accordance with the above, I gladly accept your proposal to send to the United States a representative of the Soviet Government to discuss with you the questions of interest to our countries. The Soviet Government will be represented by Mr. M. M. Litvinoff, People's Commissar for Foreign Affairs, who will come to Washington at a time to be mutually agreed upon.

I am, my dear Mr. President,

Very sincerely yours,

(Signed) Mikhail Kalinin

With the publication of this correspondence President Roosevelt announced that arrangements had been completed for an early meeting between him and Litvinoff. In a special message he indicated, furthermore, that he would personally conduct the discussions with the Rus-

sian representative, perhaps because the State Department's long record
of hostility to the Soviet Government might be a little embarrassing.
He set forth the following four principal points for discussion:

1. Russian propaganda in the United States.
2. The debts contracted by the Kerenski Government in 1917.
3. Confiscated American properties.
4. Rights of American citizens in the Soviet Union.

The impending recognition of Soviet Russia by the United States
had caused something of a sensation throughout the world. The Nazi
Government in Berlin was especially perturbed. Hitler is said to have
seriously considered preventing Litvinoff from traveling via Berlin to
the United States, but his Foreign Minister, Baron von Neurath,
strongly advised against such action. On October 25 the Wilhelmstrasse denied that there was any real basis to these "rumors."

On October 24, at an Intourist Banquet in Moscow, Constantin
Oumansky, Chief of the Press Bureau, announced that he was leaving
for Spain. The newspaper men immediately concluded that he was
going to Washington with Litvinoff, and one foreign correspondent,
annoyed at the mystification, accused him of trying to make himself
important.

Oumansky, however, was not to blame for the concealment maneuvers. Litvinoff himself had insisted on traveling incognito and refused to let any hints about his departure leak out. On October 26 at
midnight he got into a private car which was later attached to the
regular Berlin express. Only a small group saw him off, a few Narkomindel officials, and his children, Misha and Tanya. Madame Litvinoff
was not there.

The censorship was strict. When, the morning after, the foreign
correspondents enquired about Litvinoff's trip, they were told by Podol-
sky, Oumansky's deputy as head of the Press Bureau, "No comment."

This "no comment" was the leitmotiv of Litvinoff's whole journey.
He spent just one hour in Warsaw late on the evening of October 27,
thirty-five minutes of it at the Soviet Embassy in the company of
Stanislas Patek, the Polish Ambassador to Washington. When he was
besieged by newspaper men he merely said, "No interviews on political
matters."

In Paris a large crowd was waiting for him at the Gare du Nord.

The train arrived but there was no Litvinoff. Everybody was disappointed. The reporters were told by the customs officials that he had not crossed the frontier from Germany.

What had happened to Litvinoff? Had he been killed in Germany? What could the Germans have done to him? It was a world sensation. Telephone and cable lines were jammed with messages seeking to locate the elusive Foreign Commissar.

But actually there was nothing very mysterious about Litvinoff's whereabouts. He was in Berlin at the Russian Embassy discussing details of his trip to Washington with Ambassador Jacob Surich. Berlin correspondents were kept away from him and there was no publicity whatsoever. Hence the rumors.

Finally, late on October 30, Litvinoff turned up in Paris. This time only a few people were at the station to greet him. Again the one thing he said was that he had nothing to say: "No comment." The next day he received the diplomatic passports for his delegation from the United States Embassy. A conference with the French Foreign Minister, Joseph Paul-Boncour, followed.

Again he disappeared. Two ships were to sail the next day: the English *Berengaria* and the German *Bremen*. Litvinoff was a man of many surprises. Was he, perhaps, going to sail on the *Bremen*?

Newspaper men and Communist sympathizers gathered at the Gare St. Lazare where the Cherbourg boat train was leaving. But Litvinoff did not appear. And the Russian Embassy did not answer any telephone calls.

Litvinoff was already in a motor car on the road to Cherbourg, paced and followed by cars of the French Sûreté. On November 1 he boarded the Cunard liner *Berengaria*.

Again he refused to make any statement. The steamship company had reserved the royal suite for him, but he chose instead a small suite consisting of a stateroom, and a sitting room which he used as a study. Both cabins were stuffed with documents. There were 616 cases of files and papers, some of which Litvinoff intended to study during the trip. The passage was calm, and the Commissar was immensely relieved because he had been told that a trans-Atlantic crossing at this time of year could be thoroughly disagreeable, with small opportunity for work.

The only newspaper man accompanying the Foreign Commissar was Walter Duranty.

2

In the meantime the State Department in Washington was busy completing arrangements for Litvinoff's reception. There were many problems, including police protection. Another serious question was how the protocol man was to dress when receiving the Soviet Envoy? In the end, it was decided that James Clement Dunn, who was to have this part, should wear the usual morning-coat and silk topper. It was also agreed that no offense would be taken if Litvinoff should not be similarly dressed. The gentlemen hoped for the best, telling each other about occasions in Geneva and London on which Litvinoff, too, had appeared in formal morning attire.

At a second preliminary conference in President Roosevelt's study, with Hull, Undersecretary of State William Philipps, Henry Morgenthau, Jr., Bullitt and R. Walter Moor present, it was decided that Philipps, Morgenthau, Bullitt, and Moor should conduct the first negotiations and, when the initial difficulties were ironed out, the President would carry on.

On the morning of November 7 the *Berengaria* sailed into New York Harbor. She was met by two Coast Guard cutters. The cutter *Hudson* carried a group of handpicked newspaper men whom Litvinoff met at Quarantine. The cutter *Manhattan* carried the official greeters headed by Mr. Dunn. After a short ceremony Litvinoff left the *Berengaria* at Quarantine and changed over to the cutter *Manhattan*, which was to take him to the Jersey City railway station.

Litvinoff was as excited as a schoolboy. The skyline of Manhattan fascinated him. He caught sight of the Statue of Liberty and asked Dunn if it might be possible to get a closer view of the monument. Dunn arranged to have the cutter pass near the statue. Litvinoff smiled and waved his hand.

Litvinoff said that he was overwhelmed by the democratic cordiality of the reception. "It was a new experience for me," he stated. "Wherever I arrived for the first time, I was usually greeted with suspicion and it took me some time to overcome this handicap. In America it was different."

Only two foreign correspondents came to greet Litvinoff, both of them French. No English representatives of the press were present. Litvinoff thought it significant.

In Jersey City a special train, guarded by Secret Service men and a hundred police, awaited the Russian envoy. The train schedule was kept a secret by the State Department. Litvinoff dined on the train and made his first acquaintance with Virginia ham and corn fritters. He immediately gave a vote of confidence to American food.

At the Union Station in Washington the Russian was met by Secretary Hull and the President's Secretary, Louis Howe. Among the many people present were Philipps and Bullitt. Riding with Hull and Bullitt and escorted by numerous police on motorcycles, Litvinoff was at once taken to the White House.

The President, formally dressed and visibly excited, was awaiting the arrival of his guest in the Blue Room under Abraham Lincoln's portrait. There is a story that Roosevelt for a while considered receiving Litvinoff in the beautiful Red Room, but then decided to abandon the little joke.

The greeting of the two men was informal, probably to the dismay of certain representatives of the State Department. To make it even more informal, Mrs. Roosevelt appeared to welcome the guest and express her regret that Madame Litvinoff had not accompanied her husband.

Then Litvinoff was asked to step out to the White House portico where, with a broad smile, he was photographed by a host of camera men. And then, without being asked, he volunteered a statement. He said he was gratified by the happy beginning, which augured well for the negotiations to come.

From the White House Litvinoff was taken, with a motorcycle escort, to a modest building on Massachusetts Avenue where Boris E. Skvirsky lived. As chief of the Russian Information Bureau he had been functioning as an unofficial Ambassador and representative.

The following day, November 8, Litvinoff returned to the White House to begin his discussions, and lunch with the President. On the same day he also had two parleys with Secretary Hull. The next day he continued his discussion with Hull and attended a formal luncheon. He was getting on extremely well with Hull. Nine years later things were to be different. The Litvinoff of 1943 was much closer to Assistant Secretary of State Sumner Welles, and to the President, to whom he often carried his problems, than he was to Hull.

In his negotiations with the State Department, Litvinoff once more proved himself the shrewd diplomat. He told American newspaper men that as far as he was concerned all outstanding points between the United States and the Soviet Union could be settled in half an hour. When he made the statement, it was termed an incautious and undiplomatic remark and, as Litvinoff had expected, it caused considerable excitement throughout the country. Newspapers and political leaders demanded that recognition should not be a matter of half an hour of discussion, but that extensive preliminary negotiations were indispensable. Litvinoff had expected, as had the American officials, prolonged conferences, but after that remark the extensive negotiations appeared to be a compromise, a concession, on Litvinoff's part, giving him an initial advantage.

On November 11 the *New York Times* announced that the President was conducting negotiations prior to recognition of the Soviet Union in the "shrewd New England horse-trading" manner. This was exactly the sort of press comment that Litvinoff liked. Whether or not Roosevelt did show a "shrewd New England horse-trading" sense, the two men understood each other and soon became quite friendly and confidential. Roosevelt was pleased when Litvinoff, during one of their meetings, showed him cables of press excerpts from Moscow hailing the cordial reception in Washington. By November 12 Litvinoff had had a prolonged night parley with Roosevelt and, on November 17, the recognition was a fait accompli.

A number of letters, signed by the President and Litvinoff respectively, were published on November 17. They contained all the stipulations of both parties, and formed the basis of the subsequent collaboration.

Exchange of Communications between the President of the United States and Maxim Litvinoff of the Union of Soviet Republics. November 16, 1933.

The White House, Washington, Nov. 16, 1933

My dear Mr. Litvinoff:

I am very happy to inform you that as a result of our conversations the Government of the United States has decided to establish normal diplomatic relations with the Government of the Union of Soviet Socialist Republics and to exchange ambassadors.

I trust that the relations now established between our peoples may forever remain normal and friendly, and that our Nations henceforth may cooperate for their mutual benefit and for the preservation of the peace of the world.

I am, my dear Mr. Litvinoff,

Very sincerely yours,

(Signed) Franklin D. Roosevelt

———————

Washington, November 16, 1933

My dear Mr. President:

I am very happy to inform you that the Government of the Union of Soviet Socialist Republics is glad to establish normal diplomatic relations with the Government of the United States and to exchange ambassadors.

I, too, share the hope that the relations now established between our peoples may forever remain normal and friendly, and that our Nations henceforth may cooperate for their mutual benefit and for the preservation of the peace of the world.

I am, my dear Mr. President,

Very sincerely yours,

(Signed) Maxim Litvinoff

———————

Washington, November 16, 1933

My dear Mr. President:

I have the honor to inform you that coincident with the establishment of diplomatic relations between our two Governments, it will be the fixed policy of the Government of the Union of Soviet Socialist Republics:

"1. To respect scrupulously the indisputable right of the United States to order its own life within its own jurisdiction in its own way and to refrain from interfering in any manner in the internal affairs of the United States, its territories or possessions.

"2. To refrain, and to restrain all persons in Government service and all organizations of the Government or under its direct or indirect control, including organizations in receipt of any financial assistance from it, from any act overt or covert liable in any way whatsoever to injure the tranquillity, prosperity, order, or security of the whole or any part of the United States, its territories or possessions, and, in particular, from any act tending to incite or encourage armed intervention, or any agitation or propaganda having as an aim, the violation of the territorial integrity of the United States, its territories or possessions, or the bringing about by force of a change in the political or social order of the whole or any part of the United States, its territories or possessions.

"3. Not to permit the formation or residence on its territory of any organization or group—and to prevent the activity on its territory of any organization or group, or of representatives or officials of any organization or group—which makes claim to be the Government of, or makes attempt upon the territorial integrity of, the United States, its territories or possessions; not to form, subsidize, support or permit on its territory military organizations or groups having the aim of aimed struggle against the United States, its territories or possessions, and to prevent any recruiting on behalf of such organizations and groups.

"4. Not to permit the formation or residence on its territory of any organization or group—and to prevent the activity on its territory of any organization or group, or of representatives or officials of any organization or group—which has as aim the overthrow or the preparation for the overthrow of, or the bringing about by force of a change in, the political or social order of the whole or any part of the United States, its territories or possessions."

I am, my dear Mr. President,

Very sincerely yours,

(Signed) Maxim Litvinoff
People's Commissar for Foreign Affairs
Union of Soviet Socialist Republics

The White House, Washington, Nov. 16, 1933

My dear Mr. Litvinoff:

(Mr. Roosevelt replied, repeating Litvinoff's letter word for word, and then added):

It will be the fixed policy of the Executive of the United States within the limits of the powers conferred by the Constitution and the laws of the United States to adhere reciprocally to the engagements above expressed.

I am, my dear Mr. Litvinoff,

Very sincerely yours,

(Signed) Franklin D. Roosevelt

The White House, Washington, Nov. 16, 1933

My dear Mr. Litvinoff:

As I have told you in our recent conversations, it is my expectation that after the establishment of normal relations between our two countries many Americans will wish to reside temporarily or permanently within the territory of the Union of Soviet Socialist Republics, and I am deeply concerned that they should enjoy in all respects the same freedom of conscience and religious liberty which they enjoy at home.

As you well know, the Government of the United States, since the foundation of the Republic, has always striven to protect its nationals, at home and abroad, in the free exercise of liberty of conscience and religious worship, and from all disability or persecution on account of their religious faith or worship. And I need scarcely point out that the rights enumerated below are those enjoyed in the United States by all citizens and foreign nationals and by American nationals in all the major countries of the world.

The Government of the United States, therefore, will expect that nationals of the United States of America within the territory of the Union of Soviet Socialist Republics will be allowed to conduct without annoyance or molestation of any kind religious services and rites of a ceremonial nature, including baptismal, confirmation, communion, marriage and burial rites, in the English language, or in any other language which is customarily used in the practice of the religious faith to which they belong, in churches, houses, or other buildings appropriate for such service, which they will be given the right and opportunity to lease, erect or maintain in convenient situations.

We will expect that nationals of the United States will have the right to collect from their co-religionists voluntary offerings for religious purposes; that they will be entitled without restriction to impart religious instruction to their children, whether singly or in groups, or to have such instruction imparted by persons whom they may employ for such purpose; that they will be given and protected in the right to bury their dead according to their religious customs in suitable and convenient places established for that purpose, and given the right and opportunity to lease, lay out, occupy and maintain such burial grounds subject to reasonable sanitary laws and regulations.

We will expect that religious groups or congregations composed of nationals of the United States of America in the territory of the Union of Soviet Socialist Republics will be given the right to have their spiritual needs ministered to by clergymen, priests, rabbis or other ecclesiastical functionaries who are nationals of the United States of America, and that such clergymen, priests, rabbis or other ecclesiastical functionaries will be protected from all disability or persecution and will not be denied entry into the territory of the Soviet Union because of their ecclesiastical status.

I am, my dear Mr. Litvinoff,

Very sincerely yours,

(Signed) Franklin D. Roosevelt

Washington, November 16, 1933

My dear Mr. President:

In reply to your letter of November 16, 1933, I have the honor to inform you that the Government of the Union of Soviet Socialist Republics as a fixed policy accords the nationals of the United States within the territory of the Union of Soviet Socialist Republics the following rights referred to by you:

"1. The right to 'free exercise of liberty of conscience and religious worship' and protection 'from all disability or persecution on account of their religious faith or worship.' "

This right is supported by the following laws and regulations existing in the various republics of the Union:

Every person may profess any religion or none. All restrictions of rights connected with the profession of any belief whatsoever, or with the non-profession of any belief, are annulled. (Decree of Jan. 23, 1918, art. 3.)

Within the confines of the Soviet Union it is prohibited to issue any local laws or regulations restricting or limiting freedom of conscience, or establishing privileges or preferential rights of any kind based upon the religious profession of any person. (Decree of Jan. 23, 1918, art. 2.)

"2. The right of 'conduct without annoyance or molestation of any kind of religious services and rites of a ceremonial nature.' "

This right is supported by the following laws:

A free performance of religious rites is guaranteed as long as it does not interfere with public order and is not accompanied by interference with the rights of citizens of the Soviet Union. Local authorities possess the right in such cases to adopt all necessary measures to preserve public order and safety. (Decree of Jan. 23, 1918, art. 5.)

Interference with the performance of religious rites, in so far as they do not endanger public order and are not accompanied by infringements on the rights of others, is punishable by compulsory labor for a period up to six months. (Criminal Code, art. 127.)

"3. 'The right and opportunity to lease, erect or maintain in convenient situations' churches, houses or other buildings appropriate for religious purposes.' "

This right is supported by the following laws and regulations:

Believers belonging to a religious society with the object of making provision for their requirements in the matter of religion: may lease under contract, free of charge, from the Sub-District or District Executive Committee or from the Town Soviet, special buildings for the purpose of worship and objects intended exclusively for the purposes of their cult. (Decree of April 8, 1929, art. 10.)

Furthermore, believers who have formed a religious society or a group of believers may use for religious meetings other buildings at their disposal on lease by private persons or by local Soviets and Executive Committees. All rules established for houses of worship are applicable to these buildings. Contracts for the use of such buildings shall be concluded by individual believers who will be held responsible for their execution. In addition, these buildings must comply with the sanitary and technical building regulations. (Decree of April 8, 1929, art. 10.)

The place of worship and religious property shall be handed over for the use of believers forming a religious society under a contract concluded in the name of the competent District Executive Committee or Town Soviet by the competent administrative department or branch, or directly by the Sub-district Executive Committee. (Decree of April 8, 1929, art. 15.)

The construction of new places of worship may take place at the desire of religious societies provided that the usual technical building regulations and the special regulations laid down by the People's Commissariat for Internal Affairs are observed. (Decree of April 8, 1929, art. 45.)

"4. 'The right to collect from their co-religionists voluntary offerings for religious purposes.' "
This right is supported by the following law:

Members of groups of believers and religious societies may raise subscriptions among themselves and collect voluntary offerings, both in the place of worship itself and outside it, but only amongst the members of the religious association concerned and only for purposes connected with the upkeep of the place of worship and the religious property, for the engagement of ministers of religion and for the expenses of their executive body. Any form of forced contribution in aid of religious associations is punishable under the Criminal Code. (Decree of April 8, 1929, art. 54.)

"5. Right to impart religious instruction to their children either singly or in groups or to have such instruction imparted by persons whom they may employ for such purpose."

This right is supported by the following law:

The school is separated from the Church. Instruction in religious doctrines is not permitted in any governmental and common schools, nor in private teaching institutions where general subjects are taught. Persons may give or receive religious instruction in a private manner. (Decree of Jan. 23, 1918, art. 9.)

Furthermore, the Soviet Government is prepared to include in a consular convention to be negotiated immediately following the establishment of relations between our two countries provisions in which nationals of the United States shall be granted rights with reference to freedom of conscience and the free exercise of religion which shall not be less favorable than those enjoyed in the Union of Soviet Socialist Republics by nationals of the Nation most favored in this respect. In this connection, I have the honor to call to your attention Article 9 of the Treaty between Germany and the Union of Soviet Socialist Republics, signed at Moscow October 12, 1925, which reads as follows:

"Nationals of each of the Contracting Parties . . . shall be entitled to hold religious services in churches, houses or other buildings, rented, according to the laws of the country, in their national language or in any other practice, in burial grounds established and maintained by them with the approval of the competent authorities, so long as they comply with the police regulations of the other Party in respect of buildings and public health."

Furthermore, I desire to state that the rights specified in the above paragraphs, will be granted to American nationals immediately upon the establishment of relations between our two countries.

Finally, I have the honor to inform you that the Government of the Union of Soviet Socialist Republics, while reserving to itself the right of refusing visas to Americans desiring to enter the Union of Soviet Socialist Republics on personal grounds, does not intend to base such refusals on the fact of such persons having an ecclesiastical status.

I am, my dear Mr. President,

Very sincerely yours,

(Signed) Maxim Litvinoff

————————

Washington, November 16, 1933

My dear Mr. President:

Following our conversations I have the honor to inform you that the

Soviet Government is prepared to include in a consular convention to be negotiated immediately following the establishment of relations between our two countries provisions in which nationals of the United States shall be granted rights with reference to legal protection which shall not be less favorable than those enjoyed in the Union of Soviet Socialist Republics by nationals of the Nation most favored in this respect immediately upon the establishment of relations between our two countries.

In this connection I have the honor to call to your attention Article II and the Protocol to Article II, of the Agreement Concerning Conditions of Resident and Business and Legal Protection in General concluded between Germany and the Union of Soviet Socialist Republics on October 12, 1925.

"Article II

"Each of the Contracting Parties undertakes to adopt the necessary measures to inform the Consul of the other Party as soon as possible whenever a national of the country which he represents is arrested in his district.

"The same procedure shall apply if a prisoner is transferred from one place of detention to another.

"Final Protocol to Article II

"1. The Consul shall be notified either by a communication from the person arrested or by the authorities themselves, direct. Such communications shall be made within a period not exceeding seven times twenty-four hours, and in large towns, including capitals of districts, within a period not exceeding three times twenty-four hours.

"2. In places of detention of all kinds, requests made by consular representatives to visit nationals of their country under arrest, or to have them visited by their representatives, shall be granted without delay. The consular representative shall not be entitled to require officials of the courts or prisons to withdraw during his interview with the person under arrest."

I am, my dear Mr. President,

Very sincerely yours,

(Signed) Maxim Litvinoff

———————

The White House, Washington, Nov. 16, 1933

My dear Mr. Litvinoff:

I thank you for your letter of November 16, 1933, informing me that the Soviet Government is prepared to grant to nationals of the United States rights with reference to legal protection not less favorable than those enjoyed in the Union of Soviet Socialist Republics by nationals of the

Nation most favored in this respect. I have noted the provisions of the treaty and protocol concluded between Germany and the Union of Soviet Socialist Republics on October 12, 1925.

I am glad that nationals of the United States will enjoy the protection afforded by these instruments immediately upon the establishment of relations between our two countries and I am fully prepared to negotiate a consular convention covering these subjects as soon as practicable. Let me add that American diplomatic and consular officers in the Soviet Union will be zealous in guarding the rights of American nationals, particularly the right to a fair, public and speedy trial and the right to be represented by counsel of their choice. We shall be notified immediately of any arrest or detention of an American national, and that he shall promptly be afforded the opportunity to communicate and converse with such national.

I am, my dear Mr. Litvinoff,

Very sincerely yours,

(Signed) Franklin D. Roosevelt

In reply to a question of the President in regard to prosecution for economic espionage, Mr. Litvinoff gave the following explanation:

"The widespread opinion that the dissemination of economic information from the Union of Soviet Socialist Republics is allowed only in so far as this information has been published in newspapers or magazines, is erroneous. The right to obtain economic information is limited in the Union of Soviet Socialist Republics, as in other countries, only in the case of business and production secrets and in the case of the employments of forbidden methods (bribery, theft, fraud, etc.) to obtain such information. The category of business and production secrets naturally includes the official economic plans, in so far as they have not been made public, but not individual reports concerning the production conditions and the general conditions of individual enterprises.

"The Union of Soviet Socialist Republics has also no reason to complicate or hinder the critical examination of its economic organization. It naturally follows from this that everyone has the right to talk about economic matters or to receive information about such matters in the Union, in so far as the information for which he has asked or which has been imparted to him is not such as may not, on the basis of special regulations issued by responsible officials or by the appropriate State enterprises, be made known to outsiders. (This principle applies primarily to information concerning economic trends and tendencies.)"

Washington, Nov. 16, 1933

My dear Mr. President:

Following our conversations I have the honor to inform you that the Government of the Union of Soviet Socialist Republics agrees that, preparatory to a final settlement of the claims and counter claims between the Governments of the Union of Soviet Socialist Republics and the United States of America and the claims of their nationals, the Government of the Union of Soviet Socialist Republics will not take any steps to enforce any decisions of costs or initiate any new litigations for the amounts admitted to be due or that may be found to be due it, as the successor of prior Governments of Russia, or otherwise, from American nationals, including corporations, companies, partnerships, or associations, and also the claim against the United States of the Russian Volunteer Fleet, now in litigation in the United States Court of Claims, and will not object to such amounts being assigned and does hereby release and assign all such amounts to the Government of the Union of Soviet Socialist Republics to be duly notified in each case of any amount realized by the Government of the United States from such release and assignment.

The Government of the Union of Soviet Socialist Republics further agrees, preparatory to the settlement referred to above, not to make any claim with respect to:

a) judgments rendered or that may be rendered by American courts in so far as they relate to property, or rights, or interests therein, in which the Union of Soviet Socialist Republics or its nationals may have had or may claim to have an interest; or,

b) acts done or settlements made by or with the Government of the United States, or public officials in the United States, or its nationals, relating to property, credits, or obligations of any Government of Russia or nationals thereof.

I am, my dear Mr. President,

Very sincerely yours,

(Signed) Maxim Litvinoff

———————

The White House, Washington, Nov. 16, 1933

My dear Mr. Litvinoff:

(Again the President legally confirmed the understanding by a verbatim repetition of Litvinoff's letter, concluding):

I am glad to have these undertakings by your Government and I shall be pleased to notify your Government in each case of any amount realized by the Government of the United States from the release and assignment to it of the amounts admitted to be due, or that may be found to be due, the Government of the Union of Soviet Socialist Republics, and of the amount that may be found to be due on the claim of the Russian Volunteer Fleet.

I am, my dear Mr. Litvinoff,

Very sincerely yours,

(Signed) Franklin D. Roosevelt

The vexatious problem of Russian claims against the United States for the damages due to the intervention of American armed forces in Siberia between 1918 and 1922 was summarily disposed of by the following letter:

Washington, November 16, 1933

My dear Mr. President:

I have the honor to inform you that, following our conversations and following my examination of certain documents of the years 1918 to 1921 relating to the attitude of the American government toward the expedition into Siberia, the operations there of foreign military forces and the inviolability of the territory of the Union of Soviet Socialist Republics, the Government of the Union of Soviet Socialist Republics agrees that it will waive any and all claims of whatsoever character arising out of activities of military forces of the United States in Siberia, or assistance to military forces of the United States in Siberia, or assistance to military forces in Siberia subsequent to January 1, 1918, and that such claims shall be regarded as finally settled and disposed of by this agreement.

I am, my dear Mr. President,

Very sincerely yours,

Maxim Litvinoff

Before Litvinoff's arrival, Washington was a little anxious lest some unpleasant incident—even an actual assault—mar the visit. These apprehensions, fortunately, proved to be unfounded, though a certain Paul Bants, a painter, formerly a lieutenant in the Russian Imperial Guard, and well known in Russian émigré circles, made threatening remarks in a speakeasy on the day of Litvinoff's arrival in New York. When he was arrested, he even boasted to the police that if he could get close enough to Litvinoff, he would kill him. He was sent to Ellis Island and deported as an illegal resident.

During the negotiations, pseudo-patriotic and jingoistic pressure groups agitated against recognition of the Soviet Union, including one in Chicago that called itself the Paul Reveres. The American Federation of Labor continued its work behind the scenes.

Another attack was launched by Congressman Hamilton Fish and some of his friends, who threatened to vote against funds for the American Embassy in Moscow if the Soviets should not establish freedom of worship. The movement was not taken seriously. Perhaps too many people knew that Hamilton Fish had attempted to do business with Soviet Russia and when his propositions were rejected because of the unreasonable, not to say exorbitant, profits to be reserved for himself and his associates, he had threatened in revenge to make political trouble for the Russian Government.

Much more serious was an attempt by Japan to sabotage the conference in Washington, not directly, but by using Eugene Lyons, United Press correspondent in Moscow. Eugene Lyons had come to Moscow full of enthusiasm for the Soviet Union, not sufficiently distinguishing hopes from achievement. Since hell hath no fury like a frustrated doctrinaire idealist, his good will turned to a vindictive and unreasonable animosity and he was already beginning to make an inventory of all the disagreeable things he saw, could think of, or heard about the Soviet Union. He was thus an easy victim for the Japanese schemes. "News" of serious clashes between Russians and Japanese was furnished him. Russian anti-aircraft guns, it was said, had fired on Japanese planes flying over Siberia, bodies of Japanese flyers were supposed to have been handed over to the Japanese at the Manchurian border, and Russian ships equipped with cannon had presumably sunk Japanese fishing trawlers in Russian waters. The incidents appeared grave. A war in the Far East seemed imminent. The implication was that Russia wanted recognition from the United States in order to have an ally in the event of war. The United States was, thus indirectly, warned to avoid recognition in the face of impending Russian disaster.

On November 9 Lyons telephoned the Japanese story to his London office. Later, realizing that he had fallen into a trap, the author said

that he had written the dispatch in the subjunctive and had tried to kill
it an hour later. But when it appeared in the American papers, there
was no trace of the subjunctive and the story had not been killed.

Litvinoff in Washington did not mince words. He labeled the affair
a Japanese plot to wreck the negotiations, and said that the American
journalist had been used as a cat's-paw. Tokyo, incidentally, let the correspondent down by issuing a categorical denial of the whole matter.
Lyons afterwards excused himself on the ground that he had been
"framed" by the Soviet Government.

Litvinoff was certainly the best man that the Russian Government
could have sent to show the Americans that Communists were like
other people, human beings, who enjoyed eating and drinking, working and playing, were fond of their families and eager to have a good
time. This was ideally demonstrated when the National Broadcasting
Corporation proposed to arrange a two-way radio conversation between Litvinoff and his wife and children. He readily agreed that the
conversation be broadcast over the National network to enable millions of Americans to listen in.

Early on November 17 engineers of the National Broadcasting Company arrived at the White House with their equipment to prepare for
the two-way broadcast. Litvinoff spoke from the Oval Room; his wife
was at a short-wave radio station in Moscow. Her voice came over the
R.C.A. short-wave direct to New York and was relayed by telephone
wire to Washington. Litvinoff's voice was transmitted by short-wave
to Berlin and from there over regular telephone lines to Moscow.

The conversation ran:

Litvinoff: Hello!

Madame L.: Hello, darling, hello, hello! I hear you beautifully.
How are you?

Litvinoff: Please speak slowly, will you?

Madame L.: Yes.

Litvinoff: I am now in the White House.

Madame L.: Yes, I know.

Litvinoff: I have just been talking with the President, and his last
words were to give you his regards.

Madame L.: Thank you very much. I have them.

Litvinoff: Mr. Skvirsky sends you his regards.

Madame L.: Thank you very much.

Litvinoff: Everybody here is very sorry you did not come with me.

Madame L.: Oh!

Litvinoff: Also the President and Madame Roosevelt express their regret that you did not accompany me.

Madame L.: That is very kind of them.

And so on, just intimate, trivial queries or comments and replies, such as any members of a family exchange when they have an unexpected chance for long-distance communication, with nothing particular to say. Of course, there was nothing about politics. It was the kind of family conversation that the average American would perfectly understand.

Shortly before Litvinoff sailed, he had another chance to impress Americans, this time as quite a different type of man, shrewdly practical. The Russo-American Chamber of Commerce gave a dinner in his honor at the Waldorf-Astoria Hotel. Outstanding figures in finance and industry were there. Many were delighted with the recognition, which promised good business with Soviet Russia, but they were also a little anxious, fearing lest Soviet Russia might not renounce Communist propaganda in the United States, and Communism might become a powerful movement here.

Litvinoff understood their misgivings. He also realized that his assurance that Russia would honor its obligation not to disseminate propaganda would have little or no effect. So he did not broach the question directly, but spoke of his conversations with the President whom he had learned to esteem highly, and said that during pauses in the negotiations, both he and the President had brought forward arguments for the ideas and principles in which they believed. But, Litvinoff concluded, he doubted that either had converted the other.

Everyone laughed, partly because of Litvinoff's own contagious good nature. Many commented that Litvinoff had an American sense of humor. "Too bad he is a Communist. But anyhow, he is a man you can do business with."

Ten years before, Louise Bryant had foreseen the probability of Litvinoff's success in the United States: "If . . . conferences are ever held in America," she wrote in 1923, "Litvinoff might prove the most popular of the group. Any country which is satisfied with the familiar type of our middle western Congressmen will not reject an intelligent proletarian like Litvinoff. Some of our rough-and-ready Senators will surely feel . . . at home with his bluntness. . . . Litvinoff reminds one of a successful mining man from Alaska or a lumber king from the West."

Litvinoff in later years on numerous occasions proved how well he understood the American mentality by his skillful avoidance of all discussion pertaining to the non-payment of former debts, a problem that turned up sporadically, and was used by enemies of Soviet Russia again and again to disturb American-Russian relations. He would say rather innocently that being a layman in such questions he could not make any statement, blandly disregarding the fact that he had started his diplomatic career by dealing primarily with economic matters, and he still maintains this attitude, which has helped him preserve cordial relations with the United States.

Again Litvinoff showed how well he understood American senti-ments in the case of the Catholic priest, Father Braun. Braun went to Moscow with the American delegation on the insistence of Roose-velt, who wanted to prove that there was freedom of worship in the Soviet Union. Occasionally Braun ran into a little trouble with the authorities there, principally because he kept to himself the birth records of the diplomatic corps which Russian officials required from time to time as a matter of routine. Litvinoff, who had promised Roosevelt that Father Braun would never be disturbed, always smoothed out the difficulties. Braun is still in Moscow.

Similarly when someone in the Narkomindel conceived the bright idea of sending the Russian ballet (the real one) to New York and Washington for a series of performances at the time of the New York World's Fair, Litvinoff, half in earnest and half in jest, objected: "Those girls are too beautiful. The Americans will fall in love with them, they will get married and never come back here where we need them."

When Stalin heard Litvinoff's objection, he asked whom he intended to send instead of the girls. Litvinoff suggested the Male Choir of the All-Russian Army of Workers and Peasants. Stalin was impressed and congratulated Litvinoff. The Male Choir started out but the outbreak of the war interrupted the schedule and they returned to Soviet Russia.

3

With the American recognition of Soviet Russia on November 17, 1933, Litvinoff's main business in Washington was finished. Only minor details remained to be settled. On November 20 Litvinoff took up the practical question of the resumption of normal relations. He was told that William Bullitt would be America's first Ambassador. The first Soviet Ambassador to the United States was Alexander Troyanovsky (1933–1939), the second, Constantin Oumansky (1939–1941). On November 22 everything was arranged, and Litvinoff began to make the rounds, paying farewell visits to new-found friends. President Roosevelt had already left for Warm Springs, so Litvinoff wrote him:

Washington, November 22, 1933

My dear Mr. President:

On leaving the United States I feel it a great pleasure respectfully to convey to you my feelings of high esteem as well as gratitude for the many tokens of attention and friendship you have been good enough to show me during my stay in Washington.

I also wish hereby to thank the whole Executive and its various organs for their courtesies and cares.

I avail myself of this opportunity to express once more my firm conviction that the official linking of our two countries by the exchange of notes between you, Mr. President, and myself will be of great benefit to our two countries and will also be conducive to the strengthening and preservation of peace between Nations toward which our countries are sincerely striving. I believe that their joint efforts will add a creative factor in international affairs which will be beneficial to mankind.

Believe me to be, my dear Mr. President, with the best wishes for the well being of yourself, your family and of your great country,

Yours very sincerely,
Maxim Litvinoff

The President answered:

Warm Springs, Georgia, November 23, 1933

My dear Mr. Litvinoff:

I thank you for your most courteous letter of November 22nd, 1933. It has been a great personal pleasure to me to meet you and I trust that some day I shall again have the pleasure of welcoming you in America. On your return to your country I hope that you will convey President Kalinin my greetings and best wishes.

I am profoundly gratified that our conversations should have resulted in the restoration of normal relations between our peoples and I trust that these relations will grow closer and more intimate with each passing year. The cooperation of our Governments in the great work of preserving peace should be the cornerstone of an enduring friendship.

I am sorry that owing to my absence from Washington I am unable in person to say good-bye to you and to wish you a safe and pleasant journey; but I assure you that you carry with you my warmest personal regards.

Yours very sincerely,
Franklin D. Roosevelt

Litvinoff later remarked that it was clearly the purpose of President Roosevelt not merely to restore normal relations but also to promote active friendship between the two countries.

On November 25 Litvinoff, in a very happy mood, sailed on the Italian liner *Conte di Savoia*. The armored police car did not leave the pier until half an hour after the ship had sailed. Four detectives went as far as the Battery.

Litvinoff went to Naples, and from there, on December 2, 1933, he went by special train to Rome to meet Mussolini. He was greeted at the station by the Italian Undersecretary of State, Fulvio Suvich, and a number of other officials, and outside the station a huge crowd had gathered to cheer. All noted that he was in obvious good humor, smiling broadly.

On December 3 Litvinoff held three conferences with Mussolini. Close Italo-Russian collaboration was decided upon, on the basis of the Treaty of Friendship and Non-Aggression which had been concluded three months earlier. This seemed to indicate that Mussolini did not have anti-Soviet policies. Litvinoff says that at that time Mussolini definitely promised that he would never join with Hitler against the rest of the world. Up to then, Litvinoff said, he had never really trusted Mussolini; and even then he had his doubts, in spite of the Duce's efforts to convince him of his sincerity.

On December 4 Litvinoff held a lively press conference with eight foreign newspaper men, answering questions in Russian, French, English, and German, on disarmament.

"Good will among the nations would be sufficient to solve the problem," he said, "but instead, the nations are preparing for war." He was thinking primarily of Germany and Japan.

Shortly afterwards Litvinoff drove to the home of the American Ambassador, Breckenridge Long, to a luncheon that was attended by many members of the diplomatic corps. He seemed in excellent spirits, and this mood was still in evidence on December 29, when he stood before the Central Executive Committee in Moscow to deliver one of his most important speeches on foreign relations:

"We desire no foreign land, but we shall not surrender a single inch of our own land to anyone. Once we do not desire any foreign lands, then we cannot want war. As for our own land, we have every possibility of defending it and preventing any attempt at its invasion. Our growing armed forces could teach a lesson to any of our near or distant neighbors and would prevent them for decades from again attempting to invade us; but this would be an unproductive waste of our means and energies. It would distract us for a time from our fundamental work of constructing socialism.

"We are therefore doing everything possible to defend our territory by peaceful means even though this may not be a radical means for removing the threat of aggression against us. We consider that even military activities commenced outside the immediate frontiers of our Union may be a menace to us, hence we do not only continue, but are intensifying our struggle for peace, which has always been and still is the basic problem of our diplomacy. As Comrade Molotov rightly said: 'This struggle corresponds with the desire of the masses of the peoples of all countries.'

"During the last year we have extended the system of non-aggression pacts. Such pacts are now in force between the Union of Soviet Socialist Republics and not only all our neighbors, with the exception of Japan and China, but also with France and Italy. We have made a further step towards the intensification of the significance and effectiveness of the non-aggression pacts by proposing an exhaustive definition of the idea of aggression itself. This proposal of ours is already contained in agreements with a solid chain of our neighbors from

Finland to Afghanistan and with all three countries of the Little Entente.

"The definition of aggression which we have given is generally recognized to be a valuable contribution to the science of international law, and also of international practice; at the same time it forms an excellent measure for determining the absence or presence in any state of aggressive, annexationist aims. We shall, therefore, continue to struggle for the universal recognition of this definition."

When Litvinoff mentioned President Roosevelt's name the delegates burst into spontaneous applause—the first time that a Soviet Congress had whole-heartedly cheered the head of a foreign nation. He also hailed the non-aggression pacts that the Soviet Union had arranged the year before, and he had every reason for optimism, for Poland's growing concern over the rise of Nazism seemed to be bringing her closer to her eastern fellow-Slav neighbor.

Throughout the speech, Litvinoff left no doubt that he regarded Germany and Japan as the great dangers to the peace of the world:

"Germany lost the first World War long before it began when the Kaiser allowed Russia to join England and France. Hitler is helping history to repeat itself."

When the proofs of the speech came from the printers Litvinoff added a line:

"Germany has lost the second World War."

PART THREE

PEACE IS INDIVISIBLE

CHAPTER ELEVEN

Collective Security

BY THE END OF 1933, when Adolf Hitler had been in power in Germany only eleven months, he had destroyed all political parties except his own; reduced the Reichstag to a mere claque; arrested more than 100,000 opponents and had them shot, tortured or confined in concentration camps; started his persecution of Jews by law as well as by unlicensed brute force; driven into exile many thousands of democrats, liberals, Catholics, and Jews; dissolved the Trade Unions, jailed their leaders, confiscated their funds and deprived the working class of its hard-won rights; established a tight censorship, suppressed countless publications, and staged wholesale burning of books written in the spirit of freedom.

Conservative political observers in England and France, while horrified as humanitarians, decided that these were problems of internal policy, not to be challenged from abroad. Not all the Nazi developments, however, could be so easily dismissed. The Powers, though for years they had reproached Soviet Russia for distributing in other countries propaganda for its economic-political system, averted their eyes from Germany's international activities designed to undermine other governments, but no responsible statesman could disregard the implications of appointing, as Minister of Aviation, Goering, who had emphatically advocated the development of German military air-strength; nor could they be indifferent to Germany's withdrawal from the League of Nations on October 14 because her rearmament proposals had not been accepted. Foreigners traveling in Germany saw, with amazement and dismay, that her heavy industries were working at top speed, with plenty of evidence of a furious revival of arms manufacture, while the literature not only of political complaint and animosity, but of warfare itself, increased ominously. None but the simple or the willfully blind could maintain, by the end of 1933,

that Hitler was the foe only of Socialists, Communists or Jews. Quite
plainly he was already a stark danger to world peace.

2

Russia's stituation was particularly dangerous. During all his political
battles Hitler had harped on two main points: anti-Semitism and the
Bolshevik danger. In *Mein Kampf* he had made clear that he intended a crusade against Russia, and his principal party adviser on
foreign policy, Alfred Rosenberg, was a Baltic émigré who profoundly hated the Soviet Union.

When Hitler came into power, he insisted at first that his opposition to Communism was purely domestic, and even ratified the
Protocol of 1930, on May 5, 1933, providing for the renewal of the
1926 Neutrality Treaty, and approved of commercial credits for trade
with Soviet Russia.

Yet the Russians noted with uneasiness that Rosenberg was in constant touch with Ukrainian counter-revolutionaries in Southern Russia,
especially with General Pavel Skoropadsky, the man set up in 1918
by the German army as governor of the Ukraine, who had had to flee
to Germany when the Germans withdrew from that district shortly
after the Revolution. Skoropadsky established his own General Staff,
which planned an invasion of Soviet Russia and the isolation of those
western sections of the country which might be annexed by Greater
Germany.

Meanwhile, German industrialists visited their colleagues in England, France, and the United States, and busily pointed out that Hitler
was the only guarantee against the world danger of Communism.
They found many receptive ears, especially in England. Furthermore,
many minor Nazi Party officials made speeches in which the clever
distinction used by Hitler and the Nazi Party organ between German
Communism and the friendly power, Soviet Russia, was not maintained. In fact, the Nazi Party rank and file was convinced, as any
observer would be who had watched the leaders in the preceding
years, that Hitler would sooner or later make war on Russia. Under
these circumstances German-Soviet relations inevitably became "un-
recognizable," as Litvinoff put it in his speech of December 29, 1933.

Litvinoff was not for a moment deceived or confused by Hitler's gyrations. Much later (February 26, 1942) he commented on the situation in a speech before the Overseas Press Club in New York:

"We in the Soviet Union realized, the moment Nazism and Hitlerism appeared on the political areas, that this meant war—total and universal war—not halting before any frontiers, land or sea. Unlike some other people, we did not believe Hitler when he defiled the name of peace, when he traded in appeasement, but we did believe him when he spoke of war, of aggression, of the enslavement of other nations, of world domination. We did believe him when he mocked at international obligations, international ethics, when he extolled lies and false propaganda, thereby inviting us to disbelieve all his assurances, promises, and undertakings. And so we appealed for the alliance of all peace-loving countries in a powerful, common effort for the aversion of this catastrophe."

This was no afterthought, for all Litvinoff's policies and speeches during this period confirm his account. Was Litvinoff more alert, realistic, and farsighted than the statesmen of other countries? Apparently. He had a clearer perception of the mentality of politicians, sometimes an almost clairvoyant understanding of just what was going on in their minds. This talent, which most of his colleagues in other countries seemed to lack, was far more than a flair. It was the product, first, of his own coolness and detachment, an imperturbability that preserved his powers of observation and judgment free from emotional intrusion, a concentration of attention produced by long discipline in holding to essentials and a wide and varied experience with all sorts of men in all sorts of situations—an experience which his shrewd analytical mind and retentive memory put to excellent use. He was also more skeptical than the others and his unrelenting factual-mindedness protected him from confusing words and facts, from overestimating promises or protests.

He understood Hitler's mentality especially well because he lost no chance to acquire authentic information. When he was taking a walk in Berlin in 1928 he noticed in a shop window not far from the Friedrichstrasse Station a book called *Mein Kampf,* and went in and bought it.

"I began reading the book the same night," Litvinoff said, "but it was difficult going. I read it in little stages, and after I had finished it I began reading it again, and again. Soon I knew the book almost by heart." This meant that he knew a great deal about both Hitler's mentality and his plans, for never was a blueprint for drastic international action so precisely drawn and so audaciously publicized—an impudent expression of contempt for the intelligences of other statesmen that events seem to have justified. Litvinoff was convinced that if Hitler ever came to power he would try to carry out the program presented in *Mein Kampf,* and Stalin, with whom Litvinoff repeatedly discussed this, agreed.

An enquiry in Geneva in 1936 revealed that of all the statesmen regularly attending the League of Nations conferences, only Litvinoff had read Hitler's *Mein Kampf* in full. Beneš, Herriot, Daladier, Eden and others had either not read the book at all or had just glanced through it. Neville Chamberlain in October, 1938—after the conclusion of the Munich Pact—instructed the Foreign Office to translate some excerpts for him to study.

The obvious, and in fact the only effective answer to Hitler's coarse threat to world peace was to arrange for a common front to resist by united and simultaneous action any aggression against any nation —a policy later called "collective security," which Litvinoff had conceived even before Hitler came to power. His 1932 non-aggression pact with France, the treaties which he concluded during the London Economic Conference in 1933, a non-aggression pact with Italy signed in September, 1933 (which after the December discussions with Mussolini became even more important), and last but not least, the negotiations in Washington, D. C., in 1933 were all stages in the long, needlessly obstructed road to collective security.

Litvinoff's friendly negotiations with Mussolini had been a decided shock to the Wilhelmstrasse. When Litvinoff alighted from the Rome Express in Berlin on December 7, 1933, the atmosphere had completely changed. His great successes had apparently even impressed Hitler. Several editorials in the Nazi-controlled press invited him to establish closer contacts with Germany, as he had with other countries. Most amazing was an editorial by Alfred Rosenberg in the Munich edition of the *Voelkischer Beobachter* (but not in the Berlin edition), in which he called on German and Russian statesmen to forget the past. This was shown to Litvinoff immediately upon his arrival at the Soviet Embassy. He merely smiled.

Shortly afterwards an "official spokesman" let it be known over the telephone that Chancellor Hitler and his Foreign Minister, Baron von Neurath, would be happy to see Litvinoff if he should ask for an audience. It was added that the skeleton for a non-aggression pact could be drawn up on that occasion.

Litvinoff did not ask for an audience with Hitler. Neither did he see any German newspaper men. He left Berlin on the same evening without so much as telephoning Baron von Neurath. The American Ambassador to Moscow, William C. Bullitt, arrived that day in England and wanted Litvinoff to wait for him in Berlin so that they could make the rest of the trip together. But Litvinoff did not want to provide the German authorities with any opportunity to meet him. He was already convinced that he could not do business with Hitler.

3

Litvinoff had snubbed Hitler and the Nazis. In consequence their hatred of him, which had been only temporarily and disingenuously suspended, became almost pathological in its fury.

Litvinoff was a Communist; this would have been enough. Litvinoff was a Jew; this again would have been enough for the Nazis to hate him. The fact that he was a Jew and a Communist, too, made him Hitler's scapegoat par excellence. Litvinoff could not be cajoled or intimidated and this offense stung the Nazis worst, although it did not lend itself readily to argument.

The Nazi anti-Bolshevik propaganda was always full of anti-Semitic arguments. In thousands of publications, articles, pamphlets, brochures, and speeches, the Nazis pictured the Bolshevik Revolution and the Soviet Government as instigated and set up by Jews. And in almost none of these falsifications was the "Jew Litvinoff Meer Wallack Finkelstein" missing. "Finkelstein" was an invention of the Nazis. There were any number of Nazi caricatures and cartoons of Litvinoff, and retouched photographs to make him suit his newly appointed role of the Reich's Public Enemy No. 1.

Nazi agitation also assumed a pseudo-scientific disguise, using espe-

cially fraudulent statistics. Thus an official textbook by Karin Magnussen, *Rassen-und-bevoelkerungspolitisches Ruestzeug,* maintained that
under Litvinoff's leadership the People's Foreign Commissariat became
"completely Jewish": of sixteen collaborators thirteen were Jews; but
the Narkomindel had, not sixteen, but several hundred employees.

Again Hermann Fehst, Professor at the Hochschule für Politik, in
his *Bolshevism and Jewry,* which appeared in 1934, explains that Litvinoff's appointment was due to pro-Jewish motives: "On July 21, 1930,
the People's Foreign Commissar, Chicherin (Russian), was demoted
and Litvinoff (Wallack, Jew) was promoted. Krestinsky (married to
a Jewess) became his first deputy. Karakhan (Armenian) his second,
and Sokolnikoff (Jew) the third."

And "Moscow Executes Mordecai's Last Will," by Dr. Mueller-
Kronach, brought out by the official Ostmark Publishing House in
1938, includes a chapter (21) entitled, "The Disintegration Effected by
Soviet Diplomacy and the Threat to World Peace by Militant Bolshevism—League of Nations as Platform for Jewish Bolshevists," a
fair description of the contents.

Litvinoff was spared none of the adjectives in the dictionary of
Nazi-invective, of which "criminal," "murderer" and "sub-human"
are quite moderate. He was included in all the Nazi attacks against
Soviet Russia.

All this was fundamental to the Nazi program. A section in Department VII (Defense against Lies), of the German Propaganda Ministry, devoted solely to Russia and immediately under Goebbels's
direction, was headed by a White Russian named Vaatz whose job
it was to present the Bolshevik regime as Jewish, and unearth "proof"
of this. The office of Vaatz was (and probably still is) in the basement
of the Propaganda Ministry building connected with the Russien
Archiv (Russian Archives), which kept seven employees busy.

As soon as Goebbels organized the Propaganda Ministry he advised
Vaatz that Litvinoff was to be the prime focus of Nazi anti-Russian
propaganda, and then and there it was decided that Litvinoff should
never be referred to by his own name, but either as Finkelstein or
Litvinoff-Finkelstein. This trick of attacking opponents by ascribing
to them typical Jewish names had been tried out by Goebbels before
and found highly successful.

Vaatz soon discovered that the material on Litvinoff made disappointing propaganda, so more useful "data" were manufactured. The first test was made in Mexico. Goebbels ordered a considerable quantity of anti-Semitic literature shipped to certain rural districts of Mexico where he conducted an anti-Bolshevik and anti-Jewish propaganda campaign, using Litvinoff as his arch-villain.

It resulted only in making Litvinoff's name known in Mexico. Goebbels, always quick to understand his own errors, called a halt, but started something much bolder: anti-Semitic propaganda inside Russia. Anti-Soviet, anti-Litvinoff leaflets on lightweight paper were smuggled into Russia by pilots of the Lufthansa or of its affiliate the Deraluft, and German agents began to distribute them on a wide scale. Stalin learned about these leaflets through Kaganovich and called in Yagoda, Chief of the OGPU, who had little trouble tracking down the distributors. Count von Schulenburg, the German Ambassador in Moscow, who liked and sincerely respected Litvinoff, was most embarrassed and protested emphatically to Berlin about the anti-Litvinoff leaflets.

Goebbels was obliged to drop the whole scurrilous campaign as far as Russia herself was concerned, but started the same kind of propaganda in England. Here he had considerable success, chiefly by working hand-in-glove with certain of the aristocracy who were influential with the politicians. The mildest agitation consisted of explaining away Litvinoff's opposition to the Nazis as merely a Jewish reaction. This even Kerenski categorically denied in an article in *Sowremennye Sopiski* in 1934 where, while he criticized Soviet foreign policy in general, he pointed out that even if Litvinoff did take offense as a Jew at Hitler's anti-Semitism, it would not affect the Russian governmental policy.

But much of the anti-Litvinoff campaign in England was far more violent than this. Thus the Earl of Glasgow persuaded his son-in-law, Sir Thomas Inskip, who was in the Cabinet, that Litvinoff's real name was Finkelstein and he represented a so-called Jewish International in the Russian Government. This revelation was also spread by young German noblemen, who lingered in London diplomatic drawing rooms or lectured at the All Peoples' Association meetings. Even King Edward VIII, who seems to have been thoroughly prejudiced, was reached and at a crucial moment later took a stand against the Russian Foreign Commissar.

In the United States the *Deutsche Weckruf und Beobachter* published in 1937 in New York a pamphlet entitled: "Litvinoff, Terrorist, Conspirator, Jail Bird and Smuggler—now Soviet Commissar of Foreign Affairs in Moscow," allegedly by Hans Andersen from Copenhagen. The subtitle was "Portrait of a Diplomat with Six Aliases," and the cover showed a caricature of Litvinoff, toasting the English king, against an immense silhouette of Litvinoff with devil's horns, his champagne glass converted into a smoking bomb. The sources to which the pamphlet refers either do not contain the passages "quoted" or do not exist at all. Where facts are true they are misconstrued to cast responsibility falsely on Litvinoff, and not a single date or figure is correct.

4

On January 26, 1934, Stalin said:

"Our orientation in the past and our orientation at the present time is towards the U.S.S.R. and the U.S.S.R. alone. . . . Those who want peace and are striving for business intercourse with us will always receive our support. And those who try to attack our country will receive a stunning rebuff to teach them not to poke their pig's snout into our Soviet garden again."

And Litvinoff formulated the same point of view more specifically if less picturesquely and with equal vigor at the signing of the protocols prolonging the Russo-Baltic States non-aggression pacts, on the following April 4: "The Soviet State, which is a stranger to chauvinism, nationalism, or racial and national prejudice, perceives its State duties to lie not in conquest . . . not in expansion of territory; it considers that the honour of the nation demands that it should be educated not in the spirit of militarism and a thirst for blood, but in the fulfilment of the ideal for which the Soviet State was brought into existence and in which it perceives the whole meaning of its existence, namely, the building of a Socialist society. It intends, if not interfered with, to devote the whole forces of the State to this labour, and this constitutes the inexhaustible source of its policy of peace."

This was the essence of Russian foreign policy. The first and most important goal was peace. Peace could be maintained, if at all, only by collective security. The necessary pre-condition for any system of collective security was the establishment and maintenance of normal diplomatic relations with other countries. To this problem Litvinoff had devoted himself from the very start with characteristic skill and persistence, undauntedly addressing with calculated optimism even those countries that had repeatedly declined to have anything to do with Soviet Russia—Hungary, Rumania, Czechoslovakia, Bulgaria.

The Soviet policy of collective security required, furthermore, first, a reversal of Russia's former attitude towards the League of Nations, and second, a modification of the delicate and difficult relations between the Narkomindel and the Comintern. Originally the Comintern was charged with promoting world revolution—hateful and alarming to the other nations, basic and primary to the orthodox Bolsheviki, and a means of defense when those very nations which complained of the Comintern conspired to destroy the young Soviet Government, not only by armed intervention at the beginning, but thereafter by diplomatic maneuvers, cordons sanitaires and other hostile moves. For Communist counter-propaganda had been the most effective reply to the virulent and dishonest propaganda that, deliberately encouraged by most of the Powers with the help of the Bolshevik mistakes, succeeded fairly well in turning the greater part of the world against the new Russia, building up thereby stubborn prejudices and suspicions which even now plague the United Nations and help their enemies. With the eruption of the Nazi menace, however, the Comintern was given a new role of promoting collaboration with liberal forces everywhere that were fighting Fascism—a menace more real and also more imminent than Communism had ever been.

Even more immediate and conspicuous, moreover, was the change resulting from the new principle of collective security in Russian policy towards France, denounced by Stalin and other Soviet leaders only a few years before as the most dangerous and militaristic state in Europe. For when Litvinoff concluded a non-aggression treaty with France at the end of 1932 it had become evident that the international danger would not come from west of the Rhine, and Litvinoff made perfectly clear where the menace did lie when, in a speech at the

Disarmament Conference in February, 1933, after the French had ratified the treaty, he said that the French demand for security had to be seriously considered. French security had become for him an integral part of collective security.

Three months later (May 29, 1934), again speaking to the Disarmament Conference in Geneva, he summarized world developments:

". . . in the meantime political events had not waited on the close of the discussion at Geneva, but had pursued their course. In various countries Governments had changed, parties in power had changed, the ideology of parties and Governments had changed, and their methods of dealing with international questions had changed. In spite of the adoption by all States, in virtue of the Briand-Kellogg Pact, of an international undertaking to renounce war as an instrument of national policy, the world had witnessed the method of furthering national policy precisely by the development of warlike activities on the territory of neighboring States. Some States, which as yet were not in possession of sufficient forces to carry out such a policy were confining themselves, for the time being, to verbal and printed propaganda of the idea of expansion and the seizure of other peoples' lands by force of arms, obligingly mentioning the countries they were going to attack first. Was it surprising that States which were interested in the maintenance of peace had seriously taken alarm, and were displaying still greater hesitation than before on the question of world disarmament?

"Similarly the principle of equality in armaments which had already been adopted by the Conference, had been seriously shaken. No one could or would object to equality when all States showed the same active interest, even though it were in words and by adopting suitable international obligations, in the maintenance of peace. But the question had not arisen: What was to be done with States whose rulers had quite openly sketched out a program of conquest of foreign territories (of course by means of war, since no one gave up his territory voluntarily), and when the abstract principle of equality came face to face with very real perils involved in its applications. . . .

". . . He only desired to point out the new atmosphere which had developed as a result of certain political events, and which had considerably complicated the work of the Conference involved as it had been in sufficiently vast difficulties from the very beginning. And to-day, summing up more than two years' work of the Conference, it must be openly said that the difficulties which had made their appearance at the very dawn of its existence had led the Conference, in the long run, into a blind alley.

". . . would it not be politically more honest and courageous openly to admit that international life, and particularly political events in some countries during recent years, had prevented the Conference from carrying out its direct task of drawing up a disarmament convention?

". . . He was obliged to record that the futility of such a discussion on disarmament, in the absence of any proposals whatsoever which had a chance of securing universal acceptance, had been sufficiently demonstrated. After all, the Conference could not engage in discussion for the sake of discussion, or offer up prayers for disarmament. The Soviet delegation could not, therefore, close its eyes to facts, however unpleasant, and it drew the inevitable conclusions from the situation which had been created.

"From what he had said, it would seem logically to follow that the Conference itself should close down. That would be very well, taking into account merely its title. But the Soviet delegation, as he had already mentioned, continued to have in mind a wider conception of the Conference as being intended by means of disarmament to bring into being one of the guarantees of world peace. Consequently, the question was not that of disarmament itself, since that was only a means to an end, but that of guaranteeing peace. And, since that was so, the question naturally arose, could not the Conference feel its way towards other guarantees for peace; or, at any rate, might it not increase the measure of security for at least those States which, cherishing no aggressive designs, were not interested in war, and which, in the event of war, might become only the objects of attack?

"He might be asked what guarantees there were that the Conference would be more unanimous on such questions than it had been on the question of disarmament, and that the new activity which he was suggesting for the Conference would therefore be any more fruitful or successful. He would reply that, in order to achieve any degree whatsoever of reduction in armaments, the unconditional agreement of nearly every State was essential, and that the whole cause might be frustrated by the disagreement of even one more or less important Power, let alone one of the Great Powers. But unanimity was not required to realize other measures of security. The Conference must, of course, do everything in its power to induce every State to accede to such measures. He hoped that that would be the case and that consideration for their own interest would induce even States which did not sympathize with these measures not to stand aloof from the general system that would be set up. But, even if there should be dissident States, that should by no means prevent the remainder from coming still more closely together to take steps which would strengthen their own security."

The most pressing question now for Litvinoff—for the whole world —was no longer disarmament; it was security. The word loomed large in everybody's mind. Litvinoff went on to say:

"Questions of security were far from unknown to the Conference. The Conference had even created a special political commission for these questions. More than that, it had already discussed these questions, without, it was true, carrying the discussion to its conclusion. He would recall, first, the Soviet proposal for the definition of aggression, which had already been approved by one of the Commission of the Conference and which had since been embodied in a number of international treaties. The further increase in the number of supporters of the Soviet definition of aggression would considerably facilitate the application of other proposals dealing with security which had been made at the Conference.

"Litvinoff was not by any means speaking of security in contrast to disarmament. Nor did he propose to exclude disarmament from the Conference's program of work. Everything that bore upon a system of guarantees of peace, and, consequently, disarmament in particular, must receive the careful attention of the Conference. But every question ought to be taken up when it had some chance of a satisfactory solution. To-day, it might be security; to-morrow, disarmament. He apologized for so frequently using the word 'security' which, in the eyes of so many, was an antonym of disarmament. But he could find no more suitable term to express that which was understood by the word 'security.' "

5

The Russo-French rapprochement was by no means one-sided. A number of French statesmen advocated close co-operation with the Soviet Union, such as Edouard Herriot and Pierre Cot, who had both visited Soviet Russia in September, 1933, and certain members of the French General Staff also, who were impressed by Soviet military strength. But the champion of rapprochement, who went far beyond all expectations, was Louis Barthou, who became Foreign Minister of France on February 9, 1934.

Barthou was then seventy-two years old, but in spirit he was still young. All his life he had been a conservative—even a reactionary, but he was intelligent and farsighted. Neither his age nor his political views prevented him from seeing what was in store for a Europe which allowed Hitler to rearm and choose his own good time to break loose. He was a philosopher of history and a serious student of German mentality. He had written books about Beethoven and Wagner. He thoroughly understood the German militaristic spirit and its threat. He had accordingly introduced in 1913 the three-year compulsory military service in France, which was largely responsible for the outcome of the Battle of the Marne. Barthou knew that Hitler was only another representative of an eternal threat. He intended to fight this threat. He was not interested in ideas and ideals, only in peace, because France needed peace, in security—not the word—but a real security for France. And since he realized much earlier than anybody else that France alone could never be secure against an ever-growing Germany, he turned to collective security.

Speaking in Geneva one day after Litvinoff—on May 30, 1934—M. Barthou said that, after two years of laborious and loyal efforts, which, as the President of the Conference had observed on the previous day, had proceeded continuously and had involved difficulties and perhaps also contradictions, everyone, he thought, was agreed that the time had come to take a decision. He proposed to express quite clearly the wishes of the French Government. At the present time, it was not only the authority of the Disarmament Conference that was at stake; to speak plainly, it was the Disarmament Conference's very existence.

Perhaps he should add that, over and above the Disarmament Conference, which was an emanation of the Council of the League of Nations, the very existence of the League might prove to be at stake during that session. In the view of France, of the French Government, in whose name he spoke, and of the French nation as a whole, the League was a necessity to mankind. France was not one of the countries that had ever depreciated its importance nor the part it was called upon to play. From the outset France had been firmly attached to the League, and, if he permitted himself a discreet allusion to a certain great predecessor of his at the head of the French delegation, who had lent the League the support of his incomparable genius, everybody present would realize the honesty and continuity of French policy. At the present moment—on this he agreed with Sir John Simon, as, indeed, on other points—the time for reticence, for complacence, and perhaps also for compromise, was past. Plain speaking was needed.

Barthou went ahead to discuss, at some length, rearmament in general and rearmament in the air in particular, during these last years. He was of the opinion ". . . that an agreement on air or land armaments could only be achieved if the problem of national security were solved."

The recent exchange of notes between the governments concerned, as well as other indications, showed with abundant clarity that this problem was at the root of the whole question of disarmament. The President of the Disarmament Conference had defined that question very clearly, very precisely and very correctly. M. Barthou would not attempt to evade it. It was, in fact, the problem of security which was before the Commission. This problem was not a new one. He would refrain from reverting to a past with which all the members of the Disarmament Conference were more familiar than he was. He did not wish to dwell on the past, but was it not still in the chronological order of things and in the logical sequence of events and proposals to follow Sir John Simon's example? He had spoken of the meeting of October 14, 1933, and this was the crux of the debate. It was necessary to go back to the meeting of October 14, 1933, because that was the point from which to set out. What had been said at that meeting? One speaker had referred to the troubled state of Europe.

It was troubled in October, 1933. Was it not still more troubled on May 30, 1934? This troubled state required a Convention. It was necessary to speak without evasions or concealment. Difficulties must not be hidden under vague optimistic phrases. The program was an excellent one. What was wanted was a concerted plan of disarmament, promptly accepted and loyally carried out.

A plan of "disarmament" was what the summoning and conditions of the Conference demanded. Since the Conference had been in existence, that word "disarmament" had been continually in use, and on the previous day it had been mentioned on several occasions. It was therefore not surprising that it had also been mentioned on October 14, 1933, and that Sir John Simon had said that the plan of disarmament involved one essential factor. What was that factor?

"The scheme involves the principle that the Powers now under restriction of the Peace Treaties should not begin to increase their armaments forthwith but should express their willingness to conform to a time-table. The Government of the United Kingdom takes the view that agreement could not be reached on the basis of a Convention which would provide for any immediate re-armament." With the usual honesty of his nation, Sir John Simon had added that in speaking of "no re-armament," he did not mean to dispute the reasonableness of a proportional numerical increase in Germany's armaments.

Who had echoed his words? Today and yesterday, it had been the United States representative, Mr. Norman Davis. He had said that a Disarmament Convention could not properly be made an instrument for rearmament and that qualitative equality in armaments should primarily be sought through the reduction of the armaments of the heavily armed Powers and not through an attempt on the part of others to build up their own.

For the sake of brevity, M. Barthou would not quote the exact words used on October 14, 1933, by M. Bourquin, representative of Belgium, M. Beneš, representative of Czechoslovakia, or M. Politis, representative of Greece, all in support of the speeches of the United Kingdom and American delegates; while the French delegate, M. Paul-Boncour, had added: "An equally essential point was that a disarmament movement should not begin by the rearming of the States disarmed by the Treaties."

"What happened next? After Sir John Simon made his report and after he received the support which M. Barthou had just mentioned, Germany left the Disarmament Conference.

"In his telegram to M. von Neurath, the President of the Disarmament Conference said that there was no reason for Germany to take this attitude, and Sir John Simon also said just now that Germany's departure was unjustified.

"Did the Commission believe that M. Barthou was going to evade the question, that he intended to refrain from saying what was necessary, and that he had come to represent France at that meeting by maintaining a discreet and veiled reticence which would conceal reality, and hence, the very gravity of the situation? He would bring no accusation against anyone, for he was not inspired by hatred; but he had a passion for the truth. He had always thought, even before having the notable honor of speaking before the General Commission, that the truth must be spoken. He was aware that caution might sometimes be necessary and that its utterance might thus be delayed, but a moment must come when everything would have to be said. For his part, prudently, moderately but firmly, he would say all.

"Germany had left the League. Were the principles laid down on October 14, 1933, no longer valid on that account? After prolonged efforts, certain Great Powers had agreed upon a reasonable, impartial and acceptable system. Germany refused to accept it. Was it because Germany had rejected it that the system be declared unacceptable? Had matters come to such a pass that there was one Power which was both invisible and present—present, if he might be excused the metaphor, by its very absence—which was not participating in the Conference, which had left the League, which in consequence, would be faced with no responsibility and which would have all the rights without any of the corresponding duties? Was the embargo—the word was fashionable at present—of that Power to prevent the League and Disarmament Conference from reaching a solution? Had they come to the point where there was only one system to be discussed?"

Barthou, for one, was not going to dance to the Nazi tune. And he still wanted security for France.

". . . The decisions that had been reached by the General Commission for Disarmament—there was no need to specify them by their exact dates—should be borne in mind. The intentions that had been asserted in principle, subject to details of execution, should likewise be borne in mind. Moreover, why should he not say it?—the principle of equality of rights under a system of security, as it was called on December 11, 1932, should be borne in mind. What had become of the principle of equality of rights? It was being used as an argument against the Conference, as an argument against France. But what had become of the measures of security? . . .

". . . At the end of March, the German Government had published its budget. What did the budget of the Reich contain, so far as military expenditure was concerned? There were hidden, dark and still mysterious corners, into which he did not wish to look at the present. But there was also a significant, plain, irrefutable confession: the German Government was increasing its admitted military expenditure for 1934—he would repeat that he was referring only to its admitted expenditure—by 2,500 millions. What was the position at that moment? At that moment an endeavor was being made to solve the complicated problem of guarantees of execution. An attempt was being made to classify breaches of a Convention, from the smallest to the most serious, and to decide what penalties would be inflicted for such breaches . . .

". . . It was at that moment that the German Government published a budget in which its rearmament was proclaimed by official figures. That was an indirect, but perfectly plain, way of saying: 'We care nothing for all your conversations; we care nothing for all your guarantees of execution! Since October 14, 1933, when we abruptly left the League, we have resumed our full freedom, and we are making use of it; so much the worse for you who go on discussing and negotiating; we rely on our own strength, on the strength of our re-armament.' That was the situation with which they were faced, and were they to be expected to yield on that account? Must any system be abandoned which did not at once receive the unqualified approval of Germany? Apparently the League of Nations, which represented nearly the whole world, had arrived at a point where one Power, because it had abruptly, violently, left the Disarmament Conference, could command it and impose its will upon it! For his own part, he refused to accept such a position."

And Barthou showed clearly that "this Power" had not left the Disarmament Conference for peaceful purposes. He said in so many words that Hitler meant war.

". . . Germany's air budget had increased by 160 per cent. Why? Who was threatening Germany? Who were the neighbors who wished to attack her? As he had already stated he would not say anything that could in any way be taken as an accusation or an indictment. He was speaking of a country—and he hoped that it would soon return—for whose greatness he would not conceal his sincere admiration, a country that had produced a universal genius like Goethe, such musical geniuses as Bach, Beethoven, and Wagner. Who would deny that country not merely its intellectual power, but that equality which was necessary in social life and in economic life, and which it has every right to claim? Who was threatening Germany? Certainly not France.

"He would not insult his own country by defending it. It was too great to stand in need of a justification which could do no more than detract from its greatness. As he had said, France was not threatening anybody; she did not wish to attack anybody; she did not ask for anything. The Treaties had given her back her own; she asked no more. . . . "

He went on to say that disarmament without guarantees was out of the question:

". . . What we say to you is this: a reduction of armaments, a parallel reduction, a progressive reduction is all very well; but it must be a reduction of armaments accompanied by the necessary guarantees. What guarantees? Guarantees of security. To-day there is not one of you that can have a false impression. The problem of security is not solved; but it has been raised, and raised in such a way that nobody here, no country to-day, to-morrow or in the future, can evade its terms. If you wish—and we know that you all do wish—for world peace, you will tackle the problem of security. . . ."

Finally Barthou referred to Litvinoff:

"And then there was M. Litvinoff's speech. M. Litvinoff was not a man—M. Barthou would do him justice for that—who tried to please everybody. He had said, with a downrightness which was, moreover, accompanied by an increasing measure of address, things which he regarded as truths but which had not appeared in that light to the General Commission. M. Litvinoff had said that he was a practical man, and M. Barthou did not doubt it. He was a man who accepted realities. While there were parts of his speech which M. Barthou would find difficult to endorse, he had to recognize that, in M. Litvinoff's speech also, there was an idea which dominated everything—he would repeat, everything—and which he was ready to believe had inspired M. Litvinoff's whole speech—the idea of security."

This was the first time the two had come in contact since the Genoa Conference twelve years before. At that time Barthou wanted to find some mutual basis of understanding for Russo-French collaboration, but his Premier, Poincaré, had objected, and Soviet Russia, treated like an outcast, had finally turned to Germany and concluded the Treaty of Rapallo. Barthou was no more friendly towards Communism than Poincaré. He did not like Communism now any better than he had liked the Czar twenty years before. Yet he had persistently advocated an alliance with the Czar, as he now supported the strongest possible alliance with the Communists: he was a realist.

And because he was a realist, in spite of age and many other handicaps, he could assure France once more—for the last time—an active, strong, foreign policy, based on the idea of Europe as a whole. He was, in the last analysis, reviving the traditional French policy of alliances—along with Litvinoff.

Litvinoff could have harbored the same doubts about working with the old reactionary, as Barthou might have had about collaboration with Litvinoff; but Litvinoff also was a realist. Their mutual understanding was almost ideal. They built up a large-scale plan of interlocking "mutual aid" agreements, involving an Eastern Locarno Pact, a Baltic Pact, the Little Entente, and a Mediterranean Locarno, for which a Franco-Italian rapprochement was to provide the foundation.

6

At the same time Barthou began preparing the way for the Soviet Union's entrance into the League of Nations. The Soviets had not joined the League for a number of reasons. They had always stood for revision that is, for scrapping the Versailles Treaty, and the League of Nations was one result of the Versailles Treaty, founded for the specific purpose of preserving the status quo. Thus Soviet Russia could hardly have become a member during the early stages of the League.

Again, the Soviets, during their first few years of power, were committed to world revolution, although Litvinoff as early as 1920 had declared such a project impossible. Whether or not the League was "the Holy Alliance of the Bourgeoisie for the suppression of the proletarian revolution"—as it was called by the Communist International—it certainly could be counted on to oppose revolution in any country.

Moreover, on many occasions the League showed obvious anti-Bolshevik leanings. Its first session took place during the Soviet-Polish War, which was precisely the type of conflict that the League was supposed to prevent, yet the statesmen at Geneva manifested no interest in it. The delegates closed their eyes to France's help to Poland, which was against the spirit and the letter of the League Covenant. Later, the League made an effort to suggest lines of demarcation between Russia and Poland, but this was when not Russia, but Poland, was in danger—a significant difference in attitude.

Neither was the role of the League encouraging during the Russian famine of 1921 and 1922, for it did nothing to hasten help, in spite of the most urgent appeals of Fridtjof Nansen.

Subsequently, there were attempts to interest the Soviets in the League, but it was too late. The Kremlin had decided to stay out—at least until the Soviet Union had been recognized as one of the Great Powers. "Principles of Marxism" and the impossibility of co-operating with "powers definitely opposed to these principles," were mentioned in Moscow. Even Litvinoff lost no opportunity to denounce the League. In November, 1925, when it was whispered that Russia was about to join the League, he had made a statement in Moscow:

"The Soviet Government considers that the existing League of Nations . . . has not fulfilled in the slightest degree the hopes of its adherents. Not only has it failed to protect the rights and safety of small nations against the violence of military outrage by stronger powers but on the main question in which the whole of humanity is interested and which particularly interests the Soviet Union, namely disarmament, it has taken no serious steps whatsoever. . . . The Soviet Union, like the United States of America, intends as before to stand aloof from similar organizations."

Stalin himself, citing Litvinoff, gave fundamental official reasons against it: ". . . We must carry on the struggle against new wars, the struggle to maintain peace and to secure the persistence of the so-called normal relationships towards capitalist countries. The basis of the policy of our government, of its foreign policy, is the idea of peace. The struggle for peace, the struggle against new wars, the disclosing of the true nature of all steps taken with the secret design of preparing for new wars, the disclosure of the true nature of such measures as would fain mask preparations for war beneath a pacifist flag (Locarno) —there you have our task. That is why we do not want to join the League of Nations. For the League of Nations is an organisation designed to mask preparations for war. As Comrade Litvinoff has rightly said, if we were to enter the League of Nations, we should only have the choice between hammer and anvil. Now, we neither wish to be a hammer for the weak nations nor yet an anvil for the strong ones. We are for peace; we are for the disclosure of the true nature of all measures tending to promote war, however peaceful they may pretend to be. Whether in the League of Nations, or at Locarno, they cannot deceive us by window dressing, nor yet frighten us by making a great noise." *

And in 1930 Chicherin wrote to Louis Fischer: "I am and always have been an absolutely undiluted, unmixed, unwavering, unswerving enemy of our joining the League of Nations." †

Later, the situation changed. Finally the same considerations which convinced Sir John Simon—and Louis Barthou—that Soviet Russia ought to be a member of the League persuaded Russia herself, and by December, 1933, the Soviets had decided to collaborate with it. On December 25, 1933, Stalin, in an interview to the *New York Times* correspondent, Walter Duranty, in answer to Duranty's question: "Is your position in regard to the League of Nations always a negative one?" answered:

No, not always and not under all circumstances. You perhaps do not quite understand our point of view. Notwithstanding the withdrawal of Germany and Japan from the League of Nations—or perhaps just because

* Joseph Stalin, *Leninism* (translated by Eden and Cedar Paul), p. 381, New York, 1928.
† *Men and Politics*, p. 147.

of this—the League may become something of a check to retard the outbreak of military actions or to hinder them.

If this is so and if the League could prove to be somewhat of an obstruction that could, even to a certain extent, hinder the business of war and help in any degree to further the cause of peace, then we are not against the League.

Yes, if historical events follow such a course, then it is not impossible that we should support the League of Nations in spite of its colossal defects.

Under these circumstances, joining the League was consistent not only with Litvinoff's realistic policy but also with the Marxian peace ideology.

So Barthou set about the task of bringing Soviet Russia into the League of Nations, talking to one delegate after another. Many of these followed their conversations with Barthou by assurances to Litvinoff that Russia would be welcome, but some of the small nations were less easily converted from their habitual anti-Bolshevism, notably Switzerland, Portugal, and the Netherlands.

7

The Barthou-Litvinoff security plans also were running into difficulties. Yesterday's enemies were now supposed to work together. Polish, Yugoslavian, and Italian differences were far from encouraging. German diplomats, aided by representatives of certain other countries, tried their best, behind the scenes, to disrupt the whole plan.

But Barthou was not easily discouraged. He went to Warsaw, Prague, Bucharest, and Belgrade to re-establish French influence and explain the idea of the new security scheme.

Meanwhile, Litvinoff went to Berlin in June. He had no illusions about Hitler's intentions. But as he had always believed that it was useful to go on record, in March, 1934, he had proposed a treaty in which the Reich and Moscow were to guarantee the sovereignty of Finland, Esthonia, Latvia, and Lithuania. Remembering what had happened in the Wars of Intervention, Litvinoff feared especially attacks through the Baltic States, particularly Finland, since Baron von Mannerheim, who was very powerful, hated Russia and was very close to the German military clique.

In the course of the conversations, Litvinoff several times directly challenged the Fuehrer. First he told him that if Germany were sincere in her statement that she did not want to expand, she could hardly afford to stay out. Von Neurath made a noncommittal answer which Litvinoff described as "highly negative in its diplomatic phraseology." Then on another occasion Litvinoff informed him that "the policy of encirclement was a German, and not a Russian invention." Again, he let him know that, according to information in his possession, Herr von Papen had offered an anti-Soviet pact to France in the summer of 1932, and, after France declined, in the summer of 1933 when Hitler was already in power, Rosenberg had been sent to London to try to induce England to sign an anti-Soviet pact. Neurath denied everything, but Litvinoff found nothing convincing in the denials.

In the end all these conversations amounted to little more than motions; useful motions, nonetheless, for they protected the Barthou-Litvinoff plan from any accusations that it was anti-German. However, this was precisely what the Germans asserted, so not only were the Litvinoff-Neurath talks without practical result, but also Hitler immediately went to Mussolini to dissuade him from being drawn into the Franco-Soviet orbit.

Great Britain likewise proved difficult. Winston Churchill in a speech in the House of Commons on March 8 of that year had already endorsed the idea of collective security: "We ought not to neglect any security," he said, "which can derive from international conventions"; and expressed his hope that the House was "not going to be led by very easy arguments to suppose there is no validity or virtue in such arrangements." But the Government was apathetic and unresponsive. On June 27 Barthou sent London a draft of a definite proposal for an Eastern Locarno. He himself went over on July 8. At this stage the plan envisaged a treaty of mutual assistance and consultation to be signed by Poland, the Soviet Union, Czechoslovakia, Finland, Esthonia, Latvia, Lithuania, and Germany. In addition, there was to be an agreement whereby Soviet Russia would come to the aid of France if the latter suffered an unprovoked attack by Germany, supplementing the British and Italian obligations under the original Locarno Pact. France, in turn, would aid the Soviets as though France were a signatory of the

Eastern (Locarno) Pact insofar as would be "consistent with her obligations under the Covenant of the League."

Representatives of many small countries—Rumania, Yugoslavia, Czechoslovakia, Greece, Sweden—were in favor of such a security scheme. They realized that since they were too weak to stand up against the Reich individually, it was necessary to deal with Hitler collectively. But England still did not know which way to turn. During June British public opinion had taken a sharp swing away from Hitler, influenced by Berlin's refusal to sign an Eastern Locarno Pact: the German declaration of an indefinite postponement of foreign debt payments and especially by the savage blood purge of June 30, 1934, so utterly offensive to all British traditions. But Sir John Simon was not yet abreast of his people. He gave the proposed pact his Government's theoretical approval, and also accepted Barthou's proposal that the Soviet Union, since it was planning to take part in the pact, be admitted to the League; but he would not accept for Britain any further responsibilities.

Only a few weeks later Hitler made his first attempt to take over Austria. Chancellor Dollfuss was murdered (July 25). Within a few days the Austrian national "revolution," staged by Hitler agents, was consummated, and Mussolini, angry and alarmed, denouncing Hitler with the most violent epithets, swung sharply away from Germany, and on short notice sent several divisions to the Brenner Pass. Hitler knew he was checked and that he would have war on his hands unless he retreated. If, at that moment, France had marched, Hitler might have been permanently checked. But France did not march. Another opportunity was lost.

The British Government at last was beginning to see the light. On July 30 Prime Minister Stanley Baldwin, in support of measures to increase British air power, said: "When you think of the defense of England, you no longer think of the chalk cliffs of Dover, you think of the Rhine. That is where our frontier lies." This was welcome news for Paris, and finally, English statesmen went even further. For the first time since the Russian Revolution, they had a good word for Soviet Russia. Even such an anti-Communist diehard as Sir Austen Chamberlain officially praised Litvinoff's attempt to achieve collective security.

Sir John Simon was now convinced that Britain would not incur any further obligations by the act. He still, however, had a condition: Germany must at least be allowed to benefit by the mutual assistance guarantees—this, despite the fact that the guarantees had been devised only because everyone was afraid of Germany. Barthou, Litvinoff, Mussolini and the others concerned immediately accepted the qualification.

But on September 10, nearly four months after she had first been approached, Germany announced that she preferred bilateral to multilateral pacts and, in any event, equality of armaments would have to precede any security arrangements. Indeed, according to Berlin, other means of guaranteeing security should be sought, though no alternate means were specified; and then, too, the Germans felt that their security rested on their own strength, which was doubly true since no one wanted to attack Germany.

8

In August Litvinoff had been again the hero of a disappearance sensation. Equipped with a passport bearing the name Tech (who was therein described as an engineer), he had left Moscow early in the month, gone to Berlin and there, at the Friedrichstrasse Station, where an official party saw him off, had boarded the Berlin-Paris express. Everyone assumed that he was going to meet Barthou, and newspaper men "discovered" him at the Soviet Embassy in Paris; but officials there said that Litvinoff, who was traveling on purely private matters, had left. The French Foreign Ministry said that Litvinoff had gone to Italy, but no one in Italy had seen him.

Somebody pointed out that Barthou was taking a brief vacation in a secluded spot near Lake Lucerne, and Litvinoff might be with him. A few newspaper men went there for several days, but they could find no trace of Litvinoff.

Actually, Litvinoff had left the train unnoticed at the Tiergarten Station in Berlin, and there, accompanied only by his wife, had taken the train to Marienbad. He was in need of a rest and also wanted quiet to organize his ideas and make plans in preparation for the busy weeks ahead in Geneva.

The Litvinoffs went a number of times to Marienbad or Karlsbad for short vacations, always traveling incognito to avoid reporters and photographers and severing all connections with the Narkomindel. They spent their time walking, reading, and listening to music. Litvinoff likes walking, but the detectives who followed him everywhere to "protect" him are often less enthusiastic, and some of them rather dislike being assigned to watch him as much as he dislikes being watched. And "watched" is, in his opinion, only a polite word for "spied on" in some countries—but he won't say which.

Litvinoff also has always taken a mild cure at these resorts—not that he is ill, but his blood pressure is a little too high, he has put on weight, needs to live on a simple, regular diet, and is better off if he can eat a little something every second hour. Often he has interrupted an important conference for a few minutes to eat a ham sandwich, returning to continue the discussion where he had left off.

After this particular Marienbad holiday of August, 1934, he was seven pounds lighter and quite prepared in every way to resume the arduous battle for peace.

9

Five days after Germany rejected the security pact, the Assembly of the League of Nations voted to extend an invitation to join to the Soviet Union. It had taken all Barthou's political genius and not inconsiderable force of character to bring this about, and still there were seven countries abstaining, and three opposing votes—Switzerland, the Netherlands, and Poland. Old Barthou was angry at this, for he had promised Litvinoff that the acceptance would be unanimous.

Poland put up the strongest opposition. She feared that Russia might exercise her right as a League member to bring up the question of the Polish minorities (White Russians and Ukrainians). In the end she agreed to Soviet Russia's entry only on condition that future Polish-Russian relations be based upon previous treaties, not upon the League Covenant. Furthermore, Poland notified the League that it would no longer co-operate with the League on its supervision of the treatment of minorities. Finally, the Polish Foreign Minister, Beck, declared that Poland would not enter an Eastern Locarno Pact unless Germany did so—Germany having already rejected it—and unless the Polish-German

Treaty were inserted in the text of the so-called Eastern Locarno agreement.

Three days later, on September 18, Litvinoff arrived in Geneva.

He had a few conversations in the National Hotel—an old building which had been bought for five and a half million Swiss francs by Sir Eric Drummond in 1919 to house the League of Nations offices, and remodeled that same year to serve its new purpose. Only the former manager, M. Hottop, stayed on, with his St. Bernard dog called Voelkerhund (Nations' Dog), a play on *Voelkerbund,* the German word for "League of Nations."

For some twelve years the Assembly of the League of Nations had met in Reformation Hall, a long, narrow, rectangular building, next to the Victoria Hotel; but since 1932 the Assembly had been transferred to the Electoral Building, an immense structure seating about 2,000 people, gloomy and dark, badly illuminated and full of smoke; * and it was here that Litvinoff, dressed in the correct diplomatic attire, appeared at the head of his delegation. The Russians were received by Marcel Houden, a high official of the League Secretariat.

Litvinoff was told that the acceptance had not been unanimous, but if he was annoyed, he did not show it. The procedure at the League provided that the President of the Assembly should make a short speech declaring that the League accepted the new country into full membership, while the delegates of that country remained just outside. Then when the speech ended with an invitation to the delegates to enter the Assembly Hall, they were conducted to their seats down the central aisle.

The address of the President, R. J. Sandler of Sweden, was a rather dull, pointless talk that seemed never to end. The public began to cough and the delegates grew restless, but Sandler spoke on and on. Ten minutes before he ended his address, Marcel Houden conducted the Russians to their seats in the hall through a door at the rear on the right side. Only the Rumanian Foreign Minister, Nicolas Titulescu, noticed their entrance. Consequently, when Sandler at last came to the end of his speech, and raising his voice announced: "And now I invite the delegates of the Union of the Soviet Socialist Republics to occupy their seats in the Assembly and the Council," everybody looked to-

* The League of Nations palace was not opened until 1937.

wards the far end of the hall where the Russian delegates were supposed to make their entrance. But nobody entered. The delegates grew
restless, got up, formed whispering groups, the newspaper men prepared for a sensation, and Barthou rushed towards the door to look
for the missing Russians. Sandler, who did not quite know what to
do, finally repeated his last sentence, hoping that this time the Russians
would take their cue and appear. Still nothing happened. Litvinoff
then rose from his seat in the middle of the room, made a bow and
said, "Merci, merci."

That was Soviet Russia's entry into the League of Nations, a small
incident but symptomatic. It had been carefully and maliciously
planned by Marcel Houden. At least, it was a general conviction in
the League that Houden, who had disliked Russian participation, had
played the little trick to spoil their reception.

But Litvinoff was quite unperturbed when he mounted the platform
to make his first speech before the Council of the League of Nations:

"The entry into the League, in the fifteenth year of its existence, of
one of the greatest states in the world does undoubtedly call for some
explanation.

"I will speak with that frankness and moderation which many of
you, knowing me of old, will, I am sure, grant me, and which can only
be helpful to our mutual understanding and our future cooperation.

"We represent here a new state—new, not geographically, but new
in its external aspects, its internal political and social structure, and
its aspirations and ideals. The appearance in the historical arena of a
new form of state has always been met with hostility on the part of old
state formations. It is not surprising that the phenomenon of a new
state with a social and political system radically different from any
heretofore known should come up against intense hostility from without and manifested by literally all other countries in the world. This
hostility has been not merely theoretical, but has found expression even
in military action, assuming the form of prolonged attempts, externally organized, to interfere in the internal affairs of the new state for
the purpose of getting it back to the old lines. At the time when the
League of Nations was being formed to proclaim the organization of
peace, the people of our country had as yet not been enabled to enjoy
the blessings of peace. They still had to defend their internal peace with

arms, and to contend long for their right to internal self-determination and their external independence. Even after the most extreme forms of intervention in the affairs of our state were over, the hostility of the outer world continued to be manifested in the most varying degrees and forms.

"All this makes it quite obvious that the relations between the Soviet state and the League of Nations could not be other than those existing between itself and the states belonging to the League. Not only this, but the people in the Soviet Union naturally feared that these nations united in the League might give collective expression to their hostility towards the Soviet Union and combine their anti-Soviet activities. It can hardly be denied that at that time, and even much later, there were still statesmen who thought, or at least dreamed, of such collective action. On the one hand, they were inclined to underrate the internal power of resistance of the new state, and, on the other hand, to overrate that harmony of political and economic interests in the other states which, it seemed to them, the League should have embodied. They continued to believe that the World War would be the last war in the world, and that the order established by it was immutable and secure against any attempts at alteration by force. They dreamed of establishing at least temporary peace, which would, however, by no means have been extended to the new Soviet state. The history of the last ten years, the history of the League of Nations itself, the increasing conflicts of international interests, the prolonged economic crisis, and, finally, the development of the Soviet state, have shown the world how utopian were these dreams and aspirations.

"Today we are happy to be able to state that the exponents of those utopias and the advocates of the policy of ignoring and isolating the Soviet Union are no longer to be met among broadminded statesmen, among the representatives of the more important states molding international life who think along realistic lines and understand the needs of the present day, but must be searched for among narrowminded politicians unable to rise above their petty political passions and strong prejudices and deriving their knowledge of countries and people from muddy sources. It remains only to pity such people and to wish them a speedy enlightenment and a return to more reliable sources of information.

"I take this opportunity of expressing my conviction that, in the meantime, the League will see to it that such people have nothing to do with the settlement of affairs affecting the interests of the Soviet state in which impartial judgement and at least an elementary understanding of world events are necessary.

"I have already described the attitude of the Soviet Union to the League of Nations both at its formation and during the first stages of its development, and have given the reasons for that attitude. To this I must frankly add that the Soviet Government could not have agreed with all the decisions of the League at that time and that, had we taken part in drawing up the Covenant of the League, we would have contested certain of its articles. . . .

"All this, however, has not been important enough to prevent the Soviet Union from entering the League, especially since any new member of an organization can be morally responsible only for decisions made with its participation and agreement.

"In order to make our position quite clear, I should like further to state that the idea in itself of an association of nations contains nothing theoretically unacceptable for the Soviet state and its ideology. The Soviet Union is itself a league of nations in the best sense of the word, uniting over 200 nationalities, thirteen of which have a population of not less than one million each, and others, such as Russia and the Ukraine, a population running into scores of millions. I will make so bold as to claim that never before have so many nations coexisted so peacefully within a single state, never before have so many nations in one state had such free cultural development and enjoyed their own national culture as a whole and the use of their own language in particular. In no other country are all manifestations of race and national prejudice so resolutely put down and eradicated as in the Soviet Union.

"Here, as regards equality of rights, are neither national majorities nor minorities, since no nation either in theory or practice, has less rights and fewer opportunities for cultural and economic development than another. Many nationalities which seemed to have been doomed to die out altogether have received a fresh lease on life and begun to develop anew, and this in territories where, before the Soviet regime, all nationalities except the dominating Russian were being stamped out by violence and oppression. . . .

"All the nationalities in our Union are, of course, united by a common political and economic regime and by common aspirations toward a single ideal, for the attainment of which they vie among themselves. The Soviet state has, however, never excluded the possibility of some form or other of associating with states having a different political and social system, so long as there is no mutual hostility and if it is for the attainment of common aims. For such an association it considers that the essential conditions would be, first, the extension to every state belonging to such an association the liberty to preserve what I might call its state personality and the social economic system chosen by it—in other words, reciprocal non-interference in the domestic affairs of the states therein associated; and, secondly, the existence of common aims.

"As to the first condition, which we have named the peaceful co-existence of different social-political systems at a given historical stage, we have advocated it again and again at international conferences. We have managed to get it recognized by inclusion in some of the resolutions of these conferences. But further developments were necessary before this principle was able to gain for itself wider recognition. The invitation of the Soviet Union to join the League of Nations may be said to represent the final victory of this principle. The Soviet Union is entering into the League today as representative of a new social-economic system not renouncing any of its special features, and—like the other states here represented—preserving intact its personality.

"With regard to common aims, these have long ago been established in many spheres.

"The Soviet government has also not abstained from cooperation of a political nature whenever some alleviation of international conflicts and increase of guarantees of security and consolidation of peace might reasonably be expected from such cooperation. I will only mention the active part taken by the Soviet delegation in the Preparatory Commission of the Disarmament Conference and in the Conference itself, when, on behalf of the Soviet Government, it declared its readiness for any degree of disarmament, taking its stand on far-reaching proposals for the ensuring of peace, some of which have received world-wide recognition and even application. In this respect I remember, not without pride, the Soviet definition of aggression, which has been made the basis of innumerable international acts.

"It needed, however, one great dominating common aim to prove incontestably to all nations, including those of the Soviet Union, the desirability—nay, the necessity—for closer cooperation between the Soviet Union and the League of Nations, and even for the entry of the Soviet Union into the League. The discovery of such a common aim has been greatly facilitated by the events of the last two or three years.

"Thirty delegations to the Assembly, comprising most of the members of the League and representing all the big states and those of importance in international life, declared in their address to the Soviet Union that the mission of the League was the organization of peace, and that the success of this mission demanded the cooperation of the Soviet Union. They knew that the state which they were addressing had not spared, throughout the seventeen years of its existence, its efforts for the establishment of the best possible relations with its own neighbors, on the most solid foundations, for rapprochements with all states desiring this, thus making itself a powerful factor for international peace.

"For its part, the Soviet Government, following attentively all developments of international life, could not but observe the increasing activity in the League of Nations of states interested in the preservation of peace and their struggle against aggressive militarist elements. More, it noted that these aggressive elements themselves were finding the restrictions of the League embarrassing and were trying to shake them off. All this could not be without its influence on the attitude towards the League of Nations of the Soviet Government, ever searching for further means for the organization of peace, for cooperation in which we have been invited to come here.

"The organization of peace! Could there be a loftier and at the same time more practical and urgent task for the operation of all nations? The words used in political slogans have their youth and their age. If they are used too often without being applied, they wear themselves out and end by losing potency. Then they have to be revived and instilled with new meaning. The sound and the meaning of the words 'organization of peace' ought not to be different from their sound and meaning twelve or fifteen years ago. Then, to many members of the League of Nations, war seemed to be a remote theoretical danger, and there seemed to be no hurry as to its prevention. Now, war must appear to all as the threatening danger of tomorrow. Now, the organization of peace, for which so far very little has been done, must be set against the extremely active organization of war. Then, many believed that the spirit of war might be exorcised by adjurations, resolutions and declarations. Now, everybody knows the exponents of the idea of war, the open promulgators of the refashioning of the map of Europe and Asia by the sword, are not to be intimidated by paper obstacles. Members of the League of Nations know this by experience. We are now confronted with the task of averting war by more effective means.

"The failure of the Disarmament Conference, on which formerly such high hopes were placed, in its turn compels us to seek more effective means. We must accept the incontestable fact that, in the present complicated state of political and economic interests, no war of any serious dimensions can be localized, and any war, whatever its issue, will turn out to have been but the first of a series. We must also tell ourselves that sooner or later any war will bring misfortune to all countries, whether belligerents or neutrals. The lessons of the World War, from the results of which both belligerents and neutrals are suffering to this day, must not be forgotten. The impoverishment of the whole world, the lowering of living standards for both manual and brain workers, unemployment, robbing all and sundry of their confidence in the morrow, not to speak of the fall in cultural values, the return of some countries to medieval ideology—such are the consequences of the World War, even now, sixteen years after its cessation, which are making themselves acutely felt.

"Finally, we must realize once and for all that no war with political-economic aims is capable of restoring so-called historical justice, and that all it could do would be to substitute new and perhaps still more glaring injustices for old ones, and that every new peace treaty bears within it the seeds of fresh warfare. Further, we must not lose sight of the new increase in armaments in its qualitative still more than in its quantitative increase, in the vast increase of potential destruction. The fact that aerial warfare has with such lightning speed won itself an equal place with land and naval warfare is sufficient corroboration of this argument.

"I do not consider it the moment to speak in detail about effective means for the prevention of impending and openly promulgated war.

One thing is quite clear to me, and that is that peace and security cannot be organized on the shifting sands of verbal promises and declarations. The nations are not to be soothed into a feeling of security by assurances of peaceful intentions, however often they are repeated, especially in those places where there are grounds for expecting aggression or where, only the day before, there have been talk and publications about wars of conquest in all directions, for which both ideological and material preparations are being made. We should establish that any state is entitled to demand from its neighbors, near and remote, guarantees for its security, and that such a demand is not to be considered as an expression of mistrust. Governments with a clear conscience and really free from all aggressive intentions, cannot refuse to give, in place of declarations, more effective guarantees which would be extended to themselves and give them also a feeling of complete security.

"Far be it from me to overrate the opportunities and means of the League of Nations for the organization of peace. I realize, better perhaps than any of you, how limited these means are. I am aware that the League does not possess the means for the complete abolition of war. I am, however, convinced that, with the firm will and close cooperation of all its members, a great deal could be done at any given moment for the utmost diminution of the danger of war, and this is sufficiently honorable and lofty a task, the fulfillment of which would be of incalculable advantage to humanity. The Soviet Government has never ceased working at this task throughout the whole period of its existence. It has come here to combine its efforts with those of other states represented in the League. I am convinced that in this, our common work, from now on the will to peace of the Soviet Union with its hundred and seventy million inhabitants—peace for itself and for other states—will make itself felt as a powerful factor. I am convinced that, as we observe the fruitful consequences of this stream of fresh forces in the common cause of peace, we shall always remember with the utmost satisfaction this day, as one occupying an honorable place in the annals of the League."

This was Soviet Russia's advent into the League of Nations. It was a statement of great force and genuine nobility which should have thoroughly shamed the school-boy perpetrators of the shabby little trick designed to mar the dignity of the Russian reception into the League.

But only the really serious can be rebuked by seriousness. Colonel Beck, representing Poland, sneered, with superficial cleverness: "This is only the Third International being welcomed by the Second" *—for Sandler had been in the Second International. Such cynicism among men in decisive positions contributed to Poland's great tragedy.

Moreover, some of the League officials were so pleased with their first effort that they devised another incident which again revealed how trivial-minded and vindictive in the face of great issues and great responsibilities some of the League secretariat were. Every Council member was chairman of some committee. Hence, as soon as the Soviets were in the League of Nations, Litvinoff had to be given some chairmanship. There were plenty of committees which could use the talents and powers of a statesman of Litvinoff's caliber, but he was assigned to the Committee on Seaweeds. This group had to solve the important problem of how to clear seaweed out of the Atlantic Ocean in order to free coastal shipping from this impediment—an odd assignment for the Foreign Minister of a country which did not even border on the Atlantic Ocean. Litvinoff never even smiled on learning of the appointment.

Russia's entry into the League could have been construed as a decided personal triumph for Litvinoff. It marked a definite reversal of Moscow policy toward the Western nations which had been, for quite understandable reasons, suspicious and hostile. It must have taken a deal of persuasion and a very hard-headed marshalling of facts to induce the Kremlin to initiate a new era of co-operation with the Western Powers, but Litvinoff's own realism and complete devotion to the ultimate ends he had in view never permitted him to waste time in self-congratulation. In the very moment of achievement it was his habit to take stock of all liabilities and to look ahead again to the probability of new tribulations and frustrations. When after his initial speech at the League he was riding out to a distant suburb where he was staying, his companion asked after a long interval, "Why so silent?" Litvinoff replied, "I was only composing the speech that I shall have to make when we leave the League."

Now that Russia was in the League, Litvinoff saw fit to transfer his quarters from the modest Pension d'Angleterre to the Hotel de la Paix on the Quai du Montblanc. This was by no means comparable to the

* G. Tabouis, *They Called Me Cassandra*, p. 211, New York, 1942.

Hotel Bergues, headquarters of the French, or the Hotel Beau Rivage and the Hotel Carlton where the English lived, but it was more imposing than the pension where he had stopped ever since his first arrival in the little League of Nations capital. Later he went to the Richmond.

The Russian delegation lived very quietly, seldom appearing at the innumerable parties that kept the League of Nations circles so busy socially. When they did not appear at these endless affairs malicious gossip first circulated that it was because they did not know how to dress properly. One story had it that when Litvinoff arrived in Geneva in November, 1927, he went out the first day and came back to his hotel with a large parcel containing a great number of stiff shirts and collars, which he proceeded to distribute to the men in his delegation. This may or may not have been true, but it probably was true that few of the delegation had dinner clothes, for the simple reason that they would not have needed them in Moscow. Moreover, they believed that they had come to Geneva to work, not to rush around to parties—and they preferred work. Litvinoff himself, as a matter of fact, is a skilled and genial host, adequate to any social situation, even leading the ball successfully with an ambassador's wife, and Madame Litvinoff is a poised and gracious woman of the world. But people doing big jobs are apt to find play only an interruption to work.

Thus in the Russian delegation even the women worked—as women in the new Russia usually do—for while the West after years of agitation has been gingerly advancing in feminism, Russia since the Revolution has taken it for granted. Madame Litvinoff handled the delegation's public relations so successfully that she became very popular with the correspondents, and continued to translate Litvinoff's speeches. Her close friend, Madame Lunacharsky—young, blond, elegant, witty, and a successful cinema star—was very popular also. Most of the other women acted as their husbands' secretaries and they all worked long hours, and late.

CHAPTER TWELVE

What Price Peace?

Louis Barthou was delighted at Russia's entrance into the League. So were the Geneva correspondents of the world press who, ever since Litvinoff's first appearance at the Preparatory Disarmament Committee, had been greatly impressed by his character and ability and the far-reaching significance of his plans. The newspaper men celebrated the occasion with a luncheon at which Litvinoff was the guest of honor and Barthou the chief speaker.

The menu was designed by the Hungarians Derso and Kelen, unofficial cartoonists of the League. A Russian village was depicted, in which all the Geneva celebrities strolled about in Russian costumes. In the middle of the composition was a young woman called Miss Geneva, dancing with Litvinoff, costumed as a Russian general.

When Barthou made his speech, he picked up a copy of the menu and, taking advantage of the fact that it was the custom at such luncheons for all statements to be off the record, he said: "I see a Russian general dancing with a virgin . . . or let us say, with a somewhat damaged virgin (*vierge abusée*). And now that they have got together, I am quite proud that I have played the role of matchmaker. . . ." A little later in his speech he turned to Litvinoff, who was sitting at his right. "Look at him closely," he instructed the others, "does he look like a bandit? No, he does not look like a bandit. He looks like an honest man."

Litvinoff joined in the spirit of the occasion. When he replied to Barthou, he remarked: "I will gladly dance with even a damaged virgin, if I know in which direction I dance. . . ."

That luncheon and the speeches made there caused some trouble. Geneva and Swiss newspapers felt hurt by the allusions of Barthou and Litvinoff. Litvinoff again was made to feel that he was not a welcome guest in Switzerland.

This was to be Louis Barthou's last speech in Geneva. Only a few weeks later, on October 9, he went to Marseilles to welcome King Alexander II of Yugoslavia. The visit had been arranged to conclude arrangements in connection with the Barthou-Litvinoff scheme of collective security.

The King, Admiral Berthelot, the Commander of the Port of Toulon, and two Yugoslav attachés entered the first of many waiting automobiles. An enormous crowd had gathered at the Place de la Bourse and in the streets through which the King was to pass. At the Place a man broke through the police cordon, dashed up to the royal car, and began firing. One of the officers on guard struck him down with his saber, but he continued to shoot as he fell.

King Alexander II was killed instantly. Others, among them Barthou, were wounded. In the general confusion nobody properly looked after Barthou, who, much too late, was transported first to a pharmacy and then to a hospital. He had lost a great deal of blood, and complained of severe pain; but he was courageous and in the taxicab the loss of his glasses seemed to bother him more than his wounds. Yet he kept saying: *"Ce n'est pas grave, ce n'est pas grave?"* with a questioning inflection in his voice. An excited attendant applied a tourniquet in the wrong place, and Barthou's definitely good chance of recovery was thrown away. By the time he was properly cared for, he had lost too much blood. A transfusion was attempted, but it was too late. At six in the evening Louis Barthou died.

The murderer proved to be a certain Peter Kalemen, member of a Croat secret organization, *Ustashi* (led by Ante Pavelich), which existed and conspired on Italian territory. Even at that time there was little doubt that the assault on King Alexander II had been undertaken with the knowledge of Hitler and Mussolini. Mussolini later declined to extradite Pavelich, who was sentenced to death in France, but today, sponsored by Hitler and Mussolini, is the bloody dictator of Croatia.

King Alexander II was buried on October 13. Among those present at the funeral was Litvinoff. He made a short speech, as was fitting. In Barthou's death, he could not tell then and there how much he himself, how much Europe, had lost. Barthou had died before he was able to complete his grand plan of collective security, which would have rendered Hitler incapable of starting another war. He had died—leaving Litvinoff the almost impossible task of completing the work alone.

Perhaps, at that time, only Litvinoff realized that the shots of Marseilles marked the Sarajevo of World War II.

2

On March 16, 1935, Germany decreed universal military service. The whole world was dismayed, except the British who thought it unimportant. The London *Times* stated on March 17 that "if Herr Hitler's move is simply a rather crude method of asserting German equality, then no irreparable harm has been done. The negotiations can go forward."

Litvinoff took a much more serious view of the situation. On April 17 he delivered a speech at an extraordinary session of the League of Nations:

"The question we have to discuss as a result of the application of the French Government to the Council of the League of Nations is not of equal formal interest for all the members of the League of Nations. But it undoubtedly deserves the attention both of the Council of the League of Nations and of the League as a whole.

"Yesterday we heard the representatives of the States signatory to the Treaty of Versailles and who are now directly affected by the violation of the obligations adopted towards them. I, however, speak on behalf of a country which not only bears no responsibility for the Versailles Treaty, but which never concealed its unfavourable attitude towards that Treaty in general and towards the disarmament of Germany in particular.

"Our formal attitude towards the matter in hand consists in the fact that, as members of the League of Nations and of the Council of the League of Nations, we are faced with an act of violation of an international treaty by a State which is formally still a member of the League. In accordance with Article I, Par. 2, of the Covenant of the League of Nations, this act constitutes a violation of the Covenant and consequently a violation of obligations undertaken towards the other members of the League, constituting a menace to peace. The obligation of all States to observe their international undertakings occupies a prime place in the Covenant of the League, and this testifies to the tremendous importance attributed to this undertaking. And it cannot be otherwise, for one of the foundations of peace is the observance of international obligations directly affecting the security of nations.

"However, I am more interested in the substance of the matter than in its formal aspect, on which other members of the Council have dwelt in sufficient detail. We hold by the equality of nations and their indisputable right to security and to the means which ensure their security. All peace-loving States have the right to arm for the defense of their security.

"However, while calling for equality in armaments, we must base ourselves on the assumption that these armaments will be used exclusively for defensive purposes, for the protection of existing frontiers and for the security of the nation concerned.

"But what is to be done if in some given circumstance this assumption is subject to doubt and when, on the contrary, there is reason to fear that a country is arming, not for defense but for the violation of frontiers, with the idea of revenge by forcible methods, for the violation of security of neighboring or remote States, for the violation of universal peace with all its tragic consequences?

"What is to be done if a country which demands or assumes the right to arm is exclusively led by people who have publicly announced as the program of their foreign policy a policy which consists, not only in revenge, but in the unrestricted conquest of foreign territory and the destruction of the independence of whole States—under the leadership of people who have publicly announced such a program and who, far from repudiating it, are ceaselessly disseminating it and educating their people in its spirit? What is to be done in cases when a State whose leaders have such a program refuse to give any guarantee whatever that this program will not be carried out, any guarantee of the security of their neighbors, near or remote—guarantees which other States, even those which are above all suspicion of aggressive purposes, are prepared to give? Can we close our eyes to such facts? It is obvious that such cases demand very careful attention.

"Permit me, in order to explain my thought, to give the following illustration. If in a city private citizens are allowed to carry arms, abstractly speaking, all the inhabitants of that city should be guaranteed that right. But let us suppose that a certain citizen openly attacks the inhabitants of neighboring or remote streets and destroys their homes. The municipality would scarcely be in a hurry to issue this citizen a license to carry arms, or to display indifference to the fact that he had secured his arms by illegal means. One could hardly accept on good faith the promise of the truculent citizen to spare certain city quarters and to reserve to himself and his weapons freedom of action only in the other parts of the city. It is the duty of the municipality to ensure tranquillity in all parts of the city. What is more, a citizen who is capable of breaking the law and attacking the fellow-citizens may permit himself the luxury of breaking his promise as regards the object of his threats. The city would at least demand of him first of all real guarantees of good conduct, and the inhabitants of those parts of the city in respect of which the truculent citizen demands freedom of action would be especially entitled to insist on such guarantees, and of them least of all is it to be expected that they will come forward and justify his illegal acquisition of arms on the grounds of abstract principles of equality.

"What I have said in relation to one city applies, of course, to international life. The League of Nations, as it was created to protect the tranquillity of international life in all parts of the world, cannot close its eyes to facts which constitute a menace to their tranquillity.

"We would be very glad if we could discuss the question confronting us in the presence and with the participation of the representative of the State concerned. We would be glad to hear him announce an official repudiation of the program of forcible revenge and conquest, to hear him proclaim his readiness to share with us in collectively guaranteeing the security of all States, including his own, and to hear him give general and effective guarantees of non-violation of universal peace. Unfortunately, this is at present an unrealizable wish, from which we must draw our conclusions. And it is these conclusions, and not motives of a formal character, that determine my attitude towards the resolution submitted. This attitude in no way constitutes a justification of the Treaty of Versailles and its various provisions which have now been infringed. No! It is an expression of the anxiety of my Government to further the creation of an international state of affairs which would in the highest degree render difficult the violations of peace that result in such treaties."

3

The Franco-Russian Pact was finally signed on May 2, 1935. It had been the result of the joint efforts of Edouard Herriot, Joseph Paul-Boncour and, of course, Louis Barthou. The man who was to affix his signature to the pact happened to be the new French Foreign Minister, Pierre Laval.

Laval signed the pact, but he had no intention of letting it interfere with the fundamental purpose of his foreign policy, the rapprochement of France and Italy, a policy which later led to and finally necessitated collaboration with Germany. Accordingly Laval, hoping to make difficulties, conferred a number of times with the Russian Ambassador, Potemkin, in Paris between April 20 and May 1, 1935. Nothing came of these discussions except the clear indication that Laval did not want the French army collaborating in any way with the Soviet Union; that he intended to evade every realistic commitment.

While these negotiations were proceeding, French public opinion was apathetic. France was much more interested in what was going on within France herself. Ever since the Stavisky scandal had given the public a glimpse into the intricacies of internal corruption, scandals and *affaires* had continued to shock and dismay the country.

In the end the fear of Hitler—precisely the cause that had impelled Litvinoff and Barthou to embark on the venture of collective security—decided the new French Government in favor of a Russian treaty. Germany must be isolated and, above all, a German-Russian understanding and collaboration must be prevented.

Herriot, who had to explain and defend the pact in the French Chamber, rightly emphasized the open character of this pact openly arrived at, which could have been signed by Germany any time, and thus was not in any way directed against a peaceful, law-abiding Germany, but would have force only against an aggressor nation.

The pact, signed on May 2, stipulated that:

In case of any violation of the Russian or French frontiers, the Council of the League of Nations will be immediately summoned by the two contracting parties who must accept its pronouncements, unless the Council fails to reach an unanimous decision, a circumstance which will permit both parties to resume their freedom of action. In case of flagrant aggression, the two parties would not only call upon the Council of the League to meet, but would, at the same time, take steps to help each other effectively, pending the decisions of the Council.

A few days later Laval arrived in Moscow. The station was decorated with tricolors and red flags. A band played the "Marseillaise." Laval had come, however, not to discuss the pact, but to persuade Stalin and Litvinoff to silence French Communists, who for many years had been strongly critical of the French armament program. There was also a personal matter. Laval was soon to run for re-election at Aubervilliers, and he feared the opposition of the powerful Communists there.

Stalin obliged. After it was agreed that the French and Russian General Staffs should have certain conversations a few weeks hence, Stalin made a public statement in which he stressed the need for preserving and developing the military power of France. And Laval, in turn, admonished the French press to play up this statement by Stalin.

Festivities were arranged in honor of Laval, including a stupendous display of Russian air power and a special performance at the opera. Litvinoff was the Government host. At the official reception "he danced with the youngest and prettiest," * "and he dances very well." †

Laval stayed in Moscow only forty-eight hours. Then he went to Warsaw for the funeral of Marshal Pilsudski. Here he promptly started his double dealing. He had already sent a message to Berlin calming the Wilhelmstrasse about his visit to Moscow. Now at the Hotel Europe in Warsaw, he met Goering, who had also come to Pilsudski's funeral. Goering professed to be amazed that Laval should not realize what encouragement the Franco-Russian Pact would give

* Louis Fischer, *op. cit.*, p. 304.
† Joseph E. Davies, *op. cit.*, p. 364.

the French Communist Party; he also mentioned the eternal danger of the Bolshevization of Europe. Laval was impressed.

The nearer the elections drew, the more important they seemed to Laval, more important even than European collective security. The extreme Right felt the same. Georges Mandel, a member of the French Cabinet who belonged to the Right but saw the ever-growing danger of Hitler more clearly than most French politicians, said: "While there is still a strong majority for a policy of understanding with the Soviets, it is fair to assume that this majority, at least as far as its leaders are concerned, is more interested in the doctrine controlling this policy than anxious to put it into practice."

When Laval was defeated in the elections at Aubervilliers, he was all but ready to break with the Communists. He held Stalin and Litvinoff personally responsible for his defeat and thought seriously of scrapping the pact. His first move was to call for ratification of the pact by the French parliament. According to the French Constitution this was not necessary, but the application of the pact was thus delayed for some time. It did not come up in the Chamber until a month after Laval had ceased to be Minister of Foreign Affairs. All his friends voted against it. Until the last minute he himself declared that he would vote against it but finally did vote for it.

By now the pact was compromised; it had been robbed of all practical meaning; most important of all, the indispensable supplement, a military agreement without which it was just words, was lacking. As it now stood, it involved no risks and carried no guarantees. Thus the pact had not been honestly fulfilled.

4

So one year after it had begun, the struggle for collective security was almost completely frustrated. Could peace be rescued in Europe? In the world? Could Litvinoff still preserve the peace for which he had fought so consistently since 1915?

Strangely enough, in many countries not in sympathy with Soviet Russia, the general feeling was that only Litvinoff could preserve such a peace. In some it was even believed that he actually had preserved peace by his unceasing labor in this direction. In the Western hemisphere, at least two important publications came out with suggestions that the Nobel Peace Prize be awarded to Litvinoff: *The Literary Digest* (November 18, 1933), and *The Canadian Forum* (January, 1934).

The Canadian Forum stated, among other things:

> The man who obviously deserves the Nobel Prize for Peace is, of course, Maxim Litvinoff. There should be no need to recite the claims of the Soviet Commissar for Foreign Affairs: his good-tempered fight against the cordon sanitaire which the madness of the Versailles years strove to erect about the Soviet Union; his formulation of the special type of non-aggression pacts bearing his name which have done so much to pacify the small states bordering upon his own country; the forthright realism which he brought into all the endless Geneva discussions on disarmament. And now this year (1933) the achievement of American recognition, a diplomatic master-stroke designed primarily, no doubt, to benefit the contracting parties, but likely in its implications to have a steadying influence on the two great semi-outlaw powers—Japan and Germany. Litvinoff's visit to Washington may well prove to have been the outstanding peace move of 1933. But the Nobel Prize Committee is not interested, and the conviction grows that Nobel Prize committees are rarely interested in giving any credit to men of the Left.

When Litvinoff was asked about his chance of being awarded the Nobel Prize he replied that he never expected to receive it—and he did not care. He was certainly not ambitious to be honored by representatives of the liberal and socialist parties of Norway who had the deciding influence in the awards, for in his opinion a majority of them were among the most reactionary men in Europe. In any case, the suggestion never amounted to a formal nomination.

Could Litvinoff still preserve peace? At least he had not given up. In the spring of 1935 he began new efforts to establish his Eastern Locarno, the cornerstone of which should have been the Franco-Russian Pact. The Czechs were in favor, but the English no longer felt sure that they wanted to guarantee any borders in the East. The Little Entente was in favor, but the Hungarians, who still hoped to get back the territory they had lost after World War I, were strongly against any pact guaranteeing the status quo.

Most of all, the Poles were against any such agreements. The 1932

Poland-Soviet Russia Treaty of Non-Aggression which Litvinoff had hailed in his speech before the Central Executive Committee the year before was in effect nullified when on January 26, 1934, Marshal Pilsudski signed a treaty of non-aggression with Hitler. It will never be clear whether the Poles were naive enough even then to believe in a Nazi guarantee, or whether other motives influenced their government. It was, in any case, part of Pilsudski's theory that he must treat Russia and Germany as nearly alike as possible. This new treaty warned Litvinoff that he could no longer depend upon "trust and mutual understanding" with Poland if, indeed, he had ever been able to trust the Poles in the past.

He did succeed in extending the original pact of 1932 on June 5, 1934, but this was hardly more than a gesture. Stalin, in an interview with Roy Howard of the Scripps-Howard Press, said in 1936: "I do not know what specific frontiers Germany could use for her purpose of attacking Russia. But I think that those willing to lend her a frontier can be found." Stalin and Litvinoff had two countries in mind: Poland and Finland.

Litvinoff, though he personally never handled Finnish policy (there was a special Karelian Department in the Narkomindel), had every reason to feel bitter about Finland. That little country, which had become known as "peaceful" and even "democratic," had always obstructed Litvinoff's policy of assuring peace with the immediate neighbors of the Soviet Union. It had refused to take part in Litvinoff's Disarmament Conference in 1922. It had been the scene of innumerable intrigues against the Soviet Union, beginning at the end of World War I, when Finland was used by the reactionary German Free Corps as a basis for their anti-Soviet activities. Baron Mannerheim, who had played host to the Germans, had never lost contact with the German reactionary parties and was very friendly with certain Reichswehr generals. Later, Mannerheim also had an understanding with certain Tory groups in England. Little Finland was always considered the most promising jumping-off point for another war of intervention against the Soviets. All this was either not known to the world at large or was explained away by reactionary elements in all the countries which had constantly denounced the Soviet Union as an imperialist country and a potential danger to the peace of Europe.

5

On October 3, 1935, just one year after Barthou's assassination, World War II really began: Mussolini sent his troops into Abyssinia— an act of aggression that surprised no one. It had been coming for months and had been discussed at the League of Nations for weeks. In vain had Italy's representative, Baron Aloisi, brought forward certain arguments: that Ethiopia, by violating its treaties with Italy, and by countenancing within its boundaries the practice of slavery, had placed itself outside the League Covenant. Litvinoff denounced Baron Aloisi and Mussolini in no uncertain terms in his speech of September 5, 1935, at the 88th Session of the Council of the League of Nations.

"It is with deep regret that we have listened to the communication of the representatives of the United Kingdom and of France on the failure of their attempt to settle completely the conflict between Italy and Ethiopia which would have allowed us to dismiss the question from the agenda and saved each of us the unpleasant duty of passing our individual judgment. This duty is the more unpleasant for me, as one of the parties to the conflict is a state with which the Soviet Union has been maintaining invariably friendly relations for over ten years; with which it sincerely desires to continue these relations; to which it would least of all wish to cause any harm; collaboration with which, both in the League of Nations and outside it, for the maintenance of peace in Europe we highly appreciate; and, finally, a nation which enjoys in my country the deepest respect and sympathy.

"Like the great majority of my colleagues, I have to make on this occasion a statement on a question which does not directly affect the interests of our countries, but which may have the greatest consequences for the whole of international life, for the fate of the League of Nations, for the cause of general peace and consequently, sooner or later, for our own countries. That is why I am bound to declare with regret my inability to agree with the attitude which the representative of Italy wishes us to adopt. It is true that he made no proposals, but the purport of his statement amounts to an invitation to the Council to declare its disinterestedness in the conflict, its indifference, and to pass it by, sanctioning the freedom of action which he requires for his government; but in this way, while basing this proposal on the non-observance and the violation of its international obligations, to disregard the Covenant of the League of Nations on which, in no little degree, depends the whole edifice of international peace and the security of nations.

". . . We are faced by the direct threat of impending military operations between two members of the League, by a threat of aggression, which is not only denied but, on the contrary, confirmed by the representative of Italy himself. Can we ignore this threat and forget the existence of Articles 10, 11 and 15 of the Covenant of the League? Would that be not a flagrant violation of the Covenant, would not its violation by the whole Council mean the complete repudiation and negation of the Covenant?

"I may be reminded of a precedent when the Council of the League did not take all necessary measures for the prevention of a conflict between two members of the League. But this is exactly a thing to be remembered now, for we all still feel in what measure that case weakened the League of Nations, diminished its authority and contributed to the creation of the politically unstable, menacing situation in which the world finds itself and even, may be, to the rise of the present conflict. The repetition of the precedent would certainly have a cumulative effect and, in its turn, would stimulate new conflicts more directly affecting the whole of Europe. The thesis of the indivisibility of peace is, fortunately, gaining more and more recognition. It has now become clear to the whole world that each war is the creation of a preceding war and the generator of new present or future wars.

"I am sorry to say that I cannot agree with the way of arguing of the representative of Italy. I am certain that there is no one here who feels sympathy with the internal regime of Ethiopia as it is described in the documents submitted. . . . Nothing in the Covenant of the League entitles us, however, to discriminate between members of the League as to their internal regime, the color of their skin, their racial distinctions or the stage of their civilization, nor accordingly to deprive some of them of privileges which they enjoy in virtue of their membership of the League, and, in the first place, of their inalienable right to integrity and independence. . . . At any attempt of aggression, similar or other justifications will be put forward. In my mind, the League of Nations should stand firm on the principle that there cannot be justification for military operations except in self-defense, in the same way as no such justification is admitted by the Briand-Kellogg Pact forbidding war as an instrument of national policy.

"My observations are of general character of principle and are directed, if I may say so, against the unknown aggressor. . . .

"The state I represent entered the League but a year ago, with the sole purpose and with the sole promise to collaborate in every possible way with other nations in the maintenance of indivisible peace. It is this purpose and this promise only that are guiding me today when I propose to the Council not to stop short in any efforts or decisions which may avert an armed conflict between two members of the League, thus accomplishing a task which is the raison d'être of the League itself."

Nine days later, on September 14, Litvinoff delivered another speech —this time before the Assembly of the League of Nations—in which he made clear that the question at hand was not just Italo-Ethiopian relations, but rather a vital principle was at stake, indivisible peace. Aggression must be opposed, no matter from where it came, no matter how it was disguised.

"The anxiety which has been tormenting the world for the last three years is far from decreasing, but, on the contrary, is growing. It is not only the Ethiopian question that matters or that matters so much; there are other ominous dangers facing Europe and the whole world. We owe it, fortunately, to this anxiety that all peaceable countries, all sincere friends of peace, have convinced themselves of the indivisibility of peace and of the necessity of collective security. But collective security afforded by the Covenant of the League of Nations is not sufficient. Of this we become more and more convinced with every attempt at the application of the Covenant. Hence the necessity for individual states, or rather groups of states, to take additional measures of security based on the Covenant. Such measures have found their universally recognized expression in regional pacts of mutual assistance. . . .

"We know of another political conception that is fighting the idea of collective security and advocating bilateral pacts, and this now even between all states, but only between states arbitrarily chosen for this purpose. This conception can have nothing in common with peaceful intentions. Not every pact of non-aggression is concluded with a view to strengthening general peace. While non-aggression pacts concluded by the Soviet Union with its neighbors include a special clause for suspending the pact in cases of aggression committed by one of the parties against any third state, we know of other pacts of non-aggression which have no such clause. This means that a state which has secured by such a pact of non-aggression its rear or its flank, obtains the facility of attacking with impunity third states. . . .

"I might now finish my statement, but I feel that many in this Assembly may wonder why I have not spoken on the question which is worrying and exciting them most—the Italo-Ethiopian conflict. I preferred to dwell on general questions because this conflict does not shut out for me the whole international horizon with other dangers looming beyond it. I preferred to state general principles applicable to individual cases. You may be assured that, if all efforts for conciliation fail and the Italo-Ethiopian conflict comes before the Council again and before the Assembly, the Soviet delegation will pass its judgment with impartiality and also with courage, that it will not be shaken by intimidation by way of abuses and attacks of the press or by any other method. . . .

"As you know, the Soviet Government is, in principle, opposed to the system of colonies, to the policy of spheres of influence and of mandates, to anything pertaining to imperialistic aims. For the Soviet delegation there is only one question of defending the Covenant of the League as an instrument of peace. This instrument has already been somewhat damaged by previous attempts, and we cannot allow a new attempt which would put it completely out of work. We may need it more than once and probably on still more serious occasions. . . ."

As was to be expected, the speech had no influence whatever on Italy's course. Mussolini could no longer tolerate the dangers arising from "Abyssinia's threatening attitude"; his patience was exhausted.

Litvinoff's position on the Italo-Ethiopian problem was absolutely unambiguous; Ethiopia was so far away from Russia that the Italian aggression could not possibly be interpreted as a threat to any Russian interests. Clearly his protests were based on principle: first, the indivisibility of peace; second, the unjustifiability of imperialistic war.

Molotov hailed Litvinoff's stand in a speech before the Central Executive Committee on January 10, 1936:

In the Italo-Abyssinian war, only the U.S.S.R. took an attitude different in principle, alien to any notion of imperialism and devoid of any intention of colonial conquest. Only the Soviet Union declared openly that it took for its starting point the principle of equality and independence of Abyssinia which, à propos, is a member of the League, or of any individual capitalist country intending to destroy this independence and equality.

But Litvinoff was not content merely with talking. Russia acted. Four decrees by the Council of People's Commissars, two issued on September 14, and two on November 14, prohibited the export of war materials to Italy, provided for the application of financial sanctions against Italy, limited the importation of goods from Italy (gold, printed matter, and musical publications), and extended the embargo on exports to certain additional articles which could be used for war.

The Council of the League of Nations had resolved unanimously on October 7, 1935—Italy did not take part in this vote—that Italy was the aggressor. Two days later the Assembly concurred with the Council, Austria, Hungary, and Albania dissenting. On November 18, five weeks after Soviet Russia had inaugurated its own sanctions against Italy, the League of Nations also formally voted that it would apply sanctions. On December 12, fifty-three nations had decided that they would not extend loans to Italy; fifty had declared that they would send her no goods; only four states—Austria, Hungary, Albania, and Paraguay—decided that they would not take part in any sanctions; Switzerland, Uruguay, Iran, and Peru made reservations and suggestions.

Litvinoff severely criticized these states in a speech on October 19, 1935, before the Co-ordination Committee of the League of Nations:

Mild as the present sanctions are, they have not been accepted with the unanimity for which the Committee had been entitled to hope; this is a matter of regret . . . My own country, as I have stated on many occasions, has no quarrel with Italy and no special interest in the present case. By agreeing to economic sanctions the Soviet Union is exposing itself to losses, Italy having been one of her best customers. . . . It is prepared, nevertheless, to submit to these losses. . . . It does so for reasons of solidarity and because of its desire to maintain peace and to fulfill all the obligations it has accepted under the Covenant. But these obligations hold good for only so long as they are maintained and fulfilled by other members of the League. Peace can not be based on voluntary contributions: it must be based on specific obligations undertaken by all nations. That is the true spirit of the League.

The League of Nations had decreed sanctions, but too little and too late. From the beginning it had acted against aggression only half-heartedly. Consequently it had not prevented war. In his speech of January 10 Molotov made this clear:

The League may and should be criticized for not always taking sufficient measures, for instance in connection with the Italo-Abyssinian war. . . . It must also be admitted that the League did nothing to prevent this war. However, the fact cannot be overlooked that in this instance the League was hindering not those who were for peace, but those who wanted to help the aggressor. It is from this standpoint that the participation of the U.S.S.R. in the League must be evaluated, this being particularly so in regard to the economic sanctions against Italy, which was recognized as the aggressor.

The League's tardy action in the Ethiopian case was due to the French and British governments. In France, powerful politicians headed by Pierre Laval were pro-Mussolini, and against sanctions. French public opinion was anti-Mussolini, but that did not interest or deter Laval and his friends. Laval, with cynical disregard of France's obligations under the Covenant of the League, had personally promised Mussolini that he would do everything to see that he had a free hand to do whatever he wished in Abyssinia and, with the peculiar brand of honor that holds among thieves, Laval felt constrained to keep his promise.

In England, matters were somewhat more complicated. Stanley Baldwin and his Foreign Minister, Sir Samuel Hoare, would also have liked to forget sanctions, but public opinion there was very strong, almost indeed unanimous for sanctions, and the general elections scheduled for November 14 constrained them to proceed prudently.

The Conservative Party won the elections by a small margin of votes but with a large majority in Parliament, and Baldwin and Hoare therefore felt free to embark immediately on an anti-sanctions policy. On December 9 Hoare went to Paris for a conference with Pierre Laval. Laval is said to have told Hoare that Mussolini was in a desperate situation and if the League of Nations should prohibit the export of fuel oil to Italy, Mussolini would have to attack the British Navy in the Mediterranean. The French Navy, Laval is supposed to have explained, could not possibly participate in less than eighteen days which, in this case, would be much too late. The British Navy, as Laval probably knew or guessed, was not properly equipped for battle, and it was widely rumored in "informed circles" that there was not enough ammunition for more than a few minutes' firing with the big guns. Subsequent events have proved, however, that a few minutes might have been enough.

Whether or not Hoare was convinced, he and Laval prevented Litvinoff and other representatives in Geneva from including oil in the sanctions. By the middle of December there were rumors of scrapping sanctions entirely. Chamberlain had already remarked that the continuation of sanctions was but "a mid-summer's madness." The Hoare-Laval Pact, which in the interest of peace was, Munich-like, to be imposed on a crippled Abyssinia, proposed a plain connivance with international banditry. The pact did permit Abyssinia access to the sea by a narrow corridor but on which railroad construction was explicitly prohibited. It was the occasion for a superb and memorable editorial entitled "A Corridor for Camels" in the London *Times* in which the dishonesty of the pact was ruthlessly exposed. It evoked flaming and unanimous resentment and in England popular excitement rose to such heights that Baldwin was reluctantly forced to arrange for Sir Samuel Hoare's resignation. He made a lame defense in the House and left in tears. Liberal opinion in France was also outraged. A young man of great talent, Captain Anthony Eden, who had already made for himself a high inside reputation by his successes as a negotiator, successes due to his tact, frankness, and industry, was now sent to Geneva as Hoare's successor. He came out immediately for oil sanctions, as Litvinoff had done all along. But by that time it was too late.

Had England and France taken firm and consistent action, Mussolini would not have dared go on with his Ethiopian adventure, but the Western Powers were not prepared to make a decisive stand. The closing of the Suez Canal and the stoppage of oil imports to Italy or the cutting off of the shipments of water from Aden to the Italian forces in Eritrea would have forced Italy to desist.

6

Thus a relatively small group of willful and short-sighted men, representing limited and special interests, were able to thwart the first and last joint effort ever made by a considerable number of nations to render a war impossible. The fundamental idea and purpose of the League of Nations had been flouted. A request from Ethiopia that the Assembly of the League convene was rejected, thanks chiefly to the inconspicuous but effective opposition of France and England. In June, 1936, the Argentine Government made the same request. This time the Assembly was summoned. The Italian Government sent a statement asserting that it intended to "provide peace, justice, and security" for the Ethiopians.

The sad Emperor of Ethiopia then stepped up on the rostrum:

"I ask the fifty-two nations who have given the Ethiopian people a promise to help them in their resistance to the aggressor: What are they willing to do for Ethiopia—what measures do they intend to take? Representatives of the world. . . . What answer am I to take back to my people?"

What answer were the representatives of all the little nations to take back to their people? They read the handwriting on the wall. They understood that what had happened yesterday to Ethiopia could happen to them tomorrow. The Swedish representative, Miss Kersten Hesselgren, spoke for them all, spoke with foreboding and with courageous and unanswerable accusation—with a challenge that could only be met by resolute, farsighted, and prompt action.

"However can we, after this, expect that any small nation can have any hope for the future? You may say, as has been said here, that everything must be done so as not to let loose war on Europe, that for this aim it is meet that one country should die for all the others. Yes; but are you sure that you are not letting it loose just by giving in to the aggressor now? Every small country must, after this, ask itself when its time will come, and ask this with no hope in the League. You are all thinking of this possibility. It has run like a red thread through every speech. Everyone has seen the looming shadow of such an event. What are you going to do? How are you going to prevent its coming? Surely it must be by going to the very root of the evil. Try to find the sources of unrest. Try to take every dispute in hand at once and effectively; and do not let month after month go by in futile discussion."

Litvinoff pronounced a funeral oration on the murdered country, in which he set forth the principles which had guided Russian policy throughout the whole melancholy incident, gave a very specific and frank diagnosis of the weakness of the League, derided quack remedies—or those plausible solutions which tried to solve difficulties by running away from them—and ended with an appeal to stand courageously by the League's basic principle and thus make the League really work.

"We are gathered here to close a page in the history of the League of Nations, the history of international life, which it will be impossible to read without a feeling of bitterness. We must terminate an action commenced in the performance of our duties as members of the League for the purpose of guaranteeing the independence of one of our co-members, but not carried through to the end. Each one of us must feel his degree of responsibility and guilt, which is not the same for all and depends not only on what each of us has actually done, but also on the degree of his readiness to support any common action that circumstances required.

"While expressing this opinion I must state that the Government I represent did from the outset of the Italo-Abyssinian conflict adopt a perfectly clear and firm standpoint, issuing by no means from its own interests or its mutual relations with the belligerents, but exclusively from its understanding of the principle of collective security, international solidarity, the League Covenant and the duties made incumbent upon it by this Covenant.

"The peoples of the Soviet Union have nothing but high esteem and regard for the Italian people. They are interested in an uninterrupted development and reinforcement of the existing political, economic and cultural relations with Italy. Nevertheless, the Soviet Government expressed its readiness to take part in common international action against Italy, in defence of a country with which it did not even have any relations—either formal or actual. It had to say to itself: Plato is my friend, but international solidarity, the principle of collective security, upon which peace at present reposes, loyalty to international obligations, must harden our hearts to the voice of friendship. Since then, at all stages of the discussion of the Italo-Abyssinian conflict, my Government has declared that it will take part in all actions provided for by the Covenant, accepted and jointly undertaken by the rest of the League members. All the decisions of the Co-ordination Committee have been operated by my Government without exception and with the utmost fidelity.

"However, sooner than might have been expected, the moment arrived when it became perfectly clear that the measures adopted at Geneva had to be revised from the point of view of their further expedience—namely, when the resistance of the gallant Abyssinian troops was broken, when the Emperor and Government of Abyssinia left their territory and a considerable portion of the territory was occupied by the Italian army. It transpired beyond doubt that by economic sanctions alone there was no possibility of ousting the Italian army from Abyssinia and restoring the latter's independence, and that this aim could be achieved only by more drastic sanctions, military included. The question of such measures could have been raised only in case one or several States could be found which by virtue of their geographical position and special interests would agree to bear the brunt of a military clash. No such States were to be found among us, and had there been any, the rest of the States, before venturing to take any part in these serious measures, would have demanded guarantees that when other cases of suppressing an aggressor came up they could rely on similar common action being taken. These guarantees were the more necessary since certain moves and actions of a certain European State, whose aggressive intentions are quite beyond doubt and are even announced by that State itself, indicated that aggression was being prepared at an accelerating rate in more than one direction. The attitude which certain States adopted to these actions and their gracious treatment of the authors shook the belief that the guarantees I have mentioned would be immediately forthcoming. In these circumstances, even during the May Session of the League Council, I came to the conclusion that it was useless to apply economic sanctions against Italy any longer and that it was impossible to give Abyssinia any practical help by this method. Apparently, practically all the League members have come to this conclusion.

"I say that every member of the League must now realise his individual responsibility for the failure of the common action in defence of the independence of a co-member of the League, because there have been noticeable attempts in and outside the League to attribute this failure to the League Covenant, its imperfections and the present membership of the League. Hence far-reaching conclusions are being made which may have the result that the League itself will be buried together with the independence of Abyssinia. Such attempts and conclusions must be vigorously rebutted.

"We have to face the fact that the League of Nations has not been able to secure territorial integrity and political independence for one of its co-members in accordance with Article X of the Covenant, and is now only in a position to express its platonic sympathy. We cannot pass by this outrageous fact quietly and indifferently. We must analyse it and draw the necessary lessons from it in order to prevent such cases in the future. Some, however, propose a too simple remedy, saying: Do away with Article X completely. Release yourselves from the obligation to guarantee members of the League territorial integrity and independence, and then it will be impossible ever to accuse the League of Nations of bankruptcy. They also consider it a mistake that the League tries to stop aggression and protect its members at all. Such an argument can be put forward only by people who are against collective security on principle, who decry the main function of the League and the whole raison d'être of its formation and existence. There is no need to argue with people of this kind. But those who recognise the principle of collective security, who still regard the League Covenant as an instrument of peace, could attack the Covenant only in case they could prove that either the Covenant does not provide sufficiently effective measures for the support of Article X or that all such measures in the present specific case have been used to the full and have nevertheless failed to achieve their aim. But they cannot prove it.

"I maintain that Article XVI has provided the League of Nations with such a powerful weapon that any aggression could be broken if it were brought into full play. Furthermore, the very belief that it may be brought into play may discourage the aggressor from putting his criminal plans into effect. Least of all does the sad experience of the Italo-Abyssinian war contradict this statement. In the present case, either because this was the first experiment in applying collective measures, or because some people thought that this case had specific features, or because it coincided with the preparation for a more serious aggression elsewhere, to which Europe had to pay special attention, or because of other reasons, the fact remains that not only was the formidable machinery of Article XVI not brought into play, but the tendency to keep to minimum measures was displayed from the outset. And even in this limited scope the sanctions were not applied by all the members of the League.

"Four members of the League refused from the outset to apply any sanctions whatever. One member of the League, contiguous with Italy, refused to apply the most serious sanction, I mean the embargo on imports from Italy. And of those countries which made no objections to sanctions on principle, some actually did not apply all the sanctions, but pleaded constitutional obstacles, the need to study the problem, etc. Thus, even the embargo on arms was not applied by seven members of the League, the financial measures were not applied by eight countries, the embargo on exports to Italy by ten countries, the embargo on imports from Italy by thirteen countries—in other words, 25 per cent of the total membership of the League. It may be said that, with few exceptions, the countries of Latin America did not really apply the more effective sanctions. I say this by no means in reproach of anybody, but for the sole purpose of clinching my argument. Further, the proposal that certain non-members of the League should be deprived of, or limited in, the opportunity to counteract sanctions— a practical proposal—was not approved by the Co-Ordination Committee.

"With all these limitations, the sanctions could have taken effect only in case their application had been more prolonged and they had been combined with the military resistance of Abyssinia herself. The latter, however, was broken much sooner than our best-informed advisers expected. In these circumstances, we might say that, for one reason or another, the members of the League did not wish to bring Article XVI into full play, which by no means signifies that Article XVI itself has proved bankrupt.

"Some are inclined to explain the failure of the action of the League as due to its inadequate universality, to the absence of certain countries from it. We see, however, that not all members of the League took part in the sanctions. There are no grounds to expect that those States which left the League because they were against the principles of the League and the presence of Articles X and XVI in the Covenant would have joined in the sanctions. Their presence in the League would have led only to greater confusion in our ranks and would have had a demoralizing effect rather than anything else. On the other hand, we have seen in the example of the U. S. A. that, in the application of Article XVI, the League of Nations can sometimes count on the co-operation of non-members of the League and may do so the more confidently the more energetically it acts. So we see it is not in the perfections of the League Covenant nor in the absence of universality that we must seek for the reasons of the inadequate assistance given to Abyssinia.

"We have heard another argument at Geneva, too. Well, people say, let us admit that the League Covenant is quite flawless, that the blame does rest on members of the League, on certain persons. Does not this show that there is a dissonance between the Covenant and the frame of mind of those who are supposed to keep it, and for this reason alone should not the Covenant be accommodated to that frame of mind, or, as some say, to 'reality'? But this argument holds no water either. The fact is that people vary, too, and even in one and the same country not all statesmen are of the same mind on this score. To whose frame of mind must the Covenant be accommodated? Those who hold the standpoint of consistent collective defence of security, who see the best interests of all peoples in the preservation of world peace, who consider that in the last analysis the interests of each State require it and that it can be preserved only if temporary individual interests be sacrificed to the community of nations, and who are ready even to put part of their own armed forces at the disposal of this community? Or those who in principle swear by the principle of collective security, but in practice are ready to carry it out only when it coincides with the interests of their own country? Or those who deny collective security on principle, who substitute for international solidarity the slogan, 'Every man for himself,' preach the localisation of war and declare that war itself is the highest manifestation of the human spirit? I am afraid that those who argue about the need for the adaptation, or, as I should put it, the degradation of the Covenant, have in mind this category of people, for they support this argument of theirs by pointing out that the members who have left the League might come back if this were done. We are told to get back into the League at all costs those States which left it just because they regarded the Covenant, Articles X and XVI, and sanctions as obstacles to their aggressive plans. And so we hear it said: 'Let us throw Article X out of the Covenant, let us throw out Article XVI, let us renounce sanctions, let us reject collective security and then the ex-members of the League might return to our fellowship and the League will become universal.' In other words, let us make the League safe for aggressors. I say we do not want a League that is safe for aggressors. We do not want that kind of League, even if it is universal, because it would become the very opposite of an instrument of peace. At best, if we relieved the League from the functions of collective defence, we would make it a debating society, a philanthropic institution; not worth calling a League of Nations; not worth its upkeep and at odds with the aspirations and hopes which are pinned on it.

"On my part, I would propose that the Covenant be adapted not to the frame of mind of one or another category of people, one or another group of statesmen, one or another group of temporary rulers, but to the frame of mind of the millions, the masses in all countries and continents, those who are rightly called 'mankind' and demand that peace be preserved at all costs and defended with all means.

"We must educate and raise people up to its lofty ideas, not degrade the League. We must seek to make the League universal, but we must not by any means make it safe for the aggressor to this end. On the contrary, all new members and all ex-members wishing to return must read on its portals: 'Abandon all hope of aggression and its impunity all ye who enter here.'

"Let us be frank. The League is now experiencing by no means its first reverse. There have been cases of military attacks not less but more flagrant made by certain members of the League against others where the League did not react in the slightest and left the victim of aggression to face the aggressor alone in an unequal battle. However, the question of the unfitness of the Covenant or its revision was not raised then. If there were no grounds for it then, there are even less now. As for myself, I would rather have a League of Nations that tries to render at least some assistance, even if it proves ineffective, to a victim of aggression than a League of Nations that closes its eyes to aggression and lets it pass unperturbed.

"I consider that when, instead of doing nothing but bandying the discussion of the conflict from committee to sub-committee and sending committees of investigation as in other cases, the overwhelming majority of its members, undeterred by great material sacrifices, rendered assistance, though unavailing, to a co-member who had been attacked, the present League made a huge step forward in comparison with the past. In other words, as compared with the cases I have mentioned, the frame of mind of the members of the League moved a few steps higher. This permits us to hope that in the next case the frame of mind of the members of the League will rise to the high water-mark, the highest ideals of the League, and the victim will be rescued wholly from the clutches of the aggressor.

"I am far from idealising the Covenant. Its imperfections lie not so much in its articles as in its reservations and obscurities. Therefore, the thing is not to talk of reforming the Covenant, but of making it explicit and stronger. Where the Covenant is greatly deficient, I think, is in its omission of a definition of aggression, which in the Italo-Abyssinian conflict made it easy for some members of the League to refuse to take part in the sanctions from the very outset. There is no clarity in the question as to which of the bodies of the League is to certify aggression. There is no clarity as to whether League decisions are binding in the matter of sanctions. An end must be put to the situation wherein pleas of sovereignty and constitutional formalities are an obstacle to the performance of international obligations.

"Article XVI must remain intact. Economic sanctions must continue to be obligatory for all members of the League. Only if sanctions are obligatory will there be an end to mistrust, an end to the fears that if some States not affected directly by the conflict make considerable sacrifices in one case, other unaffected States will act less idealistically in another case. Assurance is needed that in all cases of aggression, irrespective of the degree of concern in the conflict, sanctions will be applied by all, and this can be achieved only if sanctions are made obligatory. In my opinion, this circumstance is the main reason why the League has failed in the Italo-Abyssinian conflict. We can imagine particular cases—rare, it is true—when aggression could be stopped by economic sanctions alone, but I think that in most cases economic sanctions must run parallel with military sanctions. In an ideal League of Nations, military sanctions, too, should be obligatory for all. But if we are yet unable to rise to such heights of international solidarity, we should make it our concern to have all continents and, for a start, at least all Europe covered with a system of regional pacts, on the strength of which groups of States would undertake to protect particular sectors from aggression; and the performance of these regional obligations should be deemed equivalent to the performance of the covenanted obligations and should enjoy the full support of all members of the League of Nations. These regional pacts should not supersede the League Covenant, but supplement it, otherwise they would be nothing but pre-war groups of alliances. It is along these lines that I conceive the perfecting and strengthening of the League of Nations, and the Soviet Government is prepared fully to co-operate with the other members of the League. I welcome the programme unfolded here by the French Premier, with which my comments to a large extent coincide.

"If I say all this in the interests of strengthening peace, I cannot do otherwise than mention the measure which the Soviet Union has always considered the maximum guarantee of peace, I mean complete disarmament. I would like to believe that mankind will not have to undergo yet another Armageddon and that all peoples have come to the same conclusion. But while this radical measure is in abeyance, all we can do is to strengthen the League of Nations as an instrument of peace. To strengthen the League of Nations is to abide by the principle of collective security, which is by no means a product of idealism, but is a practical measure towards the security of all peoples, to abide by the principle that peace is indivisible! We must recognise that at the present time there is not one State, large or small, that is not open to aggression, and that even if the next war spares one State or another she must, sooner or later, attract the longing eyes of the victorious aggressor.

"If these ideas be reinforced, broadened to the full and acted upon, we shall be spared new disappointments like those which are now our experience, new life will be put into the League of Nations and it will become equal to the great tasks which confront it. Now, more than ever before, the League of Nations is an international necessity. It must live. It must be stronger than ever."

7

On March 6, 1936, a military reception had been held at the Soviet Embassy in Berlin chiefly to show a moving picture entitled, "Russian Army Maneuvers in the Ukraine." The highest officers of the German General Staff had accepted the invitation. All the foreign military attachés were present. The Spanish military attaché, Major Beigheder, was accompanied by General Sanjurjo, who was already discussing with the Nazis the possibility of a revolution in Spain, and was buying arms on credit.

At 5:15 the German generals sent a message that they were delayed by important discussions with the Chancellor and suggested that the film start without them. At 6:00, when refreshments were being served, General Schmidt, the Belgian military attaché, drew aside a friend of the French Ambassador and said: "At this very moment the reoccupation of the demilitarized Rhineland zone is being settled. Tell the French military attaché and then come and let me know what you think about it."

The French military attaché declared such rumors to be nonsense: "The reoccupation of the Rhineland isn't as easy as that. No doubt it may happen one day, but we have not yet reached that stage." At

8:30 that evening the British and French Ambassadors and the Belgian
chargé d'affaires were requested to appear the following morning at
the German Foreign Office to hear a statement about the Locarno
Treaty.

While they were listening to the statement that Germany no longer
felt herself bound by this pact (which had guaranteed its Western
frontiers and also a demilitarized Rhineland zone), Hitler was making
a speech in the Reichstag justifying the remilitarization of the Rhineland, and German troops were marching over Rhine bridges. When
the decision was announced to General Werner von Blomberg, then
Chief of Staff, he crumbled up in a dead faint. *"Gumiwaren"* (rubber
goods) muttered a fellow officer under his breath. The American
military attaché in Moscow announced the fact to the incredulous
German attaché in Moscow with whom he was dining. The German
turned white as chalk. From a military point of view the occupation
was a piece of utter folly. But Hitler, confident that he had taken the
measure of the British and French governments, offered to commit
suicide with General von Blomberg's own pistol if there was any
serious military resistance.

In Paris the Government had been notified at 9:30 that the German
Ambassador had brought a note to the Quai d'Orsay which was being
translated; at 11:00 it could be discussed. At that time Premier Flandin
gave a general outline of the situation. The French Ambassadors in
Great Britain, Germany, and Italy were asked to come to Paris. It was
decided, furthermore, that joint action should be discussed at once
with England and the other signatories of Locarno: the Belgians and
the Italians. A note from London that afternoon informed the Quai
d'Orsay that the British Government was willing to act with France.

In the meantime, German troops had entered the Rhineland. It
was little more than a demonstration, calculated not to create a decisive effect. The first few days there was general disorder among
the advancing troops; and neither the German infantry nor artillery
had any ammunition.

The French Rightists, already working hand-in-glove with Hitler
and Mussolini, supported Hitler's claim that he was remilitarizing
the Rhineland because France had broken the Locarno Treaty by

entering into a treaty with Soviet Russia. On March 12, an editorial in the weekly *Candide* attacked the new Foreign Minister, Joseph Paul-Boncour:

As recently as January 23rd we pointed out that the ratification of the Franco-Russian alliance would automatically be followed by the remilitarization of the left bank of the Rhine. But you had the Franco-Russian pact on the brain. For the last three months you have been trying to starve Italy. You are treating Mussolini as an outcast. You are advocating a revolution against him. You are a scoundrel. Clear out!

The meeting of the Locarno signatories took place at the Quai d'Orsay. Baldwin had sent Lord Halifax along with Eden, who was well known to be strongly anti-Hitler and anti-Mussolini. Flandin, appealing for solidarity, said that all reports agreed that Germany could not possibly defend the Rhineland and could be promptly forced to a humiliating backdown by a united move from the Locarno signatories. He even suggested that the signatories authorize France to take firm military measures and thus settle the question once and for all. The German force was quite without adequate artillery and was lacking in other essential supplies. Plans had been completed for a prompt withdrawal if the French put up any show of resistance. Had the French taken the measures that Flandin and the French General Staff recommended, it might conceivably have been the end of Hitler and Nazi aggression.

The delegates were impressed, but wanted to consult their governments. More valuable time was lost. France could not act alone without losing advantage of the international guarantees in the Locarno Treaty. A few hours later, Eden informed Flandin that the British Government wanted to summon the Council of the League of Nations, which alone, under the terms of the treaty, was competent to deal with an infringement by one of its signatories. Flandin agreed and obtained a commitment from his Government that French forces would be placed at the disposal of the League, if the League should authorize France to enforce the Locarno Treaty.

England had one additional request: the League should meet, not in Geneva, but in London, and it was arranged that the Council assemble in Buckingham Palace.

8

The French delegates found when they arrived in London on March 12 that the British Government had assumed an attitude of hostile reserve. The British felt that the Rhineland was not their affair and wanted to do nothing at all about it. The public had forgotten that the Locarno Treaty had committed their Government but they did remember that Britain had been strongly opposed to Mussolini's indefensible invasion of Abyssinia and that Mussolini had been more or less aided and abetted by the French. This contributed to the anti-French sentiment and a disposition to let the French down, in their turn.

Berlin meanwhile insisted that the Franco-Russian alliance was the whole cause of the trouble, and asserted that England would have to choose between Hitler and Stalin. Every argument was in favor of the Fuehrer. This, too, made a deep impression, and members of Parliament were deluged with letters from constituents insisting that Great Britain come to terms with Hitler.

In the British Cabinet Council meeting before the arrival of the French delegation, only Eden was disposed to settle the matter in favor of France. Later, when the French delegation met with the British, Baldwin reminded Flandin that Great Britain was not armed and, therefore, could not undertake war. The Belgians followed the lead of Great Britain. The Italian envoy, Signor Dino Grandi, stated that he could not vote for sanctions since his own country had been the victim of sanctions.

Thus, France was largely isolated, except for Poland and Russia. Poland, under the resolute Pilsudski, who had correctly estimated Hitler and the Nazi menace, had suggested that it was ready to strike against Hitler—non-aggression treaty or no non-aggression treaty—if France would declare war.

Litvinoff was in a difficult position. In the first place, Soviet Russia had not signed the Locarno Treaty, so he was present only as a member of the League Council. Second, he had a powerful opponent backstage, pulling decisive strings, King Edward VIII, who is said to have contrived the transfer of the League Council to London and

Buckingham Palace, thus bringing the negotiations right into his own home.

There can be little doubt that Edward VIII was as hostile to Soviet Russia as his father had been. The late King George V never had forgiven the Communists for the death of his cousin the Czar, and the views and information (or misinformation) that he received from certain quarters confirmed and extended his prejudice. This hostility had been transmitted to Edward, now King of England, and he lost no opportunity to work against Litvinoff as the representative of Soviet Russia.

The setting facilitated interference from behind the scenes. The whole conference was intimate, as the rooms were not large enough to admit many newspaper men. Edward VIII was always somewhere near, always willing, even eager, to talk with the various delegates —not to influence them, of course, but just to tell them how he felt. And he definitely did not feel that anything should be done against Germany just then.

Litvinoff was amused and annoyed by turns at these maneuvers, but in a powerful and unanswerable speech on March 17, he reaffirmed the principles of the League, expounded its unequivocal obligations under the circumstances, exposed once more with unerring accuracy the folly of the policy of evasion and appeasement and the peril to all were it continued, and left no doubt as to where he and his Government stood in the "struggle for peace, for the collective organization of security."

The speech, clear, logical, sensible, was especially impressive as proof that a statesman, if resolute and absolutely sincere, as well as intelligent, could discern through the fears and confusions of the moment the course of affairs with some precision, and plan effective measures to check the disaster:

"In the course of the brief period of eighteen months that the Soviet Union has been a member of the League of Nations, this is the third time that her representative on the Council of the League has had occasion to express himself in connection with the violation of international obligations. The first time was on the occasion of Germany's violation of the military clauses of the Versailles Treaty; the second time was in connection with the Italo-Abyssinian conflict; and today in connection with the unilateral violation by Germany both of the Versailles Treaty and the Locarno Pact. On all three occasions the Soviet Union was formally not an interested party, owing to the fact that it had no relation to the violated treaties, such as the Versailles Treaty or the Locarno Pact, or, as in the case of the Italo-Abyssinian conflict, its own interests were not in the least degree affected. This circumstance did not prevent the representative of the Soviet Union in the past, and does not prevent him in the present instance, from taking his place among those members of the Council who in the most decisive fashion record their indignation at the violation of international obligations, condemn it and associate themselves with the most appropriate means of preventing similar violations in the future.

"This position of the Soviet Union is determined by its general policy in the struggle for peace, for the collective organization of security and for the preservation of one of the instruments of peace—the existing League of Nations. We consider that one cannot fight for peace without at the same time insisting upon the inviolability of international obligations, especially of those that directly concern the preservation of existing frontiers, armaments and political or military aggression. One cannot fight for the collective organization of security without taking measures against the violation of international obligations. We, however, do not count among such measures collective capitulation to the aggressor, capitulation in face of the violation of treaties, or the collective encouragement of such violations, and still less collective consent to rewarding the aggressor by the adoption of a basis of agreement or other plans acceptable and beneficial to the aggressor. The League of Nations, which is based upon the sacredness of international treaties, including the Covenant of the League itself, cannot be preserved if we close our eyes to the violation of these treaties or confine ourselves to verbal protests without taking more effective measures for the protection of international treaties. The League of Nations cannot be preserved if it does not adhere to its own decisions and accustoms aggressors to ignore all its recommendations, all its warnings and all its threats. No one will take such a League of Nations seriously. The resolutions of such a League will just be ridiculed. We do not need such a League. I will say more:

such a League might even be harmful, because it might lull the nations into a sense of false security, imbue them with illusions which would prevent them taking timely measures themselves for their self-defense.

"The responsibility of the League of Nations and of its guiding body —the Council—is all the greater the simpler the case of violation of international obligations under discussion. A characteristic feature of all the three cases I have just mentioned is their simplicity—simplicity in the sense that the establishment of the facts of violation of international obligations presented no difficulty and could not give rise to any disputes or differences. When I mention the absence of disputes and differences, I am not referring, of course, to the State itself which is accused of the violation of the Treaty, and which naturally will always, if not directly deny the violation, at least invent all sorts of arguments for the justification of its action. It is impossible to conceive a case in which such a State would frankly announce that it had no justification and that it alone was to blame and nobody else.

"The case we are discussing in the present session of the Council even surpasses the previous cases in its simplicity in the sense mentioned. Here we have not only a violation of treaties in substance, but also the non-observance of a special point in the Treaty which lays down the method for settling disputes that might arise in case of an imagined or actual violation of the Treaty. But before expressing a final judgment of Germany's actions, I consider it fair to take note of all that has been said by Herr Hitler in justification of those actions or in mitigation of the offence.

"The German Government asserts that France was the first to violate the Locarno Pact in letter and in spirit by concluding a pact of mutual assistance with the Soviet Union. It appealed for an opinion to the other Locarno Powers—namely, Great Britain and Italy. It must be assumed that if these Powers were in agreement with the German thesis that the Franco-Soviet Pact was incompatible with the Locarno Treaty, Germany would have made the fullest use of their conclusions. But as these Powers came to a different conclusion, Germany categorically declares that France, Great Britain, Italy and Belgium—that is, the other Locarno Powers, have wrongly interpreted the Locarno Pact and that her own interpretation is the only correct one. It is undoubtedly an extremely convenient method of settling disputed international questions, when a country, convinced of the justice of its cause, assumes the functions of judge and bailiff in its own case.

"How unfounded is the German assertion that the Franco-Soviet Pact is incompatible with the Locarno Pact, is quite clearly shown by the fact that the former pact is of a purely defensive character. All the world knows that neither the Soviet Union nor France has any claims whatever to German territory or any intention of altering Germany's frontiers. As long as Germany does not commit an act of aggression either against France or the Soviet Union, the pact will never be put into operation. If, however, the Soviet Union becomes the victim of attack on the part of Germany, the Locarno Pact accords France, as a member of the League, the undeniable right to come to the assistance of the Soviet Union. What renders the determination of the aggressor infallible in the present case is the absence of a common frontier between Germany and the Soviet Union. If German armed forces were to leave the confines of their own country, and traverse the States and seas dividing the two countries in order to invade the territory of the Soviet Union, German aggression would be quite obvious; and vice versa. This is quite clear to the German Government itself, and that is why it is in such a hurry to summon to its aid the hypothesis that the social system in France is being altered, which only emphasizes the artificial and far-fetched character of the German argument that the Franco-Soviet Pact is incompatible with the Locarno Pact.

"The German Government, having no reliance upon the force and cogency of such arguments, itself advances another justification of its action. It declares that the demilitarization of the Rhine Zone is in itself unjust, contrary to the principle of the equality of States, and constitutes a menace to the inviolability of the German frontier. This argument might sound more convincing and at any rate more sincere than the sophistry regarding the Franco-Soviet Pact. To examine this argument in detail, I would have to repeat what I said in the Council of the League on April 17, 1935, during the discussion of the complaint of the French Government that the German Government had violated international obligations in reference to armaments. As a political institution whose aim it is to organize and consolidate peace, the

League of Nations cannot decide questions, and still less justify violations of international obligations, from the standpoint of abstract principles. The chief criterion for the decisions of the League should be
whether any particular decision contributes to the best organization
of peace. In 1919 and in 1925, a large number of members of the
League, to which the Soviet Union at that time did not belong, considered that this aim would be furthered by the demilitarization of
the Rhine Zone. I do not think that the changes that have since taken
place in the ideology and the foreign policy of Germany permit us to
assert that peace in Europe would at present gain anything from the
remilitarization of the Rhine Zone, least of all when done unilaterally
and in violation of obligations Germany had voluntarily assumed.
Neither the foreign policy of the present German Government nor the
ceaseless preaching during the past three years in Germany of aggression and international hatred and the glorification of the war spirit
permit us to assert this.

"I shall not take up your time by quoting passages in support of
this from German periodicals, German text-books, German scientific
works and German song-books. I shall only take the liberty of reminding you of the political testament of the present ruler of Germany
which you will find on page 754 of the Second Volume of the Munich,
1934, German edition of the book Mein Kampf:

"'The political testament of the German nation in the sphere of
its foreign activity shall and must always declare: never permit the rise
of two continental powers in Europe. You must regard every attempt
to organize a second military power on the German frontiers, even
in the form of a State likely to become a military power, as an attack
on Germany and you must hold it not only your right but your duty
to obstruct the rise of such a State with all means, including the use
of the force of arms, and, if such a State has already arisen, you must
destroy it.'

"There, gentlemen, are the aims of Germany on behalf of which
the remilitarization of the Rhine Zone abutting on France is demanded.
It is a question of establishing the hegemony of Germany throughout
the whole European continent, and I ask: should the League of
Nations and will the League of Nations abet the achievement of these
aims? It is not a casual newspaper article that I have read you, but

a document which the author himself describes as the political testament of the present ruler of Germany, containing the quintessence of the whole foreign policy. Side by side with this document, what is the value of isolated political speeches and declarations made with a political object in view at some particular moment and adapted to the psychology of a part of some nation or other for the achievement of definite temporary aims? Such speeches and declarations bear the same relation to the fundamental document I have just read as the temporary tactical cessation of firing on some sector of a theater of war has to the fundamental strategical aims of the whole campaign.

"As for Germany's defence, if there is any country in the world that is not threatened by any danger from without, it is Germany. I do not know of a single country that has made any territorial claim on Germany, nor do I know of any literature in which a march against Germany is advocated. A State is not, and cannot be subjected to attack without preliminary preparations, without the previous presentation of territorial or other claims, the substantiation of these claims, and without raising its people in a spirit of realizing these claims. Such preparation is not going on in any country, and there is therefore no thought of encircling Germany. On the day when all doubt of Germany's love for peace, of her sincere readiness to collaborate with other European peoples in the organization of peace, vanishes, when she will cease to refuse to give the very guarantees of her love of peace which other European peoples give so willingly, the representative of the Soviet Union, which has always defended the equality of rights of peoples both great and small, but equality of rights in peace, and which continues to entertain the profoundest respect and ardent sympathy with the great German people, would be the first to come in protest against imposing upon it any inequality of rights, against depriving it of any means of armament at the disposal of other peoples . . .

"On the assumption, however, that the 'peaceable' proposals enumerated by me will not be considered adequate compensation for the violation of international laws, Germany declares her readiness to return to the League of Nations. We, as well as the other members of the League, have always regretted the incompleteness of the League, the absence of several great countries, particularly Germany. We shall welcome the return of Hitler Germany to its bosom, too, if we be convinced that she will recognize the fundamental principles underlying the League, without which the latter would not only cease to be an instrument of peace, but might be eventually transformed into its opposite. First and foremost among these principles is the observance of international treaties, respect for and non-violation of existing boundaries, recognition of the equality of right of all members of the League, support of the collective organization of security, waiver of recourse to arms in the solution of international disputes.

"Unfortunately, at the present moment the cases of unilateral violation by Germany of her international obligations and of her refusal to abide by the methods for solving conflicts prescribed by international treaties are too fresh in our minds. We have not yet forgotten that to the very last moment Herr Hitler fought most categorically against the idea of collective security. He propagates the principle, not only of race inequality, but also of the inequality of peoples for German colonization. We know that comparatively recently—to wit, on May 28, 1931—Herr Goebbels, one of the chief companions-in-arms of Hitler, wrote in his newspaper *Angriff,* that the sword was the one and only instrument with which one could carry on foreign policy, and that Herr Hitler wrote on December 9, 1930, in the *Voelkischer Beobachter,* the official organ of his party, that in the long run the sword will decide everything. Finally, I must recur to Herr Hitler's political testament, which I have already quoted, in which the German people are recommended not to permit strong States to exist alongside of Germany, and eventually to destroy them. We cannot disregard the danger that a member of the League of Nations preaching such principles will be in a position to sabotage the most valuable part of the activities of the League of Nations, directed toward the organization of peace and the enhancement of the security of all its members. Only on the receipt of convincing proof that our fears and doubts are henceforth groundless will we consider Hitler Germany's return to the League an asset in the cause of peace.

"After analyzing Herr Hitler's proposals in their entirety I come to the conclusion that, far from making good the harm that would be done to the organization of peace by pardoning the violations of international treaties, they would themselves inflict a blow upon the

organization of peace, and in the first place upon the League of
Nations.

"Gentlemen, I have taken the liberty of speaking out with entire
frankness. I felt more at ease in doing so than others of my colleagues,
in view of the fact that the manner in which Herr Hitler permits
himself to speak publicly of the Government I represent frees me
of the obligation to resort to reticence and diplomatic convention. I
am more entitled to do so since Herr Hitler's pronouncements and
proposals in the sphere of international politics amount to nothing
more or less than the organization of an expedition against the peoples
of the country I represent—the organization of an alliance of the whole
of Europe, the whole world against them. May his aggression be
actually aimed in the immediate future against other countries, may
his attack against the Soviet Union be merely a smoke-screen behind
which to prepare aggression against other States, yet the very fact
that for this purpose he singles out the Soviet Union as the target for
his incessant attacks, and that he did this once more on the occasion
of the violation of the Locarno Treaty, gives me the right to speak
openly and with special emphasis of the essence of the aggressive
foreign policy conducted by Herr Hitler. At the same time I express
the firm conviction that the proposals now made by Herr Hitler and
which spring from this foreign policy of his will never in their present
form become the basis for an agreement among the other members
of the League.

"Before finishing permit me to express the hope that I shall be
correctly understood and that no one will conclude from what I have
said that the Soviet Union proposes nothing but the statement of facts,
censure, strict measures, and is opposed to any and every conversation
and to a peaceful solution of the serious conflict that has arisen. Such
conclusions would give an absolutely wrong idea of our conception.
We are interested not less but more than others in the non-violation
of peace both to-day and for a decade to come, and not only in one
sector of Europe, but throughout the whole of Europe and the whole
world. We are decidedly opposed to everything that could bring war
nearer, if only by one month, but we are also opposed to hasty decisions dictated by fear and other emotions rather than a sober con-
templation of reality, decisions which, while seemingly removing the

causes of hypothetical war to-day, create every condition for actual war to-morrow.

"We are for international agreement, which would not only fortify the present mainstays of peace, but would if possible set up new ones. We are for participation in such an agreement of all countries desirous of doing so. But we are opposed to granting to a State withdrawing from the League of Nations, grossly violating international treaties and engaged in sword-rattling, the privilege of dictating to all Europe its conditions of negotiation, of selecting the parties to participate in these negotiations at its discretion and of foisting upon others its scheme of agreement. We are opposed to having negotiations conducted on a basis which disorganizes the ranks of the true partisans of peace and which must inevitably lead to the destruction of the only inter-governmental political organization, the League of Nations. We believe that the true adherents of peace are entitled to submit their scheme for the organization of European peace no less than those who violate treaties. We are in favor of establishing the security of all peoples of Europe as against the half-peace which is not peace, but war.

"But whatever new international agreements we may wish to arrive at, we must first of all ensure that they will be loyally carried out by all those who participate in them, and the Council of the League must declare what is its attitude to unilateral violations of such agreements, and how it intends to and can react against them. From this angle, the complete satisfaction of the complaint of the French and Belgian Governments acquires paramount importance. Taking this into account, I declare on behalf of my Government that it is ready to take part in all measures that may be proposed to the Council of the League by the Locarno Powers and will be acceptable to the other members of the Council."

Litvinoff had told his story—based on principles, substantiated with facts. But the Council was not impressed. Perhaps, though, there were some there vaguely uneasy lest the simple solution of doing nothing might prove neither simple nor a solution.

The day after Litvinoff's speech, at three o'clock in the morning, the British Cabinet finally consented to an agreement drafted by France, Great Britain, Italy, and Belgium. It provided for an appeal to the Hague Court to decide if the Franco-Soviet Pact invalidated the

Locarno Treaty; a demilitarized zone "to be established anew on German territory"; and, most important, by implication opened the way for the British and French General Staffs to confer on a plan of joint action. This was the first formal commitment in which Great Britain had engaged since World War I.

No sooner had Eden signed the document than he confessed to doubting whether or not it would be ratified by Parliament. He asked Flandin not to play up the importance of the commitment in Paris and to make no definite statement to the Chamber of Deputies on its precise scope.

The demilitarized zone on German territory was not established, and the London Conference was a complete failure. It thoroughly devitalized the Locarno Treaty, which was now but one more grave-stone in the crowded cemetery of human hopes, one more proof that in international crises words that are not the product of a resolute and thoroughly sincere intent, gestures that are not energetically implemented by concrete action are only a pious futility.

The King of the Belgians drew the perfectly logical conclusions from the feebleness of purpose, the relative indifference to the most solemn and binding commitments, that the London Conference so mercilessly exposed. If the great nations, faced with such a crude challenge as the occupation of the Rhineland, would not back up one another or stand up to the Nazi bully when they had the power and he was relatively helpless, then what dependence or hope could the small nations place on the faltering promises of the Great Powers? On October 14, 1936, King Leopold declared his country neutral. This meant that he would no longer co-operate with the French army for mutual protection. It meant that France had lost a valuable ally. It was also fair warning that the small nations no longer had confidence in France, England, or the League of Nations. And it meant, finally, that everyone was becoming more and more afraid of Hitler.

Shadows were falling across Europe. Civil war broke out in Spain on July 18, 1936. It was clearly a revolution of Fascist-minded generals, together with clerical and aristocratic elements against a democratic government elected by democratic means. The democracies of the world, especially the Western democracies, had every reason in law, ethics, and self-interest to help the Spanish Republic: it would not have been interference in internal affairs, but assistance given to a duly elected representative government. It would have strengthened the democratic idea. Furthermore, it would have been of immense military value to France and thus to England to have a Republican and democratic Spain at her back, as the French General Staff never tired of pointing out.

Litvinoff as usual saw to the heart of the matter and once more spoke out with the clarity, logical vigor, knowledge of fact, and stout hold on principle that have distinguished him above all diplomats of his time. At the Council of the League of Nations on May 28, 1937 he declared:

". . . Here we have an indisputable case of the forcible introduction of foreign armed forces on the territory of one of the members of the League of Nations. Certain international actions on practical proposals undertaken during the past year, the agreement on nonintervention in Spanish affairs, the establishment of control, the proposal for an armistice, the appeal to the belligerents, undoubtedly distort and obscure the formal aspect of the case, because they create an impression that it is a question of belligerents equal in status. But in actual fact we have, on the one hand, a Government lawfully recognized by all States without exception and by the League of Nations, formed on the basis of the Spanish constitution and a democratic election law, which not long before the event under discussion received a vote of confidence from the Spanish people, a Government which is responsible for the observance of the laws of the country, for order, for discipline in the army and fleet, and is obliged to suppress, by force if necessary, any attempt to change the existing order, any attempt upon the interests of the broad masses and every kind of rebellion and disorder. On the other hand we have a handful of generals and officers who violated their duty as soldiers, who rebelled against the lawful Government and the constitution of the country, who began hostilities mainly with the help of Moorish troops. I venture to remind you of these simple, indisputable facts because some people are beginning to forget them. They are beginning to forget that in the present case there can be no talk of the sides having equal rights. Foreign governments have the right to enter into relations with the Spanish Government, conclude with them any commercial transactions, including the sale of munitions, without violating any international principles and obligations. But relations with mutinous generals, and supplying them with war material even more, constitute a classic example of intervention in the internal affairs of another State."

Instead of helping the democratic Government in Spain, the democratic governments of France and England hastened to wash their hands of the Fascist revolution in Spain. They created a system of non-intervention, which implied that they would not allow arms or men to pass into Spain.

This would have been a strange and ill-conceived attitude under any circumstances. But under conditions as they existed it was criminally short-sighted and stupid. For there could be no doubt whatever in the minds of the men in London and Paris that the revolution of the Spanish generals had not only been supported, but had originally been instigated by the two Fascist powers, Italy and Germany. Incontrovertible information on this was in the hands of both the British and French governments, and in fact Grandi, the Italian Ambassador to London, admitted the fact rather freely—excusing it on the ground that it was not a government intervention, that Mussolini had just winked at the export of munitions to the Franco insurgents, because the Italian munitions firms felt that they shouldn't miss the chance to make a little money. These are almost the exact words that Grandi used. Several influential Englishmen to whom he talked were sympathetic and took the attitude that, "Well, boys will be boys." Thus was inaugurated one of the most pitiful and shameless tragedies of our time—a fit sequel to the rape of Abyssinia. German participation was substantial from the start: Hitler sent technicians, planes, submarines, and at least 15,000 specialists; in addition, there were the so-called volunteers. Italy sent everything she could spare: guns, munitions, trucks, planes, and men in ever-growing numbers.

Litvinoff, factual as ever, did not underestimate German and Italian help to Franco:

"If the Spanish events were confined to internal disorders, to a struggle between the Government and the mutineers, not only would the League of Nations have nothing to do with the question, but these events would have come to an end long ago. Any impartial person who knows the relations of forces must admit that the lawful Spanish Government could have coped with the mutiny long ago, Madrid and other Spanish cities would not have been subjected to devastation and destruction, and the Spanish people would not have had to mourn the deaths of tens of thousands of men, women, and children and the extinction of the best representatives of Spanish art and science and the frustration of her program for general progress which was already hopefully underway. Matters would not have assumed an international character, and order would not only have been restored in Spain long ago, but international order itself would not have been disturbed.

"Unfortunately, the published documents prove beyond all doubt that the very mutiny of the generals was prepared and organized at foreign instigation and with foreign assistance. Moreover, the mutineers began to get arms and aircraft from abroad with military instructors and aviators from the very first day of the mutiny. With the development of events, this supply has been increasing more and more, and now the mutineers are being assisted with human material as well as military."

In another speech, six months earlier (November 28, 1936) at the Eighth Congress of Soviets, Litvinoff had been equally explicit:

"Observe that Germany and Italy at that time still maintained diplomatic relations with the Spanish Government, and their intervention in the domestic struggle in Spain was a glaring violation of the most elementary international obligations. German Fascism, draped in the toga of the defender of the Aryan race, does not apparently feel any qualms of conscience when bringing non-Aryan Moors to fight against the Aryan people of Spain."

Everybody knew about German and Italian intervention from the very beginning. But the British Government went ahead with its plan of non-intervention without any apparent compunctions. Hypocrisy knew no limit. France joined in, reluctant, confused, and a little fearful. The General Staff urged and the crowds shouted, *"Des Avions pour l'Espagne."* But Blum was under tremendous pressure of all kinds from the extreme Right, and on every side there were whispers of an impending Fascist revolution that would break the moment

France did anything in support of the Spanish Government, regardless of the fact that such support would have been entirely legal and in some respects required by contract.

Germany and Italy were invited to join the non-intervention scheme, which they did because the farce did not threaten to hinder in any way their own intervening. Soviet Russia likewise was invited, and also joined because, if she had not done so, the rest of the world would have been told that her abstention was evidence that she was planning to intervene and thus light the fires of a general war.

In the speech before the Eighth Congress of Soviets, Litvinoff explained in detail why he had been willing to enter the non-intervention tragi-comedy:

"On the initiative of France and England, with the aim of preventing possible international complications threatening peace, an international agreement was signed not to intervene in Spanish affairs by supplying any war materials whatsoever to the Government of the Insurgents.

"This proposal was undoubtedly contrary to the usual conceptions in international relations, which permit the supply of any arms by one government to another government recognized by it, and prohibit such supplies to insurgents in any country with which diplomatic relations are maintained.

"Nevertheless, considering the official motives on which this proposal was based, the Soviet Government joined in it. Moreover, we consider that if this Agreement were loyally observed by all it would have done no harm to the Spanish Government, for, if left to himself, General Franco could not have prevented the suppression of the insurrection. I repeat that the obvious condition for our joining this Agreement was its loyal fulfillment by all the participants."

It is at least doubtful if Litvinoff ever really believed that the other side—the Fascists—would adhere to the non-intervention arrangement. Too much was at stake for them. Only a few men outside Germany and Italy realized in these early stages just how much Hitler and Mussolini had to win or to lose in Spain. That Litvinoff saw this clearly is proved by another passage in his speech before the Eighth Congress:

"In the case of Spain, we have the first sally of Fascism beyond its

WHAT PRICE PEACE? 395

borders. Here is an attempt at a forcible implantation in Spain from without of a Fascist system, an attempt to force upon the Spanish people a Fascist government with the aid of bayonet, hand-grenade and bomb. If this attempt were to succeed, there would be no guarantees against its repetition on a wider scale in relation to other States."

The next few years were again to prove how invariably right Litvinoff had been.

CHAPTER THIRTEEN

Into the Abyss

DURING 1935 AND 1936 Litvinoff's idea of collective security was consistently frustrated. He had met with no success, though his persistent and thoroughly competent advocacy was beginning to enlighten the minds and arouse the conscience of men of good will everywhere. In the world of events, aggression had practically always triumphed, and the aggressor in almost every instance had used the old bogey of world revolution led from Moscow. The argument was evidently not yet stale enough to have lost its appeal. To paraphrase Anthony Eden, there was still some sawdust left in that doll.

This was true not only of Europe but also in other continents. In South America only Uruguay recognized Russia, and these relations were broken off at the end of 1935. The case was symptomatic. In a speech on January 23, 1936, Litvinoff took the matter before the Council of the League of Nations. He began by assuring the League that "the interests of the Soviet Union remained practically untouched by this rupture." However, for reasons of principle he thought that the League of Nations should hear the case. He explained that in 1926, Uruguay and Soviet Russia had established diplomatic relations. In 1934 diplomatic missions had been exchanged. But suddenly there was trouble:

"Discussions between the Soviet Minister in Montevideo and the Uruguayan Foreign Office . . . concerned one Simon Radovitsky, an anarchist imprisoned in Uruguay on a charge of terrorist attempts. The Uruguayan Government, for reasons of internal politics, desired to deport Radovitsky to the Soviet Union on the plea that he was born in Russia. But since Radovitsky was not a Soviet citizen, the Soviet Government refused to admit him to the country. Somewhat surprisingly, this apparently insignificant matter caused an altogether disproportionate reaction on the part of the Uruguayan Government.

The President of the Republic himself took a personal interest in the case, repeatedly endeavoring to obtain the consent of the Soviet Minister to the deportation of Radovitsky, actually taking the refusal as a personal affront and making no attempt to conceal his resentment. . . .

" . . . in a telegram dated December 10, 1935, from M. Minkin, the Soviet Minister, I read as follows:

" 'The Uruguayan Foreign Minister tells me that the President of the Republic would consider himself compensated for our refusal to admit Radovitsky if we would buy two hundred tons or so of Uruguayan cheese. I would recommend for the improvement of relations with President Terra the purchase of a small consignment of cheese.'

"But the Soviet Government, despite the recommendations of our Minister, did not see its way to purchasing Uruguayan cheese. In this connection, M. Minkin cabled to us on December 19:

" 'The Secretary of the President informs me that our refusal to grant his request regarding cheese is interpreted as a fresh display of lack of consideration towards himself and may weaken his arguments in favor of the maintenance of relations between Uruguay and the Union of Soviet Socialist Republics.'

"I have related all this so you may see for yourself that the only grievance advanced by the Uruguayan Government, both in Moscow and in Montevideo, consisted in our refusal to admit Radovitsky and to purchase Uruguayan cheese. There has not been a single complaint of incorrect conduct on the part of the Soviet Mission in Montevideo, or of its interference in internal affairs in Uruguay or any other South-American Republic. Indeed, as I have just had the honor to read to you, on October 26, 1935, the Uruguayan Minister for Foreign Affairs assured our Minister that his Government did not share the views accusing the Soviet Government advanced by certain Uruguayan newspapers.

"All this made still more surprising the note received by the Soviet Minister at Montevideo declaring that the Uruguayan Government had resolved to break off diplomatic relations with the Soviet Union. . . .

" . . . Two facts may be regarded as incontrovertible: first, the Uruguayan Government has broken off diplomatic relations with the

Soviet Union; second, the reason advanced by the Uruguayan Government for a rupture was not submitted either to arbitration or to enquiry by the Council of the League, as stipulated in Article 12 of the Covenant. Even if the Uruguayan Government had had a real grievance, this would not by any means do away with the infringement of the Covenant, or justify its action. . . ."

Then Litvinoff came to the point. What was behind the accusations that Soviet Russia promoted revolution?

"As a matter of fact, there is not a single precise accusation, not a definite fact laid to the charge of the Soviet Government, or of the Soviet Mission in Montevideo, in the Uruguayan note. In this note, the Uruguayan Government does not actually assert anything, merely expressing assumptions, and even these mainly not its own. For instance, the note contains the words: 'It is definitely asserted' (by whom and when is not said) that 'the Soviet Government instigated and supported the Communist elements in Brazil through the agency of the Soviet Mission to our government.' I declare categorically that this assertion, by whomever it was made, is absolutely untrue. The Soviet Government neither instigated nor supported Communist elements, whether in Uruguay or in any neighboring State, for the Soviet Government is consistently true to its policy of non-interference in the internal affairs of other States. I challenge the Uruguayan Government to produce evidence, if it has any, to the contrary. And I declare in advance that no such evidence can be forthcoming.

"This is not the first time such accusations have been leveled against the Soviet Government, but never yet—never, I repeat—in one single instance has evidence of the truth of such accusations been produced, setting aside documents forged by Russian counter-revolutionary emigrants and kindred and Fascist elements. I have little doubt that either the Uruguayan or the Brazilian Government can easily obtain such documents, even at Geneva itself. Since their value on the European market has lately fallen considerably, they are probably to be bought at dumping prices, but I must warn would-be buyers that any such documents would have to undergo the most searching inspection by experts.

"Another reference to the Soviet Mission in Montevideo is to be found in the note to the effect that, 'according to the information supplied by the Brazilian Embassy and that obtained by our own government, the Soviet Legation in Montevideo has issued bearer checks for large sums for purposes which cannot be ascertained.' And so the Soviet Mission labors under the accusations of having transmitted unknown large sums at an unknown date to unknown persons, and, their purpose and destination being undiscovered, it is to be assumed that they were expended on the financing of revolts in Brazil! It seems to me that a legal training is not necessary for the comprehension of the utter irresponsibility and baselessness of such accusations. If the checks were transmitted in Montevideo, surely it ought not to be hard to find out through the Uruguayan banks on which these checks were drawn, the exact numbers, amounts, dates and so on! The Uruguayan Government did not even take the trouble to obtain and check such details, obviously because investigation would not only have shown the utter absurdity of the statements, but would have convinced the Uruguayan Government that the Soviet Mission in Montevideo, during the two years of its existence, received alto-gether for its own requirements—for equipment, the purchase of motor-cars, salaries—about 55,000 American dollars, of which sum it did not transmit any money anywhere outside Uruguay. In any case we feel entitled to insist that the Uruguayan Government produce proofs to the Council of the League regarding the only concrete fact advanced in its note."

2

On June 22, 1936, a conference opened at Montreux to review condi-tions in the East Mediterranean, especially in regard to the Darda-nelles, which naturally was of primary interest to Russia. In 1923, the Convention of Lausanne had demobilized the Dardanelles and put them under international control. The Turks resented this as a limita-tion on their sovereignty, particularly as it diminished their powers of defense. When hopes of general disarmament faded, they began to discuss revision. By 1936 this became pressing, first because of the mounting Italo-Turkish tension. This was of long standing but had been increased in 1934 by Mussolini's bombastic declaration that Italy's future lay in Asia and Africa; and Italy's fortification of the Island of Leros and Turkey's naval pact with Great Britain in January, 1936, had not relaxed the reciprocal suspicion. And in the second place revision became pressing because the four Powers who assured the "neutrality" of the Dardanelles no longer seemed able to guarantee anything collectively; Japan had dropped out of the League; Italy— since the sanctions—was definitely hostile to Great Britain and uneasy about France.

Litvinoff had good reason to sponsor and aid Turkey's request for revision. He remembered well how the Russian Black Sea Fleet had been bottled up when it was needed in the Russo-Japanese War. The Turks had been responsible for this, but since the Russian Revolution, the Russians and Turks had been on very good terms, and it was not likely that if the Russians needed to send out the Black Sea Fleet now, the Turks would object. On the other hand, if the Dardanelles remained under the control of these Powers which in the immediate past had been so persistently hostile, the situation of 1904–05 might well be repeated. Therefore, Litvinoff decidedly favored this Montreux Conference.

Italy refused to take part. The other great States had no objection to Turkey's fortifying the Straits, but Great Britain strenuously opposed the abolition of the International Commission. On this point the British delegates were in direct and at times somewhat heated conflict with Litvinoff, who was unyielding in his demand that all Black Sea Powers (which meant, of course, Soviet Russia and Turkey) be free to send their ships through the Straits without fear that non-Black Sea Powers would intervene or attempt to send naval units through the Dardanelles. An agreement finally provided that Black Sea Powers could send their ships through the Straits after notification to other Powers, while all the non-Black Sea Powers together were restricted to a maximum total tonnage in the Black Sea at any one time of about 30,000 tons. No one non-Black Sea Power could have in the Black Sea more than two-thirds of this tonnage within a period of 21 days. The 30,000-ton limit could eventually be raised to 45,000 tons, if the largest Black Sea Fleet, Soviet Russia's, increased proportionately.

The accord was signed on July 20, by Turkey, the Soviet Union, Great Britain, France, Japan, and the Balkan nations. It was generally considered to be a Russian victory. Conservative circles in Great Britain felt that in view of the close relations existing since 1921 between Turkey and Soviet Russia, the keys of the Straits had now been placed in Soviet hands. This was an exaggeration. Turkey had been put in an advantageous position, and she was able for the next few years to play one group of Powers against the others. England did all she could to please Turkey, and Germany at once sent her commercial agents to Ankara to sell building material and armaments for the new fortifications. Even Italy, which at first had felt that the Montreux agreement had been negotiated at her expense, finally decided to accede, though not very gracefully, as she did not ratify the Convention until May, 1938.

Litvinoff was satisfied. No longer could the Soviet Black Sea Fleet be bottled up, no longer could the superior fleet of another country appear in the Black Sea—at least not so long as Soviet-Turkish relations continued friendly.

Stalin, too, felt that Litvinoff had achieved an important victory, and towards the end of the Montreux Conference, on his sixtieth birthday (July 16, 1936), the Foreign Commissar received the Order of Lenin and the two highly laudatory telegrams—one signed by President Kalinin, the other by Molotov and Stalin (see p. 190).

3

William Bullitt's appointment in 1933 as Ambassador to Soviet Russia aroused high hopes everywhere—hopes which Litvinoff shared but which were not fulfilled. His early interest in the Russian experiment, which had brought him the opportunity in 1919 to serve as emissary there, might well have been further encouraged by his second wife, the late Louise Bryant, widow of John Reed and herself an ardent supporter of the new Russian regime. Consequently, when President Roosevelt named him Ambassador to Moscow, Litvinoff and his colleagues in the Narkomindel had a right to look forward to a happy collaboration.

It started out well enough. Bullitt was received with enthusiasm on his arrival, was given exceptional privileges—such as maintaining his own airplane—and all his first contacts were promising. Bullitt's daughter, Anne (the child of Louise Bryant) and Tanya Litvinoff became friends, which seemed a good omen, and the two girls remained friends for several years, playing and swimming together—

guarded by the Ogpu. The fathers seemed good friends, too. But that was only on the surface.

Litvinoff is essentially a direct and simple man. Bullitt is by no means simple. He felt that he occupied an important and historical position, and some thought that he was overinterested in this aspect and neglected serious study of the many perplexing problems that had arisen from the new diplomatic relations between the United States and Soviet Russia. Moreover, when Bullitt first arrived in Moscow, he was immensely popular. This popularity he tried rather ostentatiously to augment; but people in Moscow began to wonder why the American Ambassador tried so hard to be conspicuous. Consequently, the more effort he made, the more his popularity diminished. Soviet Russia was accustomed to statesmen completely absorbed in the most arduous tasks and did not favor the showman—and it was the role of a showman which Bullitt essayed to play in Moscow.

For example, early in the winter of 1935, the American Ambassador gave a zoo party, so called because of the animals—pigs, little bears, goats, and monkeys—let loose in the Embassy to amuse the guests. It was, to put it mildly, in bad taste, and offensive to many of the serious, hard-working guests, who objected to rough-house in an Embassy. Many of the ladies found their dresses ruined by the unwelcome attention of the animals. People pretended to be amused, but nobody was. Madame Litvinoff did not even pretend. She showed her annoyance quite openly.

Litvinoff himself does not talk about his relations with Bullitt; but his judgment is implicit in his statement to Bullitt's successor, Joseph E. Davies, "that both he and his associates in the government were very glad . . . that a man of . . . [a] type should be nominated . . . which . . . assured them a measure of objectivity and reservation of judgment in reports as to what they were trying to do and what they were accomplishing." * And Kalinin's comment that Davies's "professional training would assure objectivity and independence of judgment" † likewise hints of the impression that Bullitt had left on the Soviet authorities.

* Joseph E. Davies, *op. cit.*, p. 60.
† *Ibid.*, p. 25.

Everybody in Moscow began to wonder about Bullitt and his stunts. Nobody knew exactly what he wanted or where he stood. According to rumors, he made statements to certain Wall Street men which could only be understood as anti-Soviet. On the other hand, when he was with journalists with pro-Russian leanings or representatives of the Narkomindel in Moscow, he talked almost like a Party member. This uncertainty about Bullitt's real attitude was very disturbing, the only certain thing being that Bullitt was "ambitious and impatient"— to quote Louis Fischer.

Litvinoff began to regret that Washington had not sent a career diplomat * who, while perhaps not oversympathetic to the "cause," would have been more conventional and dependable.

The break between Bullitt, on the one side, and Litvinoff and Soviet Russia on the other, came in 1936. The American State Department protested against the attendance of American Communists at the Seventh Comintern Congress in Moscow, in August, 1935. The presence of representatives of the American Communist Party was interpreted as a breach of Litvinoff's promises to Roosevelt "not to permit the formation or residence on its territory of any organization or group . . ." constituting, in effect, an American Communist Party.

Once more Russia was being accused of interference in the internal affairs of other countries and the promotion of world revolution. Russia's answer, as always in these cases, was that the Russian Government was not responsible for the Communist Party and the Comintern was an organization of the Party.

Such notes of protest and their answers, which had been exchanged between Soviet Russia and practically every country in the world, were by now routine. Bullitt was not satisfied with routine. He wanted to do something more decisive, and accordingly he adopted a decidedly unconventional diplomatic technique. Instead of continuing the correct protest correspondence with the Narkomindel, he initiated a one-man anti-Soviet campaign from the American Embassy in Moscow. American journalists stationed in Moscow report † that he encouraged them in views and attitudes decidedly unfriendly to the Soviet Government.

* Louis Fischer, *op. cit.,* p. 303.
† *Ibid.,* p. 308.

He even made similar attempts with non-American foreign correspondents in Moscow. He conversed on the subject with other diplomats in what Soviet officials regarded as an almost conspiratorial
manner.

He thus made himself non grata, and his removal to another theater
of diplomatic war in 1936 was spoken of by some foreign representatives as a relief to the whole diplomatic corps of Moscow.

Joseph E. Davies, his successor, is a man of considerable wealth, a
former corporation lawyer, and a convinced adherent of the capitalist
system. Here was definitely an Ambassador who was not interested in
"the cause." But he was intelligent, objective-minded, and willing to
learn about a new country, its population and its philosophy of government. He set out in a very businesslike way to find out the truth,
and accomplish to the utmost of his ability the purposes for which he
was sent.

His choice ruled out any speculation that Washington might have
changed its mind about collaboration between Moscow and the Communist Party of the United States or about the other cardinal question,
the still unpaid debts. Whenever there was an opportunity, Davies
presented Washington's views quite clearly. But he was a good lawyer
and he could formulate a point tactfully so that he did not offend the
other party. And, above all, he understood what an old politician like
Bullitt should have understood even better, that this was not the time
to quarrel with Soviet Russia, that now, when Fascist powers threatened democracy all over the world, when the Soviet Union was willing
to co-operate in every possible way with the democracies, when Russia
had decided on popular fronts and common fronts, when the Comintern had instructed the Communist parties of all countries to forget
about world revolution and work with every foe of Fascism—that
now was not the time to decline Soviet Russia's proffered friendship.

Bullitt had been welcomed with open arms in Moscow; Davies, who
arrived on January 19, 1937, was received correctly but with a certain
reserve. Yet after a surprisingly short period, Davies was able to convince the authorities—and above all Litvinoff—that it was possible to
do business with him. The old Communist and the old corporation
lawyer became fast friends. Litvinoff certainly did not become a capi-

talist during the course of their friendship, which lasts to this day, nor
did Davies turn Communist. But they respect each other's convictions,
they have the same factual-minded, honest approach, they work together amiably, and they began calling each other Max and Joe.

Davies and Litvinoff achieved the goal the President had had in
mind in establishing relations in 1933: not merely "normal," but
"friendly relations," between the two countries.

4

The Uruguayan affair was hardly more than a humorous entr'acte;
the Black Sea Convention was a triumph; the Bullitt fiasco was a
minor annoyance; but the year ended with a situation ominous alike
for Russia and for Litvinoff's international hopes. On November 25,
1936, Japan and Germany signed a so-called non-aggression pact,
which was really a pact of aggression directed against the Soviet
Union. To be sure, the words "Soviet Union" were not named in the
agreement, for the signatories professed that the treaty was directed
against the Comintern and its agents, and specifically mentioned "the
Communist International called Comintern," but that the Russian
Government was at least equally its object was unmistakable. Among
other things, the pact provided that the signatories were to "mutually
inform each other concerning activities of the International, to consult
concerning measures to combat this activity and execute these measures in close collaboration." Also, "the two contracting parties invite
third parties whose domestic peace is endangered to join the Pact."

Litvinoff left no doubt in anyone's mind that he understood perfectly just what was going on. Before the Eighth All-Union Congress
of the Soviets he stated on November 28, 1936:

"As for the Japanese-German Agreement which has been published,
I would recommend you not to seek for any meaning in it, since it
really has no meaning, for the simple reason that it is only a cover for
another agreement which was simultaneously discussed and initialed,
probably also signed, and which was not published and is not intended
for publication.

"I declare with all sense of the responsibility of my words that it was precisely to the working out of this secret document, in which the word 'Communism' is not even mentioned, to which were devoted the fifteen months of negotiations between the Japanese military attaché and the German super-diplomat.

"The aggressive character of the recently concluded agreement follows if only from the fact that participating in it are three States which withdrew from the League of Nations. It is true that Italy formally still participates in the League of Nations, but her participation consists in the fact that, as M. Mussolini himself publicly declared recently, she solicitously desires its speediest possible death.

"All the three States, well known for their aggressiveness and their attempts against the territories of others, are fighting against the principles of collective security and the indivisibility of peace. This in itself lends a sinister character to these agreements and indicates their menace to universal peace, security, and the interest of many countries.

"The activity of the Fascist countries in recent times has revealed, incidentally, all the hypocrisy and mendacity of some of their political so-called program declarations and slogans. German Fascism, for example, asserted that it is opposed in principle to all international alliances and combinations, with the exception of non-aggression pacts, and these only with border neighbors.

"It concluded an agreement with Japan, situated at a distance of tens of thousands of kilometers and separated from it by several States, and which is by no means a non-aggression agreement. German Fascism vowed its adherence to the principle of the localization of war. The agreement with Japan will tend to spread a war which breaks out on one continent to at least two if not more continents.

"Italian Fascism declared after the Abyssinian expedition that its territorial appetites had been fully satisfied and that from then on it was ready to collaborate in the work of stabilizing peace; but now it has joined in a system of aggressive agreements.

"Nor will the reputation for sincerity of the Japanese Government be enhanced; this Government assured us of its desire for the establishment of peaceful relations with the Soviet Union and urged us for the sake of this to meet it in the settlement of several questions in dispute in which it was interested. Now, however, it has concluded a secret aggressive agreement with Germany. The Japanese Government also assured us that it was still considering the non-aggression pact we proposed and that such a pact might be concluded after the settlement of all questions in dispute; now, however, it has made the conclusion of such pacts dependent upon Germany's consent, lessening thereby the independence of its own foreign policy.

"The anti-democratic, aggressive Fascist countries have had their say. They have stated that they do not want to participate in general international co-operation for the organization of peace, for guaranteeing security to all nations. They issue one challenge after another to peace-loving and, in the first place, to the democratic nations. It now rests with these nations to speak."

A year later (September 21, 1937) estimating, before a plenary session of the League, its failure to deal with the Spanish question, he gave a scathing characterization of the anti-Comintern nations:

". . . What is required is that participants in any international organization or conference, however different their national interests, should be united by a common universal idea, such as the idea of peace, the idea of respecting the independence and autonomy of all people, the idea of outlawing force as a weapon of national policy, an idea underlying the League Covenant and the Briand-Kellogg Pact.

"We know three States which have dissociated themselves from this idea and have been committing attacks on other States for the last few years. However diversified the regimes, ideology, the material and cultural level of the objects of the attacks, all three States advance one and the same motive to justify aggression: the struggle against Communism. The rulers of these States naively think, or, rather, pretend to think, that they have only to pronounce the words 'anti-Communism' and all their international wrong-doings and crimes will be forgiven. Although they boast that they have managed to extirpate Communism in their own countries and have become totally immune from it, they declare in a fit of fathomless love for nations near and far that their mission is to deliver these nations from Communism. With ideological combat? Oh, no! With the help of all the air, land, and sea forces at their command. In their voluntary mission of philanthropy to all peoples, they are ready to spare no expense of the forces and resources of their own people, they are ready to curtail their elementary needs to a minimum and put them on a hunger ration, just to have enough arms for the purpose of extirpating Communism in other countries. This, of course, is an open ideology of armed intervention in the internal affairs of other people, full of contempt for their autonomy and independence. I ask you what would the world look like if other nations were infected with this ideology and went on the warpath to impose one or another internal regime on each other?

"By the way, sometimes the founders of this ideology themselves begin to doubt its cogency and acceptability as a leading international idea. Then they come down from their ideological heights and give us a more prosaic explanation of their anti-Communist slogans. Then we learn—which we will not find in the encyclopedia—that anti-Communism has also a geological meaning and denotes a craving for tin, zinc, mercury, copper, and other minerals. When even this explanation proves inadequate, anti-Communism is interpreted as a longing for profitable trade. We are told that this trade might be lost if Spain is tarred with the Communist brush. I doubt, of course, that these are the very last, exclusive explanations of anti-Communism. But we know the example of one Communist State, rich in minerals and other raw material, which has not refused to export these minerals and raw materials to other countries, to trade with them on a very wide scale whatever the regime ruling in these countries, including even the Fascist and National Socialist regimes. Moreover, these very countries have been only too pleased to get minerals and other raw material from the Communist State, and, far from refusing to trade with it, have striven to augment this trade to the utmost, proposing the most highly favorable terms. So we see that Communism is not a hindrance to international trade with any State, on condition, of course, that the latter observes at least elementary international proprieties, does not indulge in Billingsgate, does not play the hooligan or announce openly that the proceeds will be spent in increasing armaments to attack the country it is trading with. . . .

"It must be added that the anti-Communist slogan is being applied on an ever-widening plane. Nowadays, when people speak of the Bolshevik regime and the need to destroy it, they often add the words 'and suchlike regimes.' Now, we often hear it said that all democratic parliamentary countries are on the eve of Bolshevization. This is but a step away from saying that they must be philanthropized and saved from their impending doom by means of armed intervention and attack, as was the case with Spain. We have the example of China, which can scarcely even be put in the category of countries with a parliamentary regime in the strict sense of the term. Nevertheless, the attack against her is also being made under the slogan of 'fighting Communism.' We also see in Europe itself how countries which by general opinion are earmarked for the next aggression are beforehand declared to be Bolshevized or fallen under Bolshevist influence for the purpose of subsequent justification of the intended aggression. Any country which falls under the longing eyes of aggressive States might be declared suspect of Bolshevism, because no proofs are demanded, and it is enough to repeat the same thing day after day in the unified Press and official speeches, on the assumption that a falsehood might sound true if repeated often enough.

"I am sure that everybody with common sense understands the absurdity of the anti-Communist slogan and the aggressive motives behind it. But out of politeness, scarcely appropriate in the present case, they listen to this bosh and read it without saying anything. The danger is that the aggressor might construe this silence as acceptance of the excuses he gives for his aggressive intentions or actions, with all the sad consequences involved to the cause of peace. I think it is time to put an end to this dangerous agitational weapon of aggression, it is high time those who really cherish the interests of peace told the State parrots in high places that nonsense does not cease to be nonsense from daily repetition, that aggression must be called 'aggression,' whatever its ornamental slogan, that, whatever the meaning of anti-Communism, mineralogical, commercial, strategic or anything else camouflaging aggressions, armed interventions, the invasion of other States and the violation of international treaties cannot receive international exoneration. So too is it time to say that they, preachers of rabid misanthropy, dare not fight for the interests of mankind, that they, resurrectors of the most savage, outworn theory of pagan times and the Middle Ages, dare not speak on behalf of modern Europe, that they, who consigned to the flames some of the best works of the human spirit, persecutors of the most brilliant representatives of science, art, and literature, and despised for it by the whole cultured world, make themselves ludicrous when they speak of saving civilization and invoke crusades against other people for this purpose.

"The cause of peace would be done an invaluable service by statements to this effect."

5

The year 1936 had been dark, indeed almost catastrophic for Litvinoff's policy: it had brought the Ethiopian War; the betrayal of the League by France and England; Hitler's scrapping of Locarno; the Spanish Civil War, which Litvinoff understood correctly as the first experiment of the Fascist countries to turn the world Fascist; and finally, the anti-Comintern pact, which again Litvinoff had correctly understood as just another ominous step towards attempting to erase democracy from the world.

The Spanish Civil War threatened from the start to become a world conflict. Everyone knew that Italians had swarmed in to the aid of Franco, that German planes had ferried Moorish troops across the Straits at a critical moment and saved the rebellion which the Government was about to extinguish. Anti-Fascist volunteers from many countries formed an international brigade to help defend Spain against the menace of aggression which they saw threatening the whole world; their ranks included Communists and Communist sympathizers. And from Russia came men and supplies. The war had already become international and various nations were recklessly committing their interests and prestige on the outcome of the conflict. The Chamberlain government felt that at all costs the conflict must be confined and interference from without checked, and thus the decision left entirely to the Spanish people themselves. It was, on the face of it, a sensible precaution, if only it had been justly and firmly administered. At the bottom, it was hostile to the Spanish Government. There was no intention of putting up a real fight against the governmental intervention of Germany and Italy, an intervention which Hitler, and Mussolini, the most notorious liars in international history, were daily denying with unctuous words that deceived nobody—probably not even the Chamberlain government, which hoped for a Franco success. But non-intervention was worth trying as it might have been strengthened and expanded into a really effective instrument for the localization of the conflict.

The rather dreadful war went almost according to the schedule of Hitler and Mussolini. On September 9, 1936, Germany and Italy had joined in the non-intervention comedy. On November 18 they formally recognized Franco's Government. France and England still pretended that nobody was intervening, and only Litvinoff called the act by its right name in his speech of November 28, 1936:

"Germany and Italy declare without a blush that they support General Franco because they do not want to have a democratic government in Spain, a government of the United Front, and want to see there the government promised by General Franco, based on Fascist principles. It is self-evident that Germany and Italy by no means need Fascism in Spain for the sake of Fascism as such or for the declaration of any ideological doctrine. Fascism is in this case a means of achieving entirely different and by no means ideological aims."

By the end of 1936 the democracies had conceived the plan of recalling all volunteers—which meant that the Loyalists lost the help of men of all countries who wanted to fight for democracy, while Franco got more and more German help. This was aided also by the State Department of the United States, which not only had stopped shipments to Spain by urging Congress to pass an embargo act, but also warned American citizens not to serve in Spain. Germany and Italy, on the other hand, dropped all pretense in their efforts to aid General Franco. When on May 29, Loyalist planes bombed the German cruiser *Deutschland,* German battleships mercilessly and indiscriminately bombed the town of Almeria in reprisal. Only the willfully blind who would not see could continue the pretense that the war in Spain was merely a civil war.

The Spanish Government protested in Geneva against the intervention of Germany and Italy and, on May 28, 1937, Litvinoff, in the name of Soviet Russia, endorsed this protest—once more with a courageous, discerning speech that went straight to the heart of the matter and might well serve as the standard description of the whole wretched episode:

"Tens of thousands of foreigners, well trained and well armed, many of them lately in the military service of foreign States, poured into

Spain to help the mutineers, and formed a considerable military force on the territory of Spain. In some cases big battles have been fought with the Spanish Republican army exclusively by these foreign military units, under the command of foreign generals. Spanish cities are being bombarded by foreign warplanes piloted by foreigners. One quarter of Madrid, the whole city of Guernica and many other towns and villages have been destroyed by foreign aircraft. It may be said that at the present time the Spanish Republican army has to wage an armed struggle, not so much against the mutineers as against foreign invaders. Thus, one of the members of the League has been subjected to foreign invasion and the danger of violation of its territorial integrity and political independence.

"But it is not only the question of Spain. The events in Spain have created one of the greatest dangers to European and world peace. This menace arises in consequence of an attempt at armed intervention in the internal affairs of a European State, an attempt to thrust upon the people of this State an internal regime and, mainly, a foreign policy orientation alien to it; and under the cover of this intervention deprive this country of her independence and subject her to the scepter of other States. If this attempt succeeded and went unpunished, there would be no guarantee that it would not be repeated in other countries. There is no guarantee that in the very near future there will not be a new attempt to start a mutiny in another country and recognize the leader of the mutineers as the head of the Government, bring in foreign troops and foreign arms to the assistance of the mutineers there and thus commit aggression in realization of the national policy of the intervening State. There is a tendency in intervention to begin, after the example of the religious wars of the past, a series of new wars and, under cover of the rivalry of ideologies and political regimes, carry out a policy of aggression and expansion. It should not be forgotten that, at the moment of the outbreak of the mutiny, Spain had a Government which in its program resembled governments existing in many other countries.

"The Government of the country which I represent has its ideology; it would, of course, be very glad if other countries were imbued with this ideology. However, it has never tried and will never by any methods, let alone forcible ones, try to thrust its ideology on other States.

We, as a State, were little concerned with the order existing in Spain, a country with which, when the mutiny broke out, we did not even have diplomatic or consular relations, a country where there was not a single Soviet citizen at that time. All we want is that when the present events come to an end, the Spanish people may, as before the mutiny, have the government which they want and which they voluntarily elected on the basis of a constitution established by themselves. Therefore, from the outset, the Government I represent stated that it would support any action designed to remove all non-Spanish elements from the ranks of the belligerents in Spain, so that the struggle taking place there could be decided by the forces of the Spaniards themselves.

"The circumstances of the case fully justify the appeal of the Spanish Government to the League of Nations. We know that in some countries this appeal is criticized and even condemned. There are some people who consider themselves supporters of the League of Nations and who think that the League of Nations can be kept alive only on condition that nothing will be asked of the League and nothing expected, and that any appeal to the League in any serious international affair is an attempt upon the existence of the League. These people would like to change the League into a 'universal' mummy and admire its inertness and imperturbable calm. The Spanish Government apparently does not think so but, on the contrary, presumes that the League of Nations will be finally doomed to moral, if not physical, death if it will be completely ignored and will stand aside in the development of events like those now proceeding on the Iberian Peninsula.

"Spain belongs to the number of the first members of the League and has taken an active part in all the transactions of the League. She has loyally performed all her duties as a member of the League. She occupied a semi-permanent place in the Council of the League and has never abused her privilege in order to dissociate herself from the joint decisions and actions of the League of Nations or set her individual opinion against the public opinion of the rest of the members of the League. Therefore it is impossible not to be surprised at the modesty and moderation of Spain who, in spite of the misfortune which befell her in a hard time, did not burden the League with appeals, although she had the full formal and moral right to do so. And if, with this modesty, knowing how limited the assistance which she may expect from the League, without invoking any articles of the Covenant applicable to the present case, she has nevertheless now appealed to us, I would like to express the confidence that the League Council, not only in the interests of Spain, but in the interests of international justice and the preservation of peace, and also in the interests of the League itself, will throw its word into the scale and render all possible support to the Spanish people."

Litvinoff, in a speech at a Plenary Session of the League of Nations on September 21, 1937, trenchantly summarized the preposterous and tragic farce and its implications:

"The Spanish question was withdrawn from the League of Nations and submitted to the specially formed London Committee of so-called non-intervention in order to gain the collaboration of the chief culprits of the Spanish tragedy, who cannot bear the atmosphere of Geneva. This experiment has had its results, and they are known to all. Agreements have been signed and violated immediately, resolutions adopted and disregarded, schemes and plans devised only to be sabotaged and frustrated, all to the accompaniment of door-slamming on the part of certain concertedly capricious members of the Committee who keep leaving it and returning. Of course, the London Committee has not achieved even one of its purposes. While the export of arms to Spain is formally forbidden, the supplying of the mutineers on a State scale with all kinds of arms for actions by land, sea and air has not ceased. In spite of the obligation to forbid foreign citizens to go to Spain and take part in the operations, tens of thousands of men in military formations, whole divisions in full armament led by officers and generals, have been sent to the assistance of the Spanish mutineers in full view of all on the part of countries which undertook the formal obligations I have mentioned. These are not conjectures, but facts, which are not concealed by the very violators of these obligations, but are mentioned openly in their Press, facts which we know from official orders, from printed lists of wounded and killed, from the exchange of official telegrams. Add to this the fact that foreign warships are cruising round Spain helping the mutineers by scouting, bombarding Spanish ports (the case of Almeria) and even sinking neutral commercial vessels—that is, taking part in a blockade of Republican Spain—and you will understand why non-intervention in Spanish affairs cannot be spoken of any longer without irony.

"Such are the results of the activity of an organization free from the spirit of Geneva.

"I recommend these results to the attention of the apologists of universality. Let them take thought on the cause of these results, and they will see how illusory are the hopes that collaboration can be successful between States which pursue different aims, which have contrary conceptions of international life and the mutual rights and duties of nations; the hopes for collaboration between those who sincerely uphold non-intervention in the domestic affairs of other States, those who champion the right of every people to decide their internal regime independently of those who no less sincerely and openly uphold intervention in other people's affairs and the imposition of one regime or another on other States with bayonets and bombs. There can be no synthesis between aggression and non-aggression, between peace and war."

A couple of months later (November 27, 1937), speaking at a meeting in Leningrad, he permitted himself to characterize the performance of his colleagues in face of aggressor tactics with ironically cloaked frankness:

"I see it is a puzzle to you how experienced bourgeois diplomats could fail to understand the meaning of the aggressor's tactics. You think they are only pretending to disbelieve the aggressor's statements, and, under cover of negotiations for confirmations and explanations, they are groping for a deal with the aggressor. You can think so if you like, but my position does not allow me to express such doubts, and I must leave them to your responsibility. I can speak only about the official position of other States."

What did the Spanish Civil War mean for Litvinoff? What was its meaning for Soviet Russia?

The Communists were constantly being accused of wanting to establish Communism in Spain. Litvinoff called such assertions "fairy tales for little children and big fools." "Wherein lies the interest of the Soviet State in Spanish events?" Litvinoff asked.

Spain was only the first "attempt at a forcible implantation . . . from without of a Fascist system." The ultimate attempt would be made against the Soviet Union. In short, Litvinoff—like many other clear-headed observers the world round—saw the Spanish Civil War as the prologue to a crusade against Soviet Russia. It had been started by forces that wanted to destroy Communism.

Many who fought for Loyalist Spain stated this specifically. Dolores Ibarruri (La Pasionaria) said at the Plenary Session of the Central Committee in June, 1937, that the United Front against General Franco was based not only on the idea of the liberation of Spain, but also the protection of the Soviet Union.

A leader of the International Brigade of Volunteers in his farewell address of October, 1938, when the Brigade was withdrawn from the ranks of the Loyalists said: "We are leaving. But we are not departing to sit back and rest. We are going to fight. . . . We shall not rest. We are only changing the front." Almost all of the foreigners who fought for liberty in Spain felt that they were fighting a preliminary battle of the first round of the fight of Fascism against a free world, and the second round would be a war against Soviet Russia.

In his November speech Litvinoff launched into a formidable and devastating exposé of the meaning of Fascism:

"It is necessary to bear in mind that Fascism is not only a specific internal State regime, but that it represents at the same time preparation for aggression, preparation for war against other States. This is not our characterization of Fascism, but its own. Fascism shouts about its aggressiveness from the house-tops, and not only shouts about it but in certain areas is already practicing it. I ask you, comrades, to recall what I said here earlier about the substance and methods of Fascism. I told you about the suppression of discontent among the population of a Fascist country, but this is a negative program, so to speak. Fascism also has a positive program.

"By mechanical police measures alone, by muzzles, the mouths of the discontented can be gagged only temporarily; but since the causes of discontent are not removed thereby, and since Fascism is incapable of removing them by other measures, they resort to other, spiritual means, so to speak, to influence or, I would say, to befuddle the discontented citizens.

"By monopolizing the Press, the book-publishing houses, the radio, and all other means of agitation, Fascism endeavors to impress on the citizens that their people is the chosen, the best of all peoples, destined to dominate all other, inferior peoples. Stories are told them about remarkable ancestors, about their belonging to some special, higher race.

"Just as primitive people and little children used to be frightened by the alleged existence of goblins, Beelzebub, Satan, devils, imps, and other evil spirits, just so are the citizens of a Fascist country frightened by the bogey of Communists, Marxists, democrats, Jews, Masons, who must be defeated and destroyed by all means in order to gain happiness. Tempting pictures of flourishing territories such as the Ukraine, the Urals, and Siberia are being painted, as well as colonies rich in raw materials.

"The only trouble is, they are told, that these tempting territories and colonies belong to other peoples. Hence, they must be conquered, taken by force; and this requires arms, this requires a big army, a huge navy, great and varied armament. It is clear that the citizens must strain all their efforts, must suffer privations, and give up everything to the Fascist State for the creation of military might. Thus, a whole nation is imbued from day to day with the spirit of aggression, and aggression openly becomes the program of the Fascist State, while Fascism itself becomes the function of the most reckless chauvinism and imperialism.

"What I have said would seem to be quite sufficient to justify the interest with which we, as a State that unflinchingly stands for inviolable peace between the peoples, are watching the attempt at the forcible implantation in other countries of Fascism as the bearer of the idea of aggression. But this is not all.

"Fascism carries out its preparations for the achievement of its aggressive aims not only by increasing its armaments at an incredible rate, but also by releasing itself unilaterally from all international obligations binding it or by simply violating them as suits it; by avoiding all international co-operation for the strengthening of peace; by attempting to undermine the international organizations which are called upon to protect peace; by waging a campaign for disuniting other countries and preventing the collective organization of security.

"The same object is served by spreading false reports about other countries, for which purpose a special State institution has been set up called the Ministry of Propaganda, at the head of which stands a man who, to do him justice, as the author and circulator of the most absurd inventions and the most lying reports is, as the English say, the right man in the right place.

"Fascism directs its fiery arrows particularly against the Soviet State, ostensibly because the ideas of Communism are professed there, but in reality because it is the object of the predatory aims of Fascism, and also an obstacle to its aims of conquest in other directions."

6

In 1937 Litvinoff's department, the Narkomindel, along with many other sections of the Government, was blasted by the so-called purge. Three years before (December 1, 1934) the Chairman of the Leningrad Soviet, Kirov, had been assassinated. The resulting investigation, which took two years, revealed a complex and widespread anti-Government undercover organization inspired by the exiled Trotsky, with a "center" in every important town in the Soviet Union—foci of "internal aggression," in Litvinoff's own phrase.*

The plot included an elaborate and carefully worked-out program providing for many acts of sabotage and terrorism, including the assassination of a number of Soviet leaders. The economic structure of the country, both production and transportation, was to be disorganized in order to create antagonism, the chief ultimate aim being to destroy Stalin.

The first trials (August 19-24, 1936) that grew out of these discoveries, of a group headed by Zinoviev and Kamenev, who had worked with Trotsky in attempts to undermine Stalin and his policies, concerned almost wholly internal Bolshevik Party differences. But further trials in the next year and a half (January 23-30, 1937, June 11, 1937, March 2-13, 1938) had wider implications. For the treacherous network was by that time known to have been extended not only throughout the Soviet Union but beyond, to relations with agents of foreign governments. Outstanding Russian military officers led by Marshal Tukhachevsky as well as such important civilian officials as Yagoda, Chief of the Ogpu, and former Premier Rykov were involved, and many second-line government men also had taken guilty part, among them a number of Litvinoff's subordinates.

* Joseph E. Davies, *op. cit.*, p. 173.

Among those that were "liquidated" (executed, imprisoned, exiled or drastically demoted) were many of the Foreign Commissar's collaborators: ambassadors, ministers and attachés: Bogomolov, Ambassador to China; Yurenev, Ambassador to Japan; Davtyan, Ambassador to Poland; Karakhan, Ambassador to Turkey; Karsky, Minister to Lithuania; Asmus, Minister to Finland; Brodovsky, Minister to Latvia; Skvirsky, Minister to Afghanistan, who had been in Washington before the recognition; Tikhmenev, Minister to Denmark; Bekzadian, Minister to Hungary; Raskolnikov, Minister to Bulgaria; Yakubovitch, Minister to Norway; Barmine, Chargé d'Affaires in Greece; Ostrovsky, member of the Soviet Legation in Rumania; Krestinsky and Sokolnikov (who had been Ambassador in London), Litvinoff's Assistant Commissars; and Gershelman, his private secretary. Most of the Narkomindel department heads were arrested, along with a great number of secretaries and translators.* Some refused to return from abroad. Many were shot. Some were sentenced to long prison terms; others exiled; still others simply disappeared.

Litvinoff himself had insisted on discontinuing the old Ogpu surveillance of Foreign Office emissaries which might have prevented such a wide expansion of this plot. For in the first years of Soviet administration all government employees abroad, even members of Trade Delegations, had been watched. Litvinoff had been able to convince Stalin that Russian diplomats would not have the confidence and respect of their colleagues from other countries if they were constantly spied upon and subject to sudden arrest on suspicion. So all these ambassadors, ministers and other diplomatic officials had been relatively free to enter into treasonable foreign relations if they wished.

But despite this and regardless of the number of his associates now convicted, some of whom he had implicitly trusted, he did not feel personally humiliated. Scheming of this kind was all utterly alien to his own mentality. He was completely free from the personal ambitions which had seduced some of these men into treason. The doctrinaire rigidity which had played a considerable part—adherence to the theory that world revolution was essential to complete the Russian Revolution and insistence on "pure" Communism in Russia, with resultant abrogation of the NEP private enterprises and foreign concessions, and

* Cf. Louis Fischer, op. cit., pp. 495-496.

liquidation of the kulaks—seemed obviously impractical, for the moment at least, to this invariably practical man. He was entirely concentrated on solidifying the new Russia's foreign relations, protecting her from various forms of hostility and aggression, given the actual world conditions as he well knew them. Immediately pressing real problems left no room for abstract theories, and to sell out to the Nazis of all people, no matter what the ideals presumably thereby to be served, he knew only too well meant suicide. At first he was, as he has said since, amazed and bewildered, then he was disgusted.

In one case, however, he was genuinely shocked—that of his closest collaborator, Nikolai Nikolaievitch Krestinsky, who confessed to having taken money from German generals. He was willing to give him the benefit of the doubt and seemed almost happy when Krestinsky denied his original confession. But on the second day of his trial Krestinsky revoked his denial and admitted everything of which he had been accused.

For the rest, Litvinoff felt that they deserved liquidation, and on July 4, 1937, he told Ambassador Davies, whose official duty it was to follow the trials, that "some day the world would understand that . . . they were doing the whole world a service in protecting themselves against the menace of Hitler and Nazi world domination, and thereby preserving the Soviet Union strong as a bulwark against the Nazi threat." *

And speaking in Leningrad on November 27, 1937, he was more explicit:

"Comrades, the preparation of war begins in peace-time. It consists, among other things, in the formation of a web of espionage on foreign territory and numerous agencies to carry out all kinds of instructions— in short, what is now commonly called the 'fifth column.' You read a few days ago that about 1,000 spies were arrested recently in Czechoslovakia and that a serious conspiracy has been hatched against the French Republic. Our likely enemies should know by now that they will not find the line of least resistance on Soviet territory in this respect, either. They know that the creation of ammunition dumps, fortifications, dugouts, and the organization of internal squads to man

* Joseph E. Davies, *op. cit.*, p. 167.

those enterprises and use them might be possible in some places, but certainly not in the Soviet Union. They know that our People's Commissariat of Internal Affairs is very unwilling to let such plans come to fruition and that it is vigilant and strong enough to destroy the Trotsky-Fascist organizations of spies and wreckers in embryo."

As usual anti-Soviet bias the world round seized on the situation to attack the Russian Government. The treason trials were a shock and surprise to many friends of Soviet Russia. The difference in procedure from that usual in most countries, the reliance on preliminary investigations that were not public, the confessions and self-accusations so unusual in foreign eyes; the knowledge that the Kremlin had always been ruthless in the suppression of its enemies, of defeatists, of loafers, incompetents, and grafters, increased the suspicion that some of the accused had been railroaded, that they had been tortured, given mysterious will-destroying drugs, falsely promised immunity in exchange for pleas of guilt. That there was not the slightest evidence to support these fantastic charges did not inhibit rumor, suspicion, emphatic condemnation. Trotsky sympathizers all over the world reacted in a fury of resentment, organized campaigns for his defense, and with many intemperate appeals to prejudice accused Stalin and the Soviet Government of the most monstrous crimes and the most sinister motives. But Davies, a fully experienced lawyer, with no Communist leanings, but a trained judicial mind watching on the spot, found the trials convincing, as did other especially qualified observers such as Walter Duranty, Lion Feuchtwanger, the British lawyer D. N. Pritt, and a good many members of the diplomatic corps, and other correspondents, like Quentin Reynolds, summarizes the general conclusion: "That purge eliminated Russia's Fifth Column. I found no British or American correspondent in Russia who thought that the famous confessions made by Radek, Tukhatchevsky, Bukharin, Rykov, Krestinsky, Pletnov, Rosengoltz and the others had been extorted by torture." * The country as a whole was thoroughly convinced and, while shocked at first, seemed actually relieved that a great peril to the State had been surmounted. "Russia's magnificent unity today and her completely unbroken spirit after the dreadful tragedy of that German advance, is proof of the fact

* Quentin Reynolds, *Only the Stars Are Neutral*, N. Y., 1943, p. 93.

that Russia accepted the purge and approved of Stalin's 'You can't make an omelet without breaking eggs' policy." *

Soviet Russia had saved herself from disruption and civil war that might have resulted, if the plots had been even partially successful—and as foreign enemies of the Soviet Union, particularly the Nazis, were operating through some of the plotters and were fully prepared to take instant and drastic advantage of any internal disorders, the danger to the State was a very grave one—but by a bitter irony the purge had also promoted Nazi ends insofar as it had weakened international confidence in Russian strength and thus been the final solvent of any possibility of the collective security for which Russia, through Litvinoff, had been the prime mover.

Litvinoff had lost almost his entire staff with the exception of Ivan Maisky in London, Jacob Suritz in Paris and Boris Stein in Rome (who, however, was removed later),† but he never faltered. Russian foreign policy did not change. Litvinoff was alone, but he carried on; carried on in the face of conviction that there was no more possibility of saving Europe and Russia by co-operation with the Western Powers, the thesis on which he had been working for years. He knew beyond shadow of hope that "the British and French peoples are soft under leaders that are blind," that they would trudge right on, fatuously optimistic to the last, into the disaster that their own governments were obtusely helping to prepare, that France was through, and that his own country would be the last to be attacked.‡

7

One year after Germany and Japan had concluded their anti-Comintern pact, Italy joined them, as was inevitable, given the character and ambitions of the three governments. The other governments took this apparently with indifference, assuming that the pact was directed only against Russia.

Litvinoff, with his usual perspicacity, had long predicted the new alignment, was sure that it would develop into an alliance destined to

* Reynolds, *op. cit.,* p. 110.
† Louis Fischer, *loc. cit.*
‡ John T. Whitaker, *We Cannot Escape History,* pp. 267-268, New York, July, 1943.

threaten seriously the other nations, and he so warned both Britain and France. It was equally clear that the danger of joint attack against Soviet Russia was steadily growing. Mussolini's decision to combine with Hitler rather than with the Western Powers relieved the chronic German fear of encirclement. The back door to Germany thus locked, Hitler was free to plan the disposition of his forces and engage in a more effective combination of diplomatic and military blackmail.

This was an ideal occasion for the Western Powers to come to an agreement with Russia. But again the opportunity was persistently ignored by the British and French statesmen, despite Litvinoff's unceasing efforts to make clear the trend of events. But the governing circles were blinded by deep-rooted opposition and distrust, the mass of the people were paralyzed by habitual inertia and misinformation, and both were constrained to every kind of evasion by the gnawing fear of war. Only Litvinoff and Roosevelt among the responsible statesmen and nations had the courage and integrity to face the dread prospect. Consequently, no timely or effective opposition to Hitler was in sight. Soviet Russia accordingly had only one course left open to her, and that was to hasten all military preparations and check in mid-course her cherished programs for economic and cultural progress in order to put all her energies and resources into armament. It was a cruel and ironic fate for Litvinoff, who had tried so hard and so long for disarmament, to see the last hope fade and in the end be forced by the facts to approve this melancholy decision, which, he knew, only added to the certainty of war.

Three years before (April 4, 1934) he had summarized the impasse with his characteristic relentless clarity: "The threat of war that menaces all the five continents of the world is spoken about and written about daily, but we scarcely hear anything of the possibility and the means of averting this impending catastrophe. Governments and statesmen regard it with a sort of fatalism, as something that is absolutely inevitable. The only thing they can think about is a general rearmament, the race for armaments which in the past, far from averting wars, has only served as a stimulus for them."

The small nations of Europe, as they themselves were quite well aware, were in even greater danger than the Western Powers or Soviet Russia. Ever since the League of Nations had washed its hands of

China, leaving her to be crucified by Japanese militarism, ever since Ethiopia had been betrayed to Mussolini, the handwriting on the wall was clear for all who were not blinded by prejudice or diverted by superficial interpretations of self-interest. Consequently, the small nations of Europe became panic-stricken. For years they had relied on protection from the League. The faltering impotence of that Power, which had sworn to keep watch over all, completely destroyed the illusion. Naked against the blast, every little country now undertook to play its own lone game. "Collective security" was abandoned. The new motto was *"sauve qui peut."*

On October 15, 1936, Belgium renounced her treaties with France and on March 22, 1937, the King of the Belgians went to London to see his dentist. He saw his dentist, but he also saw Anthony Eden and discussed with him Belgium's desire for more effective safeguards for her neutrality.

In the middle of 1937 Sweden's Foreign Minister, R. J. Sandler, suggested that all small countries should be freed from the obligations of Article XVI of the League Covenant which required common action against any nation that the League had classed as an aggressor. Sandler's reasoning was all too clear to Litvinoff. The small nations realized that sooner or later Hitler would be named an aggressor, and they were afraid that they would be called upon to oppose a rearmed and violent Germany. They hoped that by appeasing Hitler they might save themselves—at the cost of others, perhaps. Every small country thought so; none seemed to understand that by sacrificing other countries it was only hastening its own end. Litvinoff energetically opposed any such change. He was sure that German propaganda had been at work on them and that Hitler was simply applying the technique of divide et impera. It was all part of the tragedy of failure to do the obvious,* and because he saw it so clearly, it rode Litvinoff like an incubus.

He did all he could to persuade Sandler to the contrary, actually taking advantage of a reception in Sandler's honor (July 9, 1937) to press his point in an excellent statement: "Unfortunately the forces which stand for peace are less resolute, less energetic and less united, than the forces opposing them. . . . It is not a question of forming military alliances and leagues for the purpose of pitting the force of one side against

* Joseph E. Davies, *op. cit.,* pp. 171, 546-547.

the force of another on the field of battle. The task of the moment, in our opinion, is to consolidate, if the term may be used, the potential of peace. This potential consists not only of the defensive capacity of the peaceable States, but to a large extent of such elements as the League Covenant, the Briand-Kellogg Pact, the regional pacts of mutual assistance [which Sweden opposed, preferring a mutual understanding within Scandinavia],* the ideas of collective security and the indivisibility of peace, the manifesting of the solidarity of the peaceable countries and their ability to find a common language.

"The potential of peace in its entirety plays a great part in delaying aggression. The lessening of any element in this potential means encouraging and unleashing aggression and consequently increasing the risk of war."

Underneath this opposition—so critical in its implications—there was little Sweden's old fear of the Big Bear so close to her, kept on the alert by the proportionately greater fears of the other still smaller Scandinavian countries, and perhaps also an unrecognized undertone of personal feeling, for Sandler had played an important part in the Second International, which had been obliterated by the group that Litvinoff represented.

Litvinoff pointed out repeatedly that France and England were to blame for the growing prestige of Hitler. Thus to Ambassador Davies he said: "It was a mistake to magnify Hitler's importance by engaging in discussions. . . ." † Another time he asked: ". . . why they should project notes and questionnaires and constantly stir up the German situation and thereby accentuate Hitler's importance and 'feed his vanity' into his self-conception that he [Hitler] is the dominating figure in Europe. . . . They ought," he commented flatly, "to let him 'stew in his own juice.'" ‡

Litvinoff also felt that the United States was to a certain extent responsible for the developments in Europe. In his opinion, the neutrality law and the arms embargo act, instead of solidifying the prospect of peace, had actually enhanced the prospect of war in Europe. He wondered when America would understand that she was not and could not

* *Ibid.*, p. 547.
† *Ibid.*, p. 79.
‡ *Ibid.*, p. 59.

remain isolated from world affairs. He was enthusiastic about Roosevelt's Chicago speech of October 7, 1937, in which the President said that aggressor nations should be quarantined, but doubtful that the United States would be able to obtain any real justice for China at the forthcoming Brussels conference called by the signatories of the Washington Nine Power Treaty.*

Litvinoff felt keenly about China's most cruel predicament, and presented the situation with corrosive directness at a meeting in Leningrad on November 27, 1937: "Japan is flooding China with her troops, occupying one province after another, shelling and bombing Chinese towns —in short, is doing everything that used to be called 'war.' She declares authoritatively, loudly and repeatedly, that she intends to continue her offensive until she carries out her aims and China opens negotiations with her, with the object of capitulating, of course. At the same time, she warns us that she will not brook anybody's mediation. China applies to the League of Nations for protection, referring to the corresponding points in the League Covenant. The League forms a committee, the committee appoints a sub-committee, and the latter elects an editorial committee. A paper is drafted and addressed to Japan: 'We do not approve of your offensive. Probably it is based on a misunderstanding. Please come to confirm this, and, lest you feel lonely among us, we are inviting your kindred spirit and friend, Germany.' From Japan comes confirmation that there is no misunderstanding at all, that she is on the warpath quite deliberately and agrees to discuss matters only with China and only on terms of the latter's surrender. Disarmed by this reply, the League decides to refer the question to the Powers most concerned in Far Eastern affairs, signatories to the so-called Washington Treaty, which is violated by Japan for the second time (it was violated the first time by the occupation of Manchuria). And so the Brussels Conference is called, and the Soviet Union is also invited, although she is not a signatory to the Washington Treaty. What does this conference do? Its activity was very neatly hit off in a cartoon which I saw in a foreign newspaper. This shows the honorable delegates of eighteen States, not without great effort and strain, dragging a letter to the post-box for Japan. In this letter, as you know, they again demand Japan's confirmation whether she is deliberately committing her

* *Ibid.*, pp. 59, 79, 247.

aggression in China and request her to stop and accept mediation. Confirmation is not long in coming. Japan, even with an inflection of resentment, replies that there is no need to bother her; she has repeatedly stated that she is attacking China quite deliberately and for quite definite aims. She does not need anybody's mediation; she is ready to negotiate only with China—about capitulation, of course—and the only thing the conference can do is to make China agree to this capitulation. This reply disarmed the Brussels Conference, just as the first reply disarmed the League of Nations, and the conference was closed."

And he had shrewdly estimated the range of Japan's aggressive program, for in February, 1937, he expressed the belief that America might have a problem with Japan and that, as events were moving, America could not count on isolation.*

8

Litvinoff's bête noire was not American isolationists, or any frightened leader of the small European nations, or any of the French politicians who were either corrupt and conniving with Hitler, or had lost all power of initiative; the man he rightly saw as the real leader heading the forces of reaction and evasion was the Prime Minister of Great Britain, Neville Chamberlain.

His half-brother, Sir Austen Chamberlain, had been one of Litvinoff's principal opponents during his earlier diplomatic career; but as Sir Austen grew older he had gradually modified his original views. Starting with the "little-England" conviction that his Government should remain in splendid isolation and undertake no commitments on the Continent, he had finally come to the realization that English security had to be based on French security, and he even became much more friendly towards Litvinoff.

Neville Chamberlain's development was quite the reverse. He had been brought up for business. After a sojourn in the West Indies, he had taken over the large business interests of his father, Joseph Chamberlain. He entered politics as a liberal Conservative and up to 1936 had been an outspoken anti-Nazi. His condemnations of Hitlerism both in 1935, after Hitler had introduced compulsory military service in Ger-

* *Ibid.*, p. 59.

many and 1936, after he had marched into the Rhineland, were quite explicit. He was the only one in the British Cabinet who supported Flandin and co-operation with Litvinoff.

Just then, however, representatives of extremely reactionary circles decided to win Neville Chamberlain over. The go-between was Sir Horace Wilson, a bitter anti-Labor politician who had gained a good deal of inside prestige by being largely instrumental in breaking the general strike of the twenties, and in the intervening years had lost no opportunity to incite British politicians and, to some extent, British public opinion against the "Communist danger." Litvinoff knew him well, for the Russians had long kept their eyes on this man, seeing in him a potential leader of European reaction and of a crusade against Soviet Russia. Wilson now began to supply Neville Chamberlain with a succession of atrocity stories about the Soviet Union, and Chamberlain fell easy prey to his bizarre but carefully concocted tales, some of which may have contained a bit of truth here and there, enough seasoning of reality to give the whole a plausible flavor. Before long Chamberlain had been pushed around into a complete about-face (a fact that has been curiously overlooked), so that from the end of 1936 on, he was willing to co-operate with anybody, even Hitler, whom he had hated so much, to frustrate and, if possible, defeat Soviet Russia.

Litvinoff had not been particularly interested in Neville Chamberlain as long as he was Chancellor of the Exchequer in Baldwin's Cabinet. There were few indications then that Chamberlain would eventually become the determining factor in British foreign policy. But when in May, 1937, Chamberlain succeeded Baldwin, Ambassador Ivan Maisky apprised Litvinoff in an urgent report of some surprising and disturbing events. Field Marshal von Blomberg, Hitler's Minister of War, had been received in London by Chamberlain. There were intimations that they had discussed a common front against Bolshevik Russia, and also rumors that other anti-Bolshevik circles, including the so-called Cliveden set and the group centering around the American Ambassador Joseph Kennedy, were trying to convince Chamberlain that Hitler should be given a free hand in his war against the Soviet Union.

Chamberlain's role in the Spanish Civil War finally convinced Litvinoff that the English Prime Minister would, with all the power at his command, consistently oppose every feature of the Soviet program;

that Chamberlain's basically reactionary mind had been inflamed with hostility by fear founded on ignorance and deliberately stimulated by the long course of Fascist propaganda. Influential men of the City and a few well-known English aristocrats had convinced Chamberlain that the Spanish conflict was not a civil war, but a war between Germany and Russia. By maintaining strict neutrality, he was led to believe, England would help defeat the Bolsheviki and thereby prevent their advance to the West, which would ultimately threaten the very existence of Britain.

Even in his role of Prime Minister, Chamberlain had less confidence in his own Foreign Secretary, Anthony Eden, than in his old associates in the City, or his friends among the country gentlemen, and he paid less and less attention to the reports of the Foreign Office. For nearly eighteen months he refused to see Sir Robert Vansittart, and ignored old experienced diplomats like Lord Tyrell and Sir Horace Rumbold, who knew Germany well and had correctly gauged the fast-growing menace. All this arbitrary negligence he defended by the simple assertion: "I don't believe in experts." Other men in the Foreign Office, too, first Sir John Simon and later Lord Halifax—one largely from business and financial affiliations, the other on religious grounds—seem to have been hostile to Russia and skeptical of all the warnings about danger from Germany, and their attitudes resulted in a good deal of misinformation and warped judgment.

Ambassador Maisky did his utmost to get the right sort of information to 10 Downing Street, but the hostility to Russia finally came to such a point that Maisky, who was a member of the Non-Intervention Committee, where he had conducted himself with the greatest skill and discretion, was not even receiving notices of their meetings. Sir Horace Wilson was in charge of sending out these invitations.

Each of the many reports that Litvinoff received from Maisky was more alarming than the preceding, until in one letter Maisky suggested his own recall, in order to show the British that they could not continue to treat the Russians as Chamberlain had treated them since the peculiar neutrality policy in regard to Spain had been in operation. Litvinoff, unwilling to make such an important decision by himself, went from Geneva to Moscow and conferred on the matter with Stalin, to whom he handed all the reports and notes covering the latter part of

1937 and the first months of 1938. Stalin decided against a break then, so Maisky, who had already started packing, stayed on.

From that time on, however, Litvinoff considered himself in an open fight with Neville Chamberlain. Relations became formal and cold. Chamberlain was by that time too blinded by his prejudices to take warning. He imagined that England did not need the Russians. He counted on doing business with Hitler.

The climax of his anti-Russian attitude and activity was marked by the circulation, among "friends," of "documents" concerning Russia's military strength, supposedly put together by the British Intelligence Service. Sir Robert Vansittart, however, then the unofficial chief of the Intelligence Service, not only was not responsible for them but actually learned of their existence only when he heard that they were being passed about in Chamberlain's circle. He went to the Foreign Office and offered his resignation.

Sir Horace Wilson, it turned out, had supplied these "documents," which he had got directly or indirectly from Ribbentrop, who pretended to have secured them from the Polish secret service. In reality, they had been concocted by a group of anti-Russian Poles in Warsaw. According to the figures that they contained on Russia's military situation, the Soviet Government could no longer be counted a first-class military power, especially since the elimination of Marshal Tukhachevsky and the seven generals (Putna, Yaker, Uborevich, Feldman, Kork, Primakov, and Eudeman) convicted and executed with him—a rumor that gained world circulation and was glibly repeated even by professional soldiers and military "experts" without any effort at corroboration. The whole scheme had been worked up to prove that there was no point in England's allying herself with Soviet Russia to fight Germany. In such a war, the "documents" implied, Russia would be of little or no account, and England might even have to fight it out alone. Obviously, the safe and clever course would be to get Germany to fight Soviet Russia. And this was exactly what Chamberlain now set out to do.

The clique that encouraged the Prime Minister in this project was small. Even in his own Party were men who realized with bewilderment and dismay that Chamberlain's foreign policy had brought them to the brink of an abyss, and this alarm was shared by many who had opposed Soviet Russia in the past, but now saw that Russian and English interests coincided. The strongest and most outspoken in this group was Winston Churchill. A life-long enemy of Communism, he had been an energetic and effective promoter of intervention at the close of World War I, but his lively and honest mind had been bringing him closer to facts. Consequently, he began revising his old animosities in the light of new information and his appreciation of England's need of allies in the face of the German menace, which Churchill from the beginning had correctly gauged. The magnificent rhetorical denunciations with which he had defended his former policies towards the Soviets ceased. He grew increasingly more realistic and more sympathetic, steadily drawing closer to Litvinoff.

Churchill's gradual turn towards certain of Litvinoff's central foreign policies, especially collective security, can be traced in his speeches. For example, on March 19, 1935, he said: "We are bound to act in concert with France and Italy and other powers great and small, who are anxious to preserve the peace. I would not refuse the co-operation of any government which plainly conformed to that test, as long as it was willing to work under the authority and sanction of the League of Nations"—a designation that fitted the Russians perfectly. And again on March 14, 1938, he declared: "What is there ridiculous about collective security? The only thing that is ridiculous about it is that we have not got it"—an indication that collective security was being ridiculed then in the House.

On the other hand, Litvinoff on his side also began to revise his views and find in Churchill, whom he had once considered an implacable enemy, a man that he could profoundly respect and esteem. But in this rapprochement between these two strong men, it was Churchill that moved towards Litvinoff. Litvinoff's position was essentially the same from beginning to end, with a realistic rather than doctrinaire consistency. Churchill, however, was also an emphatic realist and was never a man to be afraid of change. He once said to Sir Arnold Wilson: "To change often enough in the right direction is ultimately to arrive at perfection."

Neither Churchill nor anyone else could divert Chamberlain. The crusade against Soviet Russia had become a fixed idea in his rather narrow mind. The Russians believe that Chamberlain actually pressed

Hitler, both at Godesberg and again in Munich, to start a war against
the Soviet Union, and it was rumored that some of Chamberlain's concessions to Hitler were won only after Hitler agreed to proceed against
Russia—in due course, since he could not possibly begin such a war,
he explained, until the Czechoslovakian Little Maginot Line was in
his possession.

Even if this is only partly true, Chamberlain's policy was largely
responsible for the dismemberment of Czechoslovakia, and for loosing
on the world fearful aggression, just at the time when Litvinoff's long
battle against aggression was being applauded by public opinion in the
very England of which Chamberlain was Prime Minister.

9

In September, 1938, when the Spanish Civil War was in critical
straits, Litvinoff announced his long-established conviction that circumstances had freed Russia from the original non-intervention agreement. His reasons he had given in his speech of November 28, 1936, in
which, with characteristic vigor and forthright speaking, he exposed
the whole shameful farce:

"Weeks followed weeks and the U.S.S.R., France and Britain and
other States loyally and scrupulously fulfilled their obligations [under
the non-intervention agreement], while Germany and Italy, with that
disregard of international honor characteristic of them, secretly continued to supply General Franco with all manner of military and naval
arms, utilizing chiefly the Portuguese vantage ground for this purpose.

"This supply became a matter of common knowledge. It was written
about by the correspondents of foreign newspapers of all political tendencies, not excluding the extreme Right. It was the common talk of
numerous observers and eye-witnesses. Undoubtedly it was also known
to foreign consuls in the respective ports, whose reports, unfortunately,
have not yet been published. Finally, the Spanish Government made
formal representations, both to the League of Nations and in notes to
individual States, regarding the military supplies furnished to General
Franco, which were doubly illegal, both from the point of view of
common law and in view of the existing international agreement.

"The Soviet Government then applied to the London Committee, which we thought had been formed to ensure the observance of their obligations by all the participants of the Agreement and to investigate cases of infringement. However, we were mistaken. The London Committee understood the word 'non-intervention' in the sense that it itself was not to intervene in the intervention in Spanish events. The London Committee understood its task in the sense that it was only to ensure that States which had undertaken definite obligations with regard to the Agreement on Non-Intervention should themselves not acknowledge their infringement, and that, as long as they denied all guilt on their part, their explanations were to be regarded as satisfactory and, this done, the functions of the Committee were at an end.

"Such a decision of the Committee sanctioned in advance all future infringements of obligations on the part of the Fascist States. There remained nothing else for the Soviet Government to do than loyally to inform the London Committee, although it was by no means obliged to do this, that it did not consider itself morally bound by the Agreement to any greater extent than the other participants."

As soon as Russia thus found the non-intervention agreement by tacit consent inoperative, she began sending ammunition, planes, and men to Spain.

A year before (September 21, 1937), speaking to a Plenary Session of the League of Nations, Litvinoff had refuted with hard fact and plain talk a particularly offensive misrepresentation of Russia's participation in the Spanish Civil War, a characteristic concoction of the Fascists which unfortunately had won considerable acceptance among the credulous and misinformed who were always ready to believe anything that reflected adversely on the Soviet Union:

"A few days ago the campaign to justify the aggression in Spain was capped with a new absurdity to the effect that the Soviet Union is intent on the conquest of Spain or, at least, is out to secure political influence over Spain and thereby disturb the equilibrium in the Mediterranean. The truth was spoken here a few days ago by the Spanish Premier, Señor Negrin, who said that, throughout the Spanish conflict, the Soviet Union has requested nothing from Spain, has not tried to get anything and is making no attempt. The Soviet Union has neither mineralogical, economic, nor strategic interests in Spain, nor even interests in the so-called equilibrium. She is interested exclusively in maintaining the right of every people to decide their internal regime for themselves, without the intervention of foreign States, let alone foreign troops, and in preventing the formation of a new base of operations in Spain for aggression against all Europe. Although from the outset the Soviet Government did not recognize and still does not recognize that the sides in the Spanish conflict are of equal status, it nevertheless subscribed to all the agreements of non-intervention and to the proposal that all non-Spanish elements should be withdrawn from the military operations. In concluding an international agreement, the Soviet Government, naturally, has the right to see to it that it is not deceived in such a manner that the obligations, while being adhered to by some, will in practice not be binding on others."

Her supplies and assistance never reached the proportions of the Fascist intervention, but a dishonest press campaign throughout the world attempted to excite further fear by creating the impression of large-scale Communist participation.

The press misrepresentation obscured from all but the well informed the important circumstances that, first, Soviet Russia had had nothing to do with the outbreak of the Spanish struggle, while Italy and Germany were directly guilty; and second and even more significant, that the Russians were supporting a legitimate government, while the others were supporting a rebellion. Thus, ironically, Soviet Russia, which had always been pictured as fomenting revolts and upheavals, played its role in the first test case as the preserver of a legitimate government. This would have shown the other Powers where the world revolution was starting, had they not long since lost their capacity for clear thinking and unbiased analyses of the facts.

Aid to the Spanish Government was far more difficult for Russia than was aid to the revolting generals for the Fascist Powers, for the distance from Russia to Spain was far greater, and there was no direct route. Italy organized a watch of the Dardanelles to detect Russian supply ships bound for Spain. Russia organized a bureau in Moscow solely to devise disguises for freighters loaded with war materials for Spain. They found it reasonably easy to get by the Italian watch-dogs with cargoes of oil, ammunition, and guns, but, as Litvinoff pointed out, it was almost impossible to smuggle airplanes by boat since they showed above deck; and it was too far to fly the smaller combat and pursuit types.

When a number of Russian freighters were sunk by submarines Litvinoff, in the late summer of 1937, sent two sharp notes of protest to Rome, declaring that he had proof of Italian responsibility. The sinkings stopped abruptly.

At the same time British ships, also, were being attacked and sunk in the Mediterranean, and finally England and France were simply forced to take a stand. After a short but lively conference at Nyon, near Geneva, in September, 1937, they decided that they would maintain a naval patrol in the Mediterranean. The diplomatic phrase "unknown submarines" was used in describing the problem, but everyone knew that they were under Italian command, and British Naval Intelligence knew the names of some of the vessels and their officers. When Mussolini was invited to join the patrol, he declined. In a ringing speech Anthony Eden, who deserves the chief credit for the success of the conference, denounced the sinkings as plain piracy and declared that "the perpetrators would now meet the fate they so richly deserved."

The sinkings again stopped abruptly, the "unknown" submarines, thus warned, had vanished rather than run the risk of being attacked and sunk in turn—a demonstration, first, of what might be expected of the Italian Navy in a real war; and second, that the Fascists, deaf as they were to legal or ethical principle, did understand the language of force.

Yet, despite this, the British and French Governments still had not identified the Fascists as their real enemies, and so they used the very patrol boats that were there to protect their own ships against the Fascists, to betray to the Fascists their only effectively active opponents, the Russians and the Spanish Government, for in at least five different cases the British and French patrol reported to the Fascist Franco, ally of Hitler and Mussolini, the passage of Russian boats with supplies for the Spanish Loyalists.

The year 1937 had seen important victories for the Loyalists in spite of the superior military strength of Franco and his Fascist allies. That the sympathies of the majority of the Spanish people lay with the Loyalist Government there could not be the slightest doubt. But neither this nor the obvious importance for the democratic nations of a demo-

cratic Spain in the coming war against totalitarian aggressors made
any appeal to the governments in London and Paris. Chamberlain in
particular hoped for a victory for Franco and his Fascist allies and
could see no reason or profit in making any effort or assuming any
risks in behalf of the legitimate Spanish Government. Only one timid
step was taken in this direction, an Anglo-Italian pact signed in April,
1938, in which the withdrawal of Italian troops from Spain was agreed
upon—after the victory of Franco.

In 1938 Franco's superior arms and the numerical strength of his
imported troops began to tell. It was now obvious that the Loyalists
would not be able to hold out indefinitely without decisive outside
help. By that time the French Socialist, Léon Blum, who had been
largely responsible for the original non-intervention arrangement, was
in despair. He saw and admitted the fatal error he had been forced
into by the threat of Fascist revolt in France as well as by pressure
from Britain. But it was too late.

In December Franco started an all-out offensive along the Ebro
front with about 300,000 men and huge quantities of imported war
matériel. On January 26, 1939, Barcelona was captured and Catalonia
was in Franco's hands. It was then that a great number of quarrels
and "basic discussions" broke out among the Loyalists; political factions and parties made demands, asking more power for their own
representatives or no power at all for the representatives of other parties. The Communists have been blamed for that gloomy intermezzo
and the subsequent defeat of the Loyalist cause. A number of Spanish
Communists and some representatives of the Comintern undoubtedly
played an important role in these quarrels, but they were by no means
the only ones, and it is not true that this splitting up of the Loyalists
was the direct cause of their defeat. The quarrels came at a moment
when the Loyalists were already defeated by the Fascist Powers with
the silent but indispensable help of the non-intervening democracies.

On February 27, 1939, Great Britain and France recognized Franco.
One month later the last Franco offensive started. Madrid surrendered,
and on March 28 the war was over and the cruel aftermath of imprisonment and wholesale executions began. Franco was a merciless as
well as a short-sighted victor. Promptly on April 2 the United States
also recognized the Franco regime.

The Fascists had won what Litvinoff had early recognized as their first attempt to install Fascism in a European State by alien force. The first round went to Hitler and Mussolini, and in Litvinoff's mind it was only a question of time when the main battle—the crusade against Soviet Russia—would begin. After the Spanish Civil War, Soviet Russia was not only the Communist danger in the eyes of Hitler and Mussolini; it also represented the democratic idea. For unlike the Western democracies, Russia and Russia alone had defended the cause of the majority—that is, the democratic cause in Spain. Litvinoff had prophesied aright when he exclaimed, in November, 1936, in his speech before the Eighth Congress of Soviets:

". . . We are taking the banner of democracy, the banner of liberty, which is falling from the feeble hands" of democracy in Europe and "becoming the bulwark of democracy and freedom."

This was precisely what happened. But the collapse of European democracy meant that Soviet Russia stood alone.

10

The European democracies, in permitting Fascism to triumph in Spain, demonstrated their irresolution and abandonment of principle, and Hitler was hurrying his preparations to take advantage of these infirmities.

In March, 1938, came the Austrian invasion and Anschluss—the annexation of the entire country. France at that moment was passing through another of her recurring political crises, which at repeated intervals deprived her of any government that could act, but it is doubtful that any faction in France with power would have wanted to intervene, anyway. Chamberlain, who had dismissed Anthony Eden from his post as Foreign Minister primarily because Eden was convinced that Hitler should be stopped at once, sent Lord Halifax to Berlin, partly to assure Hitler that England had no interest in Austria. Mussolini, who four years earlier had sent his troops to the Brenner Pass to prevent the first German attempt to seize Austria, had now definitely gone over to Hitler.

Litvinoff, alarmed by Austria's fall, denounced Chamberlain as responsible, and also was extremely skeptical about the future security of Czechoslovakia, which Hitler had guaranteed on the very day he marched into Austria.

On March 23, twelve days after the first Nazi troops had crossed the Austrian border, Litvinoff outlined the immediate future of Europe and subsequent events have proved that once more he was amazingly correct. He said, in off-the-record conversations: that Hitler would attack Czechoslovakia during the summer of 1938; Czechoslovakia would finally give in because it could no longer have confidence in France; a few days earlier he had predicted that this would be the beginning of the end of France. Perhaps his prescience of the doom of France had come at least in part from Barthou, for he also had foreseen it with despairing finality: "Everything has degenerated in France, our conception of the State, of public duty, of Parliament, of our institutions. We have reached the place where we do not know what to do about it all. We cannot act any more . . . the Parliamentary régime is through in France, and the nation itself is lost." *

Litvinoff also predicted that the small countries—Hungary, Rumania, Bulgaria, Yugoslavia—would become more and more panic-stricken and willing to go to any lengths to please Hitler; the League of Nations was dead and would revive only if Great Britain changed her policy; Great Britain, far from changing her policy, would make an arrangement with Germany and Italy; the whole of Europe would be dominated by Fascism, with only Great Britain and Soviet Russia opposing; Italy would in the end desert Germany; and Soviet Russia must plan to be independent.†

In May, 1938, Hitler tried for Czechoslovakia, but had to retreat when that brave little country mobilized. The next attack was prepared more thoroughly. By the fall of 1938 the French Foreign Minister, Georges Bonnet, was playing Hitler's game. Chamberlain made his trips to Berchtesgaden and Godesberg. Then came the fatal accord of Munich.

How fatal, most of the world knew, but not the complacent, short-sighted author of this fast-spreading disaster. On December 13, 1938, Chamberlain said that he was astonished at the pessimism "which seems

---

* G. Tabouis, *op. cit.,* p. 200.
† Joseph E. Davies, *op. cit.,* pp. 290-291, 295, 301.

to possess some of our critics" and in summing up the disastrous year of 1938 in his New Year's message, he declared with fatuous optimism, "No one would have dared to prophesy that the four great European nations would have advanced so far along the road to conciliation." * It is worth noting that Chamberlain did not include Russia as one of the great European nations. It marked the end of an epoch.

It marked the end of Czechoslovakia. 1938 was the end, too, of Litvinoff's attempts to establish collective security. He went back to Moscow. From Moscow, refusing as always to be defeated by defeats, he tried to save any bits or fragments of the collective security plan that he might gather up and patch together. He undertook to work out other pacts, agreements, and treaties; but he succeeded in nothing. Even a Black Sea pact, which was to bring together Rumania, Bulgaria, Turkey, and the Soviet Union collapsed while still in the stage of preparation. On March 19, 1939, he emerged one last time, when he refused, in a note to the Reich, to recognize the partition of Czechoslovakia and the annexation of considerable territories by Germany. On the same day he attended a party in the Italian Embassy at Moscow, the first time that he had ever accepted an invitation of Ambassador Rossi's. On April 1 he signed the extension of the fishery agreement with the Japanese.

This was his last official act as Commissar for Foreign Affairs. On May 3, 1939, he resigned. Throughout the chancelleries of Europe it was agreed that Litvinoff was finished; speculation turned chiefly on his personal survival. Edouard Herriot said solemnly: "The last great friend of collective security is gone."

* Dalton, *Hitler's War* (Penguin, London), 1940, p. 86. The Munich accord.

CHAPTER FOURTEEN

Back at Work

LITVINOFF DID indeed seem to be gone. The Moscow papers explained that he had had to resign because struggles with the Czarist police forty years before had undermined his health, but nobody outside Russia believed that. The consensus abroad was that he had fallen into disgrace, that he would be thrown out of the Party, that there would be a purge trial, that he would either be shot or exiled to Siberia. Then when Litvinoff had not made an official appearance for some time, it was rumored in the Western countries that he had been liquidated. In any case, the world was certain that it would never hear of Litvinoff again.

But the full story of Litvinoff's resignation, hitherto untold, is simpler, more reasonable, and less sensational. Litvinoff's foreign policy was a logical outcome of the general Soviet Russian situation and it was as exclusively devised to serve the needs of Soviet Russia as were the Five-Year Plans. Stalin had been in close contact with Litvinoff and knew and approved everything he planned and did. When they differed in policy, Litvinoff would talk the matter over with Stalin and in many cases brought him over to his view. Stalin used to say to Litvinoff: "You know best. You are sitting at the window looking out."

Litvinoff knew best. He foresaw that with Chamberlain maneuvering to embroil Hitler in a war against Soviet Russia, the Soviet Government would sooner or later—and probably sooner—have either to seek an understanding with Germany, or else be the victim. That there was no real alternative Litvinoff had been aware of for some time. In January he had said good-by to Madame Tabouis and explained: "I have spent a lot of time, as you know, in trying to convince my country that it must base its policies upon those of Paris and London, but Moscow now realizes perfectly well that there is little it can count on from the British and French, unless it is the policy expressed by the Paris press," and he showed her a copy of *Le Matin* with an article on the front page advocating protection for France by turning Germany towards expansion at the expense of Russia; * and a year before, admitting flatly the failure of his own policy of collective security, he had made clear that if Russia was not going to be badly burned fishing British and French chestnuts out of the fire, which their own responsible officials were constantly stoking, she would have to retreat into isolationism.†

Litvinoff himself took to Moscow from Geneva proof that Chamberlain was inciting Hitler to a crusade against the Soviets. During the last negotiations of the Czech Government immediately preceding Munich there had been constant Cabinet meetings with violent debates, so violent that even, according to well-supported reports, a shot was fired (by a bodyguard of Beneš) and a Cabinet Minister of the Agrarian Party was killed. Moreover, the French and British Ambassadors in Prague exercised virtual blackmail against Czechoslovakia, not only by threatening to leave her undefended if Beneš would not comply with the wishes of Hitler (see p. 25), but also, instructed by Chamberlain, by again informing Beneš that if he refused the terms, Britain and France would join Germany in military sanctions against Czechoslovakia, to enforce the decision reached in Munich.

Litvinoff heard about this last, almost unbelievable, threat that decided Beneš to give in, and it convinced him—if he was not convinced already—that Chamberlain meant business, that Czechoslovakia was to be sacrificed because Hitler wanted it and that the last barrier against Hitler's assault on Soviet Russia was down. The only hope was to attempt a rapprochement with Hitler. Litvinoff knew that there was no place for him in a policy of collaboration with the Nazis. Even if it had been technically possible for a man who had constantly opposed Hitler to direct such a policy—which it was not—his retention in power would have been a sign to Hitler that such a policy was only a temporary expedient. Litvinoff had to go. And it was Litvinoff himself who suggested it. He knew that he was a burden now rather than an asset. He was a realist to the last.

* G. Tabouis, *op. cit.*, p. 386.
† John T. Whitaker, *op. cit.*, p. 268.

Furthermore, no time was now to be lost. Litvinoff told Stalin after his return from Geneva that the elimination of the Czech fortifications meant the loss of one of Russia's main defenses. He also predicted that Hitler would scrap the Munich agreement and march into Prague.

The resignation itself occurred in a conference room in the former Palace of Catherine in the Kremlin. There was no scene, nothing theatrical, only a conference, or rather the last in a series of long conferences. Litvinoff himself suggested his friend, Prime Minister Molotov, as his successor.

2

Owing to his resignation, Litvinoff took no part in negotiating the agreements of August, 1939, with Germany: the commercial agreement, the non-aggression pact, or any other informal understandings that may then have been effected. Nor did he have any part in the negotiations preceding or after the war with Finland. But these were vital elements in Soviet foreign policy, and the situations they created had important results that were certain to complicate and impede Litvinoff's tasks when he should return to active duty.

Both developments aroused bitter and long-persisting resentment in the Western democracies, where little effort was made to understand the point of view of the Russians, or the imperatives that dictated their course—in each case self-preservation, that motive supremely powerful in the life of nations as well as of individuals. For Soviet Russia saw her national existence in peril from the ruthless ambitions of Hitler and his Nazi hierarchy that had for years been both preaching a holy crusade against Russia and dwelling with lustful anticipation on the delectable prospect of the seizure of Soviet lands and resources which Hitler well knew would make him invincible in Europe. Hitler was convinced, and not without reason, that he needed only the control of Russian agricultural and mineral wealth and vast manpower ultimately to become master of the world. In possession of such a central land mass, truly the heartland, with all that that implies, a European blockade would mean little. The boasted resources of the British Empire plus even those of America would be less in quantity and far less concentrated. With Russia conquered and forced into real collaboration, Germany would acquire the oil resources of Baku, Persia, and Iraq and could, joined with Japan, attack India.

The prize was prodigious and to the Nazi mentality irresistible. Legal or political inhibitions were inoperative—ethical scruples, non-existent. Hitler had at his disposal a military machine of a devastating power unprecedented in history. The offensive against Russia had been the subject of border intrigues for years, as well as much detailed military planning. In 1935 Colonel Henry of the German General Staff won a military prize for detailing the best method for an overwhelming assault on Russia that would guarantee quick victory—a plan which called promptly for a swift attack through the vulnerable Leningrad area, Russia's heel of Achilles.

Russia had seen her first great outer defense, the State of Czechoslovakia, with its formidable fortifications, fall—thanks to the cowardice, confusion, and faithlessness of the democratic nations. Hitler was now pressing Poland with fury, just as he had pressed Austria. The result could not be in doubt. Russia was not ready for war with Germany. She might have been able to defend herself; in an equal battle with Germany she was confident of victory. But now Czechoslovakia had fallen; Austria was part of Germany; Hungary, Bulgaria, and Finland were moving in Germany's orbit. This was more than Russia had counted on, and she was not fully confident of her ability successfully to withstand the threatened onslaught.

Once more, therefore, she was ready to co-operate with the Western Powers, to try again some form of collective security or concerted action against the aggressor. But while she was willing, even anxious, to conclude a mutual defense pact with Great Britain and France, she could not but be doubtful of them both, and especially distrustful of their reactionary governments, for she knew only too well what bitter hatred they and the groups they represented had felt for the Soviet regime from its very beginning. How could she forget their destructive military intervention, when the new government was young and weak? How overlook their steady diplomatic offensive relentlessly maintained for years? Was it not these very Powers which had taken the lead in frustrating at nearly every turn Litvinoff's program for collective security? And had they not, despite protestations to the contrary, furtively persisted in devitalizing the League?

Russia knew she must try to work with these governments, but the needed mutual confidence was lacking. Russia had not forgotten their long consistent policy of retreat, appeasement, and surrender, from the invasion of Manchukuo on; how could she having so recently listened to their half-hearted protests against Mussolini's murderous invasion of Abyssinia, and the cruel hypocrisy of the shocking betrayal of Spain into the hands of the Nazi-Fascist group—a betrayal the more odious because of the accompanying pious protestations of non-intervention?

What faith could she have in the English Tories who had put such pressure on Blum and the Popular Front in France? What reliance on the men who had abandoned Czechoslovakia to the enemy despite pledges, insulting Russia at the same time by excluding her from the conferences in disregard of her vital interests and the treaty obligations that by international law required her participation? Nor were the Russians unmindful that Litvinoff's proposal on March 20, 1939—one of Litvinoff's last official acts—of a joint conference of Great Britain, France, Poland, Turkey, Rumania, and Russia, had been rejected under British leadership.

No, Russia could not confer with these politicians with any bright optimism. She knew that Lord Halifax and others high in the Conservative Party were still hostile, that Neville Chamberlain hoped she would be embroiled in war with the Nazis.

Conferences for a mutual defense pact could hardly have been undertaken under less propitious circumstances. Only the dangerous situation of the three nations and their need to co-operate for elemental safety offered any ground for hope.

Given the unfavorable prior conditions and the immediacy of the danger to be averted, mutual consideration and deference were essential. But when Ambassador Maisky made the reasonable request that a diplomat of major status be sent to Russia, with power to negotiate, Lord Halifax promised to take the matter under consideration, but nothing was done. Chamberlain had found time to go to Rome, apparently to congratulate Mussolini on his newly acquired African empire and, as Lloyd George charged, to promise him a free hand in Spain. To Moscow, however, he could send only William Strang, an able and conscientious man, but only a secondary Foreign Office official; he arrived after the negotiations had begun and, moreover, was without power to settle anything. Obviously, the Russians could only conclude that Chamberlain did not consider them a first-class power, or else—as they suspected—he was not overanxious that the negotiations succeed. As early as May, it was charged that it was "political snobbery" that was at the bottom of the Government's inability to come to terms with the Russians.* Again on July 23 it was charged "that the Prime Minister and Lord Halifax were responsible for the delay because of their passive attitude." (*Sunday Express,* July 23.) And finally Lloyd George stated flatly in an article in *Le Soir:* "Neville Chamberlain, Halifax and John Simon do not want any agreement with Russia." †

Furthermore, during the dreary, four-month-long struggle to reach a conclusion, it was repeatedly evident that the British really were not eager to come to an agreement. For instance, while British proposals in the course of the discussion were promptly answered the very next day by the Russians, the British replies to Russian counter-proposals took, on an average, eleven days—a dilatoriness that aroused such suspicion in Great Britain that Hugh Dalton in the House of Commons on June 12 asked: "Does the Prime Minister not realize that these long delays in reaching an agreement with the Soviet Government are causing disquiet in this country and causing doubt whether His Majesty's Government really means business at all?" And when Mr. Adams asked the Prime Minister if "the completion of a general alliance against aggression is not being subordinated to any other purpose," Chamberlain would not answer.

Some of the Conservatives were equally bitter in their condemnation of the way in which the British Government had managed the negotiations. As one of these said, "The whole story is one of muddle, bungle and blunder without parallel; and fits in well enough with the rest of the policy which has landed us, over a period of five years, from a position of absolute security into one of mortal peril." ‡

Equally symptomatic was the niggardliness of the British concessions. Indeed, Strang once cabled Chamberlain, according to a report from highly credible sources, that his concessions were "wholly inadequate." Thus, though England had guaranteed the neutrality of Belgium and

* David J. Dallin, *Soviet Foreign Policy,* 1939–42, p. 33.
† Stanley J. Marks, *The Bear That Walks Like a Man,* pp. 75-87.
‡ Hugh Dalton, *op. cit.*

Holland without their consent, Chamberlain rejected a parallel guarantee of the Baltic States, without their consent, against aggression—
a refusal assailed by Winston Churchill, who stated that: "The Russian claims that they [the Baltic States] should be included in the
triple guarantee is well founded. It is certain that if Lithuania, Latvia
or Esthonia were invaded by the Nazis or subverted to the Nazi system by propaganda and intrigue from within, the whole of Europe
would be dragged into war. Why not then concert in good time, publicly and courageously, the measures which may render such a fight
unnecessary?" *

Again, the Anglo-French military mission, in an hour of great peril
where minutes counted, came by a leisurely six-day sea trip, when
they might have arrived by plane in twelve hours; when they finally
got there, they had no power to conclude any agreement, could only
sign a convention to which the French Government reserved its approval. The realistic Russians insisted that Hitler would not be de-
terred by any amount of resolutions or paper pacts, but only by absolute certainty that prompt action would follow aggression, and their
suspicions were sharply provoked when the mission asked for military
secrets, for the Russians knew that that information would be made
available to men like Sir Horace Wilson and Bonnet who hated the
Soviet Union and were eager for co-operation with Nazi Germany.

Other incidents increased Soviet distrust. Dallin has reported one of
the most serious of these as follows: "During the third week of July
Dr. Wohltat—Hitler's best economic negotiator—arrived in London, to confer on economic problems of secondary importance with
Robert Hudson, the Secretary of the Department of Overseas Trade.
He also met frequently with Sir Horace Wilson, Chamberlain's most
trusted confidant. In these conferences a plan of a general settlement of
European problems was discussed; part of this plan was a British loan
of a billion pounds sterling to Germany . . ." †

A denial of negotiations by the British government and Chamberlain's thin and labored explanation convinced no one and the more intemperate denials from German sources were even more dubious. Russia took notice. It was also significant in this connection that Poland's

* Cf. *Morning Post,* June 8.
† Dallin, *op. cit.,* pp. 47-48.

frantic appeal for a loan of £25,000,000 for armament had been denied by Chamberlain.

At the same time the Russians were aware that the French Fascist press was repeating the same kind of arguments that they had used for the betrayal of Czechoslovakia, and were insisting that neither Poland nor Danzig was worth fighting for. Other incidents increased Russian suspicion of the complete sincerity of the Anglo-French proposals.

Acting under British pressure, despite protests from many sides, the Bank of International Settlements paid over to the Nazis $30,000,000 in gold which had been deposited by the Czech Government, Chamberlain defending the transaction on the abstract and dubious legal ground that Czechoslovakia was now German territory, although the Nazis had no more than a bandit's title to it.

Nor did the Russians relish the transaction by means of which the British Government lent Czechoslovakia £8,000,000 which was used to buy out French interest in the Skoda Works, thus making the Skoda Works entirely state property and thus simplifying Germany's seizure of it when she was ready to move in.

In contrast to these maneuvers, Litvinoff in one of his last formal acts as Minister of Foreign Affairs notified the German Government on March 18, 1939, that Russia would not recognize Germany's seizure of those parts of Czechoslovakia that had not been covered by the Munich agreement.

Chamberlain's trend toward a quite un-British personal government also disturbed Russian observers. For Chamberlain had discarded the advice of his legally appointed advisers; he had starved some of the magnificent intelligence services and at the same time paid little attention to the reports that he got. Nor did he really trust Parliament; in fact, it was reluctantly and only under pressure that he agreed to summon Parliament during August, 1939, in case of some great emergency.

All these facts combined with Chamberlain's known hostility, his constant yielding to German pressure, convinced the Russians that there was little hope for a satisfactory treaty arrangement. They felt that Chamberlain had been forced against his will by threatening circumstances and by the declared wish of the British people to undertake negotiations for, in March, 1939, a Gallup poll showed 92 per cent of the British Electorate convinced of the necessity of an immediate alliance with Russia. Then in July, when it seemed as if Germany might be backing down a bit, the Russians thought they saw signs that Chamberlain hoped altogether to avoid coming to an agreement with them.

The perplexities and difficulties which Chamberlain faced were real enough; it had been urged that a pact with Russia would alienate certain of the neutral nations, displease the Vatican, would be taken by some as justifying the anti-Comintern pact, would anger the British die-hards and the reactionaries in the French government as well and, finally, Chamberlain was apparently still hoping to make some arrangement with Germany, a hope which would be quite ruined by an alliance with Russia. There was no difficulty to think up other sundry objections. It is a characteristic of small men in great crises that they are prolific in thinking up reasons for doing nothing and inventorying difficulties that even in total are trifling compared to the more massive but remote danger. It is too soon to make a precise estimate of Chamberlain's complex intentions regarding Russia and speculation now is not profitable; but there is unpublished evidence that Chamberlain's intentions toward Russia were hostile—evidence known to the Russians and sufficient to arouse their suspicions and to induce them to raise the price of their assent to a treaty even after negotiations started.

Adding one thing to another, the Russians could only conclude that England was not offering them anything substantial except an opportunity to bear the full brunt of a terrible war with Germany, which they knew perfectly well would be at a hideous cost, leaving them with ruined provinces, wrecked cities, mountains of dead, and a perilous dislocation of their economic structure.

The Poles throughout had been recalcitrant, and the Russians suspected—without proof—that Britain was encouraging them in a stubborn rejection of Russia's offer to defend them against German aggression and send their army through Poland for that purpose. But Poland was suffering from a super-heated nationalism, proclaiming that they were not like the Czechs to give in without a fight; that they could, even on their own, defeat Germany. They had been recently even talking about colonies. Perhaps with some reason they feared that if Soviet armies entered Poland, even for its defense, the eastern part of Poland might be lost for good. The population of the region was predominantly Russian, and Lord Curzon, acting in behalf of the Supreme Allied Council, had prudently assigned that section of the country to the Russians. Poland seemed ready to risk German conquest and all its inevitable horrors rather than risk the loss of territory —to which Poland had ambiguous title—to the Russians. Poland's attitude seemed to the Russians unreasonable, unrealistic, and one more evidence that she would have to go it alone.

When Voroshilov was faced with the Polish refusal to allow Russian troops to enter Poland even in her own defense against the German onslaughts, he left the conference in a rage, for he had skillfully planned in full detail a promising two-pronged offensive that might have had important consequences.

According to a credibly sponsored story, Stalin got another proof of Chamberlain's plot to foment war between Germany and Russia from Ribbentrop when he arrived in Moscow in the summer of 1939; throughout Chamberlain's interview with Hitler in Godesberg, hidden microphones recorded every word Chamberlain uttered. Some reports say it was a conversation between Nevile Henderson and Hitler that was reproduced. Ribbentrop brought the series of disks with him, and they were played for Stalin, who made sure that the voices were those of Hitler and Chamberlain, and then had his interpreter translate the conversation. It contained suggestions from Chamberlain that Germany wage war against Soviet Russia. After hearing this, Stalin decided to accept Ribbentrop's offer.

Litvinoff has recently said that he had not known about the incident, but it would have occurred three months after his resignation, and he thought it possible and even plausible; it would be in full accord with what he had known about Chamberlain's intentions and plans and a proof that the Soviet Union had had to act quickly to counteract this conspiracy, as he had warned Stalin upon his return from Geneva.

The Russians thought that if they could secure time they could prepare an adequate defense. They had the resources, the system of training, the industries, the manpower. But if there was to be a war, they were sure that every day of delay would increase their chance of victory. So as the negotiations with the British and French dragged their dreary way, finally to bog down completely, the Soviets began considering what kind of arrangement they could make with the

Germans to buy a little precious time. They had already indicated that they might have to do this, and the democratic statesmen had no excuse for the astonishment they pretended when the Russians finally came to an agreement with the Germans. The famous speech of Stalin on March 9 published all over the world made it clear that the Russians would not be maneuvered into the position of fighting somebody else's battles or pulling anyone else's chestnuts out of the fire. They would fight for international security, and for their own existence if those were the clear objectives.

Robert Coulondre, the French Ambassador to Berlin, from the first continuously and emphatically warned his government and through it presumably Great Britain that unless the Allies came to an agreement with the Russians, there was grave danger that the Russians would make some kind of arrangement with the Germans, but Chamberlain continued in his strange optimism.

The resignation of Litvinoff on May 3 was fair warning that the Soviets were doubtful of the possibility of any collective security guarantees with the French and English governments. It obviously paved the way to a rapprochement with Germany, to whom Litvinoff was an utter bête noir. Even when they announced the negotiations for a commercial treaty with Germany, even then if the British and French had taken this last clear hint and final notification and if Chamberlain had flown to Moscow, as readily as he did to the feet of Hitler, an agreement would have been possible and the war might have been averted.

Stalin had not made overtures to the Nazis though he had plainly indicated that he might have to. It was the Nazis who suggested to Soviet Russia a pact of friendship and non-aggression. This, too, Litvinoff had foreseen: "When the Germans are prepared at last to embark upon their new adventures, these bandits will come to Moscow to ask us for a pact," he had said at the end of 1937.*

The British and French had failed because they had too little to offer, they had broken the faith too often to be fully trusted now. What proof did Stalin have, what proof could the reactionary governments of Britain and France give him that their long and vindictive hostility was in a twinkling of an eye turned into good will, confidence

* John T. Whitaker, *op. cit.*, p. 268.

and fidelity? What proof could they give that they would not, as circumstances might change, revert to their old hostility and in a pinch leave Russia in the lurch?

Russia had one final hope, that if she refused this military convention with England and France, and if she made a non-aggression pact with Germany, the war might be localized between Germany and Poland, and Europe be spared the holocaust. She did not believe that England and France would stand by Poland any more than they had stood by Czechoslovakia. Here Russia made a serious miscalculation, but her motivation ought not to be overlooked. Subsequent events gave support to Russian suspicion of England and France: they did little or nothing to impede the destruction of Poland; yet Gamelin told Edwin Murrow that for him the Siegfried Line was only "marshmallows." Had a swift and determined assault been made through to the Ruhr, part of which at one time was within French artillery range, the diversion might have helped Poland and averted the later disastrous offensive through the Ardennes Forest.

Whatever the possibilities of some kind of second front were during 1941 and 1942, a front was not made. This again confirmed the Soviets' previous misgiving that had they concluded a military pact with France and England in 1939 they might, in the hour of their desperation, have been met with the excuses that proposals for a second front were "premature" and that it could not be set up at the moment, whatever Russia's own necessities might require.

The Russo-German agreement was the product of dire necessities, the bitter fruit of twenty years of misunderstandings, suspicions, and conflict which neither the urgency of the moment nor mutual interest could fully overcome. In the preceding negotiations with the representatives of the Allied powers there were many reasons to distrust the complete sincerity of the British and French governments. In any case, the pact was promptly denounced in the Western world as a monstrous betrayal by Stalin. The Russians were wildly charged with double-dealing; they were accused of having enticed the French and English into negotiations for the purpose of extracting their military secrets, which is just what some Russians equally unfairly charged against the French and British. They were accused with gleefully touching off the war so that the rest of the world might exhaust themselves in bloody conflict, leaving an undamaged Russia to take possession of the ruins and re-create a state in her own image. Such fancies are the result of misunderstanding, of long, lingering hostility and the human necessity of always shifting blame to some scapegoat.

But there have been a few sane observers who saw clearly what had happened, and the more detached judgment of history is sure to set the whole situation in better perspective. As John Whitaker says, it was really "the failure of the democracies to cooperate with Soviet Russia that had forced this mighty people to turn to isolationism and a pact with Nazi Germany." *

Of American political writers, Walter Lippmann gave the soundest summary: "Stalin did not join the Franco-British Alliance, because he believed, correctly enough, that Russia would receive the brunt of the attack, and because he feared, not without some justification, that the western powers might be tempted to let the war become an anti-communist crusade. He made his agreement with Germany in order to avoid having to fight Germany, and out of the partnership he got at no cost all the best strategic frontier which it is possible for Russia to have. . . . " †

Sir Bernard Pares, following an astute and realistic discussion of the whole situation, concludes: "there was no alliance; the actions of the two partners to the pact were parallel and often rival." ‡

The presence of a German delegation in Moscow once more stimulated rumors concerning Litvinoff's resignation. It was suggested that he had been forced to resign because he was a Jew, the implication being that Stalin shortly would turn anti-Semitic.

There was no foundation for such rumors. On the contrary, not even while the German delegation was in Moscow did Stalin make any concessions on the racial question. It would have been counter to his deepest convictions and out of accord with provisions in the Soviet Constitution, for which he was principally responsible. Lazar Kaganovich, Commissar of Railways, who is Jewish, did not appear at the State banquet in honor of Ribbentrop; but it was Kaganovich himself who declined to go, not Stalin who requested it; and another Jewish

---

* John T. Whitaker, *op. cit.*, p. 300.

† Quoted by Stanley J. Marks, *op. cit.*, p. 76.

‡ Sir Bernard Pares, *Russia*, Penguin, N. Y., p. 216. For a fuller and very revealing account cf. Marks, *op. cit.*, and Dallin, *op. cit.*

member of the Government, Solomon Lozovsky, Vice Commissar of Foreign Affairs, not only appeared at the banquet, but was seated next to Ribbentrop, while on the other side of the German Foreign Minister sat the famous prosecutor, André Vishinsky, who had sent to their death hundreds of men convicted of being German spies.

The German Ambassador, Count von der Schulenburg, and the German Trade Representative, Schnurre, old diplomats who were far from being sympathetic with the Nazi regime, saw at once the play behind this seating arrangement and were immensely amused. Ribbentrop was not amused.

Schulenburg had hoped for real peace between Germany and Russia, and the signing of the pact should have marked his moment of triumph; but he is reported on good authority to have said to a member of the French Embassy: "Why don't they shoot Litvinoff? I have no confidence in a Russian-German pact so long as the Russians have got Litvinoff up their sleeve." Schulenburg was one of the few who understood the real situation. As one correspondent afterwards phrased it, Litvinoff had simply "been carefully wrapped up and kept on ice for another day." *

When the pact was signed, a very dramatic film, "The Fatherland Calls," had been running for some time in Russia, depicting a possible war between Germany and Russia, presenting Stalin and Voroshilov and demonstrating to the Russian people with vivid power the ever-threatening menace from Germany. Immediately the agreement was concluded, the film was suppressed in the great western cities and hence presumably throughout Russia. Did Schulenburg know that by orders from Moscow it was still regularly shown in the factories of Siberia? And that the Party line throughout Russia continued to be: "Germany is our real enemy . . . Prepare . . . "? No wonder that German captains putting in at Archangel complained that they were treated as enemies. The outbreak of the Russo-German War was a disaster for Schulenburg. He did not return to Germany, but went to Stockholm, where he has been living since.

On August 22, the Soviet-Nazi Pact was made public. In the early hours of September 1, German troops crossed the Polish frontier. The World War II had begun. On September 5 the Polish Government

* H. C. Cassidy, *Moscow Dateline*, p. 64, New York, 1943.

folded up and vanished, leaving no directive to the people. Poland was a country without a government—a highly dangerous situation right on Russia's frontiers, involving approximately 4,000,000 Russians. It was a situation which Russia had foreseen and which she could not possibly ignore. On September 17, when it was obvious that Polish resistance was only a matter of weeks, Russia marched into Poland without encountering opposition, thus setting a barrier to German expansion in the East as well as to the Southeast. The pact was already beginning to have unpleasant consequences for the Nazis. On September 28 Germany and Russia agreed on the location of their lines and defined the regions each controlled in Poland; Russia also made arrangements with Esthonia and Latvia by which she gained naval bases in the Baltic.

All these moves were devised to protect Soviet Russia as much as possible against the eventual Nazi attack.

The Narkomindel had always believed, with good reason, that Germany would attack the Soviet Union through Poland and Finland. A surprise attack by way of Poland had been prevented by the Russian annexation of part of Poland. The Finnish threat, however, loomed larger than ever. Russia knew of the intrigues in Finland and the definite plans that Germany had made for an attack on the vital Leningrad area via Finland. Hence she felt it imperative to take measures of defense and accordingly proposed to Finland cession of territories that would remove the Finnish frontier—then within 20 miles of Leningrad—considerably farther back. The cession of territory was to be compensated for by double the area in the Karelian lands in the north. Russia also asked for a lease of islands in the Gulf of Finland for defensive fortifications. For these also Russia was ready to give compensation. An agreement was almost reached, but the Finnish statesmen finally refused to yield. Russia, aware of the close contacts between Mannerheim and Nazi generals and knowing how vulnerable she was in that area and that war with Germany was inevitable, felt that, in the interest of national safety, she must act. Accordingly, on November 29, justifying herself by a quite flimsy pretext, she invaded Finland.

The world in general knew little about the Fascist element in Finland and were not aware that Mannerheim, a Swede who had been a Czarist general and had a fearful record for cruelty, was, with others of the military clique, collaborating with Hitler. Mannerheim later proclaimed that it was a great honor to fight by his side. At the time, however, the public at large in the Western nations was quite ignorant of the peril to Russia, which the ambiguities of Finnish policy concealed. All who had hated and feared Russia saw in the conflict a chance to gratify old grudges. Finland had a very plausible case and Finland was the under-dog; Russia's case was badly mismanaged. Hence it was not surprising that foreign opinion was overwhelmingly and enthusiastically on the side of the Finns, who were thus able to score a real propaganda triumph, though facts finally set it at naught. The whole Finnish episode has to be seen in the light of its previous as well as subsequent history.

When Finland complained about this attack in Geneva, the League of Nations, which had done little or nothing about the Japanese aggression, and nothing at all effective about Italy's assault on Ethiopia, or about numerous other acts of aggression, promptly expelled the Soviet Union on December 14, 1939. Litvinoff's own definition of the aggressor was invoked against Russia—the only occasion on which the League of Nations made use of the definition.

There were other serious aspects of the Finnish-Russian War that have not been sufficiently stressed. When in early February the Finns were plainly facing a complete defeat, the French and British governments begged them to keep up the fight. They offered to send immediately 30,000 soldiers and to follow them up with a much larger detachment, and also to land on three places on the Scandinavian coast and march across Norway and Sweden. On February 25, within a few days of the Finnish collapse (the peace was signed on March 12) the Allies again officially promised military aid if Finland would ask for it, and Daladier stated: "We have been awaiting a call from Finland to come to her aid with all the means and resources at our disposal," and again: "Aviation units and expeditionary forces stand in readiness to depart for the Finnish front." Even Léon Blum urged that expeditionary forces be sent to Finland via Norway and Sweden, despite the objections of the latter country that it meant forcibly violating their neutrality.

Not only did England and France agree to send military aid directly to Finland, but arrangements were made to attack Russia in the south.

Gamelin worked out in detail a plan for the bombardment of the oil fields of Baku and Batum, which was to be a joint operation of English and French air units, supported by the British fleet, if it could get into the Black Sea. More than a month after Russia signed peace with Finland, General Weygand informed Marshal Gamelin that an attack upon the Caucasus was being planned for late June or early July. "It would take from 40 to 50 days to get ready for the attack" . . . "the entire operation would take only a few days and will represent a mass bombardment of those points, the destruction of which will be most effective for the achievement of our objectives."

In short, a year after England and France had tried to persuade Soviet Russia into a hard and fast military alliance with them, in which Russia would have been taking very grave and also quite disproportionate risks, France and England were ready, with small pretexts, themselves to make war on their intended ally. It was the old game of intervention again. That Russia was trading with Germany was no excuse. America herself has vigorously insisted on the right of neutrals to trade with belligerents, and America was sending supplies in far greater volume and value to Great Britain than Russia was sending to Germany.

It was one of the most dangerous moments in history, and one of the most colossal and costly blunders ever contemplated was barely averted. Hitler signed his death warrant when he gave the orders for the attack on Russia. But had the Allies, in a moment of sheer folly, persuaded by the smoldering hatreds, by the misinformation and recklessness of certain political and military advisers, actually made war on Russia in 1940, as they had planned, their expedition would not only have been disastrously defeated, not only would they in turn have severely damaged their most important potential ally, but they would have thrown Russia and Germany together in an all-out, even if temporary, alliance that would have spelled hopeless catastrophe for the Allied cause.

It was Germany, presumably acting in her own interests, that saved the Allies from this fatuous attempt at suicide, for Germany insisted that Norway and Sweden defend their neutrality by force of arms, threatening that if they did not Germany would herself make war upon them immediately. Thus Germany saved her iron imports from Sweden and a certain amount of oil from Baku—but thus also she lost her surest chance to win the war. Like the Allies, she also had quite misunderstood the power and the character of the Soviet Union.

To ignore, misunderstand and flout Russia had for years in the European capitals been an easy way to applause, votes, appropriations and power. It could also have been an easy path to destruction. But in the fact that such a denouement as the projected war was possible, we have the historical justification for Russia's caution in not entering the projected alliance in '39, on the terms proposed by England and France.

There is good evidence that there was a secret understanding between Finland and Germany at the close of the Finnish-Russian war and that Germany definitely promised Finland that if she would sign the treaty with Russia, closing that unhappy war,* Germany would see to it that things would be made right for them later; and Dallin's important statement about Finland's renewed war with Russia provides confirmation. "On June 20 . . . the trade unions and the Finnish social democratic party together with a number of other organizations issued a proclamation demanding that Finland adhere to her neutrality. From all sides pressure was being exerted upon Helsinki to refrain from joining in the war on the side of Germany but in his speech of June 22, Hitler said, referring to Finland: 'German divisions . . . in cooperation with the heroes of Finnish freedom under their marshal are protecting Finnish soil.' " † Dallin adds, "On June 22 without awaiting for a formal declaration of war on the part of Finland, German bombers took off from Finnish territory and bombed the Kronstadt area; this was followed by infantry action on the 24th."

3

Litvinoff, who up to the end of 1939 had been rightly called Europe's outstanding diplomat and statesman, did not resent being relegated to apparent impotence and obscurity. He was not the man to suffer from wounded vanity. He had always put his work before

* Dallin, *op. cit.*, p. 198, quoting Virginia Cowles' interview with Prince Phillip of Hesse, Hitler's confidant. Cf. Virginia Cowles, *Looking for Trouble*, N. Y. (Harper Bros.), p. 346.

† Dallin, *op. cit.*, p. 379.

his personal welfare, indifferent to his own prestige. Once he had said that no Russian diplomat was indispensable. Now his time had come. He welcomed the respite.

Watching the development of World War II from his retirement, he had at least one grim satisfaction: he had been right. The first two years of World War II—the gradual disappearance of one country after another in the order and at the time Hitler chose—demonstrated beyond any doubt that Litvinoff's program for collective security had been the only sound or possible policy. Hitler's destruction of the little nations, none of which alone could defend itself against the Nazi colossus, proved conclusively that the sole chance of survival for all those countries would have been a common front against the aggressor. Litvinoff had been right.

A man who had been so right could not disappear from the world stage forever, but Litvinoff says that he was not then thinking about a return to public life, at least not in the near future; he could wait. Twenty years of diplomatic negotiations had proved that he had both inexhaustible patience and nerves of steel. By sheer endurance he had overcome untoward circumstances and stupid or vicious opposition and survived long after the political demise of many other diplomats. He could afford again to play the waiting game. He believed in the Persian proverb: Patience is the twin brother of Victory.

His retirement from the Government was genuine. Rumors said that he was a frequent visitor at the Kremlin; foreign observers reported seeing his car driving there almost daily. But he never went even once to the Kremlin; it was not his car, it was the Narkomindel car. Others, among them Molotov, used it now. Litvinoff no longer had a car of his own.

Litvinoff had retired, but he had not been purged. He still had an official position in the Party—Chief of the Foreign Affairs Information Bureau of the Central Executive Committee of the Communist Party —and had an office in the Narkomindel Building, though not his old office; there he could be reached by telephone.

He also continued to be a member of the Supreme Soviet, and went to all the meetings as deputy of a Leningrad district. He was proud of having been elected a deputy; his other offices had always been appointments.

Yet he was rarely seen in public. Occasionally he went to a concert or to a theater and sometimes he visited the various Moscow libraries. He had a vague idea that he might write his memoirs, and started working over diplomatic documents of the 20 years in which he had represented Russian foreign policy, but he never got any further than the preliminary organization of these documents and letters.

He was no longer living at the Sugar King's Palace, but at his dacha outside Moscow, and when he had to go into town Molotov, his successor and still his close friend, often took him in his car.

Madame Litvinoff had given up her teaching at Sverdlovsk and come back, so the whole family was together again. Misha was now a tall lanky young engineer, and married. Tanya, very pretty, had become an art student, and had already qualified for the Parachute Jumpers' Corps. For the first time in many years Litvinoff had time for family life (and in one aspect he is typically a family man), so his wife and children welcomed his retirement.

He loved the country and took long walks, usually accompanied by the family's assortment of dogs of all ages, led by a black spaniel called Silky and a Scotty named Me-too. Sometimes Svetlana, the thirteen-year-old daughter of the gardener, whom Madame Litvinoff called "a serious rival," would go along.

Bridge was another diversion in the dacha, and Litvinoff was even persuaded to play chess with Misha again, though Misha still beat him, as a rule. Litvinoff resumed his singing, began regular piano practice, and he and his wife exchanged advanced lessons in Russian and music. The music, according to Madame Litvinoff, went better than the Russian. The music had no grammar and the Russian had a lot.

Presently a grandson was added to the group—named Joseph but called Joe after Litvinoff's American friend, "Joe" Davies; the baby became even more of a pet than the dogs.

It was a pleasant, leisurely life and Litvinoff had earned it. He had come to the age of retirement—65—and he had had 40 years of strain, effort, anxiety, and 20 years of almost constant overwork, all self-sacrificing, though he is too big a person to have thought of it in those terms. He had won the right to all these simple yet fundamental personal values. On February 20, 1941, his public activities were still further simplified. He was dropped from membership in the Central Committee of the Party "for non-fulfillment of his obligations as a member of the Committee." This was a formal excuse, primarily designed to reassure the Germans that Litvinoff with his implacable hostility to the Nazis was no longer exercising any influence. Stalin was determined to give no offense to the Germans that could possibly be avoided. He had told Sir Stafford Cripps that he knew that Hitler would tear up the treaty at any moment that he thought it would be to his interest. Hence, as he was playing for desperately needed time, he was doubly cautious.*

But Litvinoff could not be allowed to enjoy a purely personal life for long. The world in crisis needed its best men and there were far too few of his caliber to go round. On May 1, Litvinoff was requested to stand next to Stalin while he reviewed the parade—Litvinoff's first emergence into public life since his retirement. Stalin was cordial and they exchanged a few words, though nothing about politics. Several times he seemed on the point of speaking to Litvinoff again, but always checked himself and fell back into absorbed reflection.

Litvinoff knew the reason for that reserve. Stalin was concentrating on the German threat. There had already been a significant straw in the wind. The month before, "Alexander Nevsky" had been revived. This film, on which the famous motion-picture director Eisenstein had worked for years, showed how the Russians had defeated the Germans in the Middle Ages. It had been released at about the time the Russo-German Pact was concluded, and promptly withdrawn, evidently in deference to German feelings. Now the ban was lifted, and it was even shown in the Kremlin at a special performance which received considerable publicity in *Pravda* and *Izvestia*. Afterwards Stalin patted Eisenstein on the back and said: "You are a good Bolshevik, Eisenstein." This was more than a commentary on the quality of a film; it amounted to a political demonstration. Stalin was facing the German problem again, and so on this May Day of 1941 he had almost automatically reached out once more towards Litvinoff.

* H. C. Cassidy, *op. cit.*, p. 2.

4

On June 22, 1941, German troops invaded the Soviet Union. The declaration of war followed. So did Italy's declaration of war on Russia, and a memorable speech by Churchill in which he declared that while he still was not a friend of Communism, any foe of Nazi Germany was his friend and ally.

Stalin had expected the war, but it came earlier than he had calculated. He had hoped and believed that the Germans would be held up longer in the Balkans, so that the attack on Russia would not start until the autumn of 1941. The Germans once again had surprised their victim.

But even allowing for the considerable advantage that this gave them, their victories of the first few weeks were startling. Brest-Litovsk, Minsk, Lvov fell in rapid succession. Finland declared war on Soviet Russia. On July 5, the Nazis got to the Stalin Line, 300 miles from Moscow. On the 16th they captured Smolensk, 230 miles from Moscow. By August 19 the siege of Odessa had begun. A few days later Nikopol and Novgorod were reached by the Germans, and with anguish in their hearts the Soviets blew up the Dnieprostrovsky Dam, one of the great achievements of their industrial reconstruction.

Litvinoff was in his office in the Narkomindel (his new one as Chief of the Party Foreign Affairs Bureau) when the Germans declared war on Russia in June, 1941. The attack did not surprise him. He had expected something like that for eight years, but now that it had come he felt worried and apprehensive, but he did not connect the news with any thought of his own career. On the morning of July 8, 1941, foreign correspondents in Moscow were warned to listen to the radio that night at eleven o'clock. To their surprise they heard that Litvinoff was going to speak. Actually they did not hear him, for the local radio was off at the time, but the text of his speech was cabled round the world. His statement was brief but as usual he went to the heart of the situation:

"It is all-important that Hitler should not have a moment's respite, that he should be disappointed in his hope of a de facto truce in the west. While his aim is to strike at one adversary at a time, ours should be to strike together, simultaneously, without respite, untiringly. Each blow struck now is ten times as effective, and entails infinitely less expenditure and sacrifice, than if it is delivered when any one of his adversaries become weaker."

The words "ours" and "now" were underlined in his original text.*

Thus Litvinoff's first task had been to press with all his old fervor and hard reasoning for the immediate opening of a second front. After having lost many times more than all the Allies put together, and having inflicted ten times more damage on the German military machine than England had in three years, including everything that America had been able to do, still after two years of heroic fighting, Russia still found her pleas for a second front on the European continent denied and hopes that were encouraged, deferred. What if Russia had entered the war in the summer of '39? "Would the Allies," the Russians asked, "have let us wait four years before they took up their full share of the battle?" And if the Allies could think of opening a second front against us in 1940 in regions as remote and as far apart as Finland and the Caucasus, why could they not open some kind of a second front two years later in our behalf—especially as we were fighting for them, carrying the principal load of the war and saving them lives and destruction?"

The Russians made a sacrifice to relieve some of the perilous pressure on the Allies in the first war. Answering the urgent pleas of the French just before the Marne, they undertook an invasion of East Prussia for which they were not ready. It was a sacrifice play which cost the Russians nearly half a million casualties, but created just enough diversion to save Paris.† Their proved willingness to sacrifice the immediate advantage for a larger one and the welfare of the whole coalition, the Russians felt, should now recommend a similar assistance by the Allies in World War II. One of the things that saved England after Dunkirk was that Hitler, as he said himself, had to keep so many divisions and one third of his air force on the Eastern front and what remained to him was scarcely adequate for a conclusive invasion of Britain. And this was added claim on British assistance. But the proposal for a second

* *Ibid.*, p. 64.

† At a critical moment two divisions were detached from the German Army and dispatched to the Eastern front, leaving a gap in the German line that Foch and Gallieni swiftly exploited with disastrous results to the Germans.

front was thought "premature" and "impractical" just as disarmament and collective security had been. D. N. Pritt, Labor Member of Parliament, stated that the reluctance in opening a second front sprang from powerful influences which were still hoping for reconciliation with Hitler, and for the defeat of Russia. There were also many others, both in England and America, of all stations, who had the same feeling; and others besides the Russians began to wonder about the delay.

Russia was perfectly willing to join the Allies in all-out battle against Germany, a battle in which she knew she would have to bear the brunt; but she did not want to come in until the Allies were ready and determined to put up a full battle themselves.

Under the circumstances it would not have been surprising if the Russians again began to suspect their new ally and to feel that their judgment in the '39 negotiations was once more justified. At any rate, if they did have any suspicions, they were prudently and loyally silent about them while still hoping and pleading for a demonstration that would save Russian life and greatly increase her striking power.

There was no need to look for sinister motives in the long-delayed second front, however callous to Russia's suffering and losses certain individuals in both Government and military circles might have been. The real difference between Russia and her Western Allies, a deep and almost tragic one, seems to have been in the conflicting notions of responsibility, sacrifice and the calculated risk. England and the United States apparently were willing to undertake a military operation only if it was in itself practically certain of success, and they honestly feared that an invasion of the continent would have resulted in a bloody and costly repulse. The Russians felt that such an attack would, while it might in itself be a failure, nevertheless greatly contribute to victory, that it would require a diversion of German forces from the Eastern front which would have given them just the margin of power necessary to smash through the German lines or hold them for very great losses and very little gain. The Allied commanders were probably skeptical of this as even until 1942 some of them were still disparaging Russia's military efforts and prospects. The Russians believed in the sacrifice play, they believed in taking very considerable risks, and they believed that in waiting for the absolutely sure success the Allies were taking a greater risk than an even tentative second front would have been. The British Command, made cautious by the defeat at Gallipoli in the first War and by the debacle in Flanders and the Cretan defeat in this one, and conscious of the terrible dangers involved, were conscientiously for prudence, and the American strategy was probably influenced by the demand in the United States which has amounted almost to a psychological malady in the last two generations, for security and proof, a growing trend in the national mentality due to a complex of causes. Which was right in this unhappy disagreement will have to be left to history but the delay of many months was one more disappointment for Litvinoff.

But still Litvinoff had no inkling of what was to come. When he heard, a few weeks later, that an English-American Commission under Averell Harriman and Lord Beaverbrook was to arrive, he was pleased to be assigned to the delegation of reception, though in an unimportant capacity.

The commission arrived in September, 1941. Litvinoff was invited to the Kremlin and was present at the official banquet. It is characteristic of him that although most of the discussions centered around questions of foreign policy, about which he could have told a thing or two to most of those present, he preferred to listen. The distinguished foreigners who knew him from his great Geneva days wondered what he was doing there. Someone asked him if he were acting as an interpreter. Litvinoff smiled:

"That is a very good name, indeed. I think I have always been an interpreter of the world to the peoples of the Soviet Union."

If the Nazis had attacked earlier than Stalin had expected, it was later than they themselves had planned, so they had to race against time, for they wanted to complete the Russian campaign—they were still thinking of that war in terms of a campaign of a matter of weeks —organize the new territory and get set for the invasion of England, all before the Russian winter set in.

By the middle of September they had taken Kiev. Early in October, after Hitler had composed his order of the day: "Today begins the last great decisive battle of the year"—they had taken Orel, Vyazma, and soon afterwards Odessa and Kalinin. They were a scant 100 miles from Moscow. Taganrog, Rostov, Kharkov fell. Stalin announced a state of siege for Moscow; while thousands of women and children, but by no means all, were being evacuated, every male citizen was ordered to aid in the defense of the capital.

And then, almost at the very last minute, the Soviet counter-attack was launched. Moscow was saved. The Germans were stalled—at least for the winter. The Russian "campaign" was developing into a long-drawn-out war. The Russians again refuted their detractors and gave a demonstration of courage, endurance, organization, and military skill that astonished the world. Their first winter offensive won from General MacArthur an extraordinary tribute in which he declared it to be the greatest achievement in military history. The world was equally impressed by the solidarity of the Russian people behind their government and their army—the suffering and sacrifice of all, the immense and robust morale, the magnificent achievement of the partisans and the effective participation of the women and children. The Revolution had builded well—and Stalin's severe policy of discipline, unity, production and yet more production was justified by the result. The life of the nation in mortal peril had been saved; the onrush of the most formidable engine of destruction ever forged by the evil intent of man was stayed, the myth of its invincibility shattered and its ultimate doom irrevocably forecast.

While the Russians had tried everything possible to assure peace, they were capable, now that war had come, of defending themselves—themselves, and perhaps the rest of the democratic world.

Litvinoff expressed it in a speech on February 26, 1942, which again set forth the solid realism of Russian policy and the infinite service Russian resistance had rendered the cause of peace and freedom everywhere:

"Current events are proving that the Soviet Government is entitled to claim credit, not so much for advocating collective security and international solidarity in the face of common danger, as for the measures it adopted at the same time to be in a position to fulfill the international obligations it was prepared to undertake. The Soviet Government knew that Hitler was not to be impressed by mere international declarations, pacts, mutual aid treaties, and all that, till he was convinced that these documents were backed by material forces. The course of military events has already shown that we really did prepare these material forces.

"If we had limited ourselves to talking about peace, and had not at the same time prepared for an alternative in the event of these talks proving fruitless, our Army, however numerous it might be, could never have resisted the onrush of the Nazi hordes and Hitler's monstrous war machine. And if we had not put up the necessary fight, Hitler would have been the big boss and would have added the vast riches of our country to his other big conquests. And then, it is most likely, the United Nations, every one of them, would have had a poor chance to escape defeat. We may therefore claim, with pardonable pride, that, by our preparedness, we have done yeoman service not only for ourselves but for all other peace-loving countries."

The unbelievable strength of the Russian military machine then and in the following years was a source of surprise, not only to most of the world's military experts, whose strong anti-Soviet bias had led them to underestimate the value of the Red army, but also to many of those who had watched without antagonism the Communist experiment. The history of Lenin and, incidentally, of Litvinoff, and the foreign policy of the Soviet Union since 1917, had led them to believe that Communism almost automatically produced pacifism.

And indeed the Soviet Union, especially as represented in its foreign relations by Litvinoff, had done its utmost for peace. This was primarily for humanitarian and what might be called common-sense reasons —to avoid war's shocking waste of all kinds of values. But along with these there had also been a specifically Russian motive in Litvinoff's persistent fight against war from 1918 to 1939. He knew that peace was indivisible, that any war anywhere would eventually result in a world war which would involve Soviet Russia. Soviet Russia had to be spared a war during those years of reconstruction if that could possibly be achieved, because peace was a pre-condition of success for the new regime there. Peace was important for the sake of peace, but it was imperative for the sake of Russia and her new order.

Now that war had come—an indivisible war, just as he had foreseen —it was equally imperative that Russia come through victorious. The

Russian people had toiled, suffered, hoped, sacrificed, and achieved for 24 years to remake their world for themselves and their children, for the future. A Nazi victory would not only wipe out that momentous quarter-century; it would push the whole world still farther back, and in doing so would frustrate everywhere all the finest human hopes. Hitler, and all of which he was the noisy, violent figurehead, must be destroyed.

Consequently, the State and the man who had fought more consistently for peace than any others in the twentieth century, Soviet Russia and Litvinoff, were now determined to fight just as consistently and more successfully for military and moral victory. And Stalin soon gave Litvinoff a chance to take an active part in this new, critical fight, proportionate to his great capacities.

5

During the blitz of Moscow, when the Nazis were well on their way to the Soviet capital and the government was transferred to Kuibyshev, Litvinoff stayed on in his dacha outside Moscow, and went every day to town to the Narkomindel, as though nothing untoward were occurring.

On October 31 he was as usual sitting in his office. It was late in the evening and he was reading American newspapers, mostly copies of the *New York Times,* of the last days of June, with reports on the early phases of the Russo-German War. One of the numbers, he says, contained the prediction that the war in Russia would last three to six weeks. Another had an article by a military expert advising the Russian army to retire behind the Urals. This did not surprise Litvinoff. He well knew that most military experts, and almost all American experts, had little faith in the ability of the Red army to resist.

At ten o'clock the telephone rang. Molotov was calling from Kuibyshev, to say that Litvinoff was to be Ambassador to the United States. Washington had been sounded out, and his confirmation would be handed to him in Kuibyshev by the American Ambassador, Lawrence A. Steinhardt. As a matter of fact, two months before, Davies had told Oumansky, the retiring Soviet Ambassador in Washington, who was on the point of departure, that he hoped Litvinoff would be sent to the United States.* Litvinoff was to get ready to leave quickly because he was needed urgently in Washington.

"When do you want me to go?" Litvinoff asked.

"We want you to come to Kuibyshev at once. And then we'll see about the rest, Maxim Maximovich."

Litvinoff went to his dacha. Madame Litvinoff was not at home. She was holding classes on Basic English in an air-raid shelter in the subway station on Okhotny Riyad. Misha was not at home either; he was on the night shift as an aviation engineer. Neither was Tanya, who was on duty as an air-raid warden.

Litvinoff started to pack.

He and his wife left Moscow on November 2. He arrived in Kuibyshev three days later and on November 6 it was publicly announced that he had been appointed Ambassador from the Union of Soviet Socialist Republics to the United States. This was the first that the Russian people heard of his return to public life. There was general rejoicing in the newspapers. Litvinoff was popular.

On the 6th, too, late in the afternoon, in the office of Molotov, met a conference for which Stalin had come from Moscow. Afterwards the secretary of Ambassador Steinhardt, the first Secretary of the British Embassy, and the assistant military attaché of the United States arrived to discuss certain details of Litvinoff's trip. It was decided that he would fly to Teheran and from there via Baghdad and Singapore to San Francisco. Ambassador Steinhardt told Molotov: "President Roosevelt is particularly happy that Maxim Litvinoff will represent the Soviet Union in Washington." †

Litvinoff must have smiled when he heard it. This was the second time that he had been appointed Ambassador to the United States. The first time, 23 years before, Lenin himself had made the appointment, but the State Department had refused to accept the new Ambassador, had even refused to grant an American visa. Now the President himself welcomed him.

* Joseph E. Davies, *op. cit.*, p. 499.
† *Ibid.*, p. 499.

6

From November 10 on, the *New York Times* published the following dispatches, and similar dispatches were appearing in the entire world press:

Kuibyshev, Russia, Nov. 9.—Maxim M. Litvinoff will leave here for Washington tomorrow to assume his new post as Soviet Ambassador, accompanied by Ambassador Lawrence A. Steinhardt, who is returning to the United States on leave and for consultation with President Roosevelt and the State Department.

Teheran, Iran, Nov. 10.—United States Ambassador Lawrence A. Steinhardt, Maxim M. Litvinoff, newly appointed Soviet Ambassador to Washington, and Sir Walter Monckton of the British Ministry of Information were reported tonight to be flying here from Russia. The plane was delayed by heavy weather and was expected to arrive tomorrow.

London, Nov. 11.—A Cairo dispatch to the United Press said Mr. Litvinoff was expected there by airplane yesterday.

London, Nov. 12.—(Special to the "New York Times.") No anxiety is felt here for the safety of Lawrence A. Steinhardt, United States Ambassador to Russia, Sir Walter Monckton, British Propaganda chief in the Near East, and Maxim Litvinoff, Soviet Ambassador to the United States, who are reported by Reuter's to be overdue at Teheran, Iran, on a plane trip from Kuibyshev, Russia, to Cairo. The Ministry of Information pointed out that all accounts from Allied and enemy sources said that the weather was extremely bad along that route. It was believed that the officials' plane had made an unscheduled halt owing to the weather conditions.

London, Nov. 13.—(Special to the "New York Times.")—"Some anxiety" was voiced in official quarters in London tonight for the safety of Maxim M. Litvinoff, Soviet Deputy Foreign Commissar and new Ambassador to Washington, Lawrence A. Steinhardt, United States Ambassador to Russia, and Sir Walter Monckton, director of British Information services in the Middle East, who were overdue on an airplane flight from Kuibyshev, Russia, to Teheran, Iran.

After stressing the bad weather on the route and the possibility of an emergency landing in desolate country, the bulletins, as the hours passed without word of the plane, began to show concern in place of the earlier assurances that there was no cause for alarm.

London, Nov. 13.—In commenting tonight on the lack of news from the plane carrying Maxim M. Litvinoff, Lawrence A. Steinhardt, and Sir Walter Monckton, an official here said, "We are hopeful that word may come at any minute that the plane has landed safely somewhere, but we have no information concerning it, except press reports that it is missing."

(It is possible that the plane may have taken a route that missed Teheran. Aircraft carrying official passengers through war zones operate amid strict official secrecy and observe general radio silence to keep their movements from hostile ears.)

Part of the 1,300 mile route from Kuibyshev to Teheran lies over the Caspian Sea.

London, Nov. 14.—(Special Cable to "New York Times.")—The plane carrying Maxim M. Litvinoff, Soviet Vice-Commissar of Foreign Affairs and new Ambassador to Washington, and Lawrence A. Steinhardt, United States Ambassador to Russia, has arrived safely at Baku, Soviet port on the Caspian Sea, it was officially announced tonight by the Ministry of Information.

The announcement set at rest several conflicting reports concerning the fate of the Rusian plane which had been previously reported long overdue at Teheran, Iran, from Kuibyshev, Russia. It had been believed that the plane left Kuibyshev on Tuesday, but it was said tonight that actually it had not departed until yesterday morning.

Washington, Nov. 15.—(Special to the "New York Times.")—The State Department received official word today of the safe arrival at the Caspian Seaport of Pahlevi, Iran, of Lawrence A. Steinhardt, Ambassador to Russia, and Maxim M. Litvinoff, new Soviet Ambassador to the United States. The plane taking them to Teheran, en route to the United States, was reported yesterday at Baku, about 200 miles north of Pahlevi.

———

Teheran, Iran, Nov. 15.—The Russian plane carrying Ambassador Steinhardt and Litvinoff was expected to arrive here tomorrow from the north. The pilot telegraphed that his arrival in Teheran today was delayed by cloudy skies.

———

Teheran, Iran, Nov. 17.—United States Ambassador Lawrence A. Steinhardt and Maxim M. Litvinoff, new Soviet envoy to the United States, en route to Washington, arrived here safely today after a blizzard-plagued five-day plane trip from Kuibyshev, auxiliary Soviet capital.

The trip which caught the interest of the entire world had started with a blizzard in Kuibyshev. There had been a landing in Astrakhan where the passengers stayed till the next morning on account of bad weather. At Baku they had stopped over for four nights, with the weather turning from bad to worse and making the landing field at Pahlevi unsafe for such a large plane. (It was a Russian Douglas DC 3.) Finally another stopover was necessary at Pahlevi for one night. And there was no possibility of communicating with the rest of the world. Telegrams would have been routed via Kuibyshev and Moscow and would probably have reached London and New York even later than the news of the party's arrival in Teheran.

Exhausted, Litvinoff and his wife finally got to Teheran on November 17, and were taken immediately to the Russian Embassy. In the evening Litvinoff conferred with the American and British Ambassadors in Teheran. The chances of winning the war against Hitler were discussed—in German—because this was the only language which all those present, including a number of employees of the Russian Embassy, understood. Then Litvinoff retired, expecting to leave the next morning on his Russian plane for Baghdad.

But when Litvinoff and his wife arrived at the airport the next morning, it turned out that his plane needed overhauling and that he would have to wait another day. Sir Walter Monckton and Ambassador

Steinhardt had offered to share their British plane with him, but he had declined. Now, however, he decided that he had better go with them. He approached the British plane, which was to take off shortly afterwards for Cairo. The pilot did not recognize Litvinoff and asked who he was. Litvinoff said, "I am Maxim M. Litvinoff, Russian Ambassador to the United States." The pilot said he was sorry but that there was no reservation for Litvinoff or Mrs. Litvinoff on this plane, that all space had been taken up by British officials, and that he, the pilot, had no authority to put any of them off the plane.

Litvinoff simply nodded and went back to the Russian Embassy to wait for his plane to be ready the next morning. No offense was intended and no offense was taken, as far as Litvinoff was concerned. However, the English press somehow got wind of the affair and distorted reports appeared suggesting that Litvinoff had been snubbed and slighted by British officials in Teheran. Everybody became agitated, including Mr. Buller, the British Ambassador in Teheran, who rushed to the Russian Embassy to offer his Government's apologies. He found Litvinoff mildly surprised by all the excitement. Such was the famous "Teheran incident."

Litvinoff stayed two days longer in Teheran than he originally intended, and spent the whole time either in conference or reading reports of the newest developments in the theaters of war and on the political fronts. He was particularly interested in reports which had been forwarded from the Narkomindel concerning the attitude of the Japanese.

7

On November 23 Litvinoff's plane arrived in Baghdad; on November 26, in Calcutta; on November 28, in Singapore. Here, again, he received diplomatic intelligence reports. After he had read them he was more serious than ever. The Litvinoffs were received at Government House. Madame Litvinoff had a discussion with Sir Shenton Thomas, who exclaimed: "The Japs won't get here!" Madame Litvinoff noted down: "He smiled reassuringly at me. Maxim smiled too, when I told him, but not reassuringly." Litvinoff talked to Sir Geoffrey Thomas, to General Percival and to Duff Cooper, who was about to leave for Australia. Litvinoff expressed his belief, based on a message he had in hand, that the Japanese would soon attack the United States and Great Britain. The others, with the exception of Duff Cooper, politely refused to take him seriously. Nevertheless, Litvinoff continued throughout November 29, almost to the moment of his departure, to repeat his warnings.

On November 30 the Litvinoffs arrived in Manila, where they were received by the High Commissioner and Mrs. Francis B. Sayre. They had dinner in the cool, white palace of the High Commissioner. General and Mrs. MacArthur were also present. Again Litvinoff spoke of an impending attack by the Japanese. Again, nobody seemed to believe him.

December 2 they got to Guam; December 3, to Wake Island. About 2,000 workers were busy building a small air base there. By way of Midway Island, they got, December 4, to Honolulu. Again there was a formal reception for the Litvinoffs. They were taken to the House of the Governor, where General Short and Admiral Kimmel appeared to welcome the newly appointed Ambassador. Litvinoff, as always, persistent, again talked about his conviction that the Japanese would attack at any moment. Someone answered:

"They would be fools to attack us now."

Litvinoff smiled wryly: "Yes, indeed, they would be fools. But they will attack."

These were almost Litvinoff's last words before he left Honolulu.

The Litvinoffs arrived in San Francisco on December 6. In the last few days they had covered almost the identical route which only a few hours later was to be taken by the Japanese. He had predicted that they would come soon. But everywhere the reaction had been the same: nobody believed him, because nobody wanted to believe him. It was the same old story.

On the morning of Sunday, December 7, Litvinoff's plane arrived at Bolling Field, Washington, D. C. He was received by Brigadier General Philip R. Faymonville, formerly military attaché in Moscow, now chief of the Supply Mission to the Soviet Union; by General Marshall and Admiral King, and many other officers and officials. Only with difficulty was he able to summon a conventional smile. A 25-day grueling trip had worn him out completely.

After a few formalities he was driven to the Russian Embassy, where he went straight to bed and at once fell asleep.

Four hours later he was awakened by his secretary. She was excited: "The Japanese have just attacked Pearl Harbor."

Litvinoff opened his eyes. So it had come. The Japanese had attacked Pearl Harbor.

For a while he lay still. He was too tired. He needed more rest. He had a great deal of work before him.

So he went back to sleep. He slept until seven o'clock in the evening. Then he got up and dressed and went to his desk. He wrote his first dispatch as Russian Ambassador to Washington.

His new work had begun.

Postscript

LITVINOFF, who had once been refused a visa by the State Department although he had an ambassadorial appointment, now found himself welcomed as a friend—almost a hero. Russia had become, in essence, our ally, and despite all predictions to the contrary, she was putting up a tremendous battle against the brilliantly directed and ferocious attack of the Germans. True, at the outset she had lost more heavily than we did in the sneak attacks on Pearl Harbor and Manila, but her retreating armies were still intact and were inflicting severe casualties on the Nazis. Russia was by no means safe, she was cruelly hard pressed; Moscow and Leningrad were in jeopardy and American military opinion continued pessimistic; but the public were hopeful, indeed enthusiastic.

Even more surprising, however, than this show of military power, and to many of her critics disconcerting, was her demonstration of formidable political unity. Stalin had delivered his memorable scorched-earth speech, matching in grim realism and inspiring power Churchill's Blood-Sweat-and-Tears classic. Stalin laid down the hard way, took full responsibility on himself and trusted the people, as it had been said he never could. He received back from them the most overwhelming declarations and proofs of loyalty. Russia's morale resources—and they are infinite—were mobilized and in action. It had become a people's war, but a people disciplined, united, equipped, trained and superbly organized by a government that they all believed had acted, in the too few years available for preparation, with great foresight as well as firmness. And those who really knew Russia were confident that the utter defeat of Hitler and his evil crew was now assured.

All this greatly simplified Litvinoff's work. Russian War Relief was in full swing and was an effective channel for the expression of popular sympathy and good will. Concerts, entertainments, banquets were given in his honor, and at all he received uproarious welcome. His relations with President Roosevelt were completely cordial, and old State Department grievances seemed to have been forgotten.

But however propitious these circumstances, Litvinoff's task was by no means easy. He had still to combat the large residue of suspicion and ill-will left over from the period of non-recognition. For nearly fifteen years the American Government had failed to discern the vast and growing power of Russia; to realize that the Soviets were not going to collapse as had long been fondly hoped; to recognize that they were not the menace our frightened reactionaries and applause-seeking orators, politicians and journalists had so luridly pictured; and to appreciate that it was useless to expect that Russia would make herself over in our image, as the State Department in effect urgently recommended it to do throughout the twenties.

During this long, damaging interlude of official mistrust the habit of abuse and contempt for Russia had become well established in many quarters in the United States; originally government-sanctioned, it colored speech: "Communist," "Parlor-pink," "Fellow-Traveller" were handy epithets used without discretion or meaning. More convenient than fact or reason, they could be thrown at anyone with whom one disagreed, particularly if he were liberal and forward-looking, and Martin Dies and some of his fellow-travellers rode into considerable political power, largely on the foam of anti-Communist slogans. Journals and journalists were finding profitable careers in Soviet baiting, and those most enthusiastic about Hitler and Mussolini were the most violent about Russia.

Furthermore, the existence here of a Communist Party which had confessed to aims and methods that were incompatible with the spirit, if not the laws, of the American democracy, and the American Communist habit of taking the "Moscow Line" as authoritative, whether by instruction or imitation, had kept alive suspicion and resentment, for America will not tolerate a political party which for political, racial, religious, economic or any other kind of reason looks to a foreign source for its directives. Even Russia's heroic participation in the war could not at once undo the effects of a score of years of hostility, misrepresentation and ignorance that had so dangerously magnified legitimate and serious differences, and supplemented them to boot with fictitious terrors.

Also much that had happened since the beginning of the War had created new tensions and distrusts: the Russian-Finnish war, the incursion into the Baltic States, and the Russian-Nazi pact. The deplorable conflict with Finland was promptly seized on by the habitual enemies of Soviet Russia and played up so successfully that the American public, too easily convinced, did not wait to hear the other side of the case. Our traditional sympathy for the underdog, our resentment of the bully, our notion that Finland was a democracy, our respect for her prompt payment of her so-called war debt, committed us as a nation to Finland's side. The American people as a whole were unaware of the powerful undemocratic elements within Finland that could commit the country to war, make treaties and otherwise compromise the country without the consent of Parliament—a group that had maintained close and highly improper relations with the Nazis (just as a large majority is still unaware that the debt on which Finland makes payments was not properly a "war" debt, but was incurred months after fighting ceased). Feeling against Russia ran high in the United States over the Finnish issue. Russia was savagely denounced in Congress, where concrete plans were proposed for active assistance to the Finns, while civilian agencies sent them approximately a million dollars—ninety per cent of the total that the Finns received from abroad.

Similarly, the general press and public refused to consider the relation of the Baltic States to the Nazi peril, accounting both this and the Finnish affair sheer aggression, and clamored loudly against the "treachery" and "double-dealing" of the Soviet-Nazi pact, with no consideration of the actual conditions on the Allied side which practically forced Russia into temporary compromise with her enemy. All this material was eagerly used to stoke the fires of hatred against Soviet Russia which were still hot in many quarters when Litvinoff took up his post.

Among the specific episodes that had kept alive an unfriendly or even contemptuous attitude towards Russia was Lindbergh's shockingly erroneous estimate of the Soviet Air Force, which was, of course, politically motivated and had been instigated by some of his reactionary acquaintances.* The episode was indeed disproportionately damaging to

* William R. Castle, Joseph P. Kennedy and Colonel Truman Smith could supply very interesting information concerning the inception, purpose and character of Lindbergh's visit.

Russian foreign relations. In the first place, Lindbergh's disparaging report was received in good time to support a reactionary campaign in Britain and France for a cancellation of the Franco-Soviet Treaty, one of democracy's few security anchors at the time, the abrogation of which the Nazis were demanding with vociferous impudence. In the second place, the Russians not only knew that the estimate was based only on a superficial three-and-a-half-day visit to factories and airfields around Moscow, insufficient to permit any conclusions; but they also had heard Lindbergh's expressions to his guides there (both American and Russian) of surprise and admiration at what he was allowed to see. Hence Soviet officials and especially the Russian aviators themselves resented the dishonesty and hostility manifest in the discrepancy between these statements and his subsequent report. And in the third place, though Lindbergh's anti-Russian, anti-Asiatic, pro-Nazi views have since become obvious and are now discredited, when he made the anti-Russian report he still had considerable status as an American hero so that the insecurity about Russia which he created lingered in many American minds. Americans who complain that the Soviet authorities are suspicious and do not provide full privileges to visiting Americans for the inspection of their military effort ought not to overlook the Lindbergh incident.

In their reluctance to give up anti-Russian prejudices, both old and new, Americans had by no means fully comprehended the change in policy under Stalin, a revised orientation that Litvinoff had favored from the start: the substitution for international revolution and its promotion in other countries, of a program for the full development of Russia's own resources, which was inspiring the Russian people to ever greater efforts, and laying a basis for a new internationalism which was making possible more cordial relations with foreign nations.

There were other profound changes in Russia of which American public opinion was only vaguely aware. There was the new emphasis on the sanctity of the family, legally reflected in the reversal in 1936 of abortion laws and easy divorce, and socially in the return to the serious and respectful attitude towards parents. An acceptance of discipline as a rational necessity for effective life was an important factor that the whole nation approved. There was a new sense of the seriousness of the task ahead, the rebuilding of Russia with its incalculable potentialities;

a new vision of a future more glamorous than anything envisaged at the outset of the Revolution, but more specific and more practical. All these changes which make of the New Russia something quite different from the Russia of revolutionary days were greeted by derision from some quarters in America, while others scarcely noted them and some seemed quite annoyed that their familiar arguments were outmoded and no longer relevant. These were stubborn elements in the American scene with which Litvinoff could not deal directly, and, because so unrealistic and unreasonable, he could only with difficulty interpret them to Moscow.

Nor had the United States appreciated the immense material and cultural advances that the Soviets had made in the last few years, so that there was general surprise when Litvinoff, in his first speech in New York, told how resolutely the Russians, despite their mortal peril, had maintained and even expanded their cultural services. The Americans knew, if a bit vaguely, that England had sustained and even planned improvements in her educational services and had resolutely kept clear and bright other intrinsic values; that she had even bought a costly Rembrandt for the National Gallery in one of England's darkest hours; but having themselves consented almost unanimously and much too readily to a cultural blackout, many Americans had apparently failed to grasp the thoroughly civilized policy of the Russian Government which Litvinoff skillfully stressed while tactfully omitting comparisons. For Russia is fighting, not just for her life, but for the good life, to which all the humane achievements in art, music, literature and science are essential. Consequently, her Government has never allowed artists, musicians, writers, poets or scientists to see front-line service, except on some extraordinary mission, and her archaeologists are still at work recovering traces of Russia's past and of her productive relations with Asia. All this was part of the lesson on the New Russia that Litvinoff brought to the United States.

To correct popular misapprehensions and present the real Russia to the American people were especially important because ignorance and lurking antagonism provided a fertile medium in which to breed the intra-Allied dissensions that have from the beginning been an essential aim of German psychological warfare. To this end Germany has employed well-trained paid agents, but she has needed fewer of these in

proportion as there have been short-sighted, narrow-minded citizens in
each of the Allied countries to do the dirty work for her. Old Irish
resentments, and here and there perhaps a lingering habit of twisting
the British lion's tail, were about all Hitler's trouble-makers could count
on to gnaw at the British-American bond; but there have been many
elements, especially in the United States, which have needed only a
little surreptitious German prodding to endanger our Russian relations.
The Red menace, tattered as it was, could be waved again to excite fear
and animosity; hints of Russian unreliability found ready repeaters;
sentimental or doctrinaire Trotskyites are still busy and vocal, and reactionary groups and persons have been ready to join even with their
polar opposite to further sinister ends with violent and intemperate
speech.

That Russia herself had often been to blame, in various ways flouting
world opinion, only increased Litvinoff's difficulties when he undertook
to stem all these currents of ill-will. For the ineptness of some of the
Soviets' diplomatic maneuvers and the disingenuous fantasies of some
of their propaganda had greatly increased suspicion and resentment in
the West.

And then there was the Comintern to plague Litvinoff as it had from
the very start of his diplomatic career. That the Comintern was not a
strictly Russian organization, that it was neither sponsored nor financed
by the Russian Government, that it included eight times as many non-
Russian members as Russian, and that the Communists formed legally
recognized political parties in various countries did not constitute an
effective defense. Agreements that Litvinoff himself had entered into
seemed incompatible with the continued existence of the Comintern,
and in this country forces opposed to Russia had made the most of it.
Few can know the actual facts, but it seems highly probable that one
of Litvinoff's most urgent primary tasks, in which he was no doubt
skillfully assisted by President Roosevelt, was to induce the Moscow
Government to order the dissolution of the Comintern, which gratified
even Mr. Dies, deprived Russia's enemies of their favorite weapon, and
reassured honest people everywhere.

Other problems also there were to beset the new Ambassador. The
Lend-Lease arrangements which the President promptly inaugurated
with Russia under the blanket powers that the Act gave him, did not

always run smoothly, despite Averill Harriman's and Harry Hopkins' assurances and loyal efforts to the contrary. Some of our military leaders, still dubious about Russia, feeling that we and England must be ready to fight it out alone if need be, aware of the colossal German equipment and our own unlimited need of supplies for a two-front war, saw material going to Russia with reluctance. American military shortages seemed alarming and every military commander, conscious of the live-saving value of quick and thorough victory, always believes that his supplies are insufficient to his necessities. General Eisenhower's acknowledgment that his equipment for the Sicilian campaign was ample is almost unprecedented in military history.

Litvinoff had also the problem of the second front. To induce the United States to join in and press for a second European front irrespective of its immediate success as a separate operation was perhaps his most urgent assignment, for Moscow genuinely believed that a resolute diversion somewhere on the European continent would reduce German forces in the East to such a degree that the Russians themselves could completely smash the remaining Nazi divisions there and thus shorten the war and save Allied lives and treasure as well as their own. But for reasons that have not yet been fully stated to the public, Great Britain and the United States hesitated to make this calculated risk, and apparently felt that the war must be planned to a sure victory by the efforts of the British and American armies on their own. The Russians had no doubt that a real second front was coming. But, faced by fearful losses, by civilian suffering and privation, which were beginning to threaten the nation's future, they asked, would it come in good time?

Americans who pressed for the second front were told in general terms that this was strictly a matter for military decision and no civilian was entitled to an opinion and that, in any case, the absolutely safe and sure was the only possible course. But there was a fairly widespread suspicion that those who were responsible were perhaps not sufficiently sympathetic with Russia's needs, that they were somewhat indifferent to the devastations and horrors which she was suffering—political considerations on which the nation as a whole was entitled to render opinion. The English public was more insistent for a second front than the American, for they knew too well what Russia was enduring and their gratitude for relief was too vivid to be tolerant of any indifference on the subject. But nothing happened, even Wendell Willkie's strong and reasonable challenge was ineffective.

Russia was grieved and disappointed. She was also concerned over what she regarded as Fascist sympathies high in American councils. We had only reluctantly given up the idea that we could do business with Hitler or that America needed a Mussolini to keep labor in line. Our appeasement policy towards Japan was a definite menace to Russia and her Asiatic interests. We had not stood by Loyalist Spain and had accommodated ourselves rather too easily to Franco. Our friendliness to Vichy and Pétain, our failure to appraise correctly De Gaulle and the Free French movement, our preference for devious political by-play at the expense of principle in North Africa made the Russians uncomfortable and distrustful of our aims.

The lack of clarity and vigor of our European policy was mercilessly exposed in the Italian muddle, and there were other signs that the government was not basically in sympathy with the popular movements in Europe, which began to look upon us with misgiving. Our gross discourtesy in refusing a visa to the Russian envoy in London to contact the French Committee of Liberation in North Africa—grudgingly granted at the eleventh hour—must have caused a good deal of resentment in Russia, already more than fed up with diplomatic slights; and the fact that we have frequently given passports to Fascists and Falangists, allowing them to work up mischief, particularly in South America, must have made a comparison all the more unpleasant. While the disappointment over the second front probably outweighed all other considerations, yet the cumulative effect of these discourtesies and covert hostilities, which seemed to ignore Russia's heroism, tragedy and her incalculable services to the United Nations, must have been considerable.

Litvinoff continued to press for his policies privately with the Government and publicly insofar as it was appropriate. Molotov's visit to this country, although severely confidential, should have been a substantial aid and encouragement to Litvinoff in his difficult campaign. But once more it seemed as if Litvinoff was chalking up a failure, and his recall for consultation to Russia on May 10 was thought by some to mark the Kremlin's disappointment that he had not succeeded in overcoming the hostile elements of American public opinion or in advancing the much-sought second front. Obviously, the Kremlin needed a report on American conditions and also needed Litvinoff's participation in the discussion of Russia's program for political reconstruction in Europe and the defining of its relations to its neighbors and to its allies, for Litvinoff and Maisky, who was also recalled to Moscow, probably knew the world-scene better than any other Russians. It was given out that he was remaining in Russia partly for the sake of medical tuning up by his own physician, which, at his age and after the cruelly strenuous life that he had so long been living, was a reasonable precaution. But it is clear that Litvinoff could bring back no definitely marked triumph from his eighteen months in America.

On August 22, 1943, the Presidium of the Supreme Soviet of the U.S.S.R. announced that Maxim Litvinoff had been relieved of his post in Washington, and that Mr. Andrey Gromyko, the Chargé d'Affaires, had been appointed Ambassador in his place. The announcement, preceded by the recall of Ambassador Maisky from London and his replacement by Mr. Fedor Gusev, former Minister to Canada, coinciding as it did with the Quebec Conference, created a tremendous stir in world opinion. The formation on Russian territory of a Free Germany movement had already aroused fears and even charges that Russia was going to make a separate peace with Germany, which the withdrawal of Litvinoff seemed to some to confirm. Did it foretell the beginning of divergent policy? Was Hitler succeeding in his plan to split the Allies? As usual, suspicion outran judgment and discretion. The Free German Manifesto was widely denounced by those who had not troubled to read it. The numerous free governments formed in England or in America without consulting Russia were forgotten in the demand that Russia should do nothing without our approval and consent. We permitted the formation of a Free Hungary movement that got the temporary blessing of the State and War Departments. In this Russia was not consulted and as the movement was definitely fascist and reactionary, they had more right to be offended than we with the German Manifesto, which so eloquently reaffirmed the Four Freedoms.

The full and precise reasons for Litvinoff's recall are known only to the Kremlin, but close observers of the political scene had for some time been aware that all was not perfectly happy in Russian-American relations, and when Litvinoff left on May 10 there were predictions that he would not return as Ambassador. Two considerations influence the appointment of an ambassador: Where nations are in close accord, delighting to honor one another, they send their ablest and most distinguished representative, even though he may be needed at home. In the second place, an ambassador is chosen as the one most likely to promote good will and close and profitable co-operation between the governments and peoples of both nations. If he fails in this, though it may be no fault of his own, he must expect recall.

It is a simple fact that the last six months has seen in America the increasingly noisy expression of sentiment hostile to Russia. The film, "Mission to Moscow," for example, which was a concentrated and necessarily symbolic presentation of Ambassador Davies' book, evoked a mad hurricane of protest from reactionaries and revolutionaries alike, of such virulent hostility and utter extravagance of denunciation that it was obviously a release for emotions that had been pent up by America's widespread and enthusiastic appreciation of what Russia was doing in the war.* The attack was only a prelude and signal for others, who had timidly held their peace. Some of the newspaper chains, such as the Hearst papers, attacked Russia without regard to right or truth, assailing her for not having opened a second front against Japan, disregarding the President and Mr. Churchill, who declared that such a request would have been quite unfair and contrary to our interests as well as Russia's, and ignoring the fact that we refused to declare war on Finland, although Finland had without provocation attacked Russia without declaration of war, inflicting upon her grievous damage, and was still locking up preciously needed men and material.

It would be easy to exaggerate the importance of these unfriendly expressions. They have been conspicuous, but concentrated in origin, and do not offset the massive and steadily growing respect and gratitude in which Russia is held by the majority of Americans. Newspaper circulation is no guarantee of influence.

The suspicious and excitable tried to read into the recall the condemnation of Litvinoff and there began even the whisper of liquidation. But Litvinoff, on his return to Moscow, had been received with

---

* Cf. A. U. P., "The Film *Mission to Moscow* and Its Critics," National Council of American-Soviet Friendship, New York, 1943.

honor by Stalin and is continuing as Assistant People's Commissar of Foreign Affairs.

The incident has to be seen in the light of the previous humiliations to which Russian representatives have been subjected through many years: the frequent exclusion of Russia from any participation in international affairs, the studied ignoring of Russian interests at various conferences, the "political snobbery" of which Lloyd George complained, the continued suspicion in certain reactionary quarters, and contemptuous disregard of Russian sacrifices as if there were "only Russians" being killed. Russia can no longer be treated as she was up until '39, as an outcast nation, nor, since then by some, as a poor relation.

The second front still hung fire. Russia was aware of battling two hundred divisions while we were fighting six. While admiring our performance and grateful for military assistance, it was easy for Russia to underestimate our difficulties, and also the effectiveness of our strategy in paralyzing Italy and in bombing Germany. None the less, taken in view of the total situation which did not seem to be improving much, the withdrawal of Litvinoff was about the only way in which Russia could protest, courteously but vigorously. It was clear notice that Russia was not wholly satisfied with the course of our American relations.

Had he been defeated once again? Yet there is also a sense in which Litvinoff has never been defeated and therein lies the significance of his life, though from the point of view of his efforts to promote international peace it must seem to be nothing but a series of defeats. For twenty years he worked with courage, skill and absolute devotion for a great cause. Throughout that time, despite some progress and the more or less complete reacceptance of Russia as one of the great powers, which was largely his work, he met on the greater issues constant frustration. Hoping to save his country from the shock and exhaustion of war at the very moment when she was putting the crown on her great program for rehabilitation and the new life, hoping also to see the world spared massacre, horror and ruin, he had seen each hope broken in turn; he had had to face ridicule, meanness, complacency, politically powerful and sometimes scurrilous and dishonest. He had had to face political snobbery, infuriating inertia and plain obstructionism, to contest with the faint-hearted who magnified the dangers by trying to flee from them; the indolent who would acquiesce in evil rather than fight it; the conventional-minded who thought to meet an onrushing, quite unconventional peril by fatuous reliance on sterile and unprofitable procedures, hoping with the gossamer fabric of words to bridge an infernal precipice. There were the real cynics who had no faith in any action or any cause beyond preserving their own power and privileges for the moment, always ready with "the mistimed laugh in tragic presences." The international political scene was thoroughly confused by the notion of absolute sovereignty, theoretically self-contradictory, practically prolific of disputes, fears and an ever threatening anarchy, yet stubbornly adhered to by nearly every nation. The whole scene was poisoned by innumerable irrelevant and stale animosities—many of them directed against the Soviet Union. He had to see with both anger and disquiet the evidence of hostility to Russia by countries ready to connive at monstrous aggression so long as it was turned towards Russia and away from them. Over and over again, his situation must have been almost intolerable.

No individual had ever played for more tremendous stakes, fighting not merely for human welfare but fighting against a continuous menace of two clearly envisaged wars which threatened to exterminate civilization and to deluge mankind with a torrent of utter misery. For this supremest of causes Litvinoff battled with a courage, a persistence, a cleverness and consistency that few human beings have ever brought to any effort, and in the face of odds that would many a time have crushed any but a truly great man. At the outset of his career he had been in constant physical danger, for his whole program was treason against the Czarist state; but as the struggle was transferred to the international arena he met obstacles worse than personal danger—the obstruction by the concerted action of the Powers, of the practical means for realizing the most urgent need of the hour.

Meshed in a disintegrating world, fighting, for a hopeless cause, a series of delaying actions, watching step by step the doom foregather, Litvinoff never compromised, never faltered, and whatever feelings of wrath and bitterness he might have had, they never clouded his intelligence nor dimmed the ideal which he served. He was throughout sustained by the high significance of his purpose. If the affairs of his own nation were a constant anxiety and uncertainty, if he saw its very existence threatened by the plots of the Trotskyites and their accessories, if he saw her preparations running a too close race with calamity, nonetheless it neither discouraged him nor wore him down and Munich saw him at the summit of his powers, his fighting spirit intact.

Litvinoff had compensations and allies. He was energized by the support which he enjoyed, first from Lenin and now from Stalin. The very example of the Russian Revolution which must have seemed an almost vastly more hopeless cause than international peace, for which he now fought, must have sustained his courage to hope for the unattainable. These considerations helped to equalize the contest and also Litvinoff was not alone but had political support in other countries and stout friends at Geneva. Yet his burden and his battle, despite his superhuman energy, skill and persistence, ended in defeat and once more the terror-horror of another international war broke on a suffering world. But in Litvinoff's case defeat was never final, nor is it for any great ideal. It is not yet proven that man must be forever victimized by his own folly. Moreover, Litvinoff had been expounding principles of universal validity and although rejected in the past they still have a certain validity for the future and may yet be crowned with success.

Litvinoff's whole struggle had taken on something of the character of a Greek tragedy. Here was the *magnitude* that Aristotle demanded—twenty years of battle for the highest possible stakes involving all mankind—and there was now impending disaster on a vast and almost superhuman scale. Yet it was a comprehensible magnitude. Here was a *plot*, unified and clear, and *action* which gave to the drama tension and force; here in its principal actor was that strength and greatness of *character* without which tragedy does not rise above the level of comedy. There certainly was terror in the prospect of universal destruction and the certainty that millions upon millions were to be engulfed in the last extremity of human suffering was equally pitiable. The total situation should in all normal human beings have stirred enough *terror and pity* to have *purged* away all commonplace and self-regarding emotions.

A great tragedy is more than episodes in the life of a hero. It involves the not unequal clash of universal and immense forces, for a time apparently in balance yet the scale is turned and the tragic finale ensues—

unloosed by forces that are partly inevitable and partly a compound of the base and the accidental. And so it was in Litvinoff's case.

It is not sentimental or exaggerated to see in the Litvinoff of the long battle for collective security more than a hint of the tragic hero as conceived in classical literature, for Litvinoff was not at Geneva as a person, he was speaking for a mighty people; and in their strength he was strong. He was a spokesman for a supreme cause, the proponent of an advancing world.

If thus Litvinoff appears the hero in this account, it might seem that leaders in the British Conservative Government from 1920 to 1940 were here cast in the role of arch villains; but such an impression would be an unwarranted over-simplification. Litvinoff and his government on the one hand, the British authorities on the other, represented sharply contrasting worlds and programs. Antagonism between them was probably inevitable, for back of both were powerful forces, social, economic, political, that were in many vital ways diametrically opposed. The conflict was indeed fundamental and almost irreconcilable. Conservative Britain stood for the maintenance of the status quo and all its special privileges for a relative minority—a world that justified itself by majestic achievements and rich human experience, especially the precious sense for quality, which the established order claims to have made possible; but its views encouraged a dangerous complacency and inertia; at numerous points the system it proposed to maintain intact rested upon social injustice and was furthered at the price of impoverished, insecure and frustrated lives for many; and at bottom, it sought to resist the processes of history. For these processes require a steady development of human institutions in the direction of more adequate living for all; they necessitate the breaking down of social and political barriers and compartments; they increasingly prepare for and demand the participation of all in the work of civilization which must be envisaged as a universal, co-operative project, not the prerogative or even the directive of the few.

The Conservative forces represented by British (and French) policy were challenged by the Russian Revolution, which had its roots deep in injustice and misery, in oppression and terror of the past and was now fired by a destructive and often blind fury against all forms of privilege and entrenched power.

The first program of the Russian revolutionaries was well calculated to dismay and thoroughly disturb the Western capitalistic Powers: the repudiation of debts incurred by previous regimes, the abolition of private property, the instigation of world revolution, the hostility to organized religion—indeed an alarming prospect made the worse by lurid accounts of terror, by the lack of authentic information or any adequate background in the West for the interpretation of events in Russia. All this was perfectly calculated to arouse fear and bitterest resentment not merely in the conservative classes but throughout the Western Powers generally. Virulent campaigns of hate conducted by dispossessed and embittered White Russians and sometimes financed by those who had special economic interests to serve, inflamed animosities, darkened counsel and made it almost impossible to bridge the gap opened by the Revolution.

These were some of the basic causes of the tragedy: the conflict of two worlds; the inflexibility, the blindness, the complacency and the moral weariness of the old, unable to face the great danger with the requisite intelligence and fortitude, lacking sufficient vision and generosity to co-operate with a new set of forces and ideals virile, alert, moving with the tide of Time, a world with which there was only apparent, not permanent or fundamental, incompatibility.

The play seems to end with the thunder of the guns and the pitiful cry of anguished victims, but it has only begun and the end is not yet; new affirmations and new vistas have effected rapprochements between the two most hostile forces. Their distrust has been progressively overcome by common danger—a potent persuader, a great revealer of realities, for despite the special hostility of some of the conservative financial classes in England, Great Britain as a whole gradually took a realistic attitude towards Russia. Litvinoff always believed that the consistent hostility of the Tory government and all it stood for did not represent the will of the British people, which Litvinoff felt sure was not only in favor of collective security but, if given a fair chance, would be friendly to Russia. The magnificent affirmation of Dunkirk, the British readiness to fight it out alone, if necessary, were an impressive revelation of the character of the British people which attracted an immense amount of quiet admiration and unpublicized hope in Russia and paved the way for ultimate reconciliation. And though Baldwin,

Chamberlain and a few of their associates have much to answer for at the bar of history, yet when the final demonstration came of Russia's power and determination, England was converted to friendship—swiftly and completely—and was prompt to re-examine, renovate and expunge the blind antagonism of the past and to accept the demonstration of the present. Winston Churchill's superb speech hailing Russia as friend and ally the day after Hitler's unprovoked assault on Russia was one of the most timely and constructive of recent political utterances. It guaranteed the United Nations' support of Russia and bridged a perilous moment by a bold and realistic affirmation that has set the relations of the Western democracies to Russia in a new light.

Today the British are uneasy at the unrealistic and uninformed animosities that are still recklessly vocal in some sections of the American press; and the English anxieties on this score are not without reason, for of all the nations, the record of the United States in dealing with Russia was, until the coming of the Nazis, the least creditable. Government and public alike were from the start quite certain that the Soviets were assailing the very foundations of civilization. We were intolerant, credulous, angry and alarmed; fear and ignorance, those potent sources of doubt and hatred, did their unseemly work until in the early 20's our attitude towards Russia was a deplorable compound of suspicion, hypocrisy, fantasy and active hostility. The record of those days is not encouraging proof of our sagacity or political maturity.* The State Department was continuously denouncing Russia to the whole world, and the entire country, moreover, was guilty of a long list of crude errors, beginning with the acceptance at face value of the joke about the nationalization of women, and continuing through the deportation delirium, down to the recent complete and quite unnecessary failure to appraise the reorganized and reoriented Russia and to gauge her military power and the unanimous moral force of the nation that backed it up. We cannot afford such costly mistakes; yet there are still in this country smouldering pockets of anti-Russian rage; there are individuals and groups whose habit of enmity and contempt for Soviet Russia will not give way before either fact or the nation's interest; they have been ready to gamble with the safety of the Allied cause and to jeopardize

* See especially Fredrich L. Schuman, *American Policy Toward Russia*, N. Y., 1928, pp. 125 and 171, and Louis F. Post's *The Deportations Delirium*, Chicago, 1923.

the coming peace rather than surrender their prejudices, while irresponsible politicians and journalists have not hesitated to continue their Soviet baiting.

The attitude of the American people, as a whole, however, has at last been changed, persuaded by the facts. The realistic, independent and convincing report of Ambassador Davies in his *Mission to Moscow* presented to the Government and to a large and thoughtful public a relatively new view of the Russian Government and its policies, revealing a better organized, more reasonable economic and political administration and policy than the average American had believed existed there. Russia's proof of fighting power, her innumerable demonstrations of sheer heroism and patriotism of the highest order, the incomprehensible horrors which her civilian population has suffered at the hands of the invading Nazi savages, the serious economic dislocation and frustrated progress that she has unflinchingly borne—all this has won American respect, sympathy and gratitude. The common American man now knows well that, if the war is to terminate soon and favorably, if we are to have a chance to resume the work of civilization instead of being exhausted by decades of horrible and demoralizing fighting, it is to Russian character, foresight, capacity and bravery that the fortunate event will be largely due. Nor is this to underestimate the magnificent stand of Great Britain, the steadfastness and skill with which she has pursued the war, her sublime defiance of overwhelming odds, while America was belatedly learning and leisurely preparing.

The West is thus at last coming to understand Russia. But so slow has been this comprehension, so retarded by lingering antipathies, and so disappointing to Russia have been some of the practical expressions that she could rightfully have expected, such as a more prompt second front in Europe, that Litvinoff may still have ahead as one of his greatest diplomatic efforts the persuasion of his own country to corresponding sympathy with the West.

He has considered this to be one of his principal diplomatic functions, a fundamental and productive contribution which may in the long run be his greatest service. When the Revolution was disappointed in its hopes that the world would welcome it and that peace would be promptly declared by the suffering multitudes and a new era of co-operation and good will brought in, and instead came the dreaded hostility with diplomatic offensives and military invasion, the Russians were on the whole depressed, disappointed and angry. Then after a few years they found that their plans for a world revolution evoked nothing but further antipathy which threatened disaster to the Revolution in Russia itself. Consequently, under Stalin's guidance, Russia turned in upon herself with plans for the exploitation of her own vast territories, the education and life-fulfillment of her own multitudes, finding inspiration in her own past.

This withdrawal, which was incomplete, was only slowly comprehended, was greeted with complete scepticism by others and as a relief from tension, but Russia is an indispensable part of the world economy; she has immense social capacity and a magnificent cultural productivity that has shown itself in science and in all the arts. A real Russian withdrawal from the international scene would be a calamity and might well lead to misunderstanding and ultimate conflict, which could easily be an almost final catastrophe for civilization. Litvinoff, dedicated to the Revolution, unqualifiedly devoted to its ultimate ideals, thoroughly Russian himself, has nonetheless lived in the Western world, has known first-hand its capacities, its great political, ethical and cultural potentials—values concealed from many in the new Soviet Government. He has worked to keep alive the contacts; to convince his own people that the Fascists and reactionaries of the Western world, however conspicuous or apparently powerful, do not represent the sum and substance of the Western nations. He had to try to persuade his government that Neville Chamberlain was not Great Britain; that Chamberlain would be ultimately repudiated Litvinoff was sure. But would the rejection come in time? It did not.

While Litvinoff's primary work has been planning and working for international peace, this has by no means been his whole task. He was from 1930 and actually before that the minister in charge of the foreign relations of a great country during one of the most difficult and perilous times. This office would in itself have been sufficiently inclusive and vast and complicated, but in a hostile antagonistic political and economic environment with continuous pressure and intrigue from other countries the difficulties were immeasurably increased. Yet to these responsibilities, both special and routine, Litvinoff has been amply adequate. He is not merely a thinker of superior capacity and a far-sighted planner, but a competent administrator. Prudent and exact, methodical and industrious, he operated his huge Foreign Office efficiently and well.

The principal features of Litvinoff's personality which have made him such a successful diplomat and given him world status are fairly clear. His native endowment is of the finest quality. He has been fortified throughout his arduous life by robust nervous and physical health. He was equipped by nature with a superlative intelligence and has been cultivated and disciplined by exacting experience which was itself a continuous process of education. His remarkable capacity for sustained labor, characteristic of all the Bolshevik leaders, is no new acquisition, but must date from early youth, and there are certain other qualities of his mind the elements of which are probably inherent, qualities which if listed separately are misleading since all the factors in a thoroughly integrated personality like Litvinoff's are reciprocally interactive, with a constant interplay and interchange and mutual reinforcement.

Perspicacity and flexibility, realism and reasonableness are only different terms for a central attribute. Insight is an elementary requirement for a good diplomat and Litvinoff has to a remarkable degree an intuition as responsive as that of an artist. He senses with uncanny accuracy what is going on in the minds of those with whom he is dealing; their motives stand revealed; their limitations, their habits; the total complex of influence is clearly gauged and their conclusions anticipated.

In negotiation Litvinoff is most flexible, knows when to drop the unessentials, when to give way, and when to allow his opponent the relief of strong affirmation. Skill at playing a waiting game, in which he does not waste the waiting interval but uses it for review, new planning and adjustments, is only a corollary of his intelligence and his patience.

His realism is a marked feature of his mentality. He is never led astray by his own hopes. Emotional considerations never interfere in his operations. His feeling for fact and his ability to face up to it even when most disconcerting and disappointing have been sources of great power. His capacity for discounting the sentimental or irrelevant and his refusal to spend precious time in either self-pity or self-congratulation are marks of a strong man.

This resolute realism has won for him the reputation of being a cynic, but a cynic is one who is sceptical of ultimate values, who is without faith that honest and reasonable endeavor can win. Litvinoff is not that kind of a cynic. He is a magnificent deflator of bombast, a merciless exposer of fraudulent and pious pretensions. He takes a grim delight in confronting verbal disguises with their real motives.

But above and beyond all else Litvinoff is an idealist, even if an idealist without illusions. No man could labor with such superb tenacity and such unflinching courage for great yet often temporarily hopeless causes unless he most devoutly believed in the reality and the authority of ideals. To his ideals he has given utter and selfless devotion. They are the organising principles of his life, for a great ideal vividly conceived, unreservedly accepted, guarantees power, and with it there is neither variableness nor shadow of any turning. It provides the courage, it supplies the energy, it unifies the whole life. He has proven, even though he has not himself philosophically recognised it, that loyalty to trans-individual values generates individual values, a principle which Americans seem to have forgotten in the wave of divisive tendencies, of ethical monadism, and the revival of the "each man for himself" theory which makes for personal and national weakness.

Litvinoff's ideals are deeply and characteristically Russian. The Russian national greeting, "Comrade" is no artificial imposition like the silly Nazi salute, "Heil Hitler." It expresses a normal Russian attitude, and the Russians, like the Chinese, have a vivid sense of humankind as a whole and its claims to sympathy and service.

Litvinoff is eminently reasonable, equally in small and in large affairs. His capacity for logical deduction, for seizing and clearly defining a principle with lucidity and rigorous logic, are remarkable and not approached by any other statesmen of our time. This is one of the sources, as are his combined realism and idealism, of his remarkable consistency. For here is a statesman who has never had to reverse himself, never had to explain away any statement issued. His first utterance is consonant with his last, and all in between.

The intensity and strength of Litvinoff's ideals owe something perhaps to the primary shock in early childhood when he saw caprice, dishonesty and injustice visited on his own home. It could not have been other than a shock and probably initiated that constructive reaction which ultimately canalized his native capacities into creative tendencies. Examples of cruelty and oppression and unfairness in a thousand guises flooded into his life to reinforce that original awakening. His own town of Belostok in June, 1906, saw a ghastly pogrom, carefully prepared by the State police days in advance, with precise written instructions which resulted in more than eighty deaths, countless mutilations and many destroyed homes.

His ideals and purposes having been formulated in youth, the firm and resolute control that he took of his own life has endowed him with indispensable moral integrity. Even as a young man his soul was well knit and all his spiritual battles won. He knew where his values lay. He has been spared demoralizing inner conflicts. There have been no ambiguities of aim and no wayward inconsistencies and this has saved him from the intrusion of irrelevant emotions. This freedom is one of the greatest sources of his energy and force. He has indeed won detachment from distractions rare in any human being. The psychological and ethical unity has again protected him from the pressure of irrelevancies and enabled him to hold with singlemindedness to the work in hand. Litvinoff was not one to be caught off-base by the conventional requirements of week-ends, as were the British at Rapallo. Nor has he the time-consuming necessities for recreation and amusement that have plagued many French officials, nor the need for personal publicity or political ambition which have so often seduced public servants in the United States.

His imperturbability is probably partly a natural endowment. He says himself that he was born with it. But again it has been fortified by his idealism and by the severe discipline of his dangerous and strenuous life. For years he had to withstand every kind of insult and humiliation that hostile and mean-spirited opponents could devise.

He knew the greatness of his country and the reasonableness and justice of her appeal for co-operation, and in behalf of his country he must have resented with hot rage the stupidities and pettinesses with which he was constantly affronted. For Litvinoff is capable of great rage, and of virile and pertinacious enmity against those whom he adjudges unscrupulous or in any way servants of the too numerous and potent forces of evil that afflict international relations. Yet he never allowed even righteous indignation to interfere with practical results.

His courage is limitless. There is no sign that fear has ever been a motive in his decisions or actions. It would have no chance in a life psychologically so sound and compact, in which the values are so completely placed outside temporary personal needs.

Litvinoff can be exacting, he can occasionally be as formal as any protocol-hound; but this kind of situation arises only when some greater value either absorbs him or overrules the lesser.

All these qualities that sound by themselves rather grim are suffused with a robust humor. Litvinoff is always ready with a joke; with poetic nimbleness he lights on the comic and the ridiculous and gets a continuous laugh out of life. His humor has endeared him to his associates, given him power with the press, eased many a tension, cooled many a hot argument and floated many a discussion to a successful conclusion. He uses humor perhaps artfully as Abraham Lincoln did for such purposes, yet it seems completely spontaneous and out of the depths of his own perceptions. Those waiting in his anteroom in the Narkomindel could often overhear roars of laughter when he and Schulenburg, himself a magnificent raconteur, were battling over tense and bitter issues, trying to maintain peace between two countries reciprocally hateful.

The diplomatic utility of all these qualities is obvious, and to them in his diplomatic work he adds discretion. It is part of his technique to avoid the superfluous, never to use too many words, which, as he says, open too many doors; and his honesty gives assurance that he will never betray a confidence and never resort to double-dealing or the polite sanctioned trickeries approved in many chancelleries.

The career and achievements of Maxim Litvinoff are thus of the highest character and worthy of as unqualified approval as could be given to any human being who has had to work in such confused and difficult situations. The writer also finds a great deal to approve in the policies and achievements of the Soviet Union. It has indeed, like any other nation, made its own special mistakes. There have been recessions, cross-purposes and cruelties, but these have been incidental to a vast and creative enterprise—the rescue of a nation of nearly 200 million people from oppressive and degrading tyranny, the re-creation of a shattered and exhausted country and the building of a new nation with a new consciousness, new power and new hope. This historic project started with every handicap—poverty, inexperience, administrative incompetence, impractical dogmas, unclarified aims; battled grimly for its very existence against foreign hostility that was unanimous, powerful and vindictive; was isolated in a world of suspicion and ill will. Yet by virtue of courage and tenacity, unique endurance and a fanatical devotion combined with realistic good sense, the Soviet Union has emerged in a scant twenty-five years as a genuinely great nation.

Inasmuch as both Litvinoff and Russia have been the targets of ruthless detractors who have taken the exactly opposite view, seeing the Soviet as the epitome of all evil, many will be reluctant to accept such a high estimate despite the evidence of fact and reason; for there is a common, much esteemed conviction that neither of two sharply opposed opinions can be really valid, that the golden mean in judgment as well as in conduct is the mark of truth. Aristotle is popularly thought to have sponsored this precept and no doubt it is a prudent approach, providing a safe way, for those who need it, to avoid taking sides and evade intellectual responsibilities. If this popular dictum be true, the high evaluation of the Russian achievement must be discounted in advance and some intermediate be found between commendation and denunciation.

But is the half-and-half judgment necessarily the wise, the sound? St. Paul had some rather harsh words to say about those who were neither hot nor cold; and the donkey who starved to death between two haystacks was rather overmuch committed to the middle point of view. What, too, would be the middle course between life and death, health and disease? Do those who want to avoid extremes recommend permanent invalidism as the proper way of life? What is the mean between the Nazi assumption that they have a right to starve, massacre and torture the victim peoples and our conviction that this is an unqualified abomination? Shall we find moral security in some half-way policy approving just a little torture, only a few executions and partial starvation? Is there a medium judgment concerning the world's great traitors and criminals? Are they extremists who find the noblest servants of mankind and the supreme masterpieces in art and music worthy of complete admiration, and the endless history of cruelty, vulgarity and fraud wholly detestable? No—all these cases must be decided on the facts and on their merit, without any prior weighting of judgment or predilection for any particular position in the scale of values.

So considered, Maxim Litvinoff must be given a high rating, and although a final appraisal of his whole career must be left to the future historian, nonetheless strong approbation can be justified, for certain features of his character and policies are now sufficiently clear and established.

Litvinoff's character is particularly inspiring at a time when in the Western world security and conventional modes of thinking and acting are replacing the pioneer virtues of courage, enterprise, independence and imagination; when surrender in the face of difficulty is regarded as practical, and sublime persistence, even for the greatest of causes, as fanatical. His life and work illustrate, as few do, the power of a unifying idea that absorbs and organizes all the capacities of the individual, which guarantees victory even in defeat—the victory of an idea, defiant of adversity, tested in action, of universal validity.

Although he probably never heard of it, Hegel's dictum, "Do good skillfully," might well have been a guiding precept for him, while his general approach to problems was anticipated and prescribed by a great Russian socialist, Alexander Herzen, one of the pioneers in the long contest for Russian freedom, whose writings Litvinoff knew as a youth.

But it is a noble injunction of Lenin's that most adequately sums up Litvinoff's life and character:

"Man's dearest possession is life and it is given to him to live but once. He must live so as to feel no torturing regrets for years without purpose; so live as not to be seared by the shame of a cowardly and trivial past; so live that dying he can say 'all my life and all my strength were given to the finest cause in all the world—the fight for the liberation of mankind.'"

'IF'

Yea, if ye could not, though ye would, lift hand—
Ye halting leaders—to abridge Hell's reign;
If, for some cause ye may not yet make plain,
Yearning to strike, ye stood as one may stand
Who in a nightmare sees a murder planned
And hurrying to its issue, and though fain
To stay the knife, and fearless, must remain
Madly inert, held fast by ghostly band;—
If such your plight, most hapless ye of men!
But if ye could and would not, O, what plea,
Think ye, shall stead you at your trial, when
The thunder-cloud of witnesses shall loom,
With Ravished Childhood on the seat of doom,
At the Assizes of Eternity?

William Watson.

Bibliography

THERE ARE A large number of books in English—good, bad and indifferent —on the problems of Soviet Russia. If one could read one book only, it ought to be Sir Bernard Pares' "big little book," *Russia,* in the Penguin Series. The author is perhaps the best-informed man in the Western world on Russian history—penetrating, fair-minded, sympathetic, thoroughly equipped for understanding Russia by his forty visits and two years of fighting at the front with the Russians in the first World War.

Walter Duranty's *Duranty Reports Russia* is the record of a remarkable journalistic achievement. Duranty lived in Russia for twenty years, through all the dark and complex days. His is a realistic, alert, pungent mind with a sense for fact combined with courage and generosity and competence. Duranty's *The Kremlin and the People* is an indispensable commentary on recent affairs.

His forthcoming *Short History of the Soviet Union* promises to be a work of first class importance.

Louis Fischer's two-volume work on *The Soviet in World Affairs* and his *Men in Politics* contain information of greatest value not available elsewhere. Mr. Fischer had access to very important original documents. *The Soviet in World Affairs* is definitely the most fundamental work on the early diplomatic history of Soviet Russia that we have in English.

Maurice Hindus, himself a born Russian, saturated with the life of the common people, has reflected with literary power, deep insight and courageous truth-telling both the tragedy and the achievements of the revolution. His books, *Humanity Uprooted,* and *Red Bread,* are outstanding. In a more recent book, *Hitler Cannot Conquer Russia,* he proclaimed before others imagined or the events proved the power of Russia successfully to resist invasion. His latest book, *Mother Russia,* again speaks with the authentic voice of the Russian people.

Professor F. L. Schuman's *American Policy Toward Russia Since 1917,* a lucid, firmly reasoned, thoroughly documented account of our relations with Soviet Russia during its first ten years, furnishes an indispensable basis for the understanding of subsequent events

David J. Dallin's *Soviet Russia's Foreign Policy 1939–42* is also a thorough statement of Soviet foreign policy in the last three years, well-informed, systematic, complete, scholarly.

Stanley J. Marks' *The Bear That Walks Like a Man* gives a vigorous defense of Soviet policies during the last five years; it contains valuable material and is an effective challenge to the conventionally unfavorable interpretations of Russian policy.

There are some very readable books on Russia in wartime, written by recent correspondents:

Wallace Carroll—*We're in This With Russia*
Quentin Reynolds—*Only the Stars Are Neutral*
Alexander Werth—*Moscow War Diary*
Margaret Bourke-White—*Shooting the Russian War* presents some superb photographs of significant Russian scenes, more effective than much verbal documentation.
Henry Cassidy—*Moscow Dateline*
Walter Graebner—*Round Trip to Russia*
John Whitaker—*You Can't Escape History*
Larry Lesueur—*Twelve Months That Changed the World*
Two diplomatic reports, gauged by their influence, stand out. Maurice Paléologue's three-volume *Memoirs,* which cover the years 1914–1917, is, all in all, probably the most notable diplomatic memoirs ever published. The author was a man of extraordinary brilliance, charm, and penetration and he has left an impressive record of some of the great years in human history. Its literary and intellectual merits would give it permanence aside from the significance of its content.

Joseph Davies' *Mission to Moscow* is a factual, clear-headed, honest report of a difficult assignment, convincingly carried out. Ambassador Davies was sent to get the facts about Russia, and despite the welter of conflicting reports he brought out the truth—which has been indispensable to the American government and provided much needed enlightenment to the American people.

John Reed's *Ten Days That Shook the World* is a first-hand, very detailed and convincing report of the launching of the Bolshevik Revolution; it remains the most important documentation of those fateful days.

Albert Rhys Williams, who saw the Soviet experiment from the start, has published a number of clearly written, sound and very informing books, describing Russian social and political organization, notably *The Russian Land, The Soviets, The Russians.*

John Scott, in *Behind the Urals,* provides an admirable first-hand account of the great new industrial state which Scott knew better than any American. His *Duel for Europe,* while, like the books of the correspondents, largely a narrative, is again honest and informing.

André Gide's querulous and superficial account of a few days in Russia, which is chiefly a petulant record of personal disappointments, is an excellent illustration of a whole class of books written without proper background, and without real acquaintance with the subject.

Lion Feuchtwanger's *Moscow, 1937* shows what can be done when a man is more interested in the truth than in himself.

There are several books that are written with such animosity, amounting at times to straight-out malice, that they are best forgotten. These also are records of personal frustrations, by men whose predictions, whose advice or whose sympathies were overrun by the realities; or people who, like Gide, merely universalized their own exasperation and expanded their personal discomforts into political theory.

Documentation

Albertson, Ralph—
Fighting Without a War, an Account of Military Intervention in North Russia,
New York (Harcourt, Brace & Howe), 1920. 138 pp., map, ill.

American Relief Administration—
Annual Report of the Executive Committee, April 4, 1923,
New York (American Relief Administration), 1923.

Bernstein, Herman—
The Willy-Nicky Correspondence,
New York (Alfred A. Knopf), 1918. 158 pp., frontis.

Buchanan, Sir George—
My Mission to Russia and Other Diplomatic Memoirs,
London—New York, etc. (Cassell & Co., Ltd.), 1923. 2 vols., Vol. I, pp. 91–253, Vol. II, pp. 1–248.

Bullitt, William C.—
The Bullitt Mission to Russia,
New York (B. W. Huebsch), 1919. 151 pp.

Chicherin, George—
Two Years of Foreign Policy, The Relations of the Russian Socialist Federal Soviet Republic with Foreign Nations from November 7, 1917, to November 7, 1919,
New York (The Russian Soviet Government Bureau, Pamphlet No. 3), 1920. 36 pp.

Constitution of the U.S.S.R.—
New York (National Council for American-Soviet Friendship), 1943.

Francis, David Rowland—
Russia From the American Embassy, April, 1916–November, 1918,
New York (Charles Scribner's Sons), 1921. 361 pp., ill.

Lenin, V. I.—
Speeches of V. I. Lenin,
New York (International Publishers), 1925. 94 pp.

Lenin, V. I.—Stalin, Joseph—
The Russian Revolution . . . from the February Revolution to the October Revolution, 1917,
New York (International Publishers), 1938. 303 pp.

Lenin, V. I.—Trotsky, Leon (L. C. Fraina, Ed.)—
The Proletarian Revolution in Russia,
New York (The Communist Press), 1928.

Lenin, V. I.—
The Bourgeois Revolution,
New York (International Publishers), 1928.

Litvinov, M. M.—
On Soviet Russia,
London (People's Russian Infor-
mation Bureau), 1919.

Litvinov, Maxim M.—
The Bolshevik Revolution, Its
Rise and Meaning,
Chicago (Socialist Party of the
United States), 1920. 79 pp.

Litvinov, M. M.—
"Soviet Dumping," a Fable,
New York (Workers Library
Publishers), 1931. 31 pp.

Litvinov, M. M.—
Soviet International Economic
Policy,
Current History, IV (1931), pp.
510–516.

Litvinov, M. M.—
The Soviet's Fight for Disarmament,
London (M. Lawrence, Ltd.),
1932. 44 pp.

Litvinov, M. M.—
The U.S.S.R. and the League of
Nations,
New York (Workers Library
Publishers), 1934. 31 pp.

Litvinov, M. M.—
Relations Between the U.S.S.R.
and Uruguay,
London (Anglo-Russian Parliamentary Committee), 1936. 32
pp.

Litvinov, Maxim M.—
Against Aggression,
New York (International Pub-
lishers), 1939. 208 pp.

Litvinov, M. M.—
Czechoslovakia and the World
Crisis,
New York (International Publish-
ers), 1938. 15 pp.

People's Commissariat of Justice of
the U.S.S.R.—
Report of Court Proceedings in
the case of the Anti-Soviet Trot-
skyite Centre,
Moscow (People's Commissariat
of Justice of the U.S.S.R.),
1937. 580 pp.

Stalin, Joseph (Eden & Cedar Paul,
Trans.)—
Leninism,
New York (International Publish-
ers), 1928. 457 pp., index.

Stalin, Joseph, et al.—
The Land of Socialism Today and
Tomorrow,
Moscow (Foreign Languages Pub-
lishing House), 1939. 488 pp.

Stalin, Joseph—
Marxism and the National Question,
New York (International Publishers), 1942. 222 pp.

Stalin, Joseph—
The War of National Liberation,
New York (International Publish-
ers), 1942. 61 pp.

Trotsky, Leon—
The History of the Russian Revo-
lution to Brest-Litovsk,
London (G. Allen & Unwin,
Ltd.), 1919. 149 pp.

Trotsky, Leon—
Whither Russia?,
New York (International Publish-
ers), 1926. 150 pp.

Trotsky, Leon—
The History of the Russian Revolution,
New York (Simon and Schuster),
1932. 503 pp., index, ill.

Trotsky, Leon (F. G. Wright,
Trans.)—

Lessons of October, 1917,
New York (Pioneer Publishers),
1937. 125 pp.
Werner, M. R. (Ed.)—

Stalin's Kampf, Joseph Stalin's
Credo, Written by Himself,
New York (Howell, Soskin &
Co.), 1940. 356 pp.

BACKGROUND HISTORY OF RUSSIA

Beazley, Sir Charles Raymond-
Forbes, Neville-Birkett, G. A.—
Russia from the Varangians to
the Bolsheviks,
Oxford (Oxford University
Press), 1918. 601 pp., index.
Blackwell, Alice Stone (Ed.)—
The Little Grandmother of the
Russian Revolution, Reminis-
cences and Letters of Catherine
Breshkovsky,
Boston (Little, Brown & Co.),
1919. 337 pp., index, frontis.
Kliucheoskii, V. O.—
A History of Russia,
London—New York, 1911–1931.
5 vols.
Kornilov, Alexander—
Modern Russian History, From
the Age of Catherine the Great
to the End of the Nineteenth
Century,
New York (Alfred A. Knopf),
1943. 271 pp., bibliography, in-
dex.
Milyoukov, Paul—
Russia and Its Crisis,
Chicago—London (The Univer-
sity of Chicago Press—T. Fisher
Unwin), 564 pp., index, frontis.
Milioukov, P. N.—Seignobos, C.—
Eisenmann, L.—
Histoire de Russie,
Paris (Ernest Leroux), 1932–1933.
3 vols., 1383 pp., genealogical

tables, maps, index.
Munro, Hector H.—
The Rise of the Russian Empire,
Boston—London (L. C. Page &
Co.—Grant Richards), 1900.
326 pp., dynastic tables, map,
index.
Noble, Edmund—
The Russian Revolt, Its Causes,
Condition, and Prospects,
Boston (Houghton, Mifflin &
Co.), 1885. 263 pp., index.
Olgin, M. J.—
The Soul of the Russian Revolu-
tion,
New York (Henry Holt & Co.),
1917. 417 pp., index, ill.
Pares, Sir Bernard—
The Fall of the Russian Mon-
archy, A Study of the Evidence,
New York (Alfred A. Knopf),
1939. 504 pp., index.
Pares, Sir Bernard—
A History of Russia,
New York (Alfred A. Knopf),
1939. 528 pp., bibliography, in-
dex.
Pares, Sir Bernard—
Russia,
London—New York (Penguin
Books), 1940. 256 pp.
Stepniak, Boris—
The Russian Peasantry, Their
Agrarian Condition, Social Life
and Religion,

London (George Routledge and Sons), 1905. 643 pp., index.

Walling, William English—
Russia's Message, The True

World Import of the Revolution,
New York (Doubleday, Page & Co.), 1908. 469 pp., index, ill.

THE 1917 REVOLUTIONS AND THEIR AFTERMATH

Bechhofer, C. E.—
In Denikin's Russia and the Caucasus, 1919–1920,
London (W. Collins Sons & Co., Ltd.), 1921. 324 pp., maps.

Bryant, Louise—
Six Red Months in Russia,
New York (George H. Doran Company), 1918. 299 pp., ill.

Bryant, Louise—
Mirrors of Moscow,
New York (Thomas Seltzer), 1923. 209 pp.

Graves, William S.—
America's Siberian Adventure, 1918–1920,
New York (Jonathan Cape), 1931. 363 pp.

Hard, William—
Raymond Robins' Own Story,
New York (Harper and Brothers), 1920. 248 pp., frontis.

Kalpaschnikoff, Andrew—
A Prisoner of Trotsky's,
New York (Doubleday, Page & Co.), 1920. 287 pp.

Lockhart, R. H. Bruce—
British Agent,
New York—London (G. P. Putnam's Sons), 1933. Books Two–Four, pp. 53–346, index.

Magnes, J. L.—
Russia and Germany at Brest-Litovsk,
New York (The Rand School of Social Science), 1919. 192 pp.

Melgunov, S. P.—
The Red Terror in Russia,
London—Toronto (J. M. Dent & Sons), 1926. 271 pp., ill.

Moore, Joel R.—Mead, Harry H.—Jahns, Lewis E. (339th U. S. Infantry)—
The History of the American Expedition Fighting the Bolsheviki—Campaigning in North Russia, 1918–1919,
Detroit (The Polar Bear Publishing Co.), 1920. 303 pp., ill.

Paléologue, Maurice (F. A. Holt, Trans.)—
An Ambassador's Memoirs,
New York (George H. Doran Co.), 1923–1924. 3 vols., 1016 pp., ill.

Pasvolsky, Leo—Moulton, Harold G.—
Russian Debts and Russian Reconstruction,
New York (The McGraw-Hill Book Co.), 1924. 247 pp.

Reed, John—
Ten Days That Shook the World,
New York (International Publishers), 1926. 372 pp.

Sack, A. J.—
The Birth of the Russian Democracy,
New York (Russian Information Bureau), 1918. 552 pp., index, ill.

Steffens, Lincoln—
Autobiography,

New York (Harcourt, Brace & Co.), 1931. Chap. XVIII, pp. 790–802.

ACCOUNTS OF SOVIET RUSSIA

American Russian Institute
An Outline Study of the Soviet Union Today,
New York, 1943. 86 pp., bibliography.

Arnot, R. Page—
Soviet Russia and Her Neighbors,
New York (Vanguard Press), 1927. 175 pp.

Borders, Karl—
Village Life Under the Soviets,
New York (Vanguard Press), 1927. 191 pp.

Brailsford, H. N.—
How the Soviets Work,
New York (Vanguard Press), 1927. 169 pp.

Budish, J. M.—Shipman, Samuel S.—
Soviet Foreign Trade, Menace or Promise,
New York (Horace Liveright, Inc.), 1931. 268 pp.

Callcott, Mary—
Russian Justice,
New York (The Macmillan Co.), 1935. 265 pp.

Clark, Evans—
Facts and Fabrications about Soviet Russia,
New York (The Rand School of Social Science), 1920. 93 pp.

Duranty, Walter—
Duranty Reports Russia,
New York (The Viking Press), 1934. 401 pp.

Duranty, Walter—
The Kremlin and the People,

Williams, Albert Rhys—
Through the Russian Revolution,
New York (Boni & Liveright), 1921. 311 pp., ill.

New York (Reynal & Hitchcock, Inc.), 1941. 216 pp., index.

Eddy, Sherwood—
The Challenge of Russia,
New York (Farrar & Rinehart), 1931. 278 pp.

Eddy, Sherwood—
Russia Today, What Can We Learn From It?,
New York (Farrar & Rinehart), 1934. 308 pp., index.

Farbman, Michael—
After Lenin. The New Phase in Russia,
London (Leonard Parsons), 1924. 280 pp.

Feuchtwanger, Lion—
Moscow, 1937,
New York (The Viking Press), 1937. 151 pp.

Fischer, Louis—
Men and Politics,
New York (Duell, Sloan and Pearce), 1941. pp. 46–99, 216–240, 493–532.

Fülöp-Miller, Rene—
The Mind and Face of Bolshevism, An Examination of Cultural Life in Soviet Russia,
London—New York (G. P. Putnam's Sons, Ltd.), 1927. 289 pp., bibliography, index, ill.

Halle, Fannina—
Woman in Soviet Russia,
New York (The Viking Press), 1935. 409 pp., ill.

Harper, Samuel N.—
The Government of the Soviet Union,
New York (Van Nostrand Co.), 1938. 204 pp., maps.

Hindus, Maurice—
Humanity Uprooted,
New York (Jonathan Cape & Harrison Smith), 1929. 369 pp., ill.

Hindus, Maurice—
Red Bread,
New York (Jonathan Cape & Harrison Smith), 1931. 372 pp., ill.

Hindus, Maurice—
The Great Offensive,
New York (Harrison Smith & Robert Haas), 1933. 368 pp.

Hindus, Maurice—
Mother Russia,
New York (Doubleday Doran), 1943. 395 pp.

Johnson, Hewlett (Dean of Canterbury)—
Soviet Power,
(Modern Age), 1940. 352 pp.

Ludwig, Emil—
Stalin,
New York (G. P. Putnam's Sons), 1942. 239 pp., chronology, index, frontis.

Nearing, Scott—Hardy, Jack—
The Economic Organization of the Soviet Union,
New York (Vanguard Press), 1927. 236 pp., index.

Strong, Anna Louise—
This Soviet World,
New York (Henry Holt & Co.), 1936. 301 pp., index.

Webb, Beatrice & Sidney—
Soviet Communism,
New York (Longmans Green & Co.), 1935. 2 vols., 1174 pp.

Webb, Beatrice & Sidney—
The Truth About Soviet Russia,
New York (Longmans Green & Co.), 1942. 228 pp.

Williams, Albert Rhys—
The Soviets,
New York (Harcourt, Brace & Co.), 1937. 535 pp.

Williams, Albert Rhys—
The Russians, The Land, The People and Why They Fight,
New York (Harcourt, Brace & Co.), 1943. 248 pp., index.

RUSSIAN FOREIGN RELATIONS

Cumming, C. K.—Petit, Walter W.—
Russian-American Relations,
New York (Harcourt, Brace & Howe), 1920. 375 pp.

Davies, Joseph E.—
Mission to Moscow,
New York (Simon & Schuster), 1942. 662 pp.

Dennis, Alfred L. P.—
The Foreign Policies of Soviet Russia,
New York (E. P. Dutton & Co.), 1924. 493 pp., index.

Fischer, Louis—
The Soviet in World Affairs,
New York (Jonathan Cape & Harrison Smith), 1930. 2 vols., 892 pp.

Korff, S. A.—
Russian Foreign Relations During the Last Half Century,
New York (The Macmillan Co.), 1922. 227 pp.

Post, Louis Freeland—
The Deportations Delirium of
1920, A Personal Narrative of
an Historic Official Experience,
Chicago (Charles H. Kerr & Co.),
1923. 338 pp., frontis.

Schuman, Frederick—
American Policy Toward Russia
Since 1917,
New York (International Publish-
ers), 1928. 382 pp., bibliog-
raphy, index, maps.

RUSSIA IN THIS WAR

American Russian Institute Staff—
The U.S.S.R. at War, 50 Ques-
tions—50 Answers,
New York, 1943. 48 pp.

Carroll, Wallace—
We're in This With Russia,
New York (Houghton Mifflin
Co.), 1942. 264 pp.

Cassidy, Henry C.—
Moscow Dateline,
New York (Houghton Mifflin
Co.), 1943. 367 pp., index.

Graebner, Walter—
Round Trip to Russia, Philadelphia,
New York (J. B. Lippincott Co.),
1943. 216 pp., ill.

Hindus, Maurice—
Hitler Cannot Conquer Russia,
Garden City, New York (Doubleday, Doran & Co.), 1941. 299
pp.

Kournakoff, Capt. Sergei N.—
Russia's Fighting Forces,
New York (International Publish-
ers), 1942. 258 pp.

Lesueur, Larry—
Twelve Months That Changed the
World,
New York (Alfred A. Knopf),
1943.

Marks, Stanley J.—
The Bear That Walks Like a
Man, A Diplomatic and Mili-
tary Analysis of Soviet Russia,

Philadelphia (Dorrance & Co.),
1943. 339 pp., frontis.

Poliakov, Alexander (N. Guterman,
Trans.)—
Russians Don't Surrender,
New York (E. P. Dutton & Co.),
1942. 191 pp., ill.

Reynolds, Quentin—
Only the Stars Are Neutral,
Garden City, New York (Blue
Ribbon Books), 1942. 299 pp.

Scott, John—
Duel for Europe, Stalin Versus
Hitler,
Boston (Houghton Mifflin Co.),
1942. 380 pp., maps.

Werner, Max (H. and R. Norden,
Trans.)—
The Great Offensive, The Strat-
egy of Coalition Warfare,
New York (The Viking Press),
1942. 351 pp., index.

Werth, Alexander—
Moscow War Diary,
New York (Alfred A. Knopf),
1942. 297 pp.

Whitaker, John T.—
We Cannot Escape History,
New York (The Macmillan Co.),
1943. 367 pp., index.

Zacharoff, Lucien (Ed.)—
The Voice of Fighting Russia,
New York (Alliance Book Cor-
poration), 1942. 336 pp.

Index

A

Afanasevna, Pelagaya, the Litvinoff's maid, 176

Afghanistan, concludes treaty with Russia, 1921, 172

Agrarian Party of Czechoslovakia, urges acceptance of Munich settlement, 26

Agreements and Pacts, Kellogg, 1928, 13, 240-243; of Brest-Litovsk, 1917, 132, 133; Russo-Esthonian, 1920, 158; 1934, 336; Austro-Russian Prisoner Exchange Convention, 1920, 164; Russo-Latvian, 164-165; Russo-Lithuanian, 164, 165; Baltic, 1920, 164-165, 333; Peace of Riga, 1920, 166; Russo-German Provisional, 1921, 171; Russo-Persian, 1921, 170-171; 1927, 215; Russo-Afghanistan, 1921, 172; Russo-Turkish, 1921, 172; London Agreement, 1922, 185; Czech-Russian, 1922, 188; of Rapallo, 1922, 186-188, 207, 212; Anglo-Russian, 1924, 202-204; of Locarno, 209, 211; Litvinoff Protocol, 1928, 253-255; Franco-Russian, 1930–1932, 275-276, 277; Russo-Polish non-aggression, 1932, 276; Russo-Italian, 1932, 310; Russo-French, 1934, 327; "Little Entente," 333; "Mediterranean Locarno," 333; Russo-French, 1935, 356-358; German-Polish non-aggression, 1934, 360; Hoare-Laval, 1935, 367; Montreux Accord, 1936, 399-401; Black Sea Convention, 1936, 401; Japanese-German, 1936, 405; German-Italian, 422; Japanese-Italian, 1936, 422; Russo-German, 1939, 441 ff. See also Non-Aggression Pacts. See also Trade Agreements

Alabama case cited by Litivinoff, 1924, 203

Alexander II, Czar, rise of liberal thought under, 41; liberates serfs, 41; authorizes Zemstvas, 41; increases "Third Section" secret police, 42; assassinated, 42

Alexander II, King of Yugoslavia, his assassination, 1934, 352; and Hitler and Mussolini, 352

Alexander III, Czar, his repressions stimulate revolution, 42; Lenin's brother, charged with plotting his death, executed, 46

Alexandra Feodorovna, Czarina, her opinion of Nicholas II, 66; her influence on him, 68; interferes in conduct of First World War, 115; withdraws from politics after Rasputin's death, 118

Alexandrovski, Soviet Ambassador to Czechoslovakia, gives Beneš assurance of aid, 25

Allied statesman misgauge Russian Revolution, 141-144

Allied troops, land at Archangel, 1918, 147; occupy Murmansk, 148

Alois, Baron, and Italy's invasion of Ethiopia, 361

Ambassadors, Allied, leave Soviet territory, 1918, 149

American Federation of Labor, its hostility to Soviet Russia, 1926, 217

Andreyeva, F. M., wife of Maxim Gorki, 73

Anglo-French Military Mission to Russia, 1939, failure of, 446

Anglo-Russian Conference at London, 1924, 202-204; treaty signed, 204

Anti-Semitic propaganda, German, against Litvinoff, 1933, 319-322; German, within Russia and Great Britain, 321; in United States, 322

Anti-Soviet Propaganda, in 1918, 142; in Switzerland, 1923, 197-198; and Senator Borah, 217; German, 1933, 316-317, 319-322, American, 476-481

"Arcos" and Soviet Trade Delegation raids, London, 1927, 219-221; protested by Soviet embassy, 220; Manchester Guardian on, 220

Armenia liberated, 1920, 167

Assassinations, 1895–1901, 49

Associated Press, publishes Litvinoff's statement on trade, March, 1921, 169; publishes his statement on Russian debts and Soviet wish to attend Washington Conference of 1921, 175

Austria, her banks give credits to Russia, 1921, 172; Hitler's attempt to annex, 1934, 338; invasion of, March, 1938, 7, 437-438

Axelrod, Menshevik delegate at Zimmerwald Conference, 1915, 115

Azerbaijan liberated, 1920, 167

B

Bakhmetev, Boris, Kerenski's ambassador to United States, 135

Bakunin, his conflict with Marx, 1872, 40; founder of Russian Nihilism, 41

Baldwin, Stanley, British Prime Minister, his responsibility for Czechoslovakian calamity, 5; refuses to investigate Zinoviev "letter" affair, 206; refuses to ratify Anglo-Soviet Treaty, 1925, 213; ends British relations with Russia, 1927, 221; on the Kellogg Pact, 243; suspends trade negotiations with Russia and places embargo on Russian goods, 1933, 278-279; on defense of England, 1934, 338

Balkan nations, sign Montreux accord, 1936, 400

Baltic States, Russian incursion into, complicates Litvinoff's diplomatic task in Washington, 477

Baltic Treaties negotiated, 1920, 164-165, 333

Bank of International Settlements, pays Czech gold to Nazis under British pressure, 1939, 447

Bants, Paul, and Litvinoff's arrival in United States, 1933, 304-305

Barthou, Louis, at Genoa Conference, 1922, 183; his friendship with Litvinoff, 185-186; his work and personality, 327; his Disarmament Conference speech, May, 1934, 327-333; his work with Litvinoff, 333; on Russian entry into League of Nations, 351; his assassination, 1934, 352; and Franco-Russian Pact, 1935, 356; quoted on degeneration of France, 438

Bartlett, Vernon, newspaper correspondent, and British engineers' trial, 278

Beaverbrook, Lord, in British-American Commission to Russia, Sept., 1941, 464

Bebel, August, at Socialist Congress, 1907, 93

Beck, Colonel, on Russia's entrance into the League of Nations, 349

Belgium, appeals to Hague Court on Rhineland occupation, 1936, 389-390; declares her neutrality, Oct., 1936, 390

Belinski, Vissarion, Russian critic, read by Litivinoff, 37

Belostok, Litivinoff's birthplace, described, 32-33

Beneš, Eduard, President of Czechoslovakia, his work for League of Nations praised by Litvinoff, 7; his attitude toward Soviet Russia, 24-25; submits to German demands under British threats, 441

Bernstorff, Count, cites German disarmament under provisions of President Wilson's Fourteen Points, 251

Bessarabia, its annexation by Rumania unrecognized by Russia, 167; Russian protest on, 1928, 254

Bibineyshvili, biographer of Kamo, 87

Bibliography, 500-502

Black Hundreds, anti-revolutionary group, formed, 1905, 66; in 1916, 117

Black Sea Convention, 1936, 401

Black Sea Pact, collapses, 439

Blomberg, Field Marshal von, meets Chamberlain in London, 1937, 428

Blum, Léon, mentioned, 24, and Spanish Civil War, 436; and Finnish-Russian War, 455

Bolshevik Party, Committee for organization of, 1904, 53-54; succeeds Social Democratic Labor Party, 1905, 64; Third Congress, London, 1905, 64, 71; names candidates to Fourth Duma, 81; its growth after 1905, 81-83; methods of raising funds, 82; Fourth Congress, London, 1907, 83; its First World War Program announced by Lenin, 101-102; Litvinoff becomes its London representative, 1912, 103; assumes government of Petrograd, Nov., 1917, 127

Bolsheviki, origin of name, 52

Bonnet, Georges, suggests Mussolini urge five-power conference, Sept., 1938, 24; his dishonest stratagems in Czech crisis, 26, 27; eagerness to co-operate with Nazi Germany, 1939, 446

Borah, Senator, influenced by anti-Soviet propagandists, 217; as proponent of Russian recognition, 259

Borodin, Michael M., mentioned, 215

"Boyeviki," 83

Braun, Father, mentioned, 308

Brest-Litovsk peace negotiations, 1917, 132; treaty terms accepted, 1918, 133

Briand, Aristide, saves Litvinoff from extradition to Russia, 1908, 96; succeeded as French Premier by Poincaré, 1922, 181; defends Russia against British criticism, 222; his background and personality, 236-237; suggests Pact to Frank B. Kellogg, 1927, 240

British Labor Party, urges recognition of Russia, 1924, 201

Brockdorff-Rantzau, Count, German Ambassador to Russia, 1922, 188; endeavors to strengthen Russo-German relations,

209; opposes German entrance to League of Nations, 211-212; discusses Kellogg Pact with Litvinoff and Krestinsky, 1928, 242

Bryant, Louise (Mrs. William Bullitt; widow of John Reed), quoted on Chicherin and Litvinoff, 145; quoted on Litvinoff, 1923, 307-308; in Moscow, 1933, 401

Buckler, W. H., of United States Embassy in London, confers with Litvinoff in Stockholm, 1919, 152

Budenny, Semyon M., and defeat of Denikin, 1919, 157

Bukharin, Nikolai I, editor of *Izvestia,* supports Litvinoff's policies, 241

Bullitt, Anne, 401

Bullitt, William C., emissary to Russia, 1919, 154; 1932, 280; first United States Ambassador to Soviet Russia, 1933, 309, 401-404

"Bund," Russian Jewish Socialist Group, at Second Social Democratic Congress, 1903, 52

C

"Cadets" (Constitutional Democratic Party), and Duma of 1906, 78

Cafencu, Rumanian Foreign Minister, and Russian plan for aid to Czechs, 29

Canadian Forum, Jan., 1934, suggests Nobel Peace Prize for Litvinoff, quoted, 359

Carol, King of Rumania, and Russian plan for aid to Czechs, 29; reverses favorable decision, 29

Cassidy, H. C., his *Moscow Dateline* quoted, 453, 460

Caucasus oilfields, retained by Russia, 167-168

Cecil, Lord Robert, regards Russian leaders as German agents, 1917, 128; on Russian government, 1918, 137-138

Chamberlain, Neville, and annexation of Czechoslovakia, 3; his peace policy, 4; declares his dread of war, 5; frustrates Litvinoff's plan for blocking aggression, 10; his appeasement policy, 11; at Berchtesgaden with Hitler, Sept., 1938, 17; proposes cession of Sudetenland to Germany, 17; his Godesberg conference with Hitler, Sept., 1938, 23; at Munich, 25; his fear of Russia, 27; his policy of saving England by inducing Germany to fight Russia, 27, 441; his anti-Soviet pol-

icy from 1937, 427 ff.; his background, personality, and career, 427-430; views Spanish Civil War as Russo-German conflict, 428-429; ignores anti-German advisers, 429; threatens Czechoslovakia, 441; opposes British desire for agreement with Russia, 1939, 447; his perplexities in crisis of 1939, 448

Chamberlain, Sir Austen, protests Russian gift to striking British miners, 1926, 214; "warns" Russia, 1927, 219; attempts united front against Russia, 1927, 221; meets Litvinoff at Geneva, 1927, 237-240; praises Litvinoff's efforts toward collective security, 1934, 338

Chernaia Sotnia (Black Hundred), of Czarist Russia, 35

Chernishevski, Nicholas Gabrilovich, Nihilist author read by Litvinoff, 37

Chicherin, George, released from London prison, 1917, 130; Commissar for Foreign Affairs, 144; his background and personality, 144-147; Litvinoff's respect for him recorded, 147; his peace note to United States, 1919, 152; on Genoa Conference of 1922, 181; at Genoa Conference, 182; on the Locarno Treaty, 1925, 210; opposes Germany's joining League of Nations, 1925, 212; his note of Dec., 1923 quoted, 218; opposes international conferences and treaties, 242; his failing health and retirement, July, 1930, 273; his opposition to Russia joining League of Nations, 1930, 335

China, attacked by Japan, 1931, 7, 274; Russian policy toward, 275; diplomatic relations with Russia restored, 1932, 275; Litvinoff on Japanese aggression in, 426-427

Chinese Eastern Railway seizure, 1929, provokes Russo-American dispute, 257-258

Churchill, Winston, on Neville Chamberlain, 5; on Anglo-French apathy toward annexation of Czechoslovakia, 28; on Lloyd George's pro-Russian policy at Geneva, 1922, 185; opposes British recognition of Russia, 1926, 214-215; his view of the Kellogg Pact, 243; endorses collective security idea, 1934, 337; assails Chamberlain's refusal to guarantee neutrality of Baltic states, 1939, 446; his speech of June, 1940, on British support of Russia, 461, 490

Civil liberty, discussed in Roosevelt-Litvinoff negotiations, 1933, 295-296, 301

Clausewitz, quoted, 190

Clynes, R. J., British opposition leader, on "Arcos" and Soviet Trade Delegation raids, 1927, 221

Colby, Bainbridge, assails Soviet regime, 1918, 143; opposes United States recognition of Russia, 1926, 218

Collective Security, Litvinoff's campaign for, 315 ff.; in 1932, 318; as essence of Russian foreign policy, 323; frustration of plans for, 1935-1936, 396; abandonment of, 423-424, 439

Comintern, handicaps Litvinoff's plans, 213-214; decline of its influence under Stalin regime, 256; and United Front policy, 323; Seventh Congress of, August, 1935, and United States protest on attendance of American communists at Convention of, 403; dissolution of, 480

"Communist," substitution of name for "Social Democrat," announced by Lenin, 1917, 126

Communist Manifesto, 40

Communist Party, of Great Britain, arrest of leaders, 1925, 213; of United States, complicates Litvinoff's diplomatic task, 1941-1943, 476

Communist position and policy explained by Litvinoff, Jan., 1918, 132

Conferences, international, Zimmerwald, 1915, 115; Washington, 1921, 174-175; Genoa, 1922, 181-187; Hague, 1922, 192-194; London, 1924, 202-204; Locarno, 209-211; London Economic, 1933, 281-287; for the Definition of Aggression, 1933, 284; London, 1936, 380-390; Montreux, 1936, 399-401

Confiscation of foreign property in Russia, British attitude on, 1922, 193

Conradi, Maurice, Vorovsky's assassin, 197, 198, 223

Convention for the Definition of Aggression, signatories to, July, 1933, 284; its terms, 285-286

Coolidge, President Calvin, opposes resumption of relations with Russia, 1923, 198

Coolidge, Professor Archibald, mentioned, 155

Co-operative Societies, Russian, as channels for trade with Allies, 1920, 162

Cot, Pierre, and Franco-Russian rapprochement, 277, 327

Council of People's Commissars founded, Nov., 1917, 127; imposes Italian embargoes, 1936, 365

Courier of Europe, on Father Gapon and 1905 Revolution, 63

Couzens, Senator James, and United States recognition of Russia, 286

Cripps, Sir Stafford, cited on Stalin's opinion of Germany's attitude toward her pact with Russia, 460

Cromie, Captain, his death at Petrograd British Embassy, 1918, 137

Cultural advances in Russia, 478-479

Cumming, G. K. (and Petit, W. W.), their Russian-American Relations quoted, 143

Curzon, Lord, British Foreign Secretary, his protest to Russia on alleged anti-British intrigues, Oct., 1921, 170; Litvinoff's reply, 170

Czarist debts, used to defer recognition of Russia, 174; discussed at Genoa Conference of 1922, 182

Czarist Russia, Jews in, 35; revolutionary movements in, 1856-1903, 41-44; liberation of serfs in, 41; Zemstvas in, 41; assassination of Alexander II, 42; trade unionism begins in, 42; 1905 Revolution, 60-63, 68-69; Duma established, 69; manifesto of Oct. 17, 1905, 70; people's failing enthusiasm for First World War, 1915, 114; interference of Czarina and Rasputin in conduct of war, 115; revolutionary propaganda during First World War, 117-118; chaos of early 1917, 119; Provisional Government formed March, 1917, 120; Revolution of 1917, 120-121

Czechoslovak Corps, revolts against Russia, 1918, 147-148

Czechoslovakia, annexed by Germany, 3-28; advised by Russia to mobilize, 1938, 11; its government orders martial law, 1938, 16; anti-Soviet elements in, 24; Russia's willingness to aid reaffirmed, Sept., 1938, 25; its Anti-Soviet Agrarian Party urges acceptance of Munich settlement, 26; concludes de facto treaty with Russia, 1922, 188; betrayal of marks end of Litvinoff's efforts to establish collective security, 439; threatened by Chamberlain, 441; her gold delivered to Nazis, 1939, 447

D

D'Abernon, Lord, consulted by Litvinoff, 213

Daily Herald, London, quotes Litvinoff on Hague Conference of 1922, 192

Daladier, Édouard, in Czechoslovakian crisis of 1938, 4; welcomed in Paris, 5; opposes Hitler's Godesberg demands, 23; at Munich, 25

Dallin, David J., his *Soviet Foreign Policy* quoted, 445; quoted on causes for Russian distrust of Great Britain, 1939, 446; quoted on German aid in Finland's renewed war with Russia, 457

Dalton, Hugh, on Munich settlement, 27; his *Hitler's War* quoted, 439, 445; questions Chamberlain on delays in Anglo-Russian negotiations, June, 1939, 445

Davies, Joseph E., mentioned, 23; on Molotov, 180; on Litvinoff, 191; quoted on Stalin, 266; quoted, 357, 418, 420, 424, 425, 426, 438, 468; cited on Moscow treason trials, 421, his book *Mission to Moscow* discussed, 491

Davila, Charles A., confers with Litvinoff on Bessarabia, 1928, 254

Debts, Russian, to Great Britain, and Russian counterclaims, 1924, 202-203; Franco-Russian negotiations, 1926, 216; amounts of United States claims against Russia, 218; Franco-Russian conferences on, 1927, 235; claims and counterclaims in Roosevelt-Litvinoff negotiations, 1933, 303-304

Denikin, General Anton, as Dictator in the Caucasus, 1918, 148; attacks Petrograd, 1919, 157

Denmark, Litvinoff's treatment in, 1920, 158-159

Dennis, A. L. P., His *Foreign Policies of Soviet Russia* quoted, 138, 143, 161

Deterding, Sir Henry, oil magnate and anti-Soviet propagandist, 173; obstructs Russo-American oil-trade agreement, 1926, 217

Dewey, Charles, American financial adviser to Poland, confers with Litvinoff in Moscow, 1928, 253-254

Disarmament, urged by Chicherin at Genoa Conference, 1922, 183; conference on, called at Moscow, 1922, 194; Russia invited to Geneva Preparatory Conference on, 1925, 211; First Conference on,

1926, 211; Litvinoff and First Conference on, 223-255; Russian proposals on, at Geneva, 1927, 227-231; Rykov's speech on, April, 1927, 232; attitude of delegates and press toward Litvinoff's proposals on, at Geneva Conference, 1927, 233; Litvinoff's proposals for complete, Geneva, 1928, 244-250; their rejection, 252; Litvinoff's proposals for partial and gradual, 252; Conference of 1932 on, 253; Conferences on, 1933, 1934, 324, 327-333; Barthou's speech on, at Conference, May, 1934, 327-333

Dmitri, Grand Duke, assassin of Rasputin. 118

Dobroliubov, Nikolai, Nihilist publicist, read by Litvinoff, 37

Documentation, 503-509

Dollfuss, Austrian Chancellor, his murder, 1934, 338

Dreyfus affair, mentioned, 48

Druzhelovsky, forger of Zinoviev "letter," 205

Dubrovin, Dr., head of Black Hundreds, 117

Duma, established, 1905, 69; Nicholas II's manifesto on, Oct., 1905, 70; of 1906, 78; and Viborg Manifesto, 79; of 1907, 80; of 1907–1912, 81; of 1912–17, 81; summoned, 1915, 114; suspended, 115; attempts provisional government, 1917, 120

Dunn, James Clement, and reception of Litvinoff in Washington, 1933, 292

Duranty, Walter, quoted on Lenin's return to Russia, 125; cited, 136; quoted on Lenin, 199, 200; quoted on his interview with Stalin, Dec., 1930, 218-219, 272; quoted on Stalin, 1923, 263; accompanies Litvinoff to Washington, 1933, 292; his interview with Stalin, 1933, quoted, 335-336; cited on Moscow treason trials, 421

E

"Eastern Locarno" Pact, 333, 337-338; new efforts to establish, 1935, 359-360

Ebert, Friedrich, opposes von Maltzan's negotiations with Russia, 1921, 172

"Economic espionage," discussed in Roosevelt-Litvinoff negotiations, 1933, 302-303

Economic non-aggression, pact proposed by Litvinoff, May, 1931, 273; demanded by him at London Economic Conference, 1933, 283

Eden, Anthony, British Secretary of State for Foreign Affairs, urges stopping Hitler's annexation of Austria, 10; resigns, 10; succeeds Hoare at Geneva, 367; Chamberlain's lack of confidence in, 429; denounces Italian sinkings of Russian and British vessels, 1937, 435; is dismissed by Chamberlain for his anti-Hitler policy, 437

Edward VIII, King, and German anti-Litvinoff propaganda, 321-322; his hostility to Russia, 380-381

Eichorn, Field Marshal von, assassinated, 1918, 136

Eighth Soviet Congress, Nov., 1936, Litvinoff's speech before, on German and Italian intervention in Spain, 393-395, 437; his speech before, on German-Japanese Agreement of 1936, 405-407

Eisenstein, and his *Alexander Nevsky* film, 460

"Emancipation of Labor" (*Osvobozhdenie Truda*), first Marxist group in Russia, 1883, 42

Esthonia, concludes treaty with Russia, 1920, 158; signs Litvinoff Protocol, 1928, 255; treaty guaranteeing her sovereignty proposed, 1934, 336; Russia acquires naval bases in, 1939, 454

Ethiopia, Italian invasion of, 7, 361; Russian attitude toward, 20; her request that League of Nations Assembly convene rejected, 1936, 368; Emperor of, appeals vainly to League, 368

Europe in 1902, described, 48-49

Evans, Ernestine, cited on Stalin, 263

Evening Post, New York, quotes Senator Wheeler on Russia, 1923, 198

Export trade of Soviet Russia, 1921, 169

"Expropriation," proposed as fund-raising means for Bolshevik Party, 82-83; used in 1906, 83

F

Famine, Russian, of 1921-1922, 173, 334

Facta, Italian Premier, at Genoa Conference, 1922, 183

Fascism, in Japan, 1927, in Poland, 1926, in Lithuania, 1926, 215; in Germany, 315; in Finland, 454-455; sympathies with in United States, 482

Fehst, Hermann, German anti-Semitic propagandist, smears Litvinoff, 1933, 320

Fell, Colonel Aleksander Aleksandrovitch, Litvinoff's commanding officer, 1893, 36

Feuchtwanger, Lion, his *Moscow, 1937,* quoted, 262, 266; cited on Moscow treason trials, 421

Fierlinger, Zdenek, Czech envoy in Moscow, 1938, 25

Figaro, on Litvinoff's arrest in Paris, 1908, 95

Finland, proposes peace negotiations with Russia, 1919, 158; concludes treaty, 164-165; declines to sign Litvinoff Protocol, 1928, 255; treaty guaranteeing her sovereignty proposed, 1934, 336; obstructs Litvinoff's peace plans, 360; her anti-Soviet intrigues, 360; invaded by Russia, Nov., 1939, 454-455; Fascism in, 454-455; supported against Russia by France and Great Britain, 455; German military aid to, 1940, 457; her "war" debt payments to the United States, 477

Finnish-Russian War, begins, Nov., 1939, 454-455; French and British support against Russia in, 455; complicates Litvinoff's diplomatic task, 1941-1943, 476

First International, founded, 1864, 40

First World War, 97; Russian disaster at Tannenberg and advance on Lvov, 1914, 113-114; Fall of Warsaw, 1915, 114; Russo-German armistice, 1917, 127

Fischer, Louis, quoted, 23, 25, 168, 335, 357; cited, 202, 219; his *Soviets in World Affairs* quoted, 25; his *Men and Politics* quoted on Chicherin, 146; cited on anti-Soviet elements in United States State Department, 217; quoted on Litvinoff, 223; quoted on William Bullitt, 403

Fisk, Harvey E., quoted on Russian debts to Great Britain, 1924, 202

Five-Year Plans, inaugurated, 256

Flandin, French Premier, and German reoccupation of Rhineland, 1936, 378

Fourth Congress of Bolshevik Party, London, 1907, 83

Fourth Soviet Congress, April, 1927, and Rykov's disarmament proposals, 232

France, presses Beneš to accept Munich settlement, 25; loan to Russia by, 1906, 85; opposes return of émigrés to Russia, 1917, 121; her opinion of Soviet regime, 1919, 143; opposes Russian peace settlement, 1919, 154, 156; and proposed sale of Russian naval vessels, 1923, 197; recognizes Russia, 1924, 216; not bound by British policy toward Russia, 1927, 221; criticizes Litvinoff's disarmament proposals, 1928, 251; hostility toward Russia, 1929, 257; non-aggression treaty with Russia, 1930–1932, 275-276, 277; and General Disarmament Conference, 1934, 327-333; her fear of Hitler motivates pact with Russia, 1935, 356; and sanctions invoked against Italy, 1935, 366; signs Montreux accord, 1936, 400; her warning on German-Russian accord, 1939, 450; supports Finns against Russia in War of 1939, 455; prepares military attack on Russia, 1939, 455-456

Francis, David, United States Ambassador to Russia, 1918, regards Lenin and Trotsky as paid German agents, 134

Franco-Russian Pact, 1935, 356-358; stipulation of, 357

Free Germany movement and manifesto, 1943, 483

French Committee of Liberation in North Africa, mentioned, 482

G

Gamelin, General, mentioned, 451

Gapon, Father George, and Revolution of 1905, 60-63, 68-69; his death, 63

Genoa Conference of 1922, 181-187

George V, King of England, his anti-Soviet attitude, 204

Georgia liberated, 1920, 167

Germany, supports revolt of Don Cossacks, 1918, 149; propaganda activities by Russia in 1918, 152; and Polish attack on Russia, 1920, 165; provisional agreement with Russia, 1921, 171; concludes Treaty of Rapallo, 1922, 186; her internal situation, 1923–1924, 207; joins League of Nations, 1926, 211; aids Russia in League of Nations, 213; and British policy toward Russia, 1927, 221; is sympathetic toward Litvinoff's disarmament proposals of 1928, 250-251; trend toward Fascism in, 1931, 275; in 1932, 276; and United States recognition of Russia, 1933, 290; under Hitler, 1933, 315; withdraws from League of Nations, 315; decline of her relations with Russia, 1933, 316; her hatred of Litvinoff, and propaganda against him, 319-322; Litvinoff's relations with, 1934, 337; relations with

Great Britain, 1934, 337-338; opposes collective security, 338; decrees universal military service, 1935, 353; signs non-aggression pact with Poland, 1934, 360; reoccupies Rhineland, 1936, 377-379; signs non-aggression pact with Japan, Nov., 1936, 405; signs non-aggression pact with Italy, 422; Litvinoff denounces her intervention in Spanish Civil War, May, 1937, 411-414; invades Austria, 1938, 437-438; Chamberlain's policy of inciting her to war on Russia, 441; her pact with Russia, 1939, 441 ff.; receives Czech gold through British pressure, 1939, 447; makes war on Russia, June, 1941, 456, 461; her military aid to Finns, 1940, 457; her victories in Russia, 1940, 461

Gerny, Czech Minister of Interior, member of anti-Soviet Agrarian Party, urges acceptance of Munich settlement, 26

Ginsburg, Baron, Russian industrialist, 38

Goebbels, Dr. Joseph, orders anti-Semitic propaganda used against Litvinoff, 320-322

Goering, Hermann, and Franco-Russian Pact, 1935, 357-358

Gordon, Yankel, admits Litvinoff to Social Democratic Labor Party, 1898, 38

Gorki, Maxim, finances Novaya Zhizn newspaper, 1905, 73; gives earnings to Bolshevik Party, 82; and Russian Revolution, 141

Government of Russia after Lenin's death, 201

Grain, state monopoly of, decreed in Russia, 1918, 149

Great Britain, her responsibility for European situation of 1938, 5-6; presses Beneš to accept Munich settlement, 25; promises to aid France in defense of Czechoslovakia, 27; her desire for peace shown by Munich agreement, 27; opposes return of émigrés to Russia, 1917, 121; policy on intervention in Russia, 1918, 135; trade agreement with Russia, March, 1921, 170; sustains diplomatic defeat in Persia, 1921, 170-171; at Hague Conference of 1922, 193; threatens severance of Russian relations, 1923, 197; gives Russia formal recognition, 1924, 201; and Russian debt controversies, 1924, 202-203; General Strike of 1926, 214-215; and "Arcos" and Soviet Trade Delegation raids, 1927, 219-221; breaks off diplomatic relations with Russia, 1927, 221; and Litvinoff's total disarmament proposals, 1928, 251; recognizes Russia, 1929, 259; declines to join United States in protest on Japanese aggression, 1931, 274; relations with Russia, 1932-1933, 277-280; welcomes growing German strength as offset to Russian power, 279; internal peace propaganda, 1933, 279; and collective security proposals, 1934, 337; and sanctions invoked against Italy, 1935, 366; and Hoare-Laval Pact, 1935, 367; is willing to support France in re-occupation of Rhineland crisis, 1936, 378; appeals to Hague Court on Rhineland occupation, 1936, 389-390; signs Montreux accord, 1936, 400; her hostility toward Russia, 1937, 427 ff.; causes for Russian distrust of, 1939, 446; aids German dismemberment of Czechoslovakia, 1939, 447; popular wish for rapprochement with Russia opposed by Chamberlain, 1939, 447; supports Finns against Russia in War of 1939, 455; prepares armed intervention in Russia, 1939, 455-456; and the second front problem, 1940–1942, 463; uneasiness in at United States criticism of Russia, 1943, 490

Gregory, Captain T. C. C., his anti-Soviet intrigues, 1924, 203; and the Zinoviev "letter," 204

Grinevitsky, assassin of Alexander II, 42

Gromyko, Andrey, succeeds Litvinoff as Ambassador to United States, August, 1943, 483

Guchkov, Alexander I, and Duma of 1906, 78

Gukovski, mentioned, 73

H

Hague Conference of 1922, 192-194

Halifax, Lord, British Secretary of State for Foreign Affairs, "shocked" by annexation of Austria, 10; his attitude toward Litvinoff's disarmament proposals, 1927, 233; his hostility to Russia, 429

Hardie, Keir, at London Socialist Congress, 1915, 104, 105

Harriman, W. Averell, his plans for Russo-American trade obstructed, 1925, 217; in British-American Commission to Russia, Sept., 1941, 464; and Lend-Lease arrangements with Russia, 481

Hearst Press attacks on Russia, 1943, 484

Henderson, Arthur, at London Socialist Conference, 1915, 104

Henderson, Sir Nevile, British Ambassador to Germany, instructed by Chamberlain to suggest an international conference, omitting Russia, 1938, 11

Henlein, Konrad, received by Neville Chamberlain, 1938, 11; his revolt fails, 16

Herbette, Jean, French Ambassador to Soviet Russia, questions Russian attitude toward Kellogg Pact, 1928, 242-243

Herrick, Myron, United States Ambassador to France, quoted on Occupation of the Ruhr, 1923, 207

Herriot, Edouard, and French recognition of Russia, 1924, 216, 277; 1933, 327; and Franco-Russian Pact, 1935, 356; on Litvinoff's resignation, 1939, 439

Hervé, Aimè, at Socialist Congress, 1907, 93

Herzen, Alexander, influence of his writings on Litvinoff, 37; leader of liberal thought in Russia, 41; quoted, 498

Hesselgren, Kersten, Swedish representative at League of Nations, on League's failure in Ethiopian crisis, 1936, 368-369

Hillman, Sidney, mentioned, 176

Hindenburg, Field Marshal, succeeds Ebert as German president, 208; his attitude toward Russia, 208; dismisses Bruening, 1932, 276

Hitler, Adolf, and annexation of Czechoslovakia, 3, 12; exploits Sudeten German "problem," 10; confers with Chamberlain at Berchtesgaden, 17; at Godesberg, 23; his Sportspalast speech, Sept., 1938, 24, 28; at Munich, 25; his monuments to Rathenau's assassins, 188; his rise to power begins, 1931, 275; Germany under his rule, 1933, 315; his domestic policy, 316; his Mein Kampf cited, 315, 318; fails to secure meeting with Litvinoff, 1933, 319; French and British responsibility for his power, 425; on German troops in Finland, 1940, 457

Hoare-Laval Pact, 1935, 367

Hodgson, R. M., British chargé d'affaires in Russia, 1924, 202

Hoffmann, Adolf, at Zimmerwald Conference, 1915, 115

Holland, her treatment of Litvinoff, 1922,

192; opposes Russian entry into League of Nations, 335

Hoover, Herbert, and Russian famine relief, 1921, 173; his hostility toward Russia, 173; helps to discredit Bela Kun, 173; obstructs Russo-American trade plans, 1925, 217

Hopkins, Harry, and Lend-Lease arrangements with Russia, 481

Houden, Marcel, and Russia's admission to the League of Nations, 341, 342

Howard, Roy, belittles "menace of Bolshevism" in United States, 218; his interview with Stalin, 1936, quoted, 360

Hughes, Charles Evans, his statement on Russia, 1921, 168-169

Hull, Cordell, and London Economic Conference, 1933, 284; and initial negotiations with Litvinoff in Washington, 1933, 292

I

Ibarruri, Dolores (La Pasionaria), cited, 416

Imperial Bank of Russia, given to Persia by 1921 treaty, 171

Independent English Workers' Party, calls Socialist Congress, London, 1915, 103

"Indivisible Peace," Litvinoff's slogan on, 234; adopted by Sir Perceval Phillips, 234; his League of Nations speech, on, 363

Industries, Russian, in government control, 1918, 149

Insull, Samuel, mentioned, 272

International Brigade of Volunteers, leader's farewell quoted, 416

International Conference of Opponents of the Truce, Zimmerwald meeting, 1915, 115; Kienthal meeting, 116

International Socialist Bureau, its manifesto against Nicholas II, 1905, 63; in London, 103

Intervention, Wars of, against Russia, begin, 1918, 136; 147-157; Litvinoff's letter to President Wilson on, 150-152; finally defeated, 1920, 167; as cause of famines of 1921, 173; repetition of, considered by France and Great Britain, 1939, 456

Iskra (The Spark) Lenin's revolutionary paper, 39-40, 47; its delivery to Russia organized by Litvinoff, 50; funds needed for, 82

Italy, establishes trade relations with Russia, 1921, 172; gives formal recognition to Russia, 1924, 201-202; criticizes Litvinoff's disarmament proposals, 1928, 251; concludes Treaty of Friendship and Non-Aggression with Russia, 1932, 310; invades Ethiopia, 1935, 361; appeals to Hague Court on Rhineland occupation by Germany, 1936, 389-390; Litvinoff denounces her intervention in Spanish Civil War, 1937, 411-414; joins anti-Comintern Pact with Germany and Japan, 422; declares war on Russia, 1941, 461

Izvestia, Stalin quoted in, on Soviet peace policy, 1927, 232

J

Japan, Soviet attitude toward her aggressions, 21; lands troops in Russia, 1918, 148; her attitude toward Litvinoff's total disarmament proposals, 1928, 251; attacks China, 1931, 274; signs non-aggression pact with Germany, Nov., 1936, 405; and with Italy, 422; her aggression in China, 1937, 426-427; Litvinoff's warning of her impending attack on the United States unheeded, Nov., 1941, 473

Jaurès, Jean, at Socialist Congress, 1907, 93; assassinated, 1914, 99

Jews in Czarist Russia, conditions of life, persecutions of, as means of diverting popular discontent, 35

Joffe, Soviet representative in Berlin, at Genoa Conference of 1922, 182; and Rapallo Treaty, 186

John Grafton, arms-smuggling episode, 1905, 68-69, 85

Jouhaux, Léon, at London Socialist Conference, 1915, 104

K

Kaganovich, Lazar, Commissar for Railways, mentioned, 452

Kahn, Otto H., at Hague Conference, 1922, 193

Kalemen, Peter, assassin of Barthou and Alexander II, 352

Kalinin, his message on Litvinoff's sixtieth birthday, 190, 401; his account of Lenin's death, 200; belittles importance of Kellogg Pact, 242; his exchange of letters with President Roosevelt, Oct., 1933, 288-289

Kamenev, disagrees with Lenin, 122, 124;

in power after Lenin's death, 201; and
Moscow treason trials, 1936, 418

Kamo (Ter-Petrosian), Litvinoff's associate
in arms-running into Czarist Russia, 86-
92; Litvinoff describes arms-running episode with, 87-90; and the "Tiflis Expropriation," 90-93; his death, 92

Kaplan, Fanny, shoots Lenin, 1918, 136

Karakhan, Leo, mentioned, 215; and Moscow treason trials, 1936, 419

Katiusha, girl adopted by Litvinoffs, 178

Kautsky, Karl, at Zimmerwald Conference,
1915, 116

Kellogg, Frank B., United States Secretary
of State, his animosity toward Soviet
Russia, 240-241

Kellogg Pact of 1928, 13, 240-244; its provisions, 243; Russia first country to ratify,
243

Kerenski, Alexander F., demands new system of government, 1915, 115; in Provisional Government of 1917, 120; begins unsuccessful offensive, 1917, 126;
becomes Premier, 126; proclaims Russia
a republic, Sept., 1917, 127; loses power,
127; on anti-Semitic propaganda, 1934,
321

Kessler, Baron Harry, quoted on Genoa
Conference of 1922, 183

Kienthal Socialist Conference, 1916, 116

Kirov, assassinated, 1934, 418

Knickerbocker, H. R., American correspondent in Berlin, exposes anti-Soviet
forgeries, 1929, 259

Koeves, Tibor, his Satan in Top Hat cited,
276

Kolchak, Admiral Alexander, as Siberian
Dictator, 1918, 148; his defeat, 1919, 156

Kornev, on Litvinoff, 130-131, 190

Kornilov, General, attempts coup d'état,
Sept., 1917, 127

Krasnov, General Peter, provokes revolt of
Don Cossacks, 1918, 149

Krassin, Leonard, asks Litvinoff to direct
Novaya Zhizn newspaper, 1905, 73; raises
funds for Bolshevik Party, 81-82; at
Genoa Conference of 1922, 182

Krestinsky, Nikolai N., discusses Kellogg
Pact, with Litvinoff and Brockdorff-
Rantzau, 1928, 242; and Moscow treason
trials, 1936, 419, 420

Kreuger, Ivar, mentioned, 272

Kronstadt mutinies, 1905, 71; 1917, 126

Krupskaya, Nadezhna Konstantinovna

(Lenin's wife), comes to Siberia to marry
him, 47; her speech at Lenin's funeral,
201

Kun, Bela, his regime, and The Third International, 167; discredited by Herbert
Hoover, 1921, 173

Kuropatkin, Alexei N., Minister of War, on
approaching hostilities with Japan, 1903,
57; his defeat by Marshal Oyama, 58

L

Labor, Universal conscription of, decreed
in Russia, 1918, 149

Latvia, proposes peace negotiations with
Soviet Russia, 1919, 158; concludes treaty,
164-165; signs Litvinoff Protocol, 1928,
255; treaty guaranteeing her sovereignty
proposed, 1934, 336; Russia acquires
naval bases in, 1939, 454

Laval, Pierre, mentioned, 24; and Franco-
Russian Pact, 1935, 356; in Moscow,
1935, 357; his double-dealing, 357; and
Sir Samuel Hoare, 1935, 367

League of Nations, Litvinoff's criticisms of,
7; and Russia, 20; apathy of at annexation of Austria, 21; invites Russia to
Preparatory Disarmament Conference,
1925, 211; Disarmament Conference of
1925, 211; of 1927, 223 ff.; Litvinoff on
Covenant of, 252; reports on disarmament debates published by, 253; Germany withdraws from, 315; Barthou's
speech before, May, 1934, 327-333; Barthou paves way for Russian admission to,
333, 336; Russia's entrance into, 340-
50; its attitude toward Russia, 1921–1925,
334; and Soviet-Polish War, 334; Council of, cites Italy as aggressor and votes to
apply sanctions, Oct., 1935, 365-366; and
Litvinoff's criticisms of states withhold-
ing sanctions votes, 366; rejects Ethiopia's
request to convene, 1936, 368; Swedish
representative to, on its failure in Ethiopian crisis, 368-369; London meeting
of, 1936, on German reoccupation of the
Rhineland, 380-390; Covenant of, and
small nations, 424; expels Russia, Dec.,
1939, 455

League of Nations, Litvinoff's speeches before, 6-23, 244-250, 324-326, 342-348,
353-356, 361-363, 363, 369-377, 381-
389, 391-393, 396-399, 407-410, 411-
414, 414-415, 433-434

Lebedour, Georg, at Zimmerwald Conference, 1915, 115

Leeper, Rex, and Litvinoff, 110-112

Lend-Lease arrangements, United States with Russia, 480-481

Lenin (Vladimir Ilich Ulianov), his *Iskra* article read by Litvinoff in Kiev Prison, 39-40; on Plekhanov, 42; his career described, 46-47; meets Plekhanov in Geneva, 1895, 46; his Siberian exile, 1897, 46; criticizes policy of Social Democrats, 47; calls Brussels meeting of Second Russian Socialist Congress, 1903, 51; his opinion of Litvinoff, 53; selects Bolshevik Party Organization Committee, 1904, 53-54; his 1904 letter to Litvinoff on party organization, 55-56; on Russo-Japanese War, 58; returns secretly to Russia, 1905, 71; and *Novaya Zhizn* newspaper, 75-76; opposes "expropriation," 83; returns to Switzerland, 84; on 1905 Revolution, 84; arrested at Poronino, 1914, 98; is released and goes to Switzerland, 99; breaks with Plekhanov, 100; edits *Sozialdemocrat*, Zurich, 1914–1917, 100; attacks Trotsky on his stand on First World War, 100; publishes directions for revolutionary work in Russia, 101; on Litvinoff's role in London, 103; his eight basic points for Bolshevik policy, 104; praises Litvinoff's work at London Conference of 1915, 108-109; on failure of Second International, 1915, 109; with Krupskaya in Zurich during First World War, 113; at Zimmerwald Conference, 1915, 115; addresses Swiss workmen, 1916, 118; receives news of Russian Revolution, 1917, 121; returns to Russia, 123-125; announces his ten theses on Russia's policy, 1917, 125-126; disappears, July, 1917, 126; President of Council of People's Commissars, 1917, 127; is willing to continue war with allied aid, 1918, 134; on Brest-Litovsk treaty, 134; shot by Fanny Kaplan, 1918, 136; defends revolutionary Terror, 137; appeals on Armistice Day for end of foreign interference in Russia, 148; drafts peace resolution, 1919, 160; his *Pravda* letter to English delegates, 1920, 163; adopts New Economic Policy, 1921, 171; on Molotov, 180; and Genoa Conference of 1922, 182-183; his last illness and death, 1924, 198-201; quoted on Stalin, 1913, 262; quoted,

498. *See also* Krupskaya, Nadezhna Konstantinovna

Leopold II, King of the Belgians, declares Belgian neutrality, Oct., 1936, 390; discusses Belgian neutrality with Anthony Eden, 1937, 424

L'Humanité, quoted, 143

Lindbergh, Colonel, his erroneous estimate of Russian air power, and political motives for, 477-478; used by reactionaries, 478

Lippmann, Walter, quoted on Russo-German Pact of 1939, 452

"Liquidations," in Moscow treason trials, 1936, 419

Little Entente Pact, 333

Lithuania, proposes peace negotiations with Soviet Russia, 1919, 158; concludes treaty, 164-165; Fascist putsch of 1926, 215; treaty guaranteeing her sovereignty proposed, 1934, 336

Litvinoff, Ivy, Mme, meets Litvinoff, 111; their marriage, 111; her writings, 111-112; personal data, 112-113; their children, 113, 138; joins Litvinoff in Denmark, 1920, 164; as translator of Litvinoff's speeches, 178; her life in Moscow, 1921, 178; teaches Basic English, 178; at Geneva, 1927, 238; in 1934, 350, in Moscow, 1940, 459, 468; her air journey to the United States, 1941, 469-471

Litvinoff, Maxim, in Czechoslovakian crisis, 1938, 3, 4-5; suggests international conference to block aggression, 1938, 9-10; on League Covenant and Kellogg Pact, 13; on Czechoslovakian sell-out, 23; reaffirms Russian willingness to aid Czechoslovakia, 25; plans aid via Rumania to Czechs, 28-29; returns to Russia, Sept., 1938, 29; his resignation, 30; attitude of newspaper men toward, 30; as a linguist, 31; his parents and birthplace, 32-34; early life and religious atmosphere, 34-35; education, 35; military service, 36-38; his reading, 37, 39; refuses to fire on Baku strikers and is discharged from army, 37-38; work in Baron Ginsburg's sugar factory, 38; joins Social Democratic Labor Party, 1898, 39; buys printing press for party, 39; sentenced to prison, 39; studies English, 39; first reads Lenin in *Iskra*, 39-40; his pseudonyms, 44; escapes from prison with Zinoviev and Kamenev, 1902, 45; leaves Russia, 1902,

47; approaches Lenin unsuccessfully in Geneva, 50; meets Plekhanov, 50; organizes deliveries to Russia of *Iskra*, 50; his first meeting with Lenin, 51; assigned by Lenin to smuggling contraband literature into Russia, 52, 53; recommended by Lenin for Committee of Organization of Bolshevik Party, 53-54; and *John Grafton* arms-smuggling affair, 1905, 68-69; establishes *Novaya Zhizn* newspaper, 1905, 72-77; and "expropriation," 83; organizes arms-smuggling into Russia, 85-90; on Kamo, arms-smuggler, 87-90; and the "Tiflis expropriation," 92; delegate to Twelfth International Socialist Congress at Stuttgart, 1907, 93, 94; arrested in Paris, 1908, 94; goes to London, 1908, 96; becomes a British subject, 97; represents Bolshevik Party in London, 103; at London Socialist Conference, 1915, 105-108; his business life in London, 110; his marriage, 111; his children, 113, 138, 178, 401, 459, 468; receives news of Russian Revolution, 1917, 121; is first Soviet Ambassador to Great Britain, and opens "People's Embassy" in London, 128; his letter to Trotsky on his position as ambassador, 128-129; at Workers' Conference, Nottingham, 130, 133; meets Bruce Lockhart, 131; explains Communist position and policy, Jan., 1918, 132; appointed Ambassador to United States, but American visa refused, 135; imprisoned in London, 1918, 138; returns to Russia, 1918, 138; Vice Commissar in charge of European affairs, 144; his character and policies contrasted with Chicherin's, 146; appeals to President Wilson for aid in ending foreign intervention, 1918, 150-152; his statement on Soviet propaganda, 1918, 152-153; explains suppression of opposition within Russia, 153; his aims for establishing contacts with other powers, 1919-1920, 157-158; on peace missions in Esthonia and Denmark, 1920, 158-159; quoted on Danish attitude toward his peace delegation, 1920, 158-159; begins new peace offensive, 1920, 161; named chief director of Russian co-operatives, 1920, 162; in deputation to organize foreign trade, 1920, 162; his expulsion from Denmark demanded, 1920, 164; on foreign support for Polish attacks on Russia, 1920,

165; his policy of "trade followed by recognition," 167; on disappearance of prospects of world revolution, 168; chief of all Soviet legations abroad, 168; his first note to United States, 1921, 168; his comments on Hughes' statement, 169, 170; his opinion of Von Maltzan, 172; on United States famine relief, 173-174; urges invitation for Russia to Washington Conference, 1921, 175; with his family in Moscow, 1921, 176-177; his salary, 176; his family friendship with the Molotovs, 179; on Genoa Conference of 1922, 181; at the Genoa Conference, 182-186; demands compensation for Allied damage to Russia, Genoa, 184; his friendship with Barthou, 185-186; negotiates treaty with Czechoslovakia, 1922, 188; as a diplomat, 189-191; receives Order of Lenin, 1936, 190-191, 401; his power as a negotiator, 191; at Hague Conference of 1922, 192-194; his treatment in Holland, 1922, 192; calls Joint Disarmament Conference at Moscow, 1922, 194-195; his notes to United States, 1923, 196-197; wins British and Italian recognition of Russia, 1924, 202; on calling Geneva Disarmament Conference, 1925, 211; on supplement to Rapallo Treaty, 1925, 212-213; on hope of United States-Russian agreement, 1926, 212-213; on Russo-Turkish Peace Treaty, 1925, 216; replies to Sir Austen Chamberlain's "warning," 1927, 219; and raid on Pekin embassy, 219; and Poland, 1927, 221; his negotiations with Briand, Dec., 1927, 236-237; his Geneva interview with Sir Austen Chamberlain, 1927, 237-240; his policies supported by Bukharin, 241; discusses Kellogg Pact with Krestinsky and Brockdorff-Rantzau, 1928, 244-250; his proposals for complete disarmament, Geneva, 1928, 244-250; delegates' opinions on his proposals, 251-252; his protest on Bessarabia, 1928, 254; his policy as Foreign Minister, 256 ff.; his note to Stimson, Dec., 1929, 258; succeeds Chicherin as Foreign Minister, July, 1930, 273; his regard for Titulescu, 276; and British engineers' trial, 1933, 278; and Convention for the Definition of Aggression, July, 1933, 284; prepares basis for United States recognition of Russia, London, 1933, 286; in Washington, 1933,

288-310; correspondence with President Roosevelt on recognition, 294-304, 309-310; his understanding of Hitler, 317-318; on Russian policy, 1934, 322; his work with Barthou, 333; criticizes League of Nations, Nov., 1925, 334; proposes collective security treaties with Germany, 336; at Marienbad, 1934, 339-340; in Geneva, 1934, 341; his League of Nations committee assignment, 349; on Barthou's death, 352-353; criticizes states voting against imposing sanctions on Italy, 1935, 365-366; on betrayal of Ethiopia, 369-377; his diplomatic victory at Montreux Conference, 1936, 400, 401; sees crusade against Russia in Spanish Civil War intervention, 415-416; and Moscow treason trials, 1936, 418, 419, 420; on averting war, April, 1934, 423; and Chamberlain's anti-Soviet policy, 427; denounces Chamberlain as responsible for fall of Austria, 1938, 437; prophesies immediate future of Europe, March, 1938, 438; his note to Germany, refusing to recognize partition of Czechoslovakia, March, 1939, 439; resigns as Commissar of Foreign Affairs, May, 1939, 439-442; in Moscow after his retirement, 1940, 457-460; in reception of British-American Commission to Russia, Sept., 1941, 464; is Ambassador to United States, Oct., 1941, 467; his air journey to the United States, 1941, 469-471; in Washington until his recall to Moscow, 1943, 475 ff.; difficulties of his task in Washington, 476-478; his recall to Moscow, August, 1943, 482, 483; his career recapitulated, 485-498; his work and personal qualities discussed, 492-497

Litvinoff, Maxim, speeches of, before League of Nations on Czechoslovakian crisis, 1938, 6-23; at Geneva Disarmament Conference, Nov., 1927, 224-231; at London Economic Conference, 1933, 281-282; at Moscow, Dec. 29, 1933, 311-312; at Geneva Disarmament Conference, May, 1934, 324-326; his first, before Council of League of Nations, 1934, 342-348; before League of Nations on German conscription, April, 1935, 353-356; before League of Nations on Italian invasion of Ethiopia, 1935, 361-363; before League of Nations on "indivisibility of peace," 363; before League of Nations on German reoccupation of the Rhineland, March, 1936, 381-389; before League of Nations on Spanish Civil War, May, 1937, 391-393; before Eighth Soviet Congress on German-Italian intervention in Spain, Nov., 1936, 393-395, 437; before Eighth Soviet Congress on German-Japanese agreement of 1936, 405-407; before League of Nations on anti-Comintern nations, Sept., 1937, 407-410; before League of Nations on German-Italian intervention in Spanish Civil War, May, 1937, 411-414; before League of Nations on "non-intervention," Sept., 1937, 414-415; in Leningrad, on aggression in Spanish Civil War, Nov., 1937, 415, 416-418, 420-421; in Leningrad, on anti-Soviet espionage, Nov., 1937, 420-421; on collective security, July, 1937, 424-425; in Leningrad, on Japanese aggression in China, Nov., 1937, 426-427; before League of Nations, on misrepresentation of Russian part in Spanish Civil War, Sept., 1937, 433-434; on radio, July 8, 1941, on German declaration of war on Russia, 461-462; of Feb., 1942, on Russian policy and resistance, 465-466

Litvinoff, Misha, 113, 178, 459, 468

Litvinoff, Tanya, 113, 138, 401, 459, 468

Litvinoff Protocol, agreement of Soviet Russia with Poland, Esthonia, Latvia, and Rumania, 1928, 253-255

Lloyd George, David, desires Russian settlement, 1919, 154; repudiates peace negotiations, 156; admits failure of anti-Russian intervention and proposes trade relations, 1920, 161; reveals secret Anti-Soviet agreement, 1922, 180; at Genoa Conference of 1922, 183; angered by Rapallo Treaty, 187; opposes Anglo-Soviet treaty of 1924, 204; on British opposition to an agreement with Russia, 1939, 445

Locarno, Treaty of, 209-211; signatories confer on German reoccupation of the Rhineland, 1936, 379

Lockhart, Bruce, appointed British representative in Russia, 1917, 131; arrested, 1918, 137; returns to England, 1918, 138; his understanding of permanence of Russian Revolution, 141

London Agreement, discussed at Genoa Conference, 1922, 185

London Conference of March, 1936, 380-390

London Economic Conference, 1933, 281-286

London Non-Intervention Committee, criticized by Litvinoff, 20

Longuet, Jean, at London Socialist Conference, 1915, 104

Lozovsky, Solomon, Vice Commissar of Foreign Affairs, mentioned, 453

Lubomirski, Prince, Polish Minister to United States, on Polish War against Russia, 1920, 166

Ludendorff, General, aids Lenin's return to Russia, 1917, 123

Lunacharsky, Mme, in Geneva, 1934, 350

Lvov, Prince George E., heads Russian Provisional Government, March, 1917, 120

M

MacArthur, General Douglas, acclaims first winter offensive of Russians, 1941, 465

MacDonald, Ramsay, at London Socialist Conference, 1915, 104, 105; gives recognition to Russia, 1924, 202; his government defeated after Zinoviev "letter" affair, 204; returns to power, 1929, and secures British recognition of Russia, 259

Machnik, Czech Minister of Defense, member of anti-Soviet Agrarian Party, urges acceptance of Munich settlement, 26

Madariaga, Don Salvador de, his disarmament fable, 235

Magnussen, Karin, and anti-Semitic propaganda directed against Litvinoff, 320

Maisky, Ivan, at London Socialist Conference, 1915, 104; mentioned, 422; ignored when Ambassador as member of Non-Intervention Committee, 429; recalled to Moscow, 1943, 483

Malone, Colonel Cecil, and Russian peace negotiations, 1919, 158

Maltzan, Baron Heinrich von, German diplomat, and Russian-German agreement, 1921, 171; Litvinoff's opinion of, 172; at Genoa Conference, 1922, 183; develops hostile attitude toward Russia, 1925, 208; ambassador to United States, 1925, 209

Mamontov, General Konstantin, provokes revolt of Don Cossacks, 1918, 149

Manchester Guardian, on "Arcos" and Soviet Trade Delegation raids, 1927, 220

Mandel, Georges, and Franco-Russian Pact, 358

Mannerheim, Baron, reactionary leader in Finnish Civil War, 1918, 135; his animus against Russia, 1934, 336; his anti-Soviet intrigues with Germans and British Tory groups, 360; his part in causing hostilities with Russia, 1939, 454-455

Marks, Stanley J., his *The Bear that Walks Like a Man,* quoted, 166, 445

Martov, Menshevik delegate to Zimmerwald Conference, 1915, 115

Marx, Karl, first studied by Litvinoff, 37; quoted by Lenin, 122

Material betterment in Russia, 478-479

Maxim Litvinoff Regiment, 38

May Day, its first celebration in Russia, 1905, 64

McLean, Scottish teacher, appointed Soviet Consul by Litvinoff, 1918, 137

"Mediterranean Locarno" Pact, 333

Menshevik Party, and Duma of 1906, 78; attacked by Lenin, 100; joins Provisional Government, 1917, 126

Mensheviki, origin of name, 52

Mexico, German anti-Litvinoff propaganda in, 321

Michael, Grand Duke, as Regent, 1917, 120; abdicates, 120

Miliukov, Paul, and Duma of 1906, 78; demands new system of government, 1915, 115; Black Hundreds seek his death, 1916, 117

Minkin, M., Soviet Minister to Uruguay, 1935, 397

Mirbach, German Ambassador to Russia assassinated, 1918, 136

Mission to Moscow film, controversy concerning, 1943, 484

Moley, Raymond, at London Economic Conference, 1933, 283, 284; and United States recognition of Russia, 286

Molotov, Pauline, Mme, Commissar for Fisheries, Commissar for Cosmetics, Assistant Commissar of Food Industries, 180

Molotov, Viacheslav Mihailovich, his appearance, manner, and history, 179-180; Chairman of the Petrograd Soviet, Secretary of Moscow Party Committee, Prime Minister, 180; congratulates Litvinoff on his sixtieth birthday, 190-191; hails Litvinoff's stand on Italian invasion of Ethiopia, 365, 366; mentioned, 459; summons Litvinoff, Oct., 1941, to be Ambassador to United States, 467; his visit to the United States, 1942, 482

Montreux Conference, June, 1936, 399-401; accord signed by Russia and other states, 400

Moor, R. Walter, and initial negotiations with Litvinoff in Washington, 1933, 292

Morgenthau, Henry, Jr., and initial negotiations with Litvinoff in Washington, 1933, 292

Morning Post, London, quoted, 446

Moscow, Siege of, 1941, 467

Mueller-Kronach, Dr., German anti-Semitic propagandist, attacks Litvinoff, 1938, 320

Munich settlement of 1938, 25-28, 438; its acceptance urged by anti-Soviet Agrarian Party, 26

Murrow, Edwin, quoted, 1939, 451

Mussolini, Benito, suggests five-power conference, Sept., 1938, 24; at Munich, 25; his attitude toward First World War, 99; and recognition of Russia, 1924, 201-202; meets Litvinoff in Rome, 1933, 310, 318; denounces Hitler, 1934, 338

N

Nachalo (The Beginning), Menshevik newspaper, 72

Narkomindel (Soviet Russian Foreign office), its activity in Czechoslovak crisis, 1938, 25; reports on Litvinoff as first Soviet Ambassador, 129; Chicherin succeeds Trotsky as its head, 145; Litvinoff's office at, 177; in "purge" of 1937, 418

"Narodniki" (Populists), and Duma of 1906, 78

Nashe Slovo, Menshevik newspaper published in Paris, Lenin's letter to, 1915, 103-104

Naval bases, Russian, established in Esthonia and Latvia, 1939, 454

Navy, Russian, moved to Bizerte by anti-Soviet powers, 1918, 149

Nazi abuse of Litvinoff, 319-322

Nazi Party Congress, Nuremberg, Sept., 1938, 12

Neurath, von, his discussions with Litvinoff, 1934, 337

New Economic Policy, adopted by Lenin, 1921, 171

New York Stock Market collapse of 1929, and its effects on Russia, 271

New York Times, on Litvinoff's absence from Geneva, January, 1939, 29; on Riga

famine-relief meeting, 1921, 173; on Litvinoff at Hague Conference of 1922, 193; on Litvinoff at London Economic Conference of 1933, 281-282; on Roosevelt-Litvinoff negotiations, Nov., 1933, 294; interview with Stalin reported, 1933, 335-336

News Chronicle, London, and engineers' trial, 1933, 278

Nicholas, Grand Duke, dismissed by Nicholas II, 1915, 115; expects restoration of Provisional Government, 1918, 141; appreciates gain derived from collapse of autocracy, 142

Nicholas II, Czar, ascends throne, 1894, 42; his reactionary entourage, 43; proposes world peace conference, 49; opposes reforms, 1904, 59; and Revolution of 1905, 62-63, 66-68; his character, 66, 80; diary extracts, 67-68, 79, 80; his manifesto of Oct. 17, 1905, 70; dismisses Grand Duke Nicholas, 1915, 115; is urged to make peace with Germany, 1916, 117-118; abdicates, 120

Nobel Peace Prize, its award to Litvinoff suggested by United States and Canadian periodicals, 359

Non-aggression pacts, offered by Russia, rejected by Japan, 274; between Russia and powers, 1931–1932, 277; Russian-Polish, nullified by Pilsudski, 1934, 360; German-Polish, 1934, 360

"Non-intervention" in Spanish Civil War, Litvinoff on, Nov., 1936, 411; Litvinoff's League of Nations speech on, Sept., 1937, 414-415

Norris, Senator, as proponent of Soviet recognition, 259

Northcliffe, Lord, opposes Russian peace settlement, 1919, 156

Novaya Zhizn (The New Life), newspaper established by Litvinoff in St. Petersburg, 1905, 72-77

O

Ochrana, Secret Political Police of Czarist Russia, 35; and Social Democratic Labor Party, 38; German political police collaborate with, 85

"Octobrists," and Duma of 1906, 78

Oil interests, British and American, as barriers to United States recognition of Russia, 1921, 173; British, Dutch, and American, as factor in Genoa Conference of 1922, 182; Moscow Naphtha Syndicate and Standard Oil Company negotiations, 1926, 217; and Franco-Russian debt dispute, 1927, 236; and opposition to Russian recognition, 1929, 258-259; British, and Hoare-Laval Pact, 1935, 367

Olgin, M. J., cited, 63

"Open-door" policy, proclaimed by Soviet Russia, 1919, 158

Oumansky, Constantin, Chief of Russian Press Bureau, and Litvinoff's journey to Washington, 1933, 290; Ambassador to the United States, 309

Overseas Press Club, New York, Litvinoff's speech before, Feb., 1942, 317

P

Paléologue, Maurice, his opinion of Protopopov, 117; his understanding of permanence of Russian Revolution, 141

Papen, Franz von, appointed German Chancellor, 1932, 276

Pares, Sir Bernard, his *Russia* quoted on Russo-German Pact of 1939, 452

Paul-Boncour, Joseph, on Litvinoff's peace theory, 234-235; and Franco-Russian Pact, 1935, 356; press attack on, for signing Franco-Russian Pact, 379

Pavelich, Ante, leader of *Ustashi,* Croat terrorist organization, 352; Yugoslavian dictator, 352

Peace negotiations between Russia and Allies collapse, 1919, 154-156

Peace of Riga, 1920, 166

Peace terms offered by Russia to Allies, 1919, 155

Pekin, Soviet Embassy raided, April, 1927, 219

"People's Will," Russian revolutionary organization, 46

Perlo, Anna, Litvinoff's mother, 32; her death, 39

Persia, Russian diplomatic success in, 1921, 170-171; refuses to ratify treaty with Great Britain, 171; concludes Guarantee of Neutrality Treaty with Russia, 1927, 215

Philipps, William, and initial negotiations with Litvinoff in Washington, 1933, 292

Pilsudski, Polish Dictator, as exponent of "expropriation," 83; rejects Russian peace offer, 1920, 165; becomes Dictator, 1926, 215; nullifies non-aggression treaty with Russia, 1934, 360

Pisarov, Dmitri, Nihilist publicist, read by Litvinoff, 37

Plehve, V. K. von, mentioned, 43

Plekhanov, George V, founds first Marxist group in Russia, 1883, 42; meets Lenin in Geneva, 1895, 46; on 1905 Revolution, 84

Pobiedonatzev, Procurator of the Holy Synod, his influence on Nicholas II, 68

Poincaré, Raymond, succeeds Briand as French Premier, 1922, 181; his hatred of Soviet Russia, 185

Poland, wars against Russia, 1920, 165; retires and renounces her claims, 166; suggests reducing size of her army, 1922, 195; signs Litvinoff Protocol, 1928, 254; concludes non-aggression pact with Russia, 1932, 276; opposes Russian entry to League of Nations, 340; opposes "Eastern Locarno" plan, 1935, 360; signs non-aggression pact with Germany, 1934, 360; her appeal for arms loan denied by Chamberlain, 1939, 446-447; her recalcitrant attitude toward Russia, 1939, 448-449; invaded, 1939, 453-454; regions in controlled by Germany and Russia defined, Sept., 1939, 454

Ponsonby, Arthur, British Undersecretary of State, and Anglo-Russian settlement of 1924, 203; his *Falsehood in War Time* cited, 279

Popolo d'Italia, on Czechoslovakia, 16

Portugal, opposes Russian entry into League of Nations, 336

Post, Louis F., his *The Deportations Delirium* cited, 490

Potemkin, Russian Ambassador to France, confers with Laval, 1935, 356

Potemkin revolt, 1905, 65

Pozharsky, Prince, mentioned, 177

Pravda, and Lenin, 98; Lenin's letter to English delegates, 1920, 163-164; Stalin as editor of, 262

Preiss, Yaroslav, Czech industrialist, urges acceptance of Munich settlement, 26

Prinkipo peace meeting suggested, 1919, 152; plan collapses, 154

Prisoner Exchange Convention between Russia and Austria signed, July, 1920, 164

Pritt, N. D., cited on Moscow treason trials, 421; on reluctance to open second front, 463

Proletariat, Bolshevik illegal newspaper, 84
Propaganda, discussed in Roosevelt-Litvinoff negotiations, 1933, 295-296, 301
Protest on Fur Looting, Litvinoff's, to United States, 1923, 196-197
Protopopov, his virtual dictatorship in Russia, 1916, 116-117
Provisional Government of 1917, 120; its policy, 122; increasing difficulties, 1917, 126; moves against Bolsheviks, 126
Pseudonyms of Russian revolutionaries, 44
Pudken, supposed traitor in Social Democratic Labor Party, causes Litvinoff's arrest, 39
Purishkevich, assassin of Rasputin, 118

R

Radek, Karl, mentioned, 103; returns to Russia with Lenin, 1917, 123
Radovitsky, Sinion, and Russo-Uruguayan relations, 1936, 396-397
Rakovsky, and Russo-British affairs, 1924, 202; leaves Paris, 1927, when French assail his debts report, 235-236
Rapallo Treaty of 1922, 186-188, 207; supplement to treaty, 1926, 212
Rasputin, interferes in conduct of First World War, 115; assassinated, 118
Rathenau, Walter, at Genoa Conference, 1922; and Rapallo Treaty, 186; assassinated, 1922, 188
Ravitch, Sarah, her arrest, 1908, 94, 95
Recognition of Russia, the struggle for, 141 ff.; by countries, 1920–1925, 210; United States arguments against, 1926, 217-218; Litvinoff's policies on supported by Bukharin, 241; and Chinese Eastern Railway affair, 1929, 258; by Great Britain, 1929, 259; favored by President Roosevelt, 1932, 280; negotiations for, by United States, London, 1933, 286; by United States confirmed, Nov., 1933, 294, 309; terms of, 295-296, 297-302, 303, 304; Roosevelt-Litvinoff correspondence, 1933, 294-304, 309-310; by Uruguay, 396
Red Army, strengthened by volunteers, 1918, 149; defeats Poles, May, 1920, 166; refutes its detractors in war with Germany, 1941, 464; its first winter offensive, 1941, 465
Reed, John, quoted on Lenin's return to Russia, 1917, 125; cited, 127

Reforms, political, urged by Russian industrialists, 1905, 59
Religious liberty, discussed in Roosevelt-Litvinoff negotiations, 1933, 297-301
Revolutionary Congresses of 1904, 53-56
Revolutionary movements in Czarist Russia, 1856–1903, 41-44
Revolutions, Russian, 1905, 60-71; 1917, 119, 120-121
Reynolds, Quentin, his *Only the Stars Are Neutral* quoted, 266, 421
Rhineland, German reoccupation of, 1936, 377-379; Litvinoff's League of Nations speech on, March, 1936, 381-389
Ribbentrop, Joachim von, his assurances to Hitler that France and England would not fight, 28; Russian state banquet to, 1939, 452-453
Robins, Colonel Raymond, counsels cooperation with Soviet Government, 1918, 143
Rodzianko, Michael, and Duma of 1906, 78
Roosevelt, Eleanor, Mrs., welcomes Litvinoff to Washington, 1933, 293
Roosevelt, Franklin D., President of the United States, urges settlement without war, Sept., 1938, 23-24; favors recognition of Russia, 1932, 280; his exchange of letters with President Kalinin, Oct., 1933, 288-289; his message on negotiations with Russia, Oct., 1933, 289-290; his Chicago speech, Oct., 1937, cited, 426; and Litvinoff's appointment as United States Ambassador, Oct., 1941, 468, 475-476; his Lend-Lease arrangements with Russia, 480-481
Rosenberg, Alfred, his hatred of Soviet Russia, 316; on Russo-German amity, 1933, 318-319
Rostoptchin, Count, mentioned, 177
Ruhr Valley, occupied by French, 1923, 207; act opposed by Russia, 207
Rumania, in Czech crisis, 1938, 28-29; and annexation of Bessarabia, 167, 254; signs Litvinoff Protocol, 1928, 255
Rumbold, Sir Horace, his warnings against Germany ignored by Chamberlain, 429
Runciman, Lord, sent as adviser to Prague, 1938, 11
Russian Soviet Encyclopaedia, quoted on the Treaty of Locarno, 210-211
Russo-American Chamber of Commerce

dinner to Litvinoff, New York, 1933, 307

Russo-French rapprochement and Treaty, 1934, 327; reactionaries' campaign for its cancellation, 478

Russo-German Agreement of 1939, causes for analyzed, 441 ff., 450; suggested by Nazis, 450; made public, 453; complicates Litvinoff's diplomatic task in Washington, 477

Russo-Japanese War, 57-59

Russo-Persian Treaty, 1921, 171

Russo-Turkish Treaties, 1925 and 1926, 216

Ruthenberg, Pincus, and Father Gapon, 62, 63

Rykov, on disarmament, April, 1927, 232; on Kellogg Pact, 242

S

Sandler, R. J., President of the League of Nations Assembly, his address on Russia's admission to the League, 341; on freeing small nations from obligations of League Covenant, 1937, 424

Schulenburg, Count Werner von der, German Ambassador in Moscow, on Litvinoff, 191; protests German anti-Litvinoff propaganda, 321; retires, 453

Schuman, F. L., his American Policy Toward Russia quoted, 166; cited, 490

Second Front, controversy on, 451, 481, 485; lack of, confirms early Russian misgivings on Allies' attitude, 451; D. N. Pritt cited on, 463; Great Britain's attitude toward, 463; and United States, 481-482

Second International, its first assembly, 1889, 40; Lenin on its failure, 109; denounced by Lenin, 153

Second Russian Socialist Congress, Brussels, 1903, 51-52

Second World War begins, Sept. 1, 1939, 453

Sembat, Marcel, at London Socialist Conference, 1915, 104, 105

Serfs, liberated under Alexander II, 41

Sergei, Grand Duke, assassinated, 1905, 64

Seventh Soviet Congress, Peace Resolution, Dec., 1919, 160-161

Sheridan, Clare, mentioned, 176

Shliapnikov, Alexander, mentioned, 103

Shushenskoe, Siberia, Lenin's place of exile, 1897, 46

Sicilian campaign of 1943, 481

Simms, William P., on Russo-American relations, 218

Simon, Sir John, his attitude toward Litvinoff's disarmament proposals, 1927, 233; confers with Litvinoff, London, 1933, 283; hostile to Russia, 429

Skoropadsky, General Pavel, intrigues with Germany against Russia, 316

Skvirsky, Boris E., chief of Russian Information Bureau in Washington, 293; and Moscow treason trials, 1936, 419

Slocomb, George, British journalist, and Litivinoff-Chamberlain meeting at Geneva, 1927, 237-238, 240

Slugov, Captain, his friendship with Litvinoff during his military service, 36-37

Smuts, General Jan, counsels sympathetic attitude toward Russia, 1919, 143-144

Social changes and material and cultural advances in Russia, 478-479

Social Democratic Labor Party, 38; its origins and founding, 40, 43-44; first congress of, 1898, 47; succeeded by Bolshevik Party, 64; withdraws from London Socialist Conference of 1915, 109; distributes revolutionary propaganda, 1916, 116

Social Revolutionary Party, and Duma of 1906, 78; distributes revolutionary propaganda, 1916, 116; joins Provisional Government, 1917, 126

Socialist Conference at Zimmerwald, 1915, 115-116

Socialist Congress of 1915, London, 103-110

Socialist parties of Europe, their attitude toward First World War, 99; of Russia, 100

Society of Friends, congratulate Litvinoff on his Geneva speech of Nov. 30, 1927, 231

Sokolnikov, Gregory, Russian Ambassador to Great Britain, 1929, 259; and Moscow treason trials, 1936, 419

Soviet Constitution, 267-268

Soviet Government, is ready to make peace, 1917, 122

Soviet of Workers' and Soldiers' Deputies, organized 1917, 120

Soviet Trade Delegation, Berlin, raid on, 1924, 207-208

Soviets, decline to join Provisional Government, 1917, 126

Sozialdemocrat, Lenin's Zurich newspaper, 1914–1917, 100; prints Litvinoff's report of London Socialist Conference, 1915, 105-108

Spanish Civil War, London Non-Intervention Committee criticized by Litvinoff, 20; insurgents plot with Nazis, 1936, 377, begins, July, 1936, 390; its progress, 410-412; its end, 1939, 436. *See also* Litvinoff, Maxim, speeches of

Stalin, Joseph, his activity in the Caucasus after the Revolution of 1905, 83-84; speech of Oct., 1905, 84; and Kamo, 86; and the "Tiflis Expropriation," 92; arrested and exiled, 1913, 101; and defeat of Denikin, 1919, 157; his policy for Russia, 1920, 167; Prime Minister, 1941, 180; congratulates Litvinoff on his sixtieth birthday, 190-191, 401; in power after Lenin's death, 201; approves Germany's joining League of Nations, 212; on "propaganda," 218-219; on Russian peace policy, 1927, 232; his support of Litvinoff, 259; his personal and political career and policies, 259-269; his personal appearance, 266; and the Soviet Constitution, 267; on the World Depression of 1930, 272; on France, 1930, 275; congratulates Litvinoff on his work at London Economic Conference, 1933, 287; on Russian policy, 1934, 322; on League of Nations, 335-336; his *Leninism* quoted, 336; and Laval, 1935, 357; interview with Roy Howard, 1936, quoted, 360; his speech of March 9, 1939, cited, 450; his opinion of German attitude toward the pact with Russia, 460; his "scorched-earth" speech cited, 475

Stavisky scandal, 356

Steffens, Lincoln, his interview with Lenin, 1918, 136-137; quoted on Chicherin, 144; on Litvinoff, 145; accompanies Bullitt to Russia, 1919, 154

Stein, Boris, mentioned, 422

Steinhardt, Laurence, Ambassador from the United States, mentioned, 176; and confirmation of Litvinoff as Ambassador to the United States, Oct., 1941, 467

Stimson, Henry L., and Chinese Eastern Railway affair, 1929, 257-258

Stolypin, Peter A., Minister of Interior, leads repression after 1905 Revolution,

77; and Dumas of 1907 and 1907–1912, 80, 81

Strang, William, British emissary to Moscow, 1939, 444, 445

Stresemann, reassures Russia on effects of Germany's joining League of Nations, 212

Strikes in Russia, 1902–1903, 57; 1905, 63-64, 70; 1917, 119

"Sugar King's Palace," Moscow, described, 176

Suritz, Jacob, mentioned, 422

Swiss goods, boycott of, by Russia, 1923, 198

Switzerland, her relations with Soviet Russia, 1923, 197-198; apologizes for anti-Soviet activities, 1927, 223; opposes Russian entry into League of Nations, 336

T

Tabouis, Geneviève, her *They Called Me Cassandra* quoted, 349, 438, 440-441

Talleyrand, Litvinoff's admiration for, 189

Tartarescu, succeeds Titulescu as Rumanian Foreign Minister, 276

Ten theses on Russia's policy announced by Lenin, 1917, 125-126

Terror in Russia after shooting of Lenin, 1918, 136

Third International, as outgrowth of Kienthal Conference of 1916, 116; established, 1919, 153; co-operation with non-Russian Communists, 167

"Third Section" (Secret Police), increased by Alexander II, 42

Thomas, Albert, French labor leader, at London Socialist Conference, 1915, 104; understands permanence of Russian Revolution, 142

"Tiflis Expropriation" episode, 90-93

Times of London, quoted on General Smuts' pro-Russian statement, 1919, 143-144; announces Russian peace terms, 1919, 157-158; exposes Hoare-Laval Pact, 1935, 367

Titulescu, Nicholas, on Litvinoff, 31; and Bessarabian claims of Russia, 276; replaced by Tartarescu, 276; Litvinoff's regard for him, 276

Togo, Admiral Hihashi, defeats Russian Navy, 1905, 58

Tolstoi, Leo, mentioned, 41, 48; his *War and Peace* mentioned, 177

Trade agreements, promoted by Litvinoff

as prelude to Russian recognition, 167; with Great Britain, concluded, 1921, 170; with Italy and Austria, 1921, 172

Trade Unionism, in Czarist Russia, 42

Trade, Russian foreign, 1930–1932, 273; needs cited by Litvinoff at London Economic Conference, 1933, 282-283, and recognition by United States, 286

Transcaucasia liberated, 1920, 167

Trepov, General Dmitri, his repressions in Moscow and St. Petersburg, 1905, 60

Trials, of British engineers, Moscow, 1933, 277; their release, 284; of anti-Soviet plotters, Moscow, August, 1936, 418-422

Trotsky, Leon, and First World War, 100; at Zimmerwald Conference, 1915, 115; arrested, July, 1917, 126; opposes acceptance of German peace terms, 1918, 133; Commander in Chief of Red Army, 133; invites Allies to define peace terms, 1918, 133; is willing to continue war with Allied aid, 134; chooses Chicherin to succeed him as head of Narkomindel, 145; his tactical errors, 1920, 166; opposes Stalin after Lenin's death, 201; his personality and influence, 269-270; and Moscow trials of anti-Soviet plotters, 1936, 418

Troyanovsky, Alexander, first Soviet Ambassador to the United States, 1933, 309

Tukhachevsky, Marshal, his tactical errors, 1920, 166

Turgenev, read by Litvinoff, 37; influence on him, 39; name "Nihilist" invented by, 41

Turkey, concludes treaty with Russia, 1921, 172; is sympathetic toward Litvinoff's disarmament proposals of 1928, 250-251; signs Montreux accord, 1936, 400

Twelfth International Socialist Congress, Stuttgart, 1907, 93

Tyrell, Lord, his warnings against Germany ignored by Chamberlain, 429

U

Union for the Liberation of the Working Class, founded by Lenin, 1895, 46

"Union of the Genuine Russian People," reactionary organization, and Duma of 1906, 78

Union of Unions (Soyus Soyusov), formed, 1905, 65; calls general strike, 70

United States, her responsibility for European situation of 1938, 5-6; and Brest-Litovsk peace terms, 134; intervenes in Russia, 135; fails to answer Litvinoff note, 1921, 168; her relations with Russia, 1921, 172-175; 1925–1926, 217; refuses to attend Genoa Conference of 1922, 181; and Hague Conference of 1922, 192; and Russian protests on furlooting and illegal transfer of ships, 1923, 196-197; her trade with Russia, 1927, 241; questions Russian attitude toward Kellogg Pact, 1927, 242; business interests in, for and against rapprochement with Russia, 1929, 258-259; public of, favors Russian recognition, 1932, 281; protests attendance of her nationals at Seventh Comintern Congress, 403; her responsibility for European trend toward war, 425-426; her attitude on second-front controversy, 481-482; attitude toward Vichy France and De Gaulle, 482; attitude toward Russia, 1943, 491

Uruguayan relations with Russia, 396-399

Ustashi, Croat terrorist organization, 352

V

Vaillant, at Socialist Congress, 1907, 93; at London Socialist Conference, 1915, 104, 105

Vandervelde, Emil, at London Socialist Conference, 1915, 104, 105

Vansittart, Sir Robert, his warnings against Germany ignored by Chamberlain, 429

Versailles Treaty, Russian policy on provisions of, 333-334

Viborg Manifesto of 1906, 79; and repudiation of Czarist debts, 174

Vishinsky, André, mentioned, 453

Voelkischer Beobachter, on Russo-German amity, 1933, 318-319

Voroshilov, Klementi, and defeat of Denikin, 1919, 157; and Polish refusal to allow Russian defense of her territory, 1939, 449

Vorovsky, Vaslov, at Genoa Conference of 1922, 182; assassinated, 1923, 197, 211, 227

Vorwaerts, German Socialist newspaper, its attitude toward First World War, 99

Voykov, P., Soviet minister, murdered in Warsaw, 1927, 221

Vpered (Forward), revolutionary paper edited by Lenin, 52

W

Wallach, Meer Genokh Moisseevitch, Litvinoff's original name, 32

Wallach, Moses, Litvinoff's father, 32; arrested by Third Section police, 1881, 33; released, 33-34; his death, 39

Warburg, Felix M., his plans for Russo-American trade obstructed, 1925, 217

Wars, 1896–1900, 49

Washington Conference of 1921, 174-175; Russia's exclusion from, and protest, 174-175

Weygand, General, sent by France to aid Poles against Russia, 1920, 166

Wheeler, Senator Burton K., his visit to Moscow, 198; urges resumption of United States-Russian relations, 198

Whitaker, John T., his We Cannot Escape History cited, 422, 441; quoted, 450; quoted on Russo-German Pact of 1939, 452

White government of North Russia set up, 1918, 148

Wilhelm II, Kaiser, embitters European relations with the Orient, 49

Williams & Norgate, Litvinoff's London employers, 1908–1914, 96-97

Willkie, Wendell, mentioned, 482

Wilson, President Woodrow, is willing to intervene in Russia against Germans, 1918, 135; Litvinoff appeals to him to end foreign intervention, 150-152; desires Russian settlement, 1919, 154; refuses to meet his own peace emissaries, 1919, 155-156

Wilson, Sir Horace, in Czechoslovakian crisis of 1938, 4; influences Chamberlain against Russia, 428, 429, 430; his eagerness to co-operate with Nazi Germany, 1939, 446

Witte, Sergius, dismissed by Nicholas II, 1903, 43; on Nicholas II, 66; reappointed, 1905, 71

Workers' Soviets, first session, 1905, 70; dissolved, 77

Wrangel, General, takes Kiev, May, 1920, 166; his theft of Russian Navy, 195

Wright, Charles Hagleberg, secures employment for Litvinoff, 1908, 96

Y

Yanpolska, Freda, her arrest in Paris, 1908, 95

Yudenich, General Nikolai, fails in attack on Petrograd, 1919, 156-157

Yusupov, Prince Felix, assassin of Rasputin, 118

Z

Zemliachka, Russian woman revolutionary, 53, 55

Zemstva (Russian elective representative assembly), introduced under Alexander II, 41; influence of members of, 43; proposes popular assemblies, 1904, 59, 64; protests Protopopov's appointment as Minister of Interior, 1916, 116

Zimmerwald Socialist meeting, 1915, 115-116

Zinoviev, Grigori, Lenin's newspaper assistant, 1914–1917, 100; at Zimmerwald Conference, 1915, 115, 116; in power after Lenin's death, 201; and Moscow treason trials, 1936, 418

Zinoviev "letter" affair, 204-206; document proved a forgery, 205